W9-CKQ-526

The Great Nation

COLIN JONES

The Great Nation

FRANCE FROM LOUIS XV
TO NAPOLEON 1715–99

COLUMBIA UNIVERSITY PRESS
NEW YORK

Columbia University Press
Publishers Since 1893
New York   Chichester, West Sussex

First Published in Great Britain by Allen Lane, The Penguin Press
Copyright © Colin Jones, 2002

Frontispiece: *An Allegory of the French Revolution* by Guillaume Lethière (photo: Sotheby's, London)

A complete CIP record is available from the Library of Congress
ISBN 0-231-12882-7

Set in 10.25/13.75 pt Linotype Sabon
Typeset by Rowland Phototypesetting Ltd, Bury St Edmunds, Suffolk
Printed and bound in Great Britain by Clays Ltd, St Ives plc

Columbia University Press books
are printed on permanent and durable acid-free paper
c 10 9 8 7 6 5 4 3 2 1

For Mark and Robin
Salut et fraternité

Contents

Acknowledgements

In the course of the lengthy period spent researching and writing this book, I have taught at the universities of Exeter, Stanford and Warwick, and I thank those institutions – especially the historians and *dix-huitièmistes* within them – for providing a happy and stimulating environment in which to work. At Warwick I have profited from being in the slipstream of the Eighteenth-Century Centre, run by my colleague, Maxine Berg, and also from working alongside French historians Gwynne Lewis, Roger Magraw, Penny Roberts and Emma Spary. I won't be able to list all the conversations I have had over the years concerning the ideas in the book, but I would like to record my thanks to all who have listened and offered advice in one way or another. My special thanks go to friends who have read and commented on the draft typescript: Dave Andress, Peter Campbell, Gwynne Lewis and Michael Sonenscher. I realize I have been learning from Mike Sonenscher for more than a quarter of a century now: no one has pushed me harder to think afresh about eighteenth-century France. My thanks to all of these, and to the anonymous reader kindly supplied by Penguin. The book is far better for their efforts: defects remaining are very much my own. The final stages of production were completed while I was visiting fellow at the Columbia University Institute of Fellows, Reid Hall, Paris. I gratefully acknowledge the help and support of the Institute's Director, Danielle Haase-Dubosc, along with Michaela Bacou and Maneesha Lal. Simon Winder has been a wonderfully enthusiastic yet patient publisher, and my thanks go too to Felicity Bryan for her advice and support. Jonathan White was a very effective research assistant and John Strachan an excellent indexer. The book is dedicated to my brothers and their families. Lastly, my thanks go to my wife, Josephine McDonagh, for just about everything.

Colin Jones

Introduction

In many senses, the eighteenth century was France's century. The long reign of Louis XIV (1643–1715) was widely viewed as France's *Grand Siècle* ('great century'), yet by the king's death, the country had been reduced by European war and domestic circumstance to a wretched state: its economy was shattered, its society riven by religious and social discontent, its population reduced by demographic crisis, its cultural allure contested and found wanting, its political system in the doldrums. Yet the country was able to bounce back from misfortune and imprint its influence on every aspect of eighteenth-century European life. Demographically, France was the largest of the great powers – indeed between one European in five and one in eight was French. Socially and economically, the century witnessed one of France's most buoyant and prosperous periods: though the benefits of economic growth were far from evenly distributed, the quality of life as measured by life-chances, income levels and material possessions marked a considerable improvement. Culturally, France was the storm-centre of the movement of intellectual and artistic renewal known as the Enlightenment: for most contemporaries, the *lumière* of this *siècle des Lumieres* shone from France. In terms of politics and international relations, France remained the power that other states had to take into account, to worry about, to keep if possible on their side. Although the monarchical system failed to adapt to the domestic strains and international pressures which the period produced, French courtly and administrative structures were very widely emulated down to 1789. Nor did the shift to a republic in 1792 halt the catalogue of achievement – as was widely anticipated by European statesmen. Indeed, by 1799, France had vastly extended its frontiers and its influence over much of Europe.

To think of eighteenth-century France as 'the great nation' did not rule out criticism. Indeed, writing a volume with this title invites dis-passionate rather than eulogistic scrutiny of the criteria by which 'great-ness' is judged. By the end of the period, for example, as the Revolution of 1789 was taking a more militaristic and expansionist turn, the phrase *la grande nation* was used in quite opposing ways. For many it high-lighted the world-historical achievements of republican France. Yet for others, both within France and without, it signified something altogether more sinister. The universalist rhetoric of human emancipation spouted by French administrators and generals contrasted strikingly with the narrowly materialistic, self-seeking and indeed pillaging activities which French armies were inflicting on other Europeans. The Rights of Man of 1789 seemed to be focused largely on the claims of the French to feather their own nest, and the phrase *la grande nation* often had a critical, grudging and ironic tinge.

There was, moreover, a deeper, historical irony in the use of the term by that time too. For by then the very criteria of international greatness were shifting in ways which would knock France off its perch – and instal England in its place. This was not readily apparent in 1799: indeed, while France was brilliantly constructing a European empire, England's political system was under strain, its financial strength seemed fragile, and its social fabric looked under pressure. With the benefit of hindsight, we can see that the British were by then establishing a lead in terms of economic growth, commercial strength, industrial force and political stability which would make them the world's dominant power for much of the following century. And in 1815, France would be rolled back to its 1792 frontiers in a manner that smacked of national humiliation. But that is another story.

If historians have often failed to recognize the extent of the achieve-ment of the French nation in the period from the death of Louis XIV until the advent of Napoleon, this is partly at least because the period was topped and tailed – in 1689–1713, then in the decade leading up to Waterloo in 1815 – by heavy military defeats at the hands of Britain and its allies. The lack of recognition owes much to the fact that much of the history written about this period focuses on the Revolutionary era of 1789–99. So prevalent has been the view that the 1789 Revolution was not of a piece with the rest of the century that Alfred Cobban's *A History of Modern France, vol. 1 (1715–99)*, published as long ago as 1957, remains the only history of the full period. Many historians have chosen to write as though the years prior to 1789 are only interesting insofar as they illuminate and help explain 1789. Digging for Revolutionary origins, they have tended not to look up and see the sources of strength as well as the problems and tensions within French pre-revolutionary society. The present study proceeds on the assumption that although the causes of 1789 constitute an important historical question, there are other issues about eighteenth-century France which also deserve to be taken seriously and given due attention. Many of these (the continuing power of the state, for example, France's cultural and intellectual hegemony, its economic force, the roots of national identity) were grounded in France's acknowledged strengths over this period – rather than those weaknesses which directly influenced the outbreak of the Revolution.

Although one of my aims has been to convey much that was of significance in the social, economic, intellectual and cultural history of the period from 1715 to 1799, I have highlighted political history, which provides an essential framework for understanding both the achievements and the problems about French society over the period as a whole. The work thus will reflect the remarkable revival of interest among historians in eighteenth-century politics since Cobban's time, yet do so in a way which places politics in relation to broader developments. A thread of political narrative provides the work's organizing principle; but it is heavily interspersed with analytical and contextual chapters.

I have tried to write a history which is enjoyable and instructive on its own terms and which needs no explanation. Many readers will thus be well advised to skip the remainder of this introduction, and to proceed to the opening chapters. However, I thought that fellow scholars would find it helpful if I outlined my approach, and highlighted how what I am offering reflects – but also hopes to inflect – existing historiographical trends. This is the aim of these introductory remarks.[1]

When Cobban wrote, the political history of France was in a doldrums period. The gaze of his fellow scholars fell more on social and economic than on political issues. The *Annales* tradition of French scholarship, initiated by Marc Bloch and Lucien Febvre in the late 1920s, and then carried forward from the late 1940s by a second *Annaliste* generation dominated by Fernand Braudel, eschewed both the analysis of high politics and also narrative as a descriptive mode. It placed stress on the structural analysis of social phenomena in the long term (*longue durée*) and the middle term. 'Event history' (*l'histoire événementielle*) was regarded as the least deserving of serious scholarly attention: old-style political history was adjudged to have had its day. The hegemony of social-historical analysis extended to cultural and intellectual history too: ideas and taste were viewed within the context of *mentalités* (another *Annaliste* coinage, signifying the intellectual frameworks within which thinking takes place, rather than the ideas themselves). And *mentalités* followed the tortoise-like pace of the *longue durée* and were socially determined.

The hegemony of social-historical analyses – which was most evident from the late 1940s to the early 1970s – was such that the vast majority of in-depth analyses of eighteenth-century politics on offer were those devoted to the Revolutionary decade from 1789 to 1799. The *Annaliste* preoccupation with structures rather than narrative, and society rather than politics, dovetailed with the approach of the most internationally acclaimed historian of the French Revolution from the Second World War to his death in 1959, namely, Georges Lefebvre. Lefebvre's earliest work was on the peasantry in the Revolution, and he and his pupils and admirers – amongst whom we may classify Albert Soboul and British historians Richard Cobb and George Rudé – were instrumental in developing a 'history from below' perspective which also largely depreciated high politics, save only as a reflection of underlying social and economic trends. The history of prices developed from the 1930s by economic historian Ernest Labrousse buttressed this approach, by stressing the production and distribution of grain as one of the principal determinants of the pre-modern economy. The tempo of the eighteenth century was set more by the price of bread, it appeared, than by the deaths of kings or the fall of ministers. Historians of the Revolution tended to be interested in the politics of what they lumped together into the amorphous category of the 'Ancien Régime' only in so far as this helped them understand the social origins of the Revolution.

Alfred Cobban was one of the earliest and most pungent critics of Lefebvre's pre-eminence, and, very much the Cold Warrior, spiced his critique with an acerbity based on the assumption that the current Lefebvrian orthodoxy in France was essentially a Marxist confection. Lefebvre and Soboul were avowed Marxists, and the schema and conceptual categories they offered (1789 as a 'bourgeois revolution', marking a 'transition from feudalism to capitalism') linked to Marxist interpretations of the French Revolution espoused by Soviet scholars. Yet this most polemical part of Cobban's criticism perhaps overestimated the unitary nature of Marx's views on the French Revolution (which have been shown to be changeable and complex) and it certainly under-estimated how far the so-called Marxist interpretation could be accepted by scholars right across the political spectrum, in England and the United States as well as France. The emphasis on the social grounding of politics was, moreover, something which Cobban himself shared, as he showed by developing a 'social interpretation of the French Revolution' which highlighted the role of disenchanted venal office-holders (rather than a supposedly triumphant capitalistic grouping) as the true Revolutionary bourgeoisie. He and other Anglo-American scholars who followed in his wake[2] invariably saw the eighteenth-century economy as traditionalist and uncapitalistic – a view which fitted in nicely with the 'immobile his-tory' preached by third-generation *Annaliste* Emmanuel Le Roy Ladurie.

The neglect of high politics which resulted from the hegemony of social history (plus a certain disdain for diplomatic history, one of the most unreconstructed of specialisms, which the *Annalistes* never really penetrated) meant that pre-Revolutionary political history did not attract younger scholars and consequentially lacked sparkle or dyna-mism. The first major scholarly study of Louis XV (who ruled for fifty-nine years of the century) to be published since 1945, for example, was Michel Antoine's superb 1989 biography. We still, frankly, have no synoptic study worthy of the name for the ministries of either Fleury or Choiseul, who between them held sway for three decades.

Since the mid-1970s, however, there have been signs of growing interest in politics, tributary perhaps to that 'revival of narrative' in Western historiography noted by Lawrence Stone in 1979. It has been characterized by the renewal of old approaches to high politics and also by the exploration of new ways of thinking about the political – a process on which the so-called 'cultural turn' which many historians took from the late 1980s and early 1990s has had a particularly significant impact. This refocusing of political history has been evident in a number of domains:

- *Analysis of factional alignments at court and in ministerial politics.*[3]
- *A revival of interest in diplomatic history.*[4]
- *The work of 'neo-ceremonialist' historians*, analysing political and

constitutional issues raised by royal ritual and ceremony along lines mapped out by Ernst Kantorowitz.[5]

- *The 'sites of memory'* (lieux de mémoire) *approach* – to adopt the term popularized by Pierre Nora – which combines an interest in the materiality of traces of the past (e.g. Reims, coronation site of the kings of France) with analysis of their mythologization within national culture.

- *Micro-history*, often influenced by ethnographic analysis.[6]

- *The re-emergence of religious history* not simply as a site for collective *mentalités* but also as a domain of politics, especially in regard to Jansenism.[7]

- *The renewal of cultural and intellectual history*, now emphasizing more systematically linkages with political expression.[8] This development has sometimes been influenced by the 'Cambridge School' of political ideas. It has also shaded into cultural psychology and into an analysis of discourse which owes much to the influence of Michel Foucault.[9]

- *The development of the notion of 'political culture'*. François Furet and Keith Michael Baker have been the most influential exponents in this domain, which has drawn copiously on a mixture of cultural and intellectual approaches. Political culture is conceived of as the ensemble of political practices and languages within which politics was transacted.[10]

- *Analysis of the Enlightenment in terms of a 'bourgeois public sphere'*. Pioneered by German political scientist, Jürgen Habermas, the term 'public sphere' (for historians have been rather divided over whether it was 'bourgeois' or not) developed into one of the most influential organizing concepts from the late 1980s. It designates the socio-cultural institutional matrix within which a political culture oppositional to that of the monarchy developed over the eighteenth century.

This range of scholarship has completely transformed the study of eighteenth-century politics and society since Cobban wrote. The Bourbon monarchy looks different now. This also has implications for how we think about the nature, objectives and outcomes of the Revolutionary decade. If the latter point is often lost on many historians of the Revolution, this is partly because the new political history has tended to be fragmentary in its range, focus and chronological spread. Furthermore, proponents of the different approaches have sometimes been at daggers drawn with each other. In addition to the old divisions over the French Revolution between Marxists on the Left and Cobbanite and post-Cobban 'Revisionists' (usually but not invariably) on the Right, and the bifurcation between Ancien Régime specialists and Revolutionists, the 'political culturalists' and the 'factionalists', for example, have often been mutually dismissive of each other's work.

This scholarly dissension makes the challenge of writing a political history of France in the period from 1715 to 1799 all the more exciting, compelling, urgent – and risky. Such a history involves harmonizing divergent approaches. As I hope I show, analysis of political culture and state ceremonial can, for example, complement and complicate the study of faction in fruitful ways. Similarly, micro-historical perspectives – whether on Louis XIV's legs or on the reception of Beaumarchais's *Figaro* – can enrich rather than problematize the 'big picture'. Even more importantly, the new approaches offer more fruitful ways of understanding social and cultural history than old-style *histoire événementielle* ever did. The new political history is emphatically not merely an embarrassing appendage to more cogent social developments, but an approach which seeks to embrace and find new ways of analysing the political dimension of social and cultural phenomena at every level of the past.

One particularly important side-effect of the revival of political history has been a kind of flattening-out of the century as a whole. The Revolution no longer rules the eighteenth-century roost, and pre-1789 politics is no longer the country cousin of Revolutionary developments. In this transformation, non-historiographical but intensely historical events since 1989 have clearly played a part. Many of the old teleological certainties have been exploded, and in a post-Marxist, post-Revisionist, and maybe even post-modern world, we can explore the political culture of the eighteenth century as a whole and its diverse political projects with less of a sense that 1789 was inevitable, or linked past and future in unilinear fashion, or even that it necessarily formed part of one of the founding grand narratives of Western modernity.

This new, more dispassionate perspective on the eighteenth century involves us rejecting the French Revolutionaries' version of what preceded them as the infallible guide to the history of the pre-Revolutionary period. Even many of the scholars who have opened up fresh and exciting perspectives on the eighteenth century have still found it difficult to resist seeing the pre-1789 period in terms of what happened in 1789. Cobban's classic 1957 work, for example, underplayed the period down to 1750 and then adopted a structural approach so as to explain the waiting-to-happen 1789. Symbolic of this difficulty in shaking off Revolutionist blinkers has been historians' almost universal use of the term 'Ancien Régime' or (worse) 'Old Regime' to describe that political and social system. This term, dismissively adopted by the Revolutionaries themselves from 1790 to describe the 'former' (that is, *ancien*) state of affairs they wished to expunge, has become an apparently indispensable part of the historian's lexicon, extended into a range of fields (e.g. 'the socio-economic *ancien régime*'). The consequence of utilizing the concept as an analytical category has been, first, to give the pre-1789 social and political system an implicit unity – even though, as we shall argue, the vitality of the economy ran athwart of political developments in many ways, and society was surprisingly heterogeneous. Second, it has given the air of ailing decrepitude to a political system which viewed itself – and which was widely viewed within contemporary Europe – as anything but. Even after the disastrous impact of the Seven Years War, for example, most Europeans feared a plethora rather than a paucity of French state power – which was one reason why 1789 seemed so unanticipated. Third, it has encouraged the development of a very polarized, Manichean view of the pre- and post-1789 periods, adopting wholesale the vantage-point of the Revolutionaries themselves, so that historians think in terms of a 'bad' Ancien Régime and a 'good' Revolution, or vice versa.

In the present analysis of French society and government in the eighteenth century I have deliberately not used the term 'Ancien Régime' (save only from 1790, when it becomes an irrefragable fixture in the Revolutionary imaginary). I do this so as to avoid the conceptual pitfalls indicated above, but also so as to signal a wish to understand eighteenth-century politics in terms and frameworks which were relevant to contemporaries. I doubt I will be able to wean all scholars off the use of the term – but I hope to have demonstrated its dispensability as an analytical concept. In addition, I have drawn as copiously as I could on the work of political figures, writers and memorialists, whose testimony on political events more positivistic historians have often dismissed as 'inaccurate', but which nonetheless remains an excellent guide to the pullulating projects and plans of Bourbon political culture. From the point of view of the participants in political processes, for example, the vast majority of the century was spent in dialogue with the spirit of Louis XIV and his most cogent critics, such as Fénelon, rather than with Robespierre and Napoleon. Although when reading historians' accounts of the eighteenth century it is easy to forget the fact, Robespierre and Napoleon were probably simply unimaginable for most French men and women before 1789 at the very earliest. Another advantage of this approach is that it allows us to recapture a sense of that spontaneous joy – and fear – caused by the outbreak of Revolution in 1789 and its subsequent lurch into Terror. The importance of recognizing the sense of differentness and the shocking newness of politics from 1789 onwards has too often been lost to historians seeking the 'origins' of the Revolution in pre-1789 political culture, or stressing the supposed inbuilt debility of the 'old' régime.

Also implicit in my account is an assumption that the political culture of the period from 1715 to 1789 was basically unitary. As I hope to demonstrate, the principal features of the political system remained intact between the Regency and pre-Revolution, viz.

- *The rules of the game as regards faction.*
- *The ceremonial and constitutional apparatus of power.*
- *Administrative mechanisms of the state* underpinning the personal power of the monarch.
- *The monarchy's acceptance of the need to develop a welfarist agenda,* from the 1690s onwards.
- The sense of a public which was in some way separate from the state, and *the development of 'public opinion'* as a notion to which appeal might be made as potential grounds of legitimacy.
- *A close sense of the interrelatedness of domestic and foreign policy.* Prior to 1789, wars were what kings did. Since the emergence of fiscal-military states in the seventeenth century, fighting wars involved building up the economy. Historians have found it easier to separate home and international affairs than contemporaries did.
- An enduring sense of the *fragility of the dynasty.* The kings of France were probably the most attentively scrutinized political actors in eighteenth-century Europe – and the question 'what if?' was never far away from the thoughts of the scrutineers. There was always someone

waiting in the wings, and this shaped political ambitions and alignments in ways it is easy to lose sight of. The prince de Conti's sentiment
that the crown was a Bourbon heirloom rather than a personal possession of any single ruler was a family boast – but also a political
threat to his royal cousin.[11] In the early years following the death of
Louis XIV, dynastic indeterminacy was grounded in the threat of
extinction of the monarchy through demographic process. Later on,
intra-Bourbon politicking produced a similar sense of conditionality.

By emphasizing the unitary nature of pre-1789 political culture, my
account will thus downplay the importance of a mid-century fracture in
the political culture of the Bourbon monarchy, which many historians
in recent years, following the lead given by Keith Baker, have claimed
to detect. Historiographical neglect of the period between 1715 and
1750 has allowed historians to overestimate the novelty of the languages
of political opposition that were emerging after 1750. I shall argue that
much of what was occurring after mid-century was the recycling of old
discourses, which went back to 1715 or earlier. The disaster of the Seven
Years War made it obvious – even to government itself – that some
things had to change. Yet the intellectual *bricolage* and ideological
projection which ensued, whose seriousness and whose achievements I
will stress, were characterized by very extensive drawing on the historical
record and the grounding of claims in a pre-existent repertoire of
arguments.

To contend that the principal lineaments of Bourbon political culture
ran like letters through a stick of rock from Regency to Revolution
may seem to underplay the importance of the Enlightenment and the
emergent public sphere after around 1750. It is certainly not my intention
to deny the irreducible elements of ideological novelty associated with
the impact of the *Encyclopédie*, and the writings of Voltaire, Rousseau
and the other *philosophes*. My point is that they joined in conversations
which were already taking place. As the chapter on the Enlightenment
underlines, moreover, the enlargement of the social space in which
political discussion took place in the Enlightenment was if anything
even more important than the movement's ideological freight. Political
arguments had long since evoked the wider public and 'public opinion',
for example. What was new was that that public was larger and better
informed than ever before, and that dense new forms of sociability and

exchange were allowing individuals outside the customary charmed circle to develop a sense of belonging to that public. A new kind of space was emerging which allowed new political actors to be enlisted into discussions and debates.

The role of the Enlightenment as sociological boom-box for intellectual involvement in public affairs needs to be linked closely, I shall argue, to the development of commercial capitalism. The word 'commerce' in the eighteenth century denoted intellectual communication as well as economic trading. This semantic overlap highlighted the extent to which the movement of ideas and information depended on wider economic networks – but, conversely too, the extent to which trade depended on ready supplies of information and markets open to the idea of exchange. As well as being an epochal intellectual achievement, the *Encyclopédie* – to take an obvious example – was also a commodity marketed through a superb business operation to avid consumers.

The decline of *Annalisme* has opened historians' eyes to the dynamic levels of economic growth of the French economy over the eighteenth century. François Crouzet, who cogently argued against Braudel and others nearly forty years ago that the pre-Revolutionary economy was in many respects outperforming England, has been vindicated by much recent scholarship. The state's finances may have been in bad shape by 1789, but the assumption that the same was true of the economy as a whole needs firm rebuttal. It is, moreover, not simply that the positive aspects of the French performance have been revalorized, and that the patchiness and gradualness of British economic growth have been demonstrated. In addition, the grand narrative on which British superiority was projected – that of an Industrial Revolution in which the royal road to capitalist success was the British one – has been questioned, allowing a more even-handed evaluation of economies following alternative pathways towards modernity.[12]

An emphasis on the solidity of France's economic performance over the course of the eighteenth century also brings back into the picture a grouping which for long has been the missing person, so to speak, in Revisionist inquiries into the origins of the French Revolution, namely, the bourgeoisie (who were the triumphant hero of Marxist accounts). The tendency to view the Revolutionaries as industrial capitalists set in a Marxian mould has been rightly ruled out of court by Revisionist historiography – France's industrialization process was far too complex and drawn-out to expect such a group to play a prominent political role in the eighteenth century. However, I have found it useful to keep the term bourgeois to designate that non-noble group of town-dwellers who dominated France's production and exchange in an expanding economy. (The entrepreneurial role played by the nobility, though important, has been much exaggerated.) This bourgeois grouping may not always have used the term 'bourgeoisie' to describe themselves, for their identities were fixed more by status considerations than class allegiance, but they knew who they were – not least because they intermarried, formed partnerships and socialized together. They included merchants and traders as well as manufacturers, and were buttressed by large numbers of professionals – lawyers, medical men, state officials, teachers and the like. Such individuals invariably viewed themselves as having in common a distinctness on the one hand from the nobility (even though many aspired to join it) and on the other from the lower orders of town and countryside (into whose ranks they feared falling in hard times). In broad terms, it was the bourgeoisie which had the intellectual and business skills best to exploit market opportunities and the potential for advancement offered by a developing public sphere. They were also the group to experience most intensely the claims of citizenship in a political system which had always fragmented and hierarchized social identities.

Clearly, it will not do to view this heterogeneous grouping – with its large petty-bourgeois accompaniment of small traders, shopkeepers and the like – as constituting a single, self-conscious and unified bourgeois class. Indeed, as we shall see, one of the striking features of the eighteenth century as a whole would be the divisions and fragmentations within all social groupings (nobility, peasantry, town-dwellers, etc.). Conversely, however, one of the fascinations of the study of the eighteenth century is precisely that we start to detect the emergence of a kind of subterranean collective identity of the commercial and professional bourgeoisie, who developed a growing civic sense, which would make possible much of what was distinctive and novel about 1789. By then, new forms of identity were forming as the status perquisites of the Bourbon monarchy were commodified and marketed regionally and nationally. The Revolution would provide this grouping, who were widely acclaimed as the principal beneficiaries of 1789, with a new theatre for collective action – as well as scope for disagreements whose fall-out outlasted the following century.

It has been famously said that it was less the bourgeoisie which made the Revolution than the Revolution which made the bourgeoisie. Certainly, one of the most striking differences between politics in 1715 and 1799 was precisely the appearance of such individuals as legitimate actors on the political scene. However, I hope to have shown in the present study that the bourgeoisie – who were to play such an important role in the post-Revolutionary era – had begun to make itself long before 1789. In this respect, I go part of the way with Habermas, and like him (though without many whom he has influenced), I stress the importance of the economic dimension to this process prior to 1789: the bourgeoisie made itself on national and international markets as well as on the public sphere. However, I differ from Habermas in that, while deploying the term bourgeois public sphere, and highlighting its role in opening up new spaces for cultural and political exchange, I also stress the extent to which, before 1789, these new spaces were invaded by pre-existent political actors and provided a venue for existing debates. To a greater degree than Habermasian scholars have admitted, the bourgeois public sphere was colonized by the existing polity. Similarly, the public sphere's political agenda – how could the state provide domestic prosperity and tranquillity while at the same time remaining militarily successful in the international arena? – was largely inherited from the Bourbon polity. It would, of course, be foolish to underestimate the extent to which the existence and vitality of such a public sphere put pressure on the political culture of the Bourbon monarchy. However, discourses of 'othering' and 'outsiderhood', fostered by the Revolutionaries and then, indeed, by their opponents, from the storming of the Bastille onwards, conceal the extent to which the Revolution emerged from within that political culture, not from without.

The primary focus of my story will be on the political elite. I want also to give a sense, however, of how a wide and growing array of individuals from varied backgrounds were, increasingly, affected by these processes – and how many of them came to offer their own contribution to it. It was probably this baggy bourgeois grouping who contributed more than any other to France's 'greatness' – however that term is judged – over the course of the eighteenth century. Politics differed in 1799 from how it had been in 1715 partly at least because more individuals were directly involved with it. Furthermore, only by widening the focus in this way will we be able to get much purchase on one of the century's most historic questions: how the Revolution which climaxed the century not only saw new solutions being essayed to old problems, but also how it managed to spawn a sense that the political values inaugurated in 1789 have been worth living by and dying for. That sense has subsisted both outside and inside France for more than two centuries now. And we as historians stand in awe of it.

NOTES

1 In the light of this intention, I have not given full bibliographical details of the works to which I allude. The works referred to will be found in the bibliography; see below, pp. 613–14.

2 e.g. G. V. Taylor, C. B. A. Behrens and William Doyle.

3 The doyen of the approach is Michel Antoine, though see too British scholars Peter Campbell, Munro Price, John Hardman, John Rogister and Julian Swann.

4 See e.g. Lucien Bély, Jeremy Black, T. C. W. Blanning.

5 See e.g. Ralph Giesey, Sarah Hanley, Richard Jackson, and, on the French side, Alain Boureau, Jean-Marie Apostolides and Louis Marin.

6 See e.g. Dale Van Kley on Damiens's assassination attempt, Robert Darnton on the 'Great Cat Massacre' and Arlette Farge and Jacques Revel on the 'vanishing children of Paris'.

7 See esp. the work of Dale Van Kley and Catherine Maire.

8 See e.g. for the book trade, Roger Chartier, Robert Darnton, Raymond Birn, Carla Hesse; for the press, Jeremy Popkin and the group around Jean Sgard, Pierre Rétat and Gilles Feyel; for academies, Daniel Roche; and for freemasonry Ran Halévi and Margaret Jacob.

9 Michael Sonenscher is the main proponent of the 'Cambridge School' who works on France. For cultural psychology, see esp. Lynn Hunt.

10. Of the enormous amount of work written under this banner see esp. and e.g. David Bell, Dena Goodman, Sarah Maza, Tom Kaiser.

11 See pp. 239–40.

12 See e.g. Patrick O'Brien, Philip Hoffman, Giles Postel-Vinay, E. N. White, Hilton Root.

Maps

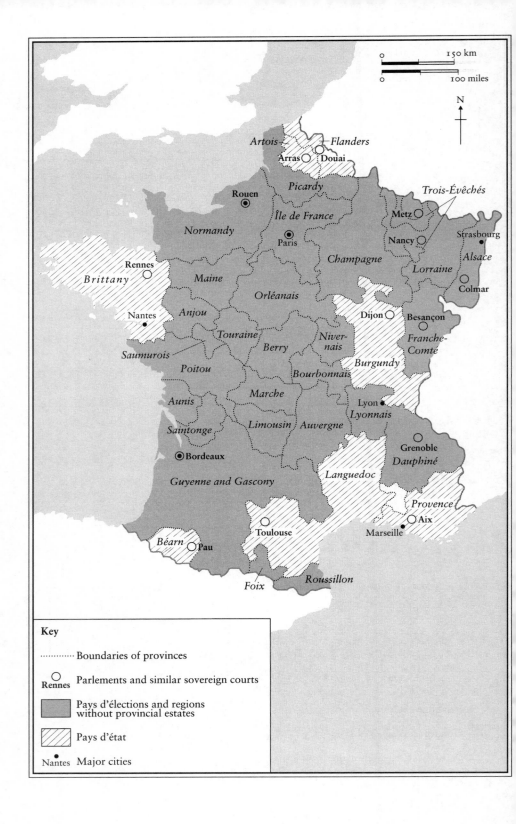

Artois — Flanders
Arras ○ Douai
Picardy
Rouen ⊙
Île de France
Paris ⊙
Normandy
Trois-Évêchés
Metz ○
Nancy ○
Strasbourg •
Champagne
Lorraine
Alsace
Colmar ○
Rennes ○
Brittany
Maine
Orléanais
Dijon ○
Besançon ○
Franche-Comté
Nantes •
Anjou
Touraine
Berry
Niver-nais
Burgundy
Saumurois
Poitou
Bourbonnais
Aunis
Marche
Lyon •
Lyonnais
Saintonge
Limousin
Auvergne
Bordeaux ⊙
Grenoble ○
Dauphiné
Guyenne and Gascony
Languedoc
Provence
Aix ○
Marseille •
Béarn ○ Pau
Toulouse ○
Foix
Roussillon

150 km
100 miles
N

Key

········· Boundaries of provinces

○ Rennes Parlements and similar sovereign courts

▓ Pays d'élections and regions without provincial estates

▨ Pays d'état

• Nantes Major cities

0 | 150 km
0 | 100 miles

N

Pas-
de-Calais
Nord
Somme
Seine-Inf.
Aisne
Ardennes
Oise
Moselle
Manche | Calvados
Eure
Seine
(Paris)
Seine-
et-Marne
Marne
Meuse
Meurthe
Bas-
Rhin
Finistère
Orne
Seine-
et-Oise
Vosges
Côtes-du-Nord
Mayenne
Eure-et-
Loir
Aube
Haute-
Marne
Haut-
Rhin
Ille-
et-Vilaine
Sarthe
Loiret
Haute-
Saône
Morbihan
Loiret
Yonne
Loire-Inf.
Maine-
et-Loire
Indre-
et-Loire
Loir-
et-Cher
Côte-d'Or
Doubs
Deux-
Sèvres
Cher
Nièvre
Vendée
Indre
Saône-et-Loire
Jura
Vienne
Allier
Charente
Inf.
Creuse
Rhône
1793
Ain
Haute-
Vienne
Puy-de-
Dôme
Loire
1793
Charente
Isère
Corrèze
Haute-
Loire
Dordogne
Cantal
Ardèche
Drôme
Hautes-
Alpes
Gironde
Lozère
Lot-et-
Garonne
Lot
Aveyron
Gard
Vaucluse
1791
Basses-Alpes
Landes
Tarn
Gers
Hte-
Garonne
Hérault
Bouches-
du-Rhône
Var
Basses-
Pyrénées
Hautes-
Pyrénées
Ariège
Aude
Pyrénées
Orientales

Corsica

Golo
1793

Liamone
1793

Key

··········· Departmental frontier 1790

▓ Frontier areas annexed 1790–99

Vaucluse
1791 Departments established after 1790 [date]

I

France in 1715: The King's Leg
and the Choreography of Power

A) THE MYTHIC PRESENT
OF THE SUN KING

The prognosis was not good. The doctors held out little hope. The patient had shown symptoms of malaise early in August 1715. By the middle of the month, gangrene had presented itself on his left leg. Over a long life – at a time in which average life-expectancy was less than thirty years – the 76-year-old had shown a doughty durability. He had survived smallpox in childhood, negotiated some youthful gonorrhoeas, learnt from adolescence to live with occasional fainting fits and in 1686 endured an operation for a life-threatening anal fistula. In the same decade, he had lost his teeth (and thanks to his surgeons part of his jawbone and palate too), and been stricken with gout. He then settled down for the remainder of his days to a regular round of recurrent fevers, rheumatism, skin ailments plus intense pain from kidney stones. The patient's physicians had always allowed him to indulge a gargantuan appetite, countering his intake and regulating his embonpoint by a heroic diet of purges and enemas. In his last years, they advised him never to put pressure on his distended belly by attempting to cross his legs while seated. Whether they should be congratulated on keeping such a plucky valetudinarian alive for so long or else excoriated for adding to his agonies seems very moot. At all events, it was a worrying symptom of this latest – and, it was to prove, last – malady that the patient was unable to eat his considerable fill. Flesh seemed to fall from his bones, as he shrank to a skeleton before his physicians' eyes. Already, the disease had started its fateful way up towards the patient's torso, turning his leg gangrenous, stinking and as black as coal.

This, moreover, was no ordinary leg. It belonged to a king – and no ordinary king.

Louis XIV, king of France and Navarre – 'the Sun King' (*le Roi Soleil*), 'Louis the Great' (*Louis le Grand*), 'The God-Given' (*le Dieu-donné*), 'Most Christian King' (*Rex Christianissimus*), 'absolute king' (*roi absolu*), the longest-serving and greatest European monarch of his generation, born in 1638, king since 1643 – had always attached importance to his lower extremities. A radiant portrait of him in 1653 dressed for a court ballet as Apollo, god of the sun, had shown him in a costume 'covered with a rich golden embroidery and many rubies. The rays that appeared round his head were of diamonds and the crown was of rubies and pearls, topped with numerous pink and white feathers'.[1] This allegorical image, which captured the exuberant athleticism, pleasure-seeking, and blithe self-confidence which attached to the king's renown in his early years, also showcased a shapely pair of legs depicted in ballet pose. Nearly half a century later, around 1700, his legs encased in the finest white silk, Louis had adopted the same dainty stance – left leg forward, toes pointed, foot arched – in Rigaud's justly famous swagger portrait of the monarch in full ceremonial regalia. The joyful insouciance of the earlier image had by then vanished: in 1700 Louis may have been at the height of his powers, but he was also in the midst of wars which would drain the resources of his country, place colossal strains upon the French state, and signally deflate his popularity. Age and anxiety were taking their toll – sunken cheeks in the Rigaud portrait revealed a monarch who had lost his teeth, while a towering wig hid well-advanced hair-loss. But the legs had stayed gloriously intact, the posture was unbowed, and the sceptre sported in the right hand evoked both the field-marshal's and the ballet-master's baton.

In 1715, with the tissue of those pristine legs, prized emblem of Louis's royal self-image, rotting and turning black, as the doctors gravely deliberated, Louis was dying – but dying a death which, political ballet-master to the last, he endeavoured to choreograph. The stage for this masterly *mise-en-scène* was one largely designed by himself and to his own measure: Versailles, some ten miles out of Paris, which he and his court had inhabited from 1683, and which he had transformed into the most magnificently appointed palace in European memory. Here, in a rigorously maintained and punctiliously ordered court etiquette, the Sun King had developed a ceremonial language of kingship centred on his own radiantly pivotal figure. The very architecture of this solar temple was profoundly and deliberately 'Louisocentric': the royal chamber lay at the heart of the palace and from it radiated the sightlines which defined the geometry of the site. Power defined itself as visibility, physical closeness to the monarch. No more crushing a statement of political nullitude could exist than Louis's famous comment about a courtier: 'He is a man I never see.' The stern symmetries of the classical gardens, which like the palace itself were extensively furnished with splendidly wrought images of him and of his elective symbols (notably the sun and sun-god Apollo), displayed even Nature seemingly brought to order by *Louis le Grand*. Spatially disposed around its sun-like centre, the Versailles court ran on Louis-time. The scheduling of court ritual was geared with minute exactitude to the daily routines of the monarch, from the 'rising' of the Sun King, in the elaborate ceremonies of the *lever*, to his 'setting' (the *coucher*). The royal chronometer was so precise, estimated the duc de Saint-Simon, the greatest memorialist of the reign, that an individual 300 leagues distant from Versailles could know exactly what the king was doing at any moment of the day merely by consulting a watch.[2] All royal acts at Versailles were played out with a public of courtiers dancing attendance. Even a visit to the royal privy formed part of the pageant, a public, humbly observed act. Fortunes were made – and unmade – in the simple act by which Louis determined who was to have the honour of being permitted to hold the candle in the *coucher*. Each of his meals was a watched display of monarchical mastication, and each royal glance was scrutinized for intent.

The ceremonial publicity of every part of the monarch's life was predicated on the assumption that the French state was embodied in his physical frame. Although it seems that Louis XIV never uttered the phrase '*L'État, c'est moi*', the sentiment was certainly his. 'The nation', he opined, 'does not form a body in France; it resides wholly within the person of the king.' 'King and kingdom', concurred d'Aguesseau, wisest of wise eighteenth-century legists, 'form a single entity.'[3] Bishop Bossuet of Meaux, Louis's most loquacious panegyrist, noted of the monarch that 'the whole of the state resides within him' ('*tout l'état est en lui*'). 'You are gods,' he enthused, of monarchs in general in 1662, claiming biblical endorsement.[4] Versailles' decor, which made a cult of the king's body, seemed to take him at his word. It depicted Louis in the character of a pagan god (Apollo, Jupiter, Mars, the God-Emperor Augustus and so on). The frescoes in the great Hall of Mirrors designed by First Painter Charles Lebrun were even more exaggerated, for they depicted Louis as the equal companion of those deities. This style inaugurated a kind of mythic present,[5] a never-neverland tense and an accompanying artistic idiom in which an ever-heroic (if anachronistically bewigged) Louis was portrayed rubbing shoulders with pagan gods, nymphs and demons.

The collective hymn of praise waxed most eulogistic over Louis's attainment of *la gloire* – the military glory which the king had achieved in his long reign, adding to French territories, strengthening its frontiers, and building up a colonial empire which made France a global power. Yet if military glory held pride of place in his '*Grand Siècle*', no act of the Sun King was too insignificant for recording – and for diffusing, since the act of commemoration was meaningless if it was not propagated and popularized, just as royal spectacle meant nothing if it was not widely observed. Versailles itself, as the epicentre of Louis's mythic universe, advertised the cult of the royal body: engravings and descriptions of its architecture were widely disseminated; Louis himself wrote a guide-book to the palace gardens;[6] and court protocols and etiquette became sufficiently well known to be slavishly copied by almost every European monarch in Louis XIV's wake who wished to emulate his prestige. The image of the ruler, in the ritual setting of Versailles, was endlessly replicated and reproduced in every conscriptible medium. There were at least 300 portraits or statues produced of Louis XIV during his reign, roughly the same number of commemorative medallions, and nearly twice that number of engravings. From the 1680s, there was a movement to have an equestrian statue of the ruler placed in the central square of every major city, as well as proposals to erect splendid triumphal arches, so as to make the ruler visible to the provincial masses. The king's pictorial pageant included not only military conquests but also hospital openings, famous diplomatic coups, acts of scientific patronage, inaugurations of monuments, the births of princes, religious rejoicings. Many of these actions of *éclat*, and the courtly ceremonials which marked them, further reverberated in public consciousness through the ceremonial celebration of Te Deums, religious rejoicings which were periodically commanded in every parish in the land to give collective thanks for the ruler's triumphs.

Louis's distinctive cultural policies were grounded in a shrewd estimation of effective styles of rule. 'People who think that [courtly rituals] are merely ceremonial affairs are seriously mistaken,' he wrote in the memoirs he destined for his son. 'The people over whom we reign are unable to penetrate to the core of things and base their judgements on what they see on the surface, and it is precisely on rank and precedence that they measure their respect and obedience.'[7] Louis therefore took pains to enlist the support of artists and writers in fashioning his cult. State-sponsored academies were established in almost every domain of intellectual and artistic activity. To the Académie française, established by Richelieu in 1635, with its brief to establish the purity of the French language, were added Academies for Painting and Sculpture (formally endorsed in 1663), and for Inscriptions and Belles-Lettres (1663), along with the Academies of Sciences (1665), Music (1669) and Architecture (1671). These bodies devoted part of their energies to acting as governmental consultants and aides – the Painting Academy under Lebrun, for example, provided the teams and programmes for the decoration of Versailles. Besides enlisting knowledge in the interests of the state's needs, the academies also acted as normative institutions, setting standards of taste in line with both the advance of knowledge and the cult of monarchy. They also functioned as channels for state patronage. For those working in the fine arts, commissions were always in the offing, as poet-propagandist Jean Chapelain noted, for 'pyramids, columns, equestrian statues, colossuses, triumphal arches, marble and bronze busts, bas-reliefs . . . [and] our rich tapestry works, our fresco-paintings and our engravings'.[8] For writers, an endlessly hyperbolic round of poems, plays, book dedications, newspapers, periodicals and scholarly works of every kind addressed, apostrophized, described, praised, panegyrized, lauded, flattered and glorified the ruler – and contributed to their authors' material wellbeing. In the new 'golden age' saluted by dramatist Pierre Corneille,[9] the Sun King was meant to dazzle – and the ascribed role of the artistic and intellectual elite on whom he showered his favours was to bring his light into every corner of his realm.

Even as he lay dying, the protocol machinery which Louis had carefully crafted to allegorize the mythic present of his reign continued, as though the tempo set by the royal ballet-master was still beating metronomically in the ears of all. The ceremony of the royal *lever* proceeded like clockwork, with the procession stopping only at the doors of the king's death chamber, while the King's Councils still met too in order to regulate business of state, with a chair left vacant at the head of the table for the absent monarch. What would happen to the state which Louis had sought to embody in his own frame, once the Sun King went into eclipse? 'Did you imagine I was immortal?' he inquired of the sobbing attendance on his deathbed.[10] And then again, as though belatedly and regretfully acknowledging his hubris in seeking to maintain his own mythic present: 'I am going away, but the state will remain.'[11]

B) THE BOURBON POLITY

Despite the brilliant inventiveness and cultural éclat surrounding Louis XIV's Versailles, the French state was far more than the king's personal creation. It constituted a palimpsest of power rituals, traditions, conventions and practices, some of which were thought to date from the times of Clovis, the leader of the Merovingian Franks, crowned king of 'Francia' at Reims in 496 as heir to the Roman imperium. Louis XIV's words contrasting his own mortality with the destiny of the state, for example, formed a kind of latterday homage to an extremely ancient constitutional adage, namely, that the king never died. He possessed two bodies, one physical, the other ceremonial, and while the former decayed and passed away, the latter was timeless and untouchable by human mortality. In the Middle Ages, it had been the practice to express this doctrine of the king's two bodies by creating a wax effigy of the defunct ruler around which the ceremonial business of state continued to be conducted, whilst his successor was hidden away, only to be allowed to partake in the full exercise of regal authority after the burial of the dead king and the destruction of the effigy. This practice had fallen into disuse after the Renaissance, partly because it made the monarchy fragile at the time of changeover of power. More crucially, the temporal schema implicit in the doctrine of the king's two bodies also clashed with Louis XIV's mythic present. In the Sun King's body politics, there was only one body, his own, which the crown's ceremonial regime and hyperbolic immortalizing rhetoric represented as beyond the reach of biological time.

Louis was a Bourbon, the third branch of the Capetian dynasty founded by Hugues Capet in 987 on the demise of Frankish power, and continued by the Valois branch from 1328 through to 1589, when the first Bourbon, Henry of Navarre, succeeded as Henry IV. The latter dynastic shift occurred at the height of the Wars of Religion which had plagued France since 1560, and it was to Henry's lasting credit that he brought these civil wars to an end, notably through allowing the Protestant (or Huguenot) minority within France rights of toleration by the Edict of Nantes of 1598. Henry and his successors – Louis XIII from 1610 to 1643, then Louis XIV – drew on pre-existent political traditions, but gave them a distinctive Bourbon twist. The Bourbon polity prided itself on ensuring tranquillity at home while fighting with vigour and determination for state expansion abroad. This entailed matching the armed forces of France's international competitors, notably the Habsburg dynasty, one of whose members sat on the throne of Spain, while another combined Austrian rule with headship of the sprawling Holy Roman Empire which covered Germanic and central European territory.

This dual task of internal pacification and external aggression required a greater concentration of monarchical authority than the Valois had been able to command, and the Bourbons were associated from the start with energetic attempts to achieve these ends through maximizing royal authority in the name of 'absolute' power. Theories of absolute monarchy had roots in Antiquity, but had again come to the fore during the Wars of Religion. Political theorists such as the humanist and legist Jean Bodin boldly asserted the 'absolute' claims of the ruler as a way out of the paroxysms of political and confessional strife which were threatening to engulf the kingdom. Bodin deemed the king of France's power as absolute in the sense that the ruler was 'absolved' by divine sanction from legally binding liens and restrictions. That 'sovereign' power, absolutism's ideologists argued, could not legitimately be challenged, let alone shared, by any human agency. *Raison d'état* ('state reason') required that all bodies and individuals within France should bow the knee, while even international powers such as the pope and the Holy Roman Emperor should acknowledge the superiority of the ruler's political rights on French territory. Rulers by divine right, French monarchs were, as Henry IV noted, 'sovereigns' who 'render account of their rule to God alone'.[12]

Part of the absolutist aura with which the Bourbons refurbished monarchical power was thus a dynastic claim to quasi-divinity. Again, this was not sheer invention on Louis XIV's part, but rested on a doctrine of divine right whose origins were lost in the mists of the Middle

Ages and which were ceremonially rooted in the coronations of French monarchs. The ancient coronation liturgy held close similarities to the consecration of a bishop: the king thereby became 'bishop from without' (*évêque du dehors*), and head of the French (or Gallican) church. As such, under terms agreed with the pope in the Concordat of Bologna in 1516 and then significantly enlarged by the Four Gallican Articles of 1682, he enjoyed wide powers over ecclesiastical affairs, including a virtual monopoly of appointment to major posts and benefices within the church. In addition, as a sign of God's mission for the 'Most Christian King', he also received the grace of healing. Monarchs were anointed with the chrism, or consecrated oil, held to have been brought down from heaven by a dove at the conversion and baptism in 496 of Clovis, the Frankish king. Miraculously moist, the chrism was kept in an ampulla in Reims cathedral where the coronations of the kings of France were held. The sacred substance allegedly accorded the monarch thaumaturgic powers over the disease of scrofula, or the 'King's Evil'. The 'Royal Touch', accompanied by the words, 'God cures you, the King touches you' (*'Dieu te guérit, le Roi te touche'*), sufficed to trigger the healing miracle.[13] The presence of pathetic files of the scrofular waiting on the royal presence thus completed the coronation rituals – Louis XIV, for example, had nearly 3,000 such petitioners for the 'Royal Touch' following his coronation in 1654 – and it thereafter passed into the king's ceremonial repertory, to be systematically practised and its representation widely propagated.

The range of prerogatives which the absolute, divine-right rulers of France laid claim to enjoy, untrammelled by the objections of their subjects and unimpeded by any other temporal power, included the right to make law (only the king passed general ordinances, and arbitrated matters of war and peace); to hold a monopoly of armed force; and to stand at the head of the administration of justice – a headship symbolized by the power to issue pardons over and above judicial process and to imprison at will, through sealed orders, known as *lettres de cachet*. These prerogatives were not, however, to be exercised arbitrarily. Bodin stated for example that the king's 'absolute' authority was subject to the laws of God and nature.[14] In the latter were grouped what Bodin referred to as 'conventions' and which from the late sixteenth century were increasingly referred to as 'fundamental maxims' or 'fundamental laws'. There was no exhaustive or agreed list of these. Some were technical points about the succession: that the crown was hereditary, for example, accorded by primogeniture, and worn by a male and a Catholic. At the coronation, kings swore oaths which stressed the fundamental laws, including the upholding of justice, the maintenance of the church in its rights, the banishment of heresy and so on.

In the absence of the kind of written constitution which was to be introduced by the French Revolutionaries later in the century (before becoming the rule for all modern states), other fundamental laws were less legislative fiats than customs, practices and procedures, hallowed by time and embedded in ritual. Their flexibility and informality meant that they could be subject to varying interpretation. Indeed, political life consisted in the ways those practices and rituals were conducted and interpreted, and the claims which they appeared to justify and legitimate.

Though sovereignty was widely represented as being located indivisibly within the physical frame of the ruler, power was in practice very widely diffused within society. The idea of centralized and personalized legislative sovereignty which lay at the heart of the Bourbon polity was balanced by complicated patterns of collective participation. Since the Middle Ages, France had developed into a 'society of orders', that is, an environment in which a complex set of institutions and corporative bodies enjoyed distinct legal status. The state was sometimes figured as a body with the king as head and the other elements of the kingdom functionally disposed within the organism. At other times, it was represented as a kind of Great Chain of Being, a complex, vertically disposed hierarchy of bodies (*corps*) from high to low, each enjoying rights enshrined in 'private laws' (*leges privatae*, or 'privileges') endorsed by the crown. These *corps* might take the form of an 'order' or 'estate': society was traditionally divided into the clergy, the nobility and the 'Third Estate' (i.e. those not encompassed in the first two orders), each of which had its own privileges. Other *corps* included territorial units (provinces, towns, parishes), professional groupings (colleges of physicians or bodies of attorneys, for example), trade collectivities (such as guilds) or institutions (universities, hospitals, vestries, cathedral chapters, etc.). All of these had varying powers of self-regulation under the overall surveillance of the monarch. The clergy's affairs, for example, were regulated by its Assembly of the Clergy, meeting quinquennially to deal with matters of common concern. Cities had their municipal assemblies, while many provinces – especially relative latecomers to the French state such as Brittany, incorporated from 1491 – retained provincial assemblies (or 'estates') of the three orders.

So thoroughgoing was the infiltration of collective rights within the polity that the bulk of the king's own bureaucracy was formed of corporative bodies enjoying their own privileges. Thus there were, for example, *bureaux* of state financial officials within a particular tax constituency (or *généralité*), while bodies of magistrates were similarly viewed as constituting *corps*. Significantly, members' rights included the possibility of treating these posts as their own private property. Under the system of venality of office which had developed in the sixteenth and seventeenth centuries, state servants purchased their posts, and in return for a small annual payment (the *droit annuel* or *paulette*) could sell them or bequeath them to their heirs like so many chunks of real estate. This secured the investment for the holder, but the system had political advantages for the state too: it ensured regular cash infusions into the royal treasury, while the emergence of a state patronage network reduced the scope for noble grandees developing private clienteles.

If with one hand the Bourbon monarchy reinforced and endorsed the corporatist mould of the 'society of orders', with the other it sought to strengthen its own powers within the corporatist realm. This entailed outright war against a diffuse tradition of political contractualism which in the past had periodically surfaced as counterweight to notions of centralized authority and indivisible sovereignty. A spasmodically convoked national parliament, the Estates General, comprising elected members of the clergy, nobility and Third Estate, had been in existence since 1302, a relic of the feudal duty of offering counsel to one's lord. Another representative body, the Assembly of Notables, a grouping handpicked by the monarch and drawn from all three orders, had also occasionally been convoked at times of national emergency. The Parlement of Paris was another body which had often claimed a representative function in the past. There were around a dozen *parlements* plus around the same number of other such 'sovereign courts' (high courts of law) in existence,[15] but none of the others had the importance of the Paris body, whose jurisdictional area covered half of the country. The Parisian *parlementaires* were individually amongst the most prestigious and wealthiest of the so-called 'Robe' nobility (*noblesse de robe*) who derived their status from royal service (in contrast to the 'Sword' nobility [*noblesse d'épée*] who had allegedly won their status by military prowess). Offices in the Parlement were among the most expensive venal offices on the market, and the institution's primacy and representative claims were augmented by the fact that the dukes and peers of the realm could sit within it for important affairs of state – a practice which they followed particularly in the ceremonial assemblies known as *lits de justice* ('beds of justice') which the king convoked so as to make known his wishes on matters of state. The sovereign courts also customarily enjoyed the right of formally registering royal edicts. They were empowered to make remonstrances (*remontrances*) if they felt that royal legislation contravened the polity's fundamental laws.

Attenuated forms of contractualism surfaced in ceremonial forms in various areas of public life. At his coronation, the ruler was customarily, after crowning, brought before the people crowded into the cathedral at Reims to seek their assent to their new monarch. A similar contractual note was struck in the *entrée* rituals accompanying the ceremonial entrance of the monarch within the walls of the kingdom's cities. These pageant-like occasions were conventionally the moment at which local rights and privileges were given royal endorsement, and when the city fathers could petition at the foot of the throne. Ceremonial and rituals of less august kinds accompanied the ruler's dealings with the whole myriad of self-regulating corporative bodies of every sort (provinces, towns, guilds, professional groupings, etc.) which claimed to represent the interests of their members. In the provinces, this was often done through the local provincial governor, the king's personal nominee selected from the oldest Sword nobility.

The idea that the polity was constituted to allow the representation of interests by elected or nominated delegates thus boasted a genealogy which long pre-dated the advent of the Bourbon line. The latter waged unremitting war against it, from Henry IV's reign, through the administrations of Louis XIII's principal ministers, Cardinals Richelieu and Mazarin, from the 1620s to the 1660s, and then, even more spectacularly from 1661, at the hands of the Sun King. For the latter, contractualism recalled the wilder excesses of the Wars of Religion. He also believed that it had served as justification for treasonous revolt in the civil wars of the Fronde (1648–53), in which magistrates of the Paris Parlement joined with discontented princes to resist the sovereignty of the Regency Council headed by Mazarin. In one of the most infamous of the scurrilous anti-governmental pamphlets known as *mazarinades* which appeared at this time, the *Contrat de mariage*, the constitution was figured not as a marriage between king and nation but as a union between Parlement and the people of Paris – a thought far too radical for the *parlementaires* themselves to avow.[16]

The political culture developed by the Sun King firmly rejected such long-established and widely dispersed notions of representation. Instead, it stressed, as we have seen, the endless enactment of monarchical spectacle, through a cyclical and spectacular 're-presentation' of the king's sovereign body for the admiration of all who glimpsed it. Highly significant in this symbolic personalization of authority was Louis's decision, following the death of Mazarin in 1661, not to appoint a successor but rather to rule as his own first minister. Henceforth, Louis sought his own counsel. His financial powers were to be untrammelled by corporative bodies: he alone had oversight and executive powers over all state expenses. He followed the examples of Richelieu and Mazarin in building up a central bureaucracy of ministers and secretaries of state rather than depending on the contractual processes of consultation and representation. In the provinces, too, he looked to a bureaucratically trained group of crown appointees, the Intendants, to counterbalance the centrifugal interests of provincial governors, venal officers and subaltern corporative groupings.

Representative claims by the cells of the corporative 'society of orders' were now brutally rejected. The Estates General was not convoked after 1614, the Assembly of Notables after 1626. Provincial estates either had their wings clipped or were simply not called: the estates of Dauphiné and Normandy were suppressed in 1626 and 1666, for example, while those of Alsace met for the last time in 1683 and those of Franche-Comté in 1704. Municipal assemblies were brought much more closely under governmental tutelage. Urban *entrée* ceremonies went into vertiginous decline. Louis XIV was markedly less itinerant than his Renaissance forebears. The most notorious example of an *entrée* was his visit to Marseille in 1660 following the city's revolt against his local representatives. The king ordered the city's principal gate – over which was inscribed the word '*Libertas*' – to be demolished and he entered the city through the resulting breach in the city's defences. Rather than confirm and extend local privileges, as was customary in such *entrée* ceremonies, Louis ordered a massive state fortress to be built here as a reminder of a new scale of priorities. While municipal freedoms were eroded by royal military power, the representative claims of the Paris Parlement were handled pretty brutally too, especially after that body flirted with outright civil disobedience during the Fronde. Significantly, after 1665 *parlements* were forbidden from calling themselves 'sovereign courts' (they became 'higher courts' (*cours supérieures*)): there was henceforth only one person in the realm with a claim on sovereignty. From 1673, the right of *parlements* to remonstrate was reduced in significance (they could issue their remonstrances only *after* registering a law). The *lit de justice* became obsolete too – the laudatory Te Deum, celebrated in the physical absence of the ruler, increasingly took its place.

Symptomatic of the anti-contractualist shift in the political culture was the fact that Louis XIV's coronation in 1654 had broken with ceremonial tradition in not allowing the common people a place in the nave of Reims cathedral. Though the doors of the cathedral were opened towards the end of the ceremony to allow the people in, this was only for them humbly to genuflect to the new sovereign – there was now no question of their being asked for their assent or being present throughout the ceremony. Breaking with tradition too, Louis refused to agree to a coronation *entrée* into Paris, whose Frondeur sensibilities he still distrusted. The ceremonial culture of Louis XIV was designed to keep the people – as indeed everyone else – firmly in their place, beneath the divinely ordained and personalized sovereignty of their absolute monarch.

c) THE KING'S NOBILITY

Louis XIV had thus shifted the workings of the French state in directions which extended royal power at the expense of the practices and the very principle of collective representation. Yet despite the flexing of absolutist muscles, Louis XIV's assault on shared forms of representation was emphatically not an attack on the corporative nature of the polity as a whole. Nor could it be. Louis took absolutist propaganda less at face value than his propagandists (and many of his historians). His relations with his nobility demonstrate a keen awareness that, although corporatism and privilege inhibited his power and made his political tasks more difficult, they also constituted the bedrock of the Bourbon polity.

The demise of contractual theory and the decline in autonomous notions of representation posed a major threat to the high nobility, which traditionally claimed to represent the best interests of the state, the *sanior pars* of the political community. High nobles regarded themselves as the monarch's natural counsellors; they, along with the provincial noblemen who were often their clients, dominated the proceedings of estates, both national and provincial; and they vaunted their right – even their solemn duty – to rebel if they felt that the constitution was not being properly upheld, and if the monarch seemed the prisoner of 'evil counsellors'. In the early seventeenth century, noble grandees had been heavily involved in popular turbulence protesting against the policies of state centralization and higher taxes introduced by Cardinal Richelieu. The nobility's objectives, up to and including the Fronde, were to resist state centralization, to oppose the system of ministers and Intendants, and to seek also to protect and further their interests by attaining high posts as of right in the Royal Council. The crown's wish to keep the papacy out of French politics also produced something of a religious backlash, and noble opposition to the imperatives of *raison d'état* often had a strong *dévot* ('devout', 'godly') coloration, and urged the need for a strong Catholic orientation to state policy.

Louis XIV's decision in 1661 to rule without a principal minister and in his own name alone was of crucial importance in changing not only the character of politics but also the grounds for opposition. It placed the royal person unequivocally at the apex of the governmental pyramid, making the rhetorical ploy of 'rescuing' the ruler from 'evil' ministers difficult to sustain. Princes of the Blood Royal (that is, direct male descendants of Henri IV), mighty generals and leading dukes and peers who had sat almost *ex officio* on the royal council were now ejected, as the king sought advice instead from career bureaucrats, drawn from less prestigious sectors of the nobility. The key officials were the secretaries of state, who divided government into functional ministries of War, Navy, Royal Household (*Maison du Roi*) and Foreign Affairs. Prior to the mid-seventeenth century, the most important royal official had been the Chancellor, who headed the judiciary. Sign of the times, he no longer sat on the highest councils as of right, and ceded ministerial pre-eminence to the so-called Controller-General of Finances (*Contrôleur-général des Finances*), effectively a fifth secretary of state, who combined stewardship of royal finances with overall policing functions.

The high nobility had thus to accept the destruction of their role in state policy-making, and to learn to live with the growth of the state bureaucracy, in the centre and the peripheries. In this work of adaptation, the Versailles court played a key role. The highest nobility were pressurized into being semi-permanently present at court and participating in the ceremonial round. The cascade of favours, pensions, titles and gratifications which the king rained down on dutiful courtiers made it impossible for any aristocrat wishing to live up to the level of his status *not* to be present, hand outstretched. This domestication of high nobles increasingly cut them off from making a military threat out of their provincial clientage networks – a process in which the concomitant growth of the ruler's standing army and the levelling of château fortifications also played a part. In any case, the worldly and (down to the 1680s at least) entertaining culture of the court had a growing appeal for nobles who seemed eager to abandon the standard of revolt for the mundane civilities of the court round. At the close of the Fronde the rebellious prince de Condé – '*Le Grand Condé*', Prince of the Blood and the most brilliant general of his generation – had joined the Spanish side in their war against France. Yet he was subsequently pardoned these earlier treasons, and ended his life a placable courtier at Versailles, paddling contentedly around the lakes of the royal gardens in a rowing-boat. The bellicose, provincially rooted warrior noble of yore was becoming the polished and urbane courtier loyally respecting the whims of his monarch.

Louis XIV's bringing the high nobility to heel did not, however, entail removing them from the ambit of power, nor did it involve an all-out assault on their collective privileges. An attack on privilege would have been tantamount to an assault on property, which rulers swore to uphold in their coronation oath. Such a step would have been viewed as withdrawing the life-blood of the body politic, and exhibiting a form of 'tyrannical' behaviour that no king, however putatively 'absolute', could contemplate. Louis XIV felt at home among his courtiers ('I have lived amongst the people of my court,' he remarked in his final illness. 'I wish to die among them')[17] – and those courtiers were nobles. He prided himself on being 'premier gentleman' of the kingdom, as fully integrated as they into the feudal nexus, under which they owed him homage. He regarded military service, the vocation of the old nobility, as the most elevated form of service, and the basis of his quest for *la gloire*. Far from marking a period of noble decline, Louis's reign offered the nobility a fresh range of challenges and opportunities – and the basis for a new partnership at the helm of the ship of state.

Nobles at all levels proved eager to accept the opportunities for royal service offered them in return for the loss of their political autonomy. The fact that the most senior figures in government were taken less exclusively than before from the highest aristocracy should not obscure the fact that the pool of trained officers and administrative personnel of which government was composed was solidly noble. Crusty old dukes like Saint-Simon who bitterly indicted Louis XIV for following the example of his predecessor and spurning the high aristocracy in favour of a governing class of 'people of lowly extraction' and 'social nothings'[18] were well wide of the mark: eminent royal servants – in the army, the church, the royal Household, the diplomatic corps – were nobles almost to a man. Among the grandees, energies which earlier had been used in a variety of ways at local level were now more focused on jockeying for place and power in the minefield of rank and precedence that was Versailles. High court-based nobles acted as conduits for requests for places and pensions from middling and lesser 'unpresented' nobles in the provinces. Many of these had resented royal inquiries established after 1668 to scrutinize the credentials of provincial nobles. Yet although this largely fiscal measure (loss of noble status entailed tax eligibility) brought about some thinning in numbers, it also strengthened their sense of difference from the rest of the population, and contributed towards a growing corporative consciousness amongst the nobility.

Significantly, the imposition of royal tax policies in the provinces often took the form of a financial deal with the provincial nobility. Analysing royal fiscal policy in Languedoc, historian William Beik has estimated that one-third of state taxes raised in the province went into the pockets of the local elite. Moreover, if the king's theoretical share was roughly two-thirds, he only actually took out of the province roughly half the tax yield, the remainder remaining in the province and being widely disbursed to the advantage of the local elite.[19] Languedocian nobles also demonstrated great energy in seizing the chance to get engaged in local business enterprises enjoying royal support. It was largely local capital, for example, which financed the building of the Canal des Deux-Mers linking the Garonne river basin with the Mediterranean from the 1680s.

Critical in bringing about this new sense of collaboration between the state and its nobility were the provincial Intendants. Hyper-loyal observers and managers enjoying the unqualified support of the king, they finessed the extension of royal prerogatives rather than imposed them willy-nilly on recalcitrant provincial society. Sheer force of numbers obliged cooperation if the king wanted to get anything done: there were maybe 45–50,000 venal officers and maybe twice as many nobles at the height of Louis XIV's monarchy – and a mere thirty Intendants. Lamoignon de Basville, Intendant of Languedoc from 1685 to 1718, knew how to be tough on the king's business – he was the brutal scourge of local Protestants, for example – but he also recognized the critical importance of cooperating with provincial governors drawn from the older Sword families, and working hand-in-hand with the noble-dominated provincial estates.

Furthermore, although Louis made a show of separating out the hierarchy of the court – in which the most ancient noble houses were most heavily represented – from the administrative hierarchy, the two worlds were never hermetically sealed one from the other. After all, both the court and the state's administrative apparatus – with the monarch himself at the apex of both – were located at Versailles. The king had his secretaries of state and his ministers for state business – but he also took advice from sagacious courtiers, including the Princes of the Blood. The Royal Councils were physically located at the centre of the court and the bureaux of government departments were only a stone's throw from the Hall of Mirrors. The tidy symmetry of state bureaucracy was subverted by the ubiquity of countervailing networks of clientage and patronage.

This intertwining of the worlds of court and government is confirmed in networks of influence and power established by key families in Louis's service. Jean-Baptiste Colbert, for example, Louis's great ministerial factotum from 1661 to 1683, used his place at the heart of government to extend the influence of his family across the whole remit of the state's activities: male relatives became ministers, bishops and generals, magistrates and Intendants, while daughters were married into high court families. Much the same was true of the Phélypeaux clan, which formed two ministerial dynasties (the La Vrillière and Pontchartrain families), which supplied royal secretaries of state from the early seventeenth to the late eighteenth centuries, spanning the worlds of court, administration, high magistracy and high finance. The clientage networks which courtiers and high administrators built up also generally crossed the Robe–Sword divide.

Rather than acting corrosively on privilege and corporatism, therefore, Louis XIV's system of government aimed primarily to reorder the functions of corporative bodies, and to integrate them more closely within the polity. The result was a Bourbon state which was a political amalgam. For all its inventiveness as regards ceremonial court culture, the crown also drew heavily on pre-existent traditions within French political culture, adding to as well as subtracting elements from what was already a complex picture. Absolutist theory allowed no space for the idea that parts of the body politic could claim some portion of sovereignty – but Louis XIV knew only too well that authority had to be negotiated all the same. His mythic present was built on the foundations of patronage, clientage and a spirit of resigned collaboration with the quotidian facts of corporatism.

If Louis submerged a wide range of elements within French political culture inimical to the theory and practices of absolutism, he failed to liquidate them. His claims to embody sovereignty did not rule out the nobility from making a contribution to the more mundane realities of power – nor indeed did those claims ever totally efface competing interpretations of legitimacy and sovereignty. The contractualism which had formerly been implicit within corporatism appeared to have gone – but it was not forgotten. Indeed, by encouraging a growing sense of corporative consciousness amongst the nobility in particular, Louis's reforms promoted the political ambitions of some of those who served him. The corporative structure of the state was, moreover, a highly appropriate location in which alternative views could hibernate – and then make a comeback. In the final years of Louis's reign, signs began to appear that a long period of hibernation was coming to an end, and that a wide array of individuals and groupings were starting to rethink political culture for a post-Louis XIV era.

D) ABSOLUTISM UNDER PRESSURE

Well before 1700, the surface glamour of court life on which the Louis-Quatorzian myth had been founded had begun to pall. The gap between representation and reality widened – dangerously so for a regime which placed importance on impressing through a show of grandeur. Louis's association with the pious widow, Madame de Maintenon (with whom he contracted a morganatic marriage in 1684) had led to a new tone of piety, even prudery, at court. The wilder festive extravaganzas of Louis's youth died out, Christian prevailed over pagan symbolism, and naked statues around the gardens of Versailles acquired strategically placed figleaves. Ageing played a part in this change in the ceremonial regime: Louis XIV had been his own Principal Dancer in court ballets down to the 1670s, but he increasingly took a spectatorial rather than a participatory role in entertainments, which became fewer and less grand. To Versailles, he now came to prefer the homelier and more comfortable adjacent palaces of Trianon and Marly. In the last decade of his life, he spent most evenings in private with Madame de Maintenon, hearing a little chamber music, reading or else chatting with a few family friends.

The growing discrepancy between the diminishing splendour of court life on the one hand and the continuing stream of displays and glorifications of the monarch outside Versailles on the other was linked to a related development, namely, the deterioration in the fortunes of the monarch in international affairs. The quest for international *gloire* had been an important component in the popularity of Louis XIV's policies: 'every petty person feels elevated and associated with the king's greatness', noted one pamphlet in 1690. 'This compensates him for all his losses and consoles him in his misery.'[20] Yet that international and military greatness seemed increasingly in question. Had Louis died at forty-six rather than seventy-six, his reputation in French history would have stood far higher: for from the 1680s to his death, he added virtually nothing to what he had achieved hitherto. The Wars of the League of Augsburg (1688–97) and of Spanish Succession (1701–13) proved disastrous for his own reputation – and for the fortunes of his subjects. The Spanish struggle, aimed to secure for his grandson, the duc d'Anjou, the crown of Spain bequeathed him by the last of the Spanish Habsburgs, Charles II (r. 1661–1700), went particularly badly. By 1708–9, with the English marshalling their European allies, France's military situation was appalling. Limited recovery thereafter meant that the Treaty of Utrecht (1713–14) ending this cycle of warfare was not as catastrophic as had seemed likely. In particular, Anjou was accepted as Spanish monarch – though only in return for Philip V (as he became) renouncing any claim to the French throne. The cost had been high, however, straining the French state's finances to the limit and placing a tax burden on the country which was made almost intolerable by the extremely harsh population losses caused by bad weather and harvest failure.[21]

France's international prestige plummeted accordingly. In 1685, the king further tarnished his international reputation by revoking the Edict of Nantes of 1598, which protected the Huguenot minority. The move, which caused even the pope to express reservations at the violence involved, had the effect of driving Protestants to leave France rather than convert. This was not only financially and economically ill-advised, it was also politically inept, for it helped to manufacture a vehement opposition to the principles of government which the king embodied. From the late 1680s onwards, Huguenot refugees in the United Provinces, England and Germany poured out a stream of invectives against the king, a chorus to which propagandists of the allied powers fighting Louis added their voices. Louis's quest for *la gloire*, it was suggested, had tipped over into *folie de grandeur*, with the ruler wishing to establish a 'universal monarchy' throughout Europe, crushing Protestant communities beneath the Catholic jackboot. Louis's turn to straightlaced piety was forgotten, and he was luridly depicted as a saturnalian debauchee from whom no virgin was safe. European printing presses highlighted Catholic atrocities inflicted in the so-called *dragonnades*, the enforced dragooning of orthodox piety by regular troops. The violent repression of the revolt of Protestant 'Camisard' rebels in the Cévennes between 1702 and 1704 restoked the fires of anti-Bourbon and anti-Catholic propaganda. In spite of a brutal campaign of counter-insurgency, moreover, which involved the wholesale extermination of rebel villages, the French government found it humiliatingly difficult to liquidate the Protestant community within its borders. Indeed, even as Louis lay dying, the Protestant community was reforming 'in the wilderness' (*au Désert*): on 21 August 1715 in the Cévennes mountains behind Nîmes, the pastor Antoine Court held the first truly national Protestant synod in France since 1685.

The emergence of an ideology of anti-absolutism came as a rude shock to a monarch who had taken extraordinary pains to control written and visual representations of his authority. The flipside of the Bourbon state's generous patronage of artists and writers was a regime of censor-based surveillance over publication of books and images. During his reign, over 170 writers, publishers and booksellers had to cool their heels in the Bastille prison for publishing offences. Affairs of state, which Louis thought of as his business alone, had become a matter of international public debate. Foreign and Huguenot critics seemed, moreover, to be taking absolutism at its own valuation, finding in Louis XIV's mythic present the lineaments of a monstrous and tyrannical despotism. Even more worrying than this international campaign against his authority was the fact that there were echoes of anti-absolutist rhetoric emerging from groupings close to the centre of the French state. A major complex of opposition and polemic was opening around the issue of Jansenism, while the reform of absolutism was under debate within the entourage of the king's own grandson, the duke of Burgundy.

'It is a great pity', noted the minor English divine Silvester Jenks, that 'so important a matter as Jansenism should be so universally talked of and so little understood.'[22] Certainly, the issues brought up by Jansenism could not easily be boiled down to a checklist of key doctrinal points – efforts to do just that in the past had only succeeded in making matters more complex and more embattled (and would, as we shall see, do so again).[23] The Jansenist current of ideas had originated in the early seventeenth century and been propagated by Cornelius Jansen, bishop of Ypres, and Jean Duverger de Hauranne, abbé de Saint-Cyran. These men drew on the example of the early church and the writings of Saint Augustine to stress the invincibility of God's grace and the innate corruptibility of human nature. They were critical of what they adjudged the morally laxist attitudes associated with the Jesuits, whose doctrines of Molinism allowed a good deal of latitude to human free will. The puritanical, inward-looking Jansenist movement, whose spiritual head-quarters became the monastery of Port-Royal outside Paris, attracted much support from the social and political elite from the middle of the seventeenth century. Louis suspected its adherents of political hetero-doxy and, with little justification, of treasonous involvement in the Fronde.

Louis's harassment of Jansenist views, which won much support from *dévot* circles, was put on hold in the late 1660s, when it was agreed that individuals who subscribed to Jansenist opinions should not be pressed publicly to declare their views either way. But further religious and diplomatic disputes in the 1680s between the king and Innocent XI (pope 1676–89) came close to causing the church in France to split from Rome. In order to restrict the influence of the papacy in French church matters, Louis formulated what became known as the Four Gallican Articles – the fourth of which stated that no papal ruling even on spiritual matters could be accepted as binding on Catholics in France without the approval of the temporal power. In 1682, the king insisted that the Gallican Articles, enunciated as a royal decree, should be formally registered by the Paris Parlement and thus become incontrovertible state law, and taught as doctrinal orthodoxy in theology faculties and seminaries.

On the warpath again by the turn of the century against a doctrine which he increasingly interpreted as being quite as disruptive of religious harmony and royal power as Protestantism had proved, Louis pestered Clement XI (pope 1700–21) into promulgating the bull *Vineam domini* (1705) which formally condemned the compromise of the 1660s over inwardly held Jansenist views. Louis's clumsy attempts to get Rome to police French consciences provoked an anti-papal backlash, for the king's actions seemed to infringe his own Gallican Articles of 1682. There was, however, no holding back the monarch, newly won to devotion and egged on by Jesuitophile Madame de Maintenon's regular bedtime diet of anti-Jansenist horror-stories. Louis stepped up persecution of prominent Jansenists, using *lettres de cachet* to imprison the most subversive, and in 1709 closed down the Port-Royal convent outside Paris, razing the site and disinterring those buried there. In 1713 he extracted from the pope the Unigenitus bull which defined and formally stigmatized allegedly Jansenist theses.

The papal bull Unigenitus was, in the opinion of the Jansenist bishop of Montpellier, Colbert de Croissy, 'the greatest event there has been in the church since Jesus Christ'. Louis had expected the papal pronouncement to put an end to disputes as confidently as he had expected the Revocation of the Edict of Nantes in 1685 to be acceptable to the Huguenot community. Instead, Unigenitus marked the inauguration of the Jansenist question as one of the most intractable political issues of the century. The body of the bull's text – which soon proved to have, as d'Aguesseau put it, 'as many enemies as readers'[24] – took the form of a step-by-step condemnation of 101 putatively heretical statements to be found in one of the most widely read religious works of the late seventeenth century, the *Moral Reflections* (1692) of Pasquier Quesnel, a Jansenist exile resident in the Low Countries. This upset many individuals, including Cardinal Noailles, archbishop of Paris, who deemed that Quesnel's work contained items well within the bounds of doctrinal orthodoxy. It was the form rather than the content of the bull which annoyed others. The pope seemed to be laying down rules of orthodoxy in a way which smacked of belief in papal infallibility and which infringed the French church's cherished constitutional independence, recently affirmed in the 1682 Gallican Articles.

The crisis was still going strong when Louis was on his deathbed: indeed, the king had been planning the convocation of a church council to force through the Unigenitus bull against a handful of bishops holding out against assent – an act which might well have resulted in schism within the church. Inept royal policies, instead of pouring oil on troubled waters, had simply inflamed the issue, and driven Gallicans like Noailles into the arms of Jansenist opponents of Unigenitus. This was all the more significant, moreover, in that Jansenism had developed faithful supporters in the highest echelons of the state as well as the church. In the eyes of the constitutional watchdog, the Parlement of Paris, the bull had raised Gallican as well as Jansenist hackles. 'Unigenitus', d'Aguesseau predicted with more than a little accuracy, 'will be the cross not only of the theologians but also of the premier magistrates of the kingdom.'[25]

Opposition to Louis's policies was not merely located, then, among Huguenot refugees and outlaws; the state's administrative apparatus and the upper reaches of the church were nurturing hostility towards royal policy and authority. Generalized dissent reached even further into the heart of the absolutist polity, moreover, for the entourage of the duke of Burgundy, second in line to the throne, was also developing a reform programme. In the late 1690s, Burgundy's grandfather had organized a nationwide inquiry through the provincial Intendants to reveal the character of the society over which the young duke, it was thought, would eventually rule. The replies to this inquiry proved to be grist to the mill of a grouping of nobles and churchmen who were acting as advisers to the young duke, led by François de Salignac de La Mothe-Fénelon, who from 1689 had been the child's tutor. Though he was exiled from court in the mid-1690s following religious disputes, Fénelon continued to develop a critique of Louis-Quatorzian absolutism from his post as archbishop of Cambrai. In writings which circulated in manuscript, he vehemently attacked wars which, as the 1698 inquiry seemed to confirm, were harmful and destructive, and suggested that the king was seriously out of touch with the needs of his suffering people.

Fénelon's austere morality of power reserved its most stinging barbs for courtiers who out of flattery and self-interest sought to blind the king to his divinely ordained regal duties.

The War of Spanish Succession provided even more ammunition for the critics of the state within Burgundy's circle, for whom Louis XIV seemed to be failing in the Bourbon task of combining international success with domestic tranquillity. Pierre Le Pesant, sieur de Boisguilbert, had in 1695 penned an attack on Louis's dirigiste economic policies, and his *Supplément du Détail de la France* (1707) further elaborated the critique. In the same year, Boisguilbert's cousin, the military engineer, Sebastien Le Prestre, comte de Vauban, who was personally responsible for much of the fortress-building which had equipped French frontiers with quasi-impregnable defences, also produced a widely and clandestinely circulated piece, *Projet d'une Dixme royale* ('Plan for a Royal Tithe'), which, in the light of the appalling conditions which he had witnessed throughout the country, urged a fairer apportionment of the costs of war. The two authors were unsparing in their attacks on financiers who, it was held, were leading Louis astray, building up colossal wealth for themselves and draining the country dry. Vauban and Boisguilbert were publicly censured in 1707, but this failed to stop the assaults. The eccentric abbé de Saint-Pierre, polymathic enthusiast for postal services, phonetic spelling and social reform, produced a *Projet pour rendre la paix perpétuelle en Europe* ('Plan for Making Peace in Europe Perpetual') (1712), which urged arbitration rather than aggression in international disputes.

The Burgundy circle assailed some of the most cherished principles of Louis-Quatorzian government: it criticized existing economic and financial policies in the name of a humane commitment to assisting the distressed peasantry; it preached peace instead of *gloire*-driven warfare, and frugal virtue over luxury; and it implied a politics which involved more than a single person, howsoever 'absolute'. In many ways this disparate movement was trying to reimagine absolutism 'from the inside'. Some of the circle – men like the dukes of Beauvillier, Chevreuse and Chaulnes – were indeed close advisers to Louis XIV. They shunned a public forum for their work – they had no wish to take on the mantle of tribunes of the people or to topple the polity from without – and operated like an in-house brains trust for innovative statesmen and faithful servants of the crown, thinking the unthinkable as Louis's impending death presaged the closure of the Sun King's mythic present. The quasi-manifesto that the group drew up in 1711 at Chaulnes's home – the so-called 'Tables of Chaulnes' – urged a reconfiguration of power so as to include the high aristocracy, who would meet periodically in local estates and in the Estates General. Secretaries of state, subservient vehicles of state centralization, would disappear, while the Intendants, centralizing agents in the provinces, would have many of their powers switched to provincial governors drawn from the high aristocracy. A similar pro-aristocratic note was struck by Saint-Simon, sometime associate of the Burgundy circle, who also began circulating position papers calling for the aristocracy to take a more significant representative role in government and to preside over a reconvened Estates General. At around the same time, another royal adviser, Henri de Boulainvilliers, penned works also calling for a greater role for the nobility in government.

The barrage of criticisms bubbling up from within the political establishment was not without an effect on government, which engaged in a number of reform endeavours in these last years. The wish that tax might be apportioned more fairly so as to cushion the needy was heeded, notably in the 1695 poll-tax, or *capitation*, paid by all from the humblest peasant to dukes and peers of the realm, and from 1710, in another universal direct tax, the 'royal tithe' (*dixième*), intellectual progeny of Vauban and Boisguilbert. Similarly, criticisms of state economic policy led to the appointment in 1700 of a Council of Commerce on which merchant lobbies were well represented. The acknowledged wish for a more rational system of administration also stimulated Colbert de Torcy's creation of a 'Political Academy' in 1712 to train diplomats, as well as influencing important legal and procedural reforms masterminded by d'Aguesseau in the Paris Parlement.

Significantly, royal decrees now muted the language of imperious demand. Louis presented himself less as the equal of the gods than as the doting paterfamilias of the national family. Commenting on the preamble to the decree establishing the *capitation* in 1695, the *Gazette d'Amsterdam* noted how the king spoke 'as a master who appears to have no need of his people's consent', yet also 'as if he is asking and trying to persuade at the same time as he commands'.[26] By the time of the War of Spanish Succession, Louis's propaganda machine had become even less triumphalistic, as it reticently stressed the need to ground

Bourbon foreign policy in legitimate dynastic claims to the Spanish crown based on respect for international law.

There were several features of this episode of court-based critique from the late 1690s onwards which were of particular note for the future. The movement of criticism demonstrated, first of all, a resurgence of interest among the high aristocracy in politics and a wish to find a new vehicle for their authority. The royal court was viewed not only as a baneful vehicle of state centralization and the personalization of power, but also as a source of moral decay which encouraged luxury, corruption and conspicuous waste. A further feature of the high nobility's revival of interest in politics as Louis XIV's death approached was a kind of rediscovery of history, as aristocratic critics of absolutism looked to the past as a means of cracking open the timeless mythic present of the Sun King. Whereas absolutist theory justified dynastic authoritarianism as a response to the anarchy of the Wars of Religion and the Fronde, its critics constructed rosy-tinted versions of an even more far distant past, less implacably saturated with absolutist values. Echoing sixteenth-century theorists whose work had been effaced by the dazzling brilliance of the Sun King, Boulainvilliers in particular claimed to locate in the Merovingian Franks the ancestors of the aristocracy, and in the Franks' warrior assemblies an alternative to the royal court as a locus of legitimate authority. Under Boulainvilliers's prism, history transmuted from being the epic recounting of the heroic, God-given acts of the ruler into the charting of a national story which was markedly different from the chronicle of royalty. King and state were no longer equated; indeed, for Boulainvilliers, the historic record seemed to show that the Franks' assemblies pre-dated the institution of kingship by Clovis. The imputation was that kings derived their legitimacy from their aristocracy, who were consequently the true representatives of the nation. Rampant medievalism thus became a channel for attacking arbitrary government, as aristocratic critics sought to replace the royal mythic present with a kind of nostalgic pluperfect.

It was in Antiquity – and an even mistier, more fictive history than that of the Franks – that the eloquent Fénelon grounded his arguments in *Télémaque*, the most influential text to emerge from the Burgundy grouping. It now seems clear that Fénelon intended *Télémaque*, which he composed between 1694 and 1696, essentially as a primer in government for the young duke of Burgundy, a 'mirror of princes' which would instruct the young man by painting a picture of the ideal monarch which would warn him of moral perils to be overcome if he was to rule in a way consonant with the spiritual responsibilities of the royal office. A deceitful copyist leaked a version of the manuscript to the publishers, who released the work in 1699, causing a wave of what one contemporary described as 'Telemachomania', as re-edition speedily followed re-edition.[27]

In a classic demonstration of how readers' reception can transcend an author's intentions, this moralistic pedagogic text was interpreted as a *roman à clef* overlaying a swingeing attack on despotic government in general and Louis XIV in particular. Fénelon consistently rejected this interpretation of his work – and certainly for a putatively anti-absolutist text it has long paeans in favour of absolute authority, punctilious attempts to legitimate it in scriptural terms and violent attacks on any form of revolt. The fictive and allegorical dimensions of the work, however, lent themselves only too easily to a more subversive interpretation. Telemachus, the son of Ulysses, follows his father around the islands of a Homeric Mediterranean, being taught precepts of good government by his tutor, Mentor, through the concrete examples they encounter on their way. In a kind of 'Golden Age' Crete, for example, they come across one king Idomeneo, whose vices have produced his downfall. His case shows, Mentor tells the youthful Telemachus, that the ideal monarch

has an absolute power (*une puissance absolue*) (sic) in doing good, but his hands are tied from doing wrong. The laws ... are there so that a single man may serve, by his wisdom and moderation, the happiness of so many men; and not so that those men should serve, by their misery and servitude, to flatter the pride and the weakness of a single man.[28]

Under the mask of allegory, political *cognoscenti* saw Fénelon as Mentor, Burgundy as Telemachus – and Louis XIV less as Ulysses than as Idomeneo. When Mentor went on to cite as the most pernicious sicknesses within a state 'luxury', which 'poisons a whole nation', and 'an arbitrary power' as 'the bane of kings', it seemed to be only too easy to detect a sly assault on the luxuriant court-based political culture of the Sun King.[29]

The existence of an audience receptive to such critical views particularly among the aristocracy fails to explain, however, the deep and enduring influence of Fénelon's master-work. Its literary and pedagogic qualities made it much admired, while its fictive form provided a model in a century in which, as we shall see, political polemic would often take the form of lightly allegorized utopias.[30] Moreover, its themes of virtuous sovereignty characterized by respect for the law and concern for popular welfare, of moderation versus luxury, of rural frugality versus urban corruption, of freedom versus arbitrary government, and of collective felicity versus dynastic aggrandisement provided an ideological matrix which would be tirelessly drawn on over the century. *Télémaque* would not only be read widely in schools throughout the century, it would also be cited approvingly in the *Encyclopédie*, cherished by Jean-Jacques Rousseau, précised by Louis XVI, and its author saluted by Robespierre as 'tutor to the human race'.[31] Fénelon had penned the perfect script for political reform, with which individuals from every political spectrum, either in power or without, could feel comfortable and inspired. After *Télémaque*, both supporters and opponents of absolute monarchy were agreed that rulers could – and should – make a difference to the welfare of their subjects. 'You should wish to be a father, not a master,' Fénelon told the duke of Burgundy in 1711. 'It shouldn't be that all belong to a single individual; rather a single individual should belong to all, so as to make them happy.'[32]

E) THE DREADED REGENCY

Beneath the automaton-like surface of court ritual and ceremony, the last years of Louis XIV's reign thus experienced a heaving world of faction, disharmony and political reimaginings, underpinned by religious discord, social distress, financial insolvency and re-emergent political ambitions. Critiques of royal authority were issuing from a wide array of positions, ranging from the geographical margins of the country to the very heart of the state, from the rugged Cévennes mountains to the antechambers of Versailles. And the attacks on Louis XIV's mythic present seemed even, as we have suggested, to be shifting the modes of self-presentation of the king himself. Bourbon political culture seemed to be ripe for a return to the drawing board: the king was being called on to attend to the welfare of his people – as well as juggling domestic tranquillity with international prestige. And if these new demands alarmed the dying monarch, they alarmed him all the more in that the period following his death was likely to be a regency.

An unpredictable bout of mortality within the royal family in the last years of Louis's reign transformed the circumstances of a succession which had looked more than adequately well supplied with suitable candidates. In a kind of princely holocaust spread over a couple of dozen months, death carried off a string of able successors, beginning in April 1711 with Louis's son and presumptive heir, the 'grand dauphin', or 'Monseigneur', a victim of smallpox. An epidemic of scarlet fever in 1712 accounted for Monseigneur's son, the duke of Burgundy, on whom so many hopes had been pinned, and his beloved wife, while a riding accident shortly afterwards accounted for the grand dauphin's other son, the duc de Berry. One of Burgundy's children, the four-year-old duke of Brittany, succumbed to the same disease as his parents. This left the even younger duc d'Anjou (1710–74; r. 1715–74 as Louis XV), who sickened but failed to die of the same illness. If on his deathbed Louis XIV did at least have the comfort of surviving legitimate issue – Anjou's nurse, Madame de Ventadour, stoutly resisted the doctors' efforts to get their hands on the child – thorny problems remained. The extreme youth and sickly disposition of the future Louis XV was a poor guarantee of political security in a society in which, on average, only one child in two reached adulthood and where – as the hecatomb of 1711–12 had shown – an aristocratic pedigree was no protection against life-threatening sickness even for those in the prime of life. Louis thus knew that power, on his death, would pass to a regent. And, for Louis, what a regent!

Constitutional convention and fundamental maxims had it that, in the absence of a queen mother, the premier eligible Prince of the Blood would accede to the regency on the death of the king. And if the little Anjou died without issue, then the throne would pass, it seemed, to the same man, namely, Philip, duc d'Orléans. Orléans was Louis's nephew, the issue of the king's perfumed dandy of a brother and the prim, superannuated tomboy Charlotte-Elisabeth, daughter of the Elector Palatine. At his birth, his mother had had his horoscope cast: her son, it was predicted, would be pope – though she herself thought a future as Anti-Christ more likely! Her son did what he could to live up to the maternal prediction, dabbling in chemistry with alchemical intent, allegedly renouncing God and invoking demons, and generally cocking a snook at conventional values. He cultivated the aura, if not quite of the Anti-Christ, at least of an Anti-Sun King, discountenancing his uncle and shocking the *dévots* by preferring the intimacy and informality of a clique of drinking companions to the formal longueurs of the courtly round, and championing sexual and intellectual freedom over against the stuffy orthodoxy of a Maintenon-dominated court. He combined young mistresses with Old Masters, collecting his own favourite artists (he owned, *inter alia*, a score of Titians, half a dozen Rembrandts and Rubenses, nine Giorgiones and three Leonardos) rather than the artists responsible for the cult of Louis XIV, and he mocked the memory of Lully, Louis's house composer. To Versailles, the duke preferred the lively ambience of Paris, where he was luxuriously ensconced in his private residence, the Palais-Royal. He never, it should be noted, totally renounced his inheritance: a critic of the court round, he benefited to the tune of a cool two million livres a year from royal largesse (which made him the wealthiest private individual in the kingdom); affable in manners, he remained intensely aware of his rights as premier Prince of the Blood; humiliated by having imposed upon him in marriage while still a teenager an illegitimate daughter of Louis XIV, Mademoiselle de Blois, he bowed and accepted as a prince should; and, though scorned for his eccentricity, he was a courageous warrior and wily diplomat, blocked in advancement only by petty court rivalries. Nothing, however, about Orléans's life – save only, sneakingly, a brio which recalled his own youth – would persuade Louis XIV that here was a future regent in whom either he or the nation could have confidence.

The adventitious disappearance of those nearer the throne than the duke had, moreover, set tongues awagging. After all, while the loss of one generation of male heirs might be understandable, the loss of three (Monseigneur; Burgundy and Berry; Brittany) suggested more than carelessness. Gossip, with a good helping of malice, transmuted Orléans's amateur interest in chemistry into professional poisoning – a claim which caused Paris crowds to hiss him in the street and courtiers to ostracize him. Only a faithful few kept him in touch, including his mother – disabused defender of her son and stern critic of 'the Old Shit' (as she termed Madame de Maintenon)[33] – and the eccentric Saint-Simon. Partly through the latter, Orléans benefited from overtures from the Burgundy circle following the death of the royal heir. In the event, however, the circle's leading lights, notably Fénelon, Chevreuse and

Beauvillier, preceded Louis XIV to the grave, further perpetuating Orléans's political isolation.

The uncertainties associated with the succession and the looming profile of this Bourbon black sheep led Louis XIV to try even harder to lay down the law after his death. It was as if the grand ballet-master, who had spent his reign getting the nation to dance to his tune and who lay dying according to his own courtly protocols, now wanted to choreograph his succession. The princely holocaust of 1711–12 had revealed a major area of constitutional ambiguity in this regard. According to many would-be constitutional experts (including even Orléans's ally, Saint-Simon), the nation's fundamental laws dictated an alternative to the duke serving as regent and even maybe acceding to the crown, namely, Philip V of Spain. The latter, son of 'Monseigneur', was Louis's surviving grandson and consequently more closely related to the Sun King than Orléans. The aged king adjudged the Spanish option, whatever its constitutional propriety, as even worse than an Orléans regency. The European powers had only allowed France to come to the conference table at Utrecht in 1713 on the specific undertaking that Philip renounced his claims to the French crown, a stipulation which had been incorporated into the Utrecht treaty (along with a counter-renunciation, whereby Orléans disclaimed rights to the Spanish throne). To allow Philip V priority over Orléans to the regency or the throne would thus infringe international law and trigger a European war which would endanger the presence of a Bourbon ruler in Spain and be disastrous to a France still recuperating from decades of damaging warfare. Even if Philip V were to abide by his renunciation, however, Louis feared that an unrestrained Orléans, who cultivated a well-known personal rivalry with the Spanish Bourbon, might get drawn into a dogfight against him, leading France into European war by another route and risking the unravelling of Louis's absolutist inheritance at home.

Louis attempted to square the constitutional and political circles in the will that he drew up in April 1714. Seeking to bolster the line of succession leading to his great-grandson, while also checking against any bellicose intent by Orléans, he stipulated that on his death the country should be governed by a Regency Council composed of the Princes of the Blood who had achieved their majority, high dignitaries of state and the ministers of state. Orléans would preside; but he would be obliged to respect a vote of council members on all issues. This strategy of the ageing king was combined with another crafty move – equally outside the framework of the kingdom's fundamental laws – which was aimed both to keep Orléans in check and to increase the likelihood of his own blood descent acceding to the throne in due time. He both legitimized and increased the power within the state of his own illegitimate issue.

In all, Louis had had thirteen illegitimate children in his sexually perky youth and had done his best by them, marrying them into the families of dukes and princes. Gender balance and premature deaths meant that by the last years of his reign, there were only two children of the thirteen who counted politically, the duc du Maine and his younger brother, the comte de Toulouse, children of the marquise de Montespan, official mistress to the king in the 1670s. Maine and Toulouse enjoyed a status lower than Princes of the Blood but higher than French dukes and peers, and, more important, benefited from the whole-hearted support of Madame de Maintenon, and a great deal of *dévot* support as a consequence. Maintenon had been governess to the children in the late 1670s before acceding to the king's favours. Far from resenting the sons of her predecessor in the king's bed, she loved the boys all the more for hating the debauched Orléans. The royal deaths of 1711–12 caused Louis to listen more attentively to Maintenon's advocacy. In July 1714 the king conferred on Maine and Toulouse the status of legitimate offspring, with the right to succeed to the throne if direct heirs were lacking, and he then elevated them in May 1715 to the rank of Princes of the Blood. These measures flew in the face of France's fundamental laws – kings in France were born, not made. Yet Louis went even further in support of the 'bastards', reserving for Maine in particular a key role in counterbalancing Orléans. He and his brother were to sit on the Regency Council and he was in addition to command the king's Household regiments during the minority and to have superintendence of the education of the young Louis XV. Maybe even responding to the poisoning rumours targeted at Orléans, Louis insisted that the child should be brought up at Vincennes, said to be healthier than either Versailles or Orléans's Palais-Royal.

If a regency threatened to be problematic for the dynasty, then, this derived not simply from the character, activities and political disposition of Orléans but also from Louis XIV's double infringement of the country's fundamental laws: the renunciation of Philip V's rights and the opening up of a route to the throne for his illegitimate issue. At least Orléans could take comfort that it was not he alone who opposed the rivalrous Maine clique: every duke and peer worthy of the title did as much, while the *parlements* shuddered in constitutionalist horror at the impropriety of the bastards' promotion.

The progress of the king's illness was the backdrop against which the succession drama unfolded. Louis was no doubt aware of the extent to which the balance of Europe as well as the fortunes of France hung on the succession, as well as mindful of his own bellicose excesses in the past. He gravely told his little great-grandson, brought mewling and whimpering to his bedside, that the child's future greatness depended on his concern for his duty towards God and his people:

You must avoid making war as much as you can; it is the ruin of peoples. Do not follow the bad example I have given you in this. I have often undertaken war too lightly and pursued it out of vanity. Do not imitate me, but be a peaceful prince . . .[34]

Louis accorded Orléans the respect which was his due, making a semi-public and somewhat surprisingly warm-hearted reconciliation with the duke. From 20 August, Orléans's antechamber, which had been spectacularly empty in the wake of the earlier poisoning accusations, began to fill with clients and well-wishers who abandoned the bed-side of the dying monarch. To the disgust of the doctors, the royal family at Versailles allowed one Brun, a wandering empiric ('a yokel', *dixit* Saint-Simon),[35] to administer a proprietary 'sovereign remedy' to the ailing monarch. Astonishingly, the king's health rallied, causing Orléans's antechamber to become deserted again as courtiers rushed back to dance attendance at the royal bedside. Quackery, however, had its limits, and by 29 August the king's death seemed only a matter of time. After joining the king to make a bonfire of confidential records (including their own letters to each other), Madame de Maintenon was despatched to the abbey of Saint-Cyr.

Faced with his own imminent death, no one was taking the mythic present in which the régime had been bathed less seriously than the king himself. Louis had done his best to choreograph his succession, and seemed now to turn his mind to playing the part of the dying Christian. Under his Jesuit chaplain, abbé Le Tellier, he accordingly followed the rituals for the 'good death' developed by the Catholic church in the wake of the Council of Trent – a complex programme of piety involving prayers, spiritual exercises, edifying reconciliations with family members, fond farewells, personal bequests and so on. The king was dying, noted Pierre Narbonne, an unremarkable police official in the town of Versailles, of the king's virtuoso deathbed performance, as 'a Christian, a king and a hero' (though he could not refrain from adding, acerbically and parenthetically 'albeit in the arms of a Jesuit').[36] Louis delivered a final *dévot* snub to the Jansenists when he made a deathbed request that his heart should be buried in the Jesuit mother-house in Paris – his body would lie with his predecessors in the abbey of Saint-Denis, for over a thousand years necropolis of the kings of France.

On 1 September, four days before the king's seventy-seventh birthday, the dance of death finally ended. The duc de Bouillon, the king's Grand Chamberlain, officiously placed a black feather in his black hat, went out on to the balcony facing over the Cour de Marbre at the heart of the palace, beneath which a large crowd had long been waiting. 'King Louis XIV is dead!' he exclaimed, before going back into the palace, replacing the black with a white feather and returning to the balcony to cry out, three times, '*Vive le roi Louis XV!*' If the 76-year-old Louis XIV had died, the ceremonial body of the French monarch lived on, now located in the frail frame of a five-year-old child, under the protection of a regent who excited less reassurance than dread.

The mortal remains of the Sun King were delivered straight away into the hands of the physicians who were widely held to have caused his death. He was decapitated on the surgeon's slab, his head sectioned, and what was left of him after autopsy and division of entrails was solemnly conveyed to the Saint-Denis basilica. Many French men and women seemed only too delighted to see 'Louis the Great' in his grave. Marquees along the Saint-Denis road past which the king's body was conveyed were filled with people 'drinking, dancing and laughing', and spitting out their contempt for the late king and his links with the Jesuits.[37] Yet the political heritage of Louis XIV would not be disposed of as easily as his biological body. His reign provided a kind of template of kingship which it was to prove extremely difficult to eradicate from the political consciousness of his successors and the statesmen who served them. For most of the remainder of the eighteenth century, politics would be conducted not at all in the anticipation of the Revolution of 1789 – as historians sometimes blithely assume – but in dialogue with Louis XIV's reign. Even though the enduring and ubiquitous popularity of Fénelon's political fable of virtuous monarchy attested a widespread wish to reform the overweening political culture of the 'Louis the Great', it would prove extremely difficult to wash the Sun King out of the French nation's hair.

2

Negotiating Stormy Weather:
The Regency and the Advent of Fleury
(1715–26)

A) HOPE BEYOND SUNSET

'The minority of kings marks stormy weather,' glumly noted one royal official.[1] Yet the auguries for the forthcoming period of regency were not all bad, and the new incumbent on the French throne carried with him his subjects' hopes for a new start, a fresh dawn after the sunset of Louis-Quatorzian absolutism. On the same day that Louis XIV's corpse was ignominiously being conveyed to Saint-Denis, Mathieu Marais, barrister in the Paris Parlement, recorded in his diary the scenes of joyous enthusiasm which greeted the young Louis XV on his passage through the capital – a mood contagious enough to be picked up by the orphan-monarch himself, who sweetly joined in the cries of *'Vive le Roi!'*. Although in time, this mood of expectation would prove a heavy burden for the regime to bear, at the outset it cushioned the stormy ride which seemed to be the likely fate of the king's uncle, the dreaded Orléans.

The first, highly dramatic, episode in the new reign would be played out with the new ruler off the set. On 2 September 1715, less than twenty-four hours after Louis XIV's death, there foregathered in the palace of justice on the Île de la Cité at the heart of Paris all the chambers of the Parlement, supplemented by the Princes of Blood and the dukes and peers of the realm, to arrange the circumstances of the regency which the new monarch's young age necessitated. The hall of the Parlement was the customary constitutional venue for such changes of regime: the regency of Louis XIV's mother, Anne of Austria, had been transacted here in 1643 (in a manner, prophetically, which had involved the tearing-up of Louis XIII's will). All now present were dressed in mourning, save the magistrates, who were clothed in their customary red work-robes as a reminder of the ceremonial immortality of a polity in which kings symbolically never died. The drama unfolded as soon as Orléans entered the hall and Louis XIV's testament, which the late king had entrusted to the Parlement, was solemnly brought forward. The duke was to make of this piece of political theatre a brilliant personal triumph – a triumph achieved, moreover, by trampling over Louis XIV's last wishes.

Orléans addessed the magistrates firmly, claiming the post of Regent both as his constitutional right and as the dying wish of the former king. 'My nephew,' Orléans recounted the latter as having said, 'I have made a will in which I have conserved you in all the rights due your birth . . . If [the young Louis XV] falls away, you will be master and the crown will belong to you.' But Orléans seemed surprised – biting his lip, he was heard to mutter, 'He deceived me' – when the exact contents of Louis XIV's will were read out.[2] The dead king's stipulation that his nephew should only chair meetings of the Regency Council and that all matters should be decided by vote reduced Orléans from regal surrogate to glorified vote-counter. The terms of the will, moreover, also favoured Orléans's rival, the legitimized duc du Maine, who now sat bathed smugly in general regard on the peers' benches. The will stated that Maine was to receive the post of superintendent of the young king's education, with command over select Household regiments – as though the young monarch needed protection against such a Regent . . .

A momentary break in the proceedings for discussions over the contents of the will allowed Orléans to regroup his forces and to frustrate Louis XIV's *post mortem* attempts to choreograph the succession. Quietly and clandestinely over the previous week, Orléans had laid the groundwork for this moment. He had imposed a 24-hour news embargo following the king's death so as to prevent couriers getting the news through too quickly to Philip V of Spain, whose claims to the crown Orléans feared. He also had planned a kind of pincer movement against his other great rival, the duc du Maine. He conducted covert dealings with the Princes of the Blood, who, like him, were ill-disposed towards the royal 'bastards'. The three leading princes of the collateral house of Condé were promised places on the Regency Council, with the 23-year-old duc de Bourbon (*Monsieur le Duc*, as he was generally known) offered the post of 'Head of the Regency Council' in Orléans's absence. Orléans opened a second anti-Maine front by cultivating opinion-leaders within the Parlement, many of whom were hostile to the *dévot* connections of the Maine–Maintenon 'Old Court' clan. The duke also did his best to reassure Jansenist and Gallican *parlementaires* and higher clergy that he would take a relaxed line on the Unigenitus bull. Select *parlement-aires* as well as members of the old Sword nobility were lobbed airy promises too about places on the new system of councils of state which Orléans said he wished to establish along lines formerly evoked by the Burgundy circle. Most important of all, he also undertook to restore to the Parlement full rights of remonstrance lost in 1673.

After the adjournment, the *parlementaires* dutifully came up trumps, ridiculing the idea of 'a regency without a regent' which seemed to be implicit in Louis's will, and invoking the need for 'a single chief who represents the monarch', before going on to acclaim Orléans Regent with full powers without the need for a vote. Maine's humiliation was consummated in the afternoon session when Bourbon rose to support the new Regent's protests against Maine receiving control of the young king's Household regiments. Maine was left blathering impotently, with his role of superintendent of the young king's education reduced to purely honorific status.

The leash which Louis XIV had planned to place on the new Regent had thus been removed. The only restrictions on Orléans's power were self-administered: he would introduce, he insisted, a system of government councils; and he stipulated that whereas he alone should have sole powers to dispense favours and rewards within the state, his hands would be bound by a collective vote of the Regency Council if it were necessary to mete out punishments. With a homage to Fénelon's hero which must have registered as clear as a bell among the assembled, he stated that – like the ideal monarch of Telemachus's Mentor – 'he strongly wished to be obstructed from doing evil, but he wished to be free to do good'.[3]

Orléans-Mentor could leave the Parlement chamber well satisfied with a day's work in which he had combined genial acceptance of the need for change with warm-hearted improvisation and lavish reassurance. Spontaneity there had been; but also a good deal of preparation and rehearsal. The Parisian streets with their cheering crowds through which his carriage now conveyed him contained some 3,000 loyal troops each with ten rounds of shot, prudently disposed by Orléans's ally, the marquis d'Argenson, the Paris Lieutenant General of Police, against the eventuality of an insurrection by the hapless Maine. In less than a week Orléans had passed from friendless pariah to sole head of government policy, with probably greater freedom of action than any regent in French history. Louis XIV's actor-managerly attempt to choreograph not only his own death but also the accession of his great-grandchild had been frustrated by some masterly stage-management by the new Regent. The overturning of the king's will showed, as Madame de Staal-Delaunay, one of the duchesse du Maine's ladies-in-waiting, noted, that even for Louis the Great it was impossible to be 'absolute beyond the grave'.[4]

B) THE POLYSYNODY EXPERIMENT

Orléans was back in the Parlement on 12 September, this time with the young king in tow, for the latter to hold a *lit de justice*, formally ratifying the momentous decisions of the 2nd. The Regent kept his word, agreeing to restore the Parlement's rights of remonstrance, and gave further details of his planned system of councils. Under the Polysynody, as the abbé de Saint-Pierre, erstwhile satellite of the Burgundy circle, later called it, the Regency Council was to be flanked by seven councils, each of which was to be headed by a grandee and to have twelve members, half from the older nobility, and half from the ranks of state officials. There were councils for religious affairs (the Council of Conscience, or *conseil de conscience*), headed by the Jesuitophobic cardinal de Noailles; for foreign affairs, headed by the marshal d'Huxelles; for the army and the navy, headed by the marshal de Villars and the comte de Toulouse respectively; for home affairs, headed by the duc d'Antin (Maine's step-brother); for finance, headed by the duc de Noailles (who thereby took over the role though not the title of Controller-General); and for trade, headed by the duc de La Force. A new deal for the high nobility – frozen out of the political arena by the ceremonial court life of Louis XIV's Versailles, and by the system of the secretaries of state – seemed to be on the cards. Members of the Robe sat alongside members of the old Sword nobility. Newcomers to high office were cheek-by-jowl next to individuals with a distinguished record of service under Louis XIV. And opponents of the Unigenitus bull jostled collegially with anti-Jansenist supporters of the 'Old Court', such as the diplomat Colbert de Torcy and ministerial veteran Pontchartrain, who were both placed on the Regency Council. The secretaries of state, bugbear of the Burgundy circle, suffered a major blow: their number was reduced from four to three, and they lost their ministerial status, as only one of them sat on the Regency Council – and he in a quasi-clerical role. The impression that the system of councils was opening up a new space within the polity seemed to be confirmed by Orléans's decision to abandon the architectural constriction of Versailles for the looser, more teeming framework of Paris. The duke would continue to be based in the Palais-Royal, while the young monarch would lodge at the nearby Tuileries palace.

Contemporaries filled the new political space with sundry musings and imaginings about the meanings and ramifications of change. There were hopes for open discussion and debate after the furtive lobbying and clandestine publication of the former reign. Some individuals, however, wanted a lot more than this. The abbé de Saint-Pierre, for example, saw in the principle of Polysynody a framework for refashioning the polity so as to make it markedly less authoritarian than under Louis XIV. Boulainvilliers went further, urging Orléans to use the councils as the first step in a more general move to shift power back to the feudal nobility, who should be primed to dominate a revived Estates General. Saint-Simon held similar views.

Yet the extent to which and exactly how Orléans was attempting to remodel political culture is open to doubt. The new Regent was a difficult man to judge. He deliberately presented a somewhat inscrutable, slightly bored, *ennui*-laden exterior to a world long accustomed to thinking the worst of him. The air of carefree insouciance which he had developed as self-defence in the antagonistic environment of Louis XIV's court was, however, the gentlemanly construction of a grand seigneur, designed to hide a ferocious taste for hard work, an elephantine memory for detail and the low cunning of a fox. The circumstances in which he found himself, moreover, pushed him towards prioritizing the short- over the long-term, and preferring inspired improvisation to sagacious foresight. Regencies were always difficult, but who, frankly, knew what the future might hold? It was far from certain, for example, that Louis XV, a relatively sickly child from an ill-starred family, would survive infancy – there were indeed a number of serious royal health scares in the early years. Were Louis to die, Orléans would presumably succeed. Would the sometime goad of Louis-Quatorzian absolutism wish to engage in the kind of power-sharing that the circumstances of a Regency entailed? Would this self-styled Mentor turn into an ideal ruler – or a tyrant-

Idomeneo?[5] Nor was it certain how strong the forces of opposition to Orléans himself might prove to be. His own accession might well trigger a counter-claim from Philip V of Spain, who under the fundamental laws of the kingdom (and despite the prohibitions stipulated at Utrecht in 1713) had a stronger right to the throne than he. And if the fundamental laws could be circumvented in this case, then could their manipulation not also allow the king's former bastards a claim on the succession? The Regency was built on sand – and shifting sand at that.

The conciliar system which Orléans sponsored from the outset did enjoy some success, even if its deficiencies were soon plain enough. The Army and Navy Councils used the period of peace to make long-overdue reforms. Toulouse in particular was an effective operator at the Navy Office, while at Finance Noailles capably filled the gap left by the non-appointment of a Controller-General, and showed considerable toughness and even some political imagination in efforts to get the kingdom's woeful finances back on track.[6] For every able administrator given his head under this political experiment, however, there were more than a few nonentities, cruising unengaged through council meetings, squabbling mindlessly about precedence issues, and leaving the hard work to the technicians. Yet any lack-lustredness about the performance of the councils owed much also to the restrictions placed upon their effectiveness by Orléans himself. The creator of the Polysynody did his best to keep the councils on a tight leash, and did not permit their existence to compromise the unitary nature of government will. From the very earliest days, Orléans made it clear that he alone retained the ex-king's powers of executive decision-making, including a monopoly of signing and settling government accounts (which Louis XIV had claimed on his accession to personal rule in 1661). The Regency Council suffered from these presumptions to the prerogatives of majesty. Orléans nodded politely towards the letter of Louis XIV's testament, by allowing council voting, whose outcome he invariably observed. Yet he was careful to make sure that no major issues went to the vote in the first place. Council members like the duc d'Antin complained that there was no real debate, since matters coming before them had been stitched up in advance.[7] The work of the other councils also tended to be consultative in character rather than legislative or executive. It could be short-circuited too, for Orléans did much business direct with council presidents and established *ad hoc* groupings for particular issues. He also used his own special advisers – notably the abbé Dubois on foreign policy and the Scot John Law on finances – in a way which undermined the system as a whole.

Nor was the Polysynody allowed to interfere with the normal functioning of subaltern domains of administration. At the centre, the secretaries of state might be in eclipse, but below ministerial level, the administrative machinery operated in much the same way as under Louis XIV. The bureaucratic support to the new conciliar system was still in the hands of the same legally trained masters of requests (*maîtres des requêtes*)[8] as under Louis XIV, and these also dominated the technical councils of state dealing with litigious matters. In the provinces, the Intendants stayed in place, their powers undiminished, belying the power-sharing hopes of provincial governors, local estates and municipal governments. Indeed, the more the anxious early days were passed and the regime stabilized, the more the old absolutist machinery became dominant. By September 1718, the Regent felt that he could dissolve the councils, and re-establish the posts of secretary of state. The abbé Dubois was appointed to Foreign Affairs, with Maurepas, scion of the absolutist service dynasty *par excellence* the Phélypeaux, taking the Navy Ministry. The Navy and Commerce Councils were provisionally maintained, but in a largely technical capacity, and they too were liquidated in 1722–3. In 1720, John Law would be appointed to the post of Controller-General, thus completing the return to the past. The Regent looked to sweeten the pill for potential malcontents among the dispossessed councils' members by nominating them to the Regency Council, whose size was increased from fourteen in 1717 to twenty-nine in 1719 (and thirty-five in 1722) – a dilation in numbers which went hand-in-hand with a dilution of real power, for the Council met less and less and played an increasingly insignificant role.

Given Orléans's character and the circumstances in which he found himself, it is probably prudent to conclude that the Polysynody was less a principled rejection of the Louis-Quatorzian heritage as Saint-Pierre would have it, or a Boulainvilliers-style 'feudal reaction', than a controlled state experiment in establishing a framework for action which did not focalize hostility on Orléans's role as Regent – and which both kept the aristocracy sweet and bought him political time. By 1718, much of that time had been effectively bought, and there seemed a growing risk that the councils might become a platform for criticism of Regency policy (particularly over foreign policy issues, which, as we shall see, were becoming fraught at this moment). Orléans had no compunction in destroying a system he had created – much as he might put down a house pet whose useful life had ended. There were to be few tears for the Polysynody. The maverick abbé de Saint-Pierre wrote passionately in their defence, but his unwise reference to the secretaries of state as 'vizirs' brought a stern rebuff from the Regent, who had him drummed out of the Académie française and had his printer gaoled in the Bastille to cool his heels. At such moments, the mantle of Louis XIV seemed to sit all too easily on this would-be Mentor's shoulders.

c) PRINCES, DUKES AND MAGISTRATES: A NEW FRONDE?

The mood of politics in the *après*-Louis XIV era was transformed by the sensation caused by publication in 1717 of the *Memoirs* of Cardinal de Retz, key player and manipulator of popular and parlementary opinion during the Fronde (1648–53). Throughout Louis XIV's reign, that episode had been a historical no-man's-land, the only licensed visitors to which had been the triumphalist recorders of the king's crushing of the revolt. Retz's account supplied a fresh and daring angle of vision on the formative days of Louis-Quatorzian absolutism – and on the past more generally. In the Fronde, royal power had been contested by individuals from every part of the political world – the magistracy, the Princes of the Blood, the peerage, the minor gentry, town-dwellers and peasants. Usually implicitly, but sometimes very explicitly, noisily and contentiously, rival theories of political authority had been voiced, only to be silenced when first Cardinal Mazarin, then Louis XIV, restabilized the polity. Louis XIV's demise now allowed many of these theories, evoked in Retz's colourful account of this tempestuous period, to emerge Rip van Winkle-like into the political day. For political critics who, even before Louis XIV's death, had been developing a historical perspective on state power, Retz's Fronde seemed like current affairs.

Retz's memoirs offered sustenance to those individuals who, increasingly disenchanted with the failure of the Polysynody to break the absolutist reflexes of the state, were attempting to reimagine the constitutional role of the *parlements* and the princes. Orléans's honeymoon with the Paris Parlement had not lasted long. By agreeing on 2 September 1715 to the full restoration of the magistrates' rights of remonstrance (and also permitting them to refer to themselves again as 'sovereign' courts), the Regent had welcomed back into the heart of the polity a body which had been a principal scourge of absolutism during the Fronde. The semblance of consultation which Orléans had allowed himself on that day, moreover, inflated the self-importance of a body which had almost disappeared from the political map. Magistrates who had exemplified dumb obedience in the latter decades of Louis XIV's reign now turned dangerously truculent – and remained so for the rest of the century. When they now opined, they did so with a sense of grievance about the way they had been treated by Louis XIV, and with a determination that their muzzling in the aftermath of the Fronde should never be allowed to happen again.

Judging itself the supreme embodiment of law, the Parlement felt it carried a vital constitutional thread. Bodies like this, noted barrister Marais, 'have long memories. Individuals die, but they never die.'[9] As we have seen, Louis XIV's absolutism had been founded on the theory that only the ruler's own body had any representational force within the state, and that no other body (*corps*) could claim to express legitimate political interests. The Parlement's progress in these opening years of the Regency highlighted its claim to be a *corps* which partook of the timelessness of the state's ceremonial body and, thereby, stood for the interests of the nation as a whole. As early as 1718, *parlementaires* were arguing that, in the absence of the Estates General, they were the sole channel through which the legitimate anxieties of all the orders of the kingdom could be authoritatively voiced.

In seeking to enlarge its prerogatives, moreover, the Parlement utilized one of the key political languages of the regime, namely ceremony. For the processions celebrating the festival of the Assumption, on 15 August 1716, the magistrates laid claim to a place superior to the Regent himself on the grounds that their corporative body represented monarchy. The Regent, always prone to *laisser-aller* attitudes on questions of precedence, which he disdained, allowed this to go ahead, though his adviser, Saint-Simon, was in no doubt that enormous political claims were riding on the case. Orléans also dismissively supported the magistrates in another case of precedence, namely, the long-running 'bonnet affair' – over, in essence, whether the presidents of the Parlement should respectfully doff their caps (*bonnets*) to any peers of the realm present during their sessions. Beneath this nugatory matter of ceremonial etiquette lurked the question of whether it was the Parlement, the dukes and peers or else the nobility as a whole which had the more legitimate claim to represent the interests of the state. Orléans's eventual adjudication in favour of the magistrates only fostered the Parlement's wider constitutional ambitions.

Jansenism proved a choice terrain for the Parlement to flex its political and constitutional muscles.[10] In the early, honeymoon days, Orléans found it relatively easy to jolly the magistrates along over Jansenism. Parlementary Gallicans and Jansenists packed the Regency Councils, the anti-Unigenitus cardinal de Noailles presided over the Council for Religous Affairs, and in 1717, the Parlement's Procureur-Général, d'Aguesseau, a staunch Gallican, was even appointed Chancellor. The Regent released imprisoned Jansenists from state gaols, and bent over backwards to prevent the hardline attitude of Pope Clement XI towards opponents of the Unigenitus bull from becoming church policy within France. A diplomatic offensive was launched to get the Holy See to devise a doctrinal statement on the bull acceptable to both its proponents and their adversaries.

Conciliation, however, was slow to bear fruit. The pope refused either to compromise or to provide doctrinal explanations for his condemnation of Quesnel's *Moral Reflections*, a text which many orthodox Catholics persisted in finding fault-free. In these circumstances, the higher clergy grew restive over the Regent's apparent acceptance of papal rulings having the force of law in France. In March 1717, the bishops of Senez, Montpellier, Boulogne and Mirepoix issued an appeal (*appel*) calling for the referral of the Unigenitus 'constitution' to a general council of the Catholic church. The demand of the *appelants* or *constitutionnaires*, as they became known, implied that papal 'infallibility' could be controlled by a temporal authority, a claim which infuriated the pope but found numerous supporters in the Parlement and throughout the ecclesiastical establishment. No theologian, Orléans nevertheless began to stiffen his resolve. He forbade discussion on the matter while awaiting the pope's view, and in December 1717, dismissed the Gallican Chancellor d'Aguesseau, and brought in as Keeper of the Seals the tough Paris Police Lieutenant, the comte d'Argenson, much liked in *dévot* circles. When the duke d'Antin inquired why he had taken this step, Orléans replied, 'Because I wish to be master.'[11]

Firmness was moreover all the more necessary in that the Parlement seemed intent on upping the ante. In particular, the magistrates were looking to extend their competence beyond religion to financial affairs – a move associated with their sniping against the growing influence in the Regent's counsels of the financial projector, John Law. When in August 1717 Orléans brought before the Parlement a package of radical financial measures concocted by Law, the magistrates issued strongly worded remonstrances, and audaciously demanded the Regent provide a detailed report on the state of government finance.[12] Though things just failed to get out of hand on this occasion, a further crisis cropped up the following summer, when the Regent took a decree on recoining to be registered not to the Parlement but to a subaltern court, the Cour des Monnaies. The Parlement erupted angrily at this jurisdictional affront, issuing a regulation (arrêt) forbidding the circulation of Law's banknotes. Seemingly mindful of the events of the Fronde as described in the works of Retz, the magistrates called for a union of all the Paris sovereign courts on the lines of the so-called 'Chambre Saint-Louis' which had initiated the Fronde in 1648, leading on to a 'Day of Barricades' in which the Parisian population had openly flouted royal authority. When on 18 August 1718 the magistrates issued a decree (very evidently targeting John Law) forbidding foreigners to be involved in the administration of the state's finances, how could they not be aware of the fact that their Frondeur forefathers had pronounced an identical measure against the Italian cardinal Giulio Mazarini?

On 26 August 1718, in a remarkable *coup de force*, Orléans crushed the political audacity and embryonic constitutional pretensions of the Parlement. A *lit de justice* secretly planned by the abbé Dubois and Saint-Simon – the latter of whom stood throughout the session hyperventilating with joy at the magistrates' discomfiture – forced through a whole series of measures which the *parlementaires* had hitherto opposed. Their rights to remonstrate were severely limited, and they were prohibited from meddling in financial affairs or linking up with other sovereign courts. Massive military preparations in the capital had in any case made certain that there would be no Fronde-like 'Day of Barricades' – and indeed it is not altogether clear whether the Parlement this time enjoyed much popular support.

This crushing *lit de justice* of 26 August was combined with an attack on the status of the legitimized children of Louis XIV. Orléans had tried to stay aloof from a long-running dispute between Maine and Toulouse on one side and the dukes and peers on the other. The dukes and peers, already embroiled with the Parlement over the 'bonnet affair', launched ferocious attacks on the constitutional legality of Louis XIV's decree of 1714 which had opened up accession to the throne to the former bastards. In July 1717, a commission established by Orléans to adjudicate the issue had emphatically denied the successoral claims of the two brothers, and the Regent declared himself in a state of 'happy powerlessness to alienate the crown's domain'.[13] Now, on 26 August 1718, Orléans followed up by reducing Maine and Toulouse to the rank of dukes and peers, and deprived Maine of his post as superintendent of Louis XV's education, which passed into the hands of the aged duc de Villeroy.

Orléans's humiliation of Maine was punishment too for the latter's increasingly open opposition to the Regent, and his apparent efforts to create an anti-Regency political alliance based around the core of an 'Old Court' faction. Maine himself was something of a political zero (as Retz would have put it),[14] and there was a strong comic-opera air about the duke's conspiratorial activities – invisible ink, coded messages, midnight assignations, swashbuckling adventurers in minor roles, and so on. Maine's wife, the Lilliputian Mademoiselle de Charolais – granddaughter of *le Grand Condé* – was a starry-eyed votary of the cloak-and-dagger, whose bedside reading included chivalric romances and Machiavelli's notes on conspiracy,[15] and she doubtless thrilled to the amazonian adventures of Frondeuses such as the duchesse de Chevreuse and the 'Grande Mademoiselle' recounted in Retz. The diminutive duchess soon emerged as the energetic heart of a conspiracy which eventually took in not just the high nobility, but also the provincial gentry, the Parisian populace and – another Frondeur touch – the kingdom of Spain. The family château at Sceaux became the launching-pad for the duchess's plots. She followed a trend already evident in the 'bonnet affair', of using printed propaganda as a means of popularizing and legitimating the princes' case. Pamphlets took the form of an appeal to the opinion of a 'public', figured as 'the Tribunal of the Nation', a kind of supreme judge of questions of legitimacy.[16] Even though the public in question was as yet tiny – the pamphlets were issued in print-runs of a few hundred, and many copies were given away – this rhetorical strategy marked something of a break from the approach of the Burgundy circle under Louis XIV which had tried to keep its criticisms under wraps. It would become widespread over the course of the century, as would another type of pamphlet attack, which had had an earlier manifestation in the *mazarinades* of the Fronde, namely, scurrilous character assassination. The *Philippiques* which the duchesse du Maine part-sponsored, part-penned herself between 1717 and 1719 targeted Orléans (the Philip in question), claiming, *inter alia*, that he had committed incest with his wild and wilful daughter, the duchesse de Berry, and was planning to poison the young Louis XV.

Orléans was well inured to attacks on his character, for the irregularity of his life made him rich pickings for *ad hominem* vituperation. Yet contemporaries were misled into seeing him as little more than a selfish hedonist. Certainly he could relax – and how! Yet it was probably less a comment on what actually occurred than on the puritanism of the age and the character of political caricature that his evening sessions with easy-going cronies, flighty aristocratic ladies and dancers at the opera – boozy and gamey though they certainly were – were dubbed 'orgies'. Partly, Orléans was taking the flak for a far more general loosening in standards of public morality which characterized the *après*-Louis XIV era: Orléans's own mother, for example, characterized Paris as 'Sodom and Gomorrah', full of men who cheated on their wives, wives who sought out lovers, spouses who took syphilis in their stride and youths who preferred homosexual liaisons to more conventional couplings.[17] Yet if there was a spirit of the 'orgy' abroad in Regency Paris, Orléans never, even his sternest critics were obliged to admit, allowed his private predilections to intrude on the business of government. The Regent compartmentalized business and pleasure – and threw himself pell-mell into both. His famous soirées took place only after a day spent glued to his desk – Saint-Simon represents him crouched low, writing with such furious concentration that his quill became entangled in his hair. His relations with the young Louis XV, moreover, were warm and respectful. His concern for the maintenance of the royal prerogatives was impeccably correct, inspiring affectionate regard on both sides.

The Maines incorporated mud-slinging into a broader political philosophy. Like the Parlement, they took advantage of the shift in political culture away from Louis XIV's mythic present to seek in the historical record crucial clues to current questions of political legitimacy, employing erudite scholars to do the scholarly legwork required to trace the hopefully glorious history of royal bastards. The resultant research was occasionally ridiculous – 'examples drawn from the family of Nimrod were scarcely conclusive', Madame de Staal-Delaunay sardonically noted, 'for that of Louis XV'.[18] Yet the pedants claimed to have discovered no fewer than twenty royal bastards who had acceded to the throne of France.[19] The circumstances of such successions suggested, it was held, that only the nation – and not simply the Regent, nor even the Parlement – had the right to adjudicate this order of constitutional claims. In ways which echoed with the arguments being deployed by Saint-Simon, Boulainvilliers and others, the Maines' apologists argued for the legal existence of the nation as separate from and autonomous of the person of the monarch and capable of expressing its wishes through the medium of the Estates General, were a dynasty to die out (a not implausible eventuality in 1717–18, of course).

That the representatives of the 'Old Court' interest, normally so identified with the undeviatingly absolutist values of Louis XIV, should be flirting perilously with contractualist theory was partly at least a sign of desperation. As they perceived themselves to be losing the legal battles in 1717–18, the Maines started investigating more forceful means of winning the arguments. Contemptuously abandoning any thought of working in collaboration with the Parlement, then in the thick of its disputes with the Regent over Jansenism and finance, the Maines looked to fortify their arguments through the military aid of the provincial nobility and the Spanish king. In the summer of 1718, agents of the Maines entered into contact with representatives of the turbulent Breton nobility, discontented with the Regent over his handling of the province's complaints about its tax burden. The two sides concocted an 'Act of Union for the Defence of the Liberties of Brittany', calling for the convocation of the national Estates General and threatening the secession of the province from the French state. Some 500–600 Breton nobles attached their signatures to the Act over the next months, and their leaders – like the duchess – began secret talks with the Spanish. King Philip V of Spain might be persuaded, it was thought, to lend force to Breton claims. As Louis XIV's grandson, he might also, with some vestige of constitutionality, lay claim to the Regency, and convoke an Estates General to uphold the rights of bastards.

The Spanish connection was, for the Regent, like a red rag to a bull, for it risked reopening questions of dynastic succession on which he had tried to effect closure in 1715. The ambiguity of Philip V's constitutional position had helped determine the Regent's foreign policy when he came to power. If at first he followed Louis XIV's latterday policy of alliance with the Spanish, plus support for the Jacobite Catholic pretender to the English throne, this soon changed to a wish to isolate the Spanish Bourbon. This policy would, it was hoped, deter Spain from aggression either against France, which was still chronically war-weary, or against the Austrian Habsburgs, who had relieved Spain of their Italian possessions at Utrecht. The defeat of the Jacobites in their invasion of England in September 1715 and the growing importance in Spanish councils of the anti-French Alberoni played a part in this policy change, which also involved rapprochement with England, and a vague Fénelonian pacifism.

While, with characteristic cunning, Orléans endeavoured to keep his options open with the English Jacobites, he was very serious about wooing an English alliance, and used the abbé Dubois as his agent in artfully concealed secret diplomacy. Son of an apothecary from Brive, Dubois was regarded by most of the political elite as a gross and revolting *parvenu* (an ill-bred ferret, was Saint-Simon's uncharitable verdict).[20] He had served as the Regent's private tutor when Orléans was a boy, and had never lost the duke's friendship and trust, while a diplomatic career developed since the late 1690s made him very much *au courant* with international affairs. He exploited the fact that the English polity was at that moment as unsteady as France's: the new Hanoverian monarch, George I, had to contend with the ejected Stuart dynasty, just as Orléans had his Spanish Bourbon rival. An Anglo–French alliance, especially if extended to other major powers, could have the effect of endorsing the Utrecht settlement and providing the foundations for lasting peace. By 1716, Dubois had crafted a defensive treaty with England, and this was extended into the Triple Alliance of The Hague in January 1717, when the United Provinces joined. Alliance with the foremost naval powers in Europe was soon shown to have its uses, for Philip V assembled Spain's largest fleet since the 1588 Armada and proceeded to invade first Sardinia, then Sicily. England and France were able to counter by concluding with the Austrians and Savoy the Quadruple Alliance of 2 August 1718. Their union bore its first fruit on 11 August, when an English fleet under Byng defeated the Spanish at

Cape Passaro off Syracuse. By January 1719, France and Spain were formally at war.

This new direction in France's foreign policy could not fail to disconcert and disillusion many political groupings within France. The 'Old Court', *dévot* faction in particular was revolted by the idea of France turning its back on a fellow Catholic power with which it now had a strong dynastic connection, in order to pursue links with the major Protestant power against which Louis XIV had spent much of the previous four decades fighting. Orléans had already been on the receiving end of Spanish manoeuvres targeting his person. Alberoni bankrolled a number of adventurers to kidnap, poison or assassinate him, and also funded scurrilous pamphlets attacking the Regency government. In addition, he put out feelers to the Maines, to the Breton nobles and to the Paris *parlementaires*, through his ambassador in Paris, the prince de Cellamare. Orléans seems to have soon had wind of these conspiratorial links (allegedly through a mistress's bedtime patter). The military success of Passaro was thus a satisfying token of diplomatic success with which to launch the *lit de justice* of 26 August 1718 against the Paris Parlement and to demote the late king's illegitimate issue.

What may have been conceived as a warning shot across the Maines' bows was interpreted by the would-be rebels as a final provocation. The duchess imprudently threatened to revenge her husband's humiliation by giving Orléans 'such a whack (*croquignolle*) as to make him bite the dust'.[21] Mindful no doubt of her grandfather Condé's yoking together of Spanish power and provincial gentry during the Fronde, she tightened her links with Cellamare, while the Spanish redoubled their efforts with the discontented Breton nobility, who in April 1719 passed under the leadership of the ferocious marquis de Pontcallec. The rebels' conspiratorial designs had already been blown, however, by the time that Philip V finally agreed to despatch troops to the Breton peninsula, and in the event French army detachments were able to clear up the vestiges of the rebellion fairly easily. Some eighty individuals were imprisoned, and four of these, including Pontcallec, were executed in March 1720.

The Breton rebels had already been isolated, moreover, by the Regent's move against the Maine conspirators in December 1718. The prince de Cellamare was expelled from France, and the Maines gaoled – only to be allowed back to Sceaux shortly afterwards to endure internal exile. Such indulgence was explicable not simply by Orléans's easy-going temperament. It was also clear to the Regent by then that the elements of a new Fronde which had threatened in 1717–19 had failed to achieve fusion. The Jansenists were troublesome, but they still only represented a minority. The Parlement's bluff had been called. The Spanish threat had remained simply a threat. Most striking of all, perhaps, was the failure of all latterday Frondeurs to attract widespread support outside the political elite. The Breton nobles failed to evoke a response from their peasants (though ironically Pontcallec's execution subsequently made him a popular martyr in the Armorican peninsula). Fellow nobles were not sufficiently disenchanted with the Regency to risk re-enacting Frondeur fantasies. The pamphleteers of Maine and Toulouse addressed a national 'public' – but one numbered only in hundreds. Would-be Frondeurs consequently lacked strength and numbers. The Parlement, rhetorically inquired d'Argenson, 'does it have any troops? As for us, we have 150,000 men. That's what it all comes down to.'[22] The Regency had retained enough of the brute force of Louis-Quatorzian absolutism to outface its critics.

D) THE FINANCIAL AND ECONOMIC CONTEXT OF THE REGENCY

From 1715 until 1720, the Regent, pragmatic through self-discipline, restrained in so many of his projects and policies, and prudent in his disarticulation of oppositional forces within the state, presided over one of the most audacious experiments in financial innovation in early modern European history. The episode – unpragmatic, unrestrained and quite imprudent – was linked to the presence in Orléans's entourage of the Scottish financier John Law. In order to understand the Regent's uncharacteristic attraction to the latter's seductive ideas, we must first map the sorry condition of the French economy and the state's finances in 1715.

On his accession to the Regency in 1715, Orléans was faced – as master of requests, Richer d'Aubé, summarized it – by 'a wretched situation [characterized by] immense debts . . . a population crippled by taxes . . . numbers diminished . . . (and) trade less flourishing [than hitherto]'.[23] Yet few doubted the country's potential for recovery. Roughly 20 million of Europe's population of 100 million were located within French borders, making one European in five a French man or woman. Spain's population was roughly one-third of France's, England's a quarter, the United Provinces' a tenth. A large population did not necessarily translate into state power, of course – after all, Poland had some 9 million inhabitants, but lacked an army and remained a diplomatic minnow. Yet what was striking about France was that over the seventeenth century it had found ways of making its numerical superiority tell, turning raw population numbers into naked military power and international dominance.

Shaped from the late sixteenth century onwards, the Bourbon political project combined a domestic programme of centralization of authority on the monarch, the removal of institutional restraints on financial policy (Estates General, provincial estates, etc.) and the development of a state bureaucracy with the build-up of a huge standing army and the creation of an impressive navy. These allowed France to undertake an aggressive quest for European hegemony and to expand France's population and wealth by extending its size. Geographically speaking, Louis XIV's annexations completed the construction of France, expanding it by nearly 10 per cent – from 470 million square kilometres to some 514 million – and bringing nearly one and a half million new subjects under Bourbon rule. There would be very little added in the eighteenth century: Lorraine was fully integrated in 1766 and Corsica was annexed in 1768, while the Revolution did some in-filling, incorporating enclaved territories such as the Comtat Venaissin around Avignon, which belonged to the pope, and the independent free city of Mulhouse.[24] Abroad too, Louis built up a colonial empire, establishing France in North America (notably in Canada, Louisiana and the West Indies) and in the south seas (at Mauritius and Réunion), and also developing trading posts in the Levant, in India and in West Africa. The achievement was all the more impressive in that expansion was complemented by the work of Louis XIV's master military engineer, Vauban, in equipping the frontiers with a *ceinture de fer* ('iron belt') of fortresses and defences which provided France with greater security than ever before from military incursions by its enemies.

These intense military efforts were, however, extremely expensive. The last serious attempt to call out the feudal levy of old, in 1674, had ended in fiasco, and thereafter everything to do with the huge standing army and cost-intensive navy had to be paid for by the state. The need to increase the country's wealth as well as its armed forces and its bureaucracy showed that the Bourbon political project had strong economic and financial as well as military, diplomatic and political dimensions. The most notable achievements in this regard occurred under the stewardship of Colbert, as Controller-General Louis's most important minister between 1661 and 1683. Colbert's aim was for the state to use all means at its disposal to mobilize the gold and silver which could put men in the field and battleships on the high seas, and could also finance the style of life to which Louis XIV and his courtiers were keen to grow accustomed. With this link between domestic and foreign policy, state subsidies were given to industry, particularly for the production of army supplies (military uniforms, weapons, artillery, etc.) and for luxury goods (mirrors, glassware, tapestries, fine cloths, etc.) which not only served the royal court but could also be an export item which would bring foreign currency into the kingdom. This was accompanied by an aggressive tariffs policy, and the chartering of trading companies to dominate European markets and begin colonial penetration. In addition, Colbert aimed to set the French to work: in the so-called 'great confinement of the poor' initiated in the 1650s and implemented from the 1670s, major cities were equipped with a poor-house or 'general hospital' (*hôpital général*) in which the needy and recalcitrant poor could be adapted to labour discipline and set to work on export commodities.

Many elements in Colbert's programme – to which historians have attached the label 'mercantilism' – were not ineffectual. A spell of peace from 1659 onwards provided a good setting for the Controller-General's work, and the third quarter of the century saw the French economy in pretty good shape. Buoyant cereal production, even in a period of generally low agricultural prices, owed something to the relaxation of war taxes. Government stimulation also aided textiles production of all kinds – woollens in Flanders, Artois and Normandy, draperies in Languedoc, luxury fabrics around Valenciennes, silk around Lyon and in the Vivarais, and lace-making around Aurillac. Government demand for luxury goods and military and naval supplies also played a part, as did the opening-up of colonial and Levantine trade through Colbert's trading companies. It was not inevitable that the return to war from the late 1670s onwards should have undercut these achievements. After all, as well as capturing new resources for the state, warfare could also stimulate important sectors of the economy, by boosting demand, encouraging large-scale production and technical innovation and help-ing market formation. It also mobilized capital and credit so that the bills of war could be paid. For this to be effective, however, war needed to be successful. In the event, the grim picture of European struggle from the 1680s to the 1710s was toxic rather than tonic for the French economy.

The heart of the problem lay on the land. As we shall show below,[25] France was still an essentially agrarian country in which poorly funded, subsistence-orientated and technologically limited peasant farming pro-duced the vast bulk of the national product – and also the lion's share of the state's tax revenue, since social privilege insulated the elite from the demeaning status of *taillable* (payer of the *taille*, the main direct tax). Neglected by government – for agriculture had entered only tangentially into Colbertist plans – the countryside was subject to violent short-term oscillations in its economic fortunes from the 1690s onwards, linked not only to war, but also to those other customary scourges of any pre-industrial society, famine and disease. The damage these caused spread like a cancer into most domains of the industrial sector as well as causing a major deterioration in national wealth – and consequently state finance.

The climate from 1680 down to 1720 was particularly disturbed, with numerous spells of exceptionally cold, wet weather alternating with unseasonal periods of drought conditions to wreak havoc with harvest yields. Bad harvests had a devastating effect on populations living close to the breadline. The effects of hunger were often conjugated with epidemic disease. Horrific mortality crises ensued as famine stalked the land. Those which occurred in 1692–4 and 1709–10 were particularly appalling. The former caused as many deaths – 2.8 million, or some 15 per cent of the total population – as World War I was to inflict on a population double the size. France, polemicized Fénelon, was nothing more than 'a massive poorhouse, devastated and without provisions'.[26] Nearly a million individuals – some 3.5 per cent of the population – were victims of the legendary winter of 1709–10, when seed froze in the ground, olive and fruit trees were blasted by killer frosts, rivers iced over, ink froze in stands, wineglasses to lips, and birds to branches.

Meteorological and epidemiological disasters could be freely ascribed to the wrath of God; yet contemporaries thought the hand of man was detectable in mass mortality too – and one man in particular, the king.

It was less the direct demographic impact of warfare – for though armies were relatively large, battles were few – than its indirect effects which stunted economic development and inhibited demographic recovery: increased tax loads, military requisitioning of food and livestock, incidental damage to the means of production, and armies' role as vectors of epidemic disease. Contemporaries who ascribed the mass poverty and high mortality to the ill-considered quest for personal and dynastic *gloire*, moreover, could add to war-related deaths the demographic losses caused by royal religious policy. The Revocation of the Edict of Nantes in 1685 led to mass emigration by Huguenots unwilling to go through the sham of becoming 'New Converts': between 1685 and 1690 roughly 140,000 individuals left France for England, the United Provinces and other destinations, and a further 40–60,000 followed their steps as part of the 'Protestant Diaspora' in the following decades of repression.

Louis had done much to bring new resources into the economy through territorial aggrandisement and had achieved an impressive level of frontier security. Yet ruling over a huge and complex kingdom and keeping armed forces and bureaucracy functioning effectively in the midst of socio-economic difficulties was a tough challenge for any king, even one as hard-working and talented as Louis XIV. When set against the indirect costs of war, the rewards seemed rather paltry – a perception which also, as we have seen,[27] was at the heart of a burgeoning critique of royal absolutism within the political elite. The strain was increasingly showing, moreover, where it mattered most: on the battlefield. French armies had won most of their battles down to the 1680s; by the 1700s they were losing more than they won, as rival armies caught up. The navy, too, sustained serious losses in the early years of the War of Spanish Succession, and the fleet never put out in anger after 1704.

The strains of war had a damaging impact on the financial machinery of state. Now that territorial acquisitions and productivity gains in the economy were no longer helping to make war pay for itself, government had to demand a larger share of what, in terms of national wealth, was a shrinking cake. Government expenditure doubled between 1689 and 1697, with war costs gobbling up three-quarters of revenue. New universal direct taxes had to be introduced in 1695 (the *capitation*) and 1710 (the *dixième*), while the burden of indirect taxes was also made heavier, with new imposts being levied on an ensemble of items ranging from playing cards to wigs. Another staple of state finance, the sale of offices within the state bureaucracy, also went into overdrive. By the end of the reign, the system of venality had been extended to bailiffs, funeral directors and oyster-sellers, and was generally believed to have reached its absolute maximum level. Despite these initiatives, tax receipts still failed to keep up, as evasion and increased levels of poverty reduced the tax take. Resort was made to extraordinary means of raising revenue. Some measures were merely symbolic one-off steps – such as the state lottery of 1700, or Louis's decision to melt down the Versailles silverware to help pay for the war effort in 1709. Recoinage was a further financial instrument increasingly desperately deployed. There were nearly forty changes in the legal value of the coinage, and the livre tournois – the country's currency of account – lost one-third of its metal value within two decades. In 1701 a further recoinage edict was linked to the recall of currency and the issue in its place of state paper notes (*billets de monnaie*), which in theory could be used in commercial transactions. They depreciated almost instantly, and were withdrawn in 1710.

The state was thus obliged to borrow increasingly massively just to keep afloat. The credit machine which the Bourbons had created strained perilously under the load. Loans were levied by selling state annuities (*rentes*). Lending was often organized through major corporative bodies such as the clergy, the provincial estates and municipal governments. In a peculiarity which said much about the baroque complexities of the Bourbon polity, the king also relied for loans on his main financial officials and the bureaucracy. Targets of choice in this respect were the individuals entrusted with farming indirect taxes (the *fermiers*) and the venal officers (known as *receveurs*) who were responsible for collecting taxes in the provinces or who were in charge of the budget in major government departments such as the army or the navy. Financiers were fabulously wealthy individuals who were able to make the tax moneys which passed through their hands work for them to build up their own fortunes. They were especially needed for short-term credits when times were tight. The state could draw on these individuals with some confidence, knowing that they would reimburse themselves from the tax loads they collected, while the high interest rates they charged also allowed them to feather their nests.

The Crozat brothers were a notable example of such specialists in financial services. From a banking family in Languedoc, they developed colossal fortunes based on an early commitment to financial office, Pierre as treasurer of the Estates of Languedoc and of the clergy, Antoine as *receveur* in the *généralité* of Bordeaux. They invested heavily in maritime trade, colonial ventures and slave trading, but also performed invaluable service during the War of Spanish Succession, and accepted Louis XIV's invitation to help finance the Jacobite rising of 1715. The king also developed a close link with another international banker, the multi-millionaire Samuel Bernard. A post-1685 'New Convert', Bernard worked out of Lyon and drew on the money-raising potential of his Protestant family and friends scattered throughout Europe. Ironically, the 'Protestant Diaspora' caused by the Revocation of the Edict of Nantes helped fund some of the key military campaigns of the war: it was the Protestant bankers of Amsterdam, for example, who in 1703 provided a 3 million livre loan to keep the French Army of Flanders in the field.

Wealth of this sort – both excessive and seemingly new – was the target for vituperative criticism which echoed the austere morality of Fénelon. Financial lobbies working hand in hand with the king's ministers were accused of placing the personal enrichment of a few dramatically before collective felicity. Lesage's popular play, *Turcaret, or The Financier* (1708) was a typically violent satirical attack. It combined an attack on corruption and luxury with a critique of the social mobility which accompanied new wealth – hence the leading character was a footman-turned-financier. Such attacks on financial milieux underestimated, however, the extent to which the scapegoat financier was in cahoots with the landed aristocracy. Besides mobilizing their own wealth and the resources of their tax constituents, financiers also nurtured close links with the political elite. Financiers provided the necessary discretion in brokering deals and acting as fronts for the landed nobility, which was keen to make money by lending to the crown at high rates of interest, but which was anxious about the laws of derogation which entailed loss of noble status for engagement in demeaning and mercantile activity. To a greater extent than contemporaries grasped, the king's aggressive foreign policy was funded by his tapping the huge wealth of his nobility, based on massive property-holding, rental income and seigneurial privileges, on highly advantageous terms for the noblemen. This subterranean linkage, in which the financiers acted as lubricant, provided another example of that alliance between a reconstructed nobility and a putatively absolutist monarchy which we have suggested was a distinctive feature of Louis XIV's political system.[28]

This world of credit in which governmental figures, financial officials and wealthy nobles seemed to be perpetually in each other's pockets formed a powerful vested interest within the state. The monarch was utterly reliant on the ability of this pivotal financial milieu to shake free money from France's social elite, from European money-markets and from the kingdom's tax-payers. The more money the king needed, moreover, the wealthier the financial milieu became. Crozat and Bernard probably ranked with the prince de Condé and the duc d'Orléans as the richest men in France. Yet the financial juggling could go spectacularly wrong. In 1709, after effectively funding all foreign transactions associated with the war for five years, for example, Bernard went bust, and had to retire from the fray to rebuild his fortune. The political credit of Chamillart, Controller-General since 1699, who had worked closely with him, was destroyed at a stroke. Chamillart's successor, Desmaretz, nephew of the great Colbert, found himself in a desperate situation, with the next three years of tax revenue already assigned to the repayment of debts. He fell back on a cartel of a dozen *receveurs* to help provide the short-term credits needed to get him through to the Utrecht peace negotiations, which he followed up with severely deflationary policies.

On coming to power in 1715, then, Orléans seemed to have only a limited set of financial instruments at his disposal for righting the listing ship of state. He could have been forgiven for looking enviously towards England and the United Provinces, which – though far less blessed than the French in terms of population size and agrarian wealth – seemed to have proved more effective in mobilizing credit to finance large-scale warfare. The innovatory fiscal mechanisms which the English and Dutch pioneered in London and Amsterdam for raising large amounts at low rates of interest seemed, however, to be heavily dependent on their political context: governments seemingly stood a better chance of inspiring lending confidence in their populations if those populations felt that they had a share in power. In France, however, sovereignty was undivided, and Samuel Bernard and Desmaretz were at one in believing that there was 'no foundation for a banking establishment . . . in a country in which everything depends on the wishes of the king'.[29] In theory, France's absolute monarch had a trump card in his hand: if he chose, he could renounce his debts at a stroke – a move which more parliamentary systems like those of England and the United Provinces could not match. The political fall-out from a state bankruptcy would, however, be intense – especially in a Regency – while it would also prove difficult to attract further loans in the short-term at least.

Initially, therefore, Orléans chose the path of orthodox financial rectitude. Sacking Desmaretz, and then working closely with the duc de Noailles, president of the new Finance Council, he followed classic methods of redressment made all the more essential by his own predilection for handing out lavish political bribes (funded partly by massive personal loans from the Crozat clan). He set about streamlining the administrative machinery of the state's finances and put auditing procedures in place designed to cut waste and maximize tax inflows. The Regent realized that, given the financial situation, war was off France's immediate agenda, and his deliberately pacifist foreign policy was combined with a continuation of the military demobilization started in 1713. Severe economies were also introduced into the court as well as the military establishment. In order to reduce the soaring royal debt, moreover, the Regent turned to a new clique of financiers, the four Pâris brothers from the Dauphiné, who had begun their rise to power in military supply after 1700. These were now called in to operate a procedure known as the 'Visa', whereby holders of state bonds had to submit them to a commission to be reviewed and (invariably) reduced. This was in effect a partial state bankruptcy, and though it helped reduce state obligations, it had a lamentable effect on public confidence, which fell to abysmal levels. Few wished to trust a government which utilized every trick in the book to escape or reduce its financial commitments.

In order to win public confidence, Noailles turned to that regular standby in such times, a swingeing attack on financiers accused of malversation of state funds. Like others which had been held in the past, the 'Chamber of Justice' (*Chambre de justice*) of 1716 performed ritualistic but largely symbolic damage on the hated figure of the corrupt state financier. The largest fines – 12 million livres overall – were levied on Antoine Crozat and Samuel Bernard, but both men lived to fight another day. In general, punishment rained down on the sprats, leaving most big fish able to swim away relatively undamaged. Over 4000 individuals were sentenced, but probably only a small proportion of the 219 million livres worth of fines which were meted out to them ever arrived in the state treasury.

Down to 1718, Orléans had shown some ingenuity in living up to his Fénelonian aim of ruling in an aura of international peace and financial rectitude and punishing fiscal wrongdoing so as to nurture an atmosphere of love and trust in his subjects. There were limits, however, to the extent to which good accountancy, even when combined with external peace, could nurture subjects' affections and restore public confidence – let alone boost an economy so severely tested by the trials of warfare. The punishment of errant financiers and the removal from the councils of state of the Desmaretz clan had done nothing to lessen governmental dependence on the financial services of cliques of private individuals and financial officials. Indeed, it may have made matters worse, for the symbolic attack of the Chambre de Justice pushed the financial milieu towards hoarding and spending rather than seeking to bail the government out. In 1717, with France shaping up to go to war with bellicose Spain, Noailles even considered convening the Estates General for the first time since 1614 to try to get out of the fiscal impasse.

The Regent had by now realized that in order to free the state from a relationship which seemed to have subverted France's natural strengths, some imaginative rethinking of power and authority was required. He seemed so boxed in by circumstances that something quite out of the ordinary was called for. A good deal of rethinking had indeed been going on in the last years of Louis XIV's reign, in the scheming of figures in the circle of the duke of Burgundy. Their interest reflected a broader concern, evident right across Europe, to find ways of living comfortably with continuing large-scale warfare, in particular by devising ways of reconfiguring the authority of states so that they could enlist their inhabitants' trust – and credit. This international debate was led by a new, cosmopolitan class of financial projectors and schemers, and it was to one of the most imaginative – or fanciful? – of such figures that the Regent now turned: the Scot John Law.

E) A SCOTTISH WIZARD IN A LAND OF TROUBLES

What became known as 'Law's System', or just 'the System' – the far-reaching attempt to establish public credit through a state bank which would receive tax revenue, keep interest rates low, boost the economy and liquidate the royal debt – would be indissolubly associated with the Regency in social memory. Contemporaries were aware they were living through an extraordinary collective experience under the financial stewardship of a man generally regarded, as one individual put it, as 'a kind of wizard [*enchanteur*] whom one day we will perhaps believe as imaginary as Merlin'.[30] The son of an Edinburgh goldsmith, who had evaded imprisonment while young for killing a man in a duel, Law travelled widely throughout Europe, gaining a reputation as a lucky gambler and as a formulator of financial schemes. His intimate knowledge of banking experiments being successfully brought to fruition in London (where the Bank of England had been established in 1694), in Amsterdam, Genoa, Turin and elsewhere gave him an air of plausibility. Affable and polite, he mixed easily in aristocratic circles and had got to know Orléans in the late 1690s. He remained in touch and was to be at hand when the duke came to power and found himself facing the financial ruin of a mighty state.

Law's diagnosis of the ailing French economy highlighted the conjunction of a monetary crisis, that is, a shortage of currency, which was causing the economy to stagnate, and a fiscal crisis, that is, enormous state debts and high interest rates caused by the state's inability to pay those debts. Releasing the state from its fiscal burden thus seemed inextricably linked to the reanimation of the economy through more credit. Law's initial proposal in 1715 was consequently simple enough: a state bankruptcy. Orléans could doubtless see the attractions of Law's arguments, but the political and financial risks they entailed made him resist falling under the wizard's spell. In May 1716, however, the Regent authorized the Scot to establish a private bank, which received deposits, discounted bills, converted foreign currency and issued notes. It was initially approved by Noailles and waved through by the Paris Parlement, but the latter was less enchanted by the pressure Orléans began to place on state officials to accept Law's banknotes in their transactions; and even less by subsequent decisions to allow tax payments in banknotes. The magistrates' quibbles failed to inhibit the success of Law's schemes, however, and the bank prospered, with its shares changing hands at well above the quoted price.

In the autumn of 1717, Law opened a second front, establishing the Mississippi Company, subsequently renamed the Occident Company, to exploit the wealth of 'Louisiana', the name for French holdings in North America from the Mississippi delta in the south to the Great

Lakes in the north. The Company's propaganda machine issued flagrant appeals to investor greed: the mountains of Louisiana, it seemed, were chockful with gold, silver, copper, lead and quicksilver; fine wool almost leapt off the backs of the native sheep; the climate allowed not one but two annual harvests of rice and tobacco; and the natives were allegedly friendly (more than friendly in the case of the women, who were said to volunteer their sexual services joyfully to all comers).

The enthusiastic public response to Law's two-track scheme helped persuade the Regent that it was worth the risks involved to give the Scot the opportunity to transform France from a land of troubles into one of milk and honey. Law was well aware that the recent record of governments arbitrarily declaring devaluations, recoinages, and financial manipulations had been more than sufficient 'to destroy trust and confidence in a state'. Constraint, he argued, 'is contrary to the principles on which credit must be built'.[31] A new blast of freedom was necessary in the state's affairs – a freedom which was an implicit renunciation of many of the axioms of economic policy in place since Colbert. The upgrading of credit should go hand in hand with a downgrading of the importance of bullion reserves, the *sine qua non* of mercantilist lore. 'Money is not the value FOR WHICH goods are exchanged', Law asserted, 'but the value BY WHICH they are exchanged'. Money should be the lubricant which helped to turn the wealth-producing wheels within society, and it should not, in the shape of bullion, be regarded as the simple embodiment of wealth. Indeed, currency would be more effective for *not* being gold and silver but fiduciary paper money. A state bank issuing the latter would stimulate foreign trade and domestic manufacture, but also centralize government income, stabilize the currency, and bring down interest rates. A prosperous, demonetized economy would also encourage population growth, and ensure that additional hands found employment: 'Let no one be idle,' Law proclaimed.[32] Furthermore, within the context of general economic growth and new-found internal confidence, the state banking scheme would allow government to tackle the repayment of the royal debt and to begin to get rid of its dependency on venality of office (officials would have their capital sums reimbursed). The mutual strengthening of state and society would ultimately help France win back European hegemony without the need for costly military ventures: France could become 'the arbiter of Europe without the use of force'.[33]

There was a strong Fénelonian undertone to the idea of being 'arbiter of Europe without the use of force': building up wealth and prosperity at home without the need for international military involvement which was hugely expensive and socially divisive was a siren's song which Orléans, whose room for financial manoeuvre was dangerously thin, found increasingly seductive. Retributive justice against financiers was reducing the government's ability to borrow, while thoughts of a bankruptcy were ruled out of court by the deteriorating international situation vis-à-vis Spain, a situation, moreover, which was worsened by the covert activities of the Maines and the Breton nobility, as well as by a resurgent Paris Parlement. Following the winding-up of the Polysynody, Orléans gave himself a breathing space by the *coup de main* of 26 August 1718. The Parlement, which had been expanding its ambitions as regards state finance, had its goose well and truly cooked, and the Maine faction was delivered a heavy blow. In the ensuing moment of calm, Orléans took Law more formally under his wing, and also gave his aide, the abbé Dubois, a freer hand in foreign affairs. The Scot's private dealings and the operations of state now became increasingly intertwined. In December 1718, his bank was made the state bank, its issues regulated by government decree. The establishment of four daughter branches in the provinces (at Amiens, Orléans, La Rochelle and Tours) highlighted the System's claims to be vivifying the economy of the country as a whole. In July 1719, Law's company was awarded the monopoly of coining and issuing money. From that autumn, his bank took on full responsibility for reimbursing the royal debt, assumed prelude to the ending of venal office. The aim seemed to be, with a wave of the wand, to switch the state's creditors into investors in the economy by encouraging them to transfer their holdings of government paper (*rentes* and such like) into shares in his Company.

The scope of Law's System was widened still further by its extension into tax-collection. From late 1718, it undertook the farming of tobacco taxes, and in August 1719 it beat off strong competition from a cartel headed by the Pâris brothers to take over control of the General Farm, which was responsible for the collection of other indirect taxes. In October, Law was entrusted with collection of direct taxes too. The commercial dimensions of Law's activities also expanded: a veritable empire was placed in his hands by integration into his Occident Company of the East Indies and China trading companies, followed soon by the Africa and Saint-Domingue companies. The new company was floated as the Indies Company (Compagnie des Indes) and its shares were eagerly purchased, with values rocketing upwards.

By late 1719, the zenith of Law's fortunes had been reached. All of France's maritime and colonial trade was effectively in the hands of his Indies Company. He ran the state's bank, holding the monopoly of issue, coinage and the printing of money; and tax-collection was under his sole control. In January 1720 (after agreeing to convert to Catholicism), Law would be made Controller-General of the Finances, the first such since the death of Louis XIV, and in the following month his bank and company were merged into a single organism. Nor had Law's ambitions and schemings reached an end. He was still hatching further plans for a unitary and universal direct tax and for a fresh burst of economic freedom.

But was the picture a little suspiciously sunny? The increased amount of paper money in circulation had produced a boom, but one that was producing its own problems: over-liquidity in the economy, fuelling runaway inflation. The whole operation could, moreover, only be sustained so long as all players retained a faith in the economic performance of the System. Here Law was longer on promises than performance. In particular, he was utterly disingenuous in everything to do with profits deriving from colonial exploitation. In 1719–20, in the midst of France's Law-led boom, Louisiana was experiencing a famine, and new recruits to the colony were dying like flies from epidemic disease. A dangerous gap was thus opening up between rhetoric and reality. Symptomatically, an ex-governor of Louisiana who on his return to Paris queried the Mississippi pipe-dream found in the Company's literature was thrown into the Bastille for his pains, while Paris police spies were primed to keep a close watch for individuals diffusing rumours and gossip which risked destabilizing Company – and government – credit.

The more the gap yawned open between Law's rhetoric and normal social expectations, the more contemporaries found the whole financial boom ridiculous, immoral, even pathological. The old world of the moral economy seemed under siege by the social forces unleashed by the System. Traditionally, an economy of a 'fair price' had tended to prevail in business operations, with profits set by custom. Corporatism frowned on social mobility, and social esteem was usually measured in property ownership rather than moveable wealth. Now, however, prices and wages were rising vertiginously fast, changing customary economic certitudes. Twelve printing presses had to run day and night to keep up with the massive demand for banknotes. The credit market was topsy-turvy, yet Company shares soared, changing hands at up to forty times their face value, allowing mega-fortunes to be made and lost on the Rue Quincampoix in Paris (between the Rue Saint-Denis and the Rue Saint-Martin), which became an impromptu stock exchange for the System's operations. The street had to be provided with gates at each end to keep trading within daylight hours, and special police patrols were organized to instil a semblance of order. The street was endlessly thronging with crowds seeking a speedy fortune – Paris was said to have swelled by some extra 200 to 350,000 individuals from all over France and Europe attracted by the hopes of windfalls. The old rigidities of rank crumbled under the pressure of new-found wealth: 'everyone', noted the Regent's mother, 'wants to surpass his neighbour in terms of carriage, table and appearances'. The Bordeaux magistrate and philosopher Montesquieu, whose *Lettres persanes* (1721) lightly clothed a critique of Louis XIV and the Regency in the form of a fictional correspondence involving Persian visitors to Paris, satirized Law's System, bemoaning a situation where 'servants are waited on today by their comrades and tomorrow by their masters'.[34] The reimposition of archaic sumptuary legislation – individuals were forbidden from wearing diamonds and pearls save with the written permission of the king – was quite unable to check a novel fluidity in fortunes and some outrageous personal destinies. A beggar was said to have made 70 million livres from his trading on the Rue Quincampoix, a lackey 50 million, a barman a cool 40 million . . .

By early 1720, with the Mississippi bubble seeming fit to burst, these anxieties and apprehensions began to crystallize into political opposition. Any wealthy private individual who had benefited from the pre-Law financial system could only resent what the Scottish wizard was trying to do. The System was, opined Pâris-Duverney, one of the props of the old financial establishment, 'preparing the ruin of the state's old creditors'.[35] Financial figures such as he – excluded from many areas of their former involvement including tax-collection – had had their heads temporarily below the parapet, but were on the qui-vive for chinks in the Scot's armour. Law's schemes also set alarm bells ringing in the Parlement. After its drubbing at the Regent's hands in 1718, the latter had consigned itself (as it put it) to 'a respectful silence [which had] exposed us to the reproaches of our fellow citizens'.[36] By 1720 it was seeing it as its duty to re-enter the fray. Law's plans for debt management and in particular his aim to end venal office discountenanced the magistrates, who had purchased their posts and regarded themselves as an important restraining influence on the crown's right to tax. The social and economic freedoms of the System seemed to be threatening the corporatist shell of the polity in ways which the Parlement felt were profoundly unconstitutional.

These critics of the System had worked ferociously to subvert one of Law's most intractable assumptions, namely, that paper money could make individuals' attachments to more tangible forms of wealth such as land, gold, silver and jewellery outmoded and unfashionable. The attempt to demonetize the economy was pursued in a bewildering variety of ways. A decree of April 1719, for example, stating that Law's banknotes were not subject to devaluation, made them more valuable than coinage. Thereafter he endlessly devalued gold and silver against banknotes in official transactions. There were twenty-eight changes in the value of gold, thirty-five in the value of silver between September 1719 and December 1720. Yet changing a traditional economic *mentalité* was an uphill task and, significantly, Law never fully disenchanted even his most intimate supporters (and maybe even himself) with customary forms of wealth: throughout the boom, he and his son bought up property as though it was going out of style, and those investing with him, including the aristocrats on whom he and the Regent showered sweeteners like confetti, did much the same.

In addition, the more resistance there was to his demonetization plans, the more Law resorted to measures of constraint, which sat ill alongside his earlier grave prognostications about the importance of avoiding force in establishing public confidence. His steps to bolster faltering confidence in his paper schemes led Law now to enthuse about 'forced credit . . . which emanates from the sovereign [alone] and not from his subjects'.[37] Absolutist regimes, he argued, even had an edge over liberal and constitutional ones when it came to schemes like his. 'I maintain', he wrote, 'that an absolute prince who knows how to govern can extend his credit further and find needed funds at a lower interest rate than a prince who is limited in his authority.'[38] As long as he acted in a rational manner which seemed neither factional nor arbitrary and provided that he had public opinion behind him, an absolute monarch could control secrecy and business corruption, command obedience, minimize financial dependence on private individuals, and maintain public order – all prerequisites for producing prosperity.

Yet as though, strangely, he were a latterday believer in the propaganda of the Sun King, Law massively overestimated the extent to which absolutism could deliver the required measure of obedience in this as in any sphere. He discovered that the more the 'absolute' monarchy had recourse to measures of constraint, the more the public doubted that the System could hold. In early 1720, Law had it formally decreed that banknotes should be exchanged at face value – even though they were generally being discounted by some 20 per cent at the time. He followed this with a state decree forbidding any individual from holding over 500 livres in specie – a chimerical wish. Worse too, the government assured its unpopularity by authorizing house searches to ensure against hoarding of gold and silver. Such attempts to use force in order to limit the option of convertibility from paper to specie provoked added pressure on paper among a nervous public unable quite to shake off attachment to more tangible forms of wealth. A gadarene rush to convert from paper to specie in early 1720, led by Law's erstwhile cronies among the court aristocracy, underlined the point. The prince de Conti needed three carts to wheel back his converted bullion from the Rue Quincampoix. He was said to have made 5 million livres from the operation – and was not untypical: the duc de Bourbon came out of the System some 20 million livres, the duc d'Antin some 12 million, richer. The courtly rats were leaving the sinking Scottish ship.

As a downward spiral started to develop, Law's efforts to contain speculation by pegging shares, now made available in unlimited quantities, at the level of 9,000 livres, were unable to forestall the drop in value. His decision to reduce the interest payments on state bonds from 4 to 2 per cent was similarly inopportune, for it mobilized against him the solid bourgeoisie of Paris, who had resisted the speculative blandishments of the System for the more traditional security of state bonds. Such individuals from 'an infinite number of middling families', were always, as the Cardinal de Retz had noted of the Fronde, 'the most to be feared in revolutions'.[39] In the face of spreading public discontent, which the Parlement now stepped in to exacerbate, and with the high nobility losing faith in the System, Orléans's faith in his Finance Minister wobbled. When in May 1720, Law tried to brazen out the crisis by an emergency 50 per cent devaluation of share prices and banknotes, public confidence sagged disastrously. What the Regent had hoped would be a restructuring of public credit turned out to be the death rattle of the System. Public fury at the devaluation edict was so intense that Orléans reversed it a week later, and removed Law from the post of Controller-General. Though the Scot remained on the councils of state, he needed an armed guard to avoid being lynched. Anyone using the word 'System', expostulated Parisian barrister Marais, should be regarded as guilty of treason.[40] Cartoonists vied with each other in portraying Law as a giant balloon, disastrously leaking air out of every orifice, or else as a dangerous lunatic deserving to be locked up for getting the state to subscribe to the economics of the madhouse. All efforts were now made to reduce the amount of paper money in circulation, and to reduce the number of shares. Paper money burnt fingers, as individuals desperately sought to get rid of it in return for more tangible assets. Banknotes and shares, stated the Regent's mother with her customary forthrightness, were now so many 'arse-wipes' (*torche-culs*).[41]

In mid-July the bank closed its doors for lack of bullion reserves, and public disturbances outside the offices of the Company in the rue Vivienne on 16 July – in which nearly a score of individuals died – were followed by Law's coach being destroyed and his coachman attacked. The Parlement waded in rather intemperately, calling for Law's dismissal. Furious at the *parlementaires*' self-promotion as guardians of financial probity and the bulwark of the small investor (and suspicious of their Frondeur intentions), the Regent banished them to the small town of Pontoise some 20 miles from the capital.

It was symptomatic of the way things were going, however, that Law was no longer the centre around which politics revolved, but was becoming a peripheral player, whose fate was linked to settlement of more pressing disputes. The decision on 15 August that banknotes with a face value of over 10,000 livres would lose currency from October, with those valued between 10 and 100 livres doing so in May 1721, spelt the end of his System. The measure was followed in the autumn by measures reducing current accounts by three-quarters of their face value, and then ending the use of banknotes in any sort of financial transaction. Jockeying for position in the political arena was increasingly controlled by the abbé Dubois, who utilized the looming disgrace of Law to engineer his own ascendancy. The Jansenist issue was also centre-stage again, with the Regent profiting from the Parlement's exile from Paris to pass a decree on 4 August 1720 forbidding attacks on the Unigenitus bull. The decree excited much fury from Gallicans and Jansenists, but opposition remained generally unfocused, and Orléans was able to go forward to broker a deal whereby in return for the Parlement's formal acceptance of the 4 August decree – plus the removal of Law from the Regent's entourage – they were allowed back to Paris. The new Controller-General Lepelletier de la Houssaye appointed the Pâris brothers to preside over the winding-up of the System, and they operated another 'Visa' procedure, annulling one-third of the value of *rentes*, and reducing the rest into state bonds at 2 per cent. The new Controller-General urged the Scot's incarceration in the Bastille as the best way of restoring public confidence, but the ever-tolerant Orléans allowed him a furtive rush into an exile from which he never returned. He died in Venice in 1729.

Parisian barrister Barbier would not give Christmas bonuses to his servants that year: having lost 60,000 livres in the Law fiasco, he could not afford to.[42] Though much contemporary comment focused on the big winners of the System, for how many respectable and middling households was Barbier's not the more typical experience? When the Mississippi music stopped, individuals left holding paper notes could only lose. Prominent among these losers were religious communities and hospitals, which suffered massively from having their investments converted into state bonds – it seemed a fitting conclusion to the episode that while a wealthy few prospered, hospitals and poor-houses had to shut their doors to the sick and needy. The post-Law mopping-up financial operations by the Pâris brothers revealed some half a million individuals throughout France claiming losses. If we use a multiplier of 4.5 to encompass all family members, then we can estimate that more than 10 per cent of the nation's population were affected by the fall-out from 'Mississippi fever'. About half of these had claims of less than 500 livres, which probably denotes their middle- or lower-middle-class status. The losers from the System thus covered all social ranks and every part of the country.

The English philosopher David Hume would later joke that Law had caused a sick French economy 'to die of the doctor'.[43] Yet he was wide of the mark. The frenetic boom of 1719–20 soon passed, but rentier losses and millionaire gains overlay more nuanced effects on the economy as a whole. The System not only gave a tremendous boost to the high aristocracy, who paid off many of their debts and enjoyed massive windfall gains; it also, at a more lowly level, gave respite to much of the peasantry. The latter's release from part of its debt burden allowed some degree of agrarian recuperation after the hard times of the turn of the century. Peasant proprietors had more money to spend and to invest. The additional demand which they represented acted as a fillip to manufacturing, which had already been boosted by the cheap credit available through the System. The property market, the building trades and the market for luxury goods were all beneficiaries of this loosening up of the economy, as were those regions associated with the colonial trades and shipping. By the late 1720s, an unparallelled burst of economic activity would launch the economy to golden years: John Law could claim some posthumous part in that story.[44]

In many ways, the biggest loser of all in the Law System was the state. Massively in debt following the War of Spanish Succession, government had been able to pay off many of its creditors in devalued paper through what was essentially a state bankruptcy. The Scottish wizard had also provided the ever-pragmatic Regent with sufficient funds to fight the Spanish in 1719–20 and, through the massive handouts he was able to make to the aristocracy, to forestall internal princely opposition to his foreign policy. The boost to the economy – whose long-term effects Orléans would not live to see – made the population more able to pay its taxes. Yet the state had also had to borrow very extensively too, so that the royal debt in 1722 was nearly three times that in 1715. In some ways, this was worse than going back to square one. The failure of Law's promises of debt management to materialize and the whole fiasco of the System made the conditions in which the state could cope with its debt in the future far more problematic.

The Law episode had been highly influential, first, in helping to form a public which was intimately involved in state politics. Whereas the 'public' interpellated in the pamphlet wars launched by the legitimized princes in 1717–19 had been tiny, the System brought state finance under the glare of a public numbering – literally, as we have suggested – millions. Though Louis XV regarded such matters as falling solely within the purview of his closest counsellors and himself, the severe impact which the System had had on private fortunes well outside narrow financial and merchant circles galvanized growing public awareness of state credit and the problem of the royal debt.

Not only did the System make a significant contribution to developing a wider public as a political force, it also, second, predisposed that public against what was now seen as an overly authoritarian strain within the state's financial policies. Henceforth, the state's issuing of paper money would be seen not as a debt-management manoeuvre aimed at reducing the burden of the state within the economy, but rather as a means of increasing the crown's political and financial independence. Law's apparent wish to do away with the corporatist carapace of the monarchy, and his moves towards constraint (conjoined with the Regent's shift away from Polysynody to a more classically Louis-Quatorzian stance), only confirmed the feeling, enunciated by Montesquieu, that the Scottish wizard was 'one of the greatest promoters of despotism that has ever been seen in Europe'.[45] Orléans and his successors would move back to a more decentralized and diffuse system of credit: the financial and political consequences of default were less than with a single credit organ such as Law's bank.

Third, the Law episode endorsed the growing role of the Parlement in defining the contours of the politically acceptable and it enhanced its stature as self-appointed defender of public interest in matters financial. Its view that currency values should not be fixed arbitrarily from above and that paper money was a dangerous thing won the day. Its claims that it rather than the government represented the best interests of the nation looked more substantially based after Law than before him. This meant, fourth, that the range of financial instruments henceforth available to the monarch had been reduced, for it was generally recognized that the Parlement and the nascent public opinion which it was helping to create were making currency devaluation, bankruptcy or paper money into policy options that it would be difficult to sustain politically. For the rest of the century (including well into the Revolutionary decade, in fact), John Law was a bogey-man, a ghastly spectre instantly conjured up as soon as structural reform of public credit appeared on the horizon. By closing down options in this way, the Law episode had made the task of organizing a rational, unburdensome and centralized system of public credit intensely problematic.

The state's failure to develop banking institutions may have impacted on economic growth – though as we shall see, France's record was not unimpressive.[46] More significant, finally, was the role of the System in confirming government dependence on networks of financial clans, with their semi-covert links to the wealthy nobility. Symptomatically, once the Scottish wizard had been put out to grass, there returned to favour the same set of individuals who had dominated state finance during the War of Spanish Succession. Law's gravediggers were Antoine Crozat, Samuel Bernard and the Pâris brothers, notably Joseph Pâris-Duverney, who retained a pivotal place at the heart of state finance down to the 1750s. The Law System had inadvertently strengthened the very forces at the heart of the polity it had been designed to do away with.

F) THE CHILDHOOD OF LOUIS XV: SIX FUNERALS AND A WEDDING[47]

What did the young Louis XV make of this extraordinarily agitated episode which had such a powerful impact on his kingdom? Very little, by all accounts. Though he presided over the Regency Council from Febuary 1720, silence was his most remarked-on contribution. In February 1723, on his thirteenth birthday – following a tradition stretching back to 1374 – he was declared a major, but his first and only thought was to conserve power in the hands of those in place: his uncle, Orléans, now ex-Regent, was maintained as effective ruler, and the duke's henchman, abbé Dubois, was kept on as Principal Minister. When finally, in 1726, following the deaths of both, Louis formally declared his wish to rule in the manner of Louis XIV – it would only be, as we shall see, deferentially to place at the centre of political affairs his tutor, abbé Hercule de Fleury.

Political listlessness on Louis's part bespoke a timidity which seems closely linked to the fact that he grew up in circumstances dominated by the deaths of those closest to him. The loss in 1711–12 of his parents and his elder brother (the duke and duchess of Burgundy and the duke of Brittany) left him a sad orphan-heir as bereft of close relatives as he was isolated from other children. It was clear from the start that he would have to live in the constant shadow of his great-grandfather. Scarcely into double figures – and his awkwardness and clumsy flat-footedness notwithstanding – he was obliged to dance at court balls 'because Louis XIV did so'.[48] Though the elderly Louis XIV had developed a fond relationship with his successor, his Sun King's death struck the child hard too, and left him prone to 'vapours' (seemingly bouts of depressive melancholia). Those into whose hands he was placed tried hard to compensate for these losses. But they were a geriatric crew, closer to the grave than to the cradle: the pompous if well-meaning duc de Villeroy, who was placed in charge of his education (which he viewed as a form of dressage),[49] and the boy's confessor, the abbé Claude Fleury, were septuagenarians, while his nurse, the duchesse de Ventadour, and his tutor, Hercule de Fleury, were sexagenarians – as was Dubois. A mere forty-one years old in 1715, the Regent would have seemed a mere stripling in comparison – had not high living and hard work raddled his health, leading to his premature death.

A child yet a king, with all that that implied in both condescension and deference from his elders, Louis was thus brought up under the direct supervision of aged adults forever fearful of his health and well-being. 'Don't try to make him handsome or clever,' Madame de Maintenon had told Madame de Ventadour as she entrusted the child to her care. 'Give him back to us healthy, that is all we ask.'[50] Highly protective – Louis wore leading strings until he was seven, a corset for his posture until he was ten – his guardians cocooned him from a wide range of normal childhood experiences. A keen and dutiful student, he shone most in technical and scientific subjects which marked some distance from sensory experience or direct communication with others: maths, geography, anatomy (he had a penchant for dissection), zoology, botany. He had fun with a little printing set – another means of making human contact less immediate. His early taste for hunting, the sport of French kings, owed more to his taste for personal athleticism than for the sociability of the chase: he showed more concern for the welfare of his hounds than his fellow huntsmen. Courtiers remarked his taciturnity which they linked to underlying timidity and fear of gaucheness, as though fear of condescension was a motivating factor. Yet he seemed immature in all he attempted. His early aversion for the opposite sex raised eyebrows, for it presented the possibility of his being drawn into an active gay subculture at court. In later years, he would do some formidable heterosexual catching-up.

His remoteness deterred even those who wished to burnish his popularity. The people of Paris had warmed to him from 1715, for example, and whenever the king got a cold, they sneezed in sympathy. Keen though he was to do right by his subjects, however, Louis lacked the common touch. His decision to shift from the Tuileries back to Versailles in June 1722 was an uncalculated but wounding snub to Parisians.

Similarly, it was unfortunate that he held his coronation in October 1723 at a time of widespread misery in northern France caused by drought. The king expected his subjects to rejoice at a time when livestock and poultry were dying in droves, bringing disaster to many households. Symptomatically, the coronation service refused to allow the people who had gathered outside the cathedral to enter the nave – a traditional ceremonial procedure which was regarded as symbolizing popular assent to the new king. The shutting-out of his subjects – his suffering subjects moreover – shocked that arch-ceremonialist, the duc de Saint-Simon, who branded it 'an enormous mistake as much against the spirit as against the constantly observed usage in all coronations hitherto'.[51]

Yet if Louis XV was exclusive, he was also excluded – and never more so than in the issue of finding him a wife, in which personal factors were wholly subordinated to state and dynastic issues, managed by Orléans and the abbé Dubois. The latter, the Regent's erstwhile secret agent, had turned increasingly into a hatchet man, who had played a key role in bringing the Maines' conspiracy into the open and in humbling the Parlement in 1720. In 1722, he also weaseled out of the reluctant *parlementaires* support for a Formulary implying acceptance of the Unigenitus constitution, thereby inaugurating a religious and parlementary truce. He was said to be driven by ambition, his anti-Jansenism allegedly a mere ploy to persuade the pope he was worthy of a cardinal's hat, which he was duly granted in July 1721. Stories were freely retailed about his humble background and allegedly obscene private life: he had procured mistresses for the young Orléans when he was his tutor, had ignoble sexual liaisons himself, was foul-mouthed (having a legendary propensity for telling members of the court aristocracy to fuck off)[52] and was famously irreligious – when receiving holy orders so as to assume Fénelon's old post as archbishop of Cambrai in 1720 it was said he could hardly remember the words of the Paternoster. Orléans smiled beatifically over his ally's excesses: Dubois was, he ruefully admitted 'the most rascally, atheistic and worst priest there has ever been'[53] – but he had more than proved his worth. As Orléans's own hectic private life increasingly caught up with him – his drinking was getting heavier, his hangovers longer, his health worse – he looked to Dubois to take up the slack, and it was the abbé who made the running in the business of finding Louis a wife – a Spanish wife.

The war which France, alongside its new English ally, undertook against Spain in 1719 had been quickly concluded. The invasion of north-eastern Spain by a small French expeditionary force brought Philip V to the conference table. Dubois did not want to alienate Louis from his Bourbon cousins, and he had Spain admitted to the Anglo-French-Austrian bloc in the Quadruple Alliance of January 1720. At the same time, Spain officially recognized the superiority of Orléans's claims to Regency over Philip V. A defensive alliance between Spain and France was signed in March 1721, by which time negotiations began for arranging what became a double marriage pact in March 1722. Philip V's only daughter, the three-year-old Maria Anna, was betrothed to Louis XV, while Mademoiselle de Montpensier, Orléans's daughter, was destined for the heir to the Spanish throne, the prince of the Asturias.

The Spanish marriages pact played as much (maybe more?) in the interests of the Orléanist dynasty than of the Bourbon state. The marital arrangements placed an Orléans within a major European ruling house, and sealed an alliance with Philip V, his feared rival for the Regency and – theoretically – the French throne. Moreover, with Philip V having renounced his title to the French throne, the choice of a child bride for Louis, by continuing the absence of a direct heir for the foreseeable future, left Orléans first in the queue for the throne. To have defused both the Franco-Spanish and the Orléanist-Bourbon rivalries at a single stroke – while simultaneously keeping on good terms with England, avoiding warfare, finding his young charge a wife of a suitable pedigree, and brightening the Regent's own hopes of succession – must have seemed to the arch-pragmatist Orléans a signal achievement to add to his others. Despite the financial vortex which had opened up in the Law System, the duke had presided over the calmest regency in French history, outfaced a potential Fronde, dampened down much of Jansenism's potential for religious divisiveness and kept a war-damaged society out of foreign engagements (the Spanish campaigns of 1719–20, involving a force of only some 30–40,000, according to one contemporary, did not 'deserve to be called a war in a kingdom such as this').[54]

One of the most striking canvases of Antoine Watteau, whose dreamily and allegorically ludic paintings became highly popular in the Regency, is entitled *Gersaint's Sign*, and it shows a painting of Louis XIV being studiously put into storage. The political allegory was only superficially apt. Despite the strong implications about turning a new political leaf in 1715, the Regent had certainly not lived up to some of the expectations placed upon him. He had not turned the clock back to a pre-Louis-Quatorzian golden age as his supporters like Saint-Simon and Boulainvilliers had demanded, nor yet moved into a principled system of counter-absolutism as the abbé de Saint-Pierre had hoped. The air of freedom and openness which came to characterize the reputation of the Regency was something of a chimera. The canons of artistic taste were more relaxed than under Louis XIV, the press a little freer, the sexual mores of the political elite more manifestly heterodox than in the prudish last decades of Louis's reign. Yet royal authority had been kept pretty well intact, and beneath the surface there were very marked continuities with the earlier reign. The would-be Mentor had failed to transcend Louis XIV's template of power. The Polysynody experiment had flattered, only to deceive, hopes of root-and-branch change, and the administrative infrastructure of absolutism developed by Louis XIV remained locked in place. The doors of the Bastille opened and closed with much the same frequency as under Louis XIV to engorge social deviants and religious and political dissidents. Despite the pamphlet wars of the mid-1710s over the princes and Jansenism, the printing industry was still under careful surveillance too – indeed, measures were taken in 1723 to tighten censorship further.

The Regency proved, moreover, a regime which took policing of public order very seriously. Demobilized soldiers after 1713 caused a major security problem in many areas, and were drawn into bandit and smuggling gangs. The most striking example of this lawlessness, the notorious bandit and highway robber Cartouche, was executed on the Place de Grève in Paris in November 1721, and much of his gang over the following months. His end marked a watershed in the move to restore internal security. The regular army had already been carefully adapted to an internal policing role, and in 1720, the paramilitary police force, the *maréchaussée*, was increased in size and given a key role in highway policing. Legislation in 1724 would assign it the further task of rounding up vagrants and tramps in the kingdom's *hôpitaux généraux*. Even before this, moreover, decrees in 1718 and 1720 had targeted city tramps and prostitutes for internment and also for transportation to Louisiana. The Parisian prostitute who was Louisiana- (and possibly death-) bound might ruefully reflect on the Regency's reputation for sexual 'freedom'.

That the velvet Regency glove contained an absolutist fist was clearly demonstrated in the government's reaction to the sudden reappearance of bubonic plague in 1720 at Marseille, after half a century's absence. The disease killed some 50,000 out of the city's 90,000 population, showing that it had lost none of its erstwhile virulence – but mortality might have been even higher without the very tough and repressive stance of the government. Operating through the War Ministry and relying heavily on the coordinating talents of the provincial Intendants, the state took extraordinary steps to pen in the disease in the south-east, disdainfully ignoring claims to freedom of action and movement by individuals and communities alike. One-third of the War Minister's correspondence at the time concerned coordination of the cordon sanitaire, and one-third of the French army spent time enforcing it, patrolling the perimeter of the infected region and crushing the skulls of potential escapees with their rifle-butts – an interesting and rather brutal early example, as Jack McManners has pointed out, of preventive medicine.[55] Uncompromisingly tough, but effective in preventing a disastrous diffusion of the killer disease, the government made much of this triumph for centralized administrative coordination of which Louis XIV would have been proud.

Continuities with the absolutist past seemed all the more striking, moreover, as Dubois emerged as a Richelieu-style figure dominating the Royal Council. This son of a Brivois apothecary walked into the Regency Council attired as a cardinal – who could by his rank claim precedence over dukes and peers – and thereby provoked his ducal enemies sniffily to stay away in protest. This gave Dubois a wonderful pretext for an Augean cleansing of the Royal Councils. Yet in the event death – once again in a childhood so marked by funereal shadows – rescued Louis XV from a Richelieu, removing Dubois from high office just as he was settling into the job. His health had been going from bad to worse, and an abscess on his bladder was diagnosed. By the time he agreed to be operated on, it was too late: five apprentice surgeons jumped on him to hold him down while the finest royal surgeons incised him from the genitals to the bladder, only to find gangrene installed throughout his lower organs. Racked in excruciating agony, he died within hours of the illness and the operation. On hearing the news, Orléans immediately sought an audience with the king to offer his services as Principal Minister, so as to forestall the eventuality of palace conspiracies. Orléans could hardly be refused. Still less than fifty years old, as dutifully committed to his responsibilities as ever and punctilious in respecting the person and the sensibilities of his teenage master, Orléans was, however, physically going downhill fast. He was in office only a matter of months before, in December 1723, a stroke carried him off.

Orléans's death, following so closely on that of Dubois, removed a vital strand of personal continuity in a royal childhood lived in the shadow of deaths of all those close to him. There remained only one link with his early childhood – his tutor since 1715, the abbé Hercule de Fleury, bishop of Fréjus. Solid, loyal, dedicated, alive to the ways of the court, no friend of the Jesuits – yet certainly not a Jansenist either – Fleury exuded dependable, discreet, trimming virtues. More than this, however, he proved to be a friend and surrogate father to the young king, who unburdened himself to him as to no other. The virtues of sympathy and support grew in resonance as death sheared the king's entourage of his other personal friendships and alliances.

Normally Fleury was a regular fixture at Louis's elbow, but he had not for once been in his presence when the duc de Bourbon broke the news of Orléans's death and blurted out a request, as senior Prince of the Blood, to be appointed Principal Minister. Bourbon was widely disliked for having benefited untowardly from the Law System, but most of all for his stunning lack of intelligence: for Barbier, he 'had a very limited mind, knows nothing and only likes pleasure and hunting'[56] (the latter allegedly so as to ingratiate himself with his monarch). In order to restrain his influence – and benefit his own – Fleury got an undertaking from Louis that he would only treat with his Principal Minister in Fleury's presence.

Bourbon might have been stupid – but he had sense enough to realize that the key political issue of the day had become getting the young king married and procreating. The three-year-old Infanta Maria Anna had entered Paris in March 1722, sitting in an open carriage on the lap of the duchesse de Ventadour and holding a doll very tight indeed. The king, who had not been informed of the plans to marry him off (but who, when finally told by his uncle, had obediently if tearfully whimpered his assent) was formally introduced and presented the princess with a magnificent new doll bedecked with precious stones, alleged to be worth 20,000 livres. With dolls so much in evidence, however, the prospect for babies looked remote. There was soon a good deal of whispering, much of it targeted at Dubois. After pulling through a period of regency in which much concern had hovered around the biological viability of the dynasty, it seemed rather perverse of the Principal Minister – or was it Orléanist calculation? – to choose for the growing king a wife who would not bear children in the foreseeable future. In 1725, the king fell ill, and even though it proved a false alarm – a digestive problem caused by cramming too much chocolate – it concentrated Bourbon's mind on the absence of a viable heir. The new duke of Orléans, son of the Regent, was a callow and shallow youth and worse still – for the house of Condé, collateral with the Bourbons, was perennially at daggers drawn with the rival Orléans dynasty – had just married and already made his wife pregnant. The Spanish Infanta was still only a child, was reckoned to have twisted hips which might present an eventual child-bearing problem and had become, moreover, the object of growing loathing by the young king. Packing her off back to Spain would place a strain on the Franco–Spanish alliance but in the circumstances, frankly, strain there would have to be. In April 1725, the Infanta was dismissed from Paris without the king even saying goodbye, and a speedy search was undertaken to find a suitable replacement for his bed.

It would not be accurate to say that the cupboard was bare. Yet frantic perusal of the lists of family members of the European dynasties found few candidates with an approximation of the key requirements for the job: to be single, healthy, young(ish), pretty(ish) and preferably Catholic. The choice eventually fell on the Polish princess Marie Leszczinska – 'what a terrible name for a queen of France!' exclaimed an appalled Marais.[57] She was the daughter of Stanislas Leszczinski, who from 1704 until 1709 had served as elective ruler of Poland, before being overthrown and spinning out the rest of his days living a modest life off pensions provided by sympathetic fellow rulers. When he had opened the letter from the duc de Bourbon asking him for his daughter's hand in marriage for the young king, he had fainted on the spot in shock, and this was only a dramatic version of the surprise which the choice evoked within France. Marie was healthy-looking rather than beautiful, six years older than the king, and hailed from essentially an aristocratic rather than a royal background. Louis was allowed only a little more say in the matter this time – though he saw only Marie's portrait before the marriage in August 1725 (with Orléans standing proxy for the monarch in the ceremony). When she arrived at Versailles, however, the auguries looked good. The two partners warmed to each other, with the king giving his new queen, it was said, some 'seven proofs of love' on their first night together.[58] Babies would soon come aplenty from the union: ten children in the first ten years, including, in 1729, a son and heir. After a decade and a half of a royal demography characterized by death, this represented a welcome infusion of fecundity – and hope.

Bourbon, architect of the royal marriage, did his best to turn the event to his personal advantage. He packed the queen's chamber with his nominees, including his own mistress, the charmingly accomplished marquise de Prie. The latter's taste for political intrigue caused nostalgia for Orléans who, it was said, might have had mistresses galore, but had not involved them in affairs of state. Nor had he been as incompetent as Bourbon. The duke failed to woo Spain back into line after the Infanta snub, and France soon seemed to be drifting towards open conflict with the combined forces of Spain and the Holy Roman Empire. In home affairs, the introduction of a new direct tax in kind, the 'fiftieth' (*cinquantième*), a 2 per cent tax on property, won almost universal opprobrium, coming as it did shortly after the one-off 'joyous accession' tax levied to commemorate Louis's coming of age. The new tax also coincided with a spell of high prices and economic difficulties caused by rain which had spoiled the harvest, triggering bread riots. Bourbon found himself being undermined in the king's counsels by Fleury. It was a clumsy attempt to put paid to the latter's influence by involving the new queen in court intrigues which stimulated Louis to lead a palace revolution against his own Principal Minister. On 12 June 1726, the duke and his mistress were exiled from court. Four days later, Louis declared that he was abolishing the post of Principal Minister and that he would rule in the manner established by Louis XIV in 1661. Yet though he stated that he wished 'to follow the example of my late great-grandfather in everything',[59] he also stipulated that the bishop of Fréjus would be present at all councils and meetings with ministers. Few – himself included – could have suspected that the 76-year-old cleric was about to embark on nearly two decades at the helm of state.

3

Fleury's France (1726–43)

A) HERCULES ON A TIGHTROPE

Everything had come late to 76-year-old André-Hercule de Fleury. His age on becoming effective First Minister contrasted markedly with that of his precedessors, Princes of the Blood, Orléans and Bourbon, who had been less than forty when they achieved political prominence. The son of a minor Languedocian tax official, Fleury had won the patronage of court grandees through precociously brilliant studies in Paris in the middle years of Louis XIV's reign. But his promise almost fizzled heedlessly away: some kind of misunderstanding with the king, who mistook abbé Fleury's affable worldliness for libertinage, led to his exile from the royal court in the 1690s. His recall produced only meagre recompense for a 46-year-old: a bishopric – but in far-away and poorly endowed Fréjus. A ringing declaration from his Mediterranean diocese in support of the Unigenitus bull, however, won him the belated approval of Louis XIV, who, just before his death in 1715, recalled the by now venerable sexuagenarian to be the tutor to the dauphin, and to begin a process of integration into the political life of the court which we have described in the previous chapter.

There were some who ascribed the rise of Fleury and his continued tenure of office down to his death in his ninetieth year in 1743 to a covert, but ruthlessly single-minded ambition. No one who saw him at close quarters could doubt that there was a tough, dogged and spasmodically obstinate streak under the benign, affable and voluble face which he presented at court. Yet Fleury's belated and improbable propulsion to the top of a greasy pole owed as much to circumstances as to his own personal goals. What was to prove the most striking feature of his tenure of high office was precisely, moreover, a refusal to commit to a single objective, a determination to remain flexible and mobile. Despite his name, there was nothing Herculean about André-Hercule de Fleury. He possessed the sprightliness of a hale and hearty geriatric, but shunned shows of strength and feats of *éclat*. His proclivity was for placable accommodation and negotiation, not for confrontation or conflict. Balance was all.

Fleury's pliable approach to policy was often – especially latterly, and sometimes with justification – taken for inaction and lack of energy and imagination. Yet such characteristics in a principal minister were not entirely inappropriate for a society and polity still feeling the aftershocks of the reign of Louis XIV. The dynastic succession was still an open issue: the birth of a dauphin in 1729 came as a relief, but it still only meant that a succession crisis opposing the house of Orléans to the Spanish branch of the Bourbons was two rather than one heartbeat away – and the hecatomb of 1711–12 was a reminder of the fragility of royal lives. The young king was still unengaged by political affairs. Furthermore, Bourbon's decision to send back the Spanish Infanta in 1725 had alienated the Spanish and threatened to drive them into the arms of France's traditional enemy, Austria. Nor was there much scope for military adventures: the army and navy had been run down under the Regency, and new taxes to fund prolonged conflict would have placed a heavy strain on an economy still groggy after the Law System. Like many of the generals and diplomats of the 1720s and 1730s, moreover, Fleury could recall too well the miseries of the Spanish Succession War of 1701–13 to wish to embark lightly on European conflict: unusually for an eighteenth-century ecclesiastic, he had personally witnessed the harsh face of war when his Fréjus diocese had been invaded by the enemy in 1707. In addition, the abbé had inherited that most delicate of issues, namely, Jansenism, and intemperate action here risked both a religious schism and a major political crisis involving the Parlement, which was vaunting itself as the movement's defender. There was more than enough here to justify a gentler and more subtle approach of the kind which Fleury could offer.

Tenure of power in the Bourbon monarchy depended to a large extent on the favour of the monarch, and the ability of the holder of power to resist attempts to dislodge that favour. The new cardinal had indeed got where he was by 1726 largely through the goodwill of the monarch, and he was never to lose it. If he never received the title of Principal Minister,

83

no one was in any doubt that this was his effective position. All ministers consulted with the monarch in the presence of Fleury, who was the king's main adviser and *de facto* executive agent on most policy matters. Once his cardinal's hat had been squeezed out of the pope in November 1726, he took pride of place on the Royal Council too. Some contemporaries imagined sinister reasons for the baffling closeness of the relationship between king and cardinal: the latter, it was whispered, had schooled his young charge in subservience to his own wishes. Stories circulated of how courtiers making unscheduled entries to the young king's chamber found schoolbooks open at the same page for weeks at a time, or else stumbled across Louis putting curling-papers into his tutor's (sparse) hair. The claim that by indulging Louis's love of pleasure, Fleury aimed to render him incapable of becoming independent seems wide of the mark, however, for he was an impeccably dutiful tutor and Louis a studious pupil. But there was indubitably an element of emotional dependency in the king's attitude towards Fleury. The apparent indestructibility of his tutor must have seemed attractive to a still-youthful monarch who had been let down by the deaths of his relatives and intimates. In the late 1730s, Louis's heir, the ten-year-old dauphin, would speak truer than he knew when he said that Fleury had 'a good window into the heart of the King [his father]'.[1] The duc de Bourbon's maxim, 'be sensible and don't quarrel with the bishop [of Fréjus, i.e., Fleury]'[2] – which Bourbon had ignored himself, and paid the full price – remained excellent advice for anyone with political ambitions in Fleury's France.

Fleury repaid Louis's unswerving trust by indulging the monarch's taste for a kind of morose hedonism. Awkward and uncomfortable in formal company, the king only felt truly at home among small groups of intimates with whom he could engage in gloomy gallows humour. These groups did not include his wife. Queen Marie Leszczinska's unfortunate involvement in the duc de Bourbon's attempt to get rid of Fleury in 1726 damaged the king's trust in her. Despite the appearance of sundry infants through to the late 1730s, sexual relations between the royal couple were becoming glacial: when asked in 1737 whether his new daughter should be referred to as '*Madame Septième*' ('Madame the Seventh'), Louis gloomily rejoined '*Madame Dernière*' ('Madame the Last').[3] Sexual relations between the spouses were discontinued at about the same time. Eschewing marital domesticity, Louis threw himself into a bachelor's life of outdoor pursuits. He maintained three packs of hounds (Louis XIV had made do with one) and was an unflagging hunter. In the period of Fleury's ministry he accounted for some 3,000 stags; and when he went shooting, his daily bag was 200 to 300 pieces of game.[4]

While Fleury compliantly worked within the gaps left by Louis XV's hunting schedule, he also showed indulgence towards the young king's extra-marital sexual activities. It was only in 1736 that the royal court became aware of a fact known to Fleury and the queen since 1733, namely that Louis was conducting a sexual liaison with the comtesse de Mailly, the eldest of the five daughters of the marquis de Nesle. From the cardinal's point of view, if Louis was to have a mistress, it was preferable that she should be someone like the plain but perky Mailly, who was devoted to Louis, solicitous for his welfare, and willing to keep clear of involvement in policy issues. This appears to have been less true, however, of Mailly's sister, Mademoiselle de Nesle, whom the king secretly took as his supplementary mistress in 1738, before she married the marquis de Vintimille the following year. The marquise de Vintimille was more interfering than her sister, but she died in 1741 after giving birth to a baby whom her husband renounced and who was widely believed to be the king's. This drove the king temporarily back into the consoling arms of Mailly – 'highly loveable', it was later recalled, when she had 'a glass in her hand'.[5] But it was not long before Louis's roving eye had included in its compass Mailly's two younger sisters, the prematurely widowed marquise de La Tournelle (soon to be made duchesse de Châteauroux) and Mademoiselle de Lauraguais. In satires which Louis is known to have seen, Parisian wags disingenuously wondered whether this studied devotion to a single family was the king's ingenious attempt to avoid promiscuity.[6]

Indulgence in the king's taste for mistresses and the hunt was one means by which Fleury maintained his position in the insecure, faction-riven world of court politics. He was also canny enough to make both of his obvious disadvantages in politics – his geriatric condition and his outsider status – work in his favour. Paradoxically, the cardinal had old age on his side. No one in 1726 believed he would be more than a stop-gap; and by the time it became apparent that he was a permanent fixture, informed courtiers realized that, such was his hold over the king, it was probably best to await the cardinal's death before acting. They therefore made their arrangements and alliances in terms of the next rather than the present ministry. Fleury's position outside and above the major factional groupings allowed him to play one off against another. Only once he had secured the neutrality of a cabal centred on the ambitious young duc d'Orléans had Fleury participated in the overthrow of Bourbon in 1726, for example, and he paid for Orléanist aid by offering ministries to Orléans's clients, including Lepeletier des Forts as Controller-General (a strictly political choice, as he was alleged not to be able to manage the simplest arithmetic).[7] Yet straight away Fleury put out reassuring feelers towards the Bourbon-Condé faction, and made it clear that the Orléanists would not be allowed on to the Royal Council. In order to demonstrate he was not an Orléanist clone, Fleury also cultivated good relations with the legitimated princes, particularly with Toulouse. He did the same with the duc de Noailles, head of the powerful and extensive court-based faction (or 'tribe',[8] as the duc de Luynes put it).

Noailles, veteran of the Polysynody, was bought off with military commands and the office of marshal of France – a good example, this, of how patronage buttressed Fleury's ability to balance faction against faction. If noble faction-leaders were to be excluded from supreme power, they required ample compensation in terms of favours, privileges and postings for themselves, their houses and their clients. Fleury could be pretty parsimonious in regard to expenditure on the royal house: he cut back on expensive celebrations over the birth of the dauphin in 1729, for example, and even packed off four of the king's daughters to a convent education in Fontevrault rather than have to foot the bill for their separate households at court. His own demands were few: as a cleric he had no extensive household to advance, and he lived frugally and made extensive charitable bequests. The meagre size of his succession would strike contemporaries as unbelievably small. Yet to the aristocracy he was highly generous, realizing – like the Regent before him – how effective patronage could be in buying off opposition. The extent of royal patronage in Fleury's hands was, moreover, colossal. All major offices at court and in government, at the centre as well as in the provinces, were under his control, as were military and naval appointments. Since 1720, Fleury had also sat on the Council of Conscience, which adjudicated ecclesiastical appointments, and from the late 1720s he had sole charge of the so-called *feuille des bénéfices* which dispensed all major nominations for the bishops' bench and the major benefices. As royal gatekeeper, he also controlled physical access to the king as well as lodgings in the royal palaces – both significant factors in a polity where propinquity to the ruler was a source of power and profit. As Postmaster-General too, he was well-placed to keep an eye on the private correspondence of ambitious courtiers.

If there was one place, however, where Fleury developed a faction of his own, it was at the heart of government, among the secretaries of state. The cardinal worked hard to keep the ministries a Fleuryite fief, as free as possible from the troubling influence of courtiers, and to have a set of ministers who owed more to him than to anyone else. The Orléanist tinge to his ministry in the early days was soon wiped out: Lepeletier des Forts was dismissed in 1730, for example. Fleury's predilection was for experienced, long-serving and competent managers, often from middling Robe backgrounds. Lepeletier's successor as Controller-General, Philibert Orry, was very much par for the course in this respect: son of a high financial official to Philip V of Spain, Orry had served in the army, and purchased a post in the Paris Parlement before being picked for royal service as Intendant in Soissons, Perpignan and Lille. Tough and with a remarked-on lack of airs and graces, Orry stayed in post from 1730 to 1745. Another former Intendant in frontier provinces, d'Angervilliers, was appointed to the War Ministry in 1728 – he died in post in 1740. The ministry contained two young Phélypeaux: 28-year-old Maurepas remained as Navy Minister, to which was added responsibility for the Household and for Paris, while 21-year-old Saint-Florentin had particular responsibility for Protestant issues. Maurepas worked closely with the Lieutenant-General of Police of Paris, Hérault, who was effectively of ministerial rank and served as Fleury's right arm when things got tough. Another by now trusted technocrat, d'Aguesseau, returned as Chancellor, initiating down to his death in 1751 landmark judicial reforms. He worked alongside the most brilliant, but also the least politically docile and most troublingly ambitious of the group, the former *parlementaire* Chauvelin. Appointed Keeper of the Seals in 1727, the latter also doubled as Foreign Minister.

Mingling administrative talent, energy, experience and, overall, political docility, this was a formidable, and relatively youthful grouping for an old man to head, especially one who knew how to conserve his energy yet stay abreast of things. When he got tired, Fleury went off to nearby

Issy to recuperate – to 'vegetate' was his own term[9] – in the country
house of the Saint-Sulpician community, confident that he could leave
these subordinates to get on with things in his absence. He went even
further along this route in 1732, when he let it be known that he regarded
Chauvelin as his assistant (*adjoint*) – a step which many (including,
regrettably for his own prospects, Chauvelin himself) regarded as a
prelude to his nomination as Fleury's successor. The latitude which he
allowed ministers was a crucial part of Fleury's balancing act. It meant
that he could at times distance himself from the policies which they
implemented. He would like to change his financial policies, he would
admit in private to some disgruntled suitor, but that Monsieur Orry (as
he shrugged and turned his eyes heavenwards) – too brutal, he couldn't
do a thing with him. Fleury was thus able to secure credit where due and
yet to divert unpopularity on to his underlings.

Fleury's singular ability to keep himself aloft on the political tightrope
even during the most perilous circumstances was also evident in foreign
affairs. The decision of his predecessor, Bourbon, to send back the
Spanish Infanta destined as Louis's bride risked driving an irate Spain –
in the unstable hands of Philip V and his queen, Elizabeth Farnese – into
the arms of an Austria which felt it had lost much international prestige
in the Utrecht settlement of 1713. Invigorated by military successes
against the Turks in 1716–18, the Austrians looked set for international
mischief, and the Austro–Spanish alliance of 1725 panicked Europe by
seeming to signal a committed move towards a war to destroy Utrecht.
England was becoming progressively more estranged from France anyway, and the latter's position in Europe seemed all the more isolated
when Prussia and Russia joined the Austro–Spanish pact in 1726. In the
Paris Peace Preliminaries of 1727, however, Fleury successfully checked
the drift to European war, and then, in the subsequent Congress of
Soissons in 1728–9, unpicked the Austro–Spanish alliance. A clause in
the ensuing Treaty of Seville in 1729 between the maritime powers of
France, England and Spain allowed the Spanish to maintain fortresses
in Italy, thus ensuring Austria's hostility. Fleury's demeanour in handling
these negotiations – realizing his own limitations on action, renouncing
sectional claims for the role of honest broker, sidestepping intractable
questions of principle and preferring the cautious and circumstantial
approach which kept open links to all sides – prefigured the posture he
would always try to adopt in European affairs. Indeed, France under

Fleury was to gain notoriety in this sphere: problems in the 1730s in Geneva, between Spain and Portugal, and then in Corsica were all referred to the arbitrational skills of French diplomacy. Political rivals sneered at Fleury's 'bourgeois policy' of evading military aggression for a pacifist strategy of seeking to live in peace with France's neighbours, but even they acknowledged that this gave a chance for France to concentrate on economic recovery – an approach which, as we shall see, bore much fruit.[10]

Though initially enjoying some measure of success, Fleury's efforts to keep the peace in Europe ran into trouble. He endeavoured to contain Austria by seeking allies within the Holy Roman Empire (notably Bavaria and Saxony) and in Italy (the kingdom of Sardinia). He also rejected the efforts of Emperor Charles VI to secure international recognition for the so-called Pragmatic Sanction – the agreement that his daughter and sole heir Maria Theresa (who as a female was ineligible to serve as Holy Roman Emperor on his death) would at least succeed to all the Habsburg inheritance. Yet England, the United Provinces and Spain all for their part accepted the Sanction in 1731, leaving the French embarrassingly isolated. Austria seemed all the more of a problem in that Francis, duc de Lorraine since 1729, was an Austrian pawn destined for marriage to Habsburg heir Maria Theresa. If the independent duchy of Lorraine, which had been occupied by French troops between 1670 and 1697, were to fall into the hands of a major potential enemy, it would pose a massive military threat to France from the east. The possibility that the duke, after marrying into the Habsburg dynasty, might be a candidate for election as Holy Roman Emperor had set French alarm bells ringing, and started a drift towards armed conflict, which Fleury's Austrophobe Foreign Minister, Chauvelin, did everything to encourage.

The *casus belli* in fact came from elsewhere. Augustus II of Saxony, regnant king of Poland, died in February 1733, leaving the strong possibility of the election as his successor of the father of the queen of France, Stanislas Leszczinski, who had ruled the state from 1704 to 1709. Support for his claims sprang from the sense that dynastic *amour-propre oblige*. A French squadron smuggled Stanislas into Poland, and managed to get him elected by the Polish Diet. At the same time, however, Russia and Austria secured the counter-election of the dead monarch's son, Augustus III of Saxony. War was inevitable. Fleury's earlier German diplomacy proved sterile: Saxony was in cahoots with Austria, while Bavaria stubbornly refused to join the French cause. Fleury managed, however, to secure English and Dutch neutrality, then formed an alliance with Spain and Sardinia. Under the first so-called 'Family Compact' of 1733 with Philip V, France allowed Spain to launch an attack on Naples, drive out the Austrians and put Philip's son, Don Carlos, on the throne of the Two Sicilies. Sardinia meanwhile helped France inflict damage on the Imperial forces in Lombardy. Developments in northern Europe were less rosy. Austrian forces supporting Augustus of Saxony marched on Warsaw, forcing Stanislas, protected by a French expeditionary force under the comte de Plelo, to fall back on Dantzig. Skirmishing outside the city resulted in Plelo's death and a French defeat, and in June 1734 Stanislas fled for his life. Though French armies made solid headway on the Rhine and in northern Italy, forcing an increasingly isolated Charles VI to sue for peace, the Polish fiasco precluded French rejoicing.

In the circumstances, France did remarkably well out of the War of Polish Succession, and what it achieved was a vindication for the shrewd and balanced diplomacy of Fleury over and against the militaristic approach urged by Chauvelin. The image of the humiliated Stanislas was a useful totem to brandish in peace talks, which Fleury did his best to prolong. Under terms of a deal, eventually struck in 1737 and ratified in 1739, Augustus of Saxony was confirmed as Polish ruler. The other key elements of the arrangements related to the balance of power in western rather than eastern Europe: Charles VI's daughter Maria Theresa married Francis, duc de Lorraine; but the latter was accorded reversionary rights to the duchy of Tuscany as part of a bout of dynastic swapping and counterswapping involving Sardinia and Austria. And Lorraine was handed over, as a consolation prize, to Stanislas Leszczinski, and would pass to France on his death (which eventually occurred in 1766).

The Lorraine arrangement, locked in place by France's agreeing to Charles's precious Pragmatic Sanction, was quite a coup. It was made clear that Stanislas would govern the duchy of Lorraine through an Intendant chosen in concert with France: the candidate selected was Chaumont de La Galaizière, Intendant of Soissons, and brother-in-law of Controller-General Orry. The Frenchification of a German-speaking province which had formed part of the Holy Roman Empire for eight centuries and which was France's largest territorial acquisition since

Franche-Comté in 1674 proceeded apace. The stroke was all the more remarkable, moreover, for being achieved with very little military, financial or manpower expenditure, and for being magicked up out of a mediocre international position. Fleury's policy of keeping bridges open to all sides had been triumphantly vindicated: once Austria had been squared, there were surprisingly few grudges for other powers to bear. To some degree too, the province was a dividend payable on Fleury's record of honest brokerage in international affairs. As the marquis d'Argenson had once noted, Fleury's 'pacifist and moderate mask . . . is worth two armies on our side'.[11] Just as Stanislas would have been less generously treated had he been less pathetic, so France would have been given less had it shown itself more aggressive in international diplomacy over the previous decade.

Lorraine represented a signal victory both for Fleury's sense of realism and his imagination. He had been realistic enough to accept that it would be extremely unlikely for France to gain the province by force of arms; yet sufficiently imaginative to conjure the acquisition from the most unpromising of international circumstances. The arch-tightrope-walker had carried off a significant prize. And he had done so while simultaneously experiencing the most severe political crisis of his ministry, over the Jansenist issue.

B) TRIDENTINE THEMES . . .

In 1720, Catholic France acquired a new hero: Henri-François-Xavier de Belsunce de Castelmoron, archbishop of Marseille, who was suddenly projected into public awareness by his conduct during the epidemic of bubonic plague which appeared in his home city in that year. French men and women recoiled with horror at lurid tales, served up in a *flambée* of sensationalist publications, of buboes cascading polychromatically from the body of the afflicted, of the breakdown in public order and the cessation of trade, of corpses lying in piles in the gutter, rotting and gnawed at by stray dogs or else being carted away pell-mell, rich alongside poor, to mass plague pits. In the midst of this Boschian horror strode the saintly figure of Belsunce, his cassock sleeves rolled high, a sponge of aromatic herbs under his nose to keep the stench of putrescent flesh at bay, offering alms, comfort and confession to the sick and dying. This ambulatory and seemingly invulnerable oasis of redemptive sanctity – eleven out of his twelve attendants were stricken and died at his side – assumed the role of community leader, pulling the city out of the crisis, at the height of which he dedicated his fellow townspeople to the cult of the Sacred Heart. As the disease drew to a close, it would be Belsunce who led the penitential processions, touring the bounds of the city, bare-headed and barefoot, with a torch in his hand.

Belsunce had self-consciously modelled his conduct – as was generally realized – on one of the great saints of the Counter-Reformation, Saint Carlo Borromeo, archbishop of Milan, who in 1576 had broken with the more customary episcopal option of speedy flight from a plague-infected area, and remained to tend the spiritual needs of his diocesans. In his long episcopacy in Marseille between 1709 and 1755, Belsunce was to follow many other features in the life of Borromeo, who had been among the most enthusiastic implementers of the precepts of the great Council of Trent (1545–63) which had rallied the Catholic church following the Protestant Reformation and defined the principal doctrines of what became the Counter-Reformation. The church still lived under the Council's shadow, and its bishops revered Borromeo. Just along the Mediterranean coast at Fréjus, Fleury himself had had the same source of inspiration during his episcopate from 1696 to 1715. Indeed to a very considerable extent, the French church as a whole in the late seventeenth and early eighteenth centuries was still acting a part in a Tridentine script, a script moreover which accorded a key role to bishops in the Borromeo mode.

Though supra-national religious orders such as the Jesuits initially took a highly prominent role in the work of Counter-Reformation, Trent had placed great emphasis on the role of bishops in implementing its precepts. This element became more evident over the course of the seventeenth century. Bishops worked to eliminate heresy and spiritual ignorance and to generalize a new style of Christian living among the lower clergy and, through them, to 'Christianize' the population at large. The aim was not only to combat Protestantism but also – as the eminent bishop, Grignion de Montfort of La Rochelle, put it – 'to renew the spirit of Christianity among Christians'.[12] A crucial element in this project – the establishment of diocesan seminaries for the training of the priesthood – had only been fully implemented in France between roughly

1650 and 1720: Paris, the most important diocese in the French church, for example, had only got one in 1696. Staffed by an array of post-Tridentine religious orders, notably the Jesuits (who had trained Belsunce), the Lazarists (who ran the Marseille institution) and the Saint-Sulpicians (who were probably the best of the lot), the seminaries of France's 128 dioceses[13] were by 1715 pouring forth cohorts of young priests with much higher levels of theological, spiritual and pastoral training than hitherto.

Post-Tridentine pastoral thinking foregrounded the need to imbue in the priesthood a sense of vocation and standards of personal integrity which set them over and above the laity. If they were to Christianize the laity, *curés* had to set a moral and religious example, leading decent, sexually continent lives, eschewing gambling, excessive drinking and other worldly pursuits. The emblem of this recharged vocational state was clerical uniform. The cassock had been relatively rare in the reign of Louis XIII, but under his two successors it became standard issue for the lower clergy: 'to be embarrassed by it and take it off', the bishop of Nevers was to warn in 1768, 'is tantamount to being a deserter and fugitive and declaring oneself unworthy of wearing it'[14] – a remark whose language coincidentally highlighted the quasi-military disciplinary sense which the episcopate was developing in its lower clergy. The bishops expected obedience from their diocesan clergy – and, moreover, had state-endorsed means of exacting it. Most bishops had extensive rights of patronage within their hands, including power of appointment to ecclesiastical benefices and diocesan posts, and this was supplemented by powers of correction and punishment which the crown endorsed in 1695. Indeed, after 1698, errant clerics, whether regulars or seculars, who strayed from required standards of conduct risked their bishops imprisoning them by *lettre de cachet*.

A further mechanism of episcopal control over the diocesan clergy was the parish visitation – another technique propagated by the Council of Trent, pioneered by Carlo Borromeo and studiously copied by Belsunce and his ilk. Bishops became more assiduous in this respect: parishes received a visitation from their bishop or his vicar-general on average every twelve years in the seventeenth century, and every eight years in the eighteenth. Visitors performed a kind of spiritual audit, punctiliously checking the life, morals and dutifulness of clergy and parishioners. The Council of Trent had stressed the role of the parish clergy in providing a ceremonial encasement to the everyday life of their parishioners from cradle to grave, most notably through the sacraments of baptism, marriage and burial and also through the festivals and rituals of the liturgical year. Visitations ensured that new-born babies were baptized swiftly – within twenty-four hours after 1698. The marriage ceremony was given primordial significance over folkloric pre-marriage engagement rituals and wild charivaris. And the last rites were viewed as the ubiquitous accompaniment to death, itself – as Louis XIV's demise had shown[15] – the subject of a whole panoply of rituals and practices. More generally, there was also an insistence on the laity's eating fish on Fridays, observing abstinence in Lent and Advent and taking regular communion, most crucially in the form of the Easter duties of confession and communion.

Post-Tridentine worship was in essence a baroque piety[16] which expressed itself in florid ostentation and which used all the media of communication and the material culture of worship to make a powerful sensorial assault on the life of the spirit. A still lively tradition of hell-fire preaching aimed to elicit holy terror in congregations: the famous Jesuit Bridaine, for example, utilized *commedia dell'arte* and ventriloquistic techniques to achieve almost Grand-Guignol effects in his sermons. Other forms of church art were similarly conscripted to produce a powerful emotional response: music was grander, with organs and choirs becoming more numerous and proficient, while painting and sculpture were profusely utilized in funeral monuments, altar screens, and the like. Baroque piety found rampant didactic expression too in the festivals and ceremonies in which the post-Tridentine church revelled. Baroque piety was an everyday, quasi-universal phenomenon – even abject paupers wanted candles carried at their funerals, with monks and nuns following the bier. The funeral ceremonials of grand personages were massive and theatrically ordered spectaculars with casts of thousands, while special events such as religious missions or the ceremonies which Belsunce organized to mark the passing of the plague in 1721–2 wrung every emotion, causing hysterical outbursts of mass weeping.

The episcopate also endeavoured to root a new spirit of godliness in their dioceses through the institutionalization of forms of voluntary and associational devotion, which proved a receptive medium for baroque piety. Confraternities of penitents, of the Holy Sacrament and the Sacred Heart (the latter boosted in fact by the 1720 plague dedication) elicited an enthusiastic popular response. The cult of saints – seen in Marian devotions, for example, in collective pilgrimages and in ex-votos invoking saintly intercession for sickness – still also enjoyed widespread esteem. This was supplemented by a growing market for rosaries, prayer-books, lives and images of saints, prie-dieux, crucifixes and the like, which brought the material culture of Catholic piety into the homes and everyday lives of the humble.

The pedagogic mission of post-Tridentine Catholicism placed a strong emphasis too on the practice of catechism. Catechisms began to assume a question-and-answer format as an accessible way of teaching doctrine. Bishops, true to their Tridentine role as guides to faith, often wrote one themselves – Bossuet produced one for Meaux in 1687, for example, and bishop Colbert of Montpellier a much-utilized one in 1705. Steady sellers on what was a buoyant market for religious publication of every sort, they formed a staple ingredient too in schools, to which the church was increasingly committed, and over which local *curés* had surveillance (and bishops, authority). Royal declarations of 1698 and 1724 urged the creation of primary schooling in all parishes, with compulsory catechism classes.

Few other groupings within eighteenth-century society had as powerful an impact on the conduct of their fellows as the episcopacy. As a group, however, they were far less saintly a bunch than their seventeenth-century forebears. It did not require personal sanctity to achieve the effective and disciplined running of dioceses. Educated, classically, at the Saint-Sulpice seminary and the Sorbonne in Paris and then trained in a post of episcopal vicar-general, many bishops had made worldly compacts. Fleury or Dubois were only the most important of those numerous prelates who played major administrative roles in public life. This was particularly evident in the *pays d'état*, such as Languedoc, where the dominant role of bishops in regional administration was legendary. A royal edict of 1695 which had released bishops from the duty of residence in their dioceses (which had been enjoined on them at Trent) encouraged some to seek a higher political profile elsewhere. An age of Counter-Reformation saints was being replaced by an era of bureaucrat-bishops and bishop-statesmen, who impressed more by their authority and efficiency than by their sanctity. Indeed, the higher clergy mistrusted unvarnished sanctity: self-immolating, poverty-loving and flea-infested figures such as saints Jeanne Delanoue and Benoît Labre raised more than a few episcopal eyebrows. There was a growing scepticism among the upper clergy too about the presence of the miraculous and the supernatural in everyday life: individuals attacked by peasants for being witches were viewed as misguided cranks or charlatans; and bishops supported more scrupulous monitoring of alleged miracles.

The episcopate cut a decidedly aristocratic figure, as indeed befitted the most highly prestigious and the most privileged of corporative groupings within the French state. They enjoyed fabulous levels of wealth, for the church owned between 6 and 10 per cent of the nation's cultivable land and collected a tithe on all property, which averaged between 8 and 12 per cent of agrarian income. Since the Concordat of Bologna with the pope in 1516, kings of France had held effective powers of appointment to bishoprics and the major ecclesiastical benefices, and they – or rather their ministers, such as Fleury – had used this as a form of patronage to shower the church's wealth over the most important families of the realm. From the mid-seventeenth century down to the Revolution of 1789, around thirty families of the aristocratic elite – prominent among whom were the Rohan dynasty (who held the Strasbourg bishopric for a century), the Noailles (of course), the Luynes, the Choiseuls, the La Rochefoucaulds and the Fitz-James – held the lion's share of the most prestigious and wealthy posts. Although a talented provincial outsider (though very rarely a commoner, for bishops were invariably nobles) sometimes broke into the charmed circle, it was birth, wealth and connection at Versailles which counted most: on the eve of the Revolution, more than three-quarters of the episcopate traced their ancestry back to the sixteenth century or earlier. These were princes of the church who consequently found it very easy to live like princes: though some of the tiny dioceses of the Midi produced little in the way of revenue, the big appointments such as Cambrai, Paris or Narbonne generated a fabulous income. The superb court held by successive Rohans at Strasbourg was legendary. Baroque piety seemed to mix easily with baroque indulgence, even for prelates renowned for preaching austerity. Jansenist martyr Soanen, bishop of Senez, possessed episcopal jewellery bearing a galaxy of precious stones and lived in some little luxury. Fellow Jansenist bishop Colbert of Montpellier slept every night in a room richly appointed in crimson damask, trimmed with gold, ate off expensive silver plate, and was forever on the look-out for costly *objets d'art*. At Cambrai, the richest diocese of France, the austere apostle of simple virtue, Fénelon, maintained a table groaning with a calorific overload of meats and wines. Episcopal diet was too rich and grand to include humble vegetables – the bishop of Lodève even contracted scurvy!

This highly, even anarchically individualistic group of men, all-powerful within their dioceses, also possessed collective weight within the state through their domination of the General Assembly of the Clergy. Meeting every five years (and on an *ad hoc* basis when the state required), the Assembly was the only corporative body – except, arguably, the royal court – of truly nationwide dimensions. This gave added resonance to its deliberations on matters managerial and fiscal as well as doctrinal. The Assembly negotiated direct with the crown over the *don gratuit* – the ill-named 'free gift' which the church made in lieu of paying normal royal taxes, which averaged between a measly 1 and 3 per cent of its total income. The Assembly subdivided the sum among the dioceses, which then held diocesan assemblies, presided over by the bishops, to allocate the load around the parishes and benefices. Though it usually worked harmoniously with the crown, the Assembly did on occasion flex its muscles – and get results. In 1725, for example, it killed in their cradle the duc de Bourbon's plans to extend his new *cinquantième* direct tax to clergy and nobility alike, invoking the authority of the pope in the defence of ecclesiastical immunity. One of Fleury's first acts, on his appointment as Bourbon's successor in 1726, was the withdrawal of the *cinquantième*, which he accompanied with a ringing endorsement for the tax immunity of the clerical order. The cardinal knew how to manage the church as he did every other institution of state.

Notwithstanding numerous personal peccadilloes, the episcopate were instrumental in driving through the Council of Trent's Christianization project. All the indices of religiously motivated practice that lend themselves to measurement – performance of Easter duties, for example, observance of the church's teaching on baptism and the respect for the last rites – were in triumphant ascent from the late sixteenth to the early eighteenth century. There was much evidence too to suggest that the changes signified real attitudinal and behavioural transformation. Extremely low levels of illegitimacy and pre-bridal pregnancies and a slump in conceptions during the abstaining months of Advent and Lent demonstrate an almost universal acceptance of the church's teaching on the sacrament of marriage, which was new. It was assisted no doubt by the moral policing of private life performed by the zealous, vocationally committed and seminary-trained parish clergy. Yet in return, there was greater pressure from the laity for better and more seemly conduct from its priesthood – less drunkenness and, in particular, less sexual hanky-panky – which showed a rising line of expectation on their side too.

English visitors frequently mocked the baroque piety characteristic of post-Tridentine French Catholicism which the administratively proficient episcopate did so much to promote. They viewed it as so much popish mummery, revealing ignorance and superstition rather than spiritual awareness. Many Catholic clerics were equally condemnatory about levels of piety among their charges. Christophe Sauvageon, for example, parish priest at Sennely-en-Sologne in the Orléanais from 1675 to 1710, lugubriously qualified his parishioners as 'baptized idolaters', who were 'more superstitious than devout'. Though 'highly zealous for the externals of religion', they mixed genuine belief with a heavy dose of superstition and paganism such as belief in witches and spirits. Even apparently Christian practices were turned to profane ends: religious confraternities became ribald drinking associations, for example, while devotion to saints descended into a kind of crude bargaining for health and fortune, with acts of penitence being viewed as means of buying off the ire of God and the saints.[17]

It is possible to read Sauvageon's critique of his parishioners – and other similar attacks – as showing how basically unChristian much of rural France remained. There would be no shortage of outlandish stories of peasant superstitions and basic religious ignorance well into the nineteenth century. Yet though it is tempting to see in play here solely a conflict between Catholicism and religious ignorance, it is as likely that the jaundiced testimony of clerics like Sauvageon witnessed more to their own high standards than their parishioners' lack of them. One of the major targets of Sauvageon's ire – the externalism of peasant religious beliefs – in fact reflected the practices of the baroque piety prized by and diffused by the post-Tridentine church. Sauvageon's was not a lone voice in reminding the church that baroque piety needed to be viewed as a means of the internal acceptance of the Christian message rather than as a surrogate for it. The heyday of baroque piety in the late seventeenth and early eighteenth centuries was indeed also characterized by unparalleled efforts to clarify and to explain Christianity – through schooling, catechisms, religious publication and the like. The eighteenth century was, as we shall see, to witness many famous conflicts between Christians and unbelievers – yet the church too was riven with dissension and debate. Many of the bitterest criticisms of externalized piety were in fact to come from within the church. The Jansenist critique of the moral and spiritual laxity of Jesuit Molinism was the most celebrated of a far more general concern that the church should be winning hearts as well as changing practices. And the middle decades of the eighteenth century were to be the period in which Jansenism passed from being the proclivity of a handful of elite souls to the status of popular belief system.

c) . . . AND JANSENIST VARIATIONS

The wellsprings of Jansenism lay, as we have suggested, in the theological dilemmas of post-Tridentine Catholicism, and in anxiety about doctrines associated with the Jesuits which were held to imply that formal observance of rituals and practices was sufficient to achieve God's grace. Jansenists' puritanical stress on Augustinian austerity had brought it into conflict with Rome which it freely attacked as a 'New Babylon', and Jansenists called for ecclesiastical affairs to be regulated by a general council of the church. Conciliarist anti-papalism was combined with a call for a more democratic power-structure within the church. Many Jansenists followed the precepts of the seventeenth-century theologian Edmond Richer, embraced by Quesnel, which viewed each priest (rather than the bishops alone) as the formal descendant of the original apostles. This view was occasionally extended to a call for a quasi-presbyterian running of parishes and a reading of scripture in the vernacular reminiscent of Calvinism.

Fleury's reputation as a pro-Jesuit ultramontane – 'a 24-carat Molinist' was Noailles's acidulous comment[18] – owed much to his ringing support for the Unigenitus bull in 1713. Yet in fact the cardinal supported the bull not out of pro-papalism but because, as a good Counter-Reformation prelate, he regarded opposition to it as a threat to the principle of authority in church and state alike. He loathed what he saw as Jansenism's in-built drift towards disrespect for secular as well as spiritual authority. The cardinal did not go as far as Louis XIV in seeing Jansenists as republicans, but he was firmly opposed to their infractions of obedience. In particular, he felt that the Paris Parlement since 1715 had hidden its political claims behind a Jansenist smokescreen. In addition, he was particularly suspicious of the prophetic and miraculous tendencies within the movement from the 1720s onwards, which Jansenists brandished aloft as signs that God was on their side. Despite the fact that running through all the manifold guises of Jansenism was an obstinate refusal even to consider leaving the Catholic church, Fleury saw the movement through the prism of French Protestantism. Following an alleged Jansenist miracle in a former Protestant stronghold near to his birthplace in Languedoc, he commented to the bishop of Lodève, that 'there is only too much connection in this respect between Jansenists and Protestants, and we must avoid anything which could help to unify them further'. With a nod back to the Camisard War of 1702–4, he opined that Jansenist miracles 'derived from the fanatics of the Cévennes' and constituted 'a fanaticism which is only too contagious'.[19] He feared that Jansenism might develop into a schismatic movement strong enough to provoke a new bout of religious wars, in which Jansenists would ally with the Protestants.

The fear of driving Protestants and Jansenists together also determined Fleury's rejection of violent confrontation against either. He preferred a subtler, more oblique approach (to which he was temperamentally suited anyway). His attitude towards 'New Converts' was rather relaxed. Although thirteen Protestants were sent to the galleys in 1727, only a further thirty committals were made between 1727 and 1744 (under Louis XIV the annual figure had often exceeded 100). As regards the Jansenists, Fleury's control of the Council of Conscience and then the *feuille des bénéfices* allowed him to use ecclesiastical patronage against avowed Jansenists, and he developed a taste for appointees who were solidly anti-Jansenist, but not too close to the Jesuits. He also pressurized bishops to insist that all applicants for posts should sign the Formulary of 1722 rejecting Jansen's ideas.[20] In order to 'destroy all the schools where error is taught',[21] he had Jansenists ejected from universities, seminaries and cathedral chapters, a task which was made easier by his own appointment in 1729 as provisor of the Sorbonne. Firm but discreet action to turn off the Jansenist taps was combined with some tough measures, notably rigorous press censorship and, with the help of Hérault, the Parisian Lieutenant-General of Police, action to root out recalcitrants. Hérault – the 'French Great Inquisitor',[22] as the Jansenists called him – imprisoned nearly a hundred activists in Paris alone between 1726 and 1731.

Fleury's instinct was to focus his attacks on Jansenism at the top as well as at the bottom of the movement. He therefore placed enormous time and personal energy into securing the adhesion to Unigenitus of Cardinal de Noailles, who as archbishop of Paris was spiritual father to the clergy in the French city most thoroughly in thrall to Jansenism. Noailles was more of a Gallican than a Jansenist, and in October 1728 he succumbed to Fleury's pressure, signing a 'pure and simple' acceptance of the Unigenitus bull and allowing Jesuits to preach in the diocese for the first time since 1719. Noailles's death in 1729 allowed Fleury to appoint in his place Gaspard-Charles de Vintimille du Luc, a career bishop who had served twenty years in Aix and who, besides being of Fleury's vintage, combined a Fleuryesque mixture of congeniality, discretion and firmness. The new archbishop continued the cardinal's strategy, directing ecclesiastical preferment to anti-Jansenists and neutrals, closing down Jansenist teaching centres, and working with Hérault on select repressive measures.

The cardinal used a different tactic – exemplary punishment – towards Soanen, bishop of Senez, who in early 1727 followed up his co-authorship of the Jansenist *appel* of 1717 by issuing a second *appel* in the form of a pastoral letter vigorously attacking the supporters of Unigenitus. The 1725 Assembly of Clergy had urged the meeting of provincial councils chaired by the metropolitan archbishop, and in 1727, Archbishop Tencin of Embrun was primed by Fleury to establish such a meeting, to call Soanen to account. In what Jansenists were soon calling 'the brigandage of Embrun', Soanen was replaced by a pro-Unigenitus vicar-general and sent into life-long exile at the remote Auvergnat fastness, La Chaise-Dieu.

Fleury's episcopalist strategy as exemplified in the cases of Noailles, Vintimille and Soanen did seem to demoralize the Jansenists, whose numbers were perceptibly thinning within the clergy: thirty of France's bishops and 7,000 ecclesiastics (nearly a quarter of the episcopate and around 5 per cent of the clergy as a whole) had signed the *appel* launched by Soanen, Colbert and their *appelant* peers in 1717–18. The new *appel* of 1727 was a relative failure in comparison: only a score (some 15 per cent) of bishops and around 3 per cent of the clergy signed. Appearances were deceptive, however – and Fleury was indeed deceived into thinking that the movement was in fatal decline. Judging the moment was ripe for a terminal blow, on 24 March 1730, he had a royal declaration issued stating that the Unigenitus bull was now a law of state; and that all ecclesiastics should accept it 'purely and simply' on pain of being removed from their benefices. When the March declaration was enacted by *lit de justice* on 3 April 1730, magistrates in the Parlement mouthed familiar arguments about Unigenitus subordinating the French king to the whim of papal infallibility. But the Parlement seemed something of a paper tiger: it had kept itself aloof from the political crisis of 1725 caused by the *cinquantième* tax and the 1727 uproar caused by 'the brigandage of Embrun'. What brought it in now was essentially the affront to its jurisdictional eminence which it adjudged implicit in the 1730 declaration, and which it defended tooth-and-nail over the next two years in what rapidly became the most serious political crisis in Fleury's long ministry.

To understand the intensity of the political struggles of 1730–32, we need to appreciate the ways in which Jansenism was being reformulated – even reinvented – in the early decades of the century. Much of the credit for this lay with a small grouping associated with the Oratorian seminary of Saint-Magloire in Paris. The classes on the Old Testament which Jacques-Joseph Duguet conducted there in the first decade of the century allowed a group of around sixty activists to emerge – including Vivien de La Borde and the abbé d'Etamare – who with Duguet would develop a 'Figurist' exegesis of the Bible which purported to give meaning and purpose to Jansenist struggles. At around this time, as we have seen,[23] critics of Louis-Quatorzian absolutism had sought inspiration in the medieval past, but it was in biblical history that the Figurists located the necessary key for unlocking the secrets of the present. They saw the biblical past as a prefiguration of the present and the future, so that contemporary events were 'figures' of episodes in sacred history. They attached great importance, for example, to Louis XIV's destruction of the monastery of Port-Royal in 1709, which they claimed had revealed and replicated the biblical time of troubles. The Jansenist/Jesuit struggle was thus only the latest example of a perennial struggle within the church which pitted the holders of sacred truths against their opponents. This interpretative schema gave the group an adamantine certainty in their own mission as heirs of the defenders of the true faith within the church. Their conviction that they constituted 'the sacred depository of the truth', heirs of the beleagured early church, was matched by an acceptance that – in accordance with the cyclical nature of 'figures' – the remainder of the church was bound to oppose them and persecute them. This helps to explain the uncompromisable belief among them that Unigenitus was error incarnate.

In seeking to preach their distinctive theology of resistance – and also to justify it – the Figurists placed growing store on appealing to the people. At the same time that the bastard princes were invoking public legitimation, the Figurists started issuing pamphlets which made a similar appeal to the notion of the public as an arbiter of the validity of their claims. The *appel* of 1717 was clandestinely organized by this group who did their utmost to attract public support for its four episcopal 'authors'.[24] The relative failure of the 1727 *appel* to attract as much support within the church may have been one inspiration behind a new initiative, namely, the establishment of a low-cost newspaper, the *Nouvelles ecclésiastiques*. This too invoked 'the Public' as 'a judge that [the Jesuits and supporters of Unigenitus] have not been able to corrupt'.[25] Offering a populist brew of editorial pieces, news, book reviews and eloquent Jansenist obituaries, and vilifying the Jesuits in a way which resonated positively with a latent anti-Jesuit feeling in the capital, it was destined to become the morale-boosting organ of the Jansenist movement as a whole. Published weekly without cessation down to 1803, with a print-run rising to 5,000 or more (and with a readership far, far more extensive), the *Nouvelles ecclésiastiques* avoided police censorship by means of an ingenious clandestine production and distribution system which was soon extended into the provinces: the Paris basin, Troyes and the east of France, as well as the diocesan capitals of the most recalcitrant bishops (such as Montpellier and Senez) proved especially receptive. The Jansenists' first marked success in incorporating a greater lay element was in 1727, when the harsh treatment meted out to bishop Soanen of Senez triggered support from the Parisian order of barristers. In October 1727, some fifty barristers attached to the Paris Parlement issued a pamphlet denouncing the Embrun verdict on Soanen as illegal. Widely distributed in the provinces as well as in the city, and swiftly copied by Jansenist upper and lower clergy, the pamphlet injected a stronger legal basis and lay element into the movement.

Growing public support for the Jansenist cause had been accentuated in a quite different way, moreover, by the appearance of a popular cult around the tomb of a recently deceased young deacon, François de Pâris. Scion of a well-off parlementary family, Pâris had renounced his family wealth for a life in the Faubourg Saint-Marceau distinguished by voluntary poverty, manual labour and Jansenist humility. He died of his privations in 1727 with the local reputation of a saint. Soon, reports circulated that sick individuals who had come to pray on Pâris's tomb in the cemetery of the Saint-Médard church had been miraculously cured. The tomb swiftly became a place of pilgrimage for the halting and the lame. Those who witnessed healing miracles diffused the news, and the example of Pâris spread with his relics, as Fleury noted, like a 'contagion', reaching Jansenist communities throughout the land. Jansenists claimed that Vintimille had blocked investigations into the miraculous character of the incidents instigated by a repentant Noailles, which only confirmed them in their own self-portrayal as persecuted holders of divine truths.

Fleury had thus chosen a most unpropitious moment at which to try to make the Unigenitus bull the law of the land. Focusing as was his wont on the upper clergy, within whose ranks he was achieving marked success in stamping out Jansenism, his eye had missed the growing popular support for the cause and the incipient reinvigoration of the Parlement of Paris as defender of the Jansenist cause. Destined as the *coup de grâce* to a moribund Jansenism, the declaration of 24 March 1730 acted as a *coup de fouet* whipping into frenetic action the new elements within the movement.

The nub of the quarrel with the Parlement came to be the legal instrument known as the *appel comme d'abus*. This appellate procedure allowed judgements made under religious authority – for example the disciplining of putatively Jansenist priests – to be referred to the jurisdiction of the *parlements*. The magistrates viewed the *appel comme d'abus* as an essential guarantee of their own status as the ultimate legal resort within the realm. Yet to an episcopacy which had been accorded wide-ranging disciplinary powers over its clergy, particularly after 1695,[26] the *appel comme d'abus* constituted unwarranted secular interference in the internal life of the church, and an affront to their own status and prerogatives.

It was in the defence of one such *appel comme d'abus* case, involving several *curés* from Orléans that, in October 1730, forty Parisian barristers issued what was immediately adjudged to be an inflammatory pamphlet in the form of a legal consultation (or *mémoire judiciaire*) on the case. The authors stated that

According to the Constitution of the Kingdom, the Parlements are the Senate of the Nation, [and] render in the name of the King, who is its leader, the Justice that he owes to his subjects on behalf of God. The Parlements . . . are the depository of public authority . . . Laws are veritable conventions between those who govern and those who are governed.[27]

This was fighting talk. It resuscitated a contractualist language which Louis-Quatorzian absolutism had set out to destroy, and purported to make the Parlement the safeguard of the public rather than the expression of royal authority. It also highlighted the shift of Figurist argument into political discourse: just as the Jansenists claimed to be 'the sacred despository of [divine] truth', so the barristers were setting up the Parlement as 'the sacred depository of public laws'. The rhetorical leakage was to prove of enduring significance. Furthermore, the publicity which the case attracted also showed the Jansenist issue spreading well beyond the church and the legal profession. As a gage of the independence of the law, *mémoires judiciaires* were the only printed texts not subject to routine government censorship, which gave them a potential for widening political issues to the reading public – and mobilizing their support for the Jansenist cause.

The convergence of the Jansenist cause with the Parlement's legal and constitutional position was facilitated by the presence within the institution of a small but highly zealous religiously motivated grouping which had links to the Figurist groupuscules in Paris. Approximately a score of barristers, prominent amongst whom were Charles-Jacques Aubry and Charles-Joseph Prévost, and just over a dozen members of the Parlement, were convinced Jansenists. Many in fact were probably theologians *manqués* who had entered the law faculty because a religious career was barred to them by their beliefs. Numerically weak – they amounted only to around 10 per cent of the active membership of each body – the Jansenist group was not even well-situated within the Parlement's internal hierarchy: most of them sat in the junior *enquêtes* chambers rather than in the senior Grande Chambre, where the most important business was transacted. It says a great deal about the ability and dedication of these men, and the shrewdness of their choice of the *appel comme d'abus* as the issue on which to rest their opposition, that they had the impact they did. To sway the Parlement as a whole, as well as the wider public to whom they also addressed themselves, they penned legal briefs and pamphlets, ghostwrote speeches for parlementary interventions, and composed copy for the editors of the *Nouvelles ecclésiastiques*. Furthermore, the more influential they became, the more the Figurist rhetoric of 'the depository of the truth' influenced the magistrates' view of themselves as guarantors of constitutional rectitude, 'sovereign depositories of the fundamental laws of the state', as one of them put it.[28] As the term 'depository' became more systematically used in parlementary remonstrances from this period, the implication that the Parlement had a representative function vis-à-vis the nation as a whole became more acceptable to the magistracy as a whole.

In March 1731, Fleury attempted to impose a law of silence on the issue, and he sought to pour oil on troubled waters when disputes arose by using the procedure of *évocation* which transferred Jansenist cases involving an *appel comme d'abus* away from the Parlement to the Royal Council (where, in Fleuryite style, the cases usually vegetated). Resentful at having their authority endlessly circumvented without their arguments being heard, the magistrates took heart from the barristers, who had gone on judicial strike over the treatment of their *mémoire judiciaire*. On 7 September 1731, the Parlement issued a decree restating the four Organic Articles of 1682 on relations between church and state and adding new clauses, including one stipulating that ecclesiastical authority was inherently inferior to the Parlement's. Confusion ensued. The king formally required the expunging of this decree from the Parlement's registers, and skilfully dodged the Parlement's manoeuvres to express their remonstrances to him. In January 1732, Louis – through Fleury – convoked a delegation from the Parlement to Versailles and had the Chancellor read them the riot act: it was to be as if nothing they had done since 24 March 1730 had taken place; and the royal decree was to be enforced forthwith. 'This is my will', the king informed them with as much Louis-Quatorzian disdainful relish as someone who had just celebrated his twentieth birthday could manage. 'Do not force me to make you feel that I am your master.'[29]

The humiliation of the Parlement in January 1732 was not sufficient to end the crisis, however, which was unexpectedly reanimated by the Jansenist cult developing around Pâris's tomb in the cemetery of Saint-Médard. From July 1731, events at the cemetery had taken a hysterical turn: miracle-seekers on Pâris's tomb began to experience bodily convulsions. Fits and contortions were accompanied by wild prophesying and cries for help (*secours*). Bystanders stepped in to untangle the twisted bodies by pulling and tugging and even blows. A whole dramaturgy began to evolve in which convulsionaries acted out, in ways which owed much to Figurist biblical exegesis, episodes of the Passion, biblical history, or the events of the Jansenist movement. Convulsions thus became embodied representations of the persecution of true believers – and the *secours* took on more dramatic form as blows with objects, jabs with swords and so on represented the persecutory 'tortures' inflicted on the faithful. The more violence there was, the greater the divine grace, the sweeter the individual's spiritual relief. These theatricalized happenings took on ever more dramatic forms, with convulsionaries mimicking the lives and sufferings of Christ, the drunkenness and fornication of sinners, the conversion of the Jews, and so on. One performance involved an individual eating the Bible. Crowds grew in size and enthusiasm as performances became ever more colourful, and sensationalist accounts of the events were soon circulating widely in pamphlet form. Some thirty pedlars selling iconic portraits of Pâris were arrested in the second half of 1731 alone. There was a problem of public decency and public order here (police reports noted women baring their breasts and rolling around on the floor with their skirts up) and government was worried too about the movement drawing support from the middle and upper classes. Though anti-convulsionary propaganda represented the whole episode as dominated by hysterical plebeian women (and certainly women were in a majority among the individuals experiencing miraculous cures) in fact nearly half of those attending convulsions to provide *secours* were from literate and well-off families, and a majority were men.

Fleury redoubled repression and mobilized the medical faculty to 'prove' the unmiraculous nature of Jansenist healing against those doctors of the church and the faculty who had sworn on its veracity. Yet the parish of Saint-Médard was becoming unruly and ungovernable. The *curé* sent in to replace the Jansenist incumbent removed by Vintimille in 1730 was powerless to stop the cemetery turning into a fairground-like shrine, and the Rue Mouffetard leading to it became blocked with the carriages of pilgrims and spectators. Parish governance turned into farce: even an endless stream of government *lettres de cachet* failed to expunge

Jansenist influence. Finally, Fleury acted decisively, on 27 January 1732 ordering the closure of the Saint-Médard cemetery. Two days later soldiers moved in, bricking up all approaches (it would only be reopened under Napoleon). The action was accompanied by a wave of arrests and police harassment aimed at notorious convulsionary sympathizers.

The Paris Parlement, however, was not for closing. Indeed, the magistrates and barristers were simmering with growing resentment at the way Fleury consistently blocked their moves to try to resolve the Jansenist question through the courts. They were also critical of his use of police powers to bypass the magistrates' role in the maintenance of public order. Following an incident in which archbishop Vintimille took action against twenty-one Parisian *curés* who refused to read out in their churches an episcopal prohibition on reading the *Nouvelles ecclésiastiques*, the Parlement took a leaf out of their barristers' book and went on strike in May 1732. Forced back to work by government pressure, and with the Jansenist ringleaders in their midst being continually picked off by *lettre de cachet* the Parlement took the extraordinary step on 20 June 1732 of collectively resigning their posts – a move saluted by supportive Parisian crowds as the act of 'true Romans'.[30]

By bringing the administration of justice and the registration of laws to a halt, the collective resignation was seemingly aimed to bring about a ministerial crisis which would cause the dismissal of Cardinal Fleury, the rock on which parlementary manoeuvres and Jansenist tactics had been breaking. The next six months saw a kind of political arm-wrestling taking place between Fleury and the Parlement. The *parlementaires* dribbled back to work in July, but Fleury overplayed his hand on 18 August 1732 by trying to reserve delicate political and religious matters to the purview of the Grande Chambre and restricting the Parlement's right to persist in remonstrances against royal decrees. This triggered a further strike, loudly supported by the Parlement's barristers and its attorneys (*procureurs*). Fleury attempted to override it, exiling over a hundred obstreperous magistrates, but failed to end the affair. Negotiations between the two sides finally resulted in a sustainable compromise on 3–4 December 1732: the 18 August declaration was revoked, and the chastened *parlementaires* returned to normal work.

There were magistrates who saw the final outcome as clearly in the Parlement's favour. Yet though it had climbed down from its more extreme positions, Fleury's government had survived a real challenge to its existence in the summer of 1732, and done so in a way which brought the Parlement back into line and restored tranquillity. This triumph for political management – always Fleury's forte – had been given added acuity by the cardinal's realization that European war was not far away. From spring 1733 the Polish Succession issue, and from October full-scale war, brought the Parlement into a more docilely patriotic frame of mind. The magistrates made only gentle remonstrances against the imposition of a *dixième* to fund the war.

The *aggiornamento* with the Parlement from 1733 was facilitated too by growing divisions within the Jansenist movement. A conflict between Parlement and barristers in 1735 over precedence matters split and weakened the Jansenist grouping, which had been breaking apart anyway over credence in the Saint-Médard 'miracles'. In February 1733, Fleury passed a decree prohibiting convulsionary sessions in either public or private – and the Parlement supported him, and failed to block a decree in May which took jurisdiction of Jansenist cases out of their hands. The magistrates were now content to leave the convulsionaries to the far from tender mercies of the Paris police: cells in the Bastille were soon filling up with Jansenist extremists. In January 1735, thirty Paris physicians, all known Jansenists, formally attacked convulsionary cures as impostures. The baroque extravagance of the convulsions was increasingly revolting many Jansenists, whose preference was for austere rather than floridly ostentatious forms of piety. The single *parlementaire* who tried to keep open a link to the convulsionaries was Louis Carré de Montgeron, who held convulsionary sessions in his home. He had a choice morsel of alleged miraculous cures printed and bound, along with fascinating illustrations, and in July 1737 journeyed to Versailles to place a copy into the hands of the monarch. The consequences were predictably dire: Carré ended up in the Bastille, the book was banned, the hunt for convulsionaries redoubled, and the Parlement reiterated its protestations of loyalty to the government. The convulsionaries themselves were becoming split too: most opted for prudence rather than provocation, meeting secretly in increasingly fissiparous conventicles, thus losing the imitation effect (or 'contagion') which had been the strength of the movement in the Saint-Médard days. The convulsionaries consequently fell into discredit, and the *Nouvelles ecclésiastiques* came out against them in 1742.

Divisions within the Jansenist movement thus deprived the Parlement of its favoured stick for belabouring Fleury's government. Even though the magistrates had more freedom to manoeuvre when the War of Polish Succession ended in late 1735, the late 1730s witnessed only petty skirmishes against the government – the kind that Fleury was particularly adept at handling. The crown consistently evoked potential *appel comme d'abus* cases to the royal council (notably attempts to refuse Jansenists the last rites if they did not make a deathbed renunciation of their beliefs), and pitilessly censored Jansenist and extreme anti-Jansenist writings alike. Moreover, the subtle undercover erosion of the position of Jansenists within the church through a policy of non-preferment was shifting the ecclesiastical balance of power. Openly Jansenist bishops were the now ageing exception – Colbert of Montpellier died in 1738, isolated even within his own diocese, Soanen in 1740. It would be left to Fleury's successors, however, to come to realize that Jansenism as an issue had not gone away and that management of the Parlement plus an episcopalist strategy within the church would not suffice to kill it off as a force of political and religious opposition. But for the meanwhile at least – from the mid-1730s – all seemed quiet on the Jansenist front.

D) THE KING'S INFORMATION: NEWS, VIEWS, SECRETS, LIES

Do you know the number of men who compose your nation? How many men, how many women, how many farmers, how many artisans, how many lawyers, how many tradespeople, how many priests and monks, how many nobles and soldiers? What would you say of a shepherd who did not know the size of his flock? . . . A king not knowing all these things is only half a king.[31]

Fénelon, the author of *Télémaque*, panegyrist of virtuous monarchy, writing in 1702 with the ill-fated duke of Burgundy in mind, was in no doubt: to be virtuous, a king needed to be well-informed. Fénelon's implied criticism of the level of information which even an absolute monarch like Louis XIV had in his possession for making decisions for the good of the state and the welfare of his people was highly apposite. French monarchs had a poor sense of even such basic facts as the size of their territories and the number of their subjects. Louis himself had joked that the map-makers had lost him half of his kingdom, when it was discovered that Marseille was 15 leagues and Brest some 30 leagues closer to Paris than had hitherto been thought, and much topographical uncertainty persisted well into the eighteenth century. Similarly, it was widely believed that France's population was far inferior to what it had been in Ancient times: writing in the 1720s, Montesquieu argued that the contemporary level of 14 million contrasted with a level of 20 million in Roman times; later still in the century, the Physiocrat Quesnay estimated population size as 24 million around 1650, 15.5 million in 1715, and 16 million in 1755. As far as we can now judge, this latter figure was an underestimate of some 8 to 9 million![32]

Reliable and disinterested information was at a premium within the political system. Representative estates and assemblies tended to defend local interests, while the capacity of other administrators was limited by the fact that, through the system of venality, they regarded their posts as much as private property as public function. The tendency of the crown to alienate parts of its activity to private bodies – such as tax farmers to collect indirect taxes – could also be a problem. No monarch was entirely sure of his annual budget before the Revolution. There was always a danger, moreover, that officials who were asked for information would provide the government with what they thought it wanted to hear. The inquiry into the state of the country launched in 1697 for the young duke of Burgundy was classic in this respect: one would hardly know the misery many provinces were then suffering, to read the glowing accounts of some Intendants who eschewed statistical accuracy for a kind of temperamental geography of their territories, which played into age-old stereotypes (Normandy was 'industrious', Provençals were 'lazy'). More common than flattery in vitiating government information, however, was fear. Peasants in Languedoc in 1705 refused to provide information about their livestock because they were apprehensive lest the data should trigger a rise in the salt tax. The failure of appeals to local people in the diocese of Le Mans around the same time for information on population was due, one parish priest claimed, to the 'false terror that these sorts of descriptions will tend to increase taxes'.[33]

Such perceptions were far from ill-founded. The history of statistics – and indeed of cartography – in early modern France is closely linked to the history of state formation and the development of tax-raising potential. Plans to establish a census in the 1660s, in the 1690s and then under the Regency were overtly guided by a desire to cut back on tax-evasion. Efforts to secure geographical information were similarly partial. Cartography was an instrument of power, a weapon of government. Map-makers prioritized military frontiers and areas of civil unrest – wonderful maps were drawn of the Cévennes, for example, during the guerrilla conflict of the Camisard Wars, purely for counter-insurgency reasons.

The eighteenth century was to see far more concerted and continuous efforts by the state to improve the quality and volume of information which it received to inform decision-making. This was done less through startling innovation than through adjusting and perfecting existing administrative bodies, improving the professionalism of their members and widening their sphere of competence. At the heart of government, following the failure of the Polysynody experiment, for example, there was some degree of streamlining of the form of the Royal Council inherited from Louis XIV. The State Council, whose remit was major affairs of state, and membership of which the king reserved to highly distinguished servants of the state, remained the major strategy body. It was flanked by a Council of Despatches which from Fleury onwards increased its share of domestic policy issues, and more functional committees such as the Council of Finances and the Council of Commerce, re-established by Orry in 1730.

Conciliar forms were, however, increasingly subordinated to the interests of the ministries, or secretaryships of state, back in all their pomp following the demise of Polysynody. Continuing a trend already evident under Louis XIV, the Controller-General of Finances remained the linchpin of the executive activity of government. Since the middle of the previous century, he had squeezed out of the limelight the Chancellor, quondam head of government, and over the eighteenth century the Controller-General's authority also strayed well within the remit of the councils of state. His office also acted as a nub of domestic information, including the generation of statistical materials: in a mere two decades, for example, it conducted national inquiries into wages (1724), charitable institutions (1724), administrative officials (1725) and paper manufactories (1728), plus census inquiries in 1730 and 1744. Archival management techniques were developed so as to allow the establishment of a kind of documentary memory bank which could guide decision-making.

The councils were serviced and staffed below the level of state dignitaries and ministers by some eighty-eight masters of requests who handled other business of government, including a growing amount of routine legislation, through a sprawling collection of committees and commissions under the general title of the Private State Council (Conseil d'État privé). Wealthy Robe nobles, usually with a Parisian background, who had purchased their offices and whose families frequently intermarried, the masters of requests constituted a career-oriented administrative cadre whose strong *esprit de corps* proved a significant factor of cohesion within government. It was from this milieu that were selected the provincial Intendants, or *Intendants de finance, justice et police*, to give them their official title. The term *police* signified not simply the maintenance of order (in which Intendants certainly played a major role) but more generally a kind of rational and informed administration, a 'science of government',[34] as one of its enthusiasts later put it, which extended to all aspects of regional life: alongside market regulation, the term comprehended collective health and hygiene, observance of religious worship, manufacturing and retailing, urban improvement and public works. The Intendants worked partly on their own initiative, partly through supervising the local workings of finance and justice, and monitored other local agencies such as estates, *parlements*, provincial governors and municipal administrations. 'This kingdom of France is ruled by thirty Intendants,' John Law had commented, in astonished admiration, 'on whom depends the prosperity or wretchedness of their provinces, their abundance or their sterility.'[35] If anything, their competence increased the more the century wore on.

The Intendants were the most important agents of *police* beyond the walls of Versailles, though there were other relatively effective and disinterested agents of the royal will: notably the Lieutenant-General of Police created for Paris in 1667, and policing agencies based on this post which were extended to the main provincial cities. The Intendants were also assisted by a couple of hundred subdelegates, unpaid assistants, who were located in most major towns, and also by the country's 30,000 parish priests. The post-Tridentine *curé*, primed for obedience and dutiful to his charge, was an admirable local administrator and information conduit. He was consulted, for example, over population statistics (where his stewardship of registers for births, marriages and deaths made him particularly well informed) and in poor relief and public hygiene matters. *Curés* were an important part, for example, of the battery of local authorities galvanized by the 1720 plague outbreak at Marseille.

Food supply was high on the priorities list of these police bodies. Preventive operations aimed to pre-empt popular turbulence caused by high bread prices. Severe grain riots in Paris in 1725 led Lieutenant-General of Police Hérault to develop a resilient method of keeping Paris happy in bad times: with the Controller-General's authority behind him, he bullied provincial Intendants into prioritizing the needs of the capital over their own regions, built up emergency granary supplies, made price-fixing arrangements, organized road-building and developed international links for grain supply. A key part of the new system was intelligence about the state of the harvest – the data was pooled in the Controller-General's office. The system proved effective: extremely poor harvests between 1738 and 1741 did not result in disturbances in the capital though conditions elsewhere were grim. Controller-General Orry, opined the marquis d'Argenson, 'would sacrifice a hundred days of famine in the provinces against one troublesome afternoon in Paris which might put him out'.[36]

Technical agencies offering expert advice and opinion on request, and developing a systematic body of data on which policy-makers could draw, comprised a further link in absolute monarchy's information chain. One important form of this was the learned corps of savants. The concern of the Académie française with the purity of the French language was mocked by contemporaries for its mind-numbing pedantry, but the Academy of Sciences founded in 1666 offered a more dynamic and utilitarian model. Reorganized by the abbé Bignon in the 1690s, it was primed to be not only a regulator of legitimate scientific knowledge but also an initiator and technical innovator with a practical bent: characteristically, firearms, surveying equipment and nautical instruments headed the list of inventions which received state privileges on the Academy's recommendation down to the middle of the eighteenth century.[37] The Academy of Inscriptions and Belles-Lettres, originally founded in 1663 as an arm of Louis XIV's propaganda machine, was revamped in 1716 and hencefoward operated as a state historical, archaeological and archival service. Other seventeenth-century academies – like those for Painting and Sculpture and for Architecture – had geared their activities around setting criteria of public taste, but utilitarianism would be the hallmark of eighteenth-century creations: there were academies for Surgery (1739), Naval Affairs (1752) and Agriculture (1761), as well as provincial academies located in the major cities and designed to relay the efforts of the Paris-based institutions.

The practical bent of Fleury's government was also shown in the support which it gave to civil engineering in the form of the Ponts et Chaussées service established in 1716 out of a hitherto ill-organized bridges and highways service. A director, reporting to the Controller-General's office, and aided by an inspectorate, headed a hierarchy of engineers dispersed in the *pays d'élection* under the authority of the Intendants. It was Controller-General Orry – who had had experience of road repairs as Intendant of Soissons in the 1720s – who took the service in hand, increasing its budget fivefold against 1700 levels and then in 1738 imposing on all inhabitants the *corvée*, or compulsory labour service on the highways. Orry was phlegmatic about the unpopularity of the *corvée* among the peasants who bore its brunt: he preferred, he stated, 'to ask them for use of their arms, which they have, rather than money, which they don't'.[38] The fortnight's annual labour on the roads, directed by Ponts et Chaussées engineers, according to standardized techniques and road dimensions, constructed the finest set of major roads in Europe. The policy of improved communications was also witnessed by Controller-General Orry bringing to final fruition the Cassini map of France in 1744.

The Ponts et Chaussées went from strength to strength after the appointment in 1743 as its director of Daniel Trudaine, who in 1747 secured the erection of the service into the École des Ponts et Chaussées. The new school, within which a surveying and cartographical service operated, offered a highly professional training, fostering a strong *esprit de corps* and an open-ended approach to scientific research and development. Other technical services also received a boost. A nationwide corps of factory inspectors developed to promote quality production in the nation's manufacturing sector on related lines. Military engineering received similar treatment through the creation of the École de Mézières in 1748.

The period of the Regency and Fleury's ministry thus showed a keen awareness in government circles of the extent to which knowledge and expertise could be linked to state authority in a powerful new synergy. Government attitudes towards the exchange of ideas highlighted this shift. Under the system inherited from the 1690s, the state accorded privileges to produce and distribute only works which had passed its censors, but accorded 'tacit permissions' to circulate works whose content was questionable but which did not quite deserve repression. A more liberal policy was evident from the late 1720s. 'Nothing', stated Chauvelin in the early 1730s, 'is more deleterious to the trade in books than an excess of severity.' The average annual number of tacit permissions trebled between the 1720s and the 1730s – and rose faster still thereafter.[39]

Yet this liberal and indeed enabling approach to freer communication was countered by an inherited assumption that many forms of knowledge were essentially, as contemporary parlance put it, *le secret du Roi* ('the king's secret'). The penchant for secrecy reflected the view that accurate information relating to the key factors of the state's strength – manpower, economic resources, scientific innovation – was a legitimate monopoly of the royal person. The great 1698 inquiry sponsored by the duke of Burgundy's circle, for example, was purportedly for his future majesty's eyes only: 'what you send me', Beauvillier had informed the Intendants, 'is not to be made public: on the contrary'.[40] Extracts of the reports were only to be published in abridged form by Boulainvilliers in the late 1720s. The writings of Vauban and Boisguilbert on political economy in the last years of the reign of Louis XIV had been adjudged to cross the bounds of state secrecy: Vauban died in disgrace, Boisguilbert was exiled for his pains. The issue of public knowledge of political information had been given disastrous illumination, moreover, it was held, in the John Law episode, where the whole of the state's finances had become an object of public scrutiny and speculation: 'Monsieur Law', ruminated Chancellor d'Aguesseau in 1731 during the stand-off between the government and the Parisian barristers, 'ruined everything by teaching the world the intrinsic value of money; is this any less dangerous than revealing the mystery of the intrinsic value of power?'[41] Beneath the liberal veneer, therefore, knowledge was still to be regulated and controlled by the sovereign – or those who ruled in his name. There had been four royal censors in 1624 working under the aegis of the Chancellor; by 1741 there were seventy-nine (and by 1789 nearly 200), according or refusing authorization to everything published and distributed in France.

This view that the state should keep crucial information out of the gaze of a broader public was not confined to government: the Parisian barrister and diarist Barbier, for example, praised the Regent for not talking to his mistresses about matters of state, and eulogized Fleury's government for controlling all government information through the state gazettes during the War of Polish Succession. Fleury's penchant for secrecy was a personal character trait – no one was ever quite sure what he was thinking – as well as a policy conviction. It left no room for discussion by private individuals of public affairs. In the late 1720s, for example, there was an effort to create a semi-public forum for political debate and discussion, the Club de l'Entresol, on the model of English political clubs. Under the dual animation of the abbé d'Alary and the eccentric veteran of the Burgundy circle, the abbé de Saint-Pierre, the club grouped together individuals from Robe and Sword nobilities, financiers and Intendants, members of the academies and a sprinkling of foreign luminaries such as Horace Walpole, and met weekly to debate digests of international and domestic news and to hear papers read on current political and diplomatic issues. Their ambition to become a state-sponsored political academy on the lines of the Academy of Sciences stood little chance of success. Jealous court factions assumed that the club was a machine designed to launch its members into government, and accused it of stirring up the public. Fleury's frown, not long in coming, killed the association off in the early 1730s, and though a few members tried to prolong the experiment in secrecy, it passed into obscurity.

Fleury was predictably hostile too to another form of vaguely political sociability which began to appear in Paris from 1737 onwards, namely the free-masons – or *frimassons*, as Barbier colourfully called them.[42] Masonic rituals seemed blasphemous, their secrecy and their aristocratic membership a threat to the state, and they were consequently outlawed, forcing them deeper underground. The cardinal's penchant for secrecy in state affairs was also evident over the Jansenist controversy. The increasingly public orientation of Jansenist agitation was utterly antithetical to the secrecy-based political culture which Fleury cherished. The cardinal became hot and bothered even talking about Jansenists, and his efforts to impose silence at key junctures on the controversy revealed a sense of quiet desperation about their infractions of state mysteries.

Yet notwithstanding Fleury's integral adherence to mysteries of state, his government was also increasingly drawn to participating in and trying to shape public attitudes. The John Law episode had highlighted the issue of confidence at the heart of state credit. Credit was malleable and elusive and could not be sustained simply by government fiat in the minds of those whom the government wanted to tax and from whom it wanted to borrow. Keeper of the Seals Chauvelin maintained that the state's budget should be as secret as the king's personal accounts: 'anything which is too well known is despised or is even no longer held in veneration, an attribute which is however necessary in attracting confidence'.[43] But the marquis d'Argenson's view was more sanguine: 'opinion governs men', he confided to Fleury. 'It is by opinion that men rule, and with more or less power.'[44] By this token, opinion and, if need be, information needed to be managed – maybe even created.

The idea that government could act through propaganda to influence the king's subjects in his favour was hardly new: Louis XIV had been past-master at governing by show. The tendency from the 1690s of the monarchy to style itself as a regime committed to the welfare of its subjects also propelled the state towards explaining and justifying its views, and from the 1720s onwards the government worked more assiduously in the direction of manipulating opinion in its own interests. Fleury's government seemed to acknowledge that opinion was there to be manipulated, not ignored. Even the king – who maliciously liked to set hares running – engaged in 'playing' opinion. In 1729, for example, he allegedly paid the well-known charlatan and tooth-puller, *le Grand Thomas*, a regular fixture on Paris's Pont Neuf, to yell out his conviction that the queen's forthcoming baby would be a son and heir. (It was – and Thomas was duly rewarded.)[45] Similarly, in 1738, Hérault paid a crowd of fishwives to yell 'Long live the King! Long live our good M. le Cardinal!' on the conclusion of the European peace-talks.[46] News relating to public disturbances was systematically massaged: government tried to keep up a pretence that everything in Marseille was being handled effectively during the plague epidemic of 1720, even though people were dying in their tens of thousands; and during the high prices and bread shortage of 1738 to 1741 it displayed icy calm, even though Louis privately admitted that maybe one-sixth of the population had died of hunger. Nor did government shy away from news-creation and even active disinformation. In the early 1740s, for example, the Paris police funded the chevalier de Mouchy to run an intelligence bureau which reported on the state of Parisian opinion but which also acted as a sounding board for government plans by floating rumours. And in 1744, Orry ordered Intendants to sow rumours about tax increases so that his intelligence network could weigh the strength of the reaction before he finalized his financial strategy.

At the heart of Fleury's government, therefore, was a paradox. Fleury's traditionalist line, that politics was essentially what took place within the king's (and his cardinal's) head, and that the information on which government made decisions should remain state mysteries, beyond the reach of a broad public, clashed with the practices of his government, and on social and political conditions he was helping to create. Realizing that it could not count on unqualified obedience, government worked to influence opinion and manufacture consent. In addition, his government's progressive communications policy not only promoted a general policy of openness, but also, by boosting trade and exchange, assisted in the emergence of a commercial society. As we shall see,[47] the disjunction between secrecy and opinion would grow wider and more problematic as the century wore on, as the material preconditions of a broad and active public were being assembled, and as the world of print became too sprawling and tentacular to be controlled by the censorship technology available to the Bourbon state. Secrecy was becoming a chimera as government joined the game of shaping opinion, while the mystique of state was coming progressively under the microscope of a public whose views on news required more than secrets and lies.

E) THE WILTING CARDINAL

An important shift in the personnel and balance of power within Fleury's government took place in 1737, as the cardinal was emerging triumphantly from the War of Polish Succession with Lorraine as his trophy, and with Jansenist turbulence under control: Chauvelin, Keeper of the Seals and Foreign Minister, was peremptorily dismissed and exiled to the provinces.

The exact causes of the brutal exclusion from power of a man whom Fleury had dubbed his 'alter ego',[48] and who was widely tipped to succeed both him as effective Principal Minister and d'Aguesseau as Chancellor, were not divulged. The shift after 1737 towards a more pro-Austrian policy was unpopular with the Foreign Minister, a noted Austrophobe. It may have been as simple as that, though with a character as secretive as Fleury, one can never be sure. Personal rivalry may well have been a factor. Though contemporaries sometimes assumed Chauvelin, veritable workhorse of the ministry, was the senior partner in the relationship, this was a Fleuryite ruse. During the War of Polish Succession, for example, Fleury allowed Chauvelin to compose alliances in Germany and Italy, while he himself nurtured English friendship and worked behind his Foreign Minister's back for peace negotiations. Chauvelin probably felt that, with Fleury's death surely not far off, he should act pre-emptively to secure his own succession. He seems to have been developing links out to the Parlement and to the court, and possibly to Spain too. Even more serious than this, he may also have made independent approaches towards the king. Exclusive political intimacy with Louis was the ark of the cardinal's covenant and he would not tolerate any meddling from a rival.

Whatever the exact reasons for Chauvelin's dismissal, the fall from grace had opened up the question of Fleury's successor at the same time that it drew attention to the fact that even the apparently indestructible cardinal must be approaching the end of his days. A serious illness in 1738 had courtiers rubbing their hands in glee, but the wilting octogenarian bounced amazingly back. Thereafter, however, the signs of decrepitude became more and more apparent – he needed more rest, he consumed patent medicines by the drove, he absented himself from court more frequently, and he seemed increasingly shrunken and shrivelled, diminishing in stature from five feet eight to some five feet one, resembling now an exhumed monkey, now a desiccated mummy.[49]

The choice of replacements for Chauvelin underlined Fleury's customary priorities. The cardinal chose to reassert his primacy by ensuring that the ministers were not only his own men but were totally impervious to any influence at court save his own. There was to be no new Keeper of the Seals, for Fleury allowed the erudite but politically null d'Aguesseau to resume the plenitude of the Chancellor's powers. As Foreign Minister he chose Amelot, whose training was in finance and administration, who avowedly knew next to nothing about foreign affairs and who stuttered to boot – an extraordinary deficiency in a diplomat. Strong on administrative competence, the ministers as a group were united in their indebtedness to Fleury and in a collective mistrust of any putative successor from the court.

One of the keys to Fleury's long-lived success had been a more hermetic segregation of court from administration than even Louis XIV had achieved. It was a symptom of the decline of the cardinal's system that uncertainty over his successor reduced his ability to manage developments which did not respect this division, and he proved unable to prevent the habitués of the royal bedchamber re-emerging into the circle of ministerial power. His conduct of foreign policy at this time stimulated the formation of factions. Developing friendship with France's age-old enemy, Austria, including acceptance of the Pragmatic Sanction, seemed to offer the best means of consolidating the new province of Lorraine in the wake of the War of Polish Succession. But it excited much discontent in sabre-rattling court circles which regarded Austrophilia as the most un-French of diplomatic perversions. A new generation of bellicose nobles, too young to have had experience of warfare under Louis XIV and feeling starved of chances for advancement under Fleury, began to make their voices heard, notably in the entourage of Louis's mistress, the duchesse de Châteauroux. A serious grain shortage following bad harvests in 1738 and 1739 causing popular discontent outside Paris offered fresh opportunities for criticizing Fleury's ministry. The bishop of Chartres indignantly informed the king that his diocesans were dying like flies and eating grass like sheep, and indeed both the king and Fleury got a fright when their coaches were stopped in the Paris countryside by peasants crying out 'Famine! Bread!' rather than '*Vive le Roi!*'[50]

The court atmosphere was all the more febrile in that no obvious successor to the ageing cardinal was presenting himself, while Fleury himself remained as inscrutable as ever. The deaths of the ducs d'Antin, du Maine and Bourbon and the comte de Toulouse between 1736 and 1740 and the progressive religious eccentricity of the duc d'Orléans temporarily eclipsed the faction wars of the princes, but other courtiers took their place. Chauvelin in political exile, for example, retained friends at court who believed in and worked for his return. He was held to have links, for example, with a political combination which involved the king's mistress, the duchesse de Châteauroux, and the duc de Richelieu – a reprobate who had almost defined the term *roué* under the Regency but who had since developed a powerful military and diplomatic career. Another candidate for the reversion was Tencin, archbishop of Embrun, then Lyon, and from 1739 cardinal, who worked closely with Fleury on religious and foreign policy. The Parisian salon that his sister, Mme Tencin, ran in Paris acted as a recruiting office for a growing, *dévot*-orientated faction. Fleury brought Cardinal Tencin and another *dévot*, the comte d'Argenson, into the state Council in 1742, but seemingly only to strengthen his own position tactically rather than to give the nod for the succession to either man.[51] The coming star on whom all eyes were increasingly trained, namely, the marquis de Belle-Isle, was grandson of Louis XIV's disgraced Finance Minister Fouquet. He had finessed himself an enormous fortune and maintained ambitions to match. As well as enjoying links in the royal court, he was said to stipend some 200 individuals in the city of Paris to spread favourable news stories about himself.

Major developments on the European stage in 1740 – notably the succession in Prussia of the war-like young Frederick II and then, in the autumn of the same year, the unexpected death of Emperor Charles VI – further stimulated faction-fighting, and weakened Fleury's hold on power. A war party urging France to tear up its support for the Pragmatic Sanction and to profit from the circumstances began to crystallize around Belle-Isle. Fleury tried to be non-committal, and approved Louis XV's preference for staying on the sidelines 'with his hands in his pockets'.[52] The king agreed to allow Maria Theresa to inherit the Habsburg lands but also sought to oust the Habsburg dynasty from any link to the elective post of Holy Roman Emperor, for it did not relish the idea of ex-Lorrainer Francis, Maria Theresa's husband, acceding to this powerful position. Almost immediately the ground shifted under the cardinal's feet, however, for in December Frederick II invaded the Austrian province of Silesia, claiming it for Prussia, then going on to crush Austrian troops at Molwitz in April 1741. The extreme discomfiture of Maria Theresa only exacerbated demands within France to move in for the kill and to amass tangible trophies of war over the prostrate body of Habsburg power.

Fleury moved slowly at first in a manoeuvre which would end with him throwing a lifetime of diplomatic caution to the winds. He appointed Belle-Isle ambassador in Germany with instructions to seek the election to the imperial crown of Charles-Albert, elector of France's traditional ally, Bavaria. Within months, Belle-Isle had negotiated a treaty with Frederick II, whereby Prussia could retain Silesia in return for Frederick's vote for Charles-Albert as Emperor. Fleury had thereby allowed an underling to drag him into a war – formally declared in May 1741 – a war, moreover, which soon mushroomed dangerously in scale: the exigencies of the Family Compact required that France support Spain in its struggle against the English, while Sweden attacked Russia. Belle-Isle led one French army into Bohemia, one of the heartlands of Austrian power, and by January 1742 managed to get Charles-Albert elected in Frankfurt as Emperor. The Habsburg corpse, however, stubbornly refused to lie down and die. Maria Theresa rallied the Magyar nobility to her cause, and, as newly crowned queen of Hungary, made a spirited come-back, occupying Bavaria, winning support from England, and disengaging Prussia from the war, albeit at the cost of acceding to the loss of Silesia. Thrown on to the defensive, Belle-Isle and the French army under his control were besieged by Austrian forces in Prague. In December 1742, they were instructed to evacuate and to return towards France, as Maria Theresa celebrated her triumph over the Bavarian pretender.

With the architect of the war policy ignominiously humiliated out in the field, Cardinal Fleury lay dying. Visibly failing from the late summer of 1742, he was nailed to his bed out at Issy for most of December 1742 and January 1743. It would have tried the resource of this great tightrope-walker to keep his balance in this grievous situation which was so unlike the usual circumstances in which he liked to work. The peace-lover was at war, and committed to operations which were being fought at a distance from French soil, making logistics problematic. The diplomatic initiative had passed out of French into other (notably Austrian and Prussian) hands. His popularity had suffered too: in the late 1730s, the Parisian diarist Barbier had commented favourably on Fleury's 'great, judicious and gentle' administration – but such views disappeared in the context of the German fiasco.[53] The secrecy of public affairs which Fleury so prized, moreover, was also becoming a thing of the past. From the summer of 1742, Paris police spies were reporting a city pulsating with stories, rumours, panics, jokes and critiques. Barbier noted the existence of an Austrian lobby among the Parisian public, and mocked the government's attempts to harass denizens of cafés and parks into silence by sending to the Bastille writers and pamphleteers who overstepped the line. How, he wondered, can you stop Paris writing ditties (*chansonner*)?[54] And doing so, he might have added, both pertinently and saucily. One pamphlet, for example, cheered 'Fleury is dead! Long live the King!'[55] – a nice ironical homage to the doctrine of the king's two bodies.

For nearly two decades indeed, Fleury had indeed acted much like the king's ceremonial body. The spare but spry frame of the cardinal had allowed Louis XV to neglect his political and administrative role in favour of a life of private pleasures and occasional state ceremony. Even the very way that Fleury operated – making a show of being above faction (while working strenuously to balance factional groupings), ensuring that his underlings shouldered the blame for unpopular policies while he took the credit for any successes, intuitively preferring the authoritarian option, prizing secrecy and discretion in government – shadowed the usual role of a king. Acting as surrogate monarch had inclined him to a conservative approach to politics, and he allowed no winds of change to trouble the Louis-Quatorzian system still at the heart of government.

Maybe towards the end old age was showing: the reflexes of a Tridentine bishop were not well attuned to the emergence of a public sphere of debate. Louis seemed, moreover, increasingly to resent the quasi-infantilizing tutelage of a figure who seemed from another age – contemporaries recorded royal sulking fits, petty asides and tantrums in order to have his own way on minor matters (Fleury called them 'His Majesty's little huffs' (*enfantillages*)).[56] But the king bided his time, and his general appreciation for Fleury's shielding was apparent to all at court. He was deeply moved by the death of his old tutor, and gave him impressive funeral honours. The cardinal had indeed achieved much – managing the Parlement and the Jansenist issue with some skill, improving France's position within Europe and, as we shall see in the following chapter, giving the economy a chance to grow. Yet with the body of the cardinal in its grave, the time was ripe for the body of the other king, the crowned one, to emerge from the shadow of Fleury and to rule in his own name – as he claimed to have been doing since 1726.

4

Unsuspected Golden Years
(1743–56)

A) HEROD 'THE WELL-BELOVED'?

Royal nicknames were not always flattering nor apt. Louis XV was never going to be 'Louis the Great' – his predecessor had sewn up that claim, providing a template of royal authority which the new monarch would always envy. The sobriquet 'Louis the Well-Beloved' (*le Bien-Aimé*) which Louis XV acquired in 1744, shortly after his passage to sole rule without the guidance of Cardinal Fleury, was certainly more seductive than, say, Charles the Bald or Louis the Fat. Even so, it was ill-starred: his predecessor *Bien-Aimé*, the fourteenth-century monarch Charles VI, had also been known as Charles 'the Insane' and had witnessed his kingdom torn apart in some of the most tragic episodes of the Hundred Years War with England. Louis XV's sobriquet proved unable to inspire popular affection. Even though French society was beginning to expand and boom after the hollow years at the turn of the century, certain of his subjects were almost at once after 1744 ironizing about the title of 'Well-Beloved', and comparing Louis with Herod. In many circles, Louis XV would be 'the Ill-Beloved' (*le Mal-Aimé*) down to his death in 1774.

Louis had been chafing at the bit in Fleury's last years, and he was encouraged in his determination to take command by the dusty letter which Noailles now laid before him which Louis XIV had entrusted to the duke (now also marshal) on his deathbed with orders that it be given to Louis XV when he assumed sole power. 'Do not allow yourself to be governed; be the master,' Louis XIV had written. 'Never have a favourite or a prime minister . . . Listen to and consult your council, but you take the decisions.'[1] Louis needed little prompting to revere 'my greatgrandfather . . . whom I want to imitate as much as I can'.[2] As if to signal his intentions, he reacted swiftly to an attempt by the exiled Chauvelin to wheedle himself back into office, confirming the ex-minister's banishment. He then moved to break up the sprawling patronage empire which Fleury had enjoyed: the post of royal chaplain went to the old cardinal's nephew, the abbé Fleury, while the politically null bishop of Mirepoix took over *feuille des bénéfices*. No one was allowed to occupy Fleury's position as junction-box for patronage and access to the king. Louis, moreover, kept his cards close to his chest and exalted almost as a passion the secrecy in policy-formation which the inscrutable Fleury had exemplified. The king kept clandestine a good deal of advisory consultation with Noailles in the early years, and also a long-running correspondence he began with his cousin from the Condé house, the prince de Conti, on foreign policy matters (the so-called *Secret du Roi*).

There was no more fitting example of Louis's wish to emulate his predecessor while also showing that he was his own man than his decision to go to the front to lead his armies. The War of Austrian Succession had not been going well. The anti-Bourbon alliance of Austria, England and Sardinia meant that France and her allies had to prosecute the war on several fronts. Conflict was hottest in Germany, and it was thither, appropriately, that the ruler directed his steps in May 1744, taking with him the wise counsel and strategic guidance of Noailles and the comte (soon marshal) de Saxe. By assuming the mantle of warrior, Louis gave the lie to those who joked that he only fought against stags and boars. When it went well, as Louis XIV could attest, war could be incredibly popular in early modern Europe, attracting to the ruler's person a set of immensely powerful images of the monarch as valorous defender of his subjects. Louis XV would, moreover, prove himself a worthy soldier in this Bourbon tradition, displaying considerable sangfroid on the field of battle and helping in (or at least not obstructing) the victories of his generals. His concern for the welfare of his troops and the civilian population – he visited hospitals, tested bread quality, consoled the sick and dying – also won widespread approbation.

The effect was ruined, however, by Louis's decision – echoing Louis XIV's earlier campaigning jaunts – to be accompanied by his mistress, the duchesse de Châteauroux, along with her sister, the duchesse de Lauraguais (who was Louis's occasional sex-partner rather than a fully fledged royal mistress). Matters came to an unexpected pass in Metz, which the royal party had entered in some grandeur in early August. The king became very sick; by 11 August, royal physicians were warning that his life was in danger. Chastened by Premier Royal Almoner, Fitz-James, the bishop of Soissons, Louis stopped blowing kisses to his mistresses and, reflecting darkly on the state of his soul, called for absolution. For someone with such an active extra-marital sex-life, Louis was a good, even superstitiously good, Catholic: he attended mass almost daily, though he did not confess or take communion and since 1738 had abandoned the ritual of touching for the King's Evil on the grounds that thaumaturgic power would not function through an unabsolved vessel. The bishop of Soissons now began a kind of spiritual extortion on the ailing monarch, playing on the king's sense of guilt to effect a renunciation of his marital irregularity. He refused to minister to Louis until he had not only banished the mistresses from his bedside but also had them driven, as 'concubines within the gate', out of Metz. Urged on by courtiers who were suddenly aware of the possibilities of *dévot* resurgence, he compelled the king openly to make honourable amends for his past life. An explosion of popular enthusiasm welcomed this change of heart: the mistresses' coach, its blinds down, came close to attack as it left the city.

As news reached Paris, Queen Marie Leszczinska could scarcely believe her luck and set out for her husband's side, despatching the young Dauphin towards the front too. Furthermore, the king's sexual repentance and subsequent, quasi-miraculous recovery caused an explosion of popular joy. When he returned from the front via Paris, where he spent a week in November, everything conspired to show, chroniclers recorded, the 'love and attachment of the people' for the king: newspapers and pamphlets were full of glowing accounts, corporate bodies (down to humble carters, water-carriers and coal-porters) jostled to organize celebratory Te Deums, and the sobriquet *le Bien-Aimé* was coined as a symbol of the general enthusiasm.[3]

Louis had raised popular hopes, however, only to dash them. His renunciation of his mistresses had seemed to mark a commitment to his people's welfare. The reinstallation of Châteauroux by late November was thus not only a shock but also a kind of snub, which was made all the more forceful for being associated with vengeful punishment meted out on the *dévot* clique which had conducted the Metz masquerade. His ire further raised by the sudden death of Châteauroux in December 1744, Louis dismissed the bishop of Soissons from his entourage, exiling him to his diocese, while other Household officials who had supported the prelate were banished from court. The queen too was rapidly sidelined.

By rejecting the version of kingship on offer at Metz in this way, Louis forfeited a good deal of popular acclaim. He had always had a problem with popular expressions of enthusiasm. Crowds made him feel uncomfortable. Courtiers had witnessed the recuperating monarch being chased around Laon in 1744 by a crowd crying '*Vive le Roi!*', like a character from a Molière farce trying to dodge an enema.[4] 'He does not like great ceremonies,' Barbier recorded on noting the king's embarrassed demeanour during a visit to Paris in 1751 marking the birth of a boy-child to the dauphin.[5] This discomfort extended to court life too. Louis maintained Louis XIV's Versailles traditions of the public *lever* and *coucher* and the meals in public, and could cut an imposing ceremonial figure: one of his physicians passed out in fright when he met him for the first time, and a Turkish ambassador being presented to him in 1742 disgraced himself and had to borrow an unsoiled pair of breeches.[6] Yet Louis circumvented court ceremony by absenting himself more and more from the Sun King's palace. Between 1736 and 1738, for example, he had averaged nearly 250 nights a year at Versailles, but by 1750 and 1751 he was down to one night or so a week, preferring smaller châteaux and country-houses in the environs. In Versailles too he built smaller apartments, which he lavishly decorated and in which, when present, he could lead a less ceremonial and more private life, cutting himself off from the habitual palace throng of courtiers, petitioners and Parisian day-trippers and tourists.

A consequence of his carving-out from the ceremonial royal life, established by his predecessor, a more private, intimate sphere to which he felt more temperamentally attuned was that Louis's reputation for secrecy and remoteness, both physical and psychological, was amplified. Cutting himself off from the public in this way risked making him personally invisible: significantly, following the Flanders campaigns of 1744–5, he virtually never again ventured outside the palace circuit within the Île-de-France. He knew his kingdom more from his beloved maps and history books and from administrative correspondence than from personal experience. His visits to Paris (which he had not allowed his son to visit until he was a teenager) became less frequent too: he never over-nighted there, for example, after 1744.

His insouciance, his penchant for secrecy and his fear of having his innermost feelings and intentions penetrated by others were further complicated by a commitment to an active sex life from which the Metz episode failed to deter him. There was nothing unusual, it is true, in a king of France having mistresses. In his own court it was generally thought that all grandees had one, with the exception of the *dévot* duc d'Orléans, widely scorned for his uxorious fidelity. The post-Metz debate was less about the fact of royal mistresses than who they were, the power they wielded and the way in which they seemed to symbolize failings in the royal will. It was a debate which found its immediate focus in the beautiful person of Jeanne Antoinette Poisson, Madame d'Étiolles – soon to be known as Madame de Pompadour. Born, bred and married in high financial milieux, Madame d'Étiolles seems to have set her cap at becoming the lover of the king as he was casting off moroseness caused by the death of the duchesse de Châteauroux. Their affair is said to have started at a masked ball in February 1745 (Louis was dressed as a yew tree, 'Pompadour' as a shepherdess). By the time Louis set off on campaign again several months later, she was installed as official mistress and lodged in Versailles. In the autumn a separation from her husband was arranged and a handy marquisate – Pompadour – located to give her requisite status.

The young marquise was witty, cultured and accomplished – and also had a calculating head on her shoulders. Unlike her predecessors in the mistress role, she showed unfailing respect for the queen. She encouraged Louis to do so too, and also to develop warm, paternal feelings for his children – an ingenious way of reducing his propensity for sexual and marital guilt. The king's dizzy infatuation with his new mistress was not long in passing – they seem not to have had sex after 1750 but, again unlike her predecessors, she was able to use the period of grace to make herself indispensable to the king. She became mistress of royal pleasures, keeping Louis's gloom at bay by an unceasing round of evening entertainments, gambling parties, musical soirées and plays in which she and other guests acted the parts. As Louis's sexual interest in her began to wane, moreover, she winked at (and may well have colluded in) the supply of a series of 'little mistresses', usually daughters of obscure noble families, to allow Louis's sexual energies an outlet. She worked hard to ensure that the king's relations with these women was strictly sexual – any attempt to develop something more substantial was crushed. A score or so of royal bastards resulted and all, like their mothers, were dealt with discreetly and generously, without any thought for the process of legitimation which had caused so much political trouble with Louis XIV's bastard issue.

In a way, too, Madame de Pompadour became Fleury's successor as gatekeeper and private adviser to Louis XV. Indeed, she prided herself on being 'a Fleury and a half',[7] and was widely accounted to play a major part in government business. Though she lacked the cardinal's portfolio of posts and appointments, she could – and did – become a major influence on royal patronage. Where Fleury's system had been founded on the need to keep separate the spheres of government and the royal court, however, Pompadour disregarded such divisions. She was influential enough, for example, to secure the dismissal in 1749 of the long-serving and reliable Secretary of State Maurepas, whom she felt had insulted her, and her influence was also detectable in the replacement of Feydeau de Marville by her protégé Berryer as Paris Police Lieutenant in 1747. Though other post-Fleury changes were less directly her doing – Amelot had been sacked by the king in 1744, for example, and Orry retired of his own free will in 1745 – the dismantling of Fleury's old team allowed her considerable room for manoeuvre. She used it to advance the interest and careers of kin, friends and clients. It was widely believed that she was the daughter of either Le Normant de Tournehem or Pâris de Montmartel, wealthy financiers both, who managed to do well out of her rise to influence. The latter put up the money for the king to pay for the marquisate of Pompadour for her in 1745 and was to be rewarded – to mention only the most outstanding gifts – by Pompadour arranging for him to become a marquis and marry the daughter of a duke. In 1746, Le Normant was given the influential post of Director of Royal Buildings, Arts and Manufactures (the Bâtiments du Roi), which on his death in 1751 passed to Pompadour's younger brother, the marquis de Marigny.

These appointments typified several traits about Pompadour's influence. She clearly wanted her own men; but these were not thereby necessarily bad appointments – the tenure of Le Normant and then, down to 1774, Marigny at the Bâtiments du Roi was marked by a productive flurry of architectural and artistic activity. Characteristically, Pompadour's eye for talent was particularly sharp as regards cultural matters: the future cardinal de Bernis, for example, was a humble cleric from an obscure Languedocian noble family making his way as a writer when Pompadour gave him his break. Similarly, it was her influence which helped get Voltaire elected to the Académie française in 1746, and she showed a general goodwill towards the *philosophe* movement developing within Parisian salons.[8] Her artistic patronage was most evident in architecture and decoration. Fleury's famed frugality was now a thing of the past, and Pompadour was the moving spirit in the elegant refurbishment of most of the royal residences, and in the development of a number of minor residences such as Crécy, Bellevue and the Trianon, in all of which she indulged the king's penchant for intimacy and privacy.

Someone as influential on royal patronage and as culturally ambitious as Pompadour was bound to be attacked by the envious and disgruntled. On the death of the king's ex-mistress, Madame de Mailly in 1751, the Parisian chronicler Barbier noted: 'People praise her for having loved the king and having asked for nothing nor thought about her own fortune,' adding sombrely 'which is quite a contrast with the one who is nowadays in place'.[9] Many courtiers put her self-promotion down to her insufferably 'bourgeois' origins: the Nesle clan had been irreproachably aristocratic and though Pompadour's family was probably wealthier, its non-noble status and its orientation around the much-hated world of high finance made it the object of aristocratic disdain. She was thus a soft target, who was accordingly much aimed at. An important anti-Pompadour grouping, with a powerful *dévot* tinge, developed around the queen, the dauphin and the other royal children, grounded in resentment against this impostor who seemed to be keeping the king from living righteously as a good husband and father, and as a good Catholic. Nor were court cliques above encouraging attacks on Pompadour by pamphleteers and polemicists. There was soon quite an anti-Pompadour literature – the *Poissonades* – drawing on a tradition of anti-court writings which dated back to the Regency at least (and in some respects back to Suetonius), and dealing in equal measure in gossip, scurrility and self-righteousness.

The role of Madame de Pompadour in distancing Louis XV from his kingly duties as mapped out at Metz became an issue, moreover, just as the government was running into criticism following the end of the War of Austrian Succession in 1748. As we shall see, France gained far less in the Peace of Aix-la-Chapelle than had been anticipated.[10] Bad harvests and then post-war demobilization caused widespread social disturbances and economic troubles in 1747–9, and made a poor backdrop against which the government sought to recoup the costs of war. Popular discontent crystallized damagingly on the person of the king in the episode of the so-called 'vanishing children' of Paris in 1749–50. Rumours that young children were being kidnapped by Parisian police officials provoked widespread panic in Paris and other cities. Parisian glazier Jacques-Louis Ménétra later remembered being met from his primary school by his father, along with 'seven strong cooper lads each carrying a crowbar over his shoulder'.[11] Rioting in Paris against would-be abductors left up to twenty dead, and there was a good deal of looting. Much popular indignation was aimed at the new police Lieutenant, Berryer (known to be a Pompadour appointee), who had ordered his men to be ruthless in their arrest of vagrants and demobilized soldiers. It also, however, targeted the person of the king. Barbier noted the belief that the kidnapping was the work of agents of 'a leprous prince whose cure required a bath in human blood, and there being no blood purer than that of children, these were seized so as to be bled from all their limbs'.[12] In accounts which circulated widely at court and which reached the ears of the king himself, that leprous prince was metamorphosed into the morally and spiritually unclean and sexually debauched Louis XV.

'The wicked people . . . are calling me a Herod,' whined le Bien-Aimé, now transformed into the instigator of the massacre of the innocents and archetype of regal wickedness.[13] In the event, the Herod reference would only be a passing one. But the matrix of belief and suspicion out of which that accusation had developed would prove more long-lasting. The vanishing children rumour was significant not because of its veracity or non-veracity but because it was so widely believed. It was as though people were choosing to trust even rumours more than government news accounts. This failure of government to explain itself and to engender credibility stimulated criticism of Louis in particular and monarchy in general. The monarch had turned his back on the royal vocation sketched out for him at Metz, and opted to live in a state of mortal sin, in which his mistress and nebulous financial interests allegedly influenced the exercise of royal patronage. Louis unwittingly allowed the royal court to be sketched out as a closed space shut off from the wider public, a place of sin and perdition, luxury and self-indulgence, where manly virtues were ensnared by female wiles, and where royal duty was subverted by financial interest groupings. Notions of civic virtue were at that moment changing,[14] in ways which would make of Louis's alleged vices an incubus on the back of the monarchy. This was all the more damaging, moreover, in that the state was perceiving the need to undertake extensive reform, so as to maintain its rank in an increasingly competitive international arena.

B) THE BALANCE OF POWER AND THE GLOBALIZATION OF WARFARE

The difficulty which Louis XV experienced in adjusting to the template of authority inherited from Louis XIV was evident in foreign as well as domestic policy. War under Louis XV was less about the unbridled pursuit of *la gloire* than had been the case under his predecessor. Even the Sun King had seemed to accept, in his last years, that he had warred too much. The Regent, Dubois and Fleury had also each in turn renounced thoughts of preponderance in Europe, and largely accepted the notion of a balance of power, which the Utrecht Treaty – through seeking 'to confirm the peace and tranquillity of the Christian world through a just equilibrium of power' – enshrined. Louis XV had thus to adjust the popular image of the warrior-monarch to fit the shifting complexion of international relations in which the need to fight and the nature of warfare had changed.

A general acceptance of the notion of the balance of power as the idiom within which international relations were conducted after Utrecht reflected an estimation of the relative limitations of France's strength, and the strength of its friends and foes in the aftermath of Louis XIV's extensive wars. The rejection of foreign adventurism derived partly from an awareness of the dynastic vulnerability of the Bourbon line, partly from the country's economic as well as its military fragility – and partly too from the increasingly evident limitations of France's traditional international allies. In the sixteenth and seventeenth centuries, France had pursued its struggles against the Habsburgs by fostering friendship with states in northern and eastern Europe which after 1715 were in serious decline. Sweden never recovered from defeat at the hands of Russia in the Great Northern War (1688–1721), while Poland was escaping French influence and falling increasingly under the hegemony of Austria and the new military and naval power of Russia. Another customary ally, Turkey, victim of Austrian expansionism in south-east Europe, was also less of a player in international relations than hitherto. The Hungarian and Transylvanian noble dissidents whom France had earlier cultivated were being progressively integrated by the Austrians. In Germany too, France's traditional friends – notably Bavaria and the Rhine princes – had failed to break through to great power status, and were being eclipsed by the emergence of bellicose Prussia, a natural opponent of Austria, but one which France was to find unreliable.

If prolonged warfare down to 1713 had exhausted France and reduced its foreign policy options, at least it had had much the same effect on the state's traditional opponents. Spain was now under a Bourbon (Philip V) rather than a Habsburg – even though that Bourbon had gone native, and adopted the autonomous interests of the Iberian state. Most European states after Utrecht saw Austria, France's long-term opponent in European power politics, rather than Spain, as the most powerful threat to international peace. In the event, the Habsburgs tended to direct their energies towards consolidating their hold on the Italian peninsula and building up their south-eastern territories. Dynastic weakness – as in France, and indeed in Hanoverian England too – restrained Habsburg aggression: Holy Roman Emperor Charles VI gave high priority to securing the succession for his daughter Maria Theresa through the Pragmatic Sanction, and he failed to expand the Habsburg power-base in Germany. The financial toll of decades of warfare on another of France's foes, the United Provinces, was also showing, and the Dutch economy failed to match the pace of change set by its rivals, England and France. The Hanoverian connection and the perennial threat of Jacobitism induced England too towards prudence. Under the Fleury-esque Robert Walpole (in power from 1721 to 1742), the English eschewed Continental entanglements, aiming only to give the balance of power a few tweaks when this seemed absolutely essential.

Utrecht thus prefaced a phase in international relations in which states were pulling in their horns out of a fear of continuation of generalized European conflict. A system of five great powers – Britain plus, on the Continent, Austria, Prussia and Russia as well as France – was slowly emerging, with no single state being able to assert itself without producing countervailing opposition from the other great powers. Europe was not locked into stasis – the 'system' was always breaking down under the impact of events such as dynastic extinction, and diplomacy was not always up to the task of preventing the resort to arms. The balance of power had become a kind of mantra to which all deferred. There seemed a growing sense that international power politics had become in fact a zero-sum game in which territorial gains inevitably produced compensatory adjustments. States thus sought to extend their influence marginally and incrementally, and by negotiation and diplomacy rather than full-scale war if at all possible. Although between 1610 and 1792, every one year in two was a war year somewhere in Europe, between 1713 and 1740, France was at war only one year in five.

Given the dwindling strength of France's customary allies, the limitations of its foreign policy options, and the major financial implications of fighting wars, one can understand Orléans, Dubois, then Fleury, being attracted by means of maintaining grandeur through economic development rather than military manoeuvrings. This entailed a prudent tendency to favour friendship with England. The Entente Cordiale which developed between the two powers after 1715 was never the best of all possible worlds, for there was strong economic and colonial rivalry between the two powers, notably over commercial influence in Spain's American colonies. Yet given that war was unthinkable in France's situation, friendship with England aimed at containing and reducing potential hostility seemed the surest guarantee for the pursuit of state objectives.

The Entente Cordiale did not, however, last long. Distinct signs of chilliness were evident by the late 1720s. Walpole's rapprochement with Austria in 1731 meant that Fleury had to work hard to keep England out of the War of Polish Succession. By late in the decade, England was resentful of the French acquisition of Lorraine and was anxious about its growing influence in Continental affairs, especially as France's commercial prosperity contrasted with the sorry state of its own balance of trade at that moment. Growing clamour in England for a more aggressive policy towards France's ally, Spain, triggered the Anglo–Spanish 'War of Jenkins's Ear' in 1739, which seemed certain to bring in the French on Spain's side.

In the event, Jenkins's ear proved a turning point around which Anglo–French relations failed to turn. This was less due to the diplomatic skills of the ever-plausible Fleury – for the cardinal was losing ground to a war party in Versailles and Paris just as Walpole was doing the same in London. Rather, the unexpected death of Holy Roman Emperor Charles VI in 1740 sparked off an international crisis which placed

Anglo–French rivalry in a different context. As we have seen,[15] France's efforts to put the Bavarian ruler rather than a Habsburg client on the throne of Holy Roman Empire, coming on top of Prussia's seizure of Austria's wealthy province of Silesia, gave a rude enough shock to the Continental balance of power to worry the English. The novelist and journalist Henry Fielding was not alone in England in surmising that these steps presaged 'the scheme of universal monarchy, framed by the House of Bourbon'.[16] Carteret, Prime Minister following the fall of Walpole, pieced together a wide-ranging European alliance against France, its Spanish ally and the endlessly unreliable Frederick II's Prussia. The Anglo–Austrian victory over the French at Dettingen in May 1743 was accompanied by alliance between Maria Theresa's Austria and Sardinia, which opened up an Italian front against the 'Gallespani' (Franco-Spanish forces), while the death of the Bavarian Holy Roman Emperor left the road clear for Maria Theresa's husband, Francis, to succeed to the imperial title. The queen of Hungary was now inclined to cut her losses, and in December 1745 she signed the Treaty of Dresden with Prussia, ceding the contested province of Silesia.

Dresden terminated hostilities in central Europe, but not elsewhere. In the Low Countries, the French came out unequivocally on top: Saxe's brilliant victory at Fontenoy in May 1745 against Anglo–Dutch–Hanoverian forces under the duke of Cumberland opened up the road into the Austrian Netherlands. Virtually the whole of the region fell to Saxe's ingenious generalship. His task was, it is true, made easier by the need of the English to remove troops to put down the 1745–6 Jacobite Rising, which the French had subventioned. The '45 Rising' was comprehensively crushed, and following defeat at Culloden in April 1746, the 'Young Pretender', Jacobite Charles Edward Stuart, took refuge in France. In Italy, where France, Spain and the Two Sicilies matched up against English, Austrian and Sardinian forces, the issue swayed one way then the other. In 1747, Philip V of Spain died and his successor Ferdinand VI sought peace. In the same year, Belle-Isle had to be sent down to repulse Sardinian incursions into Provence – the only military invasion of French soil between 1715 and 1792.

The Anglo–French struggle was also taking place in the colonies, marking a new, and enduring, globalization of warfare. The inhabitants of England's North American colonies outnumbered French Canadians some ten to one, but the French were tough, fur-trapping frontiersmen who posed a considerable military threat. It took a combined operation between the American colonists and the Royal Navy to seize the strategic centre of Louisbourg on Cape Breton in 1745, which the French spent the rest of the war trying to win back. The English and the French were also locked in combat at the other end of the world – in India, where Dupleix, Governor-General of the French trading ports, outclassed his opposite numbers from the English East India Company, capturing Madras in 1746.

Although colonial and commercial issues were starting to make themselves felt, the achievement of a balance of power in Europe was still the highest priority of European statesmen. After his mixed fortunes posturing as military campaigner defending his people, moreover, Louis accepted the more restricted foreign policy goals inherited by Orléans, Dubois and Fleury. Even though by 1748, France was holding all the Austrian Netherlands and a number of Dutch frontier strongholds, and had occupied the Sardinian possessions of Nice and Savoy, the king was willing to trade them in and return to what was in essence a return to the *status quo ante* 1740. The marquis d'Argenson, Secretary of State for Foreign Affairs between 1744 and 1747, opined that France had become 'too big, too rounded off, too well-placed for trade to prefer territorial acquisitions to a good reputation'. The king sacked d'Argenson for maladroitness, but seemed to share some of his views, presenting the restitution of French gains in the Treaty of Aix-la-Chapelle as his own wish to act magnanimously – he claimed to eschew unseemly haggling and to be making peace 'not as a merchant but as a king' – the ruler of a great nation.[17]

There was a good deal of shrewd strategic thinking behind this approach. France, now encamped behind Vauban's *ceinture de fer*, could be thought of as a 'satisfied power':[18] gains in the Low Countries would imply perpetual (and expensive) conflict not only with the Austrians but also with the English and the Dutch, who would regard French acquisitions as a threat to their own trading and strategic interests. The attempt to wrap up this policy in bland Fénelonian language did not, however, go down well with the public. More used to the diplomatic quest for glory of Louis XIV, the French people had also suffered severe privations during the final stages of the war, and many were appalled to see France – seemingly naively – handing back most of its conquests. News-sheets railed incontinently against France having 'fought for the king of Prussia', who by managing to hold on to Silesia was the biggest gainer from the peace, and they coined the phrase *bête comme la paix* ('as stupid as the peace'). One clause in the treaty had obliged France to expel the Jacobite Pretender, Charles Edward Stuart, and when the latter, who had turned himself into a popular icon in Paris, was bundled into a carriage by policemen as he was coming out of the Opéra and thrown out of the country, there were riots and expressions of outrage at the indignities performed by the government. Furthermore, if the French had airily waved away one potential *casus belli*, more than enough causes of potential conflict remained embedded in the Aix-la-Chapelle Treaty. In particular, Austria felt humiliated and was already planning to get its beloved Silesia back. In addition, there were still numerous outstanding colonial and commercial matters at dispute involving France, England and, to a degree, Spain. The French had restored Madras to the English in return for Louisbourg, but these exchanges solved nothing. As war ground to a halt in Europe, it continued in the rest of the world.

The Treaty of Aix-la-Chapelle thus revealed the prioritization which European statesmen still accorded European power politics, and also signalled the growing centrality of Anglo–French conflict within international relations and the world stage on which that conflict was now taking place. One reason why the French – for all Louis XV's altruistic claims – had hastened to the conference table in 1748 was the economic pressure which the English had been applying on them from 1746 onwards. The Newfoundland cod fisheries and the Canadian fur trade had made a longstanding and growing contribution to France's trading position, but in the first half of the century this was being demoted in importance by the explosive impact of the Caribbean sugar islands (Saint-Domingue in particular, plus Martinique and Guadeloupe). England was a rival and competitor in these markets, as well as in the trade in slaves into the region. Similarly, the Indian subcontinent and through it the Chinese and south-east Asian markets were also a theatre for economic rivalry. The importance of these trading sectors in the broader French economy was highlighted by the English harassment of French trade which the War of Austrian Succession opened up. In 1747, the Royal Navy blockaded French ports against the return of the Newfoundland fishing fleet, and fears were soon being expressed lest the same fate be visited on the merchant vessels involved in the sugar trade. French trade was losing out to the English – only 149 slaves were landed in Saint-Domingue in the last three years of the war. In deciding to press for peace in 1748, France was as much moved by apprehension that things could only get strategically and commercially worse outside Europe as by a conviction that France had no possibilities of gaining territory within Europe on to which it could hope to hang. This was a difficult message, however, to sell to a public opinion which was becoming increasingly vocal.

The globalization of the Anglo–French conflict was further in evidence even before the ink was dry on the 1748 treaty. Indeed, England and France were to all effects still at war outside Europe. In India, Robert Clive's appointment to head the English forces swayed the fortunes of the struggle England's way. Rather than relying on local rulers to do the English's fighting for them, Clive took to the offensive, shaking Dupleix's complacency. Meanwhile in North America, the establishment by the French of a line of forts southwards from Canada towards France's Louisiana possessions irritated English colonists by appearing to set limits to the latter's westward expansion. Anxious about possible encirclement by the French, they became involved in a number of clashes with them in the early 1750s. Though England at first tried to keep aloof, French successes were seen as strategically threatening, and from 1754 the English government was moved to levy regiments of regulars in America to halt French expansion. The French riposted by embarking an expeditionary force of some 4,000 troops, but the Royal Navy intercepted it. The troops were imprisoned, and the English went on to impound some 300 French merchantmen. At the same time, they also deported 8,000 'disloyal' Acadians from the erstwhile French possession of Nova Scotia. By the mid-1750s, a fuller resumption of Anglo–French conflict seemed to be in the air. War, however, had its costs.

C) FLEXING THE SINEWS OF WAR

War had always been the most expensive item in any European monarch's pocket-book. The early seventeenth century had inaugurated an arms race amongst the main European powers which continued down to the late eighteenth century. France's army grew from an earlier maximum of 50,000 men to a standing force of a quarter of a million towards the end of the seventeenth century, and around 400,000 during the War of Spanish Succession. Admission to the club of the great powers was thus very costly – especially if, as was the case with a would-be great nation such as France, one also wanted a powerful navy.

As with its civil administration, the state sought to reduce military overheads by alienating government functions to underlings. Thus, regimental commands in the army were – as with the judiciary or the financial bureaucracy – venal posts, which were purchased, bequeathed and sold among the nobility. This meant that anyone without an impressive noble pedigree found it difficult to get on in the army. In the last years of Louis XIV, around one officer in fourteen had been a commoner – yet for most of the eighteenth century the figure hovered around one in a hundred. The financial stakes were so high that even many country gentlemen of ancient noble stock felt themselves excluded. It was to palliate such individuals that Louis created the École militaire in Paris in 1751, in which 500 scholarships were designated for noblemen able to prove four degrees of noble status.

The crown expected the aristocratic officers not only to equip themselves but also to handle recruitment. Normally, proprietary colonels handed this responsibility over to semi-professional recruiting sergeants, who developed a range of recruiting techniques from bribery and corruption through to press-gang violence. Soldiers tended to be seen as desperadoes, butchers and villains, and this image was to a certain extent self-confirming: the army ended up as a refuge for social outcasts (including, interestingly, a disproportionate number of Protestants, for the army was one of the few careers in which they were not systematically disadvantaged), vagrants and the mentally unstable. Areas near to the northern and eastern land frontiers produced fair numbers of recruits, but the south and west were rather recalcitrant. Breton recruits were notorious for suffering from *la nostalgie* – a mortiferous form of homesickness. Where regimental recruiting-sergeants failed to produce the goods, foreigners filled the gap. At mid-century, around a quarter of the army was non-French, with the Swiss and the Germans producing the largest contingents, followed at some distance by Italians (including Corsicans), Irish, Hungarians and others. A final fall-back was the militia. Abolished in the aftermath of Utrecht, then re-established in 1726, the militia was not a frontline battlefield arm, though in time of war militia-men could be called up as ancillary forces. Men in each parish drew by lot for service – a few, bitterly resented, days of military training each year.

Despite the continued resort to the farming-out of many essential functions, the state was also taking a growing part in the arming, supply, training and sustenance of its armies. In 1717, the government decreed the use throughout the army of a single type of musket, and from 1727 took over from its colonels the task of supplying arms. Decent bread, meat, wine and clothing rations supplied from state-run storehouses now provided the soldier's wherewithal. State welfare services too – military hospitals, regimental surgeons, and so on – were developed so as to conserve the state's investment in human capital. The state also played a greater, and increasingly expensive, role in the training of its troops. The shift on Europe's battlefields to linear battle formations in broadly disposed ranks three to four men deep required high levels of military discipline. Governments sought to inculcate it through the drillground and in military exercises: Frederick the Great of Prussia reckoned it took five years of such training before a soldier could be committed to the frontline without flinching. Frontal fire in these massive new armies was spectacularly deadly too, so that commanders were inclined to conduct 'petticoat wars' (*la guerre en dentelle*), preferring siege and manoeuvre, marches and counter-marches, to committing expensive troops to immolation in battle. Most generals took pains to evade face-to-face conflict if at all possible, and to campaign in ways which placed attritional strain on their opponent's ability to pay for keeping troops mobilized. 'The masterpiece of an able general', Frederick the Great held, 'is to make his enemy go hungry,' while the marshal de Saxe was perhaps exaggerating but not entirely joking when he remarked that the sign of truly great generalship was to go through one's entire career without having to fight a single pitched battle.[19]

No commander worth his salt allowed his men to forage for themselves. This would risk raising the already very high incidence of desertion to unacceptable levels, and, through gratuitous looting, damaging the tax-paying capability of the civilian population. Rather than living off the land at the population's expense, armies were increasingly provisioned from state-run supply systems, and, in order to keep discipline intact, commanders endeavoured to keep their troops as insulated from the rest of the population as they could: there was a drive from 1719 onwards to house troops in barracks where they could be kept out of harm's way and subjected to round-the-clock discipline. By 1742, some 300 localities had military barracks.

The relative cost of security was thus higher in the eighteenth century than before, partly because changes in the conduct of war and the composition of the army were making fighting soldiers a weightier investment than in the previous century. A further dimension to the problem was the extension of the European arms race to navies as well as armies. If France was serious about containing, let alone combating the commercial strength of England and the United Provinces and maintaining the status of the greatest of the great powers, it needed a strong navy. The French had made an enormous investment in naval forces in the seventeenth century, but there was no French ship-building worth speaking of over most of the War of Spanish Succession. The Regent, then Fleury, were not of a mind to commit scarce resources in this direction, so that France accepted the *de facto* superiority of the Royal Navy – which made the costs even higher once the government determined, in the 1740s, to reinvest in naval might.

The European arms race, military and naval, meant that it was very expensive for the French state merely to keep the sinews of war duly toned in conditions of general peace. The armed forces remained the major item on which the state spent its revenues. They towered over other items of state expenditure – including court festivities and pensions, which remained rather meagre in comparison, despite the switch from the stinginess of Fleury to the prodigality of Pompadour. In the late 1720s, with the John Law episode over, upkeep of the armed forces cost the state 65 million livres (the army took 57 million, the navy 8 million) – around one-third of a total spend of 182.3 million. Yet a further one-third (61 million) out of the latter sum represented debts contracted for the most part in Louis XIV's wars. By 1751, following the War of Austrian Succession (which cost roughly 1,000 million livres), the figures for the armed forces were 105.7 million (army 76.9; navy 26.8) out of a total of 256.3 million – and debt service had risen to 71.8 million. Thus, between the advent of Fleury and the aftermath of the War of Austrian Succession, overall state peacetime expenditure increased by over one-third. The share of the armed forces (especially as a result of the naval build-up) in total government spend remained extremely high.

Analysis of state expenditure down to the early 1750s thus suggests not only a growth in war-driven expenditure, but also a tendency, detectable in the rising proportion of expenditure devoted to debt service, for regular state income not to cover expenses except by borrowing. The bulk of regular royal income derived from a bewildering array of taxes. Since 1439, French kings had had the right to impose direct taxes on their population. In 1726, such levies accounted for roughly half of state income (88.8 million livres out of 181.0 million), and in 1751, proportionately, slightly less (116.6 million from 258.5 million). The main royal tax was the *taille*, a tax on landed wealth, distributed among the *généralités* and assessed and levied in a variety of ways, and it was supplemented by a range of other direct taxes (*taillon, supplément d'hiver*, etc.) paid according to the same schedules. Most French provinces were administratively classified as *pays d'élections*, which meant that these direct taxes were collected through royal tax officials, the *élus*, under the supervision of the local Intendants. But the *pays d'états* had retained local assemblies, which negotiated with the crown a contract for the collection and payment of an agreed sum. This arrangement favoured the *pays d'état*, whose relative tax burden was rather low. The same was true of the other major grouping to negotiate its tax liability in this way, namely the clergy, whose *don gratuit* ('free gift') made to the royal treasury, in return for the legal fiction of tax immunity, was a pitifully small proportion of their total wealth.

The theoretically universal obligation to pay royal taxes was thus shot through with arbitrariness and variability. In the areas classified as *pays de taille personnelle*, assessment was on the appearances of personal wealth, as estimated by local collectors – but only commoners paid. In the areas of so-called *taille réelle* (in the south, in particular), privilege attached to property rather than persons: assessment was based on usually out-of-date land surveys, and property therein classified as 'noble land' was exempted from tax (even if owned by a commoner). If the nobles, the clergy and the *pays d'état* were the most fiscally protected social groupings, other corporative bodies also enjoyed tax immunities. Most major cities, for example, were exempted from paying the *taille*. In addition, powerful individuals were able to use their social influence and patronage links to reduce their tax liability. The *capitation*, or poll-tax, for example, which had started out in 1695 as a tax on revenue applicable to all classes, soon became merely an adjunct to the *taille*, and was widely ignored, especially among the nobility. Tax-evasion was a quintessentially aristocratic point of honour – but one which all social groups aspired to emulate.

The ways in which direct taxes were assessed and levied made them notoriously inelastic. Though the clergy and provincial estates could be pressurized into paying more in time of war, it was always difficult to squeeze extra moneys swiftly out of the *taille* and *capitation*. From the War of Spanish Succession onwards, the crown was obliged periodically to resort to emergency taxes on income rather than property. From 1710 to 1716 this had been the *dixième* – a 10 per cent tax – but a 'twentieth tax', or *vingtième*, was levied on top of the customary taxes from 1733 to 1737 to finance the War of Polish Succession and between 1741 and 1749 to cover the cost of the War of Austrian Succession. These demands were extremely unpopular – though in fact the light-handed system of self-assessment still left the door open to massive under-estimations of tax liability.

Eighteenth-century monarchs were less heavily dependent on direct tax income than their predecessors, since they were able to rely on indirect taxes bringing in a solid, and growing, ancillary income. Indirect tax revenue grew from 88.6 to 116.6 million livres between 1726 and 1751 (while income from direct taxes progressed, roughly proportionately, from 79.9 to 109.0 million). There was as little uniformity in the enforcement of indirect as there was in direct taxes. Salt, for example, was a state monopoly, and the tax on it – the much-detested *gabelle* – was levied at six different levels in the various regions, producing a sense of social outrage and a propensity to smuggling and black-marketeering in equal measure. While certain small enclaves, usually close to the coast, were totally exempt from the tax, a number of provinces had redeemed part of their obligations in the past and paid at a lower rate than the so-called *pays de grande gabelle*, which covered most of northern France. There were equally flagrant anomalies and exemptions as regards the other main indirect taxes, the *aides* (covering drinks, meat, fish, metals, oils, soap, paper, etc.) and the *traites* (which covered taxes on internal circulation and movement of goods and operated largely through tolls). Since 1726, the collection of *gabelle*, *aides* and *traites*, along with the tax on tobacco (which was a lucrative royal monopoly) and a number of other fiscal dues, was placed in the hands of the 'General Farm', or Ferme générale, a company of some forty wealthy private financiers. Every six years, the Farmers General negotiated the collection franchise with the crown, aiming to set the price at a level which guaranteed themselves a profit over and above the costs of collection and the annual payment to the royal treasury. It was widely believed that the first such contracts massively favoured the Farmers General. The latter's often draconian efforts to compel payment from the population at large through an army of excise-men – they employed some 30,000 individuals overall – won the *gabelous* never-failing popular hatred, and smugglers never-ending support.

One of the most striking characteristics of the royal tax system, reaffirmed after the failure of John Law's System, was the extent to which the crown was willing to outsource its putatively 'absolute' power in this domain to a range of privileged social groupings (rather than seek to rely on a single credit source as had been attempted so catastrophically under Law). While the private company of Farmers General looked after indirect taxes, direct taxes were alienated either to privileged corporative groupings such as the clergy and the *pays d'état*, or else placed in the hands of financial officials who had purchased their posts. Though the sale of venal offices in the state administration never reached the salad days of the early seventeenth century (when they had accounted for nearly half of state income) or the wars of Louis XIV, it comprised a solid alternative means of raising revenue when times were hard. There were 50,000 venal offices or more for most of the century, roughly 4,000 of which ennobled their owners.

Over the century, these administrative practices began to be vociferously criticized for administrative and financial inefficiency. Yet it was a system which had advantages for those skilled enough to understand its intricacies. A particular advantage was that it allowed the state to tap the income and the credit of the most wealthy groups within society – precisely those who were most effective in evading direct taxation. Corporative bodies like the General Farm as well as certain categories of venal office-holders – as well as the clergy, the *pays d'état* and major municipalities – could, for example, be inveigled into arranging loans for the crown. (The cost of the state borrowing in its own name might require double the interest rate involved.) Furthermore, tax farming, for example, kept administrative overheads remarkably low, and supplied the state with tax revenue even before the tax was collected. It was not only the sale of offices, but also the manipulation of the terms of office ownership which offered extractive possibilities. Thus at the heart of the financial maelstrom of 1714, the government had ordered all salaries to venal officers to be reduced from 5 to 4 per cent of their nominal value. Thus again, at the outbreak of the War of Polish Succession in 1733, Orry decreed the venality of municipal officials, and in 1743, as the costs of the War of Austrian Succession were rising, established the heredity of notaries, attorneys and court ushers – at a price. The government was not above using such veiled extortion either in discussions with the Farmers General at the moment of their six-year negotiation over the terms of the extension of their lease on indirect tax-farmers. As they bargained with the state over raising their annual contribution to the state treasury from 92 million livres (in the period from 1744 to 1750) to 101.1 million for the period down to 1756, the Farmers General proffered outright gifts of 2 million livres to the princesse de Conti, 2.4 million to Madame de Pompadour, and 0.3 million to Controller-General Machault. With venality, outright corruption was rarely far away.

That the arcane system could be made to work effectively was underlined by the achievement of Orry, Controller-General from 1730 to 1745, in balancing the accounts in 1739–40 – an event worthy of record in the annals of royal finance. Yet its intricacies made the task of financial management extremely fraught, even at the best of times. Orry's successor, Machault d'Arnouville, in place from 1745 to 1754, was prudent, but his task was made very difficult by the heavy cost of the War of Austrian Succession, compounded with the general feeling of dissatisfaction which the Treaty of Aix-la-Chapelle had produced. A tough-minded administrator whom service as an Intendant had fashioned into an ultra-loyal crown servant, Machault determined to seize the opportunity for introducing more structural financial reform, namely, a new universal direct tax on income. In May 1749, he announced that from January 1750 the *dixième* (or two *vingtièmes*) put in place in 1741 for the duration of the war would be replaced by a less onerous single *vingtième* – effectively a 5 per cent rather than a 10 per cent levy on incomes – revenue for which would go into a special fund to help pay off the national debt. But there was little spirit of generosity implicit in this reduction: for the tax was given no terminal end-point, and it was declared that it would be levied throughout France not by the customary venal fiscal officers but by new tax officials responsible to the Intendants, who were empowered to ask for justification of individual tax declarations. It was thus hoped that the tax, even though levied at half the rate of the *dixième*, would actually produce more revenue for the royal exchequer.

The secrecy in which the royal finances were immired meant that the government was unable to demonstrate the fiscal prudence of this measure. In addition, the *vingtième* seemed constitutionally dubious. The medieval tradition of the king 'living off his own' survived only as a pious wish by the eighteenth century: the royal domain accounted for only a few per cent of the state's regular income. Yet even so, there was a widespread feeling that extraordinary state demands were only justified by the extraordinary state of war. The attempt in 1725 by the duc de Bourbon to levy a *cinquantième* (a 2 per cent tax on incomes) in time of peace had created the political furore which led to his disgrace and dismissal. In 1749, Machault, dubbed *Tête de fer* ('Iron-Head'), tried hard to live up to the sobriquet in facing down protests against the *vingtième* emanating from many provincial *parlements* as well as the Parisian body. Squeals of protest were also heard soon enough from two other groupings which enjoyed extensive financial privileges, namely, the clergy and the provincial estates. The Assembly of the Clergy in June 1750 set in motion an orchestrated campaign in defence of the church's traditional immunity from tax obligations over and above the legal fiction of the *don gratuit*. The Assembly's wish to make a constitutional issue as well as a moral dilemma out of the reform (one bishop even comparing the church's situation to that of Thomas à Becket) was echoed when provincial estates in the *pays d'état* joined the fray, notably in Languedoc, where local bishops held the whip hand. Machault, however, combined the support of the king (who added the post of Keeper of the Seals to his Controller-General's portfolio in December 1750) with support from the Pompadour lobby, which disliked the way in which the church's case was winning favour with the *dévot* grouping clustering around the queen. The Controller-General sent the members of the Assembly of Clergy off packing to their dioceses, and dissolved the Languedoc Estates (who did not meet again down to 1752). Nor did he shirk from taking his case on to the field of public opinion which the privileged orders were seeking to agitate: he hired pamphleteers (including Voltaire) to mock the church's arguments.

In the event, despite the running which Machault had made in both consolidating royal authority and in widening the state's tax base, Louis XV would manage to snatch defeat out of the jaws of victory. The strong government position which Machault had achieved was frittered away as a consequence of neither financial crisis nor court faction, but as a result of the resurgence of the Jansenism in the so-called *billets de confession* (confession certificates) affair. In December 1751, the king – against Machault's better judgement – caved in to the Assembly of the Clergy's plea to be exempt from the *vingtième*, so that the government and church were singing from the same hymnsheet as they girt their loins for a renewal of the the Jansenist struggle.[20] The episode highlighted the fact that in the absolutist polity, a strong financial position was always hostage to the vagaries of the government's political fortunes.

D) VITAL SIGNS IN RURAL FRANCE

In the political crisis of the early 1750s, the opponents of the crown invoked the misery and distress of the common people as justification for their criticisms. Yet in fact, although short-term problems caused by harvest failure still occurred, the economy generally was doing rather well – far better, in fact, than many contemporaries suspected.

There was a widespread assumption that the peasantry on whom so much of the country's wealth was based lived within an economy of self-sufficiency which left little room for change or improvement. Just as the conventional wisdom had it that the king should 'live off his own', so the ideal of rural living was the household which was at once a unit of production and consumption, and which possessed the substantial wherewithal to look after most of its own needs. Most peasant family heads spent most of their time producing enough food for themselves and their families to live on. The staff of life was bread, and home-produced tasted sweetest. Political arithmeticians regarded the daily ingestion of between 4 and 5 livres of it by each adult male as an irrefrangible universal need. In the peasantry's lexicon, *gagner son pain* ('to earn one's bread') was synonymous with *gagner sa vie* ('to earn one's livelihood, living, or life') and people had as many names for bread as the Eskimos for snow and the Bedouin for sand, each richly encrusted with connotations of nutritional quality, geographical provenance, economic status and social aspiration. Thus the rich might afford white, wheat-based loaves; the hard-up a black, unleavened loaf of rye and barley or a maize-based porridge; and the very poorest – like the disinherited paupers of the Vivarais – a practically indigestible chestnut bread which comprised, one village proudly boasted, 'our aid, our principal foodstuff, the wherewithal on which we nourish our families, our servants, our pets, our livestock, our poultry and our pigs'.[21]

The wish to maintain and perpetuate the domestic unit was accompanied by an equally thoroughgoing commitment to local autarchy. Most peasants conducted the majority of their lives within a 5–10 mile radius of their birthplace. Where they could not satisfy their family's needs from their own production, they looked to their neighbours, their village and their locality – their *pays* – to supply them. The *pays* contained the local weekly market for the exchange of goods, as well as encompassing most other needs – the services of a notary or of a surgeon, for example, or a local royal court. Peasants' homes were built and furnished very largely with local ingredients, their bread-based diet was, wherever possible, home-grown and their clothes, tools and furniture were similarly either made at home or passed down across the generations. Three-quarters of young men and four-fifths of young women even found their marriage partner within the *pays*. *L'esprit de clocher* – 'loyalty to one's local steeple' – was an instinctive reflex among France's peasants, and to find the hated foreigner one did not have to cross the Channel or the Pyrenees: *l'étranger* was not infrequently the denizen of a neighbouring village or an adjacent *pays*, who was instantly identifiable by an alien dress or accent. Roistering youths patriotically defended the honour of their village in violent pranks and pitched battles against their neighbours.

The scale of household priority was etched on the face of the landscape: polyculture targeted at supplying local needs was the rule, and pride of place in the fields was taken by cereal cultivation. The *ager*, in the terminology inherited from the Romans – the cultivated land – predominated over the other main components of the rural landscape: the peasant *domus* or home, around which the garden (*hortus*) provided a further site for cultivation; and the *saltus*, the mixture of meadows, heathland, woods and wasteland stretching indeterminately around cultivable and inhabitable zones. The preponderance of the cereal-producing *ager* was most apparent in the north and north-east. In these so-called *pays de grande culture*, in which open-field farming was the rule, the *ager* formed between two-thirds and four-fifths of the acreage of communities. Vast cornfields growing rye (for local consumption), oats (for local livestock) and wheat (for the towns and the rich) stretched away as far as the eye could see. Fields were unenclosed and often in medieval strip formation, and followed a rotation system which left at least one-third of the cultivable land fallow each year. The lack of *saltus* left little room for grazing, and the shortage of livestock produced a chronic insufficiency of dung, the main fertilizer, thus keeping crop yields low. The function of the *saltus* in providing ancillary means of subsistence was met in this region by practices such as *glanage* and *vaine pâture*, whereby after harvest the fields were turned over to all members of the community for gleaning and grazing.

There were fewer open fields outside this classic *pays de grande culture*, the interplay of local geographical and meteorological conditions, legal situations and historical differences producing a more varied, polycultural landscape – and, in consequence, a more varied local diet. In both the south and west, the *ager* was broken up into smaller plots by fields and hedges. Cereal quasi-monoproduction was replaced by more varied cultivation: pastoral farming in Normandy and elsewhere; vines in the Bordelais, Burgundy and along the Loire valley; olives and fruit-trees in the Mediterranean south; hemp, flax and linen in the coastal areas in the north and west; and salt in southern and western marshland areas. The palette of cereals, normally grown here on a biennial rotation, was wider too: there was a good deal of buckwheat in the west, for example, while maize, imported from the New World in the sixteenth century, had installed itself widely in the sunny south-west. Gardens tended to be larger and more extensive in many of these southern and western areas, allowing crop diversification and a good deal of experimentation in fruits and vegetables – garlic, tomatoes and aubergines in the Midi, for example, alongside more classically northern peas, beans, cabbages, carrots and onions. Zones of *saltus* between areas of cultivation were more extensive here too – they made up to half of farmed land in the Massif Central, for example, as against a paltry 4 per cent in northern Artois. The produce of the *saltus* provided animal litter, fuel (wood, fallen branches, etc.) and dietary alternatives (berries, mushrooms, etc.).

The autarchic tendency within French peasant agriculture, staked out around polycultural usage of the *ager*, *hortus* and *saltus*, was underpinned by poor agrarian technology and inefficient communications. While in England and the Netherlands there was a vibrant trade in publications on agricultural improvement, there was simply no innovatory work on agriculture published in France from Olivier de Serre's paean in praise of the self-sufficent farmer, *Théâtre d'agriculture et ménage des champs* ('Theatre of Agriculture and of Field-Management') (1600) down to the middle of the eighteenth century. Technical archaism was widespread: the light plough used in the Midi, for example, differed very little from its Roman forebear. The agrarian innovations with which its neighbours were beginning to experiment made little ground in France. Although, as we shall see, external and colonial trade was starting to boom,[22] internal trade was still relatively sluggardly. Distance-times were unimpressive – between 30 and 40 kilometres a day by land, and though water-borne transport had the edge over mule-back terrestrial carriage, traffic was sparse and subject to delays caused by flooding, low water levels and the like. Hardly surprisingly, grain prices in – for example – Toulouse showed a completely different profile from that of Paris, highlighting the localism of markets. Early eighteenth-century France was, rather than a single national economy, a collection of quasi-molecular economies, all of which nervously depended on the state of the harvest.

In the context of poor agrarian technology and communications and over-dependence on cereal crops, localism spelt periodic famine at worst, hunger at best when there were harvest shortfalls caused by bad weather. Seventeenth- and early eighteenth-century France was wracked by spas-modic 'mortality crises' which saw the number of deaths in a locality spiral upwards three-, six-, even tenfold, under the impact of hunger and famine. In the *pays de grande culture* in particular, the price of grain acted as a kind of demographic barometer, high prices caused by bad harvests sending the number of deaths spiralling upwards in so-called 'steeples' of mortality. Though the more variegated cultivation and diet of the south and west acted as a demographic cushion, no locality was immune from this deadly mechanism. Peasants starved in their droves in the final years of the '*Grand Siècle*' of Louis XIV, as we have seen.[23] For every nationwide catastrophe, moreover, there were numerous local crises, and the poor state of communications often meant that peasants in areas of shortage could sicken and starve without redress while adjacent areas enjoyed a period of plenty.

Famine was not death's only calling-card. Peasant households were visited with unfailing regularity by infant mortality, which carried off on average one child in every three or four before his or her first birthday, and granted new-born babies only a one-in-two chance of attaining puberty. This kind of inbuilt, quotidian mortality was accompanied by famine's companion scourges, war and disease. Life-threatening epidemics could operate independently of the state of the harvest – the Marseille plague of 1720 had emerged from the bluest of economic skies – but in practice often reinforced the impact of hunger and malnutrition. Starving peasants ate anything to hand – unripe fruits and berries, weeds and nettles, and even, according to one seventeenth-century Alsatian chronicler, 'rats, mice, the corpses of hanged criminals and rotting carcasses'.[24] The breakdown in normal economic relationships in time of bubonic plague, moreover, had a similarly deadly effect: contemporary physicians argued that the disease was not contagious and that deaths ascribed to plague were caused by starvation. The deadly cocktail caused by epidemics and hunger in combination was even more fatal when mixed with the impact of war, as the terrible crises of 1692–4 and 1709–10 attested.[25]

Given the range of catastrophes, man-made and natural, which could rain down on the peasantry, it is perhaps surprising that France's population in the middle- and long-term was relatively stable: between the fifteenth and the early eighteenth century, it oscillated between 17–18 and 20–21 million. Though poorly adapted to sustained growth, the molecular structure of peasant France was highly resilient and durable under the harshest of attacks. High mortality – roughly forty deaths per annum per thousand head of population – was matched by fertility at roughly the same high level, which suggests, incidentally, a systematic ignorance of contraception. Mortality crises were characterized by a sharp drop (often up to 50 per cent) in the marriage rate and the number of conceptions, but when the number of deaths fell there was a recuperatory rush down the aisle and a comforting spurt of conceptions. This pattern was linked to the prevalent system of household formation. It was normal to establish a separate household on marriage, for which the partners saved in advance – a factor which had the effect of deferring the age of marriage far beyond the biological minimum, and producing a large pool of available celibates. Limits on the availability of land, moreover, meant that marriage was invariably deferred until death produced either an inheritance or a new niche in the land market from which frustrated celibates could profit. Young women married in the early to mid-twenties, men when they were getting close to their thirtieth birthday.

The strength of the self-equilibrating, homeostatic mechanisms operating on population size in the middle and long term underlined the extent to which the economy was geared essentially around the peasantry's conservation and survival. In addition, peasants had to operate within a social and juridical system – seigneurialism, or *féodalité* ('feudalism') in contemporary parlance – which also inhibited innovation. With the exception of a few enclaves of completely freehold ('allodial') land, notably in the south, all property was subject to the dues and obligations levied within some 50,000 seigneurial estates. Around half of these were owned by noblemen, and the rest were under the control of the bourgeoisie, the church or collective owners such as village communities, and they ranged in size from fractions of a village to huge expanses of territory. Conventionally, seigneuries were divided between, first, the domain land which included the manor and which was owned and farmed direct by the seigneur, usually by his steward supervising its leasing out under share-cropping (*métayage*) or leasehold (*fermage*) arrangements; and, second, the tenures (or *censives*) which were divided among the peasantry and others. Overall, allowance made for enormous regional variations, peasants owned maybe 30 to 40 per cent of the cultivable land, as opposed to the nobility's share of some 25 per cent, followed by the bourgeoisie with 20 per cent and the church with between 6 and 10 per cent. Peasants holding tenures paid their seigneurs a whole array of dues, whose form differed from area to area. Most paid a *cens*, or cash quitrent, though some had commuted this into a due in kind, and many into the unpopular *champart* (or seigneurial tithe), which hovered at around 10 per cent of produce. They could sell and buy, exchange and donate, receive and bequeath largely without hindrance – but only at a price: they also paid transfer taxes on the sale, inheritance or exchange of land. The *lods et ventes*, for example, were a particularly onerous purchase tax on *censives*.

Classic medieval-style feudalism was not widespread: only in the main within recently acquired areas like the Franche-Comté were there serfs who were tied to the land, had few rights upon it and performed labour-dues for their lords. Yet *féodalité* remained a key notion of reference in the peasant's mind-set. In it were embodied not only the range of dues and services owed, but also the rights of justice and policing which lords enjoyed throughout their seigneurie, and which were often emblematized by acts of personal homage and a wide array of other honorific rights and customary entitlements: seigneurs had their own pew in church, their coats of arms on the church weathervane, first claims on grazing rights, the right to a manorial dove-cote, symbolic labour-dues (*corvées*) of various kinds, and so on. Though some of these ancillary rights were honorific, others were more financially productive than strictly seigneurial dues, which formed only a minority of the income of most lords. Many seigneurs, for example, derived large sums from the *banalités* within their estate – the right to insist that all peasants (or vassals, to use the archaic vocabulary still in use) used their wine-press, mill or bread-oven. Seigneurial tolls were another moneyspinner: between the source and the mouth of the river Loire, one of the most utilized channels of communication, there were no fewer than seventy-seven tolls. Even when not financially productive, seigneurial rights could be mightily resented – because seigneurs enjoyed a monopoly of hunting rights on their lands, for example, peasants had to bite their lips in frustration as their lord's doves gorged themselves on springtime seeds.

The weight of the seigneurial system on peasant farm output varied from place to place. In some areas, village communities were strong enough to stand up to their seigneurs, and whittle away their powers. This was particularly the case in the Midi, where village communities had often purchased the seigneurial function, and where the seigneurial burden was usually less then 10 per cent of the peasant product. Elsewhere, however, notably in Burgundy and Brittany, figures ranging up to 25 per cent were not uncommon. The seigneurial burden was all the heavier when taken in conjunction with other peasant outgoings: the church took a tithe on all produce (apart from new crops and those cultivated by gardening) which usually worked out at between 8 and 12 per cent in kind. Then there were local taxes for maintenance of communal property, and so on, and of course state taxation. Overall perhaps one-third or more of the peasant product could be creamed off in these ways in an average year. There were, however, no 'average' years for peasants working within an economy so dependent on the vagaries of the climate, in which the grain yield could fluctuate by a factor of two each year, where impositions varied erratically and where one-fifth or so of the harvest had to be retained for sowing the next year. Peasant families perforce adopted an 'economy of makeshifts'[26] within the household, combining work of all family members (for richer farmers, this might be in textile manufacturing or rural industry) with migration, begging and petty crime, and where necessary borrowing up to the hilt.

Considering the demands made on the peasantry, it is perhaps surprising that there were relatively few signs of overt collective resistance. There were, as we shall see,[27] grain and market riots in years of high prices and grain scarcity, and a powerful undertow of petty crime (poaching, theft, arson, etc.), plus a good deal of peasant litigation. But this was small beer when compared with the first two-thirds of the seventeenth century, when the three- or fourfold increase in state taxation had triggered a whole panoply of anti-governmental riots and popular revolts throughout France, often supported by seigneurs who resented the state siphoning off a greater part of the peasant surplus. A slowdown in the rate of increase in direct taxes under Louis XIV's rule attenuated fiscal pressure, and combined with a tougher policy of government repression of rebels to bring docility back to French countrysides – a process in which the post-Tridentine-trained parish clergy, who acted as a moral policing agency, also played a part. Also of import was a tightening-up of already draconian laws against vagrancy, a streamlining of the rural police force, the *maréchaussée* (backed up when called for by the army), plus concerted efforts from the 1680s down to the 1730s to institute a 'great confinement of the poor', forcibly placing deviant and destitute groupings in 'general hospitals' (*hôpitaux généraux*), where they could be both punished and moralized back into the ways of social and political conformity.

If eighteenth-century peasants were rather more docile than their ancestors, this was also due to a degree of erosion of the sense of local community on which the earlier riots and revolts had been predicated. Seigneurs found themselves being marginalized within the rural community. The numbers living on the land shrank: the life of great nobles revolved around Versailles and Paris; middling nobles were more based in provincial towns; and many poorer nobles – *hobereaux* ('little hawks'), as they were called – either kept a low profile or else simply collapsed into the peasantry, especially once governments started to crack down on tax-dodgers among putative country gentlemen. Established patterns of provincial patronage frittered away: by 1750, a ducal absentee landlord, for example, preferred a capable bourgeois steward on his estates rather than a flock of resident noble dependants and commensals looking to him for preferment. The functions of seigneurs within their community also dwindled. The role of the lord's château in offering physical protection to peasants in the times of war and invasion was also being attenuated by the security success of Vauban's *ceinture de fer*. The peace-keeping services of the seigneur were in decline too. Peasant communities were often effectively self-policing, while the newly reorganized *maréchaussée* served as an ancillary peace-keeping force. Seigneurial courts which in the past had coped with the bulk of local litigation were, moreover, increasingly bypassed by royal courts. Though the cost and pettifogging longueurs of royal justice made many peasants continue to rely on seigneurial justice for arbitration of minor and urgent matters, the state often seemed to offer a more genuinely impartial service.

There was less and less love lost between peasants and seigneurs. The services which the latter had provided for the peasant community in the past had diminished in value. Seigneurs were less likely now to recycle seigneurial dues back into the community in the form of charity. And whereas in the past they had drawn most of their consumption from local sources, offering employment and custom to the locals, this too was in decline. The noble Roncherolles family in Pont-Saint-Pierre in Normandy, for example, were typical in abandoning indigenous tastes of the *terroir* for imported foodstuffs – champagne, oysters, widely assorted fruits and vegetables, coffee and so on. Seigneurs were increasingly resented for draining money and produce out of the village and putting very little back in – a criticism which was also levied against the clergy over the tithe, which in nine cases out of ten left the community to end up in the hands of eminent ecclesiastics in the towns. The lack of interest shown by most seigneurs in agricultural improvement – they allowed their tenants only short leases, and rarely invested in agricultural production themselves, preferring venal office and other investment channels – seemed only to confirm the view that most seigneurs regarded their peasants as a collective milchcow providing sustenance for their own increasingly cosmopolitan tastes.

If the sense of solidarity between peasant and seigneur was breaking down over the early eighteenth century, social and economic change was also bringing a broader sense of differentiation within the peasantry itself, and making the assumption of universal peasant autarchy as ridiculously archaic as the notion of the king 'living off his own'. The period from the middle of the sixteenth century down to around 1720 had witnessed a major shift in landholding patterns. Small and middling peasants were adversely affected by low grain prices and high state taxes and were forced into indebtedness and thence, via a notoriously slippery slope, expropriation. Nobles and urban bourgeois tended to snap up the choicest morsels close to the towns – ownership of the expansive cereal-growing areas to the south of Paris, for example, was monopolized by these groups, plus the clergy.

Peasant indebtedness caused by tough times offered opportunities not only to the social elite, however, but also to other peasants. The structure of the peasantry thus became increasingly steeply hierarchical. At the apex of the pyramid was a minority of well-off farmers who were edging into the bourgeoisie, and who produced enough to feed themselves and their families even in hard times. In the average village there would be two or three peasants who owned a plough and draught animals (for their own use and for renting out to their social inferiors), a cart to take their surplus produce to market, land-holdings over 10 hectares in extent, herds of livestock and a house and garden with the incipient trappings of gentility. In the *pays de grande culture* in particular, such peasants, who might be the only fully literate members of their village, often combined farming with the job of acting as seigneurial steward or collector of dues, plus a little dabbling in money-lending. These *coqs de village* ('village cockerels') were heartily resented by those less blessed with land, literacy and good fortune, for they seemed the embodiment of that model of household independence to which all peasants aspired yet which very few achieved. Most villages also had a solid phalanx of peasants who possessed between 4 and 10 hectares of land and who hovered on the threshold between economic dependence and independence: in good years, they prospered and produced enough for themselves to eat, but a bad harvest (and all the more a run of them, or too many children, or chronic sickness) could lead to borrowing, land sale and family impoverishment. Below this grouping were large numbers of peasants with only very little land or with no land at all. These individuals, who comprised over two-thirds of the inhabitants of many villages, relied on salaried work for seigneurs or richer peasants, the village community's collective rights and the other expedients which constituted the peasants' economy of makeshifts. From their ranks sprang another perennial component of the rural world, the hordes of beggars and vagrants who roamed the highways seeking employment or sustenance.

The last years of the reign of Louis XIV had been tough on the least secure and the least protected of the peasant community – most dramatically in the mortality crises of 1693–4 and 1709–10. Yet out of the seemingly bottomless cauldron of misery in the late seventeenth and early eighteenth century there emerged a number of developments which by around 1750 were already transforming some of the most perdurably gloomy features of rural France. Considering the scale of the demographic damage caused by mortality crises between 1690 and 1710, the process of recuperation was remarkably swift and complete. A population level of some 21.5 million in 1690 had swelled to some 22.6 million in 1710. Large numbers of deaths in these years had opened numerous gaps in the pattern of landholding, which were eagerly filled by young, assiduously procreating couples. Though the economic troubles of the last years of Louis XIV's reign and then the Regency seem to have halted the upward movement, John Law's famous System was a blessing in disguise for many peasants, whose indebtedness was reduced to nugatory proportions by the massive depreciation of the early 1720s. The wiping clean of many slates was combined with a denser provision of employment, not only in agriculture but also in industry which, as we shall see in the next section, was making important headway at this time.

This economic upturn coincided, as chance would have it, with the diminution in the effects of the three great demographic scourges of early modern France. War-related population losses were less devastating even under the last years of Louis XIV, partly because most campaigns were conducted outside French borders, but also because the French army – like its European peers – was developing better military supply systems which reduced the need to live off the land. Killer disease was in retreat too. Bubonic plague had been in relative abeyance since the 1660s, and its explosion into Marseille and Provence in 1720 confirmed the ability of government, through quarantines and cordons sanitaires, to hem the disease in and prevent its diffusion across the country. Other diseases would take up the demographic slack left by the disappearance of the plague: smallpox, dysentery and typhoid fever remained particularly damaging. But none of them had the plague's ability to kill 90 per cent of those affected and to cut the size of a major city by half.

War and epidemic disease were losing their demographic sting, and, in the favourable economic atmosphere of the 1720s and 1730s, allowing population to grow at an unprecedented (and, by contemporaries, unsuspected) rate. Population levels rose from 22.6 millions in 1720 to some 23.8 millions in 1730 – an increase of over 5 per cent in a decade, which added another 1.2 million to France's population, to which the 1730s in turn contributed another 0.8 million. Famine too was becoming a thing of the past. The tightening of grain markets over the early decades of the century played a part in this, but so too did government policies of famine relief. This was strikingly evident in 1739–42, when appalling weather caused a series of harvest failures which some contemporaries maintained were more severe than those of 1709–10. The central government utilized its Intendants to provide intelligence about harvest shortfalls, and to mobilize charity, locate surplus grain on the world market and coordinate famine relief in the areas worst affected. Some areas – notably Brittany and Anjou – were hard hit nonetheless, but population losses never reached the scale of earlier such mortality crises, and the overall population level was maintained down to 1750, before another spurt of growth occurred. Life expectancy at birth was maybe two years more in 1750 than it had been in 1700 or 1650 – and rising. Though largely unsuspected by a political elite still mainly fixated on the unchangeability of peasant miseries and beset by depopulation fears, the vital signs of rural France were surprisingly strong.

E) HEALTH AND WEALTH BY STEALTH

The grim canopy which death had cast over the last years of the reign of Louis XIV was thus beginning to lift. The social and demographic scene was now marked by dynamism, not stasis. Mortality crises were becoming less of a threat to life and limb; life expectancy was increasing; and population was growing. As a long demographic cycle drew to a close, moreover, the stirrings of durable economic expansion were detectable, linked not only to demographic buoyancy and rural recovery but also to advances in trade and manufacturing. From the death of Louis XIV down to the Revolution, France's population would grow by one-third, from 21.6 million in 1715 to 28.6 million in 1789, while its trade with Europe increased fourfold and that with its colonies expanded tenfold – a record that no other European power, even England, its perennial competitor, could match. Although it was very precisely in the period down to the 1750s that some of the most impressive changes were occurring, contemporaries down to mid-century showed only a patchy and flawed perception of these dramatic, almost subterranean transformations and the steady advance of commercial capitalism. Health and wealth were achieved by stealth.

Partly, the improvement in France's economic performance was recuperatory after the bad last years of Louis XIV's reign. Even before 1715, however, there had been silver linings in the black clouds, including the emergence of the most dynamic sector of France's economy over the eighteenth century as a whole: colonial, and particularly Caribbean, trade. The tonnage of France's commercial shipping was some three and a half times higher in 1715 than it had been in 1667, and ports such as Saint-Malo and Dunkirk had profited from engaging wholeheartedly in privateering, which helped to recircuit English and Dutch trading commodities into France. The sugar trade based in the West Indies was also beginning its brilliant career. As recently as 1685, there had been no sugar plantations at all on Saint-Domingue, forthcoming jewel in France's colonial crown; by 1717 there were over 100 plantations, and the black slave workers within them, shipped across from Africa, rose from 9,000 in 1700 to 24,000 in 1715. By 1730 they numbered 80,000. The island's sugar production – 7,000 tonnes in 1714 – had sextupled by 1742 (and would increase tenfold by 1789). France's other two main West Indian colonies – Guadeloupe and Martinique – also saw their slave populations quadruple between 1686 and 1720. The sugar islands engaged in the production of indigo dye and a little tobacco and cotton as well, though production of the latter substances never reached the levels achieved elsewhere in the Americas. From the late 1720s, Martinique in particular added another commodity, coffee (which had hitherto entered Europe from Arabia). The value of imports of sugar and indigo from Saint-Domingue alone increased seventeenfold between Utrecht and the outbreak of the Seven Years War in 1756.

The buoyancy in international trade was helped by the fact that the serious currency depreciation and low wages current in the last years of Louis XIV made French manufacturing exports extremely competitive against European rivals. The same was true of those sectors of the agrarian economy geared to cash-crop rather than cereal production, such as viticulture. Once peace had been established, the total of French exports doubled in less than a decade, only to go on to double again by the early 1740s. The rate of export growth down to 1748 – roughly 4 per cent annually – was overall more striking than in the following period (down to 1789 it averaged less than 2 per cent). This pattern was matched in the demographic sphere: the highest annual population growth rates in the century were achieved from the 1710s to around 1740.

This strong performance also highlighted the fact that, despite the grim final years of Louis XIV's reign, structural damage to the economy was limited and the bases of expansion were still intact. France's agrarian riches were complemented by an impressive range of industries, which Colbert's mercantilist policies had done much to develop. Though few regions were totally without some form of industry – the autarchic reflex died hard – the provinces of Normandy, Picardy, Flanders and Champagne in particular had a strong manufacturing orientation. Although there was a good deal of industrial concentration, much of the productive process took place in the countryside, 'proto-industry' adding to the resources at the disposal of a peasantry emerging, as we have suggested, from relative torpor in the late seventeenth and early eighteenth centuries. Woollen textile manufacturing was present in all the main textiles areas, as also in the Lyonnais, Touraine, the Maine, Auvergne and along a crescent running from upper Languedoc and the Vivarais through to the Pyrenees. Linen textile production was well developed in the north-west and in the Dauphiné, and the manufacturing of silk cloths around Lyon and Nîmes. France's coal deposits – exploited notably around Saint-Étienne, Carmaux, along the Loire, near Valenciennes and, from the 1730s, at Anzin – made less of an impact on the supply of power than in neighbouring England, which also eclipsed France in iron working. France's metal-production was most concentrated in the east and north-east, but there were outposts in Flanders, Normandy and the Pyrenees. Other specialisms of note included the paper industry, which was dispersed around Troyes, Orléans, the Perche, Auvergne, the Limousin and the Angoûmois, and glassworks at Saint-Gobain. Limoges and Nevers specialized in ceramics and pottery, while the porcelain created at the royal manufactory at Sèvres (which Louis XV placed under the tutelage of Madame de Pompadour) was becoming a world leader by the late 1750s.

Sèvres illustrated a particular feature of French production which won it eminence on world markets, namely, its orientation around fashionability. From the late seventeenth century, Lyon silk merchants had developed a fashion-driven production cycle by which they launched new goods at high prices, and then, as industrial competitors began to copy and emulate their styles, they junked stock at bargain-basement levels, at the same time launching a new style, to which competitors again took time to react. 'Fashion's empire'[28] fitted neatly with the spirit of novelty, variety and surprise which were intrinsic to the rococo decorative style prevalent over the first half of the eighteenth century. It spread to the full range of the luxury goods for which the French became famous on world markets: silks, fashionable clothing, silverware, mirrors, furniture, fine wines and brandies, chinaware and the like.

France's distinctive fashion-driven production cycle was envied by foreigners and had been praised by Colbert, who noted that 'fashion is to France what the gold mines of Peru are to the Spanish', as well as by John Law.[29] In the period between Utrecht and mid-century it constituted an important element in the good times enjoyed by numerous sectors of French industry. The traditional textiles industries boomed: wool production doubled at Amiens and tripled in Beauvais over these years, and Lyonnais silk production doubled too. Cotton – the greatest textiles success story of the century – was by mid-century already beginning to displace woollen and linen cloths both within France and on foreign markets. Restricted before the 1720s and 1730s to the Rouen area, the production of light cotton cloths spread thereafter in Normandy and western France, with production doubling between 1732 and 1766 – and accelerating thereafter. Heavy industry also made substantial progress, while the luxury goods in which France excelled maintained their pre-eminence too: the fancy glassware of Saint-Gobain, for example, doubled output between 1715 and 1739. French goods generally were strong on quality: merchants and manufacturers endlessly bemoaned the restrictions placed upon them by factory inspectors – but a concern for quality control gave French goods cachet on home and international markets.

One of the hallmarks of France's vibrant economic performance over the century as a whole was its thoroughgoing engagement with the sea, an engagement which contrasted with the country's habitually terrestrial orientation. The French state's long-term geo-political strategy and the economy's sturdy, subsistence-orientated agrarian base gave a landed look to a country which in fact had an exceptionally long sea-coast.

Much of France had turned its back on the sea, regarding littoral communities as alien bodies, full of godless heathens (the Counter-Reformation had made notoriously little impact on sea-going superstitions), whose experiences transcended the normal round. As late as 1701, a Bordeaux ship's captain was able to persuade his employers that he had lost his cargo off Newfoundland to a fire-breathing dragon looming out of the deep.[30] The call of the sea was the call of trade – and in the seventeenth century the Bourbon state had done much to heed it, and to push the French towards forsaking their distrust of blue water. Under first Richelieu, then Colbert and Louis XIV, the government established a global trading network. The rationale behind commercial and colonial ventures was that the wider world provided agricultural products and raw materials, in return for the home country's manufactured goods – a transfer which would boost home industries at the expense of commercial rivals. (European statesmen regarded mercantile wealth as relatively inelastic, so that anything one state gained would necessarily disadvantage her international competitors.) What had been achieved by 1700 was undeniably damaged by the wars of the last years of Louis XIV's reign. The English and the Dutch – those other classic seventeenth-century interlopers – increasingly gained the upper hand over France, and at the Utrecht peace settlement the French received some telling blows. The Asiento – the valuable monopoly of provisioning Spain's New World colonies with plantation slaves – had been placed in French hands by Bourbon Spain in 1702, but in 1713 was awarded to the English. France also lost at Utrecht Nova Scotia ('Acadia') and the far north, which was held by England's Hudson Bay Company. But it held on to its main North American colony, Canada, and the Caribbean sugar islands.

Sweated slave labour in the Caribbean producing exotic commodities formed the nub of a complex set of worldwide systems of exchange involving all the major colonial powers. Characterized as 'triangular trade', the complexity of the patterns of exchange often belied simple geometry. One notable triangle involved the shipping of cheap and gaudy trinkets, pots, cloths and firearms (plus on occasion New World-produced rum) from the mother country to West Africa, where they were exchanged for slaves. Across the Atlantic, these were sold to planters in return for colonial commodities which were then shipped back to Europe. But the story did not end there, since a good deal of colonial imports – three-quarters of sugar, for example, and four-fifths of coffee – was immediately re-exported. The most notable destination for France's colonial goods was northern Europe. France had long sustained substantial trading links with this area, exchanging manufactured and luxury goods, plus salt, wine and spirits against Baltic timber, iron, naval goods and Polish and Ukrainian – surprisingly perhaps – grain (for despite agriculture's massive commitment to cereal farming, France was a net importer of grain). Although England consumed around one-third of all sugar imported into Europe, it was France which took over the north European provisioning, working through Amsterdam, Hamburg, Bremen, Stettin, and Saint Petersburg. By mid-century, France had begun to supply northern Europe's coffee requirements too.

Other ambiguously triangular sets of trading relationships involved France, Canada and the sugar islands. Canada's fur trade – crucial to French hat production – was based on the French supplying native Indian tribes with alcohol, firearms, woollen goods and trinkets in exchange for the furs. But the colony also produced grain, leathers, timber and iron which were traded in the Caribbean. The sugar islands also took some of the cod fished by French fleets off Newfoundland. Though slave populations did not offer much in the way of demand, Canadian farmers and trappers, native American populations and planter populations had more disposable income. The French formally required them to spend this on French or Canadian produce: thus Saint-Domingue planters, for example, ate white bread made of European grains and dressed their wives in the latest Parisian fashions. Overall, however, France was far less successful than England in developing its own colonies as outlets for its manufactured goods. Emigration to its colonies was not a mass phenomenon in France: over the century, it involved probably far less than 200,000 French individuals – a figure which bore scant comparison with the quarter of a million Huguenots expelled after 1685, the huge numbers of intra-European migrations, or the 2 million Spanish and the 1.8 million English people who emigrated to colonies. Canada's population swelled to around 60,000 by 1761, the white population of the French West Indies hovered at around 50,000 – yet the English North American colonies had a population of some 2 million by mid-century, 3 million by its end. This constituted a far broader and more economically stimulating demand base than French colonies could offer.

To France's considerable irritation, moreover, its West Indian colonies were also illicitly supplied in many of their requirements by England and its North American colonies. This was only one example of a generalized disregard for monopolistic trading arrangements within the Americas. France was as guilty as anyone, supplying England's North American colonists with cheaper sugar than British islands such as Jamaica could manage, and flouting Spain's restrictions on trade with its own colonies almost as brazenly as did the English. The English had signed the Methuen Treaty with Portugal in 1703, which allowed them to edge into the trade in gold which had been mined in considerable quantities in Brazil from the 1690s. French interloping was aimed at both this and also – rather more successfully – at trading with Spanish American colonies selling manufactured goods so as to secure Mexican silver, the other main metallic product of the Americas.

The close trading links which France built up with Spain from 1715 down to 1750 helped French penetration of the Spanish American market. Lyon and Marseille were the main generators of activity here. Marseille was also the key port for trade with the Levant, which had been building up even during the last years of Louis XIV's wars. Alongside sundry luxury goods and silks from Lyon and the Vivarais, woollen goods from the Rouen area, Champagne and Languedoc were much appreciated commodities, exchanged for light Levantine cloths. France proved able to eject British competition from this Mediterranean market as successfully as it was concurrently doing in northern Europe.

The Levant had traditionally acted as a staging post for commodities coming from the Far East, but the latter region was accessed increasingly in the eighteenth century by sea routes. European demand for Asian goods and commodities diversified – Indian cotton cloths and muslins, Persian carpets, precious woods and lacquered goods, porcelain, camphor, tea and rice joined the peppers and spices which had been the region's main export commodity in the sixteenth and seventeenth centuries. France developed Île Bourbon (Réunion) and Île de France (Mauritius), into which slave populations were also introduced, as serviceable staging posts of the eastern trade. The trading partners did not provide a strong demand for European products in return – China in particular was most sniffy in this respect – so under another 'triangular' trading arrangement, the silver and gold which had been gained from Spanish and Spanish American trading and interloping made up the shortfall.

France had established trading posts on the Indian coast from the late seventeenth century onwards, utilizing, like its European competitors, chartered trading companies to penetrate the region. The Indies Company (Compagnie des Indes) had had tough times under Louis XIV and then John Law, but was totally reorganized in 1731 and proved a potent force in Indian political and economic life, with the Company's Governor-General Dupleix building up a powerful political bloc in the region prior to the 1740s, often at the expense of the English.

'All France's wealth', stated the Italian wit and *philosophe*, abbé Galiani, in 1770, 'is concentrated on its frontiers, all its big opulent cities are on its edges and the interior is fearfully weak, empty and thin.'[31] This was an exaggeration – but an understandable one. While the population of Paris grew relatively slowly over the century from about half a million in 1700 to 650,000 in 1789, the growth of peripheral cities was more impressive: land frontier cities such as Lyon (97,000 to 146,000), Strasbourg (26,500 to 50,000) and Lille (57,500 to 62,500) did well, but were outstripped by port cities linked to booming overseas trade: Nantes grew from 42,500 to 80,000, Marseille from 75,000 to 110,000, and Bordeaux from 45,000 to 110,000, while the combined forces of Rouen and Le Havre rose from 72,000 to 91,000. Bordeaux had impressed Turkish envoy Mehmed efendi in 1720 as incomparable in terms of wealth, trade and buildings among the provincial cities he visited, and on the eve of the Revolution the English agronomist Arthur Young – usually a harsh critic of the French economy – was dazzled by the 'commerce, wealth and magnificence' of the city, which owed its grandeur to massive involvement in the slave trade, sugar exports and re-exports, and the export of its own wines and spirits.[32] The value of the city's external trade expanded from 13 million livres in 1717 to over 50 million in the 1740s, by which time it was concentrating around one-quarter of all French foreign trade.

Galiani's remark highlighting the supposed centrifugality of the economy, with a coastal France looking outwards and plugged into world trading patterns on one hand contrasting, on the other, with a backward and sterile rural France, was another of the myths about French social development which – like the issue of 'depopulation' – comprehensively fooled contemporaries (and subsequently many historians). The comment signally underestimated the extent to which France's external trade-driven economic performance down to mid-century profited the country as a whole, blurring the contrast Galiani noted. The volume of overseas trade was always small when set against the kind of transfers associated with the everyday business of subsistence at home: the grain trade, for example, dwarfed colonial trade in volume and value, while between three-fifths and three-quarters of France's total trade was with Europe. Nevertheless, the profits to be derived from global commerce were very high and of great potential benefit to the wider economy. Despite the tendency to re-export colonial goods as soon as they reached French shores, colonial commodities were finished and processed in the hinterland – even quite some distance into the interior. Sugar refineries studded the Bordelais, for example, but probably the biggest such works were located at Orléans, accessible from Nantes along the Loire river. Similarly the production of cloths for the Levant was located well into the interior behind Marseille, which monopolized the trade, in regions like the Vivarais and the Cévennes which to the outside eye seemed immired in archaic farming practices. The good river system which irrigated each of the period's most dynamic ports – Nantes, Bordeaux, Rouen-Le Havre, Marseille, which together dealt with some 90 per cent of the Atlantic trade – was a further guarantee of the productive uses of commercial capital. The very wide geographical spread of proto-industrialization in rural areas throughout France also gave Galiani the lie.

What seems to have been a steady rise in demand for manufactured goods after 1715 testified to the buoyancy of the whole economy, and not simply the performance of regions most directly tied in with booming colonial trade. Rising population produced steady pressure on land – with the result that income from agricultural rents started growing steadily from the late 1720s onwards, allowing the disposable income of the social elite to grow accordingly. What was, however, most impressive about the volume and shape of demand in the decades after the 1720s and early 1730s was the solidity of demand for manufactured products – more varied clothes, shoes, pottery, cutlery, tools, soap and the like – from a middling and even lower middling sort constituency. Wages were generally not keeping up with the rise in prices over the period – but the fact that there was more work about because of commercial and indus-trial recovery meant that even many poorer households received waged income from more of their members, and thus packaged together a family budget which left some surplus for spending on non-subsistence commodities. This was perhaps truest of the town – but the development was far from unknown in many rural areas. The trend towards a steady rise in the price of agricultural produce from around 1733 onwards meant that many peasant families which had been forced below the breadline in the tough years of the late seventeenth and early eighteenth centuries came up into a situation where they had money to invest or to spend. The nefarious John Law had been helpful to many such families too, by allowing debts to be repaid or annulled and mortgages redeemed. While the rise in prices and the drop in their purchasing power put many peasants into difficult circumstances, many middling and upper peasant households began to do something whose rudiments they had almost forgotten: to prosper.

Little credit was generally given to the state for these novel, optimistic and even somewhat baffling developments. 'We understand trade in France', crowed Voltaire, 'better than anyone knew it from Pharamond [first mythical Frankish king] to Louis XIV,'[33] but the general sense was that this had come about despite rather than because of the government. 'This empire govern[s] itself,' was the opinion of anti-court polemicist Toussaint,[34] reflecting a more widespread conviction that France had become a global trading power in the early eighteenth century in a fit of absence of mind. Certain contributory factors to the changed economic situation were beyond even the knowledge of the state – the booming population growth, for example – while others, such as the beneficent effect of the John Law imbroglio in debt-clearance, were far from intended. Yet it would be wrong to imagine that the state made little contribution to economic growth. Though European power politics lay at the heart of the government's diplomacy, commercial factors did count. Fleury re-established a royal Council of Commerce and though it met only rarely, it served to register merchants' interests at the heart of government. It also acted as a bulwark for the maintenance of the monetary stability of the livre, which had been set in 1726. Perhaps most important of all in this respect was a very dynamic communications policy, exemplified most brilliantly, as we have seen, by the work of the Ponts et Chaussées department. By 1739, English visitor Lady Mary Wortley Montagu was commenting favourably on the prosperous transformation which had overcome the face of the countryside since she had last visited the Continent in the aftermath of the Treaty of Utrecht: 'the roads are all mended, and the greatest part of them paved as well as the streets of Paris, planted on both sides like the roads in Holland . . . It is incredible the air of plenty and content that is over all the country.'[35]

Indubitably the most crucial contribution which government made to boosting economic performance after 1713, however, was its avoidance of expensive warfare. Peace had been, in many respects, the big idea, the prime strategic objective, of both the Regent and Fleury – and one to which, at Aix-la-Chapelle, even Louis XV seemed to be paying grudging, if transient adherence. It provided an appropriate context for economic recovery, if only because in conditions of expensive state-maintained standing armies and a European arms race, war was simply too expensive for an economy beleaguered by Louis XIV's wars to contemplate. Peace meant that tax was light and rose only slowly down to the 1740s – it was probably roughly half the per capita tax load being paid by the English, for example, and in these buoyant economic conditions was probably declining as a share of average income. Fleury and his self-effacing ministerial team thus deserve a good deal of credit for providing the political and economic circumstances in which recovery and growth could take place from the second quarter of the century, inaugurating golden years in France's economic history.

Even the venerable Hercule, however, had his Achilles's heel: namely, the navy. Fleury was doubtless prudent to prescribe a goodly dose of peace as a means to achieve economic prosperity, but he failed to appreciate the extent to which the development of the overseas trade sector depended on French merchant vessels receiving adequate protection from rival trading powers – especially the English. He largely endorsed the Regent's decision to renounce earlier ambitions of maintaining parity in navy size with the English, even though Navy Minister Maurepas perennially made the case for catching up. 'Protection', the latter urged the king in a memorandum in 1730, 'is absolutely necessary for trade.'[36] Only as a result of the navy's poor performance against the English in the War of Austrian Succession was the message heard, and large sums started to be poured into ship-building. The global dimension of that war had also set alarm bells ringing: if it highlighted the need for better naval protection for trade, it also underlined the importance of resisting economic vulnerability in these circumstances by building up the indigenous economy, especially in the countryside. A wave of 'agromania' was triggered by the sudden appearance in the immediate aftermath of the peace of Aix-la-Chapelle of numerous tracts on improving farming – after more than a century of conspicuous silence on this front. Agrarian self-sufficiency was a virtue again.

It was very worrying, therefore, that by the mid-1750s, France seemed to be drifting towards a further global conflict against the English whilst still at a signal disadvantage as regards the security its navy could provide for its merchants, and without there having been a sufficient time-gap for agrarian reforms to have strengthened France's rural economy. The Seven Years War was to prove a come-uppance for decades of naval neglect. It would place a question-mark against France's commercial performance and international position. And it would provide a knock to the great nation's confidence in itself as a major power, providing a fertile terrain for critics of government on a developing public sphere.

5

An Enlightening Age

A) THE MOMENT OF THE *ENCYCLOPÉDIE*

Topsy-like, the *Encyclopédie* just grew and grew. Some seventeen volumes of text appeared spasmodically between 1751 and 1772, with eleven volumes of plates intercalating from 1762 to 1777. When complete, the 'Reasoned Dictionary of the Sciences, Arts and Trades', to give it its full title, the work of around 150 known and an indeterminate number of anonymous authors, contained over 70,000 articles and nearly 3,000 plates.[1] Contributors included many – even most – of the greatest writers of the century: Voltaire, Rousseau, Montesquieu, Condillac, d'Holbach, Buffon, Quesnay, Turgot, Morellet, Duclos, Jaucourt, Grimm. Between 4,000 and 5,000 copies of the original folio edition were published, but with re-editions, supplements and reprints, around 25,000 sets of the work had been sold through Europe as a whole by 1789, roughly half of them within France. By then, its canonical, even mythical, status was assured, as the master-work of the French intellectuals and writers known as the *philosophes* ('philosophers').

The financial backers who originated the *Encyclopédie* project in 1745 had had no idea about what they were getting into. They planned a far less ambitious venture – a four-volumed French translation of Ephraim Chambers's *Cyclopaedia* (1728) – but did not reckon with the flair and vision of their product manager, Denis Diderot. The 32-year-old Diderot had renounced an artisanal background, preferring to live off his wits rather than by his hands. Alliance with the equally youthful Jean-le-Rond d'Alembert, tyro mathematician of genius and darling of the Parisian salons, led to the two men commissioning articles for the new venture straight away, and scheduling the launch of the first two volumes for 1751.

Had Diderot known what would be expected of him over the next two decades he would have written a job specification for himself at the outset which itemized the courage of a lion, the vision of a Conquistador, the ambition of a Caesar, the daemonic energy of a fury and the hide of a rhinoceros, to say nothing of a dazzling range of other diplomatic, financial, polemical, organizing and intellectual skills. Almost at once the enterprise came close to collapse and it would be endlessly dogged by trials and tribulations. In 1749, Diderot was imprisoned by *lettre de cachet* in the state prison at Vincennes for writing a work – his 'Letter on the Blind' – which was adjudged irreligious. The same year that the first volumes appeared, the *Encyclopédie* was almost caught up in a scandal caused by the abbé de Prades, a friend of Diderot who had contributed an article on 'Certitude', and who was condemned by his ecclesiastical superiors for atheistic writings. In February 1752, a royal decree forbade the sale of the first two volumes of Diderot's work – a decision which proved less damning than it sounded partly because most copies were already under subscription rather than on open sale. The *Encyclopédie* had won enough friends and supporters to continue publication, but it attracted a good deal of hostility too, not simply from established authorities but also from other writers, including the prestigious figure of Jean-Jacques Rousseau, who contributed a few articles, but then turned against the whole enterprise in general and d'Alembert in particular.[2] D'Alembert was in fact feeling the strain, and withdrew altogether in 1757, as the sixth and seventh volumes appeared and just as attacks were growing more venomous. The *Encyclopédie*'s enemies were able to get the work implicated in the furore caused by the publication of the openly atheistical *De l'Esprit* by Helvétius (who, though a *philosophe*, had not actually contributed to the *Encyclopédie*). In February 1759, the Parlement of Paris ordered the burning of both works, and the Royal Council officially revoked Diderot's licence to publish, and later that year the work was placed on the papal Index. The *Encyclopédie* pulled through this crisis mainly through the amical assistance of Malesherbes, councillor in the Paris Cour des Aides, a member of the Lamoignon clan, and official Director of the Book Trade. The latter had already shown a tolerant attitude towards Diderot's enterprise, on one occasion warehousing copies in his own house out of the way of prying police officials. Once the fuss was dying down, Malesherbes awarded Diderot a 'tacit permission' to continue publishing, and finessed the neutrality of Paris Police Lieutenant Sartine so as to allow the remainder of the text to appear in 1766. Although the work soon achieved international renown, the enterprise always retained a sulphurous scent and problems recurred: in 1770, some 6,000 copies of a subsequent edition were impounded in the Bastille and only released in 1776.

The *Encyclopédie* was a major capitalist venture, its production involving probably 20,000 workers and mobilizing over 7 million livres. Given the risks and dangers inherent in its distribution, there was safety in numbers – in regard to patrons, readers and authors. Malesherbes was strategically important in securing the enterprise sympathetic treatment within the political elite. With the help of the young abbé de Bernis, he acted as a liaison with Madame de Pompadour, who was generally well-disposed towards the *philosophes*. Choiseul, the most important minister of state from the late 1750s, was another crucial prop. These contacts helped popularize the enterprise, so that members of the very bodies which condemned the work – such as the church and the Paris Parlement – purchased and read it. Any work of similar scale in the past had relied on state patronage – something that the risqué nature of the *Encyclopédie*'s contents put out of the question. Though subscription was not new – it was particularly widespread in England, for example – the *Encyclopédie* was the first major work to rely so heavily on attracting a public to invest by subscribing to the ongoing work of production. This meant that when Diderot was imprisoned and harassed for his writings, bringing the viability of the whole enterprise into doubt, support and protection came from powerful subscribers wanting their investment brought to fruition.

A spirit of inclusiveness and collaboration was thus at the heart of the *Encyclopédie* enterprise. Marshalled and quality-controlled by Diderot, the work represented a triumph for collective authorship. Even Homer nodded, of course, and some dull drudge reached the page, particularly in the later volumes, when Diderot was getting jaded. Yet in general the standard of writing and editorial work was very high, involving as it did acknowledged authorities such as Daubenton of the Jardin du Roi for the natural history sections, Le Roy for astronomy and watch-making, Bourgelat for veterinary matters, Blondel for architecture and Véron de Forbonnais for finance and economics. In addition, Jaucourt, who became the enterprise's jobbing author, writing maybe as many as 5,000 pieces, was an interdisciplinary all-rounder and synthesizer of rare talent, as were Diderot and d'Alembert themselves, who also did much in-filling.

The *Encyclopédie* aimed to bring knowledge of all disciplines within the grasp of the intellectually curious. They also extended the range of what the intellectually curious *should* be interested in. Notably, true to Diderot's dictum that there was 'more intelligence, wisdom and consequence in a machine for making stockings' than 'in a system of physics or metaphysics',[3] they included a great many descriptions of machines, inventions and methods of organizing production, also devoting numerous plates to precise visual depiction of such manufacturing. The inclusion of subjects traditionally seen as 'low' and 'ignoble' was justified on three grounds. First, there was the firm conviction that the measure of all knowledge was mankind. The *Encyclopédie* supplied an all-inclusive road-map of knowledge, which demonstrated 'the order and linking together of the sciences'. 'Man is the single term from which one must begin, and to which all must be brought back,' Diderot argued, implicitly criticizing transcendent or divinely based conceptions of knowledge. 'Make an abstraction of my existence and of the happiness of my fellow human beings and what will the rest of nature matter to me?'[4] As this quotation suggests, human value was the critical yardstick of knowledge employed. The *Encyclopédie*'s notion of inclusiveness involved a radical critique as regards anything which did not conform to the editors' notion of utility as grounded in the 'social'. Indeed, the *Encyclopédie* popularized the terms 'social', 'society' and 'sociability' as justification for the exclusion of topics and subject-matters otherwise adjudged ignoble. The work performed a kind of utilitarian audit of all forms of knowledge, with theology in particular, erstwhile 'queen of the sciences', being found sadly wanting as a 'social' form of knowledge, and placed close to the black arts on a remote twig of the tree of knowledge. Philosophy in contrast was lauded as 'the most extensive [and] the most important science' – precisely because it was the most 'social'.[5] Institutions and individuals were criticized in much the same way as bodies of knowledge. Thus, the church was subjected to pitiless lampooning: its knowledge claims were vacuous, its cherished baroque piety was nonsensical, and much of its personnel were (like the nobility, for that matter) idle and socially parasitic. Utility enabled social improvement – the third reason why technical forms of knowledge were accorded such prestige in the *Encyclopédie*. In his 'Preliminary Discourse', d'Alembert specifically looked back to Francis Bacon as an early exponent of the empirical, inductive approach the *Encyclopédie* championed, in contrast to a priori approaches, whether derived from scriptural sources or even from Cartesian rationalism. He cited approvingly the empiricism of John Locke and the scientific method exemplified by Isaac Newton (*Encyclopédie* history tended to be of the 'great man' variety) as offering the critical approach which the *philosophes* had honed into a powerful instrument of analysis. 'What progress has not been made in the sciences and the arts?' he asked. 'How many discoveries today were not foreseen then?'[6] And what hopes there were for social improvement through the use of human reason!

Implicit in this view of progress was a very particular view of history, and the role of the *Encyclopédie* within it. In his article, 'Encyclopédie', Diderot claimed that the aim of his enterprise was

to assemble the knowledge scattered over the face of the earth, to expound its general system to the men with whom we live, and to transmit it to the men who will come after us; in order that the labours of past centuries will not have been in vain for the centuries to come; and that our children, becoming better instructed than we, may at the same time become more virtuous and happy and that we may not die without having deserved well of humankind.[7]

The collective enterprise was thus serving a humane, improving task. The progress of reason had not all been plain sailing, and indeed the past was invariably dramatized as a bitter struggle between reason and superstition. The engraving on the frontispiece of the *Encyclopédie* depicted Reason pulling a veil from the eyes of Truth, while dark clouds receded to brighten the skies. This Manichean allegorization made of history a chronicle of the progress of the human mind, represented as a process of incremental illumination. It made of the *philosophes* in general and the *Encyclopédistes* in particular the secular apostles of the project of Enlightenment, casting in the role of villain any idea or institution which threatened to inhibit the critical light of reason.

The crimes of organized religion – intolerance, fanaticism, persecutions, auto-da-fés, etc. – were described in loathsome detail, with the church routinely indicted as prime obstacle to the cause of improvement. Although the editors had to be more circumspect about temporal power, implicitly the state too was not exempt from criticism. Some of the work's most coruscating pages – Turgot on ecclesiastical foundations, for example – were attacks on the corporatism which lay at the heart of the Bourbon polity and which ran counter to social utility. 'Even the names of princes and great personages', d'Alembert noted, 'have no right to be in the *Encyclopédie* except by virtue of the good they have done for science . . . It is the history of the human spirit, not of men's vanity.'[8] This stern intellectual hygiene extended even to a precursor of the collective endeavour of the *Encyclopédie*, namely, the royal academies which the Sun King had established to channel and promote scientific research. The *Encyclopédie*'s editors devoted much energy to highlighting the intellectual and organizational deficiencies of the academy tradition. The Académie française's notorious failure to bring to fruition its dictionary was hardly an example to follow. Government hindered rather than helped such projects: 'if the government gets involved it will never get done', Diderot claimed, not least because 'a new minister does not as a rule adopt the projects of his predecessor'.[9] The academies in any case, he argued, were dominated by noblemen who had no real interest or humanitarian commitment to science: something like the *Encyclopédie* was required because it contained 'a great number of men from all the classes of society, men of value but to whom the doors of the academies are no less closed because of their status'. If anything, the *Encyclopédie* had a preference for merchants, traders and artisans, to whom empirical method came more naturally.

Intellectual collaboration was extended not simply to the 'society of men of letters' producing the *Encyclopédie* and the 'skilled workers' who served as consultants. In addition, the work was inclusive enough to enrol its readers in this joint project and challenge. This was evident in the rhetorical technologies utilized. The requirements of the censors obliged the work's editors to encourage its readers to read against the grain, to engage the same critical spirit on the knowledge embodied in the pages of the *Encyclopédie* as the work was itself deploying on the field of human knowledge. Learning thus became an interactive, associational activity with the reader invited to reject pre-ordained meanings in favour of a more dynamic construal of meaning.

This strategy was particularly evident in regard to religion. The bulk of the *Encyclopédie*'s attack on Christianity was made through winks and nudges rather than by frontal attack. Due lip-service was paid to the proprieties, but the editors encouraged their readers to enter into collusion. Allegory played a part here, and so did the strategy of placing the harshest attacks where they were least expected: the article on the pagan goddess Juno was the site of an acerbic attack on Marian devotion, for example; that on 'Siako' (the Japanese emperor), for an assault on the papacy; and the plant *Agnus Scythicus*, for a ridiculing of the doctrine of the incarnation.[10] A related technique was the subtle use of cross-reference, made necessary by the alphabetical ordering of the volume (itself an implicit rejection of hierarchical presentation of fields of knowledge with theology in first place). Diderot regarded the cross-reference as having profoundly heuristic and hermeneutic (rather than merely instrumental) value: cross-references, he maintained,

clarify the object, indicate adjacent relations with those that touch them closely and remote links with others which appear isolated; they recall common notions and analagous principles; they strengthen consequences, connect the branch to the tree and give everything this unity which is so favourable to the establishment of truth and persuasion . . . they will attack, shake and secretly overturn certain ridiculous opinions which we would not dare to insult openly.[11]

Thus, at the end of the article on cannibalism ('*anthropophagie*') the editors had put '*See* eucharist, communion, altar, etc.' – a subtle dig at the doctrine of transubstantiation. Truth lay in such coded connections, rapprochements and juxtapositions – processes in which the reader's involvement was vitally necessary.

The *Encyclopédie* extended the parameters of the knowable and used a critical approach to outpourings of the intellect with the aim of producing socially useful knowledge. That the light of Reason should be preferred to the Light of the World or the radiance of the Sun King was already a radical step. Yet in many ways the most striking aspect of the epistemological revolution on offer within the pages of the *Encyclopédie* was the collusive collective relationship it proposed and exemplified between writers and readers, within a network of *lumières* ('lights') putatively held together by a unitary and rational project of enlightenment. Communication was posited not only as the basis of society but also the way in which knowledge was constructed and in which human beings were changed. At the heart of the *Encyclopédie* lay a yearning for a new kind of politics appropriate to a 'century of lights' (*siècle des lumières*), and new, empowering forms of sociability driven by the critical and self-reflexive use of reason. It aspired to nothing less than to embody 'the power to change men's common ways of thinking', so as to make a 'revolution [. . .] in the minds of men and the national character'.[12]

B) POINTS OF LIGHT

Diderot and d'Alembert dreamed of a network of points of light, nodes of critical reason, facilitating a *commerce des lumières* ('commerce of lights') in which a self-reflexive virtual community, united through the medium of print, could pursue the 'revolutionary' collective mission of societal improvement. Yet the dream only made sense, and could only possibly be enacted, within a society in which those points of light – those *lumières* – were already numerous and dense, and provided an audience and a recruiting-ground for the project of enlightenment. Happily for them, the *Encyclopédistes* were not preaching in the wilderness, but rather within a cultural milieu and public sphere which already accepted the improving potential of enlightened sociability and in which the social practices of communication and exchange were firmly established. As the century wore on, and as Paris increasingly took over the role of cultural pace-maker from Versailles, it became increasingly evident that the public sphere on which the *lumière* of the *philosophes* was projected was not easily accommodated within the purview of the royal court. Intellectual exchange – *le commerce des esprits* – worked best among the literate and urbane social elite and in the kind of commercial society which France was fast becoming.

The notion that communication and exchange were integral to intellectual life and scientific advance did not originate in the eighteenth century, but had venerable roots in natural law theory and in theories of politeness and conviviality which had prospered under Louis XIV. A key institution in this respect was the salon. Aristocratic women had held gatherings in their homes in which men and women, usually from a lower social status, read aloud from their latest works. Such salons became social fora, but also institutions which set the artistic and intellectual agenda and dictated polite patterns of behaviour. The salon in the following century which most resembled this was that hosted by the duchesse du Maine at Sceaux, on the outskirts of Paris, from the Regency period down to her death in the early 1750s. In general, however, the major salonnières of the eighteenth century came from a broader and less exclusive background. Madame du Deffand was the wife of a financier with a scandalous past, albeit one less colourful than Madame de Tencin, sister of the cardinal, and mother of d'Alembert (whom she abandoned as a baby). Madame Geoffrin, wife of a financier, and Suzanne Necker, who was married to the Genevan millionaire statesman, were rather more sedate, though Julie de Lespinasse achieved notoriety as d'Alembert's lover. The social provenance of those who attended the salons also became more wide-ranging. Madame de Geoffrin received the great and the good – including Gustavus III of Sweden, for example, Stanislas Poniatowski, former king of Poland, and numerous distinguished visitors to Paris and foreign ambassadors – but also men of letters from lowlier origins. The range of topics discussed in the salons also widened. Open discussion on politics was invariably taboo – indeed, those salons which tried to specialize in it (such as the Maines' Sceaux meetings under the Regency or the Club de l'Entresol in the 1720s) were forcibly prevented from doing so. Yet history, philosophy and political economy now figured alongside the belles-lettres in which the seventeenth-century salon had specialized.

The salon provided a receptive context for the message of Enlightenment. So too did the academy. The latter's traditional format was much mocked in the post-Louis XIV era. Even before the *Encyclopédie* waded in, Montesquieu had poked contemptuous fun at the members of the Académie française – 'a body with forty heads, all full of figures, metaphors and antitheses' – in his *Persian Letters* (1721),[13] and guyed their assumed mission as relays for the glory of the ruler. The academies survived and even prospered by subtly changing their role – and their location. The Paris-based academies established under Louis XIV were supplemented by a host of provincial institutions. Fifteen in 1715, there were nineteen by 1743 and thirty by the 1770s, by which time all major cities had one. Each was formally and hierarchically organized under the patronage of the king, who accorded them charters. They gathered together the intellectually and culturally concerned from local elites, often meeting in their own premises and funding a library. Devised as top-down institutions, designed to endorse the authority of the national institutions in conferring epistemological legitimacy and setting aesthetic standards, many developed considerable autonomy and took pride in reflecting the interests and concerns of local society. This caused a little nervousness in Paris: in 1750, the Académie française's prize essay was on 'Just how far should the proliferation of learned societies be allowed to go?'. Like the salons, moreover, their agenda widened to take in a much more utilitarian set of issues, extending beyond literary or narrowly scientific matters into social questions and the applications of science. This shift was reflected in their prize essay competitions, which stimulated public interest at national level. Characteristic post-1750 topics were the extinction of begging, wet-nursing techniques and drainage systems. This functional and practical edge was also evident in the work of the royal societies of agriculture established in many localities from 1760 onwards.

The changes which salons and academies underwent over the course of the eighteenth century were congruent with the open, collective and utilitarian values espoused by and exemplified in Diderot and d'Alembert's *Encyclopédie*. As with the latter, they represented forms of learning couched in the vernacular. Since the *Grand Siècle*, French had taken over from Latin as the *lingua franca* of polite discourse to which Europe's intelligentsia aspired (a tendency which was also served by the post-1685 Protestant diaspora outside France). Salons and academies also worked together to nurture the idea of a republic of letters, comprising any individual of wit, intelligence and cultural accomplishment – who could speak and read in good French. Other associational forms which developed over the course of the century also helped to develop this inclusive public sphere of intellectual sociability outside the corporatist parameters of the state. The first masonic lodge in France had been founded in Dunkirk in 1721, for example, and the first Parisian one in 1725 or 1726. Despite the fulminations of the pope and Cardinal Fleury in the late 1730s, they began to spread widely within the urban milieu. A period of rapid growth in the 1760s was followed by efforts to reorganize the national framework of lodges in the 1770s into the Grand Orient of France under the grand mastership of the duc de Chartres (subsequently duc d'Orléans). A further spurt of foundations followed in the 1780s. By the end of that decade, there were perhaps as many as 1,000 lodges throughout France containing between 50,000 and 100,000 masons. Perhaps as many as one published writer in ten was a freemason. Exactly what the lodges got up to behind their closed doors and besides their arcane rituals was shrouded in mystery, but it was clear that they too breathed the same spirit of polite sociability and the same wish for human betterment.

Less clandestine but equally convivial was the coffee-house culture which evolved over the century. The first coffee-house had been established in Paris in 1672. By 1723 there were 380 of them and they probably tripled or quadrupled in number by the 1780s. The phenomenon spread in other cities, making of what had been a rare medicinal substance a banal commodity of everyday living. The more boisterous culture of the bar, tavern and billiard-hall supplemented coffee-house sociability. Subscription to a range of newspapers and journals facilitated and promoted public debate. 'They hold academic session,' ironized the writer Louis-Sébastien Mercier in 1782 of the denizens of Parisian coffee-houses. 'They pass judgement on authors and plays, and they assess their standing and judgement . . . The chatter endlessly revolves around the newspaper.'[14]

Mercier's remark on the place of newspapers in coffee-house culture highlighted the critical importance of print as a lubricant for the mechanisms of Enlightenment sociability. The oral sessions of salons and academies had been relayed through a dense 'epistolary commerce'[15] – a decent postal service was the *sine qua non* of Enlightenment sociability. Yet, as the example of the *Encyclopédie* showed, nothing could match print's capacity for allowing associational life to occur 'virtually' – that is, without the physical presence of those involved – and thus building an immeasurably larger audience than salons and academies could ever manage. The audience for printed works expanded prodigiously. The annual output of publications roughly tripled: around 200 works were authorized each year in the last years of Louis XIV, and this grew to about 300 by 1750 and 600 by the late 1770s. These figures include authorization by 'tacit permission' – the stratagem employed by government to allow publication which left the door open to subsequent repression – but it omits the dark number of works published without full government consent. There was a massive black-market in books of this sort. In Paris, 120 licensed pedlars traded in illegal works, many of them finding semi-immunity in privileged sanctuaries beyond the direct reach of the Paris police, such as the headquarters of the Order of the Temple and, to some extent, the Palais-Royal. Illegal works (including most titles in the flourishing pornography market) were normally printed just across the French border in places such as Liège, Amsterdam, Bouillon, Neufchâtel and Geneva, and smuggled into France on muleback along secret mountain paths.

Foreign printing houses also made an important contribution to the market for periodicals and newspapers, which boomed as never before. There were fewer than a dozen titles available to the reading public in

1715 and around a score in 1750; by 1785 there were eighty-two. A great many periodicals were literary, philosophical or special-interest organs, but from mid-century there was substantial growth in current affairs-oriented publications: in 1750 there had been five political newspapers, four of which were published abroad and circulated by informal government agreement; by 1770 there were twelve, and by 1785, nineteen (sixteen of which were still published abroad). The official *Gazette de France* supplied all the news that government censors saw fit to print, but it had to compete commercially with foreign-based newspapers like the *Gazette d'Amsterdam* and the *Gazette de Leyde*, which despite government warnings showed increasing editorial independence. They were supplemented by one of the big newspaper successes of the post-1750 period, the provincial advertiser cum news-sheets, or *affiches*. Down to 1789, these retained their air of a print bazaar for buyers and sellers of everything from venal offices to horse-manure, from châteaux to billiard-tables and from seigneuries to patent remedies and false teeth. Yet as their number grew – originating in 1751, there were sixteen in existence in 1770 and forty-four in 1789 – they expanded their remit to include reportage of current affairs – sometimes necessarily politically coded.

The buoyancy of the book trade and the newspaper network highlight the emergence of an urban sector increasingly open to national and international affairs. As we have seen,[16] towns boomed as the economy started to expand from the 1730s. They grew in size: by 1789, over 5 million individuals – roughly one French person in five – lived in a town. (As a comparison, it should be noted that although a higher proportion – perhaps 40 per cent – of neighbouring England's population of 6 million lived in towns, this meant France had numerically nearly twice as many town-dwellers as its more urbanized neighbour.) Whereas a very high proportion of English city-dwellers were Londoners, the distinguishing characteristic of French urban life was the solidity of a middling band of towns with between 20,000 and 60,000 inhabitants (only Paris, with around 650,000 and Lyon and Marseille, with 120,000 each, were significantly larger than this). Even more striking than their population growth were changes over the period in urban physiognomy. The Bourbon monarchy's standing army and Vauban's *pré carré* had rendered obsolete the massive ramparts which had enclosed cities since the Middle Ages. These were now demolished, leaving liminal open space which was developed as boulevards, squares, promenades and piazzas. Physicians applauded the removal of city walls for allowing the freer circulation of urban air and light. Most towns still retained much of their dark, tortuous medieval street-system and enough of their noisome smells to shock genteel English travellers, yet a host of other types of micro-improvement in urban public health were changing the feel of urban living: the relocation of cemeteries, for example, hospital rebuilding, vast improvement in waste removal and street cleanliness, paving and lighting schemes, marsh and ditch drainage, purer water supplies, tighter policing of trades producing noxious waste (butchers, tanners, etc.) and the like. Some of this far-reaching campaign of environmental micro-engineering was state-directed: the Intendants in particular played an important stimulant and shaping role, notably in the demolition of urban ramparts, the compensating erection of royal garrisons and barracks, the decoration of the offices of the provincial authorities and the development of a central square as a *place royale* in which the statue of the ruler could be shown off to good advantage. Change also testified to a growing demand from town-dwellers themselves for a reworked urban environment. Much rebuilding focused on the beautiful private residences of the great, which played an important role in the cultural life of the town by hosting salons, circles, exhibitions of paintings, theatrical representations and concerts. The building of theatres towards the end of the century reveals growing support for and also sophistication in provincial urban culture. The culture of the outdoors also evolved: the old hierarchically disposed public processions, dominated by the church and local corporate bodies, gave way to open-air mass spectacles, festivities and sports events (horse-racing, rackets, boules, etc.) in which all could savour 'the charms of equality'.[17] Public gardens on the English 'Vauxhall' model were very popular as centres for promiscuous social mixing, and events staged within them were often topped off with fireworks – a more than appropriate spectacular form for an enlightening age.

Open space, the incursions of commercialism and the growing prestige of polite society produced an urban environment increasingly consonant with the voluntaristic collective culture of the *philosophes*. Madame Geoffrin once refused admission to her salon to the powerful duc de Richelieu, arguing that wit rather than social rank was the passport for admission into her circle. This was the kind of action which made sense in an urban culture less heavily dominated by a corporatist ethos than hitherto, where like-mindedness between equals rather than rank within a pre-ordained social pyramid acted as the prime form of solidarity and identity. In theory at least, the points of light of the *siècle des lumières* were class-blind. The main Enlightenment authors were of very mixed social provenance. Diderot's father was a master cutler, Rousseau's a watch-maker, Morellet's a paper-maker and Marmontel's a tailor. At the other extreme, Jaucourt and Condorcet were of ancient feudal lineage, while d'Holbach was a hyper-rich baron and Helvétius and his scientist colleague Lavoisier were both Farmers General. The highest echelons of society were not in principle ruled out from this world – but they entered in it on terms which were not those of the corporatist hierarchy. Overall, moreover, the intellectual elite was probably drawn more from the middling groups of the professions than from the ranks of wealth and poverty: Voltaire was the son of a notary, Turgot was from a distinguished Robe family, La Mettrie and Quesnay had medical careers, while Maupertuis was a soldier. The professional orientation of the grouping extended into the church: Condillac, Raynal and Mably, for example, were clerics (at least of a sort).

If the *philosophes* were a mixed bunch, so were the other adherents of the urban public sphere. The organs of enlightened sociability had a cross-class and mixed-sex ambience, as did participation in print culture. A certain degree of intellectual cultivation was required. So was a decent amount of leisure-time – a factor which signally reduced the number of individuals with mercantile and business careers involved in these activities. Clergy and nobles dominated in the bodies most closely linked to the culture of the state: 20 and 40 per cent respectively of provincial academicians, for example, were from the first two orders, and court nobles were heavily over-represented in the salons. The more remote institutions were from the influence of the royal court, however, the weaker noble involvement was. In general, the sociology of the public sphere which bore enlightened culture aloft was solidly of the middling sort: lawyers, state officials and medical men, along with smaller contingents of other professional groupings such as engineers, teachers and non-titled military men and ecclesiastics. Less than 40 per cent of provincial academicians came from these ranks, but the figure was higher in the case of subscribers and collaborators to the *Encyclopédie* (50 and 84 per cent respectively), of active authorship (59 per cent), of masonic lodges (78 per cent) – and doubtless even more of the informal organs of sociability such as coffee-houses and bars. In sociological terms at least, even though the nobility were proportionately over-represented, this was a public sphere that was predominantly bourgeois. Despite the female governance of the salons, it was predominantly male too.[18]

One of the fundamental values of the bourgeoisie back to the Middle Ages had been a punctilious concern to differentiate itself from the manual and working classes. The public sphere was bourgeois in this respect too, despite the fact that the popular voice was increasingly equipped to make itself heard. Literacy rose over the course of the century: male and female literacy rates, which had stood at 29 and 14 per cent under Louis XIV, rose to 47 and 27 percent respectively by the 1780s. Rural fastnesses, especially in the Midi and the far west, had much lower levels, but conversely literacy rates in the north and north-east generally were roughly three-quarters and a half for men and women respectively, and there seem to have been very few Parisians beyond the scope of the written word. The Enlightenment project envisaged the gradual enlightening of the masses in the long term; yet in the short term, the *philosophes* were pessimistic about making much impression on the brute masses. Diderot praised the ingenuity behind the invention of the silk loom, but noted of its operative that he 'moves the machine [without] understanding anything, knowing anything or even dreaming of it'. Although Diderot acknowledged the intellectual potential of an aristocracy of enlightened labour, the *Encyclopédie*'s plates often displayed enthusiasm for the potential of mechanization under technocratic management to reduce the input of skilled labour.[19] Workers did not need minds.

The class distinction which lay at the heart of the collective identity of the *Encyclopédistes* was also apparent in regard to popular education. Gains in popular educational provision owed nothing to the *philosophes* and everything to their putative opponents. The *philosophes* mocked the externalism of post-Tridentine baroque piety, and tended to be highly suspicious of popular education for encouraging religious vocations among people who ought to have their hands on the plough. It was ecclesiastics and charitably minded *dévots* rather than they who put the printed word within the reach of the popular classes, notably through charity schools and religiously staffed primary schools. Above primary level too, the religious orders proved receptive to the updating of syllabi. The Jesuits in particular, who were responsible for around half of all secondary schooling in France and who numbered amongst their ex-pupils many of the *philosophes* (Voltaire, La Mettrie, Helvétius, Turgot, Morellet, etc.) were alert to the utilitarian twist to curriculum development. The decline of Latin at the hands of French as a language of instruction also testified to a more utilitarian pedagogic outlook.

What also became increasingly evident over the century was that a strong demand for education was developing which transcended the social desiderata of the *philosophes*. The primary school syllabus was confined to religious verities, moral precepts and the three 'R's; but an ability to read and reckon at very least equipped the individual for participation in public debates in the medium of print and in the market economy on which that was based. In the hide-bound universities, the call for the modernization of teaching came from the students themselves, who realized the career potential involved in the inculcation of professional skills. The traditional format of primary schools, colleges and universities was, moreover, complemented by a diverse assemblage of ancillary institutions – military academies, technical schools, schools of art and design, business schools, public lecture courses and so on – created very largely to respond to popular and middle-class demand.

The debate on the value of education shed interesting light on the claims of *philosophes* and *Encyclopédistes* to embody the forces of improvement within society. Philosophic demands were highly congruent with the commercialization of society and a growing respect for mental labour and professional training. Conversely, however, the popular demand for education showed that there was now in play more than a single version of modernity – and indeed enlightenment. The new public sphere was more pluralistic than – and not always as polite as – the *philosophes* might have wished.

c) CIVILIZED MAN, NATURAL WOMAN

In his inaugural speech in the Académie française in 1787, the historian Rulhière looked back to 1750 as the eighteenth century's turning point. His criterion was not the conclusion of a famous peace nor an act of monarchical *éclat*. Rather, he highlighted this as the moment when the *philosophes* had established their intellectual hegemony over the royal court in the realm of public opinion.[20] The historian simplified; historians do. Yet in much the same spirit, the marquis d'Argenson mused in 1751 about 'revolution' blowing in the 'philosophical wind'. And it was the same epoch that Voltaire had in mind when he declared in 1767 that 'in the past fifteen years or so a revolution has occurred in people's minds'.[21] The moment of the *Encyclopédie* etched itself deeply on the collective memory of the enlightening age.

One of the striking aspects of the mid-century which Rulhière evoked was a changed view of history in many of the key works which appeared around that date. As we have seen, historical research had been utilized as one of the means by which the mythic present of Louis XIV's reign was opened up to critical scrutiny around 1700.[22] The discipline retained a polemical edge, and the years around 1750 highlighted fundamental new concepts and practices within it. Crucial here was the philosophical history enshrined in the *Encyclopédie* and championed in the 'Preliminary Discourse' of 1751, which represented history as the unfolding triumph of enlightening reason. Other works published around this time exemplified – and sometimes complicated – this quasi-triumphalist account. There was, for example, Voltaire's cultural history of the reign of the Sun King, *Le Siècle de Louis XIV* of 1751; Montesquieu's *De l'Esprit des lois* ('On the Spirit of Laws') of 1748, which provided an analysis of the environment and values of political cultures in different regimes in the past; the rather divergent historical account offered by Jean-Jacques Rousseau in his 'Discourse on the Sciences and the Arts', which appeared in 1750 (to be followed in 1755 by a second discourse, 'On the Origins and Foundations of Inequality'); and the natural historical dimension to chronology offered by Buffon, the first volumes of whose multi-volumed *Natural History* appeared in 1749. Whatever their differences, all exhibited a historicist sensibility which transcended orthodox views of the past promoted by church or state.

The article on 'history' in the *Encyclopédie*, penned by Jaucourt, offered as a definition, 'a narrative of facts taken to be true', in contradistinction to 'fable' which was based on falsity.[23] All these foundational mid-century texts evinced open scepticism about the possibility of revealed religion – only recently acknowledged as the prime epistemological yardstick – contributing to the establishment of sound, socially grounded historical knowledge. God and his earthly representatives, it seemed, could provide no clue to the implicit rules behind the workings of past societies. Buffon used fossil evidence and physical experimentation, for example, to underpin his contention that the world was far more ancient than the Genesis account was held by the churches to suggest (Louis XIV's bishop Bossuet, for example, had dated the Creation to 4004 BC, with Noah's Flood cutting in in 2348 BC). Rousseau, in sketching out an account of human history since earliest times, took his examples from classical Antiquity rather than scripture. Similarly, Montesquieu's quest for 'the spirit' (or the mind) of laws excluded from the start the possibility of a single divine plan: 'First of all, I have examined men,' he announced in his Preface, 'and I have come to believe that, in the infinite diversity of their laws and customs, they were not solely led by their fantasies.'[24] He drew on the growing ethnographic record contained in travellers' tales about extra-European societies to develop a stadial view of human evolution according to which each society passed through the stages of hunting, pastoral life, farming and trading – a schema which had no place for scriptural precept.

With the striking exception of Rousseau (to whom we shall return), this cohort of mid-century historians largely subscribed to the progressivism implicit in d'Alembert's 'Preliminary Discourse'. This was certainly the case, for example, with François-Marie Arouet de Voltaire, poet, dramatist, wit, essayist, historian and all-round *belles-lettriste*. A celebrity at twenty-four under the Regency when his play, *Oedipus* (1718) won him massive fame, Voltaire was a success in all the genres – save only that of courtier. Briefly thrown in the Bastille for some crude jokes at the Regent's expense, and then again for seeking to get his own back on the chevalier de Rohan who had had the poet beaten by his lackeys for lack of respect, Voltaire's attempts to be accepted within the courtly ambience of the state sadly fizzled out: despite Madame de Pompadour's backing, his tenure of the posts of Royal Historian and Gentleman of the Royal Bed-Chamber in the 1740s was a flop, while his subsequent acceptance of an invitation from king Frederick II to serve as royal philosopher-in-residence in Prussia also ended in tears. After his return to France in 1753, he chose to live close to the Swiss frontier, from 1759 at Ferney. Participating in the Republic of Letters through his numerous letters and publications, Voltaire wrote furiously and brilliantly enough to become the first French writer to make a living solely from the pen.

Voltaire's most celebrated historical work was his *Le Siècle de Louis XIV* (1751). It was a latterday contribution to the great seventeenth-century debate over the Ancients and the Moderns, with Voltaire coming down powerfully on the side of the latter, arguing that the great cultural achievements of Louis XIV's France marked a signal advance on Antiquity. His rejection of 'the endless detail of wars, and the attacks on cities, taken and retaken by force of arms' in favour of a history of 'the genius and manners of men'[25] chimed very harmoniously with the *Encyclopédie*'s downgrading of 'the conquerors who have desolated the earth' in comparison with 'the immortal geniuses who have enlightened it'.[26] Voltaire's fulsome praise for the Sun King in this volume contrasted with the attitude of many of his peers: Montesquieu had satirized the king, in his *Persian Letters*, as 'the great magician', while the abbé de Saint-Pierre freely compared him with Nero, Attila and even Satan.[27] This Voltairean encomium was also at odds with his own more habitual views, which had a strongly liberal, English flavour. A spell spent in England out of political prudence in the 1720s had transformed his outlook, opening his eyes to issues of personal freedom and material progress. His *Philosophical* (or *English*) *Letters*, published in 1734, under the guise of travel literature, constituted a coded and wittily ironic attack on French mores. The English had an open and secular approach to science, in which Newton's inductive approach and Locke's empiricism were exemplars, while the intellectual life of the French, Voltaire more than implied, was dominated by the Catholic church, with Cartesian rationalism inhibiting Lockean and Newtonian approaches. English people enjoyed the right to personal and religious freedom, enshrined in the English constitution; the French suffered under *lettres de cachet*, brutally enforced confessional unity and press censorship. The English had a truly representative and patriotic Parliament; the French had to make do with a corporative, sectional and legally pettifogging Parlement (which indeed lived up to Voltaire's stereotype by having the *Lettres philosophiques* ostentatiously burned by the public hangman). The English traded and prospered and were happy; the French valued land over commerce, esteemed social rank over wealth, and had a poorer quality of life. 'In England', Voltaire claimed, 'commerce, by enriching the people, has extended their freedom and this freedom has in turn extended their commerce and furthered the greatness of the state.'[28]

That a virtuous circle could be set up so as to conjoin trade, freedom and civic virtue in a new configuration of national greatness was an idea which in principle at least should be applicable to the French, whom

Voltaire adjudged 'the most sociable and the most polite people on earth'.[29] And indeed, this kind of thinking had started to gain in intellectual currency within the social elite as well as among the *philosophes*. Cardinal Fleury's age of peace had helped to kick-start French economic growth, and to promote more positive views of the commercial sector.[30] Like many others, Voltaire was influenced by *The Fable of the Bees* by the English-based Dutch writer, Bernard Mandeville (1723). The work's subtitle, *Private Vices, Public Virtues*, indicated the disjuncture between private and public morality which explained its notoriety. A radical revalorization of individual self-interest, Voltaire argued, could serve as an agent of social improvement; the individual quest for material happiness was perfectly congruent with wider, societal felicity. Voltaire's favourite economist was Jean-François Melon, 'a man of intelligence, a citizen and a philosopher',[31] he stated, who had at one stage served as John Law's secretary, and who produced an influential *Political Essay on Commerce* in 1734. Melon offered a diluted Mandevillianism, shorn of its more outrageously cynical topnotes. Luxury might be spiritually undesirable, Melon held, yet in moderation it supplied a key to collective material improvement: it stimulated trade, exchange and communication which refined the senses, produced greater sociability, and engendered more wealth. Developing a critique of France's commercial and industrial performance which went back to Boisguilbert in the final years of Louis XIV's reign, Melon argued against the notion that one person's luxury was his or her neighbour's impoverishment; rather, he held, the more luxury there was in society the more likely it was that essential needs were also met. Luxury was, moreover, a dynamic rather than a static concept, and was evolving in ways which demonstrated historical progress:

What was luxurious for our fathers is nowadays commonplace and what is luxurious for us will no longer be so for our nephews. Silk stockings were a luxury in the time of Henry II and porcelain is as much a luxury compared to ordinary earthenware as fine china is compared to porcelain.[32]

In the luxury debates which Melon's work helped to stimulate, the *philosophes* came down firmly on the side of material improvement. Voltaire's *Le Mondain* of 1736 was a kind of anti-*Télémaque*, a principled rejection of enforced frugality as a route to virtue and happiness. 'Luxury is an extremely good thing,' Voltaire commented on another occasion, 'so long as it doesn't go to ridiculous lengths.'[33] Montesquieu (who had met Melon in the Bordeaux Academy) thought frugality an estimable republican virtue, but regarded commerce and restrained indulgence in luxury as a positive force for harmonious social interaction: 'everywhere there are gentle mores there is commerce' (and vice-versa).[34] 'There is luxury in all states,' concurred the *Encyclopédie*. The article on 'luxe' distinguished between 'lazy and frivolous luxury' (which was bad) and 'polite luxury [*luxe de bienséance*] which always serves utility'; in general, it seemed clear that luxury 'adds to the happiness of humanity'.[35] Support for a degree of luxury came from the Jansenist camp: so fallen was man, so far distant was God from material creation, in the eyes of influential seventeenth-century moralist, Pierre Nicole, that it became acceptable to believe that good could be achieved through individuals following their self-interest to achieve communal felicity. Other ecclesiastics – including many of the Jansenists' sworn enemies, the Jesuits – were similarly accepting of a space for purposive and beneficent human action and betterment in a disenchanted world. Human freedom and social betterment seemed to depend on economic growth: significantly, the first author to use the term in which such debates were subsequently to be couched – *civilisation* – was the political economist (*économiste*), the marquis de Mirabeau, writing at mid-century.[36] Trade and culture, commerce and enlightenment, were never far away from each other in the *siècle des lumières*.

By the time that Mirabeau wrote, however, giving an enduring name to that hybrid process of material improvement, progress and sociability which *philosophes* and *Encyclopédistes* had already enshrined at the heart of their project, the face of the luxury debate had been transformed. Luxury and indeed civilization were given an altogether more negative, even sinister reading (and one which cast history in a totally different light) by one of the *philosophes'* own, Jean-Jacques Rousseau. This son of a Genevan watch-maker had had a desperately unhappy childhood and peculiar adolescent sexual dalliances before entering Paris's Grub Street in the 1740s, becoming friendly with Diderot and other *philosophes*, writing poetry, developing musical interests and penning articles for the *Encyclopédie*. In 1749, he made a splash in the Republic of Letters through one of its characteristic literary channels, the academy prize essay. The essay question proposed by the Dijon Academy, whether the re-establishment of the arts and sciences had contributed to the purification of morals, struck him with uncommon force. Rejecting the progressivist narrative of his fellow *philosophes*, he answered with a resounding no: the wealth and luxury which accompanied the progress of the sciences had corrupted a pristine innocence in man. Man's conscience seemed to tell him that the contemporary world was corrupt.

Rousseau's prize-winning efforts might have remained a witty and not particularly original or influential *jeu d'esprit*. His central thesis resonated with sub-Fénelonian criticisms of luxury and corruption, for example, while his privileging of the inner voice had been pre-dated by François-Vincent Toussaint's acclaimed and controversial *On Manners* ('*Les Moeurs*', 1749). What made a difference was Rousseau's throwing himself body and soul for the rest of his life into exploring the perception the First Discourse had embodied. The first return on this intellectual and emotional investment was a further prize-essay submission, the 'Discourse on the Origin and Foundations of Inequality among Men' of 1755. The 'Second Discourse', as it is usually known, took the form of a dazzling thought experiment, starting from the premise that the first men, once they had emerged from an animal state, were innocent, robust and healthy, and with an instinct to remain solitary rather than become sociable. He then imagined himself and his readers through the different stages involved in the making of modern man – the acquisition of language, the advent of private property, and so on. 'I dared to strip man's nature naked,' he later wrote. 'I compared man as he made himself with natural man, and showed that his supposed improvement was the true fount of all his miseries.'[37] Far from being the source of human felicity, luxury was an unnatural bane of society and an insult to suffering humanity.

Rousseau's two Discourses were arrows aimed at the heart of the *philosophe* movement. Even a group as tolerant of divergent opinions as they, who found much to admire in the author's erudition, historical research and rational argumentation, found Rousseau difficult to digest. 'I have received, Monsieur, your new book against the human race,' Voltaire wrote to him with savage irony on receiving a copy of the Second Discourse, 'and I thank you. Never has so much intelligence been seen to try to turn men into beasts.'[38] The banter of the salons and the cut-and-thrust of polemical debate (plus disapproval voiced by the church establishment, furious at his rejection of the doctrine of original sin), stung the thin-skinned Rousseau to the quick. In 1756, he left Paris somewhat theatrically for a more solitary, back-to-nature life in a 'hermitage' in the Île-de-France (his *philosophe* antagonists imagined him down on all fours eating grass). He followed this up with a definitive break with his erstwhile friends, sealed with a highly personal attack on d'Alembert. By 1760, he was solemnly writing to Voltaire, 'I hate you.'[39]

Rousseau thus spurned obvious and available connections to the incremental social improvement looked for by the *philosophes*, his two Discourses comprising a credo which on the surface seemed deeply pessimistic about the present and the future. Yet though the sickness which Rousseau diagnosed in contemporary society seemed terminal, hope did remain. Just as certain poisons taken in limited quantities constitute an effective antidote, so there were seeds of possibility which provided an opportunity for human regeneration in the paths of virtue. *Pace* the taunts of Voltaire and others, Rousseau was not seeking to return humanity to a state of nature, but rather to explore how society could be reimagined in terms of that condition, albeit evidently at a higher level. This became more apparent in Rousseau's writings in the early 1760s. His *Social Contract* of 1762, with its ringing opening peroration – 'man was born free but is everywhere in chains' – was a half historical, half prophetic analysis of a form of government in which citizens could be both free and happy in their virtue.[40]

It was, however, the human and emotional – rather than the overtly political – aspect of Rousseau's writings which won him fame and celebrity for the rest of his days. The two novels he published in the early 1760s – *Julie, or La Nouvelle Héloïse* (1761) and *Émile* (1762) – were enormously widely read over subsequent decades. In them he created a new authorial voice, integrally dipped in heart-rending sentimentality, which touched the deepest emotions of his readers, who reacted as though they were born again into ecstatic inner turmoil. In a century which liked a good cry, Rousseau's readers broke all records. Readers were moved to communicate their feelings to the author in purple-passaged prose, reporting 'delicious tears' and 'delicious outpourings of the heart'. The litany went on, 'one must suffocate . . . one must weep, one must write to you choking with emotion and weeping', and 'You have overwhelmed my soul. It is full to bursting and it must share its torment with you . . .'[41] It was less Julie's story itself – a tale of requited and unrequited passion, with the heroine dying melodramatically at the dénouement – than the intimacy and frank transparency of the emotional relations between the principals which struck a chord, along with the intimacy which the novel appeared to establish between writer and his readers, many of whom had difficulty in believing that such portrayals were fictional. The novel seemed to offer a new recipe for virtuous living and earthly happiness which highlighted the role of conscience and the need for emotional honesty and transparency in the creation of selfhood. While Voltaire remained Voltaire and Diderot was Denis only to his intimates, *La Nouvelle Héloïse* transformed Rousseau into everyone's friend, loveable (if difficult) 'Jean-Jacques'.

The brilliant literary success of *La Nouvelle Héloïse* – which had buyers queuing round the block and libraries lending out chapters by the hour – was matched the following year by Rousseau's *Émile*. Although it was dressed up as fiction, the work was, to a considerable degree, a pedagogical tract, and one which made a matching pair with the two Discourses. While the latter had imagined natural man anterior to society, *Émile* was organized around the Lockean premiss that the education of a young boy (the eponymous Émile) could be structured around manipulating his sense impressions in such a way as to develop a moral personality and a capacity for natural happiness and transparent social relations. The core of the novel was the quest to fashion individual virtue, but Rousseau's aim was not to strip away societal accretions to reach the 'natural' man in the manner of the two Discourses. Rather he strove to imagine a pathway towards the making of a virtuous citizen in a necessarily corrupt society. Civic virtue, it seemed, could be worked at, and a new, more natural personality structure could be created which transcended the artifices of contemporary society. He avowedly sought to up-date *Télémaque*, and the work is crammed with Fénelonian touches. Crucially, however, the virtue he described was to serve as goal for the citizen rather than, as had been the case with Fénelon's work, a mirror for princes. *Émile* was *Télémaque* for the bourgeois public sphere.

The issue of 'natural' virtue was given added substance by burgeoning debates over the meanings derived from the practices of exogenous societies revealed to an avid reading public by traders, travellers and missionaries. In the past, a great deal of this literature had endorsed the technical, religious and therefore, it was believed, moral superiority of Western Europe. The civilizing project of the *philosophes* and the *Encyclopédistes* was indeed predicated on a contrast between the light of contemporary reason and the dark times of savagery and barbarism. Since the times of the Spanish conquest of the Americas, however, there had always been a subjacent stream of travel literature which had queried the civilizing function of Western penetration of such societies. In the eighteenth century, this was instantiated in writings which developed the view that 'savages' exhibited more virtue and moral nobility than their conquerors. Rousseau wrote more against the idea of the 'noble savage' than for it, and was not without his own ethnocentric prejudices (thus, Émile had to be brought up in a temperate European climate since in hot and cold climes 'the brain [is] less well-organized').[42] Nonetheless, his writings had the effect of encouraging many contemporaries to locate natural virtue within other, more exotic and more primitive societies than their own. A developing humanitarian critique of the institution of plantation slavery on which much of France's colonial and economic wellbeing was based played a part in this trend. So too did the exploration from the middle years of the century of the South Pacific, Enlightenment Europe's 'New Found Land'. Of particular significance were chronicles of life in the island of Tahiti retailed by James Cook and the French savant Bougainville in the early 1770s: Tahiti was portrayed as a living utopia, an Edenic vision of what must once have been the state of Europe. The reception of Rousseau's work in the decades after their publication was strongly inflected by this current of thinking, which further dramatized the contrast between natural virtue and civilized corruption.

Émile was a boy's story about civic virtue – with very important consequences for girls. Whereas the centre of the fiction was the moral perfecting of the young Émile, the fate ascribed to his marriage partner, Sophie, seemed to suggest that women were nature-bound to play second fiddle. A woman's education, Rousseau stipulated,

must be planned in relation to man. To be pleasing, to win his respect and love, to bring him up as a child, to tend him in manhood, to counsel and console, to make life pleasant and happy – these are the duties of women for all time.[43]

Whereas Émile's personality was in some sense malleable, there seemed to be an ahistoric, 'natural' aspect to women's characters which constrained such moulding. This motherly domestic role involved a rejection of women's own rational activity in favour of that of their partner's: 'all that tends to generate ideas is not within the compass of women; all their studies must deal with the practical'.[44]

Rousseau's views on women directly contradicted the theory of communicative and egalitarian sociability which was at the heart of the *philosophe* vision of knowledge. Salons run by women offered not only a venue for social mixing but also a key epistemological site for the polite and reciprocal exchange of reason. In the salon, men subjected themselves to the formal direction of a female, who umpired debate and policed the frontiers of polite discussion. French civilization could pride itself on being so much more advanced than other nations, it was held, precisely because of the polishing of manners and honing of intellects which occurred under female governance. Very much in line with this liberal view of women, a number of the *philosophes*, from the abbé de Saint-Pierre to Condorcet, criticized the inferior legal and social status of women, while Jaucourt, in the article on 'Woman' in the *Encyclopédie*, went so far as to argue that the husband's authority within a marriage was 'contrary to natural human equality'.[45]

'I am very far from thinking', Rousseau had stated in a footnote to the First Discourse, 'that [the] ascendancy of women is in itself an evil.'[46] Indeed, his view of women as 'the moral sex' par excellence[47] highlighted a firm valorization of what women could offer society. Yet much of his work was read by contemporaries as endorsing precisely the opposite sentiment, for which, from mid-century, there was a growing amount of support. In Sparta, Rousseau approvingly noted, women had been confined at home and forbidden entry on to the public arena on which (male) public life took place. The history of ancient Rome, Renaissance Italy and many other societies, Rousseau claimed, showed that as soon as women began to influence political affairs, corruption and decay wheedled their way into the polity. The symbol of a naturally ordered polity was a mother breastfeeding her offspring within her home (rather than hiring the child out to mercenary wetnurses). By the same token, the symbol of a disorder and corruption was a woman on the public forum, in the palace, in the street – or in the salon. Rousseau marked his passage into open opposition to the *philosophes* by venomous attacks on this quintessential enlightening venue. The salonnières were so many 'tyrants of [men's] liberty', who, he alleged, 'do not know anything, although they judge everything',[48] and therefore needed to be directed and kept under control.

Rousseau's works were to have an enormous influence on the moral economy of gender in the last half of the eighteenth century. Rousseau had opened up debate on the extent to which eighteenth-century man was civilized and virtuous, but those who drew inspiration from his ideas seemed to foreclose on any discussion of a positive role for women in social change by confining them within an atemporal version of their 'nature'. The 'natural' social arrangement on which emphasis was placed as the site for the inculcation of civic virtue was the domestic family in which only the men did the thinking and public acting. Women, in contrast, were confined to a subordinate, ancillary and supportive role in mental work, and were restricted from participation in public life. This approach was endorsed by medical men who were tending to locate gender difference more strictly in terms of biological incommensurability between the sexes. Pierre Roussel's influential and much republished *Système physique et moral de la femme* ('Systematic Overview of Women as Physical and Moral Beings') (1775), for example, drew freely on current debates in physiology and anatomy, and ended up blaming women's distinctive nervous system for limiting their intellectual development ('Their delicate organs will feel more keenly the unavoidable ill effects that [serious study] involves')[49] and saw the child-bearing capacity inscribed on to their bodies as grounds for believing in their essential difference from men. Their inherent propensities should be allowed to blossom in the work of reproduction, breastfeeding (which became highly fashionable), child-care and husband-nurturing. This view also dovetailed with political economists' fears of depopulation: societal prosperity seemed to rely on women doing the procreative work which should have come naturally. And Nature was increasingly seen as the grounds for human happiness.

D) RE-ENCHANTING A DISENCHANTED WORLD

The *philosophes* aimed to disenchant the world, that is to say, to evacuate nature of magical or spiritual powers and to present a version of material reality over which forces inaccessible to rational understanding had no sway. Like their sometime enemies, the Jansenists, they had a sense of a world in which God's intentions were illegible and beyond the reach of human reason. Unlike the Jansenists, they sought to ground the meanings of human life in 'society' – a term which only began to be widely used in the early eighteenth century, and whose resonance derived from a rejection of transcendent spiritual values and a linked belief that cultural meanings were socially grounded. It was not that the *philosophes* disregarded the deity. Indeed, as the English philosopher, David Hume, implied, even in fashion-crazy Paris it was rarer to find someone who believed in atheists than an individual who did not believe in God.[50] The baron d'Holbach and some of his philosophical intimates verged on outright disbelief, as did Diderot, spasmodically. Yet many whom their contemporaries regarded as outright atheists protested their belief: even La Mettrie, author of the ultra-mechanistic, soul-denying *L'Homme machine* ('Man the Machine') (1747), left the door open to the possibility of God's existence, while Voltaire died within the bosom of the church (though not without some stage-managed anti-clerical touches).

Down to mid-century (and in many cases beyond), the *philosophes* tended to take their cue from Voltaire, who popularized the purportedly Newtonian metaphor of God as watch-maker, with the internal machinery of the universe operating according to some not empirically obvious design. The natural philosopher thus operated from a stance of epistemological modesty, eschewing any insight into the mysterious operations of the deity, who was the first cause of all creation, and restricting himself to issues pitched at the level of secondary causation. The only things about God which seemed to be knowable were that he had removed himself from his creation once it was complete, and that he had set up the mechanism of the human world in an essentially beneficent manner. His lack of intervention in the material world meant, however, that the whole substance of revealed religion – the Bible, the church, the record of miracles – must necessarily be fraudulent. Individuals who preached an interventionist God were consequently charlatans and scoundrels who conspired to keep the people in a state of foolish ignorance and dark prejudice from which the *philosophes* were now striving to free them. Voltaire's celebrated slogan, '*Écrasez l'infâme!*' ('Crush [religious] infamy!') was directed not against the Deity but against the priesthood which claimed to speak in his name. Diderot too struck a militantly anti-clerical note:

This is our device: no quarter for the superstitious, for the fanatical, for the ignorant or for fools, malefactors or tyrants. I would wish to see our brethren united in love of virtue, feeling for beneficence and taste for truth, goodness and morality – a rather more valuable trinity than the other one. It is not enough for us to know more than Christians; we must show that we are better than they, and that science makes more good men than divine or sufficient grace.[51]

The *philosophe* belief in a distant deity was thus combined with systematic hostility to all those who claimed to be his interpreters. What got the *philosophes*' goat – and helped them score some of their most telling propaganda points – was the apparent hypocrisy of the Catholic church's claims to provide a model for virtue. The *philosophes* contrasted their own irenic calls for tolerance with the church's historical record as the perennial source of cruelty and fanaticism. They constructed an image of the regular clergy in particular as essentially irreligious, driven by their own appetites, and socially useless: monasteries were, for Voltaire, 'the repair of disorder [and] enmity' and 'monkish sloth'.[52] The ostentatious lifestyle of the upper clergy, the church's obstreperous refusal to contribute proportionately to national tax loads, its greedy insistence on a tithe of all agricultural produce – all were held to highlight the clergy's lack of commitment to the social good.

Yet despite the growing ferociousness with which the *philosophes* conducted the campaign to eradicate *l'infâme*, most of them did not exclude a role for the church within society. This was to be grounded, however, not in the clergy's claimed access to transcendent values and meanings, but in their usefulness to society. Belief in a deity who punished wrongdoers and promised rewards for good behaviour was a pillar of social order. And that belief had to be nurtured by the clergy. 'If God did not exist,' was Voltaire's celebrated view, 'it would be necessary to invent him.' The quip highlighted the extent to which the *philosophes* were seeking a *via media* between what they saw as the morally and intellectually impoverished tradition of Christian revelation and its embattled polar opposite, a sceptical materialism which left no space for a moral sensibility which the *philosophes* regarded as essential in any virtuous and happy human society.

Intriguingly, the *philosophes*' argument for religion on grounds of social utility was also one which was increasingly espoused by their opponents. Partly, ecclesiastics were thereby responding to anti-clerical taunts of their alleged social parasitism, but partly too this reflected important shifts in religious thinking. The Catholic church's grafting on to its post-Tridentine pastoral mission an acceptance of the state's need for docile and obedient subjects had encouraged a tendency to prioritize moral issues over spiritual concerns. 'True devotion', announced the abbé Dinouart, 'is exactitude in fulfilling one's duties.'[53] The figure of the *bon prêtre* – the good parish priest who placed pastoral care above theological niceties and served as a natural, tolerant, peace-loving and ultra-charitable spokesman and arbitrator for his community – proved a seductive advertisement for the church, even in *philosophe* eyes. It did indeed represent a reality in many locations, for, as we have suggested,[54] the parish clergy was more committed, more zealous and better educated than at any time in the history of the French church. The hard-working, under-appreciated and yet socially useful *bon prêtre* found a female equivalent, moreover, in the Daughter of Charity, the religious nursing sister whose vocational commitment and humane compassion in the face of soul-destroying tasks made even Voltaire dewy-eyed.

The valorization of the *bon prêtre* as more socially useful and spiritually admirable than the upper clergy gave many parish priests ideas well above their station. From the 1750s, rumblings of discontent began to be heard in a number of dioceses, notably in Nancy, Provence and Dauphiné where, despite formal royal prohibition, the lower clergy formed diocesan assemblies to protest their cause. There was often a Jansenist twist to their complaints: many *curés* were attracted to the doctrines of the seventeenth-century Augustinian, Edmond Richer, who had held that the successors of Christ's disciples were not the episcopate but the whole body of the clergy. They argued that church decision-making ought to be done in democratic diocesan synods. There was, moreover, an economic as well as a spiritual edge to their militancy: the pitifully low *portion congrue* (the clerical stipend on which much of the lower clergy had to live) had failed to keep up with increases in the cost of living: set at 300 livres for *curés* in 1690, it was raised to 500 in 1750, and then to 750 in 1786 (with 300 for parish subalterns). The lower clergy resented how sorry these figures appeared when set against the prodigious incomes of the prelates. Even though Richerists amongst them would have been appalled to think of themselves as being influenced by the *philosophes*, their protests were increasingly couched in a language of civic virtue and social utility which reflected Enlightenment debates.

If forces within the church increasingly warmed to the utilitarian gospel preached by the *philosophes*, this sprang partly from growing anxiety and concern about the church's impact on the laity. From the second quarter of the century, deep cracks were starting to appear across the face of the country in the façade of religious conformity. After mid-century, those cracks developed into an abyss. Perhaps the most striking feature of this thoroughgoing transformation of *mentalités* related to the florid set of beliefs and practices clustered around the deathbed, centre-piece of post-Tridentine baroque piety even, as we have seen, for a king.[55] The traditional kind of last will and testament – replete with charitable and religious bequests, intricate funeral instructions and spiritual invocation of God and the saints – went into steep decline. In Provence more than 80 per cent of testators had written the traditional kind of will at mid-century; by the 1780s, only half did so. In Paris, the shift had taken place even earlier and was even more extensive. It was as though most French people were starting to forget how to die – or at least to die like Catholics. The rate of religious and charitable giving fell starkly, worsening the financial state of hospitals and charitable institutions. Characteristically, the burial spot, perennial theatre of much baroque funeral pomp, was under attack on utilitarian, sanitary grounds: in 1776, burials inside churches were forbidden as a health risk; and the transfer of the sprawling Cemetery of the Innocents graveyard at the heart of Paris to a more remote spot signalled a move towards suburban graveyards which would become the norm early in the nineteenth century.

Other indices of religious commitment were in parallel, sometimes vertiginous, decline. Religious titles dropped from around one-third of all books published in 1720 (the figure had been even higher under Louis XIV) to a quarter by 1750 and one-tenth in 1789. Religious vocations also seemed in free fall for most of the century, with a marked acceleration after around 1750: they dropped by a quarter down to the 1780s. A quarter of a million strong in 1680, the clergy was only half as large in 1789. The unpopular regular clergy were the worst affected. Their numbers had been dropping from the 1720s, and the raising of the age of vows in 1768 to twenty-one for men and eighteen for women completed the rout. From the 1760s, moreover, the church itself was looking to eradicate failing institutions – the 'Commission of Regulars' established in 1768 closed down around one-sixth of all monasteries over a period of two decades. Lay confraternities also entered a phase of decay: churchmen deplored the tendency of these to become centres of collective profanity, and deplored members seeking out company and profane pursuits in coffee-houses and masonic lodges. The sociability of the public sphere offered a seemingly more attractive model than religious association.

The moral teachings of the church were also increasingly ignored. Ecclesiastical censors worked overtime but could not prevent the spread of philosophical works whose message believers were enjoined to despise. (Indeed, many works on the papal Index also found their way on to the bookshelves of French ecclesiastics.) Those within the church who held fast to the theme of religious unity proclaimed by Louis XIV in the 1685 Edict of Fontainebleau were downcast by the lack of repression of Huguenots after mid-century, and by the growing sense in government as well as philosophical circles that toleration was inevitable. Church attendance and, in particular, Easter duties were no longer the occasions for community togetherness which once they had been: priests bewailed the opening of bars, the playing of *boules*, and the raucous cracking of jokes during divine service. Belief in miracles, attendance on pilgrimages, participation in missions and the vitality of religious art all went into decline. The church's teachings on sexual matters had been remarkably faithfully observed at the high water-mark of post-Tridentine influence – but here too there was plentiful evidence of deterioration. Illegitimacy rates rose by nearly 50 per cent from the 1740s down to 1789: though the towns maintained their reputation as sinks of iniquity, with much higher levels than the countryside (around a third of births were illegitimate in Paris, for example, and nearly 40 per cent were so in Nantes), in fact the rate of increase was probably more pronounced in rural than urban areas. There were rises too in the rate of pre-nuptial pregnancy and in child abandonment: the latter increased 100 per cent between the 1740s and the 1780s. Shocked confessors reported the growing evidence of the use of coitus interruptus too – in rural localities as well as in the towns.

It would be quite wrong to imagine that this erosion of religious belief was universal and across the board. As with average wage rates, average rates of religious observance obscure very great divergences from the mean, and complex patterns of difference. The towns had been the leading edge of post-Tridentine Catholic zeal, but in the eighteenth century their piety tended to wane, and it was rural areas, slower to receive the post-Tridentine message, who tended to stick with it. Here, community peer pressure often acted in the direction of conservatism and homogeneity, especially in remote mountain areas more cut off from the lively interchange of ideas and commodities of valleys and plains. Certain regions – Nice and Upper Provence, Alsace-Lorraine, the Velay, the Vivarais and parts of Brittany were good examples – even bucked the secularizing trend altogether, and showed greater religious vitality in the eighteenth century than in the seventeenth. Gender was a further line of differentiation: in general women were more likely to retain their religious beliefs than their menfolk. In addition, there were signs of at least partial recovery from the 1770s: the number of religious vocations rose, and a flurried revival of spiritual activity in publishing too: changes in laws of literary ownership in 1779 led to a spurt of religious publications. More than a million religious works were sold, the field being led by the bestseller, *L'Ange conducteur* ('The Guardian Angel'), which went into fifty-one re-editions, selling over 100,000 copies in a decade.

Ecclesiastics were swift to blame the *philosophes* for the erosion of religious uniformity and the growth of spiritual indifference over the century as a whole. This was a case of shooting the messenger. The Enlightenment project did seek to change attitudes and did indeed impact on the behaviour and innermost convictions of much of France's elite and most of its intelligentsia. Yet it was also very much a product of the wider social, economic and cultural transformation which was taking place in eighteenth-century France, linked to the development of commercial capitalism. The shift in *mentalités* which necessitated coming to terms with a remote Deity and grounding religious values in the material world involved many individuals besides the *philosophes*. It also had more to do with a changed society than with the anti-clerical views of the *philosophes*, who, moreover, acknowledged God's existence, valued rather than depreciated popular religious belief and retained a place in their universe for the moral teachings of the church. The latter was, moreover, in the throes of a spiritual reform which sought a more purposive social dimension for religious action. Furthermore, the popular classes did not look to the *philosophes* for their social values. It is possible to detect in the writings of the *Bibliothèque bleue*, which provided the literary pabulum for the popular classes, some reflections of the values of the enlightened elite – there was less astrology and prophesying, as the century wore on, and more popular science and civility. Yet in general, the common people shared their priests' and community leaders' suspicions of the *philosophes*. It was widely believed that the most characteristic feature of the latter was sexual deviancy: in popular parlance, *le péché philosophique* – 'the philosopher's sin' – was sodomy, while pornographic and obscene writings were commonly dubbed *livres de philosophie*.

Furthermore, although the *philosophes* were a useful whipping-child for a beleaguered church, some of the reasons for the transformation of religious mores lay within the church itself. Some of the bitterest denunciations of popular piety, for example, came from purist clerics like Christophe Sauvageon, scourge of what he saw as the spiritual lip-service his parishioners paid to the Christian verities.[56] Despite the wish of many clerics to tailor their faith and to transform their lives to the demands of a more secular age, the fact remained that the church was a house divided, and its divisions reduced its efficacy against *philosophe* attacks. Doctrinal battles within the church – uncertain counsels on strategy as regards the *philosophes*, the fierce anti-Jansenist struggles, and the social critique which the Richerists were starting to mount – reduced its overall effectiveness. So too, from the late 1750s, did the campaign to expel the Jesuits, who had formed the shock-troops of the early Counter-Reformation. Diderot commented to his mistress Sophie Volland on how ecclesiastical tergiversations over the expulsion of the Jesuits in 1762 'g[a]ve the *philosophes* a good laugh'.[57] The Jesuits were often criticized for being too accommodating with the sins of their flocks. On the other hand, Jansenists' often austere rigour in the con-fessional and their wish to purify popular beliefs of allegedly pagan accretions alienated many of their would-be supporters, swelling rather than thinning the ranks of unbelief.

Just as the *philosophes* distinguished between attacking the church and denying the existence of God, so too, many of the individuals manifesting religious indifference did not reject an overarching belief in a beneficent providence, belief in which had calculable social benefits. Providence was, for many, clad in the garb of Nature. For some of the more radical *philosophes*, the *siècle des lumières* had knocked God off his pedestal and installed Nature in his place. In his scandalously materialist *System of Nature* (1770) – published abroad under cloak of anonymity – d'Holbach presented Nature as an alternative, more authentic and more attractive deity than the Christian God: 'Return to

Nature!', he apostrophized his readers. 'She will console you, drive out from your heart the fears that hobble you, the anxieties which tear you ... the hatreds that separate you from Man, whom you ought to love.'[58] This was an extreme version of a view which Buffon voiced more moderately towards the end of his life: 'I have always called the Creator by his name; but it is only a short step to removing this word and putting naturally in its place the power of Nature.'[59]

'Nature', the Encyclopédie noted (supplying no fewer than eight separate meanings to prove the point), was a 'vague term', and vagueness was part of its appeal.[60] While semi-atheists might rejoice in God's displacement by Nature, a great many orthodox Christians also held that Nature constituted a transcendent source of goodness which offered guidance to right living. Voltaire had drawn on Newton to demonstrate an allegedly divine orderliness in the natural world which left no space for God's intervention in human affairs, but as the century wore on it was Christian apologists who utilized a version of this argument from design to demonstrate the necessary existence of God. Nature was taken to form a Great Chain of Being, established by the deity, with mankind at the top and the other forms of life disposed beneath it in interlinking patterns so hierarchically complex that they necessarily implied a hidden designer. The master text in this respect was abbé Pluche's *Spectacle of Nature* (1732–50), a pedagogic compendium framed as a polite conversation about nature's wonders, which went into dozens of editions, selling more than 20,000 copies. The cult of nature as 'sugar-coated spectacle'[61] was further boosted by Rousseau's writings from the late 1750s onwards: the critic of cities, courts, commerce and civilization only felt at home in settings as far removed from their corrupting influence as possible.

Jean-Jacques thus helped engender vigorous enthusiasm for pastoral settings and mountain scenery where the corrupting hand of humankind was less apparent. After 1750, moreover, a growing sense among natural philosophers that Nature was not just pre-assembled passive matter but also an energizing force in its own right which was determining as well as determined placed pressure on the Newtonian-Voltairean conception of the universe as finished artefact. Though Maupertuis, Buffon and others flirted with moving away from the fixity of species towards a more evolutionist position, the Great Chain of Being stayed in place, seeming testament to God's master design. The master metaphor with which Nature was described, however, passed from the watch, an intricately mechanical artifact, to the natural organism, capable of growth and development. Nature, Buffon stated, was 'a ceaselessly active worker, able to make use of everything'.[62]

'Nature elevates the soul by way of the truths one discovers by contemplating it.' This guileless sentiment, testament to the widespread attachment to natural history of the last half of the century, were the words of a middle-ranking factory inspector.[63] Perhaps indeed, it needed a culture as thoroughly rooted in urban and commercial values as the Enlightenment to make a cult of nature, mingling intellectual curiosity with nostalgia for a world which many town-dwellers had lost or feared losing. Devotees of the cult often stayed at the level of contemplation and enjoyment of nature in all its forms – especially as prettified in the contrived pastoralism of artists like Boucher. Yet a striking feature of the cult of nature in the eighteenth century was the number of individuals who strove to enter the machine-room behind the unfolding spectacle (the metaphor was Pluche's). Using a wide and varied set of methodologies, unified by a politeness of approach inculcated in salons and academies, they sought to survey, comprehend, collect and taxonomize nature's epiphenomena. Underlying these activities was a touching Enlightenment faith in the social utility of their activities. When Réaumur spent long evenings motionless in the dewy grass of his garden spying on the nocturnal perambulations of caterpillars, he nurtured a belief that there might well be industrial products (lacquers, dyes, etc.) which could result from a better knowledge of that world. Bazin's erudite and semi-anthropomorphic studies of bees were guided by a determination that advanced apiary could stimulate the national economy. Physicians throughout France checked their barometers and thermometers and tirelessly visited hospitals and the homes of the poor to record patterns of morbidity, mortality and meteorology, out of a firm sense that a healthier world would be a happier place. In Buffon's Burgundian château, badgers warmed their toes by his hearth and hedgehogs defecated in his cooking pots, for the great naturalist's efforts to comprehend the mores of the animal realm involved building up a menagerie of creatures, to whom he gave the run of his premises. He combined his natural history with experimentation in a whole range of utilitarian fields, including animal husbandry, chemistry and electricity, which he hoped would further enrich him and boost national production.

Front-line naturalists were important not only for what they did but also for allowing others to experience nature vicariously. A veritable passion for collection was combined with moves to present inventorized and contextualized works of nature for the visual delectation of a large public of amateurs. Academies, public institutions and private individuals all took a part in this. The Jardin du Roi in Paris under Buffon's stewardship from 1739 to 1788, for example, became a show-case for exotic naturalia. The private residence in Paris of the Languedo-cian financier Bonnier de la Mosson was in all essentials a museum in which visitors could wander, contemplating in turn a chemistry labora-tory, a pharmacy, a collection of precision tools, a cornucopia of stuffed and pickled animals, and one of the finest collections of mechanical objects in Europe. Despite the frequent bric-à-brac dimension to such collections, these theatres of nature invited an appreciation of nature rather different from the Renaissance *Wunderkammer* which had pre-ceded them. Whereas the latter had foregrounded the freak, the pro-digious and the monstrous, the Enlightenment cabinet stressed the order and regularity of nature, and sought rational systems of classification for presenting them (taxonomy being the invariable reflex of Enlightenment science, as Michel Foucault noted).[64] By a similar logic, Buffon devoted only three pages in the forty-odd volumes of his great *Natural History* to monsters. Science's laws were more impressive in their performance than in their transgression.

New technologies were available – and were further developed – to encourage and enthuse this multiform wave of polite science. The superior glass-manufacture for which the French were famed supplied better telescopes for the study of the superlunary and better microscopes for the sublunary worlds (to use an Aristotelian language which was fast becoming *démodé*). For every savant lovingly devoted to his or her science, there were a score of amateur naturalists doing their bit for the glorification, the progressive revelation and the use-value of the natural world. A useful role-model in this respect was Tremblay, whose minute observation of pond-life hydra revealed a baroque sex-life which called into question the most fundamental views of reproduction: one could espy secrets of the Creator in one's own back-yard. Besides entomology, the measurement of climate, astronomical observation and the study of rocks also became voguish pursuits, but all were surpassed, as domains of this kind of domestic scientific observationism, by botany. Shorn of its earlier medicinal orientation, the discipline developed cult status, which was further validated by Rousseau's *Rêveries du promeneur solitaire* ('Reveries of the Solitary Walker') (1782), in which Jean-Jacques depicted himself wandering contentedly through the countryside, in his hand a magnifying glass and, under his arm, a copy of Linnaeus (the Swedish naturalist whose system of plant classification achieved canonical status).

Alongside the natural history cabinet, the garden was a further example of a site in which public tastes for science and nature were satisfied. The regimented gardens of Versailles, in whose stern geometry Louis XIV had taken such a strong personal interest, no longer provided the model to emulate. The more naturalistic English garden, along lines popularized *outre-Manche* by William Kent and 'Capability' Brown, provided a more appropriate setting in which to indulge a taste for the force of nature (rather than nature under human force, as at Versailles). Gardens in the *maisons de campagne* which much of the urban elite were building were also ordered in such a way, with serpentine lines, lakes, follies, bosks and the like. They inspired and projected the emotions (even a fashionably gothic melancholia) in the same way that unspoiled landscape did for anyone who had read Rousseau. Gardens were almost didactic in their orientation, providing a site in which the individual could commune with nature, perhaps intuit the hand of God, and through exploration of the palette of emotions seek out the parameters of his or her selfhood.

Engineering technology also played a big part in this new appreciation of the intricacies and wonders of the natural world and the concomitant quest for 'natural' selfhood. Better, faster roads, along with modernized public transport and the development of a burgeoning hospitality industry, made it possible for the town-dweller to indulge a taste for the wild 'natural' scenery which was so much to Rousseau's taste. Classical civilization had abhorred the vacuum of wildernesses, deserts and mountains, but with a little push from Jean-Jacques, such denuded sites now came into their own. No collector could put an Alp in his cabinet; but the new tourist infrastructure allowed mountains to be visited and explored, in some comfort and style, and with a groaning bookshelf of guidebooks in tow. It was a gesture highly characteristic of the age that, when the adventurous naturalist de Saussure achieved the first ascent of Mont-Blanc in 1787, rather than admire the view he rushed through a sequence of thermometrical and barometrical readings, took the pulse of his companions, and built a fire to check on the boiling point of water. And when he descended, taking rock samples as he went, he wrote up his experiences as a scientific best-seller.

Probably the most critical technology in diffusing and popularizing the taste for nature in the eighteenth century remained the printing press. If for every *philosophe* savant there were twenty amateur naturalists, for every amateur naturalist there were scores of readers who consumed 'the life sciences' (to use an anachronistic but helpful term) at one remove. Massive editions of often lavishly illustrated works of natural history – Pluche, Buffon, Réaumur (on insects), the chevalier de Lamarck and the Lorraine naturalist Buc'hoz (on flora) – invariably financed through the subscription method pioneered by the *Encyclopédie*, were enormously popular. So too were dozens of humbler works, often in small format to allow carrying when out walking. Science books and novels were the most important genres in private libraries by the 1780s, with theology – the core of most seventeenth-century collections – well down the list. Science periodicals also began to blossom: the ending of the Jesuits' famous *Journal de Trévoux* in 1767 left the field wide open for the development of a specialist science sector. The general press took up the baton too: the *Journal de Paris*, for example, regularly reported on the flowering of exotic specimens in the Jardin du Roi. Pastoral poetry (of an often excruciatingly awful quality), novels set in rural locations, historico-geographical accounts of provinces and natural phenomena, guide-books of every description and aimed at every pocket, supplemented by engravings which carried the naturalistic landscapes of Vernet and Hubert Robert beyond the walls of the art collector, provided further elements within this highly buoyant market.

The commodification of nature through the book trade highlighted the role of commercial capitalism in fuelling the taste for the picturesque and developing a wide audience for the life sciences. The capitalistic element within such public science caused some anxiety in a world of polite inquiry which saw itself as peopled by gentlemen scientists. Though they themselves benefited enormously from the development of cultural markets, scientists and their patrons resisted entrepreneurial attempts to play too flagrantly to popular taste. The role of the academies, the scientific academician Fontenelle held, was as much to 'disabuse the public of false marvels as to report on true ones'.[65] There was particular concern over cases in which the diffusion of science had a performative element. Enlightenment scientific heroes – from Boyle and Newton through to Lavoisier and Priestley – inspired the public demonstration of science. Provincial academies, salons and private individuals proved eager to stage such events. Yet it was thought that the frontier between practical instruction and popular entertainment needed careful policing. A limiting case was the physicist abbé Nollet, who claimed to be gratifying 'the most reasoned curiosity' of his public, and who spoke out harshly against any 'spectacle of pure amusement'[66] – yet who laid on highly theatrical demonstrations of electricity in which circles of soldiers, then 300 monks, were simultaneously propelled vertically into the air by an electric shock. Nollet retained the necessary gentlemanly politeness, however, whereas many who followed his lead were essentially businessmen seeking profits. Beneath the thinnest of scientific veneers and the most implausible claims of social utility, scientific entrepreneurs offered sheer escapist entertainment at a price. Paris and other major cities swarmed with anatomical freakshows, talking horses, magical tricks, illusionary stunts, magic lantern performances and the like, which irked and embarrassed polite science – but attested to the vitality of the taste for science outside the social elite.

The bitterest such dispute occurred over the public demonstration in Paris in the early 1780s of the putatively scientific doctrine of animal magnetism espoused by the Viennese physician Franz-Anton Mesmer. Mesmer had a great deal going for him – an orthodox medical pedigree, a stress on 'natural' cures, exotic scientific apparatus, humanitarian and utilitarian justifications – but the movement he promoted signally failed to live up to expected standards of gentlemanly politeness. A government commission stuffed with the most celebrated scientists of the age (including chemist Lavoisier, astronomer Bailly and physicist Benjamin Franklin) roundly condemned Mesmer and all his works. He was accused of keeping his craft as an arcane secret beyond public scrutiny by fellow scientists; of bamboozling money out of the gullible sick; and of producing, through the bodily stroking which the treatment involved, orgasmic states in female patients (thought rather ungentlemanly behaviour). Yet the strength of the support his movement attracted – including from within the medical and scientific establishments – highlighted the fragility of the *philosophe* claim that the age of Enlightenment was tolling the death-knell of public credulity. Mesmer's emphasis on his therapy as 'natural' showed that nature was still open to widely varying interpretation, while also demonstrating – in the eyes of his critics – that the public sphere could nourish rather than extinguish the age of wonder and miracles.

Rousseau's influential writings of course had been based on a wholesale rejection of urban and commercial values. Whereas the *philosophes* stressed the role of towns in civilization's progress, for Rousseau, 'towns are the abyss of the human race', while Paris, *philosophe* city of enlightenment, was nothing but 'noise, smoke and mud'.[67] Yet even he, after decades of hermetic living and wanderings in rural locations, returned to live for the last eight years of his life in the human goldfish bowl that was Paris. Transgressing his own rule that his nature was 'to write and [then] hide',[68] he strolled the streets clad 'naturally' (and oh!-so-anonymously) in eye-catching Armenian dress. His quondam disciple Mercier offered an even more characteristic 'enlightened' response: he recorded how in his youth, inflamed by Rousseau's writings, he had set out to live in the state of nature in the wildest forests – only to find that such a life was dull and boring, and to return forthwith to Paris.[69] Most writers would cheerfully have subscribed to the abbé Galiani's view that he would rather be a pumpkin or a cucumber than renounce the pleasure of living in Paris.[70]

In spite of the anti-urban rhetoric which clothed it, commercially marketed changes in urban taste played a key role in the popularization of nature through science. The exotic plants and shrubs in domestic gardens – Bougainville's bougainvillea is an apt example – were silent testimony to the outreach of French colonial and commercial power. The coffee served in coffee-houses, as well as the tea and chocolate consumed in salons and academies, had been turned into everyday beverages by the transforming power of the market. The 'natural' wonders (waterfalls, lakes, mini-Alps, follies, ruins, etc.) within Enlightenment gardens were created using engineering and hydraulic technology developed by the Ponts et Chaussées officials. Those high priestesses of fashion – Madame de Pompadour and Louis XVI's queen, Marie-Antoinette – both designed 'naturalistic' English-style gardens within the Versailles enclosure, with Marie-Antoinette developing an arcadian little hamlet close to the château in which she played the role of shepherdess and milkmaid, and spawned a whole *à la bergère* fashion trend. Nature in the age of Enlightenment was thus far more comfortable with the values and practices of commercial capitalism than its Rousseauist rhetoric implied. The Great Chain of Being was underpinned by a Great Chain of Buying and Selling which commodified Nature for a growing middle-class and elite audience, and thereby helped re-enchant an increasingly disenchanted world.

E) THE CONTESTED POLITICS OF THE PUBLIC SPHERE

'Happiness', the chilling ideologue of Terror, Saint-Just, was to proclaim in 1794, 'is a new idea in Europe.'[71] Yet the idea of terrestrial happiness as the product of purposive collective action was an Enlightenment, not a Revolutionary invention. The *philosophes* devoted an enormous amount of energy to imagining a legitimately grounded national community in a disenchanted world, in which public felicity could be found not in the afterlife but on the bedrock of a reordered society constantly on the march towards improvement.

The progressivist norms of the Enlightenment project were, however, intensely questioned from within. From mid-century – at the very moment at which the Enlightenment project seemed to be gaining intellectual hegemony – key terms such as 'reason', 'nature', 'civilization', and, indeed, 'enlightenment' (*'lumière'*) were vigorously contested. And as the century wore on, there was a growing sense of the fragility of the optimism prevalent at the *Encyclopédie* moment. Rousseau's systematic questioning of the value, meaning and direction of progress played a critical role in this, but there were other straws in the wind. The Lisbon earthquake of 1755, in which 30–40,000 died, dramatically confronted Voltaire with the problem of evil in the world, for example, and his tale *Candide* (1757) was a savagely ironic attack on the facile philosophy of the 'all for the best in the best of all possible worlds' variety. Histories of the Roman Empire by Montesquieu (1734), then Gibbon (1776–87) helped foster an awareness that civilizations could decline as well as rise, a perception that was also in play in a wide-ranging dispute, framed particularly around nature and humankind in the Americas, over whether Europe was in fact degenerating. The Mesmer affair also dramatized the persistence of credulity even in Paris, the heart of enlightened reason. This sense of fragility about the Enlightenment project was heightened by the fact that the *philosophes* found themselves frequently under attack – and, just as frequently, divided amongst themselves.

The shadow of the Bastille loomed over the persons and the productions of the *philosophes* right down to 1789. Individual ecclesiastics may have been attracted to the doctrine of social utility, but the church's watchdogs maintained a watching brief for any philosophical work which overstepped theological orthodoxy and public decency. Despite the liberal tenure of Malesherbes as Director of the Book Trade in the 1750s and 1760s, the government always monitored writings, while the Paris Police Lieutenant subjected authors, printers and booksellers to spasmodic repression – an activity in which the Paris Parlement was often only too pleased to join.[72] As if this were not enough, fellow writers – and not simply the apologists and defenders of the church – also gave the *philosophes* a sharp reminder that they did not monopolize the world of print and that critical reason could be used against its champions. Rousseau's noisy defection from the *philosophe* camp caused a durable split, and the year 1757 also saw the forces of a kind of counter-Enlightenment develop substance in the world of letters, as Palissot, Fréron and Moreau launched a variety of attacks on the faction of the *philosophes*. Moreau's allegorical *Mémoires pour servir à l'histoire des Cacouacs* ('Memoirs which Serve as History of the Cacouacs') attacked the *philosophes* for irreligion, vanity, intellectual elitism and inhumanity, tellingly using against them their own arms of humour, light-heartedness, fantasy and irony. The literary periodical *L'Année littéraire*, which Fréron directed for over twenty years down to 1775, served as a perennial pricker of the pretensions of the movement, and this task was continued by the *Annales politiques* (1777–92) of the disbarred barrister and maverick journalist, Linguet, harsh critic of 'the wretched *Encyclopédie*' and its editors.[73] Even in the salons, the *philosophes* were not immune from attack: when d'Alembert deserted Madame du Deffand for Julie Lespinasse, the former sneered at 'our lords and masters the *Encyclopédistes*' and imbued her sessions with a strong anti-*philosophe* flavour.[74]

These strains and tensions gave the *philosophes* a highly embattled air. Embattled they were – but they also often played this theme for all its worth, highlighting the extent to which they were part of a movement which had political clout yet which had grown up despite rather than because of the purview of the royal court and the world of corporatist privilege. Yet in practice many of their number were more tightly integrated within the political establishment than their standard 'outsiderist' rhetoric and subversive squibs gave to understand. A number were, by social origins or employment, already within the socio-political elite, while the salons provided a channel through which men of letters of lowlier origins could come into contact with the social elite, and develop patterns of friendship, clientage and dependence. These were often grafted on to existing factional alignments. Madame de Pompadour served as an important link of friendship for much of the *philosophe* faction, so that in 1749, when Controller-General Machault was looking for a polemicist to pamphleteer against the Parlement and in favour of his *vingtième* tax, he was able to draw along the lines of the royal mistress's client-base to acquire the services of Voltaire.[75] There were other faction-leaders who also showed themselves especially able to exploit and to patronize the *philosophes* in this way. The prince de Conti, for example, Pompadour's sworn enemy, who passed into Frondeur-style opposition to the king in the late 1750s, also cultivated men of letters. Prior of the largely honorific Order of the Temple, he placed its headquarters in Paris, which were outside the jurisdiction of the ordinary police, at the disposal of subversive printers and writers. After Conti's death in 1776, the duc d'Orléans followed a similar tack, and his residence, the Palais-Royal leisure complex, became a safe haven for clandestine authors and presses. Other senior political figures with strong *philosophe* links were Choiseul – effectively main minister from the late 1750s through to 1770 – and Turgot. When the latter, an *Encyclopédiste*, was appointed Controller-General in 1774, he revoked the licences of Fréron's and Linguet's anti-*philosophe* journals – an action which demonstrated that even *philosophes* were not immune from old-fashioned political spite and that, as often as not, there was little love lost between *lumières*.

That the movement of the Enlightenment was more pluralistic and divided than the unitary, progressivist face which the *philosophes* often presented to the world was particularly apparent as regards the politics they espoused. It did not take much nous to realise that 'enlightenment' (whatever that was held to be) could not be expected to spread beatifically over the nation without significant institutional change; nor to appreciate that traditional political arrangements did not offer the best nor even the most appropriate means for the kind of transformation they had in mind. Yet how to formulate a politics of enlightenment would remain perennially problematic. To simplify – but helpfully – it seems possible to delineate three types of political account of what needed to be done within French society to improve it according to the general precepts of the *philosophes*.[76] First, there was a view, associated particularly with Montesquieu and taken up by the *parlements*, which stressed the importance of the legitimacy of traditional law. Second, there was a view, to which Voltaire in particular subscribed, but which was also highly influential within government itself, which highlighted the capacity of a recharged state to produce happiness through rational and ordered action. Third, there was a Rousseauian diagnosis of society's ills which linked up with civic republican ideology and stressed the importance of collective political will.

All three scripts for social improvement straddled the space between the bourgeois public sphere and the political and corporative establishment. The latter was less refractory to the political aims of the Enlightenment than the *philosophes* often gave to understand, and the bourgeois public sphere whose organic intellectuals they aspired to be maintained strong links of deference and allegiance to established authority. To a greater degree than historians have often appreciated, the political projects of the *philosophes* overlapped with the kinds of problems which had long concerned existing political elites: the relationship between state authority and public welfare; the nature of public law; religion in a disenchanted world; the state as a confessional unity or as rationally driven administration; the arguments between Jesuits and Jansenists – and in the European theatre, between Protestantism and Catholicism; the economic agency of the state and the morality of trade and consumption; the place of the nobility in the state and society; and so on. Just after the *philosophes* collectively joined these long-running political conversations – roughly speaking, the moment of the *Encyclopédie* – the state, moreover, was thrown into crisis and demoralization by the defeats of the Seven Years War, raising the political stakes and adding colour and drama to political discussion. The *philosophes* thus discovered rather than invented politics. They were as likely to be the agents of existing political elites as their critics, and the scripts for change with which they were associated as often as not overlapped with pre-existent positions.

The juridical perspective on change was set out most influentially by

Montesquieu, magistrate of the Bordeaux Parlement and author of the best-selling *De l'Esprit des lois* in 1748. Montesquieu, whose contribution to the political debates of the Enlightenment was immense, provided an influential taxonomy for understanding political systems which was both historically and environmentally grounded. His insight that climate influenced forms of government was linked to a wider historical awareness of the way in which the sequential stages of civilization impacted on political forms. He proposed a threefold typology of republics, monarchies and despotisms. Each governmental form, he argued, was characterized by a dominant value, whose perpetuation was essential for a regime's good health: republics required virtue; monarchies, a cult of honour which united the ruler and his aristocracy; while despotisms were motivated by fear. This relativistic classification had a diachronic aspect, for Montesquieu also proposed laws of internal evolution of all regimes based on the idea that corruption in the core principle of any of the regimes would necessarily trigger overall decline.

Eighteenth-century France fitted into Montesquieu's typology as a monarchy with a powerful aristocracy imbued with a sense of honour. That honour was, however, threatened by internal corruption which risked the monarchy degenerating into a despotism. Degeneration was partly the result of honour being compromised by the competing tug of luxury and greed in a commercial society – for Montesquieu's celebration of trade's benefits[77] was matched by an awareness of its drawbacks. Partly too he saw degeneration occurring as a result of growth in the power of the ruler at the expense of his nobility. His *Persian Letters* of 1721 had displayed republican sentiments, but he was too much of a stadial developmentalist to believe that the clock could be put back so as to allow the Roman republic to re-emerge in the modern age of big commercial monarchies. The contemporary polity for which Montesquieu cherished affection was post-Glorious Revolution England. Voltaire's idealization of England had been grounded in its commercial successes breeding a respect for individual freedom and a spirit of tolerance. Montesquieu too valued individual freedom from constraint as the desirable outcome of governmental forms. Yet, though he did not deny the role of English commerce in loosening the hierarchical bonds of society, he felt that the key to England's success was its divided system of sovereignty. The English constitution, Montesquieu held (in a view which had as shaky a hold on current English political practice as

Voltaire's), was based on the separation of judicial, legislative and executive powers. Like Newton's description of the universe, Montesquieu's idealization of the British constitution stressed the harmony achieved by the balancing of countervailing powers.

Montesquieu's political position was never made wholly explicit in *De l'Esprit des lois*, but his criticism of the growth of the power of the monarchy and the state was pretty apparent. The call of this Bordeaux *parlementaire* for royal power to be balanced by intermediary authorities was close enough to the traditional oppositional discourse of the parlements to be picked up and exploited by the courts almost at once. The crown was charged with systematic disrespect for fundamental laws on which the ancient constitution was based. Successive monarchs had removed representational forms such as provincial and national estates, reduced *parlements'* legitimate rights of remonstrance, and built up a secretive and unaccountable 'bureaucracy' (the word which was beginning to be used) which attacked customary property rights and removed public affairs from the judicial to the closed, administrative realm. In sum, the absolute monarchy had so tarnished the honour of its aristocracy and launched such an assault on corporative freedoms that 'despotism' lay just around the corner. Though *parlementaires* sometimes metaphorically clothed themselves in the toga of virtuous Roman republicanism, more characteristically they followed the arguments of Montesquieu (as well as of Boulainvilliers) that the legal rights of intermediary bodies like the *parlements* were grounded in an ancient constitution which had originated in the dark forests of the Frankish invaders of Gaul in the fifth and sixth centuries. Fundamental law pre-dated – and therefore had priority over – the French monarchy.

Many contemporaries might be unkeen to accept the full burden of historical legitimation adopted by the *parlements*, but still value the check which the magistrates offered to the abuse of sovereign power. Yet many *philosophes* – in total contrast – were vehemently opposed to the *parlements*, which they held to be, in Diderot's words, 'the irreconcilable enemy of philosophy and reason'.[78] A good many of them looked to the undivided sovereignty of an absolute monarchy as the best medium for enlightening French society. Such a view had important antecedents, which again had a historical, or meta-historical, dimension. In his *Histoire critique de la monarchie française* (1734), for example, abbé Dubos had supplied a vigorous riposte to Boulainvilliers by arguing that the Frankish kings in the fifth century had inherited the full extent of prior Roman imperium. Consequently, according to this 'Romanist thesis', to which royal propagandist and arch-anti-*philosophe* Moreau also subscribed, Clovis was as absolute as Louis XV. Voltaire, for his part, had argued in *Le Siècle de Louis XIV* that the reign of Louis XIV had represented the acme of civilization thus far, and that rulers should seek to imitate and surpass the Sun King's efforts at centralization if they were to augment human happiness. Also particularly significant in this respect was the natural law tradition refurbished in the seventeenth century by Hobbes, Grotius and Pufendorf, who had argued that, as a result of the horrors of primitive life, early societies had handed over sovereignty to their rulers as the best guarantee of communal welfare. This anodine variant of contract theory highlighted the duty of the monarch to sustain the welfare of his charges. Voltaire, who had more than his fair share of entanglements with *parlements*,[79] was unconvinced that wealthy venal magistrates would be more disinterested and non-sectional than a monarchy well accustomed to standing above the fray of human interests and developing policies in the interest of all. Like many of his fellows, he largely disregarded the sacral aura in which the acolytes of Louis XIV had sought to envelop the ruler: in a disenchanted world, Voltaire held, the royal mission should be directed by the guiding light of reason.

Many *philosophes* were encouraged in their belief in absolute monarchy's capacity for improving communal welfare through the implementation of reason by the successes of an increasingly professional state bureaucracy. Contemporary rulers looked enviously at the latter's administrative competence, which allowed a very personalized monarchy to govern, in a rational, disembodied and objective manner, a political system of baroque complexity. The notion of 'police' – that is, rational administration – was seen as a historical force which could bring civilized improvement to societies. The idea that a transformed monarchy committed to the rule of reason was more likely than a restoration of the ancient constitution to bring about human happiness was, moreover, underpinned by a set of established practices and procedures. The royal Intendants, for example, were playing a growing role in the social and economic development of the provinces under their administration. So too the civil engineers of the corps of Ponts et Chaussées were providing a highway system which made viable the

Enlightenment ideal of ease of communication and exchange. Although parlementary discourse excoriated such figures as clandestine despots of public life, the service ethic and the professional expertise which they embodied seemed to many to be a highly attractive paternalistic model.

This kind of welfare agenda for the crown was mapped out in the 1690s, but it was especially from the 1750s that it began to make real headway. Though most state servants were less willing than the *philosophes* for the crown to renounce traditionalist positions and sacral claims, government from the 1750s proved increasingly responsive to a secular concern with society's material wellbeing. Conversely, many *philosophes* were drawn into the circuit of a government which many of their peers attacked.

A strikingly good example of the potential for symbiosis was the grouping who became known as the Physiocrats (or 'Economists'), and who included the marquis de Mirabeau (father of the Revolutionary), the colonial administrator and publicist Mercier de la Rivière, the royal surgeon and physician Quesnay, the administrator and journalist Dupont de Nemours and the magistrate and then royal intendant (and eventually Controller-General) Turgot. The Physiocrats espoused a professional service ethic and, in the interests of societal welfare, sought to establish laws of political economy and social relations. This new science of government, like all science, should be open and public, rather than secretive and confined as in the past. And it should reach out to develop the country's material wealth which the Physiocrats viewed as a *sine qua non* of happiness. Their slogan on all that related to trade, industry and exchange was *laisser faire, laisser passer*. They criticized the mercantilist economic policies espoused by government since the time of Colbert. Government should step back and allow market forces free rein in everything regarding production and distribution – an approach which was instantiated in the call for free trade and the removal of internal tolls and tariffs. Though they fought to remove the corporatist carapace of trade and industry, they regarded both sectors as less important to France's economic fortunes than the land, which they made the focal point of their analyses. Their emphasis on agriculture was far distant from the egalitarian frugality preached by Fénelon (and, as we shall see, by Rousseau). Like Montesquieu, who had written in favour of 'solid luxury founded not on the refinement of vanity but on that of real needs', they criticized excessive luxury (*luxe de décoration*), but regarded considerable inequality in wealth and a certain *luxe de subsistance* as prerequisites for spurring a spirit of enterprise and innovation within the economy.[80] They reckoned that the class of comfortable and wealthy property-owners – and in their eyes, this meant landowners – was the group whose well-being would do most to re-energize the economy. They thus welcomed the boom in production of agricultural manuals which spread the gospel of English-style agrarian improvement; urged complete freedom in the grain trade as the best means of enrichment; developed distinctive politics for education and state finance; and played with new forms of political representation which would be dominated by the landed interest, irrespective of which of the three estates landowners belonged to.

The influence which the Physiocrats were able to wield owed much to the cogent range of strategies they deployed: substantial correspondence with opinion-leaders in the provinces and abroad; extensive publication; the establishment of a house journal in 1765 (the *Ephémérides du citoyen*); and the currying of royal favour at court through Madame de Pompadour, to whose health surgeon-physician-economist Quesnay attended. Yet that influence also derived from the assistance they seemed to offer political elites rethinking state power during and in the aftermath of two sobering wars – the Austrian Succession War of 1740–48 and the Seven Years War of 1756–63 – which had highlighted the need for change, and the dangers of over-reliance on international trade at the expense of a strong rural economy. The Physiocrats were as much instruments of power as critics of it.

They did not, consequently, carry all the *philosophes* with them. Indeed, the Physiocrats' influence on the liberalization of the government's grain-trade policy in the 1760s led to a bitter polemic amongst men of letters. The wittily urbane abbé Galiani led the charge against Physiocracy, accusing its exponents of a quasi-religious belief in the veracity of their own faulty theorems, and an inhumane and disastrous experimentation with what was literally a life-and-death issue for much of the population. Yet though the Physiocrats were accused of placing a specious mask of reason over the face of root-and-branch despotism, many of their accusers were as committed as they to the idea of monarchy as generator of utilitarian reform, and this remained a political option long after the Physiocrats' fall from grace.

The attack on Physiocracy also signalled the entry into the political domain of the third strand of political criticism emergent from mid-century, namely, the republican tradition, as renovated by the writings of Jean-Jacques Rousseau. It would be fair to say that no one – not even Rousseau himself – thought a republic worth having was within the compass of viability for a state like eighteenth-century France. Montesquieu had consigned republican virtue to a distant past, and indeed republican states in contemporary Europe, such as Venice and the Netherlands, were generally adjudged corrupt and unworthy of imitation. Whereas both the juridical and the rationalistic critiques of monarchy were grounded in the conviction that the modern state could be improved as it stood, the republican critique was entirely negative in this respect: as Rousseau's First Discourse had shown, corruption seemed to be an adhesive component of modernity from which even republican institutions could not escape.

If the republican discourse thus offered no political blueprint, it still developed enormous influence as an idiom of criticism antagonistic to modern monarchies based on bureaucracies, standing armies, high finance and commercial engagement. Even before Rousseau, Fénelon's rural arcadia had been framed in such terms, while Boulainvilliers and the Paris *parlementaires* also drew fitfully on the classical republican repertory. It was Rousseau, however, who added new and explosive components to this approach. Civic virtue, he argued, was necessary to restrain the passions and appetites of humankind and to fireproof the polity against a drift towards despotism. Civic virtue was, moreover, inalienable: Rousseau took over and gave a democratic twist to the natural law tradition which had previously had an absolutist cast, and argued that attempts – whether by a king, a *parlement*, or any other political entity – to represent the interests of the citizen constituted an unwarranted infraction of a natural individual right inherent in citizenship. For Rousseau, civic rights were essentially anterior to rights grounded in legal entitlement. Whatever the legal precedents, political decision-making was only legitimate if it emanated from the collectivity of citizens and was expressed as an act of the general will of the whole community.

The general will as a disembodied state was more easily imaginable in small direct democracies such as ancient Sparta or the early days of the Roman Republic, when political decision-making could be made in a face-to-face context. Even here Rousseau made a distinction between the (rather inferior) majority of wills on one hand and on the other a 'general will' which represented the objective and moral best interest of the community as a whole, as judged by individuals making decisions purely according to their conscience. Rousseau's intense political pessimism saw 'no acceptable middle ground', he stated regretfully, between 'the most austere democracy' and (in a reference to Thomas Hobbes's apologia for a powerful centralized state) 'the most perfect hobbism . . . the most arbitrary of despotisms imaginable'.[81] His fatalistic political outlook about the present was, however, conjoined with an intense self-belief which was, as we have suggested, infectious amongst his readers.[82] The impact of his writing was to strengthen the existing classical republican strand of political thought, and to moralize, melodramatize and individualize it. In that it was impossible to imagine Rousseau's general will as an operational construct in a sprawling state like France (though Jean-Jacques himself did reflect on the rather different situations in Poland and Corsica, as well as keeping a torch lit for his native Geneva), conventional politics could only be blackened as the quest for civic virtue became an individual rather than a collective quest.

Rousseau's rejuvenation of the republican tradition stimulated other authors to imagine the transplantation of civic virtue into current political forms – in critical as well as constructive dialogue with his work. Mably and Morelly, for example, called for state regulation of wealth and the reimposition of sumptuary legislation as a means of levelling wealth. Other radicals looked for inspiration to England again – though, interestingly, neither to Voltaire's commercial nor Montesquieu's constitutional paragon, but rather to the seventeenth-century Commonwealthmen. Yet the resultant political writings remained intellectual curios rather than influential texts. Republican ideology had no obvious institutional focus and ideological carrier as was the case with the discourse of reason (the monarchy) and the discourse of law (the *parlements*). In some senses, however, that weakness was its strength, for it meant that it could insinuate itself into a wide range of situations and contexts.

Rousseau's strengthening of republicanism was achieved less through suggesting concrete means of political actualization (about which he remained consistently pessimistic) than through his providing a lodestar of individual civic virtue which made people feel differently about themselves and their political context. The individuals in question, moreover, were not – as in both the parlementary and Physiocratic versions of political change – property-owners. Any sentient being – any member, that is, of the bourgeois public sphere – could feel interpellated by Rousseau's stirring invocation of civic virtue.

Just as, around 1750, the *Encyclopédie* seemed to be marking a new crystallization of ways of understanding and acting upon society in the interests of all based on the use of human reason, the field of reason, we are suggesting, began to fragment and fissure along a number of divergent tracks. Politics felt different after mid-century because of the growing influence of men of letters and writers who subscribed to the light of reason. But that influence was thrown behind a wide range of scenarios and strategies and pointed in no single direction. There was certainly no incrementally rising tide of reason in the years leading from 1750 through to 1789: different fractions within the philosophical movement faded into and out of the complex and evolving landscape of the Bourbon polity; certain ministries responded to parts of the movement, while others ignored them altogether. The *philosophes* offered recipes for change, but those recipes drew on pre-existing political problems and dilemmas – even if governments felt under no constraint to cook by them.

What did, however, have a real impact on the political map after 1750 was the way this complex ensemble of debates and arguments was projected on to the screen of a burgeoning public sphere. Louis XIV and Cardinal Fleury had been past masters of political manipulation of the public, as we have suggested, while the invocation of the public in political argument was a rhetorical strategy which had pre-dated Demosthenes and had been given a fresh lease of life under the Regency. Yet, as we shall see, after around 1750 – starting with disputes over Jansenism and then over the difficult issue of popularizing an unsuccessful war – there was a growing tendency for government to take its cause more systematically out on to the public sphere on which the *philosophes* and men of letters had established their pitch. This made the old government strategies of regarding all politics as essentially 'the king's secret' or else commanding silence through religious injunction seem hopelessly archaic. In addition, the quest for public justification transmuted almost insensibly into a stress on 'public opinion' – what, tangibly, ordinary citizens thought, said and (most important of all) printed – as the impeccable and objective source of political legitimacy.

It would be in prison, facing certain death at the height of the Terror in 1794, that the latterday *philosophe* the marquis de Condorcet would pen his *Esquisse d'un tableau historique des progrès de l'esprit humain* ('Sketch of a Historical Account of the Progress of the Human Mind'), which revealed an irrefragable confidence in the onward and upward march of humanity, guided by reason. With fond hindsight, he spied the gradual emergence during the Enlightenment of public opinion as 'a tribunal, independent of all human coercion, which favours reason and justice, a tribunal whose scrutiny it is difficult to elude, and whose verdict it is impossible to evade'.[83] This phenomenon had started to occur well before it was fully theorized: as late as 1766, the *Encyclopédie*'s entry on 'opinion' reflected earlier usage, defining opinion as 'belief based on probable motive or a doubtful or uncertain mental judgement', and then again as 'a feeble and imperfect light which reveals things only by conjecture, leaving them always in uncertainty and doubt'.[84] Yet by then, as we shall see, the appeal to a public opinion viewed as a kind of moral highest common denominator cancelling out the partiality of individual views was well on the way to becoming a staple of political argumentation not only by men of letters but also by *parlementaires*, ministers and government propagandists.

The change in the feel of politics from mid-century onwards was not just about the entry of a new, 'virtual' reality, namely, public opinion, into the field of political argument. What also counted was the growth in the sociological referent behind that linguistic marker. The public – ignored by the Burgundy circle, but apostrophized by the legitimized princes in the 1710s and by the Figurist Jansenists – now had an immeasurably broader social outreach.[85] Symptomatically, moreover, political forms and genres also evolved so as to bring within the aegis of public opinion the middling and elite membership of the bourgeois public sphere. Under the rules of the political game that was evolving, the arguments which played best in the court of public opinion were those which this kind of audience already took pleasure in digesting as a leisure pursuit. Thus, the love of travel literature, nature writing and fictional depictions of faraway places encouraged men of letters to use the utopia as means of getting their message across – especially, in Montesquieu's *Persian Letters* or Mercier's runaway best-seller 2440 (1771), where the 'exotic' location visited by aliens was in essence a rational version of eighteenth-century Paris. The allegorical reading which these texts encouraged marked their authors' wish to protect themselves against the censor, but also showed a confidence in the capacity of that audience to understand the character of political coding. The same was true of another enormously influential kind of political text, the legal brief, or *mémoire judiciaire*, which from mid-century onwards utilized the sentimental repertoire of Rousseau's lachrymose fictions, the theatre's 'bourgeois dramas' and Greuze's melodramatic domestic paintings to fashion powerful rhetorical arguments about abuses of power. Writers also exploited the niche market for pornography to develop a highly dangerous but also very remunerative genre of political pornography, satirizing the royal family's sexual high jinks (or, as was to be the case for Louis XVI, his lack of them).[86]

Politics from mid-century onwards were increasingly modified so as to cater for tastes developed out in the public sphere. And it was on that public sphere that the Enlightenment showed itself to be more pluralistic, more divided, more anxiously troubled and more reflective of existing political divisions and dilemmas than the brash unitary confidence of the moment of the *Encyclopédie* had suggested.

6

Forestalling Deluge (1756–70)

A) DAMIENS'S EPIPHANY

On the freezing evening of 5 January 1757, the eve of the Epiphany, *la fête des Rois*, Louis XV suffered an assassination attempt. He was leaving Versailles to return to the Trianon after paying a visit to his influenza-stricken daughter, Madame Victoire. As he descended the palace steps to join his carriage, a figure clad in riding-coat and hat muscled past the Swiss Guards and stabbed him in the side. Bringing his hand to his side and seeing blood, Louis exclaimed, 'Someone has touched me.' Then, spotting the lowering figure of his assassin wiping his knife-blade, he ordered, 'Arrest him and do him no harm.' Louis was bundled upstairs, and dutifully acted out the role of dying monarch, summoning his Jesuit confessor, entrusting power to the Dauphin, and making public amends to his wife and daughters for his scandalous life.

Then the surgeons discovered the wound was not life-threatening.

The chance for crying *'Vive le Roi!'* for *le Bien-Aimé* was still there, but few found it worthwhile to make the effort. Courtiers felt that Louis was making more of the incident than it deserved, and the episode caused little concern (or even interest) in Paris.

The would-be royal assassin, who spent his Epiphany having the soles of his feet burned in torture under the accommodating eye of 'Iron Head' Machault, was an unemployed, forty-something domestic servant originally from the Arras region called François Damiens. He had, it seemed, used the shorter, three-inch penknife blade on his weapon, and this, and the heavy muffling the king had worn to keep out the cold, made the blow between the king's ribs cause little more than a flesh wound. Throughout his interrogations and trial, Damiens gave the impression of being a loner, who had acted out of his own, rather confused motives. Yet if he was a nobody, he was, as Dale Van Kley has noted, 'a nobody not unknown by some pretty important somebodies'.[1] His career as a servant had taken him through a wide range of noble households, including those of several Jansenist members of the Paris Parlement, where he had observed and listened enough to develop a sense of 'religion' which he cited as his main motive in making the attack. He had been moved to act, he elaborated, by royal taxes and the misery of the people; he did not seek to kill the king but to 'touch' him (an ironic reversal of the Royal Touch, from which the king had long desisted), so as 'to prompt him to restore all things to order and tranquillity in his states'.[2] Nobody could quite believe he was not a tool of faction. The Parlement and the Jansenists claimed that he had been put up to it by the Jesuits (who had supplied Ravaillac, the murderer of Henry IV in 1610); while just about everyone else thought that the finger of blame pointed at the pro-Jansenist *parlementaires* in whose homes Damiens had devised his odd exercise in political bargaining by assassination attempt.

All this was intensely embarrassing for the Paris Parlement, which in January 1757 was in the midst of a stand-off with the government – the second major political crisis in which it had become embroiled in the 1750s. The roots of these crises – in 1752–4, then 1756–7 – lay in the ongoing and venomous atmosphere in church–state relations caused by the so-called *billets de confession* issue. Christophe de Beaumont, appointed archbishop of Paris in 1746, had launched a spirited attack on Jansenism in his diocese, culminating in his orders for parish priests to refuse the sacrament of the last rites to any individual who failed to produce a *billet de confession*, that is, a notice of spiritual orthodoxy signed by a priest who had publicly subscribed to the Unigenitus bull. The Parlement objected to this refusal of sacraments, on the grounds that it offended individuals, threatened public disorder and implied that the church rather than the law had final say over matters of conscience and law. The magistrates' opinion found favour with a majority of the Parisian population – including Damiens, who claimed that he had formed his plan to attack the king at 'the time of the first refusals [of sacraments] by the archbishop'.[3] Following an incident in March 1752 in which a particularly devout and popular Parisian priest called Lemerre was denied the last rites by his confessor, the Parlement weighed in, condemning outright the practice of *billets de confession*, and on 18

April it issued an *arrêt* which prohibited their use within the city. The crown scolded the *parlementaires* for overstepping the line between the temporal and the spiritual arms, and decreed silence on all Unigenitus issues – that favoured procrastinatory, Fleuryite response – while the king awaited the report of a special royal commission established to examine the question. Silence, as Fleury had well known, however, needed to be managed: it never happened of its own accord, as the government now appeared to believe. Tension soon built up with a string of sacrament refusal cases, not simply in Paris but also in other northern dioceses under the jurisdiction of the Parlement. In December 1752, the latter struck back against archbishop Beaumont, ordering the seizure of his property and inviting the peers of the realm to join them in his impeachment. When the king blocked this step, issuing Letters Patent warning the Parlement off, the latter reacted by drawing up Grand Remonstrances (*grandes remontrances*) to justify their position.

The quasi-contractualist logic of the Grand Remonstrances – 'subjects owe their ruler devotion and obedience', the text ran, '[and] the ruler owes his subjects protection and defence'[4] – ensured the king's stern rebuff. Faced with deadlock, the Parlement voted, on 5 May 1753, for the suspension of its normal services. The government acted with a *coup de force*, exiling individual *parlementaires* to cities and places of confinement all over France, then transferring to Pontoise the Parlement's most senior arm, the Grande Chambre (and subsequently exiling it to Soissons). In this game of bluff and counter-bluff, the *parlementaires* calculated that their absence – which entailed much of the country being without an appellate jurisdiction – would force the government to treat for terms. Yet ministers only tightened the screw, establishing a handpicked 'Royal Chamber' in September 1753 to attend to judicial business usually handled by the Parlement. Subaltern courts recognized the new body – but did little business with it. In fact, the king's treatment of the Paris Parlement stimulated a nationwide support campaign on the magistrates' behalf involving the important Paris Châtelet court and a number of provincial *parlements*. Eventually, on 2 September 1754, following negotiations brokered by the prince de Conti, the king recalled the Parlement and reissued a Law of Silence, enjoining all parties to the dispute to refrain from discussion of the refusal of the sacraments.

The government's attempts to resolve the conflicting interests of church and Parlement in the 1752–4 crisis were short-lived, not least because the Law of Silence accorded the Parlement an important policing role, which the truculent *parlementaires* gleefully deployed against the archbishop. When in early December Beaumont publicly approved a refusal of the sacraments, they forced him into exile forthwith, and followed this up by issuing a decree on 18 March 1755 denying the Unigenitus bull the character of a rule of faith. The government proscribed this decree, quietly beginning negotiations with pope Benedict XIV, through the careful diplomacy of the comte de Stainville (future duc de Choiseul), to secure a papal ruling which could defuse the situation. The Parlement, however, was growing boisterous over other matters too. It framed a hostile response to royal attempts in 1755 to give the docile Grand Conseil court powers of enacting legislation without the endorsement of the Parlement – a move which the latter feared was the thin end of a wedge aimed at reducing its powers. And it was unprecedentedly critical of the government's tax measures to finance the incipient war against Prussia and England. When the country was faced by war, the Parlement usually passed such measures unopposed. Yet in July 1756, it remonstrated pointedly, and was only brought to heel by a royal *lit de justice* on 21 August forcing the financial edicts through.

The arrival from Rome in October 1756 of the papal encyclical, *Ex Omnibus*, on the refusal of sacraments issue only worsened matters, triggering the second major political crisis of the 1750s. Paradoxically, the pope's ruling largely endorsed the view of the Parlement over *billets de confession*, envisaging the refusal of sacraments only in the outlandish circumstances of recalcitrant sinners. This demobilized the posture of Beaumont and the *dévot* interest. Yet even this was not good enough for the Parlement. The magistrates took umbrage less over the content of the encyclical than over the way in which the crown seemed to be implementing it within France without referring the document, in true Gallican spirit, for parlementary ratification.

The Parlement's decision on 7 December 1756 to outlaw the papal encyclical led court factions marshalled by Keeper of the Seals Machault to spur the king into radical action. Silencing the Parlement would help bring religious peace and also mute criticism of the government's financial policies. Consequently, on 13 December, Louis held a *lit de justice* in the Parlement to enforce registration of an 'Edict of Discipline' (dated 10 December): the gist of the *Ex Omnibus* encyclical was enacted;

the powers of the Parlement to remonstrate were more carefully regulated; the institution's authority to interrupt the proceedings of justice and to create political protest were limited; organizational changes increased the power of senior magistrates at the expense of the more radical younger ones, known as the *zélés* ('the zealous'); and two chambers of the Parlement – approximately ninety posts out of the full parlementary contingent of around 500 posts – were abolished. The latter reduction was not necessarily unpopular, since the price of office within the Parlement had been falling (possibly because of the reduction in the amount of judicial business the court handled) and so the suppression could have boosted office prices and protected magistrates' investment. In this particular context, however, the parlementaires saw in the Edict of Discipline only a concerted effort to reduce their power, combined with a victory for Beaumont and his minions. With the judicial strike now made illegal, some 140 magistrates resigned their offices.

Damiens's Epiphany gesture in January 1757 thus struck in the midst of a severe and multi-layered political crisis. The latter's resolution was consequently complicated by the fact that the Parlement, the focus of opposition to the crown, was also trying (and would eventually convict) the would-be king-killer. The legal process became a show-trial. Though collectively engaged in a political stand-off with the king, the magistrates protested their eternal loyalty and their horror at the acts of the hapless regicide. The presence at the trial of the prince de Conti – seemingly fishing in troubled waters – further complicated its character. Ultra-loyalist sentiments also served to divert attention away from evidence which highlighted the role of parlementary opposition in the formulation of Damiens's crazed plans. Official accounts invariably skated over the turbulent political context in which the act had occurred, yet the Parisian chronicler Barbier was not alone in thinking that Damiens's act had its origins in 'the Jansenist system', and, 'the impression with which this party has affected the public and troubled people's minds'.[5]

Damiens played out his part as ceremonial fall-guy in the horrifying act of his execution in March 1757 on the Place de Grève in Paris, which the Parlement had insisted should replicate that of his more effective predecessor, Ravaillac, assassin of Henry IV. An ornate set of symbolically retaliatory tortures – burnings, rippings of flesh, breaking of bones – proceeded with quasi-liturgical exactitude, climaxing in the efforts of four champing horses to pull Damiens's limbs out from his body (in a gruesome twist, his body stubbornly refused to be depieced and had to be further chopped and battered by public executioner Sanson).[6] This act of judicial theatre – played out before a full and appreciative crowd – symbolically countered the would-be assassin's pathetic act of violence by an overpowering expression of the coercive force of the wounded sovereign. Designed by the Parlement, the grisly *mise-en-scène*, which horrified many *philosophes*, was intended to wipe the Parlement's slate clean of any putative stain of anti-monarchism.

Diderot once summed up the political tactics of the Parlement as being 'for the king against the king', and this was certainly the case over the Damiens trial and execution.[7] There were pragmatic reasons for an oblique stance under an absolute monarchy, in which disloyalty and opposition were only a hair's breadth away from outright treason, and where subservient mouthings of absolutist maxims consequently served as self-protection. Beneath the formalities, however, the bases of a much more formidable political opposition were evolving in the 1750s whose tenets countered those customarily embodied in absolutist theory. At the heart of the revitalized parlementary discourse was a concern to restrict the prerogatives of royal authority save when these were grounded in the nation's fundamental laws whose custodian the Parlement claimed to be. Over and against absolutist dogma's emphasis on the indivisibility of royal sovereignty, lodged in the ruler's corporeal frame, the parlementaires now argued that political harmony depended on the cooperation of 'sovereign authority, the law and the ministers of the law'. '[T]he king, the laws and the magistrates', they continued, 'are one, an indivisible whole.'[8] The magistrates highlighted the primacy of law, rather than that of the king himself, deploying historical arguments which foregrounded the ancient constitution in ways evoked by Boulainvilliers and Montesquieu, and now crystallized in the *Lettres historiques sur les fonctions essentielles du Parlement* ('Historical Letters on the Essential Functions of the Parlement'), penned in 1753 by the crypto-convulsionary barrister Louis-Adrien Le Paige. Drawing on punctilious archival research, and deploying arguments which had surfaced occasionally in the past at moments of crown–Parlement dispute, Le Paige established a legitimation for the Parlement's authority which was part history, part romantic fiction, and part political wishful thinking. The *parlements*, it was claimed, were as ancient as – indeed, even more ancient than – the monarchy, for they originated in the Germanic assemblies described by Frankish chroniclers as forming the basis of Merovingian political culture. The authority of the Parlement in 1753 was, for Le Paige, 'precisely what it was in the time of Clovis', namely 'a wall of bronze' against any diminution of the force of law.[9] 'Sire,' the Parlement had remonstrated in 1755 over the Grand Conseil issue, 'for the thirteen hundred years that the monarchy has existed your parlement, under a variety of denominations, has always formed the same tribunal and exercises the same functions within the state.'[10] The bewigged and red-robed *parlementaires*, sage advisers to Louis XV, were thus consubstantial with Clovis's hairy-chested sixth-century Merovingian warriors forming the 'Court of France' on the *Champ de Mars*.

The Parlement thus increasingly prided itself on being the 'depository of the laws', the protector of constitutional rectitude. This formulation, as we have seen,[11] with its strong link to the theological language of Figurism, had crystallized in the parlementary disputes over Jansenism in 1730–32, and it had received further endorsement from Montesquieu's *De l'Esprit des lois*, published in 1748. Given the inconstancy of monarchs and aristocrats, the Bordeaux *parlementaire-philosophe* had argued, a 'depository of the laws is necessary . . . There must be a body which ensures that the laws come forth from the dust in which they lie buried.'[12] Le Paige now pushed this doctrine even further: the Parlement was the 'depository of the laws', embodying 'the primitive and essential constitution' of the nation in much the same way that he saw the Jansenist sect to which he belonged as the heir of the early church and 'depository of truth' in a persecuting world.

There were thus Jansenist fingerprints all over the contestatory language of opposition which the Parlement developed in the 1750s. As the marquis d'Argenson noted, moreover, the Parlement's arguments implying that 'the nation is above kings just as the universal church is above the pope' had a quasi-conciliarist ring to them.[13] The Parlement was not simply representing the laws to the king, but also seemed to imply that they rather than the monarch now represented the body of the 'nation'. The latter term (like 'state'), d'Argenson noted, '[had] never [been] uttered under Louis XIV' [but] was now replacing the more archaic 'subjects' or 'peoples' in parlementary discourse.[14] As the remonstrances of the Rennes Parlement put it in early 1757, 'the Parlement only ever speaks to the nation in the name of the king, and similarly, it only addresses its king in the name of the nation. The remonstrances are the remonstrances of the nation.'[15] This rhetorical polarization of 'king' and 'nation' – with the parlements purporting to play a vital mediatory role – was formally antithetical to the Bourbon view that state and nation were embodied in the corporeal frame of the ruler.

After the débâcle of the Convulsionary episode, Jansenists remaining associated with the Parlement had sought integration and the pursuit of their spiritual goals by tying their religious arguments even more tightly into the jurisdictional claims of the court. Their numbers were comparatively small – maybe only a score of the 250 of so magistrates normally involved in parlementary business in the 1750s were committed Jansenists. These *zélés* owed their impact, first, to their cooperation with another energetic minority of roughly the same size comprising the Jansenist barristers led by Le Paige, and, second, to the extraordinary energy they displayed. Besides concerting parlementary strategy and seeking to squeeze their religious demands within the jurisdictional corsets of their more sedate fellow *parlementaires*, these groupings were also responsible for spreading the Parlement's line of arguments outside Paris. This development was a particular feature of the crises of the mid-1750s. One of the jurisdictional arguments on which Le Paige and others insisted was that the original Frankish assemblies of which the Parlement was continuator had been unjustly subdivided in the past. In consequence, all the *parlements* really formed elements (or *classes*) of the same body – 'the diverse classes of a single and unique *parlement*, the various members of a single and unique body, animated by the same spirit, nourished in the same principles and concerned with the same object', as parlementary remonstrances put it in 1756.[16] The idea of the 'union of classes' (*union des classes*) justified a more rumbustious and daring involvement of provincial *parlements* in political disputes than at any time since the Fronde of 1648–53. In 1753–4, the Parlements of Aix, Bordeaux, Rennes and Rouen remonstrated in support of the exiled Paris institution. Chancellor Lamoignon responded by convoking groups from the protesting institutions for formal admonition – yet the provincial magistrates took advantage of their visit to the capital to rub shoulders and develop solidarity with the barristers and other supporters of their Parisian *confrères*. By the mid-1750s, the Parlements of Toulouse, Bordeaux, Metz, Grenoble and Aix were invoking Frankish history to legitimize their remonstrances in support of the Paris Parlement, while the Rennes court was developing a jurisprudence grounded in the laws of the reigns of Charlemagne and Louis the Pious. Mutual support by the *parlements* extended to financial as well as religious and jurisdictional issues.

Important elements in the shift in political culture occurring in the 1750s were the strong and increasingly concerted provincial dimension to parlementary politics and the crystallization of fragments of political arguments, both old and new, both Jansenist and parlementary, into a resilient body of oppositional discourse. With the growing public sphere acting as voice-box, languages of contestation resonated more widely and more subversively than at any time in the century. In 1714, royal propagandist Jean-Nicolas Moreau noted, the Jansenist issue had simply been 'a matter of knowing whether Father Quesnel had explained the nature and effects of grace in a very devout and rather boring book'. By the 1750s, at issue was '[the] matter of knowing whether the king was master in his realm'.[17] The question was all the more pressing, moreover, in that the state had in 1756 embarked on a European, and global, war.

Problems were exacerbated by a shortage of political management skills at the very top of the political tree. Consistency in government policy was undermined by the king's personal mixture of authoritarianism and spiritual contrition which seemed to make it difficult for him to get a grip on events. As even the scourge of anti-Jansenism, Le Paige, quizzically noted, the Royal Council was 'sometimes for the clergy, sometimes for the Parlement and sometimes in between'.[18] Without Fleury to depend on, the king proved no abler at controlling court faction than at managing the *parlements*. His backing-down from confrontation with the church over the *vingtième* in the early 1750s left his valiant Controller-General, Machault, very much a lame duck. Machault lingered on, for Louis XV trusted him, but in a ministerial reshuffle in mid-1754, he exchanged the post of Controller-General for the Secretaryship of State for the Navy (though he also was retained as Keeper of the Seals). With 'Iron Head' increasingly a political lightweight, destabilizing factional power-struggles started to re-emerge. The *dévots*, grouped around the queen and the dauphin, with War Minister d'Argenson and a majority of the episcopacy behind them, formed an unofficial opposition, which, though chastened by Beaumont's routing in the *billets de confessions* issue, still launched numerous attacks on the faction focused around Madame de Pompadour, whose influence was probably stronger in the mid- and late 1750s than at any other time.

Her opponents portrayed her as keeping the government together by ceaseless patronage, but this was only one weapon in her armoury. Despite her very real political skills, on which Louis was heavily dependent, her status as royal mistress restricted what she could achieve.

Just when Louis needed support from the Parlement, moreover, he alienated the body, exiling sixteen magistrates, on 27 January 1757, with an imperiousness which set the whole institution against him. He followed this on 1 February 1757, by dismissing Machault, reputed framer of the 1756 Edict of Discipline, and a Pompadour man who had blotted his copybook with the mistress by suggesting she leave court at the time of Damiens's assassination attempt. At the same time – as if every tit should have its tat – the experienced *dévot* War Minister, d'Argenson, was also dismissed. The ministers who took their place were, moreover, nonentities – and only moderately competent nonentities to boot. In the event, Madame de Pompadour filled the policy void, promoting the cause of one of her protégés, the abbé de Bernis, a key figure in government since his role as architect of the Diplomatic Revolution of 1756, which, as we shall see, had been the prelude to the outbreak of war.[19] Trusted by the church, Bernis also had the sense to realize that the Parlement needed mollifying if it was to be prevented from becoming a political obstacle to the financing of the war. Fleury-like, he worked assiduously behind the scenes to find a compromise, building up a pro-government faction – or *parti ministériel* – in the Parlement, and then finally persuading the king in September 1757 to decree that the Edict of Discipline should not be implemented.

Bernis's adroit political skills temporarily appeased the Parlement. Yet within weeks the government found itself in the midst of a profound political crisis, though one with military rather than parlementary roots: on 5 November 1757, Frederick II of Prussia inflicted on French forces in the battle of Rossbach one of their severest defeats in the eighteenth century, calling into question the military substance of the state and seeming to constitute, for the anxious marquis de Caraman, 'the signal for the approaching destruction of our monarchy'.[20]

B) THINGS FALL APART:
THE SEVEN YEARS WAR

'Après nous, le déluge.'

Madame de Pompadour's notorious remark – which historians have been perhaps too quick to see as a prophecy of 1789 – is alleged to have been uttered in 1757, one of the most depressing years in the reign of a depressive monarch. The Damiens episode had left deeper scars on the king's psyche than on his body – contemporaries noted the prevalence of black-dog moods, and an English secret intelligence source even suggested, in a coded report to London in August of that year, that Louis '[had] lately frequently burst into tears; and at times discovered an inclination to resign the crown'.[21] Maybe the English spy was taking too seriously royal expressions of weariness with the strains of office, which were not infrequent. Yet the circumstances in which the king found himself in that year were particularly grim – and would deteriorate. The severe domestic difficulties which the government had been having were overlaid by engagement in a war which – as the Rossbach defeat highlighted – humiliated the régime and presented a tough challenge which would have made rulers far abler than Louis XV flinch.

The gloom of 1757 was all the gloomier for contrasting with the rather hopeful outset to the war the year before, following a startling realignment of international relations in a process of alliance reversals which historians term the Diplomatic Revolution. The latter's most striking feature consisted of France's alliance with the Austrian Habsburgs, who had been the almost uninterrupted target of French aggression for more than two centuries. The initiative behind the shift came from Vienna, and in particular from the Austrian statesman Kaunitz, who from 1749 estimated that alliance with France offered the best chance for Austria to regain Silesia, lost to Frederick II's Prussia in the War of Austrian Succession. The task of winning over Maria Theresa to the idea was a long one, and one which Kaunitz refined in his spell as Austrian ambassador in Versailles between 1750 and 1753. It was his replacement, Starhemberg, who in 1755 made a secret approach from the Empress to Louis XV, symptomatically routed via Madame Pompadour. An initially sceptical Louis XV put Pompadour's protégé, Bernis, on to the case. Working in total secrecy, Bernis and Starhemberg met in sundry shifting locations around Bellevue, Madame Pompadour's residence. Their negotiations were given added pertinence by the Westminster convention in March 1756 between England and France's erstwhile ally, Prussia. Despite Frederick II of Prussia's protestations that he was 'the most faithful, most zealous and most grateful ally in the world',[22] he had proved unreliable to France. An Anglo-Russian convention of 1755 whereby the Russians agreed to provide troops on England's side if Hanover were subject to foreign aggression had made him calculate that he had much to gain from a mutual guarantee of possessions with the English.

Though the public disclosure of the First Treaty of Versailles in May 1756 linking France and Austria in formal alliance caused consternation and amazement, this complete break with hallowed diplomatic tradition made a good deal of sense. Austria was no longer the all-threatening, would-be hegemonic power of yore. It had failed to turn the Holy Roman Empire into a unitary Habsburg state. The War of Austrian Succession had shown that the customary theatres of Franco–Austrian conflict – the Low Countries and northern Italy – were no longer target zones for Austrian expansion, and that France seemed 'satisfied'[23] with what it had. Once-Habsburg Spain was in the hands of a Bourbon too, so that French fears of encirclement seemed otiose. The Habsburgs were now primarily concerned to consolidate their possessions in south-east Europe and to win back Silesia. France, for its part, had reasons to value Habsburg friendship. Fleury had correctly grasped the wisdom of forestalling possible Austrian *revanchisme* over Lorraine, while France's biggest international problems emanated from England, its commercial and colonial rival on the global stage. Alliance with Austria could thus herald an era of continental peace and allow France to concentrate on its global commitments against an England with which it was already virtually at war in North America and India, and which it had just deprived of its main continental ally. Domestically, alliance with another great Catholic power would palliate the discontent of parts of the *dévot* faction. All this could only be achieved, however, if France resisted Austria's gung-ho enthusiasm to lead an assault on Prussia to get Silesia back. The Versailles Treaty was therefore a defensive alliance, which neutralized the Low Countries, while also ruling out Austrian aid for France in the Americas. It was followed by the decision of Russia – infuriated by the Convention of Westminster – to break with the English and conclude an offensive alliance with Austria, and to seek France's friendship.

The odds had stacked up curiously: Catholic Europe seemed to be opposed to the Protestant powers of England and Prussia. It was less piety than pragmatism, however, which led Frederick II, fearing encirclement by Austria and Russia, and keen to get his retaliation in first, to invade Saxony in August 1756 as a stepping stone towards Austrian Bohemia. This brought France into the fray on the side of its Habsburg ally. It was anticipated that war would be short and sweet: Prussia had a strong army and a brilliant commander, in the person of Frederick, but seemed very light on the scales against the combined military forces of France, Austria and Russia. With only 'perfidious Albion' as aide, Prussia's 3.6 million inhabitants seemed a poor match for the 70 million to be found in the domains of the allies. Seeking a swift termination of continental struggle, France threw money at the war effort: there were big subsidies for Russia, Sweden and Saxony, while a second Treaty of Versailles promised larger subsidies to Austria plus more than 100,000 men in armed support, in return for various gains and rearrangements in the Low Countries. Early campaign successes in Germany set Prussian forces on the defensive, while the conflict with England also opened very promisingly, and looked likely to redress the considerable indignities the French had suffered at English hands over the two previous years.[24] England's attempts to bring land war to the continent failed – assaults and attempted landings in Normandy and Brittany were repulsed – and in May 1756, the French seized Minorca, which had been in English hands since the Peace of Utrecht. The government followed up by negotiating with Genoa the right to establish naval and military outposts on Corsica. In the Americas, the French commander, Montcalm, deployed his meagre military forces effectively alongside settlers and Indian tribesmen, completing a bad year for the English.

1757 could be said to have been the year that things came apart for France – had things not got worse in 1758 and worse still in 1759. Frederick II transformed the character of the war, with a brace of brilliant victories in lower Germany: at Rossbach over French and imperial forces on 5 November, and at Leuthen over the Austrians on 5 December. Rossbach was immediately perceived in France as a most terrible humiliation. 'The King has the worst infantry under the sun,' was the conclusion of the veteran comte de Saint-Germain, while the army's leadership was pilloried even more viciously.[25] With far fewer troops at his disposal, Frederick had out-generaled and out-manoeuvred the flower of Austro–French chivalry – and out-strategized it too, for the victory consolidated Prussia's links with England and called into question the military wisdom of the Franco–Austrian alliance.

So powerful was the blow to French morale that there was some thought of moving swiftly to sue for peace. The government was in too deep, however, to make that a viable option. Ominously, the Austrian compulsion to regain Silesia seemed to be dictating the way forward. Although sheer strength of numbers over Prussia made it seem that Austro–French victory could not be far away, lack of military co-ordination, plus some pretty poor generalship (which the brilliance of Frederick II made all the more glaring) consistently prevented this. Over the next years, Frederick would lose more battles than he won, as each campaigning season the allied forces swept down on him from two directions, east and west. Yet he proved able to achieve crucial victories at key moments over his numerous foes, keeping Prussia in the game as all the combatants fought themselves to a standstill.

The single-minded focus on the armed struggle which Frederick exemplified was not matched in France. Indeed, even in 1757 it had become apparent that there were still major problems in the formation of strategy at the heart of government. Besides the dismissal of Machault and d'Argenson, the retirement in 1756 of the aged Noailles from the Council of State removed an experienced hand. In swift succession there followed the defection of one of the policy advisers on whom the depression-prone and secrecy-obsessed Louis XV had most relied, namely, his cousin, the prince de Conti. Meeting regularly in secret since the early 1740s, Louis and Conti had developed a parallel diplomacy to state international strategy, the so-called *Secret du Roi*, focused initially around moves to have Conti elected king of Poland. Conti had never got on with Madame de Pompadour, however, and relations between the two worsened as the mistress consolidated her authority.

The Diplomatic Revolution came as a severe shock to Conti, who had been left out of the information loop. The refusal of the king (or was it Pompadour?) to allow him either continuing participation in the *Secret du Roi* or a compensatory military command threw him among the regime's malcontents. 'The crown belongs to us all,' he once insouciantly remarked of the Princes of the Blood. 'Our most senior member wears it.'[26] This dynastic stirrer was soon shaping up as unreconstructed Frondeur, creating a political bloc of support in ways which emulated the conduct of his eminent forebears who had participated in the 1648 Fronde. He had developed links to the Paris Parlement through the crises of the mid-1750s, and the Parlement's principal apologist, Le Paige, after 1756 was working out under Conti's wing in the Temple precincts, a safe haven from direct police censorship. The prince made the Parlement's causes his own: he supported the right of the magistrates to invite the dukes and peers to their meetings in 1755, and he took a wilfully prominent role in the trial of Damiens. As Pompadour's links with the *philosophes* became less intense, Conti developed good relations with them (notably with Voltaire, Diderot and Rousseau) and he also dabbled in freemasonry. In 1757, moreover, rumours reached the king's ears that Conti was seeking to profit from Louis's post-Damiens depression to put together plans for Protestant revolt conjoined with an English landing in western France. The Diplomatic Revolution had been a blow to 'New Convert' hopes for greater religious toleration, for by 1757 the war was taking on the aspect, as the marquis d'Argenson put it, of 'a general crusade of the Catholic party against the Protestants in Europe' (adding, in a sly reference to France's heavy commitment to financial subsidies, 'with France as treasurer').[27] Conti's plans for revolt – if plans there were – came to nothing, but the king redoubled his distance from his erstwhile confidant.

The passage of Conti into oppositional politics – where he remained, on and off, down to his death in 1776 – was a severe blow, all the more so with the state at war, and in a condition of perpetual governmental crisis, with ministers being changed as rapidly as scenery at the opera.[28] The ministerial replacements for Machault and d'Argenson lasted only a year: the War Ministry passed through the hands of the marquis de Paulmy to the ageing Belle-Isle in 1758, while at the Navy Office, Machault's successor, Peyrenc de Moras, was succeeded in turn by the marquis de Massiac, then Pompadour's protégé, Berryer. There were no fewer than five incumbents of the crucial post of Controller-General between 1754 and November 1759, a rate of turnover partly due to the sheer incapacity for the job of a number of the incumbents. The most durable figure in power was one of the least talented – Chancellor Lamoignon, widely viewed as less animated than Vaucanson's famous automata which were being shown at court around this time.

Faction and royal whim were instrumental in the fall from power of Bernis, the figure who represented a measure of continuity in the mid-1750s and who had gamely tried to keep the ship of state afloat. The prestige which he had acquired first by orchestrating the Diplomatic Revolution, and then by defusing post-Damiens parlementary opposition led to his promotion to the Ministry of Foreign Affairs and membership of the Royal Council, then election to a cardinalcy. Yet he overplayed his hand. He formally resigned Foreign Affairs to the comte de Stainville in late 1758, offering the latter his continued service for relations with both the clergy and the Parlement, a role for which he had some flair. This was to raise the prospect of a duumvirate – 'two heads in the same hat', as Bernis quaintly put it.[29] The king, for his part, clearly felt one would do. Resistant since the death of Fleury to the idea of a principal minister, especially one who risked inspiring ministerial jealousies, the king abruptly dismissed Bernis from the State Council in December 1758 and exiled him from court. Fortunately for the monarchy, he now turned to the comte de Stainville, from 1758 duc de Choiseul, whom he appointed to the Foreign Affairs portfolio as Bernis's successor.

Choiseul entered a State Council which was relatively denuded of talent through deaths, political exile, and poor ministerial choices, and at a moment when the state's fortunes were in a singularly deep trough. A first step along the road to recovery was the rehabilitation of the appalling financial position in which the government found itself in the late 1750s. State finances had not been in bad shape at the outset of the war: Machault's *vingtième* had done a good job in bringing post-1748 debts under control, and, despite protests from the Parlement, a second *vingtième* was imposed in July 1756 for the duration of the war. From then onwards, the state looked to loans (and in particular the highly uneconomic life-annuity loans, or *rentes viagères*) rather than taxation, to finance the war. The cost of credit rose, moreover, the longer the war continued, and the more remote the prospect of a satisfactory peace became. It became apparent that the war was running at nearly twice the cost of its predecessor, the War of Austrian Succession. A state bankruptcy looked a real possibility. 'A government which is short of cash', the marquis de Mirabeau warned, 'abdicates legitimate authority and renounces its primordial essence.'[30] Desperate measures were consequently tried for these desperate times. In 1758, an annual 'free gift' (*don gratuit*) was imposed on all towns and bourgs for six years, yet the following year, the shortfall in government revenue was still some 200 million livres, roughly equivalent to one year's normal state revenue. In September of that year, the new Controller-General Silhouette tried a more radical approach. His composite plan for a 'General Subvention', which was forced through the Parlement by *lit de justice*, included the imposition of a third *vingtième*, and wide-ranging taxation on luxury items, from tobacco through to carriages, lackeys, wallpapers, silks and gold and silver plate. This atavistic act in what was an increasingly consumerist age[31] produced almost universal condemnation by the social and political elite. Louis tried to rally to his minister's support by sending court gold and silver plate to the mint – a grand, Louis-Quatorzian gesture which backfired spectacularly by frightening potential lenders to the state. The impending collapse of credit obliged Louis to sack Silhouette. The latter's successor, Bertin, dropped the taxes on luxury but salvaged what he could from the 'General Subvention', notably the third *vingtième* for the duration of the war. He also imposed a doubling of the *capitation* for individuals who were exempt from the *taille*. These measures rekindled the opposition of the *parlementaires*, who as *non-taillables* were personally affected by the measure.[32]

War prospects were poor. By aligning itself too closely for its own good to Silesia-obsessed Austria, France had failed to keep the fighting in Europe short. The perpetuation of campaigning in Germany with the commitment of more than 100,000 men plus high subsidies to allies made it difficult to divert funds to the global conflict with England. Despite the deceptively bright start in North America, French forces failed to stop the English from opening up the Saint Lawrence seaway through Louisbourg, which fell in 1758, and French fortresses along the Ohio river passed seriatim into English hands. It was a sign of desperation that Choiseul got the king to agree to the organization of an amphibious landing in England for 1759. Aimed to coincide with a Jacobite rising in Scotland, the scheme would, it was hoped, relieve pressure in North America and perhaps drive the English to the conference table. This was combined with a scaling-down of France's financial commitments to Austria in the third Treaty of Versailles in March 1759. The Treaty markedly reduced what France could expect to gain at the peace – but in the circumstances this was the least of the French worries. Lack of realism about the invasion scheme, however, was punished by crushing naval defeats which the Royal Navy meted out to the French Mediterranean fleet off Portugal in August and to the Brest fleet at Quiberon Bay in November. Hopes for invasion collapsed.

The Royal Navy ruled the waves. For the remainder of the war, it delivered reinforcements of supplies and men to give England local superiority in all global theatres of conflict. Even had they been able to afford it, or to organize with the zeal which Prime Minister William Pitt was displaying in England, the French were henceforth blocked from invading England and denied access to the extra-European world. French overseas commanders were consequently at a consistent disadvantage. In Canada, Montcalm's 3,000 men had defeated some 15,000 English troops at Fort Carillon in 1758, but given this kind of numerical imbalance it was asking too much to expect a string of victories. In September 1759, Quebec fell to armed assault by English forces under Wolfe comprising 76 vessels, 13,500 sailors and 9,000 soldiers. A year later it was the turn of Montreal, where 2,000 Frenchmen were outnumbered by 17,000 English troops. The situation was much the same at the other end of the world: 22,000 English troops besieged the French Governor Lally-Tollendal with 700 men under his command for some months at Pondicherry before the key Indian trading post fell in January 1761. Naval supremacy allowed the English to pick off other French outposts throughout the world, which started falling like plums into the English lap.

The efforts of Choiseul in particular to mitigate the scale of the disasters raining in on the Bourbon polity were serendipitously helped by dynastic changes in Europe's ruling houses. In 1759, Ferdinand VI of Spain died and was replaced by the more energetic Charles III, who was determined to counter the trading dominance which the English, through trade, force of arms and privateering, had achieved in the New World. Charles approached France for an alliance, which resulted in the second 'Family Compact' of August 1761 conjoining the Bourbons of France, Spain, Naples and Parma. Secret clauses committed Spain to join the war on France's side on 1 January 1762. The impact of this shift in the balance of forces was attenuated, however, by two factors. First, the English continued their rash of naval victories, taking the key Spanish centres at Havana in the Caribbean and Manila in the Philippines and thereby threatening the overall integrity of the Spanish empire; and second, a change of ruler in Russia made Frederick II's proverbial luck seem quasi-miraculous. In 1762, the Prussian ruler was given unlooked-for relief by the death of Empress Elisabeth of Russia and the succession of Peter III, a deranged Fredericophile, who immediately switched sides in the war, restoring Russian-occupied East Prussia to Frederick. By now, all parties to the conflict seemed to have reasons for ending it – even England, where the bellicose Pitt had been replaced by the more emollient Bute. Peace talks began in earnest in November 1762 and on 10 February 1763 produced the Treaty of Paris, followed five days later by the Treaty of Hubersburg ending the continental war.

The intervention of Spain in 1762 had changed the terms under which peace was agreed: difficult though it may be to imagine, peace conditions would probably have been even worse for France in 1761. On the bright side was France's retention of its main sugar-producing islands in the Caribbean (Saint-Domingue, Guadeloupe, Martinique). Among other small mercies for which the French could be grateful, the defeat had produced less genuine hardship within the country itself than many other wars: the campaigns had been conducted in Germany or in the wider world, so that the effects of warfare, though serious, were neither first-hand nor materially devastating, and left a decent margin for recovery. All the same, the 1763 peace was extremely punishing for France, which gained nothing in Europe for the expenditure of its men, money and efforts over seven years: the main clauses of the Treaty of Aix-la-Chapelle of 1748 were confirmed, with Silesia remaining in Prussian hands – and indeed Minorca passing back to the English. On the global stage, the scale of loss was huge and humiliating, worse even than Utrecht. With the exception of the tiny Saint Pierre et Miquelon islands, France lost all North American and Canadian possessions, merely retaining fishing rights off Newfoundland. Its Louisianan territories were given – seemingly in some kind of chivalrous family gesture – to Spain, to compensate the latter for the loss of Florida to the English. There were losses in the Caribbean too, while, with the exception of Gorée, Senegal passed out of French hands, and in India, France was cut back to five trading stations.

Some made light of the situation. The retention of the sugar islands more than compensated, in the eye of most contemporaries, for the loss of Louisiana, land of John Law's pipe-dreams, and of 'a few arpents of [Canadian] snow', as Voltaire put it in *Candide*. Yet most contemporaries adjudged the peace as massively humiliating for the institution of the monarchy, whose most cherished values and structures had been wounded. Its armies had been shown to be ineffectual, its navy of nugatory value. Its aristocratic officer corps had been exposed as weak, while its bureaucracy had been hampered by factional squabbles at the heart of government. Above all, the honour of the state – that indefinable entity with which Louis XV had proclaimed his magnanimity at Aix-la-Chapelle – had been as palpably compromised as at almost any moment in the annals of the monarchy.

The recovery of that honour would be the task that Choiseul assigned himself. Down to his fall from power in 1770, he would shuffle the key Foreign Affairs, Army and Navy portfolios in various combinations, building a wide power-base for his growing dominance. He needed to have his wits about him, for the political context in the 1760s was changing fast: respect for the king was at an all-time low; the prince de Conti was reopening dynastic politics; critical political discourses were evolving, notably in the Parlement, which questioned the customary values of absolutism; and a public sphere of debate and discussion had opened up on which the government was finding it difficult to put a lid.

Over the next years, Choiseul utilized his position at the heart of government to lead the state through a process of reform and restructuring in the wake of humiliating military defeat and political demoralization. In the event, his efforts would be crowned by success – but only subsequent to his removal from politics: the happy outcome for France of the American War of Independence would have been unthinkable without Choiseul's reforms.

C) CHOISEULIAN SCAPEGOATS: *DÉVOTS* AND JESUITS

Once upon a time, royal commands in a *lit de justice* had been regarded as non-negotiable. 'When the king is present, the magistrates [of the Parlement] have no power,' noted Loyseau, early theorist of Bourbon power, 'just as the sun extinguishes the stars.'[33] This was no longer the case – at least in the sublunary world. On 3 May 1763, Louis XV ceremoniously insisted on the registration of a package of financial edicts drawn up by Controller-General Bertin, originally decreed on 24 April, which aimed to redress the state's finances in the aftermath of the Seven

Years War. The measures decreed that the third *vingtième* established in 1760 and the doubling of the *capitation*, confirmed in 1761, should end in January 1764, but that the second wartime *vingtième* should be maintained for a further six years – well into time of peace. The urban *don gratuit* established in 1758 would also be continued for the same period. The package included a new stamp tax – the *centième denier* ('hundredth penny') – plus added indirect taxes. Plans were also announced for a cadastral survey which would allow a more equitable imposition of direct taxes. The latter measure – a perennial tax-payers' bogey – transformed a solid means of facing up to the state's financial problems into a surefire method of alienating parlementary and popular support.

The 3 May *lit de justice* was 'badly received by the entire public'.[34] That royal ceremonial was losing its entrancing power to command obedience was reflected in a current debate on this form of expression of the royal will. In 1756, arch-Jansenist publicist Le Paige produced, under cover of anonymity, a *pièce d'occasion*, the *Lettres sur les lits de justice*, which argued, on the basis of impressive antiquarian research, that the ceremony was in fact heir to ancient Frankish assemblies at which the Merovingian rulers had sought the advice and counsel of their subjects; only the passage of time and the workings of an indefinable 'despotism', he argued, had turned it into a purely ritualistic royal pronouncement. When the Parlement duly remonstrated about the *lit de justice* of 3 May, they complained not only about the content of the royal edict but also about the form of the ceremonial: authentic Frankish experience would have required that the views of the *parlementaires* were genuinely sought, and that the magistrates could intone their views out loud rather than being summoned to give a consensually deferential nod.

Following the principles of the *union des classes*, this kind of ceremonial contestation was also taking place within provincial *parlements*. Outside Paris, the *lit de justice* took the form of the king's personal representative (aristocratic provincial governor or lieutenant-general) reading the monarch's communication, which was supposed to be registered forthwith. By the early 1760s, this automatic response was eroding: parlementary stars were refusing to be eclipsed by rays of royal sunshine. From 1758, the Parlement at Besançon had been in conflict with government over the appointment of the Intendant of Franche-Comté, Bourgeois des Boynes, as its First President, and in 1760 there was a mass resignation of magistrates. Conciliation resolved the matter here, but further disputes blew up elsewhere in the provinces over the 1763 financial package. In Rouen and Toulouse, the efforts of the king's lieutenant-general to enforce the registration of the legislation by a *lit de justice* were rudely contested by the Norman and Languedocian *parlementaires*. In Rouen, the dispute led to the collective resignation of the magistrates, and in Toulouse to the enforced house arrest of the entire membership, while in Dauphiné related protests led to the exile of the Grenoble Parlement.

The development of new strategies of opposition thus coincided with the increasingly evident failure of royal ceremonial to work its sacral magic within the polity. The meaning of absolutist political practices was being subverted, as the state divested itself of some of the mystical vestments with which it had hitherto clothed itself (witness, for example, Louis's desisting from the Royal Touch). Indeed, the person of the monarch might seem less sacral than pathetic. Parisians, for example, had been both tickled and irritated by another recent royal ceremony, on 23 February 1763, at which – with the ink on the ignominious Treaty of Paris scarcely dry – a new equestrian statue of the monarch was put in place at the centre of the Place Louis XV (later, Place de la Révolution, then Place de la Concorde). In the worst catastrophes of war, Louis had not left Pompadour's side nor sundry mistresses' beds to go to the front, and his most bellicose act, as Barbier noted, had been hunting and killing roughly a thousand stags in the duration of the war.[35] This martial and equestrian representation was too much to stomach for many Parisians, who proffered ribald jokes about Louis being held up by four *grues* (cranes, but also whores) before being lowered gently down in place. The reports in the official state *Gazette* were, in contrast, widely acknowledged to be little more than fiction: they described 'celebrations' and 'great acclamations of joy on the part of a numberless multitude', whereas in fact the whole event had been washed out by a rainstorm.[36]

An additional blow to the sacral basis of absolutism was the developing campaign against the Jesuit Order. Spearhead of international Counter-Reformation, the Jesuits had also proved highly adept at acclimatizing to the specific character of the states in which they served. In France they proved an invaluable bulwark of the *dévot* connection at the heart of the state, and won the respect and support of much of the higher clergy, which had once been their severest critics. Their place near the heart of the polity made them a prime target for a renewed Jansenist campaign of denigration in which the *philosophe* movement also played a part.

Leading Jansenists had been working behind the scenes in Rome to persuade Pope Benedict XIV to withdraw support for the Unigenitus bull. The pope's sudden death and his replacement in July 1758 by Clement XIII, who refused outright to attack Unigenitus, led Jansenists to switch their strategy to more careful plotting against the Jesuit order within France. Partly to cover their own tracks in the Damiens affair, Jansenist *parlementaires* had been claiming that the king's would-be assassin – like Ravaillac in 1610 – had been put up to the job by the Jesuits, and this feeble, unsubstantiated charge was given greater credence by the attempted assassination of King Joseph I of Portugal in September 1758 – an event which the king's principal minister, Pombal, exploited by making an outright attack on the Jesuits. In 1760, the indefatigable Le Paige produced a *Histoire générale de la naissance et des progrès de la compagnie de Jesus* ('General History of the Birth and Progress of the Company of Jesus'), which received further amplification in the Jansenist house-organ, the *Nouvelles ecclésiastiques*. The Jesuits, it was charged, championed a laxist theology which encouraged rather than deterred sin; they had amassed enormous wealth; they were personally vicious; they perverted young boys, imbuing them with the precepts of regicide; and they had been founded by a foreigner and were essentially anti-French. Le Paige's trump card, however, was the assertion that the constitutions of the order were 'despotic' – very much a buzz-word in Jansenist and Gallican circles: their Superior in Rome ruled over French subjects with no concern for their rights as subjects of the French crown as if he were a tyrant in Turkey, Persia or Mongolia.[37]

Most unwisely, the Jesuits themselves brought the issue to a head. One of their number, La Valette, had built up a considerable fortune in Martinique. Two of his creditors, Marseille-based merchants Lioncy and Gouffre, had gone bust when a cargo from La Valette in Martinique had been seized by English vessels in 1755. La Valette was consequently sued and when the court stipulated that recompense should be made out of the coffers of the Jesuit order as a whole, the Jesuits appealed the case to the Paris Parlement, the trial beginning on 31 March 1762. The Jesuits were on a hiding to nothing, and in May, the court found for the

Marseille merchants and ordered 1.5 million livres to be paid to them by the Jesuit order. In August, using the *appel comme d'abus* procedure, the Parlement held the French attorney-general of the Jesuits personally responsible for the order's 'despotism' and its 'anarchical, murderous and parricidal doctrines'. The order in France was prohibited from recruiting and imposing vows; its congregations, associations and provincial framework were dissolved; and its colleges were ordered to be closed.

A half-hearted plan – which had Louis XV's support – to get the Jesuits to reform themselves as a national congregation failed, partly through the intransigence of the new pope. By now the assault on the Jesuits had developed a national dimension – virtually all the provincial *parlements* swung behind the Paris institution, in a celebration of the *union des classes*. The movement was gaining international profile too: the order had been expelled from Portugal in 1759, and would be so from Spain and Spanish colonies in 1767. In November 1764, Louis XV formally suppressed the Company, though allowing its 3,500 French members to reside as private citizens within France. In 1773, Pope Clement XIII would abolish the order as a whole.

Louis begrudged the decision: he had supported the abolition of the Jesuits, he told Choiseul, 'for the sake of the peace of my kingdom', but all the same 'against my will'.[38] It was the view of the *dévot* dauphin from the late 1750s that Choiseul (whose sardonic impiety he detested) was deeply implicated in a machiavellian anti-Jesuit conspiracy. Even if he never actually plotted the downfall of the Jesuits, Choiseul, in these desperate times, was certainly prepared to sacrifice the Order on the altar of political stability and parlementary alliance. 'One cannot pay armies with remonstrances,' Voltaire once noted acidulously,[39] and indeed there was a pressing need to keep the Paris Parlement sweet given the financial requirements of the state in the midst of the Seven Years War. *Aggiornamento* with the increasingly truculent magistrates was a major plank of Choiseul's recovery strategy for the state. The duke's purview over the Ministries of War, Navy and Foreign affairs put him in the best possible situation to realize the damaging effect that internal domestic crisis would have on the tottering war effort.

Choiseul's attitude towards the abolition of the Jesuits helped to consolidate a developing atmosphere of détente between government and *parlements*, in which much of the *philosophe* movement also participated. Cooperation with the magistrates now seemed the order of the day: by 1760, for example, Controller-General Bertin was clearing financial policy with a select handful of *parlementaires*. Choiseul prudently sought to buttress his position against the the undying hatred of the *dévot* faction at court in a number of ways, including the promotion of close relatives and clients within the establishment. His cousin, the comte de Choiseul, was put in charge of Foreign Affairs in 1761, with the award of the title of duc de Praslin. A rump of fellow Lorrainer aristocrats including Beauvau and du Châtelet supported him at court, while he also kept a direct line open to his friend, the Farmer General and court banker the marquis de La Borde. In addition, he appointed one of his brothers to a bishopric, promoted another (who had been a serving Austrian officer) within the army and married off his sister to a duke. This wedge of support helped secure his position, for, despite his wide-ranging influence, Choiseul was never granted the title of Principal Minister, and his relationship with Louis was ambiguous.

Alliance with the *parlements* would always be unsteady, and Choiseul proved particularly adept at manipulating any moments of friction in the relationship in ways which redounded to his own political interests. He was helped by the support of Madame de Pompadour, who liked his attitude towards the *parlements*, which recalled that of her favourite Bernis. When – as we noted above – Bertin's tough financial policies, guided through by *lit de justice* in the Paris Parlement in May 1763, triggered off a welter of protests from *parlements* across the land, Choiseul used the ensuing political crisis to weaken the position of his rivals in government. The crusty old Chancellor, Lamoignon, long-standing prop to the *dévot* cause, was disgraced and sent into exile. He refused to surrender his post on the grounds that the chancellorship was traditionally held until death, so Choiseul countered by appointing the former First President of the Paris Parlement, René-Charles de Maupeou, to the newly coined post of Vice-Chancellor, at the same time making Maupeou's son, René-Nicolas-Charles de Maupeou, the Parlement's new First President.

The organic links developing between the ministry and the Parlement were further strengthened by changes in financial policy. In November 1763, Bertin's fiscal reform programme was largely withdrawn, and the following month he was replaced as Controller-General by a Paris *parlementaire*, Laverdy, who had made a name for himself in the campaign against the Jesuits. This appointment was made quite deliberately,

Choiseul informed the prince de Conti, 'to put the Parlement beyond excuses',[40] and it was followed by conciliatory moves to bring back into line the recalcitrant *parlements* at Toulouse, Besançon and Rouen, who returned to their functions amid wild popular rejoicing. 'This is the start of a new order of things!', enthused the Dijon Parlement at the beginning of the year of 1764 in the light of this new wave of government-*parlementaire* cooperation.[41]

Choiseul had no major rival at the heart of government now, and his position was further eased by the dissolution of current factional groupings following a string of adventitious deaths. Belle-Isle, the most powerful figure on the Royal Council, died in 1761. Even more crucially, the premature deaths of, first, the dauphin in 1765 and then, in early 1767, the dauphine, followed a year later by that of Queen Marie Leszczinska, knocked the stuffing out of the *dévot* faction. More worrying for Choiseul was the death of Madame de Pompadour in 1764 – she was only forty-three, and court factions were soon lining up the candidates as her successor. The king's favour in the end fell on Jeanne Bécu, illegitimate daughter of a monk, whose beauty and wit had won her quite a reputation in Parisian *roué* circles. She was duly reinvented as an aristocrat grand enough to be presented at court in early 1769 and provided with a spouse who conveniently decamped. Choiseul regarded the new mistress with displeasure: he had lined up his own sister, the duchesse de Gramont, for the honour, and was aware that du Barry was closely linked to his court rivals. Initially, however, Madame du Barry was keener on jewels and fashion than on political meddling.

Choiseul looked down contemptuously on Madame du Barry; but then he looked down contemptuously on just about everyone (including, his memoirs later suggested, Louis XV). Royal mistresses were going down in the world just as royal ministers were on their way up. Pompadour's origins had been excoriated as bourgeois, but du Barry's were positively plebeian in comparison, while Choiseul's rise to power in the 1760s formed part of a pronounced upward shift in the social composition of government personnel. There was nothing new about high nobles dominating the state: indeed what was more worthy of remark were the very few cases (Dubois, Fleury and, later, Necker) of commoners who achieved high office. The whole political establishment was still overwhelmingly noble. With very few exceptions, moreover, it was becoming harder to enter the ambience of the monarch: from the late 1750s, court etiquette began to insist that nobles wishing to be presented at court should be able to display a noble genealogy going back to before 1400. What was also new after the 1750s, moreover, was a tendency for the highest and most prestigious nobility to permeate even the more technical services of state. Fleury had taken his cue from Louis XIV in trying to keep courtier (Sword) and bureaucratic (Robe) hierarchies as separate from each other as could be managed. The abbé de Bernis, scion of an ancient minor noble family from the Vivarais, set something of a precedent, therefore, when he accepted the habitually Robe post of Secretary of State for Foreign Affairs in 1757. In the event, he was merely the first of what was to become a flood of appointments from among the ancient *noblesse de race*. When the duc de Belle-Isle (grandson of a Robe Surintendant des finances, Nicolas Fouquet, though he tended to overlook the fact) had been appointed War Minister in 1758, concern was expressed that somehow the post implied a derogation of ducal status ('as though governing a great kingdom was unimaginably below some kind of dignity', scoffed Bernis).[42] In fact, the Belle-Isle, Bernis and Choiseul appointments marked the breaking of a social dyke at the heart of government. Under Pompadour, the influence of court faction had become increasingly apparent among the secretaries of state. Now, with Choiseul, the aristocracy were definitively taking on these functions, and the ministries down to 1789 would be dominated by high aristocrats – and, *ergo*, by high aristocratic faction. 'These posts', confided the duchesse de Praslin, 'have passed into our hands ... these *petits bourgeois* [she meant, breathtakingly enough, highly distinguished Robe families] will meddle no more.'[43] Although the Cinderella post of Controller-General, still run by legally trained Robins, remained outside the aristocratic charmed circle, a *cascade de mépris* had installed itself at the heart of government.

D) THE MONARCHY RETOOLS

Choiseul's Olympian and aristophilic hauteur did not mean that he was out of touch with the needs of government. On the contrary, he used his lofty ministerial perch during the dark days of the Seven Years War as a vantage-point from which to survey the full range of the state's activities, and form plans for root-and-branch reform. While it rebuilt and planned to exact revenge on the English, France would need, Choiseul informed Louis XV, 'to take precautions against [England] and to defend ourselves' against a country which was 'aim[ing] for supremacy in the four corners of the world'.[44] It therefore needed to avoid like the plague an imprudently hasty return to war. In diplomatic terms, this meant binding France to the Austrian alliance. Choiseul accepted this out of pragmatic expediency rather than enthusiasm: by keeping its powder dry in Europe, France could focus its energies on the global stage on which English power had to be encountered. Realizing that France needed the help of the Spanish fleet if it was to be a match for the Royal Navy, Choiseul combined the Austrian alliance with underpinning the Family Compact which since 1761 had united the interests of the Bourbon rulers of France and Spain.

The cost of this diplomatic orientation was reduced influence on major changes in European power politics. Hence in 1763, France had to permit the election to the Polish throne of the Russian candidate Stanislas Poniatowski – a feeble return for several decades of manoeuvring by the *Secret du Roi*. Similarly, vicarious attempts to counter Russian influence in central and eastern Europe by encouraging the Ottoman Turks to attack Russia led, annoyingly, to Russian successes in the Russo–Turkish War of 1768–74.

Significantly, though France expanded under Choiseul, it was by hereditary reversion and diplomatic agreement rather than by force of arms. Following the death in 1766 of Louis XV's octogenarian father-in-law, Stanislas Leszczinski, Lorraine, first of all, passed fully and definitively into French hands, under the terms of the international agreement brokered by Fleury in 1737. Stanislas had allowed his duchy to be governed quasi-directly from Paris, and his death merely tightened France's grip. As a frontier province, Lorraine passed under the general surveillance of the War Minister – namely, Choiseul, himself a Lorrainer. Like most such, he did not mourn the loss of a status which was far less independent than it appeared. The local inhabitants in Choiseul's second acquisition, however – namely, Genoan Corsica – posed more of a problem. As Fleury had realized, the acquisition of Lorraine consolidated France's eastern frontier. Corsica, for Choiseul, provided valuable cover against the invasion of Provence (which had suffered incursions in the Wars of Spanish and Austrian Succession), as well as offering good ports and better access to Italian markets. The French had stationed troops in

Corsica in the Seven Years War, but found the island turbulent and rebellious, with Pascal Paoli leading an independence movement against Genoa. The Genoan government accepted the French offer to pacify the island, agreeing that it could revert to France if Genoa proved unable to pay the costs of the operation. The French needed to deploy 25,000 troops to bring the island to order in 1768–9. With Genoa washing its hands of the island, it became French. By the end of the decade, Paoli was in exile, and most Corsican notable families – such as, for example, the Buonaparte clan – had rallied to French authority.

Though Choiseul did a great deal to consolidate France's international situation through diplomatic craft, he also faced up to the prospect of revenge against England by major investment in the armed forces, which had suffered such humiliations in the Seven Years War. Some 100,000 men were demobbed in 1762, and the trimmer army was overhauled with new-found thoroughness. Recruitment passed out of the hands of independent recruiting sergeants into state control for the first time. The number and composition of regiments were changed too, and in 1763 the purchase of infantry regiments was ended, with regiments now, significantly, being named after provinces rather than their colonels, and with soldiers being obliged to take a loyalty oath to the king. More standardized supply of uniform and arms was introduced; chains of command were formalized; there was a further push to locate troops in barracks and garrisons; and Prussian-style disciplinary codes were introduced. The draconian was mixed with the benevolent: better pay scales were established; pensions for long-serving and disabled veterans were revamped; and there were moves to improve the quality of food supply and medical provision. The performance of the artillery in the Seven Years War had been dire, and Gribeauval, appointed Artillery Inspector by Choiseul, was encouraged to think boldly: he brought in lighter, more mobile guns and innovated with flexible forms of deployment on the battlefield which would remain standard down to 1825. The navy attracted even more attention and investment. Though a Lorrainer, Choiseul was no landlubber – his grandfather, indeed, had been enslaved by Barbary Corsairs under Louis XIV, served as commander of Saint-Domingue and the Turtle Coast and died in a sea-battle at English hands – and the duke realized the importance of a strong navy as a means of combating England and of offering protection to French merchant vessels. In 1763, he set himself the target of a fleet of 90 ships and 45 frigates before France went to war; by the early 1770s the fleet stood at some 66 ships of line, 35 frigates and 21 corvettes, nearly all of which had been built since 1762.

The attention to quality and expertise which was a hallmark of Choiseul's reforms in the armed services was particularly in evidence in regard to officer recruitment. His recent predecessor as War Minister, the comte d'Argenson, had widened officer recruitment away from the high nobility, but Choiseul returned to the systematic favouring of the *noblesse de race* – very much one of his gut reflexes. This caste favouritism possibly owed something to the feeling that the poor performance of the officer corps in the Seven Years War was due to *nouveaux riches* and wealthy, recently ennobled families buying themselves high commands. His moves were also associated with a more general revalorization of the poor provincial nobility, who were being increasingly mythologized as the seedplot of military commitment and the cult of honour, particularly following the publication in 1757 of *La Noblesse militaire, ou le Patriote français* ('The Military Nobility, or The French Patriot') by the Chevalier d'Arc (illegitimate son of Louis XIV's bastard, the comte de Toulouse). While attacking court luxury and the corrosive effects of wealth on traditional values, Arc urged the state to support its impoverished country gentry, making a powerful case that caste and breeding were efficacious stimulants of military professionalism – an analogous approach to that employed by Choiseul as regards government personnel.[45]

Arc's work played a part in a more general recommitment to the systematic favouring of the *noblesse de race* within the army. In 1758, confirmation of ancient nobility was required of aspirants to high rank, while the closure of infantry regiments to the practice of purchase in 1762 was, partly at least, a bid to prevent the corrosive influence of monied *arrivistes* within the officer corps. The comte de Saint-Germain – ex-Jesuit, international soldier of fortune, and enthusiast for Frederick the Great – was to take the process further as War Minister from 1775 to 1777, closing all military posts to purchase. There was greater stress now on the need for young officers seeking career advancement to know something as well as someone.[46] Under Choiseul, the ex-Jesuit college of La Flèche was remodelled as a prep-school for bellicose eight-year-olds wishing to advance to the École militaire. The late 1760s also saw reforms in the teaching at the artillery school at Mézières – and this too took an increasingly more elitist attitude towards recruitment. The multi-talented Duhamel du Monceau, agronomist and naval engineer, also revitalized teaching at the École de Marine for navy officers at Brest (from 1769 officially a royal institution).

Despite the patrician allure of much that Choiseul attempted, a renovating, technocratic spirit was abroad during his tenure of office which sought to rationalize and revivify government service, so that the state could strengthen the country's infrastructure and stimulate its economy. A role model here was the Ponts et Chaussées service, generator, as we have suggested,[47] of an ethic of loyal state service which prized the values of exchange in unlocking productive resources and stimulating social improvement. Motivated by reason and enlightenment, the enlightened civil engineer was to work unstintingly at his task of improving roads and building bridges for the good of humanity. A quasi-militaristic system of service and advancement by merit helped heighten the school's *esprit de corps* – admission was by competitive examination, and from 1772 pupils wore uniform. They applied an acute sense of order and discipline not only to themselves but also to the workers they used under the system of the *corvée* and over whom they exerted a tough, quasi-military authority. The École des Ponts et Chaussées founded in 1775 served as a model for both military training establishments and other civilian establishments such as the École des Mines, founded in 1783 for mining engineers.

The spirit of experiment and innovation spread out from central government from the late 1750s and early 1760s through the capillary action of provincial Intendants. Many of the latter stuck to their traditional areas of expertise – three-quarters of the business of the Intendants at Aix-en-Provence concerned financial matters, for example – but a great many showed themselves altogether more versatile and imaginative and in tune with Choiseul's modernizing project. Saint-Priest, for example, Intendant in Montpellier from 1750 to 1786, cooperated fruitfully with the score of bishops who dominated the Languedoc Estates in the economic development of what was becoming by the eve of the Revolution one of France's most heavily industrialized provinces. Similarly, before being elevated to the post of Controller-General in 1774, Jacques Turgot, inveterate salon-goer, covert contributor to the *Encyclopédie* and friend of Voltaire and Diderot, had served from 1761 as Intendant of the poverty-stricken region of the Limousin

('Siberia', as he dubbed it, only half-jokingly). He modernized the mail service, improved communications, introduced free trade in grain and encouraged the adoption of new farming methods and manufacturing techniques. One of his characteristic concerns was the quest to innovate in a way which might relieve poverty among the local population and also stimulate productivity: he investigated means of making tax assessments less burdensome on the poor; arranged for a system of replacement for unpopular militia-service; set up charity workshops in times of dearth; gave tax remissions for needy families; proselytized for the humble potato, a cheap and healthy grain substitute; enthused over a new type of rat-trap he had found in Paris; and sponsored the latest public health fads. He also funded the midwifery classes of the king's roving obstetrical emissary, Madame du Coudray, who claimed to be saving babies through reducing midwife incompetence and ignorance, and thus being 'useful to my *Patrie*'[48] – a motto any Intendant could take for his own.

The humanitarian, patriotic language which Intendants utilized to validate their initiatives was also evident as regards state encouragement to agriculture. Duhamel du Monceau's *Traité de la culture des terres* in 1750 was, it has been argued, the first original work on agronomy published in France since Olivier de Serre's writings in the early seventeenth century, and it triggered a rash of subsequent publication, which drew heavily on English and Dutch innovation. The developing cult of agromania owed much to realization in political circles of the need to build up domestic production of food, given the vulnerability of global trading networks to British naval hegemony. From 1760, Bertin encouraged the formation of local agricultural societies, on the model of the provincial academy, to diffuse best practice and encourage innovation and emulation in farming techniques. Sixteen such bodies, scattered through the provinces, were established between 1761 and 1763, and provincial intendants were specially charged to nurture them. The foundation in the 1760s of veterinary schools at Lyon and at Alfort, just outside Paris, showed a related concern for maintaining livestock quality. The schools were very much the brainchild of Bertin, and although the latter was ousted from the post of Controller-General by Choiseul in 1763, he was continued by the king as a fifth secretary of state: the so-called 'little ministry' (*le petit ministère*), over which he presided down to the early 1780s, had responsibility for general economic issues, and spawned not only a wide-ranging set of initiatives but also a clientage network which included some of the great technocratic figures of the reign of Louis XVI, such as Lavoisier, Trudaine, Condorcet, Vicq d'Azyr and Turgot.

This emphasis on agriculture was linked to the impact that the doctrines of Physiocracy were having in government circles. In 1763, the *Journal économique* noted how 'the genius of the nation turns almost entirely today to the side of the economy'.[49] The Physiocrats took much of the credit for this. Though their doctrinaire adhesion to themes of support for agriculture and property-owners, free trade and liberalization of the economy won them criticism from the philosophic circles in which they had originated, the grouping was well placed to have an impact on government policy. Well connected both at court and (through Bertin) in administrative circles, they promoted cliques of true believers throughout the land in *parlements*, provincial estates, agricultural societies, academies, chambers of commerce and the like.

Though Choiseul personally detested Quesnay, the Physiocrats' emphasis on breaking the shackles under which the economy was labouring appealed to the duke, whose retooling of the state presupposed a reinvigoration of the economy which would allow the government to go to war without bringing the country to penury. He consequently adopted a hands-off policy towards the Controller-General, the *parlementaire* Laverdy, whose appointment had formed part of Choiseul's policy of accommodation with the Parlement, and who liked the idea of economic liberalization. In 1763–4, Laverdy passed decrees freeing the grain trade, as a means of boosting agricultural production and enriching big landowners (among whom primacy of place was taken by commercially minded high nobles). In 1767, the laws on noble derogation were lightened, so that nobles could engage in banking and manufacturing without losing their status and its associated privileges.[50] The latter measure owed much to the influence of the abbé Coyer's *La Noblesse commerçante*, published in 1756. Coyer argued against Montesquieu (and, subsequently, the chevalier d'Arc), maintaining that to allow the nobility to enrich themselves would not kill off the sense of honour necessary in a monarchy: indeed it would mean that the state did not have to subsidize impoverished *hobereaux*, and had more to spend on professionalizing the armed forces.

Choiseul and Laverdy may have been attracted to the idea of a business nobility, but they were also attentive to the economic aspirations of commoners, and the 1760s witnessed the introduction of a wide range of other liberalizing measures, justified at some length in the language of reason, nature and humanity. In 1762, for example, urban guild privileges were cut back by a decree permitting manufacturers to locate in the countryside – a measure which gave a signal boost to rural industry. In 1763, Choiseul also heeded the request of Atlantic port merchants to relax the restrictive regulations on trade, and in 1769 he abolished the Compagnie des Indes, whose monopoly of trade beyond the Cape of Good Hope had been violently attacked by Marseille and Saint Malo business interests. From 1764 onwards, Laverdy introduced major reforms in municipal governance allowing a greater degree of participation by local inhabitants: the preamble to legislation in 1765 cited election as 'the most appropriate means of fructifying incomes, reducing expenditures, [and] recalling the order and economy necessary in all public administrations'.[51]

Choiseul was not excessively enamoured of Laverdy's municipal reforms, whose political liberalism was not to his patrician tastes. Nevertheless, the spate of economic liberalism over which he presided through the 1760s contributed to a very spirited revival of the national economy in the aftermath of the losses and failures of the Seven Years War. Colonial trade, significantly, boomed prodigiously between 1763 and 1778 despite the losses enshrined in the Treaty of Paris, and highlighted the revival in economic fortunes that Choiseul's ministry had achieved.

E) LANGUAGES OF PATRIOTISM: THE JUDGES JUDGED

In 1765, Paris, then Versailles, then France, were lit up by Calais Fever. Buirette de Belloy's play *The Siege of Calais*, staged at the Comédie-Française, won a quite unparalleled reception throughout the land, sparking a wave of patriotic enthusiasm. The play depicted an episode during an earlier Anglo–French conflict, the Hundred Years War, when Edward III of England, besieging the Channel port, ordered the death of six burghers whose stoical acceptance of their fate in the name of their country (later to be immortalized by Rodin) moved even the dastardly English monarch to repent. The play was unusual in making an episode in French, rather than Greek or Roman, history the focus of the action, and in portraying the bourgeoisie as demonstrating faultless devotion to their monarch when faced by the military incursions of their English neighbour, whose monarch was laying claim to the French crown.

This was a stirring patriotic allegory for a sensitive period of *après-guerre*. De Belloy's fellow-playwright, Collé, noted with some envy how the play was endlessly performed to enthusiastic crowds, with one show being given gratis so that the common people of Paris could share in the patriotic paeans: 'The marketwomen and the common people . . . cried out for the author, and when he appeared shouted out "*Vive le Roi et M. de Belloy!*"'[52] The court joined in the enthusiasm, and following frequent stagings at Versailles, the king awarded de Belloy a thousand *écus* and a golden medallion. He also allowed the playwright to dedicate to him the printed version of the text, which was soon selling like hot cakes. The play toured the provinces – Calais accorded de Belloy the freedom of the city – before being played to rhapsodic colonial audiences in Saint-Domingue.

The Siege of Calais was emphatically not to the taste of all. Theatre-lovers applauded the sentiments and the characterization, but deplored the lame versification. There was indignation too at the story that Choiseul had been so taken by the patriotism that the play had evoked that he ordered de Belloy to write more in the same vein, 'as though one gave orders to a genius as to a pastrycook'. More significantly, many courtiers resented the popular shows of patriotism. The comte d'Ayen snootily called it 'a tragedy fit only for cobblers', and he was not alone at court in resenting the fact that the hero was a militaristic ruler, that the villain of the piece was a French aristocrat of the highest breeding (the turncoat Frenchman, the duc d'Harcourt) and that the play focused on the six 'martyrs of the *Patrie*' who were bourgeois. The mayor of Calais stirringly addressed the burghers:

> *Défenseurs de Calais, chefs d'un peuple fidèle*
> *Vous de nos chevaliers l'envie et le modèle.*
> [Defenders of Calais, leaders of a loyal people,
> Envy and model of our knights.]

Many of the *philosophes* found this patriotism disquieting too: one of the play's most famous lines – *plus je vis d'étrangers, plus j'aimais ma Patrie*' ('the more foreigners I saw, the more I loved my fatherland') –

offended their inherent cosmopolitanism and made their customary anglomania look decidedly odd. D'Holbach's salon was said to have condemned it outright on the grounds that 'love of the *patrie*' was 'a prejudice'. Yet the articles on '*patrie*' and '*patriotisme*' which appeared in the volume of the *Encyclopédie* which appeared in 1765 caught the jingoistic mood.

The *Siege of Calais* phenomenon demonstrated that the reconstruction of the monarchy could be popular. Government did not have to rely on its ancient ceremonial mystique and its sacral sheen (both facets of monarchy which the hyper-materialist Choiseul disliked anyway). Enlightened values of reason and humanity were the monopoly of neither the *parlements* nor the *philosophes*. Ministers had long been in the habit of informing and shaping opinion, hiring barristers (even Jansenist ones on occasion) and literary hacks to pen government propaganda and anti-*parlementaire* attacks or else circulating favourable views through coffee-houses, public parks and other sites of Parisian polite sociability. The bourgeois public sphere offered an enlarged and more alert theatre on which the ministry could develop a collective sense of identity throughout the kingdom, centred on and symbolized by the person of the king. Government propaganda in the Seven Years War had exceeded itself in proto-racist attacks on the English nation, whose alleged 'savage' and 'barbaric' character contrasted with the gentler and more loveable mores of the French.[53] By 1766, the pamphleteer Basset de la Marelle was arguing that one of the striking features of French (as opposed to English) patriotism was its orientation around obedience to their ruler: 'the love of the French for their sovereign is the strongest support of the state, the unshakeable basis of the power and glory of the monarchy'.[54] A population which could be moved – by a mere play – to transports of patriotic attachment to its king had evidently retained a residual fondness for the ruler which might be appealed to over the heads of the nobility and the *parlements* and even of the *philosophe* movement. Patriotism could be simultaneously plebeian and monarchical, even (in a desacralized way) absolutist – a point which writer Louis-Sébastien Mercier had in mind when, in his best-selling 1771 science-fiction novel *2440*, he berated patriotism as 'a fanaticism invented by kings and baneful to the universe'.[55]

A further element in this phenomenon were government-sponsored efforts to reground royal authority in an absolutist version of the national past. One of the striking features of the political battles of the 1750s had been the way in which parlementary critics – and most notably the Jansenist *érudit* Le Paige – had through painstaking anti-quarian study provided more convincing accounts of national history than the crown was able to mount. From the late 1750s, in contrast, the government began to institute procedures to build up its own archival resources and to constitute what Keith Baker has called an 'ideological arsenal' which allowed the historical arguments of the *parlementaires* – which occasionally had a more than fanciful aspect – to be met on their own ground.[56] Under the patronage of Controllers-General Silhouette, then Bertin, the former Jansenist pamphleteer Jacob-Nicolas Moreau, at first alone, and from the late 1760s with an academy-style grouping called the Cabinet des Chartes, began to compile the documents which would form the state's official memory. By the eve of the Revolution, it contained over 50,000 documents drawn from 350 archival repositories. It allowed the government to make powerful historical arguments which made up in energy what they lacked in scientific objectivity: the *Preuves de la pleine souveraineté du Roi sur la province de Bretagne* ('Proofs of the Full Sovereignty of the King over the Province of Brittany') published under Laverdy's name in 1765, but in fact penned by Moreau, was a highly partisan absolutist polemic which sought to dismantle the histori-cal arguments for relative autonomy being bandied about by Breton notables.

Choiseul's government increasingly played to this nationalistic pro-gramme, which allowed the doctrines of inflexible absolutism to be mixed with the milk and honey of rational debate and beneficent human-ity. Following a trend detectable, as we have suggested, from the 1690s,[57] the preambles to royal edicts and other documents of monarchical authority used the language of 'public welfare', 'beneficence' and 'patri-otism', and demonstrated a more systematic quest to explain and to 'enlighten' as well as to command.

Absolutist reflexes, however, died hard. The adjustment which the monarch and the state apparatus had to make to their customary ways of doing things was a difficult one. The government had long dictated the formal grounds on which public discussion occurred, and feared being seen to enter the field of debate too overtly, and having to win arguments where once the king commanded unreflective assent. The lawyer Barbier, for example, was pleased to note on one occasion that the publicly diffused remonstrances of the Parlement were greeted by 'replies by the king', which were 'strong and well-written'. Significantly, however, he added 'sensible people found it indecent that the king, for laws or taxes which he wishes to create, should be obliged to plead against his Parlement'.[58] As we have seen,[59] government regulated the number of printshops throughout the realm, policed the book trade, ran the only newspaper cleared to report political news (the *Gazette de France*) and enforced censorship throughout the land. It took the function of that censorship to uphold religious faith and public morals extremely seriously: a royal edict in 1757 promised death to anyone involved in the writing, publication or circulation of writings which threatened to injure state or religious authority and sought to trouble public order. Although the death penalty was not much invoked in practice, censorship and state interference comprised a quotidian threat for authors, publishers and readers.

The monarchical version of patriotism required more attention to public taste, more ease of manners, and more rational control over his demeanour than Louis XV was able to muster, for it implied a willingness to listen as well as to orate. 'Whatever we say', Miromesnil, First President of the Rouen Parlement, remarked to Controller-General Laverdy in 1765, 'the king must speak to us ceaselessly in the language of reason and never that of anger.'[60] Chance would be a fine thing: *parlementaires* and officials given an audience with Louis XV were invariably dismayed by his imperious air, his studied disdain for discussion, and his wilful impetuousness, which came close to brutal contempt. In a famous clash with the Paris Parlement in 1766 on the festival of the day when Christ was scourged (and consequently known as the *Séance de la Flagellation* ('The Scourging Session')), the king outlined the pristine character of royal absolutism, against those who dared to question it, in an arrogant, ahistorical manner which Louis XIV could not have bettered:

It is in my person alone that sovereign power resides . . . it is from me alone that my [sic] courts hold their existence and their authority . . . public order in its entirety emanates from me, and my people forms one with me, and the rights and interests of the nation, of which people are daring to make a body separate from the monarch, are necessarily united with mine and repose only in my hands.[61]

To thrust the point home, Louis ordered the publication of the speech in the *Gazette de France*, and its diffusion to all the sovereign courts and to the colonies – indeed, some thought the speech was aimed less at the *parlementaires* than at the general public. Yet such behaviour could backfire. President de Brosses of the Dijon Parlement was not alone in reacting angrily to such a performance, which seemed both grotesquely anachronistic and constitutionally threatening: 'It's the cannon with the biggest calibre: oriental despotism and barefaced tyranny.'[62]

Such bravura royal displays failed to turn the tide for *le Mal-Aimé*. As we have seen, the ceremonial rituals and courtly ostentatiousness of yore were failing to do their job, and monarchical authority was losing its sacral sheen. Yet Louis still invariably preferred to look back to the template of an idealized Louis-Quatorzian absolutism, with some Fénelonian touches, rather than forward to a more popular style of 'patriotic' monarchy of the kind that Choiseul was designing. Although de Belloy claimed, in his dedication to the *Siege of Calais*, that 'Calais recalled Metz', Louis XV showed little sign of reclaiming his erstwhile status as *le Bien-Aimé*.[63] Indeed it was from the mid-1760s that the rumour of the *pacte de famine* began to circulate widely, to the effect that the king had made secret deals with speculators and grain-merchants to raise the price of grain so high that famine killed off much of the population while the heartless ruler enriched himself prodigiously.

The monarchy's patriotic credentials were, moreover, being increasingly questioned and criticized on the forum of the public sphere – particularly by the *parlements*. At the height of the anti-Jesuit campaign, an apologist for the Order had accused the magistrates of deploying a 'jargon of patriotism mixed with the language of rebellion', while the Toulouse Parlement, for example, claimed that the Jesuits were 'insensible to the impressions of the national spirit'.[64] This tendency to couch their oppositional discourse in patriotic terms was increasingly evident in disputes from the late 1750s onwards over state finance. Judging finance the government's Achilles heel, the Paris Parlement was increasingly seeking to make something traditionally seen as the king's private business into an issue of rightful concern to the sovereign courts. As Barbier noted in 1760,

The Parlement is right to profit from the circumstances to extend its authority, all the more in that the people, borne down with taxes and forewarned about the administration by rumours and complaints, looks to find some moderation through the resistance of the Parlement.[65]

Yet accepting advice on financial matters, even from his *parlements*, was something to which the king found it hard to warm. From the late 1750s Physiocracy had become *mode du jour* in government circles, assisted by the liberalization of censorship by Book-Trade Director Malesherbes.[66] When in 1760, at the height of the Seven Years War, however, the marquis de Mirabeau, one of their number, published a *Théorie de l'impôt* ('Tax Theory') which stated that taxes should only be imposed with popular consent, claimed tax on landed income to be the most equitable of impositions and called for the abolition of the General Farm, the author was imprisoned in the Bastille, then exiled to his family estates. In May 1763, the government's *lit de justice* introducing reforms to re-establish the state finances at the end of the Seven Years War[67] seemed to mark a liberal change of tack, for it also formally encouraged individuals to proffer proposals for reforming the national taxation system along more rational and productive lines. Yet this was soon shown up as a charade. There was an outpouring of writings calling for radical reforms of the tax system – 'everyone at the moment is meddling at being a reformer', noted the *Journal encyclopédique*.[68] Roussel de La Tour's scandalous *La Richesse de l'état* ('The State's Wealth') called for the abolition of all but a single unitary tax, while the barrister Darigrand's *L'Anti-financier* mounted a swingeing attack on the Farmers General. The scale and radical character of the print output frightened the government back into repression. As part of its accommodation with the Paris Parlement in November 1763, it was agreed that a committee of *parlementaires* should receive and process fiscal proposals, and by March 1764 a new ban had been put on them.

The course and the outcome of this episode spoke volumes about the problems of taking absolute monarchy out on to the public stage. By oscillating between the traditional repressive line and a sometimes almost shame-faced liberalism, Louis XV hoped to have the best of both worlds. He ended up with the worst. Government censorship was not repressive enough to be effective, yet the freedom it encouraged only made its censorship look more open to criticism. Parrot cries for silence on delicate political issues sounded increasingly archaic – and were quite unable to stem the rising tide of parlementary critique.

The *parlementaires* trained their fire on the tendency of the state to trample over legal propriety in financial affairs. For most of the 1760s, tax innovations *per se* were less at issue than what the *parlementaires* saw as the government's progressive expansion of its administrative powers in financial matters. A prime target of parlementary critique were the unaccountable and 'despotic' local tax officials who were always seeking ways of 'subjecting taxpayers to their petty authority and enveloping them in their fiscal science',[69] through more efficient collection and assessment procedures. The excise-men of the General Farm attracted similar criticisms. The Farmers General were probably the most unpopular men in the country, but their local agents – portrayed as greedy, grasping and unmindful of personal freedoms – were not far behind. The Farm's special tribunals for dealing with smuggling were particularly harshly attacked for arbitrariness and inhumanity.

The Intendants – the main provincial exponents of 'fiscal science' – also came under attack. Architects of schemes of humanity, beneficence and patriotism by their own account, they were roundly assailed by others for their 'despotic' and 'unpatriotic' tendencies which, the *parlements* argued, overstepped constitutional bounds. Besides lending support to grasping local tax officials, the Intendants also organized the road-building *corvées*, which were another bone of contention. The Ponts et Chaussées engineers who supervised this work were tinpot dictators, who pulled peasants off the land to build roads whose utility, it was claimed, remained to be proven. Intendants also organized the drawing of lots for militia-service – another form of royal service which won the *parlements'* opprobrium. As seigneurs too, many parlementary magistrates disliked the efforts of the Intendants – notably in Burgundy – to protect peasant communities against seigneurial encroachments, as a means of ensuring that a greater part of the peasant surplus went into state coffers in the form of royal taxes. The government's economic liberalization measures came under attack from certain *parlements* (others were more accepting), as did the policy of free trade in grain which the Intendants enforced locally. There was much criticism too of the tough new laws on vagrancy which Laverdy instituted between 1764 and 1767. At one stage the introduction of a parishional poor-rate to deal with local paupers was considered, and though this was dropped as a result of the Paris Parlement's hostility to new taxes, a new network of state-funded *dépôts de mendicité* was created throughout the land for the incarceration of beggars and vagrants. The *dépôts* triggered provincial outrage for being expensive, ineffective and infringing personal freedoms: in Languedoc, for example, the Estates complained bitterly that a bonus-hungry *maréchaussée* was making almost indiscriminate arrests and damaging the local economy which was dependent on influxes of migrant workers at key points of the agricultural year.

The measures for which the *parlements* were calling from the late 1750s – fewer fiscal levies, greater economy in the state establishment, a simplified tax system, more local accountability of tax officials through the *parlements* – did not form a consolidated and coherent programme of reform. What was perhaps more striking than their piecemeal, uncoordinated and *ad hoc* content was the patriotic idiom in which these ideas were clothed. Parlementary ideas invariably evinced that most thoroughgoing national miserabilism which had impressed poor Damiens: harmful and unpatriotic government demands were driving the country to despair and depopulation. Parlementary protests were also increasingly lodged as appeals to the gallery. Just as the kings increasingly appealed to public opinion, so too the magistrates made as if to look over the shoulder of the monarch, who was the formal recipient of their remonstrances, towards the opinion of a wider public which could weigh up and adjudicate the force of their arguments and the strength of their high minded attachment to the welfare of the nation.

Policy issues were thus becoming patriotism debates, with disagreements taking the shape of a trial by propaganda, with the approval of the public as the prize. The *parlementaires* were ceasing to confine their invocations within the walls of the *palais de justice* and were striving more systematically to extend them into the burgeoning public sphere. The *basoche* – the world of law including barristers, attorneys, clerks, bailiffs, ushers and the like who worked within the *parlements* and the other royal courts – played an important role as the cultural intermediaries of the *parlements*, diffusing the magistrates' views through urban society. The links forged in the *union des classes* also provided a national dimension to disputes. But the means *par excellence* for the popularization of public debate was the printed word. The Parlement's remonstrances had been regarded in the past as private documents which, if not quite for the king's eyes only, were certainly not viewed as public documents. From the early 1750s, however, it became current for remonstrances to be published and circulated in thousands, even tens of thousands of copies – despite strong royal injunctions to the contrary. They jostled alongside other print forms for conveying parlementary views to a wider public – the censorship-exempt legal brief (*mémoire judiciaire*), the clandestine distribution networks of the Jansenist house-organ, the *Nouvelles ecclésiastiques*, the fertile, multiform output of Le Paige, and the increasingly well-briefed foreign press, such as the Dutch-based *Gazette de Leyde*.

The *parlements* thus played a leading role in extending the parameters of public debate, grounding their arguments in terms of their would-be representative role as regards the wider society and invoking the public as a kind of patriotic supreme court whose opinion was arbiter of justice and legitimacy. Yet their position towards the involvement of a wider public in politics was highly ambivalent. Beneficiaries of the liberalization of the terms of public debates at mid-century, and artful circumventors of censorship regulations, the *parlementaires* cast doleful and nostalgic glances back to the old 'mystery of state' days, and were not at all averse to falling back on repression and constraint. The magistrates were jealous not only to maintain the right of the workings of the law to be open, but also to safeguard from government their customary right to condemn published works. It was they, for example, who had drafted the 1757 edict stipulating the death penalty for publishing offences, and they similarly made great play, in 1758, of condemning Helvétius's atheistical work *De l'Esprit*, which had slipped past a dozing censor. Characteristically, the crusading Jansenist radical Le Paige was particularly outspoken in his criticisms. In 1759 they followed this up by publicly condemning the first seven volumes of the Bible of the Enlightenment, Diderot's *Encyclopédie*, while in 1762, it would be the turn of Jean-Jacques Rousseau, whose novel *Émile* achieved the rare distinction of uniting the Paris Parlement and Beaumont, the archbishop of Paris, in full-throated condemnation. The ambivalence of the Parlement's position was evident in their attitudes towards open discussion of financial reform after the Seven Years War: the farrago produced by permitting open debate on tax reform ended in 1764 with the Paris Parlement openly conniving with the government in the limitation of public debate. A related case around the same time saw the famed liberalizing Director of the Book Trade, Malesherbes, in his role as magistrate in the Paris Cour des Aides, meting out an exemplary punishment to the Secretary of the Burgundy Estates for publishing offences. The sovereign courts wanted to extend the forum of debate – but not too far.

Magistrates often gave the effect of wishing to replay the Fronde, and continued to play the traditional game of bluff and counter-bluff with the government, drawing on their customary panoply of obstructive devices, speaking loudly then quietly compromising its positions. This showed only a limited sense of how the context and significance of their actions was altered by the quite different framework within which this political game was now being played. Court, government and *parlements* were no longer the only players. The Parlement's ambivalence over the openness of political debate served as a reminder of the limitations of the claims of the *parlementaires* to 'represent' the people – or rather a sign that their version of representation incorporated outright repression of dissident views. The 1760s not only witnessed the promotion of parlementary squabbles to national political issues but also the elaboration of powerful critiques of the *parlements*, as the magistrates themselves came under closer scrutiny from the public to which it had so insistently appealed.

The public which magistrates ceaselessly invoked was not simply a figure of speech; it had begun to achieve a new sociological consistency and was beginning to find a voice of its own. Malesherbes later recognized this development, highlighting the formation of a rational reading population, whose judgement had precedence even over the magistrates of the Parlement:

Knowledge is being extended by printing; the written laws are today known by everyone . . . The judges can themselves be judged by an instructed Public, and that censure is much more severe and equitable when it can be exercised in a cool, reflective reading.[70]

We would want to add to Malesherbes's analysis the role of improved literacy, economic growth, improved communications and greater social mobility in producing a flesh-and-blood public with rational faculties and powers of analysis. But there is no denying the critical role of the Parlement – and in particular the energetic Jansenist lobby within it – in transforming the character of politics from the 1750s and 1760s onwards. The judges could now themselves be judged, as Malesherbes noted – and in many respects they had only themselves to blame.

If, as we have suggested, the king often got the worse of both worlds, being seen as both too repressive to be liberal and yet proving too liberal to be effectively repressive, much the same was true of the *parlements*. A good example of this was the so-called Calas affair, which brought a cloud of international opprobrium over the Parlement of Toulouse in particular, and sullied the reputation of the *parlements* in general. In October 1761, Marc-Antoine, the depressive son of Protestant shopkeeper Jean Calas of Toulouse, had been found dead. It was initially assumed that the son had committed suicide, but rumours were soon circulating that his parents had murdered him in order to prevent him converting to Catholicism. Despite protesting his innocence under torture, the sexagenarian father was condemned by the Parlement in March 1762 to be broken on the wheel, a fate which he bore with stoical fortitude. To a degree, this severity was out of line with a general drift of indifference towards anti-Huguenot legislation throughout France. The Seven Years War, which pitted Catholic Spain and France against Protestant powers England and Prussia, however, reactivated older reflexes. South-west France was the particular theatre for these: the region had been riven with rumours of Protestant risings in 1755–7, with the Toulouse region involved in an incident in 1761 which had led to the execution of a Protestant pastor. The traditional annual ceremony which celebrated the delivery of the city from the Protestants in the Wars of Religion took place two months after Calas's execution, and was a particularly strident celebration of Catholic unity – the police guards were bought new uniforms, relic shrines were specially repainted, the customary fireworks display was particularly magnificent, and Pope Clement XIII offered extra indulgences for church visits.

The Calas case became the Calas *affair* through the good offices of *philosophe* Voltaire. As soon as he heard the news of the trial and execution, he summed up the incident as a monument to Catholic intolerance, meridional superstition and judicial bigotry – and he decided to do something about it. This involved taking on both the *parlements* and the church. His successful embracing of the Calas cause highlighted how multi-levelled and complex politics had become by the 1760s. He was well enough connected to seek out money for the wronged Calas family from his court friends and his patrons across Europe (including Frederick II of Prussia and Gustavus III of Sweden). He was in cahoots with Parisian barristers who published best-selling legal briefs based on the arguments he provided. But most significantly of all, he took the case on to the public sphere, invoking that 'public', that 'nation', for whose support king and *parlements* seemed to be competing. He told the Calas story as a narrative of bigotry no fewer than six times in literary productions of different forms. The movement of opinion he provoked was such that in March 1763 the royal council decided that the case should be brought before the king for reconsideration. In June 1764, the Toulouse Parlement's judgement was overturned. And on 5 March 1765, three years to a day after the execution of Calas, the latter was formally declared innocent. Voltaire worked through Choiseul to get Louis XV himself to offer major compensatory pensions to the Calas family, engravings of whom became best-sellers throughout Paris. Voltaire put one above his bed.

Voltaire would take up cudgels on behalf of the oppressed on a number of other occasions – he was appalled by the chevalier de La Barre case in 1766, for example, in which the Paris Parlement upheld a decision of the court at Abbeville that the young noble should have his tongue pulled out, his right hand cut off and be executed for silly juvenile pranks involving blasphemy. Such cases not only showed the political uses to which public opinion could be put. 'Opinion governs the world and in the end the *philosophes* govern men's opinions,' was Voltaire's view. They also highlighted the injustices and bigotries inherent in the legal system, and in the *parlements* in particular. The comte de Creutz, Danish ambassador in Paris, noted of the La Barre case that 'everyone is surprised to see magistrates who wish to be the protectors of the people and to rein in authority demonstrate such a dark spirit of persecution'.[71] On the public sphere, the *parlementaires* were not immune from some severe judgements by the very public they claimed to represent.

F) FROM THE BRITTANY AFFAIR TO THE MAUPEOU REVOLUTION

The political and ideological struggles of the 1750s and 1760s had changed politics from being the preserve of the royal court or, more simply, what took place inside the king's head. To know what the king thought – even about *la patrie* – was no longer sufficient to love it and obey it. Contestation and debate were in the air, and it seemed difficult for *parlements* as well as government to stay in control.

The détente which Choiseul was able to effect with the Paris Parlement had doused down the subversive dimension of public debate in the years immediately following the end of the Seven Years War. The end of the decade, however, was to witness the detonation of one of the most severe political crises of the century – the so-called 'revolution' of Maupeou. This involved the overthrow of Choiseul, and it resulted in the outright abolition of the *parlements* of the realm and their replacement by a judicial machinery more directly responsive to royal authority. It was the most dynamic and forceful attempt to reorder the state so as to pre-empt that 'deluge' which Louis XV's Madame de Pompadour had forecast for France. The crisis highlighted many of the changes to the nature of politics wrought over the 1750s. Significantly, for example, it originated not at the heart of the royal court nor even in the Paris Parlement, but out in the country's periphery, in the province of Brittany.

Brittany was one of France's most heavily contrasted regions. English agronomist Arthur Young – a perceptive, if one-eyed observer – characterized it as the home of 'privilege and poverty'.[72] Its population grew slowly over the century, its agrarian economy not even much energized by the construction of a *corvée*-driven road network. The province's identity was fixed on traditionalist and historical attachment to particularist privilege. Brittany was a *pays d'état* and while the province's elite of ancient Sword nobles controlled the Parlement at Rennes, its provincial estates were dominated by its extensive poor nobility, grandsons of the *hobereaux* who had signed the 'Act for the Defence of the Liberties of Brittany' during the Cellamare conspiracy of 1719. If the parlementary *union des classes* helped guide this self-proclaimedly backward province towards the networks of the public sphere, so too did the presence of three of the most dynamic ports engaged in colonial trade, veritable hives of commercial enterprise and bustling prosperity – Lorient, Saint-Malo and slave-trading Nantes. The mercantile elites of those cities were eager to take provincial issues out to a wider public sphere less dominated by their noble betters.

The agreement of 21 November 1763 which had watered down Bertin's tax programme may have marked the basis of a new beginning in relations between the Paris Parlement and Choiseul's ministry,[73] but it caused a good deal of resentment in Brittany. Changes in indirect taxation were said to infringe Brittany's provincial liberties. Although the Rennes Parlement was eventually browbeaten by government into accepting the measures, the provincial Estates, meeting in October 1764, rejected them outright. The crown's representative in Brittany, Provincial Commander d'Aiguillon, played a leading role in strong-arming resistance, and next spring, the bulk of the Parlement's magistrates resigned en bloc in protest against the way they were being treated.

From Versailles, this conjunction of opposition between *parlement* and estates looked like conspiracy. Secretary of State Saint-Florentin's suspicions fell on the Parlement's high-profile Procurator-General, the marquis de Caradeuc, sieur de La Chalotais, a friend of Quesnay and the Physiocrats, renowned anti-Jesuit and anti-clerical pamphleteer, and a man known to have political ambitions. It is possible that Saint-Florentin believed that La Chalotais, besides being the author of insulting anonymous pamphlets directed against the king, was also engaging in political blackmail through private letters in his possession from the king to Mademoiselle de Romans, one of the royal 'little mistresses'. At all events, in November 1765, the government girded its loins, and arrested six magistrates from the Rennes Parlement, including La Chalotais and his son, and imprisoned them in the Bastille. The Rennes Parlement was exiled, and the government launched a campaign of black propaganda against Breton claims of autonomy.

The Paris Parlement had been too deeply immersed in its post-1763 honeymoon with Choiseul and Laverdy to give much initial support to the cause of their Rennes colleagues. The decision of the government to try La Chalotais and his fellow 'conspirators' by special government commission, and then to establish a new Parlement more loyal than the last, finally alerted Parisian magistrates to the gravity of the issues at stake (especially since government was also in the process of reconstituting the Pau Parlement at roughly the same time). The new Rennes Parlement, painstakingly assembled by d'Aiguillon and a team of imported government hatchet-men including future Controller-General Calonne and future Paris Police Lieutenant Le Noir, met for the first time in January 1766. Instantly dubbed 'd'Aiguillon's bailiwick' (*le bailliage d'Aiguillon*), the new body triggered remonstrances from the Paris Parlement and other provincial bodies attacking the government's assaults on the independence of magistrates and local privilege.

It was in direct response to parlementary protests that, on 2 March 1766, Louis XV held the *Séance de la Flagellation*, in which he roundly asserted the principles of an unbending absolutism which had no truck with the claims of *parlements* to represent the nation or with the theory of the *union des classes*.[74] Yet in the continuing crisis, government showed itself unfailingly incapable of living up to these big words and proud sentiments. The government was increasingly split, as a major rival to Choiseul's pre-eminence at court emerged, the pivotal figure around whom the Brittany Affair would now revolve, namely the duc d'Aiguillon.

D'Aiguillon had a hawkish, no-nonsense approach to provincial dissidence. 'I think the government has to be firm', he opined privately, 'in order to do the work of the state and to keep everyone in his place.'[75] By 1766, however, he was becoming disenchanted with the government's failure to provide consistent support for such a policy. Ministers changed their minds on several occasions as to who exactly should try La Chalotais, each time leaving loyalist Breton supporters in the lurch and exposing them to local hostility from those supporting the parlementary cause. The king decided to use his powers of *évocation* to refer the case from Rennes to the Royal Council, yet followed this up in December 1766 by dropping all charges against La Chalotais – 'I no longer want to find the guilty,' he stated grandiloquently.[76] D'Aiguillon also felt that Choiseul was covertly encouraging the cause of the *parlements* by allowing the rumour to circulate that the old Rennes Parlement might be recalled to take the place of 'd'Aiguillon's bailiwick'. The Commander was exposed to the taunts of local *parlementaire* supporters – who were claiming that he had always been a covert supporter of the Jesuits, and that the whole Brittany affair had been caused by his inability to control secret Jesuit caballing. D'Aiguillon's plans to reform the provincial estates to make them more amenable were also cold-shouldered in Versailles. His resignation as Provincial Commander in Brittany in August 1768 was followed by outright governmental capitulation: the old Parlement was restored, and the six imprisoned Breton magistrates were released from the Bastille – only La Chalotais being made to stay in exile, this time in Saintes in the south-west.

D'Aiguillon's departure from Brittany brought back to court a powerful and hostile critic of Choiseul and Choiseulian policies. The duke became the focus of a *dévot* faction which was beginning to reform following the deaths of the queen, the dauphin, and the dauphine. Links with the *dévots* derived less from any conspicuous personal devotion on the duke's part than because of his entanglement with the Jansenist *parlementaire* lobby and on account of his family relationships – the *dévot* faction included his uncle by marriage, Secretary of State Saint-Florentin, and his cousin, the ageing duc de Richelieu. The *dévots* seemed to be making a habit of striving for virtue through accommodation with vice, for Richelieu was a famous *roué*, while the king's last mistress, the comtesse du Barry, also came to be associated with the grouping.

Choiseul had thus to cope with the re-emergence of hostile factions at court, and also within the government (where 'little minister' Bertin also proved a *dévot* supporter), just as the limitations of his domestic policies were becoming apparent. The policies of modernization and economic liberalism had achieved much; but they had also brought problems. Although the economy had recovered remarkably well from the strains of the Seven Years War, freedom in the grain trade had produced consumer hostility. There were food riots sporadically from 1764 onwards right through to 1770, and by then it was also becoming clear that the strategy of boosting the economy had failed to solve the government's financial problems, which looked increasingly dire. In 1767, Laverdy had been compelled to seek the Parlement's approval for the prolongation of the 1763 *vingtième*: wanting a four-year extension of the tax, he and Choiseul lavished patronage and outright bribery on the magistrates, yet still had had to settle for only a two-year extension and endure pious *parlementaire* homilies on the need for state economy.

Choiseul's policy of placating the Paris Parlement – first through the expulsion of the Jesuits, then through assiduous conciliation and lobbying – had won the government space and time when it needed it, during and in the difficult aftermath of the Seven Years War. Yet by the late 1760s – as the *vingtième* issue suggested – it was beginning to look as though this policy had whetted rather than assuaged the magistrates' taste for politics. In 1763, the First President of the Parlement of Toulouse had claimed that the political crisis was caused by 'ten hotheads in each Parlement [who] claim to rule the state'.[77] By the end of the decade, in contrast, views which had been the preserve of radical minorities were being shared by the bulk of the magistrates. In Paris, for example, the rump of the old Jansenist grouping had been augmented by new blood, comprising magistrates who were noticeably more outspoken than those from longer-serving parlementary families. Prominent amongst them was Michau de Montblin, who from 1765 was running a kind of think-tank for like-minded colleagues, the *Conférences sur le droit public de la France* ('Lectures on French Public Law').

State finance was increasingly the target for parlementary remonstrances, while the Paris Parlement was also developing ever-closer links with court faction. Its tactic of inviting attendance from the princes and dukes and peers to discuss critical matters of state – daring when first used in 1755–6 during the debates in the Grand Conseil affair[78] – was becoming commonplace. They made the same call in both 1766 and then again in 1768, over further government efforts, eventually thwarted, to revive the Grand Conseil. Although the king dissuaded his relatives from taking up the offer of attendance, it was clear that all the Princes of the Blood – with the sole exception of Conti's son, the duc de La Marche – were increasingly warm in their support for the *parlements*. There was cooperation between Sword and Robe out in the provinces too, in opposition to Laverdy's municipal reforms of 1764–5. Choiseul had never been very keen on the elective element in these measures, and he was not moved to obstruct grandees with provincial authority – such as Condé in Burgundy, Soubise in Flanders and Noailles in Roussillon – who caballed against the local introduction of the reforms: Soubise even turned on Choiseul over them, accusing him of 'damaging the constitution [sic] of this country . . . and depriving it of its privileges'.[79] In 1769–70, the reforms were being quietly laid to rest.

Choiseul's inability to keep a lid on parlementary and provincial politicking was brought into stark relief by the turn of events in Brittany. The newly restored Rennes *parlementaires* seemed less moved by gratitude at their reinstatement in 1768 than egged on by resentment that La Chalotais was still not among their number. In March 1770, they solemnly determined to reopen the criminal investigations of 1766, but this time with d'Aiguillon as prime suspect rather La Chalotais (who had, after all, been declared innocent by the king himself). Proceedings started in Rennes, but d'Aiguillon sought the right to trial by his peers in the Paris Parlement. He wished to clear his name, but also to strike a blow against an institution which, he told the king, was seeking 'to destroy the ancient form of government in order to substitute an administration to their own liking in which they will have the principal part'.[80] 'I consent, but you wait and see what happens!', was Louis XV's doleful response.[81]

The king's foreboding proved well grounded. Though Chancellor

Maupeou had supported the idea of a trial because he felt d'Aiguillon would be exonerated and his name cleared, the legal proceedings developed into a mare's nest of accusations and counter-accusations. D'Aiguillon was even alleged to have planned to assassinate La Chalotais, and the Parlement formally stripped him of his rank of peer. Feeling things had gone too far, Louis convoked a *lit de justice* on 27 June 1770 which formally absolved d'Aiguillon of blame. To pardon La Chalotais was one thing, however; to do the same for his hated opponent, ignoring the evidence that the Parlement had accrued, was another. The magistrates were furious, and refused to regard d'Aiguillon's exoneration as legal. Though their efforts to get the Princes of the Blood on their side were frustrated, it was clear that the latter were also alarmed at the maladroitness of the royal action. The provincial *parlements* swung into line, those at Bordeaux, Metz, Dijon and Rennes vehemently protesting against the *lit de justice*. Yet Louis attempted to ride out the crisis, arresting a couple of Breton magistrates for overstepping the mark, and then on 3 September 1770, descending in person on the Paris Parlement to scold them, stipulating that he would regard correspondence with other *parlements* as evidence of 'a criminal confederation against his authority and against his person'.[82]

The ministry was in a state of chaos, with Choiseul, the major figure in the King's Councils for more than a decade, in manifest difficulties. Already weakened by the recrudescence of the *dévot* lobby around d'Aiguillon at court, he also fell out with his erstwhile ally, Chancellor Maupeou. Controller-General Maynon had framed a radical set of financial reforms to set before the Royal Council in December 1769 in order to extricate the state from 'the horrible state of ruin' which it faced. Maupeou was instrumental in having the plans sabotaged, and when Maynon resigned, was able to prevail on the king to replace him not with Choiseul's nominee but with his own, his long-term political ally, abbé Terray, a Paris *parlementaire*. A magistrate with a record of 100 per cent proof royalism, Terray also had links – worrying for Choiseul – to the meddlesome prince de Conti, on whose private council he had served. The financial policies on which Terray at once embarked further weakened Choiseul. The new Controller-General made big cuts in the main high-spending departments, the Army and Navy Ministries, run by the Choiseul cousins, thus damaging their patronage networks. Terray's decision to implement a partial state bankruptcy in February

1770 also hit hard the court bankers whom Choiseul favoured, notably the financier La Borde.

Choiseul's fate was sealed when he finally and irrecoverably blotted his copy-book over his conduct of foreign affairs. The trust which Louis XV had placed in him since the late 1750s had been grounded in the fact that both men had regarded the maintenance of peace as the first priority, though both also concurred over the need for the refurbishment of the armed forces. Yet the king's hostility towards warfare was more deep-dyed than his minister's. By late 1770, Choiseul was coming desperately close to giving Spain a *carte blanche* to resist the English settlement of the Malvinas (or Falkland Islands) in the south Atlantic. There seemed a chance of France being dragged into war when its armed forces were still insufficiently prepared, when its financial position was abysmal, and when it was the king's express wish to remain at peace. '*Monsieur*,' Louis XV glacially remarked to Choiseul days before the dénouement, 'I told you that I did not want war.'[83] Choiseul's dismissal on 24 December 1770 was accompanied by personal missives from Louis to Charles III of Spain assuring him of the solidity of France's intention to maintain existing alliances but also making it clear that this would not involve going to war with England. The king personally directed foreign policy for the next six months.

Choiseul's dismissal threw Paris into a spin, not least because a major political crisis was already in train. On 3 December 1770, the Parlement had examined a royal Edict of Discipline, issued on 28 November, which Terray had drafted and about which Choiseul, significantly, had not even been consulted. The edict forbade correspondence between the *parlements*, and prohibited any protests against royal orders and *lits de justice*. This was strong stuff. Stronger still was the edict's lengthy preamble, in which Maupeou twisted the knife into parlementary pretensions to be 'representative of the nation, the necessary interpreters of the king's will, and overseers of the administration of public affairs and the acquittal of the debts of the sovereign'.[84] The *parlementaires* were not disposed to take all this lying down, and within days they and the government were locked into a toe-to-toe conflict which seemed to offer either side precious little room for manoeuvre. Efforts to seek a compromise whereby the Parlement retracted its protests in return for the king withdrawing the Edict of Discipline came to nothing. Government hamfistedness only made matters worse: on the night of 19–20

January, every member of the Parlement was awakened by musketeers who asked them – yea or nay – whether they would agree to resume judicial service. Thirty-nine proffered a yea, but in the less isolated atmosphere of the Parlement's session next day they recanted, and the body reaffirmed its collective opposition to the crown's policies.

What followed was the beginnings of what contemporaries would call the 'revolution' of Maupeou, a new and distinctive turn in royal policy after the Choiseul years. During the night of 20–21 January, all the *parlementaires* who the previous night had refused to resume service were served *lettres de cachet* exiling them to grim locations throughout the country. Their offices, it was made clear, would be confiscated to the profit of the king – a quite unheard-of gesture. Maupeou, the author of this startling coup, clearly meant business. Within a year, aided and abetted by Terray at the Control-General and d'Aiguillon as Foreign Minister, he had dismantled the Parlement of Paris; broken up its sprawling constituency into a network of more compact jurisdictions; put a new, more malleable remonstrating body in the Parlement's place; and accompanied all this with a programme of other important socio-legal reforms. The very juridical fabric of the Bourbon monarchy had been ripped open. The price of Maupeou's 'revolution' was the expression of dissent more furious and more turbulent than any in Louis XV's reign. An affair which had started in peripheral Brittany ended up mobilizing the full force of national opinion.

7

The Triumvirate and Its Aftermath
(1771–84)

A) MAUPEOU'S REVOLUTION

With the blandly untroubled benefit of hindsight, historians have sometimes categorized the years between 1770 and 1774 as witnessing the
last chance for absolute monarchy to reassert itself in the face of the
parlements. In this scenario, Maupeou – central member of a 'Triumvirate' which comprised Controller-General Terray and, from June 1771,
the duc d'Aiguillon as Foreign Minister – emerges as a far-sighted,
statesmanlike figure vainly seeking to remove a persistent thorn in the
flesh of absolutism and to restructure the state's administration and
finances in ways which would pre-empt the Revolution of 1789. Only
the unexpected death of Louis XV in 1774 and the decision of his
successor, the young and inexperienced Louis XVI, to dismiss the Triumvirate prematurely ended what was – through no fault of Maupeou's –
'a failed revolution'.[1]

Despite Madame de Pompadour's fatalistic invocation of the forthcoming 'deluge', government did not sit and wait for the regime's collapse, and the Maupeou period represents only one of a number of
attempts to manage the political system and to reform the state in the
period following the Seven Years War. Considering the appalling state
of the monarchy in the dark days of that conflict, there is indeed some
merit in viewing the period overall as marking less a record of inevitable
terminal decline, than a chronicle of patchy recovery in which a variety
of statesmen offered differing reform pathways. The Maupeou years
were not necessarily the most politically promising of the manifold
initiatives of the period. Nor was Maupeou himself cut of a different
cloth from other statesmen in his position: his principal motivation
appears to have been personal ambition to topple Choiseul and the

wish to establish himself as Principal Minister. Far from setting out perspicaciously to renovate the political system, he stumbled backwards and unintentionally into the limelight, overthrowing the delicately balanced Choiseulian system and triggering a widely ramified political crisis with more than parlementary dimensions at a moment when the regime was faced with the severest financial and economic crisis of Louis XV's reign. Although the Triumvirate was able to face down opposition and the regime live to fight another day after the Triumvirs' demise, the 'Maupeou revolution' stirred up and radicalized public opinion, making state-driven reforms without public consultation more contestable.

The years from 1769 to 1771 represent the forgotten financial and economic crisis of the eighteenth century, whose severity in many respects bears comparison with the more epochal years of 1787–9. Bad harvests from 1768 onwards produced a doubling in the price of grain, with the cost of bread reaching its highest levels since the famine years of 1709–10. Middling and large grain producers made their fortunes – though at the expense of consumers and small producers. Failure of the wine harvest produced widespread misery too, while the manufacturing sector also experienced bankruptcies and labour lay-offs. Unlike in 1709–10, demographic fall-out was limited – there were more births than deaths throughout the crisis – but this only meant that more individuals survived to vent their anger. That anger was targeted at government. The state legislation on free trade in grain which had been introduced in 1763–4 was widely unpopular and fanned the flames of rumour, reigniting belief in the state's complicity in a 'famine plot' (*pacte de famine*). Predictably, the tax take plummeted, causing a shuddering impact on state finances. So severe was the shortfall in revenue that tax farmers and major tax officials whose short-term credit customarily helped government through such sticky moments found themselves stretched and several went bankrupt.

'Necessity', Terray explained to Louis XV, 'led me by the hand.'[2] An improviser through and through, the new Controller-General proved adept at the fiscal trouble-shooting the crisis required. The raft of measures he introduced in 1769, involving arbitrary reductions of interest on certain government financial obligations and suspension of payment on others, drastically reduced state outgoings. There was an outcry in some circles – the *nouveau riche* Voltaire claimed to have had his nails 'cut to the quick' in the operation, for example.[3] Yet Terray acted nimbly to support the credit of those financiers on whom the state most depended and he also took care to protect rents on the Paris Hôtel-de-Ville, in which most parlementary magistrates as well as a great many middling Parisian families had substantial investments. Despite this clever footwork, the worsening economic crisis of early 1770 necessitated harsher measures, which the *parlements* would be sure to block. The impulse to crush the *parlements* thus owed less to strategic astuteness or reforming zeal than to short-term personal and political goals. The Paris Parlement stood as the major obstacle in the pathway to power of the ambitious Maupeou and in the political future of the harassed duc d'Aiguillon. It now also inhibited the introduction of financial reforms on which Terray's tenure in power depended. Choiseul's customary strategy of leaving an avenue open towards the Parlement looked quite out of the question for each man. Indeed, deep-dyed hostility towards the magistrates acted as a political adhesive, glueing Maupeou, d'Aiguillon and Terray together in a united mission of destruction.

A Parisian *parlementaire* himself, Maupeou marked his striking conversion from poacher to gamekeeper in February 1771 when he followed up his exile of the Paris Parlement by introducing an edict which, formally chastising the magistrates for treasonous disobedience, set about restructuring the whole administration of higher justice. The Parlement's sprawling jurisdiction was fragmented among six new 'higher courts' (*cours supérieures*), situated in Arras, Blois, Châlons-sur-Marne, Clermont-Ferrand, Lyon and Poitiers, each of which would judge civil and criminal cases on appeal. Though only the Paris Parlement was permitted a role in registering royal legislation, its powers of remonstrance were severely circumscribed, and its membership much reduced. Even more striking was the stipulation that magistrates in the new courts were not to be venal office-holders, but salaried state appointees, promised progressive ennoblement for long service. The old magistrates were offered reimbursement for their lost offices. Many, assuming that Maupeou would eventually crack under pressure and restore the *parlements*, refused to go through the formalities for this and launched a coruscating assault on the new system.

The Triumvirate's attack on the Paris Parlement was merely the capstone of what became an even more ambitious reform programme. The collegial complaints of provincial *parlements* against the harsh treatment meted out to the Parisian institution gave Maupeou little option but to bring them too into his line of fire. With the exception of docile Pau, all were remodelled, and four (troublesome Rouen, plus Douai, Metz and Dombes) were abolished. Parlementary jurisdictional authority was split among 'higher courts'. These benefited by receiving the attributions of a number of other courts which were also dissolved (including the Cour des Aides, the Grand Conseil and the Amirauté courts in Paris, and the Lyon Cour des Monnaies and the Clermont Cour des Aides). These measures were intended to produce a more rational and efficacious judicial map, but it was also hoped that the dissolution of such courts would free up judicial personnel to staff the new institutions. Judicial officials were offered promotion and sundry sweeteners, as state functionaries throughout France fished for loyal recruits in much the way that d'Aiguillon had done at the start of the Brittany crisis in 1766.

The rational, innovatory and meritocratic flavour of the new arrangements was much trumpeted by Maupeou and Terray, as was their abolition within the new courts of *épices* (the emoluments – or 'seasonings' – which plaintiffs paid for judgements). The measures were prized as part of a more general royal campaign to make justice 'prompt, pure and free'. Such claims were, however, little more than window-dressing for reforms whose underlying rationale was narrowly financial and political. The 3,500 (mainly judicial) posts made non-venal as a result of the reform of the *parlements* accounted for only around 2.5 per cent of the total number of venal offices. Terray did seriously consider a long-term campaign to reimburse all venal office-holders, but the spectre of John Law deterred any kind of commitment in this area. The notion was more than offset, anyway, by short-term financial pressures to strengthen rather than diminish the prevalence of venality. Terray's ministry saw a larger number of creations – at the lowest estimate, around 9,000 posts – than at any time in Louis XV's long reign. In November 1771, for example, municipal officials in all incorporated towns, which since Laverdy's reforms of 1764–5 had been electable, were made venal once more. This was viewed as a nakedly cynical ploy to squeeze money out of the townships, which were encouraged to buy the right to continue election. A similar ploy was evident in Terray's decision to make a certain number of masterships in trade guilds both hereditary and venal. The Parisian attorney, Régnault, wryly noted that 'it was certainly not the good and solace of the people [which] were in view' in such measures.[4]

Terray also showed great ingenuity in making the existing venal network more financially productive for the state. An edict rationalizing office-holding in February 1771 decreed that venal officers should themselves assess the value of their own posts. Office-holders were restrained from inflating them (and thus securing a larger return on the investment) by the Controller-General's cunning insistence that the valuations should form the basis of tax liability: a new 'hundredth penny' (*centième denier*) tax was extended to all offices, bringing in high yields. A greater degree of standardization was also introduced into the ways in which office-holders were paid. In addition, individuals utilizing venal office-holding as a ladder into the nobility were required to pay a higher premium for the privilege. Terray extended this new spirit of rationalization into remodelling the structures of the state's financial management. More efficient, more centrally controlled financial institutions were developed which reduced state outgoings and increased revenue. The silencing of the *parlements* allowed the Controller-General to issue an unopposed decree in November 1771 that one *vingtième* should become a permanent tax, while an additional one should be continued until 1781. In regard to direct taxes, Terray was convinced that 'every owner of capital, rich and poor, must contribute as much as possible in the same proportion'.[5] With the *parlements* now safely out of the way, he also accentuated the trend, established by Machault, of using royal Intendants to revise (or 'verify') tax assessments in a way which squeezed more money out of the landed elite.

In the context of parlementary nullity, Terray's ruthless squeeze on both tax-payers and venal office-holders – who found themselves rueing the king's 'prompt, pure and free' justice – pulled the state through its financial crisis. In 1772, the budget came close to balancing – a remarkable achievement less than a decade after the Treaty of Paris. By then Terray had also survived the worst effects of the country's economic woes. No minister could expect popularity in time of high grain prices, but Terray's decision in July 1770 to abandon doctrinaire adhesion to free trade in grain took the bile out of popular attacks on the government. The export of grain was now abolished. Though promoting free trade within the kingdom, Terray even attenuated this when the Intendants, on whom he relied for economic and social data, claimed that it was threatening the social fabric. There were grain riots in parts of the south-west in 1773, but by then economic recovery was well on its way, drawing the claws of popular discontent.

Terray's strategy of staying well-informed and utilizing administrative remedies to forestall problems was typical of the Triumvirate's policies more generally. D'Aiguillon was an arch-pragmatist as regards foreign policy. If very little was achieved in this area, this was mainly because very little was attempted. As the Malvinas crisis of 1770 had underlined, war with England was off the agenda. The collapse of Choiseulian grand strategy also highlighted the limitations of France's options in Europe too, especially in the east. The Francophile Poles whom Choiseul had nurtured were unable to prevent the First Partition of Poland in 1772 by Russia, Prussia and France's ally, Austria. In addition, the Turks, whom France had urged into war with Russia in 1768, suffered a drubbing, and in the Treaty of Kainardji in 1774 conceded that the Russian fleet could be given access to the Black Sea. D'Aiguillon's attempts to reconfigure France's alliances in northern Europe were unproductive: friendly approaches to England were rebuffed, while attempts to use the dynamic Swedish monarch Gustavus III to counter the growing power of Prussia and Russia had produced little fruit by 1774.

D'Aiguillon's rejection of an adventurist foreign policy was whole-heartedly endorsed by Louis who, as he approached the seventh decade of his reign, showed every sign of having religiously heeded his great-grandfather's deathbed injunction to avoid wars. He may well have felt that he had to leave a peaceful and tranquil country to his own grandson and heir, the duc de Berry, whom in 1770 he had married to Marie-Antoinette, daughter of Austrian empress Maria Theresa, in ceremonies of unparalleled splendour. Thoroughly disenchanted with the Choiseul-ian spirit of compromise with the *parlements*, as he grew older, Louis was also becoming (again, very much like his great-grandfather) more open to *dévot* influence at court. Louis retained his taste for hunting and mistresses and was developing a penchant for a certain kind of grandeur: he gave the green light to the extensive remodelling of the Versailles palace, for example, and followed up the marriage of Berry with similarly lavish ceremonies for the marriages of his two younger grandsons, the comtes de Provence and Artois. The king was finally seeming more at ease on the State Councils. The political dinosaurs of earlier periods had died or (like Choiseul) been exiled, and the growing aristocratization of government clearly suited him. The disgrace of Choiseul and his brother, Praslin, meant the loss of two dukes, but this was balanced by the arrival of the hyper-elitist d'Aiguillon at the heart of government. He was joined, moreover, by another courtier, the marquis de Monteynard, appointed War Minister (though he – like the jurist Bourgeois de Boynes, who made a far from competent Navy Minister – was a political non-entity).

The key policies of the Triumvirate were very much the king's. At the *lit de justice* of 13 April 1771, at which he formally registered the decree establishing the new Parlement on the ruins of the old, he ended his short speech with the words, 'I will *never* change [my policies]', with a vehemence which sent shivers through his audience.[6] When in the ensuing political fracas, the opponents of government tried to argue that the king had been misled by his ministers, he countered, 'You say that I have not been fully informed; nothing is more false.' This personal identification by the king with the policies of the Triumvirate was the strongest card in his ministers' hand. In particular, it helped contain factional mischief at court. The Princes of the Blood had developed numerous links of patronage with *parlementaires* over previous decades, and the Parlement's demotion in status reflected badly on the princes who had come to vaunt the political role which their right to attend the Parlement's Court of Peers had given the institution. Led by the perennial irritant, Conti, and using arguments culled from Le Paige, the princes made formal objections to the government's attack on the Parlement. When they made their complaint public in the *Gazette d'Utrecht*, the king exiled them from court for their pains, only allowing them back in 1772. Similar toughness was shown to court-connected provincial dignitaries – such as the duc d'Harcourt and the prince de Beauvau, Commanders of Normandy and Languedoc respectively – who endeavoured to show solidarity with princes and *parlements*. A delegation of Norman gentry boldly requesting in 1771 the calling of the Normandy estates (which had been abolished in 1666) was despatched prestissimo to the Bastille.

Royal endorsement helped the Triumvirate overcome opposition to their reforms. The new Parlement of Paris, installed by *lit de justice* in April 1771, and its provincial analogues, established between August and November, were primed to start work before Christmas. Start work they did. Doggedness and ruse, arm-twisting and political bribery brought sufficient new magistrates into the fold, and also helped crush the opposition of the Parisian barristers, who had been amongst the most vocal defenders of the *parlementaires*. The presumption that all the *parlements* of France would stand shoulder to shoulder in the *union des classes* thus proved unfounded. Furthermore, although parlementary propaganda invariably portrayed the legal cohorts flocking to Maupeou's banner as low-born, technically incompetent, politically spineless and Jesuit-supporting careerists, this damning description simply did not fit. Differing less from their predecessors in terms of experience and social background than in ideological commitment, they formed an incipient 'king's party' relatively secure from the blandishments and polemical stances of the old *parlementaires* and willing to be mobilized by ministers and provincial Intendants.

The Triumvirate's achievement was all the more impressive in that it also involved outfacing one of the most turbulent and vehement public outcries in the eighteenth century thus far. 'Political questions have become almost the sole topic of conversation at court, in society, in the city and indeed in all the kingdom,' the Austrian ambassador, the comte de Mercy, informed Maria Theresa.[7] Repression was a key part of the government's strategy in dealing with this public outcry. Censorship was tightened up, and police spies worked overtime in a crack-down on 'dangerous' books, authors and publishers, many of whom were soon languishing in the Bastille. The famous prison had to have special new storerooms built to house growing mountains of seditious literature seized from printshops and peddlers (and among which figured 6,000 copies of the new edition of the *Encyclopédie*, which had got caught up in the crossfire). The editorial team of the official *Gazette de France* was replaced by a more compliant crew, and unprecedented pressure was also put on foreign-based newspapers such as the *Gazette de Leyde* to ensure that they did not support the parlementary cause.

The government also looked to influence the public debate in creative as well as repressive ways. By late 1771, over 100 pro-government pamphlets had been penned by a wide variety of authors, including Voltaire, who deserted the *philosophe* team to support a government he regarded as the lesser of two evils. The ageing veteran of the Calas affair had had too many tangles with the *parlements* to hold them in much esteem: 'I would prefer to obey a good lion, born stronger than myself,' he noted, 'than two hundred rats of my own kind.'[8] He also warmed to rumours that Maupeou was planning a sweeping codification of the laws as well as introducing major educational and welfare reforms. The bloodless royalist *coup d'état* performed against his Riksdag by enlightened ruler Gustavus III of Sweden in August 1772 gave credence to the idea of a European wave of reaction against the excesses of representative government.

In the royalist legitimations of Maupeou's policy, there was a remarkable absence of strong religious themes. The government did not lack for *dévot* support (and indeed was assailed by its opponents as ardently Jesuitophilic). Yet there was little dwelling on the claims of divine right. The expectation of deferential obedience was grounded in historically derived, social utilitarian arguments which reflected the enlightened temper of the times, and not on the basis of theological doctrine. The materialist turn to political discourse evident since the Seven Years War thus proved an enduring legacy of Choiseul's ministry. The king's own propagandists were divesting him of his sempiternal sacral aura; Fénelon's virtuous utilitarianism was winning out over Bossuet's intimations of royal divinity.

Pamphlets provided a secular sanctification of the king as the friend of the needy and the benefactor of the nation, whereas the nobility in contrast was comprehensively demonized. For all their self-serving talk of 'fundamental laws', the Robe nobility and the sovereign courts were viewed as being quite as obstructive as the ancient aristocracy of the Sword in acting as a check on social improvements engineered by the beneficent monarch. The *parlements'* opposition to Maupeou was represented as resistance to the social good of free and cheap justice, and the crushing of selfish nobility as a hopeful harbinger of national felicity. Voltaire and the other pamphleteers mixed absolutist rhetoric with examples from the historical record to demonstrate that the crown's claims to political legitimacy were more solidly grounded than the Parlement's. Claims that, as one irate pamphleteer bemoaned, 'the government wants to make us all happy by bringing back the Dark Ages' were countered by the view that 'France was never happier or more tranquil than when her kings were most absolute'.[9] More absolutism, the slogan seemed to go, more happiness.

The welfare rhetoric of the embryonic king's party was forthrightly challenged by opponents of the Maupeou coup. Published anonymously, smuggled from hand to hand and under the cloak and read in secret, anti-governmental pamphlets vaunting a quite distinct version of patriotism beat the censor and the police official. Outnumbering those of their opponents three or four to one, they received the tacit support of the magistrates and barristers and drew sustenance from right across the political spectrum, including court aristocrats and Princes of the Blood and a good sprinkling of individuals from the *philosophe* movement, such as Helvétius, Raynal, d'Holbach and Mercier. Many of the most assertive voices belonged to lawyers who comprised the vestiges of the old *parti janséniste*, which, one well-informed pamphleteer asserted, having disposed of the Jesuits, had now managed 'to turn themselves into a party of patriotism', with Le Paige, still in his Temple lair, very much in the thick of things.[10] Roughly half the anti-governmental pamphlets of the Maupeou years were authored by Jansenists, and around one-third of arrests and police interrogations of suspects for publishing offences were of Jansenists. Unsurprisingly, the historically based arguments, which Le Paige and his ilk had familiarized over the decades of the Jansenist struggle and which Montesquieu was held to have endorsed, were staples of patriot propaganda. Maupeou's attack on the *parlements* – heirs of the representative institutions of the Merovingians – was viewed as an assault on the nation's fundamental laws which even the monarchy, in the past, had admitted it was in a state of 'happy powerlessness' to change.[11] The Triumvirate was 'ministerial despotism' incarnate.

There were some emergent themes which stood out against this familiar backcloth. One fresh element within anti-government discourse was its lack of religious resonance. Just as the king's party rarely deployed the language of divine right, so these quondam Jansenist enthusiasts rarely utilized religious argumentation. The abolition of the Jesuits had removed the classic Jansenist scapegoat, and a new spirit of secularism was abroad in the patriot as well as the Maupeou camp. A second distinctive feature of patriot propaganda was the way in which their demands transcended the corporative interest of the sovereign courts and hovered as yet still tentatively around the supra-corporative notion of the nation. A good deal of patriot polemic followed the ringing appeal of Malesherbes, for example, who, in the remonstrances he penned in 1770 on behalf of the Paris Cour des Aides, had gone so far as to call for the meeting of the Estates General. This august forum, which debated matters of national importance, had last met in 1614 – and its quasi-permanent recess was coextensive with the reign of the absolutism which now was under attack.[12] Notions of national sovereignty and a national 'general will' were starting to appear.

A third feature of the Maupeou polemics was a particularly intense contest over the meanings and implications of the most basic terms in the political lexicon, facilitated by the fact that patriots and their opponents shared much the same vocabulary. 'The war of the pen is beginning,' Madame d'Épinay wrote to the abbé Galiani in April 1771, 'heads are in ferment, the dictionary is changing and we hear nothing but big words like "reason of state", "aristocrat" and "despotism".'[13] The ubiquity of the word despotism was very much a case in point. While royalists maintained the traditional distinction between 'absolutism' and 'despotism', many of their opponents attacked practices and prerogatives which a few decades previously would have been regarded as uncontestable truisms about the monarchical constitution. Despotism was evident, it was held, not only in the policies of his ministers, Intendants and police and tax officials but also in the personal life of the ruler. Personalized and often openly pornographic attacks on Louis XV, his mistresses and his ministers – such as Thévenot de Morande's *Le Gazetier cuirassé* ('The Armour-plated Gazetteer') – purported to bring under the public gaze the immoral and corrupt realities of court life. A good king should be a faithful and virtuous servant of the nation's interest: Louis XV, it seemed, was the polar opposite. Despotism was also allegedly detectable in lack of respect for individual 'freedoms' – and this too was another word whose meanings were being contested. Though the sense of freedom as historically validated and legally enforcible privileges – such as the liberties of the provinces, cities and other corporative bodies, including the *parlements* – still remained intact, there was a growing tendency to give a more positive and universalist spin to the term, in ways which echoed Rousseau and the natural law tradition.[14] Thus, the exile of individual *parlementaires* by *lettre de cachet* was viewed as symptomatic of a more generalized lack of respect for individual freedom. In much the same way, the government's tough stance on censorship was interpreted as an assault on a 'natural' right of free speech and freedom of conscience. The Maupeou debates thus registered a sea-change taking place in the political culture and vocabulary of Bourbon France. Absolutist verities were not only being challenged in more systematic and more daring forms than hitherto; the parameters of political debate were also being widened by both government and its critics.

The apparent strengths of the patriot movement were only a light veneer, however, over its many weaknesses. However many arguments the patriots won, it proved impossible to mobilize the public opinion whose support was endlessly evoked. This was all the more the case in that the vague and baggy language which the patriots spoke obscured rather than clarified very different interests of the individuals – princes, *parlementaires*, lawyers, *philosophes*, or whoever – who used it. A notable diminuendo in pamphlet production from 1772 highlighted the growing efficiency of the state's policing operations and the erosion of public support for the patriot cause. Although the bumptious Beaumarchais would make effective fun of the new Paris Parlement in several best-selling pamphlets in 1773, the patriot movement had by then seemingly failed to cut the political mustard.

Maupeou thus seemed triumphant, while Terray – though endlessly ridiculed for corruption – had come close to balancing the state budget in 1772 and by 1773 had ridden out the worst of the economic and financial crises he had faced on coming into office. Yet those who lived by faction in the Bourbon polity risked perishing by it. Despite the considerable political credit they had amassed by 1774 for outfacing parlementary and popular opposition, the Triumvirate's situation was still fragile. One of their great strengths had been their unity and cohesion. Strapped tightly to each other by their collective need to do down the Paris Parlement in 1770–71, the three members had less in common once that threat had been exorcized. More fissiparous tendencies started to develop between them. Relations between Maupeou and Terray went from the cool-but-cooperative to the distant-cum-glacial, while d'Aiguillon started to develop his own agenda, cosying up in particular to the Princes of the Blood. This seemed like treason to Maupeou, since the refusal of the princes to attend his new Parlement (and thus to confer on it the prestige of being a Court of Peers) was in his eyes a continuing weakness in the institution.

Although rumours were abroad in 1774 that Maupeou's ministerial days would soon be over, the support of his ruler did not waver. Yet if Louis's strength of commitment never failed, his body did. Taken ill while out hunting, the king was diagnosed as suffering from smallpox –

though he himself was the last to know, realizing what was happening to him only when he glimpsed his own pock-ridden hand. At once he sought to use the decay of his physical body to demonstrate the eternal value of the monarch's ceremonial body. 'Now I know what is going on,' he told Madame du Barry, 'we must not start up again the scandal at Metz . . . I owe myself to God and my people.'[15] The mistress was despatched from court at once and Louis set about dying like a Christian in imitation of his great-grandfather, whose image and representations had dogged every aspect of his long reign. Though the contagious nature of the disease ruled out the attendance of the dauphin for deathbed advice, other court ceremonials played out mechanically around the increasingly hideous figure of the ruler, nailed in suffering to a campbed in the midst of the royal chamber at the heart of the solar temple of the Sun King. Louis's belated rallying to piety won him some small measure of public sympathy, chroniclers noticed, but this meant little to the factional vultures gathering for the royal demise. The stock of the Choiseulists rose, while *dévot* activists like Richelieu and d'Aiguillon, who had composed with the now-exiled du Barry, cast round desperately for allies. With its mainstay and prop on his deathbed, the ministry looked as ripe for removal as the monarchy for a new direction.

B) THE TURGOT EXPERIMENT

The Triumvirate had already begun to disintegrate before the death of Louis XV and accession of his adolescent grandson, the duc de Berry, destroyed it altogether. The new ruler had never been emotionally close to his predecessor, away from whose contagious dying body he had been studiously kept. Dauphin at eleven following the death of his father, the 'grand dauphin' in 1765, and still (just) a teenager on his accession, the new Louis XVI had not even progressed to sitting on the State Council, and felt he was too young to have the burden of rule thrust upon him. Even though – following the example of Louis XIV, whose memory he venerated – he was determined to rule without a Principal Minister, he realized he needed help. An avid enthusiast for Fénelon's *Télémaque*, he looked desperately around for a Mentor to start him on his political odyssey. He could expect nothing from his own family – he shared the view of his father that the Condé and Orléans cadet branches were political troublemakers. Though in the early 1770s he had congratulated Maupeou for having 'put the crown back on the head' of Louis XV,[16] Maupeou's rather limited reforming zeal looked played out by 1774, and his ministry was widely unpopular and stood accused of despotic arrogance and corruption.

In the end, Louis fastened for a Mentor on a ministerial has-been whose main credit was grounded in three decades of royal service and an extensive knowledge of government, namely, the gouty septuagenarian Maurepas. The latter's disgrace from Louis XV's court in 1749 (before Louis had been born) as a result of an intrigue orchestrated by Madame de Pompadour had not lost him credit in the eyes of the grand dauphin, who on his deathbed in 1765 had commended him to his son. 'I am king', Louis now wrote to Maurepas, recalling him to take up a place on the State Council, 'and am only twenty years old and don't have all the knowledge I need.'[17] Maurepas had no other brief in government than to be around for regular consultation with the king, and this awkward position made him initially vulnerable to factional sniping, notably from Choiseulites clamouring for the recall of their patron. He strengthened his position, however, by persuading Louis to dismiss both Maupeou and Terray in a court putsch on 24 August (d'Aiguillon had been ousted a little earlier). The other beneficiaries of this ministerial reversal were ex-Intendant Turgot, recently appointed Navy Minister and now promoted to the post of Controller-General, and the Norman *parlementaire* Miromesnil, a Maurepas client, who was made Keeper of the Seals. The career diplomat, Vergennes, took over Foreign Affairs, the heroic, gnarled veteran, the comte de Saint-Germain, took the War Ministry, with Paris Police Lieutenant Sartine appointed Navy Minister. This cleansing of the Maupeouian political stables owed much to the background influence of Maurepas, but a good deal of public attention focused on the person of Turgot, the most dynamic of the new ministry and, in the astonished acclamation of the abbé Galiani, that rare bird, 'an *Encyclopédiste* who's made it!'[18] Turgot's appointment gave the new ministry a philosophical and secularist hue which mortally offended the *dévot* faction – the duc de Croÿ, for example, called Turgot's appointment 'the greatest blow to religion since Clovis'[19] and huffed and puffed in vain against the apparent seizure of government patronage by the *philosophe* faction. The *dévots* were further discomfited by the subsequent appointment in 1775 as Minister for the Royal Household of the liberal ex-censor and friend of the *philosophes* Lamoignon de Malesherbes, who as President in the Paris Cour des Aides had been amongst the most virulent opponents of the Maupeou coup.

'I helped [Louis XV] win a case which had lasted three hundred years,' Maupeou, evoking his dissolution of the *parlements*, oracularly pronounced on returning the seals to the crown, '[Louis XVI] wishes to resume the case. He is the master.'[20] And indeed one of the first things the new ministry did was to negotiate the recall of the *parlements*, popular support for which had swollen in the weeks following the collapse of the Triumvirate. Maurepas, a scion of the Phélypeaux clan, which had provided royal ministers in an unbroken line for nearly a century and a half, was not unsympathetic to the plight of his fellow Robins in the *parlements*. His aphorism, 'no *parlements*, no monarchy',[21] however, highlighted a lack of appreciation of how political rhetoric and practices had changed since his last encounter with power. The Paris Parlement was triumphantly reinstated in its pre-1771 form in early November, and provincial *parlements* were recalled over the next year or so.

The recall of the *parlements* was seen as heralding a new start which would bind the nation together following the despotic divisiveness of the Maupeou years. The move highlighted the young monarch's agonized desire to rule in ways which won the acclaim of his subjects. This wish to please was moral and political principle as well as personal quirk. His tutors when he was a boy, the duc de La Vauguyon and the ultra-royalist publicist Moreau, had inculcated in him a strong sense of the need to be a virtuous ruler responsive to the interests of his peoples. When he was twelve he had written (and published on his own little printing press) a work entitled *Moral and Political Maxims Drawn from 'Télémaque'*, which was thoroughly suffused with Fénelonian principles. From his wide reading of works of history, moreover, he culled examples of good kings who were to be imitated, bad ones to be despised: a good reign was one in which the people were happy, and this required a high level of personal morality in the ruler – solicitude for the less fortunate, openness in dealings, tolerance of diversity, and an absolute commitment to royal duty. This equation between private and public goodness was one reason why, as Dauphin, Louis had found it difficult to stomach the vices of his *roué* grandfather, and one of his first acts as king was to declare that only persons of 'recognized morality' would henceforth be presented at court. Louis also detested his predecessor's crushing insouciance towards public opinion. 'I must always consult public opinion,' the new king had once noted in his schoolboy notebooks, 'it is never wrong.'[22] Initially at least, he was as good as his word: 'It may be considered politically unwise', he observed, defending his decision to recall the *parlements*, 'but it seems to me that it is the general will [sic] and I wish to be loved.'[23]

In his quest to inspire his people's love, Louis felt he had found a soul-mate in Turgot. This did not derive from Turgot's notorious indifference to religion – which indeed jarred with the religious inspiration the king drew from the example of his painstakingly pious father. Yet Louis's moralistic view of politics chimed harmoniously with Turgot's lofty commitment to humane reform. The Controller-General promised his young monarch greater prosperity for the population, which he aimed to achieve with, as he put it, 'no bankruptcy, no tax increases, no borrowing' – a slogan diametrically opposed to the unpopular and, for Louis, immoral policies of the Triumvirate. Turgot was an odd mix of a thinker and a man in a hurry (the linguistic legacy of his spell in power, fittingly, would be the *turgotine*, the speedier and more streamlined public carriages he introduced). An intellectual who kept abreast of discoveries across the sciences, he was convinced, his admirer, Condorcet, noted, 'that the truths of moral and political science are capable of the same certainty as those that form the system of physical science, even in those branches like astronomy that seem to approximate mathematical certainty'.[24] Yet Turgot was more of a pragmatist than this chillingly hubristic quotation suggests. Though his name was closely linked to that of the Physiocrats, he was less an armchair intellectual like Quesnay or the elder Mirabeau than a doer in the vein of Bertin and Trudaine, with, like them, a thorough administrative savvy, honed in his case in more than a decade as Intendant in the Limousin. He had no shortage of big ideas but he lacked either time or inclination to persuade anyone that they were right. Galiani was exaggerating when he said that Turgot would run France like a slave plantation,[25] but the new Controller-General certainly preferred the exposition and implementation of his ideas to dealing with the messy irregularities of dissent.

Turgot held that the key to unlocking the economy's potential, producing greater prosperity and happiness, was an economic freedom he defended with the passion of the true believer. 'The freer, the more animated and the more extensive trade is,' he argued, 'the more swiftly, efficaciously and abundantly can the people be supplied.'[26] A reduction in market regulation would let the mechanisms of supply and demand work in ways which would bring landowners profits and consumers affordable foodstuffs. Similarly, state and corporative regulation of labour and production needed to be removed, since it acted as a block on output and inhibited the ability of the poor to make their own livelihoods in freedom. The government needed to stand back from the economy, intervening only in marginal cases where it seemed that the play of vested interests and human passions might adversely affect collective felicity. What set Turgot apart from other individuals who had preceded him at the levers of governmental power was his quintessentially *philosophe* view that society could and should be reconstructed on the basis of human reason rather than through divine injunction or jurisdictional legality. With exemplary energy and relish, he set about his self-assigned task of delivering to his ruler a prosperous and happy society without recourse to higher taxes, government loans or state bankruptcy, cresting the wave of post-Maupeouian popularity to drive through a radical programme of reform attuned to the rational principles associated with the Physiocrats.

On 13 September 1774, Turgot removed all regulation of grain markets, liberalizing the grain trade along lines essayed in 1763–4, and subsequently abandoned. In February 1775, a further package of reforms – the 'Six Acts' – was introduced, including the abolition of trade guilds and the ending of the *corvée* (the peasant labour tax used for road-building), which was to be replaced by a new property tax payable by all but the clergy. These radical reforms brought howls of protest – both from that public whose opinion Louis in theory so esteemed (and whose support Turgot took for granted), and from within the social and political establishment. Turgot was blinkered as regards the good faith of political opponents, and ascribed hostility to his views as deriving from ignorance or knavery. Yet free trade in grain would never be a popular reform in a country in which, despite the sizeable incursions of commercial capitalism, the molecular multiplicity of physical, geographical and institutional obstacles to freedom of movement inevitably produced pockets of grain shortage when harvests were poor. Fear of the *pacte de famine* had become an inescapable datum of social and political life. Turgot was unlucky, moreover, in that the introduction of his liberalization measures coincided with a grain crisis caused by bad weather in 1774, which doubled bread prices. Market disturbances, originating in Burgundy in late 1774 and then rippling outwards through much of the remainder of northern France the following year, produced numerous attacks on bakers, rich farmers, hard-hearted seigneurs and other alleged 'monopolists'. There were also episodes of *taxation populaire*, in which angry crowds stopped convoys of grain moving out of dearth-affected areas, and sold off the grain at what was adjudged a 'fair price'. In late spring, the rioting wave had reached Paris and Versailles. *Laisser-faire* in economics, tender in social outlook, Turgot proved politically tough when hordes of grain rioters challenged his policies. The young king gave him the force he needed to meet popular violence with armed repression, and by May the so-called 'Flour War' (*'guerre des farines'*) was brought to a close in a flurry of intimidatory public executions.

The popular violence of the Flour War was less of a threat to Turgot's position than the way in which it opened him up to attack from sources within the political nation antagonistic to reform. The liberalization of the grain trade had been combined with reductions in the privileges of the General Farm, and the financial milieux affected were quick to encourage opposition to the ministry. Particularly prominent was a grouping orchestrated by the Swiss millionaire banker, Jacques Necker, whose overtly anti-Turgotian *Essai sur la législation du commerce des grains* ('Essay on Grain-Trade Legislation') in 1775 took the fight out into the public sphere. (Turgot responded by launching Condorcet and Morellet against the Genevan upstart.)

The reinstated *parlements* also joined in the fun of discomfiting the opinionated Controller-General. The Parisian magistrates had shown no gratitude towards the young ruler for bringing it back from the dead. The *lit de justice* of 12 November 1774 which restored them had struck quite the wrong note: Louis presented the recall as an act of royal grace and pardon rather than a belated act of monarchical submission to the majesty of France's fundamental laws. Administrative changes made at the same time, slimming down the number of parlementary chambers, increasing the powers of the Présidial courts, limiting the remit of parlementary remonstrances, and threatening the use of a 'plenary court' as a means of imposing discipline on the courts, caused further resentment. In addition, the freeing of the grain trade was also ill-viewed by the magistrates for trampling over their own customary powers of regulating markets in the interest of consumers. By mid-1775, moreover, they were becoming aware of further major reforms in the government pipeline. Turgot was reputed to want to introduce elective representative assemblies within the provinces, for example, as well as wishing to reform the system of *lettres de cachet* and maybe to give freedom of conscience to Protestants and to permit the redemption of feudal dues.

Magistrates viewed the Turgot ministry as being so hell-bent on far-going reforms that the very corporative structure of the state was under threat – a view also held by the Princes of the Blood, who, with the irrepressible Conti to the fore, had lost no time in taking their seats amongst the magistrates. The Parlement's defensive posturing was particularly outspoken in attacks on the legislation on the *corvée* and over the abolition of the guilds. (They managed to make the latter measure sound as though it infringed the most fundamental nerve of the state – even though under Colbert the Parlement had inveighed furiously against the creation of guilds!) 'Any system which, in a well-ordered monarchy, under the guise of humanity and beneficence', their remonstrances stated, 'tends to establish an equality of duty between men and to destroy necessary distinctions would lead to disorder; a consequence of absolute equality would be the destruction of civil society.'[27] 'Necessary distinctions' were taken to include juridical ones: the *parlementaires* highlighted the crucial constitutional importance of the three estates, each of which had different rights and responsibilities. In this light, the introduction of a general tax like the commuted *corvée* was only the thin end of the wedge of a ministerial despotism which might go on to annihilate France's historic corporative hierarchy. Turgot seemed even more dangerous than Maupeou, not least because he appeared to believe his own propaganda.

The Parlement's remonstrances were not effective, and the Six Acts were enforced by a *lit de justice* in March 1776. Yet they had taken much of the shine off Turgot's erstwhile popularity: the welcome new broom had become the hatefully despotic scourge of constitutional rectitude. Furthermore, there was much displeasure in the court at the economies which Turgot was making in state expenditure on the royal household. In particular, the mountain of military reforms introduced by his colleague, Saint-Germain – who seemed even more a man in a hurry than he – amplified suspicions of the government's intentions. Saint-Germain's efforts to rationalize the structure of the army led to the disbanding of a number of regiments (with a consequent loss of commands for courtier generals), the abolition of venality for military posts and a meritocratic privileging of technical competence which many found threatening.[28]

If ever there was a time when Turgot needed the confidence of his monarch it was now. But Louis was not to prove good at steadfastness. Faced with burgeoning waves of discontent among the *parlements* and in the royal court, and with his ministry unable even to dominate the Parisian salons and public opinion, which had formerly been one of its strengths, Louis went into the indecisive mode which was to become his forte. Neither as unintelligent nor as indolent as he has often been portrayed, Louis invariably floundered when circumstances called for intestinal fortitude. The comte de Provence famously represented conversing with his royal elder brother as like keeping two oiled billiard-balls in the palm of a hand.[29] The wily Maurepas had spotted this temperamental deficiency, and played it to his own interest. He had become alarmed at the way that his colleague Turgot's reforms were stirring up discontent at all levels of the state, and was attentive to parlementary arguments that the very soul of the Bourbon polity was in the balance. Keeper of the Seals Miromesnil also shared with the magistrates a deep-dyed hostility to anti-corporatist reforms which cut against the grain of jurisdictional hierarchy, and he quietly cultivated links with the most vocal *parlementaires*. Also now working against his ambitious colleague was Foreign Minister Vergennes, who viewed Turgot as a rival and also regarded as irksome the Controller-General's adamantine opposition to French support for England's rebellious American colonies: 'the first gunshot', Turgot had dramatically pontificated, 'would drive the state to bankruptcy'.[30]

Black propaganda by courtiers and by Turgot's fellow ministers weakened the king's commitment to a statesman with whom he had seemed to share so much, but whose lack of respect for tradition was proving irksome. He was furious at the Enlightenment progressivism Turgot exemplified in one of his reports which, in the king's eyes, sought to condemn 'venerable institutions which the author claims to be the product of centuries of ignorance and barbarism, as if the reigns of my three predecessors could be equated with those of the dark ages'.[31] True to the precepts of those predecessors, Louis also disliked the way that Turgot was assuming the airs of a principal minister. 'Monsieur Turgot wants to be me', he darkly reflected, 'and I do not want him to be me.'[32] On 12 May 1776, Louis consequently dismissed his reformist Controller-General, who had been so scornfully condemnatory towards the hallowed traditions of the Bourbon polity. Turgot was replaced by the altogether more anodine Clugny, another former Intendant. By the end of the year, all Turgot's reform programme – the liberalized grain trade, the abolition of guilds, the ending of the *corvée* – had been rescinded.

Louis XVI's backing for a renovatory and radical ministry had frittered away when placed under the strain of factional tugs and personal ambitions. The limitations of the new monarch's view of public opinion as a lodestar of policy had been ruthlessly exposed (though he clung on to it no less determinedly). His recall of the *parlements* had been predicated on a spirit of *aggiornamento* in political culture which had patently failed to happen – the magistrates, with the Princes of the Blood in tow, had instantly resumed the obstructive and difficult habits of yore. Added to the obstacles which reforming ministers like Turgot (and indeed Maupeou and Terray before him) now had to face was the king's havering inconstancy.

Louis XVI's problem was less an attachment to principles than the inconvenient fact that those principles – fidelity to his historic legacy as ruler, a devotion to ethical rule and an enlightened regard for public opinion – often conflicted with each other. His coronation in June 1775 proved a supreme example of the mutual incommensurability of his good intentions.[33] In a briefing document in late 1774, Turgot had urged the king to modernize the ceremonies for an enlightened age. Holding an abbreviated and updated ceremony in Paris rather than Reims, he argued, would be less costly, attract more revenue from visitors, and provide a more satisfactory and open ceremony in which the king would gain 'new calls on the love and gratitude of his peoples'. A monarchy grounded in popular assent rather than divine right, Turgot held, did not require archaic ceremonial to be played out in all its increasingly anachronistic detail. The coronation ceremony, rock of monarchical tradition, seemed suddenly to be exposed to the corrosive power of the public sphere. Radical pamphleteers argued that the coronation offered a chance for king and people to seal a solemn pact of alliance, rehearsing the social contract. Others – among whom one might even class Turgot himself, who privately expressed the view that the coronation represented 'the most useless and also the most ridiculous of all the useless expenses' – mocked the 'absurd ceremony' as 'a political charade'.

Louis made some concessions to Turgot and there were a few 'enlightened' gracenotes in the ceremony. Yet overall, the king was more guided by those of his prelates who saw the coronation as a religious rite of renewal in which the monarch could make a sacred, even missionary pledge in an age of irreligion. It was held according to immemorial custom in Reims, and its liturgy was resolutely medievalist and theocratic. It concluded, for example, with the new sacred monarch touching some 2,400 paupers for the King's Evil – the first time the ceremony had been held for more than a generation. The part of the coronation oath calling for the extirpation of heretics was retained (to the intense annoyance of Protestants and *philosophes* alike) on the grounds that Louis XIV was its author and that therefore it would be unseemly, as Louis put it, to 'displace the traditional limits [. . .] where wisdom [had] placed them'. The construction of theatre benches in the nave of the cathedral, the unseemly theatrical applause which greeted key parts of the ceremony, and the manifest difficulty of many participants apart from the king himself to keep a straight face gave the event, despite flashes of timeless majesty which impressed even Voltaire, the air of comic opera. But it was comic opera with a dark message: the common people were kept out of the cathedral, and the customary part of the ceremony in which the monarch was presented before the people in his regalia for popular acclaim was removed altogether for fear that it be interpreted as incipient contractualism. In the changed discursive universe of the late Enlightenment, in which political debate had been increasingly secularized, and in which even Louis XV had regarded evocations of divine right as off limits, the coronation seemed unwittingly – and to the blithe unconcern of the new monarch – to be inventing new forms of religious sectionalism and political conservatism.

C) PATRIOTISM À L'AMÉRICAINE

Despite the failure of the Turgot experiment, the young king still retained goodwill in the country at large – indeed, so unpopular had the Controller-General become by late 1775 that his dismissal gave Louis's popularity a fillip. Despite the rumblings of reaction in the coronation, the move for reform and the mood of political renewal which had pre-dated Turgot post-dated him too. This owed a great deal to the influence of Maurepas, whose position in the king's favour had been strengthened by Turgot's removal – and much also to the policy issue which dominated these years, namely, France's involvement in the War of American Independence. The ferocious sideswipes which the war allowed France to make against its traditional enemy, England, stimulated the recrudescence of a popular patriotism focused on the monarch.

Louis was still a big clumsy bear who needed licking into political shape, and he lacked any relish for rule. Though he retained much of the court etiquette inherited from his idol, Louis XIV, the young king invariably seemed more awkward on ceremonial occasions than his courtiers. His moralizing view of politics impelled him towards a style of self-presentation which stressed the humane rather than the remote and disdainful. This often emerged in a preference for a homely, familial ethos – indeed, he appeared to take most simple pleasure far removed from the stately ceremonial round, in the guise of loving husband or bourgeois paterfamilias. The duc de Croÿ recorded how, once, the king and queen and their entourages, out riding separately, chanced to encounter each other in the Bois de Boulogne. The queen 'threw herself down from her horse, and [Louis] ran to her and kissed her on the forehead. People applauded, at which [the king] gave Marie-Antoinette two good kisses on her cheeks.'[34] This informal style was sometimes rather awkward – for Louis's natural shyness made spontaneity a bit of a problem – but was undoubtedly assisted by Marie-Antoinette's own distaste for protocol. The queen's patent boredom at court ceremonials was widely commented on: the Anjou priest Besnard who made a tourist visit to Versailles to witness the king's public dinner noted the king filling his face ('and drinking quite a bit') while the queen scarcely opened her napkin and fiddled with her food with conspicuous ennui.[35] Marie-Antoinette preferred pleasure within the ambit of a more restricted audience of courtiers and intimates. The weekly balls she organized each spring were famous – and famously exclusive. Many of the festivities in which she engaged were indeed located in the less publicly accessible royal residences such as the Trianon, where attendance was even more recherché. 'Except for some favourites, designated by whim or intrigue', the duc de Lévis later tartly recalled, 'everyone was excluded:

no longer were rank, service, esteem, or high birth fitting qualification to be admitted into the intimacy of the royal family.'[36]

The value which the royal couple accorded domestic intimacy fanned the flames of aristocratic resentment and encouraged intrigue and faction. During Louis XV's reign, court faction had often tended to crystallize around the king's principal mistresses. Louis XVI's lifelong marital fidelity erased royal mistresses from the political landscape, yet by some kind of perverse and arcane political logic, faction came to hover instead around the person of Louis's queen. A year younger than her husband and just as politically unformed, Marie-Antoinette offered political protection after his fall to Choiseul, the architect of both the Austrian alliance of 1757 and her own marriage in 1770. Choiseul's recall to power was not at all out of the question, and many of his would-be followers – such as the ambitious archbishop of Toulouse, Loménie de Brienne, and the baron de Breteuil, who tried to displace Vergennes as Foreign Minister throughout the late 1770s – drifted towards the queen's milieu. So did Choiseul's supporters in the ambit of the prince de Conti, who died in 1776. In the 'queen's party' were also to be found pleasure-seeking, horserace-loving young aristocrats such as the ducs de Guines and de Coigny, and the baron de Besenval; exotic foreign imports such as the dashing comte de Fersen from Sweden; close personal female friends such as the princesse de Lamballe and the comtesse de Polignac; as well as, sporadically, the maturing younger princes, Provence, Artois and Orléans's heir, the duc de Chartres (who succeeded his father in 1785). The grouping was a loose one, which had no homogeneous views, but it did exude a certain oppositional ambience – support for Austria, the royal court and the high Sword nobility – which put it at odds with the ministry. This emergent 'queen's party' could moreover boast at least one early scalp – it had a hand in 1774 in bringing down d'Aiguillon, whose scepticism over the Austrian alliance was aggravated in the queen's eyes by his friendship with Madame du Barry.

It says a good deal about Maurepas's skills of political management that he was able to master the king's continuing political immaturity and to keep the emergent queen's party in check. In 1776, the king gave him the largely vacuous title of *chef du conseil royal des finances* ('Head of the Royal Finance Council'), which helped strengthen his moral position over other ministers. He was also now allowed to sit in on the departmental business which each of the ministers transacted with the king, while rearrangements in the layout of the palace of Versailles allowed him informal access to the king via a secret passageway. He also altered the conciliar complexion of government, diverting most decision-making away from the unwieldy state council towards ad hoc committees which he found easier to manipulate. In addition, he aimed to propel Marie-Antoinette's energies into non-political channels. He enjoyed more success with this task than had been his fate with Madame de Pompadour thirty years earlier: by the late 1780s the queen had developed into a major patron for great swathes of court, diplomatic, military and ecclesiastical appointments, and had become fashion-leader in haute couture and music. Maurepas's masterly containment of factional pressures allowed him to piece together a relatively unified ministry. Indeed, an unanticipated era of government stability opened up after Turgot. Vergennes was to remain as Foreign Minister and Miromesnil as Keeper of the Seals until 1787, and Sartine stayed at the Navy until 1780, as did Montbarey, Saint-Germain's successor at the War Ministry. Amelot, Malesherbes's replacement in the Royal Household, lasted from 1776 until 1783. Following the death in office of Controller-General Clugny in 1776, the key role in finance from 1776 down to 1781 was taken by the Genevan banker, Jacques Necker.

What united ministers was not merely the fact that Maurepas had picked them. Following the fall of Turgot, there developed a foreign policy approach – and a financial strategy for implementing it – in which the ministerial principals found themselves in general agreement, and in which the king concurred. One of the few things on which Louis XVI complimented his royal predecessor was his restrained and unaggressive foreign policy. The young monarch was shocked by, and wished to reverse, the decline in the mores of international relations signalled by Frederick the Great's seizure of Silesia in 1740 and by the Partition of Poland between Austria, Prussia and Russia in 1772. He disassembled the machinery of the old king's *Secret du roi*. 'Honesty and restraint must be our watchwords,' he told Foreign Minister Vergennes, and the latter was in agreement that France should 'fear rather than seek out territorial aggrandisements'.[37] Both men were highly suspicious of the expansionist diplomacy of Emperor Joseph II, and refused to back the Austrian ally's struggle against Prussia over the Bavarian succession in 1778.

Yet despite their principles, both Louis and Vergennes were resentful at the way in which England had, since the Seven Years War, eclipsed much of the international prestige of France and diminished the *éclat* of the Bourbon house. Consequently, they did not take much persuading to ditch their virtuous principles when, from 1775 onwards, they were served up on a platter with a golden opportunity for redressing the international balance in France's favour, namely, the rebellion of England's American colonies. Maurepas – a former Navy Minister and a pronounced anglophobe – was also game for engagement, though action was initially blocked by Controller-General Turgot, who was wary of submitting recuperating state finances to the demands of outright war. Turgot's dismissal eased the drift towards military involvement. Extra resources were committed to Sartine for a naval build-up, while Vergennes worked hard to convince other European powers of France's determination not to upset the balance of power on the Continent – the aim was only 'to ruin [England's] commerce and sap [its] strength'.[38] While pacific protestations winged their way across the Channel with more sophistry than political moralists should have been able to manage, Vergennes and Louis began providing covert aid to the American rebels. Money, arms and provisions were supplied through shadowy front organizations such as the business run by the entrepreneurial playwright Beaumarchais out of Lisbon; grants of leave were made to French army officers which allowed them to cross the Atlantic to fight against the English; and permissions were given to rebel privateers to use French ports. Finally, in February 1778, the government signed a Treaty of Alliance and Commerce with the rebels, secret clauses of which agreed French recognition for a new post-bellum American state.

Anglo–French hostilities began in the summer of 1778. The bulk of France's early efforts were taken up with drawing Spain into the alliance and then preparing for an amphibious landing in Britain and for the conquest of Gibraltar. In 1780, an expeditionary force of some 6,000 soldiers under the comte de Rochambeau was shipped out to America. Combined activity in 1781 around Chesapeake Bay between Rochambeau, the French admiral de Grasse and the rebel commander George Washington penned in an English army under Cornwallis at Yorktown. The ignominious surrender of the British forces had a powerful impact in Europe: it electrified French public opinion, caused a change of administration in England, and made moves towards peace inevitable.

The war continued on the American mainland, in the Caribbean and in India, and England even went some way towards righting its situation by the Battle of the Saints in the Caribbean in 1782, which left over 20 million livres worth of French shipping on the ocean bed. By then, however, the overall outcome was already clear: the thirteen colonies had gained their independence.

Anglo–French peace preliminaries in February 1783 were followed by the formal Peace Treaty of Versailles in September. France's allies did well: the American colonies won their independence, and Spain was rewarded with Florida and Minorca. French territorial gains were far from great, however, amounting to a handful of colonial gains and restitutions – nothing like the reconquest of pre-1763 Canadian or Indian possessions. Yet military and naval success had done wonders for the repute in which France was held internationally – with a strong minister at the helm, its strength and prosperity would be unequalled, opined the Austrian ambassador, the comte de Mercy.[39] The war had also proved popular, and allowed the king to pose as patriot monarch in much the same way as his grandfather had done in the 1760s. The great nation seemed to be back in business.

The French people, an anonymous news-sheet recorded at the outset of the American War, 'can only talk and dream war', and 'breathes nothing but war and vengeance'. The aim was 'to humiliate English pride and to give up to France its equality and superiority on the seas'. A new 'Rebel' hairstyle allegorically representing the war caught on furiously, though it had to be banned from court because the snake representing England was so lifelike that it risked causing fits of nerves among the ladies.[40] With anglophobia driving out anglophilia, the king – as during the Seven Years War – came to represent the very cynosure of patriotic zeal. A gala showing of the *Siege of Calais*, de Belloy's patriotic, anti-English hit of the 1760s,[41] had been put on specially for Louis and Marie-Antoinette, on the first occasion on which they visited Paris together in 1773, and de Belloy's death in 1775 allowed his obituarist to remind readers how the playwright had 'revealed to the French the secret of their love for the State and taught them that patriotism did not belong to Republics alone'.[42] The circumstances of war allowed Louis to bathe in the reflected glory of warrior and protector, and also to indulge that paternal streak of concern for the welfare of his people which lay at the heart of his political philosophy. Louis's personal virtues only seemed to make his radiance more appealing. Popular prints, pamphlet accounts, newspaper articles and cheap engravings propagated the image of the 'good king' as humane private individual, benevolent, tolerant and utterly committed to his patriotic duty. He was depicted taking walks with his children, making acts of charity to the needy, or featuring in anecdotes which highlighted his affability and good humour. Marie-Antoinette's childbirths, illnesses, festivities and life events were also eagerly followed through the popular prints and engravings. A royal visit in 1786 to the new naval defences being constructed on the Channel at Cherbourg highlighted the patriotic fervour which encompassed the young monarch and the wider public. A kind of mass hysteria focused on the person of Louis, with the enthusiastic crowds yelling out, 'Vive le roi!' and the king, getting into the mood, rejoining, 'Vive mon peuple!' The militaristic context allowed the fusion of popular royalism with quasi-Fénelonian paternalism: Louis addressed the crowds as his 'children' at this moment of rapture 'in the midst of his family'.[43]

The media exposure of royalty, evident since the times of Louis XIV, and now given added vitality on the bourgeois public sphere, made the the king's domestic as well as his public life more widely known about by his subjects than at any time in the history of the French monarchy. Yet it was accompanied by a marked diminution of unmediated contact between king and people. Neither Louis nor his queen strayed much from the well-trodden circuit of royal palaces, making even the relatively palace-bound Louis XV seem a veritable vagabond in comparison. Indeed, the Cherbourg visit was the only occasion prior to the Revolution on which the king ventured beyond the Île-de-France. The Versailles palace gates were still open for the wider public to come and gawp at the person of the king – English tourists were shocked at some of the unsavoury types they found prowling round the corridors and gardens. But just as king and queen found it more congenial to cut themselves off from their aristocracy, they were even more committed to their privacy as regards the population as a whole.

There were dangers with this kind of peekaboo style of monarchical presentation. Familiarity, for example, might breed contempt. It was the view, not of some stuffy courtier, but of the enlightened Intendant and literary figure Sénac de Meilhan, for example, that 'it is good for the monarch to come close to his subject, but this needs to be through the exercise of sovereignty and not by the familiarity of social life . . . This familiarity allows too much to be seen of the man, and reduces respect for the monarch.'[44] Furthermore, the taste for news and information on the domestic doings of the royal couple which royal propaganda stimulated could not necessarily be kept within homely and cosily domestic bounds. Thus, a whispering campaign began very early in Louis's reign about his alleged inability to consummate his marriage to Marie-Antoinette as a result, allegedly, of a malformation of the penis (though possibly as a result of a psycho-sexual malfunction).[45] The problem had disappeared by 1778, when babies started appearing: first, a girl, then, to popular acclaim, a dauphin in 1781. Yet doubts and innuendoes about the sexual life of the royal couple would never disappear. An even more vitriolic whispering campaign – started by the anti-Austrian court faction – was also directed against Marie-Antoinette, who was represented at first as maritally unfaithful, then as sexually voracious (with young aristocrats, maybe even with the king's brothers) and finally as polymorphously perverse (notably in alleged lesbian relationships with the comtesse (later duchesse) de Polignac and the princesse de Lamballe). Long before the Revolutionary pamphleteers got their hands on her, Marie-Antoinette had become an unwitting star of underground pornography.

The political risks inherent in the media packaging of Louis XVI were particularly intense over the years of the American War: after all, a *soi-disant* absolute monarchy was assisting a would-be republic to achieve its freedom from tutelage by a constitutional monarchy. Vergennes led moves to smooth over and explain away this apparent contradiction. As Foreign Minister, he had authority over the circulation of the foreign press on which the French public had come to depend for its political and international news, but he extended his influence more generally to develop a veritable news-management machine. Censorship was tightened up: the *Gazette de France* did not carry any mention of the American Declaration of Independence, and even downplayed rebel victories such as the battle of Saratoga of October 1777. He used the police to harass journalists and writers who threatened not to toe the line. He also provided doctored briefings to the international press, bribed editors and journalists and was not above financing a new newspaper, the *Affaires de l'Angleterre*, with the specific task of countering republican sentiments which surfaced elsewhere in the press.

Pro-government organs portrayed French aid to, then alliance with, the thirteen colonies as a purely instrumental means of achieving age-old anti-English goals: the American alliance was an epiphenomenon of a visceral and enduring anglophobia. In addition, the American alliance was also presented as a masterwork of political beneficence, with Louis lending a characteristically generous and fatherly arm to a young people. To be politically anodyne, the latter argument depended on representing the colonists' political aspirations as qualitatively different from those of French men. And indeed, government propaganda placed great emphasis on the Americans as 'a new people', locked into an earlier stage of societal organization, trying to establish the kind of polity which European societies had long enjoyed. Thus the American envoy to Paris, Benjamin Franklin, with his homespun manners, beaver hat, farmer's suit and straggling hair, cut a conveniently archaic, even primitive figure among the powdered wigs and fashionable dress of the court and of polite society.

France was far from immune, however, from the ideological contagion which Vergennes and the king feared. One conservative writer questioned Vergennes's strategy of putting 'into the mouth of a king of France or his minister paradoxical assertions concerning *natural liberty, inalienable and inadmissable rights of the people and its inherent sovereignty*'.[46] Although successes in the Americas accrued to the patriotic glory of the ruler and highlighted the reinstatement of France at the pinnacle of the international system, there were many who were willing to regard the Americans' struggle for freedom as an allegory which might one day be transported from the New World to the Old. While readers of government propaganda were encouraged to see Franklin as only one step up from the noble savage, for example, others grasped the more immediate relevance of the humane virtues he embodied. Some were moved to view the quest for American freedom as a prelude to transplanting liberty within France. Particularly prominent among the latter group were the career soldiers who served in the War of Independence, either as volunteers in the late 1770s or else with Rochambeau's forces after 1780. The political outlook of individuals such as the marquis de Lafayette, for example (who had married into the archi-ancient Noailles clan), the Lameth brothers, or Rochambeau himself was transformed by their involvement in the struggle for American freedom. They saw the Americans less as uncivilized semi-primitives than as France's political pedagogues.

The American sauce with which patriotism was so cheerfully consumed from the late 1770s could thus be confected in a variety of ways. Patriotism had broken out of the juridico-theological Jansenist straitjacket in which it had before been confined to become a more manifestly secular ideology. Even so, it was still open to miscellaneous construal. On one hand, it denoted enthusiastic support for a populist monarch, the patriotism of a Fénelonian ruler seeming to incarnate the patriotism of his social body. On the other hand, the word could also evoke fraternal sympathy with fellow liberals transforming their political culture. The term would, moreover, be placed under further semantic pressure as the American War ended and as France woke up to the fact that patriotism had to be paid for. The American War had severely aggravated the state of the nation's finances and produced circumstances which would make the word 'patriotic' synonymous with 'revolutionary'.

D) THE PRICE OF PATRIOTISM

In November 1781, news of the brilliant Franco–American victory at Yorktown was brought to the bedside of the dying Maurepas, who was too mortally ill to take it in, or to understand the wild rejoicings outside his windows. In fact, by then it was becoming apparent that military involvement had not been without its costs. A financial crisis was looming; court factions were active; and, with Maurepas dying, the ministry was far weaker than it looked. Any remedy to the government's problems would be all the more difficult to swallow, moreover, in that France's involvement in the American War of Independence had been thus far, financially speaking, virtually painless for the population at large. From 1781 onwards, pain was on the horizon. Yorktown was a signal that the kissing had to stop, not start.

France's financial passage through most of the American War had been steered by one man: Jacques Necker. Turgot had seemed a relative outsider to the political establishment, yet Necker was infinitely more so. The only political role the forty-four year old had played was as Genevan ambassador in Paris, an honorific post served up to him in gratitude by his fellow Genevan burghers for all the profits he had brought them by wheeling and dealing on their (as well as his own) behalf, notably as Director of France's Compagnie des Indes. The

Genevan had political ambitions, and these lay in France: he used his wife's Parisian salon as a propaganda weapon; developed business and leisure links to the political as well as the literary elite; and wrote polemical anti-Turgot economic tracts. In the early 1770s, he had helped out Terray with some important loans, and the fact that he knew how government finance worked was not lost on either Vergennes or Maurepas, who realized that France's involvement in America required some fancy financial footwork. Necker's foreign and Protestant status forbade him the title and status perquisites of a Controller-General, and initially he was appointed Director of the Royal Treasury under Controller-General Taboureau des Réaux; in 1777, the latter disappeared and Necker was promoted Director-General of Finance – *de facto* Finance Minister. Despite his promotion, Necker's was not to reason why; his function was to produce the bullets which others would fire. This instrumental view of him as a technician rather than a fellow statesman was symbolized in his exclusion not merely from the State Council, which his Protestant faith made problematic, but from the ceremonial *grandes entrées* (which gave those present the right to sit in the king's office to discuss state affairs).

Down to his overthrow in 1781, the Genevan seemed quite as much of a financial wizard as his Scottish predecessor John Law had done to an earlier generation. He accepted the terms which Louis XVI had agreed with Turgot in the much less stressful atmosphere of peace – namely, no state bankruptcy and no new taxes – and managed to stick to them during a war which was to prove as expensive for France as the Seven Years War. The extension in 1780 of a second *vingtième* for five years brought in only roughly twenty million livres, and virtually all the rest was achieved through borrowing. Necker utilized tried and tested methods – state lotteries, borrowing from provincial estates, and so on – but relied especially heavily on lifetime annuities or *rentes viagères*. A good deal of this borrowing was handled by the Discount Bank (Caisse d'escompte) which Necker's Genevan financial rival, Isaac Panchaud, had founded in 1776 to provide cheap credit for economic expansion. Necker ejected Panchaud and put on the board bankers and financiers who allowed him to tap international money-markets, notably through the Protestant financial diaspora which had formed in Geneva, Amsterdam, London, Cadiz and elsewhere following the Revocation of the Edict of Nantes.

'If he can finish the war without departing from this system', Vergennes commented privately in 1777, before his disenchantment with the Genevan had set in, 'he will be a very great man in his field'.[47] There were important political gains as well as financial benefits to be derived from not relying on the reflex of imposing new taxes. In particular, the strategy helped to tranquillize the *parlements*, which were still somewhat chastened by the experience of the Maupeou years. From 1774, Maurepas and Miromesnil proved adept at the kind of parlementary management which had gone out of style under Maupeou, developing a friendly *parti ministériel* through cultivating senior *parlementaires*, staying well informed, distributing pensions to buy off potential troublemakers, and so on. 'The magistracy has not made a fuss since I have been in office,' Miromesnil boasted in 1782.[48] Calm on the parlementary front was also helped by the absence of issues out of which the magistrates could make political capital. Even the extension of the second *vingtième* in 1780 passed without a hitch. Necker's financial stewardship also accrued to the credit of the king, and further burnished his patriotic credentials. By turning his back on 'arbitrary finance' under Necker's instruction, Louis truly appeared, according to Edmund Burke, in a masterly back-handed compliment in 1780, 'a Patriot King'.[49]

The capstone of Necker's system which allowed this novel phenomenon in French history – a war without new taxes – was public confidence. Public confidence could be boosted, first, by renouncing the tax option. It was accepted that the state would rather increase tax revenue than declare a bankruptcy which risked durably alienating cheap credit: tax-payers were always likely to be sacrificed on the rentiers' altar. If, then, Necker could refrain from introducing new taxes, he would keep both state rentiers and tax-payers happy. Confidence was boosted, second, by a public relations campaign to highlight Necker's financial wizardry and (coincidentally) his humanitarianism. As his writings on the grain trade showed, the Genevan was far less confident than Turgot that the hidden hand of the market would bring general prosperity and happiness. Analysts were just realizing that France was experiencing not depopulation but strong demographic growth, and Necker felt that population increase risked producing larger numbers of paupers, and that the state should take a proactive role to avoid popular misery and revolt. He brazenly deployed his own wife as virtual minister of health and public welfare, reforming hospitals, visiting the sick, encouraging the streamlining of charitable institutions and so on. Her efforts were flanked by other humane measures designed to keep Necker's image in the public eye: the ending of serfdom on royal domains in 1779, for example, and the abolition of judicial torture in 1780.

Necker's utilization of publicity aimed to benefit the crown as well as himself of course. This was particularly evident in his quest to draw provincial opinion into a closer and more sympathetic relationship with the crown through a dose of political representation in the form of provincial 'administrations' (a term he employed so as to avoid comparison with Turgot's much-excoriated plans for elective assemblies). Necker was confident that these could develop into important agencies for both testing and shaping public opinion. In a confidential memorandum to Louis in 1778 he stressed their advantages for the crown over the self-ascribed representative functions of Intendants and provincial *parlements*. The latter in particular, Necker argued, should be cut back to purely judicial functions. The king was, however, lukewarm, and Necker's original plans had to be watered down. Only two such assemblies were introduced, by way of trial, in the provinces of Berry and Haute-Guyenne. They had powers over tax-assessment and oversaw roadworks under the surveillance of the local Intendants. The assemblies retained the hallowed division into three estates – one-quarter of the members were ecclesiastics, one-quarter nobles and a half from the Third Estate – and were constituted through a mixture of royal nomination and cooptation rather than election (which led Turgot sourly to remark of them that they resembled his own projected elective assemblies 'as a windmill resembles the moon').[50]

Finally, Necker aimed to boost public confidence in his financial management by providing more transparency in this area than any previous ruler or minister had dreamt of. He estimated that the mystery which surrounded the state's financial affairs could act as a deterrent to lenders, and that there were benefits to be gained in opening the books to show that the king's finances were healthy and that bankruptcy or new taxes were not just around the corner. In February 1781, therefore, he published a *Compte Rendu au Roi* ('Account for the King') which – belying its name – was not a confidential memorandum to his ruler but purported to be a public disclosure of the state of royal finances. The work was, courtier de Croÿ ruefully admitted, 'a great political stroke' (though the wickedly sardonic Maurepas hailed it as being 'as true as it is modest').[51] An overnight best-seller – 100,000 copies were sold – it certainly did the trick of reinforcing the minister's credit and personal popularity.

Though Necker's book-keeping techniques would be subject to pitiless criticisms by his successors (and subsequently by historians), the *Compte Rendu* purported to show an average year of ordinary expenditure which left some 10 million livres surplus in the state's kitty after around 400 million expenditure. It did not, however, crucially, indicate the full extent of the extraordinary expenditure to which the American War had committed the state. Insofar as we can reconstruct Necker's thinking on this point, it seems that he made a fundamental distinction between ordinary and extraordinary state expenditure, and worked on the assumption that the state could borrow as much as it liked in wartime provided, first, that it could manage to pay the interest on loans from its ordinary accounts without them going into deficit; second, that wars were neither too protracted nor too frequent; and third, that a vigorous campaign of retrenchment kept normal expenditure under constant review.

A policy of economy was indeed an important dimension of Necker's programme. He continued Turgot's work of cutting sinecures within the Royal Household, but went far further down the line of administrative rationalization, launching a full-scale attack on venality in financial adminstration. The aim was not only to reduce the state's outgoings in the form of fees and perquisites but also – as Terray had indicated – to make efficiency gains by turning posts staffed by amateur officials, who regarded their places as a form of private property which should make a return for their investment, into positions staffed by a smaller and more loyal contingent of salaried officials. An early step was the buying out of some 481 venal receivers and controllers in the royal domains and forests department and their replacement with a minuscule staff of state officials. Similarly, a score of financial officials in the Royal Household was replaced by a single treasurer-paymaster-general. When the six powerful mandarin-like *intendants de finance* who ran government departments made objections to the swathes that Necker was cutting through the bureaucracy, he abolished them forthwith, following this up with the abolition of the four *intendants de commerce*. In 1780, he abolished forty-eight receivers-general of taxes between whose hands between one-third and one-half of the state's taxes passed. Where venal officers survived, moreover, they were subjected to closer scrutiny. Day-to-day monitoring of accounts was enforced so that venal officers holding state revenues did not profit from their position by lending that money to the state – a widely practised form of financial graft. The great court officers were forbidden from selling subordinate offices within their departments – a move which was rigorously applied even to figures of the stature of the prince de Condé, Grand Master of the King's Household. Nor was the General Farm immune from Necker's improving scourge: in 1780, the Genevan reduced their workload, putting the collection of royal domain revenue and *aides* in the hands of salaried officials.

Necker was too much of a pragmatist not to avail himself occasionally of the advantages of venal office for putting cash in the government's hands – his decision in 1780 to make the posts of auctioneers venal raised some 7.5 million livres for the state treasury. More characteristically Neckerite, however, was his drive to increase revenue from the *taille* by insisting on more careful monitoring of individual tax returns – an issue on which the Paris Parlement became hot under the collar. This kind of revenue-raising move, like that of establishing a leaner and more efficient tax machine, was designed to ensure that the state's ordinary accounts were healthy enough to bear the additional burden of interest payments on loans.

Necker's strategy of administrative rationalization implied a novel degree of central control over the state's finances. The word budget had only entered the French language as late as 1764, and the practice it denoted had not yet become an accepted government procedure. Fearing the fall-out from another John Law imbroglio – when the state had suffered political catastrophe through over-dependence on a single financial provider – Fleury and his successors had deliberately built decentralization into the state's accounts. Finance ministers consequently did not have a single revenue fund or the bureaucracy necessary to ascertain exactly even how much money was coming in and going out. The 'royal treasury' was composed of two quite separate treasurers. Many royal funds – notably those relating to the big spending departments (War, Navy, Household) as well as expenditure on Ponts et Chaussées, the provinces, the factory inspectorate and so on – did not pass through the hands of the two treasurers at all but were dealt with in separate accounts. Annual auditing was a farce, and since the Chambre de Justice had fallen into disuse after 1716, judicial checks on financial maladministration were non-existent.

Necker's move in the direction of a modern, more centralized financial bureaucracy was not something which his ministerial colleagues welcomed. Sartine at the Navy Ministry, for example, faced with the task of bringing the French navy up to virtual parity with the Royal Navy following the decay of ship-building under Terray's stringent financial stewardship, was the ultimate big spender. The annual outlay on the navy had more than quadrupled between 1726 and 1775 – passing from eight million to 33.2 million livres – and between a quarter and a third of the money the state borrowed in the course of the American War went on naval expenditure. Necker was hyper-sensitive, then, when in 1779 and 1780 Sartine started to spend funds for which he had no authorization. The two ministers were so much at loggerheads that (Maurepas being temporarily indisposed) the king had to step in and adjudicate between them. Louis frankly concluded that Necker's financial skills made him 'more useful to us',[52] and Sartine was summarily dismissed.

By 1780, however, Necker's financial strategy, designed for short rather than long wars, was feeling the strain. He had been permitted to put out peace feelers to England, but Foreign Minister Vergennes had persuaded Maurepas and the king that France needed to stay in the field to obtain the fruits of military intervention. Yet the extension of the war and the rising cost of borrowing was threatening Necker's strategy of keeping the state's ordinary accounts in credit. Evidence was accruing that the annuity loans (*rentes viagères*) which accounted for around half of government borrowing had become needlessly expensive. Rates of interest – on average 8 per cent, rising to around 10 in the early 1780s – were simply not sufficiently sensitive to improving patterns of life expectancy. In addition, the practice of allowing lenders to name a person on whose life the annuity was based had permitted financial speculators – ironically, Genevan bankers most of all – to nominate as their 'life' particularly healthy, virginal young girls who had survived a bout of smallpox. By the 1780s, literally millions of livres in *rentes viagères* were riding on the lives of thirty 'immortal Genevan maids'.

Necker's increasing sensitivity to the need to limit spending was, however, impaired by the lack of fiscal discipline shown by his ministerial colleagues. He won the battle with Sartine, who was replaced as Navy

Minister by Necker's nominee, the marquis de Castries. The Director-General of Finances also gained in authority within the ministry as a whole when pressure from the queen's party, which was re-entering the political game at this time, had Montbarey replaced at War by the marquis de Ségur in 1780. Yet these two appointments disrupted the harmony of the ministry which Maurepas had so carefully constructed. Maurepas resented Necker's growing influence, as did Foreign Minister Vergennes, who had ambitions to succeed the royal Mentor (now nearly eighty). In addition, tension with fellow ministers over Necker's policies gave comfort to factions within the royal court, as well as to venal office-holders and financial interests, who resented his parsimony, his brutal insistence on accountability and his taste for administrative rationalization.

In this context, it is possible to see Necker's publication of his *Compte Rendu* in February 1781 as a slightly desperate move in terms of both his financial and political fortunes. The clarity of the royal accounts would silence the doubters and lay the groundwork for further hefty loans which the continuance of the war necessitated. And so it proved. In addition, the work was intended to buttress Necker's weakening political position by summoning up behind him public opinion and the reform constituency which he was amassing in the country at large. Yet although the *Compte Rendu* boosted his position among the public, it weakened his chances of political survival. The idea that the state's accounts should be anything other then the 'king's secret', veiled from public gaze, appalled government servants of Maurepas's vintage and of Vergennes's natural conservatism. Necker had drawn scandalized attention, moreover, to the amount of money spent on pensions for royal favourites and courtiers, making himself some durable enemies.

In April 1781, the king's brother, the comte de Provence, signalled his advent into the world of faction by a striking act of malice, the leaking of the memo which Necker had written to the king in 1778 supporting the idea of provincial assemblies. The document included passages in which Necker had favourably compared such bodies with the *parlements* and the Intendants. Uproar broke out in Paris, among the *parlements* and at the heart of the royal administration. A pamphlet war was joined, in which sundry doubts were cast on the reliability of the glowing figures in the *Compte Rendu*. At this juncture, the king asked Vergennes to provide him with reasoned arguments about the desirability of the

Compte Rendu. Vergennes poured withering scorn on the document as a Genevan – worse, British – manoeuvre and, twisting the knife, condemned the 'innovatory spirit' of Necker's whole ministry.[53] Necker tried a last throw of the dice to bolster his position. On 16 May 1781 he petitioned the king for entry into the State Council, and control over spending on the armed forces and the navy. It was asking too much. Had Louis granted the request, he would have effectively placed his Finance Minister over and above fellow ministers, and lost the king the unqualified support of Vergennes and Maurepas. Louis said no. Stunned at the refusal, Necker resigned on the spot.

Historians remain divided as to how serious the problems of the royal finances were at the time of Necker's fall. What seems unequivocal, however, is that in the immediate aftermath of Necker's dismissal they grew far worse. In the two years down to the conclusion of the war in 1783, virtually as much was borrowed as Necker had managed in the five years down to 1781. The rates of interest on the new loans tended to be higher, thus increasing the load to be borne on the ordinary accounts. By 1783, the American War had added 1,000 million livres to the state's debts, which represented additional annual expenditure on interest payments of some 100–130 million. This was becoming almost impossible to sustain, given that Necker's immediate successors renounced the policies of retrenchment and administrative rationalization on which the Genevan had relied in order to pay for additional interest charges.

Necker's successor, the distinguished crown servant, Joly de Fleury, had far less freedom of manoeuvre than his predecessor, and was accordingly appalled to discover a much less rosy picture than Necker's *Compte Rendu* had painted: Necker's 10 million livres 'surplus' on the ordinary accounts seemed in fact to be a deficit of 15 million; and extraordinary borrowing had been so extensive, Joly de Fleury reckoned, that even if it were amortized over the following decade, the state would still be running an annual deficit of over 50 million livres. His own family links in the Parlement and every corner of the Robe proved invaluable in preparing the ground for new taxes. The French naval setback at the Battle of the Saints in 1782 served as a pretext for presenting to the Parlement an edict, couched in terms of pressing military urgency, proposing the levying of a third *vingtième* for three years. The Parlement scarcely jibbed. Joly de Fleury was also by then reassuring financial and administrative milieux that the days of floating loans in the cosmopolitan world of European banking were over. He sought instead to draw on the indigenous credit of venal office-holders, and to this end he embarked on a policy of wholesale restoration of the venal posts which Necker had suppressed (and indeed even some posts which had disappeared under Terray and Turgot). The forty-eight receivers-general for the *taille* were a spectacular early resurrection, and many others followed. The closer scrutiny of high Household officials was removed, and the monitoring of accounts was also relaxed. The restored officials proved sufficiently grateful to be back in business to be generous in their provision of loans, but even this was not enough for a beleaguered royal treasury.

Within a year of Necker's dismissal, Joly de Fleury had moved far away from his predecessor's policies of financial retrenchment, centralizing rationalization of financial administration and the rejection of new taxes. One of Necker's main headaches – indeed the occasion for his resignation – was the Finance Minister's lack of control over the spending patterns of other ministries, and this problem did not disappear. Post-Maurepas, factionalism doggedly militated against a unified ministerial policy on finance – as indeed on anything else. Navy Minister Castries in particular felt that he had no duty to declare his accounts to anyone but the king. This was all the more serious in that naval expenditure was colossal, even following the peace with the English. Castries regarded the peace as utterly unsatisfactory and sought to maintain the navy on a war footing, ready for a re-engagement with the British which he felt was just around the corner. The case highlighted the swift erosion of the ministerial unity which Maurepas had coordinated since the fall of Turgot. Maurepas's influence had been in decline some time before his death. His failure to prevent the appointment of Ségur and Castries in 1780 had placed at the heart of the government two court aristocrats with a powerful contempt for mere 'Robins' and with strong links to the factions swirling around Queen Marie-Antoinette. The demise of Maurepas's system allowed the queen's party to burst out of the sphere of court patronage where Maurepas had managed to contain it since 1776 and to re-emerge into the political arena.

Although there was a good deal of continuing stability at the level of government personnel down to the late 1780s, this hid a growing fragmentation within the ministry. Foreign Minister Vergennes, who was the closest that Maurepas had to a successor, proved quite unable to pour oil on troubled waters in the Maurepas manner, and indeed seemed more disposed to act the role of faction-leader than to serve as supra-ministerial coordinator. The king respected Vergennes (for most of his ministers he by now displayed something like contempt), but he was keen not to be seen as having a principal minister, and so Vergennes was given little by way of ministerial priority. He did not sit in on individual ministers' business sessions with the king, which meant that he lacked coordinating oversight over the ministry such as Maurepas had, and he never enjoyed influence over ministerial appointments. Much of the influence he did amass, moreover, he expended on feathering his and his family's nest. Hated by courtiers as a *parvenu*, Vergennes had come from a lowly social background, and sought to use his position to place members of his family in prominent positions throughout the political establishment.

Characteristically, Vergennes's efforts to bring the chaotic and unruly accounting procedures of the big spending ministries under control exacerbated rather than mollified the divisions within the ministry. In February 1783, a 'finance committee' was established, composed of himself – now with the title of *chef du conseil royal des finances* – plus Keeper of the Seals Miromesnil, Finance Minister Joly de Fleury and the king himself. All ministries would bring regular accounts to the new council for approval. Ségur and Castries, seeing themselves as engaged in a battle to the death with their Robe colleagues, were endlessly obstructive. A couple of months later, when Joly de Fleury failed to get the king's support in an inter-departmental battle with Castries about unauthorized navy spending, he resigned in frustration.

Joly de Fleury's successor, the young but experienced financial official Lefèvre d'Ormesson, enjoyed a reputation for honesty which the king – always keen on political virtue – commended: 'you have morals', he intoned, 'and are not an intriguer.'[54] But integrity proved insufficient either to deal with the financial morass or retain the favour of the fickle monarch. In addition, Vergennes seemed to make his colleague's job more rather than less difficult: d'Ormesson was appalled to discover that the Foreign Minister was drawing on his ministry's accounts, without giving any notification to the Controller-General's office, in order to purchase the palace of Rambouillet from the duc de Penthièvre on the king's behalf. The two ministers made their peace on this issue, and Vergennes backed d'Ormesson's plans to undertake reform of the collection of indirect taxation, which involved moving from a system of tax farming to a more direct form of administration (the *régie*). This led to a head-on confrontation with the General Farm, which orchestrated a run on the Caisse d'escompte, on which the government depended for short-term credit. Vergennes cravenly backed down, offering up the well-intentioned d'Ormesson as sacrificial lamb to the world of high finance back into whose clutches the state had fallen since the overthrow of Necker.

The task of d'Ormesson's successor as Controller-General, Charles-Alexandre de Calonne, had been made immeasurably more difficult as a result of the costs of the American War (for which Necker was partly responsible) and because of the political dispute which now hovered around the royal finances as a result of the *Compte Rendu* (for which the Genevan bore full responsibility). Necker's had been a brave attempt to construct a model of the royal finances out of the figures he derived from what was still, despite his best efforts, a very dispersed and chaotic accounting system. As his political rivals were swift to point out, however, Necker was not a disinterested analyst, but a player with much to lose from accounts which looked anything but glowing. After his fall, there was no way that claims and counter-claims about the state of the royal finances could be adjudicated in an impartial manner. It remained uncertain, therefore, whether the *Compte Rendu* represented a window of transparency or a crude, self-serving political fable. Ambiguity over the issue was magnified by the fact that, following his dismissal, Necker chose to stay in politics, while the king, following Vergennes's advice to distance himself from any Neckerite 'innovatory spirit', clammed up totally, acting as though financial affairs were his business alone. Necker's successors as Finance Minister would thus always have their task enormously complicated by the Genevan wizard and the whole of the literate public looking critically over their shoulders. However much the king disliked the fact, the state's management of its finances had become a talking-point on the public sphere.

E) FIGARO'S MASTERS

Over and above the earnest anxieties of ministers and royal treasury officials, above even the jubilation occasioned by the victorious American peace, hovered the buoyantly ambiguous figure of Figaro. It was known that Pierre-Auguste Caron de Beaumarchais had swiftly followed up his spectacularly successful 1775 play, *The Barber of Seville*, with a sequel, *The Marriage of Figaro*, which related the fortunes of the eponymous manservant-cum-factotum. The new play was, however, believed to be too politically explosive to perform. The light-hearted satire of human frailties in the first play had become, it was rumoured, something altogether more mordant, including an attack on *lettres de cachet* and the state prison, the Bastille, which was fast coming to have almost totemic value in debates over political despotism. Figaresque Beaumarchais knew, moreover, whereof he spoke: quite as multi-talented as his creation, in a career as inventor, businessman, speculator, adventurer, government spy, pamphleteer, publisher, aide to the American rebels and much besides, he had experienced the insides of a state prison. His new play's plot was peopled by characters ruled by a panoply of moral defects: hypocritical Basilio, lustful Bartholo, fickle Cherubino, venal judges, mindless or drunken peasants and, at its core, a noble seigneur, count Almaviva, who was a cynical libertine. Vengeful, grasping, pathologically unfaithful to his loving wife (he attempts to impose a feudal *ius primae noctis* ('right of the first night') on his valet's fiancée) and – unkindest cut – very stupid, the noble count was a figure to whom, as Beaumarchais put it, 'the author has had the generous respect to lend . . . none of the vices of the people'.[55] The play's resolution sees love, which the count initally disparages as 'a fairy-tale of the heart', conquering all, even the vices of a grand seigneur. Not, however, before Figaro, deliciously engineering his master's return, out of the arms of his own fiancée, into the bed of his loving Countess, has apostrophized him in his absence:

Because you've been born a grand seigneur, you think yourself a great genius! . . . Nobility, wealth, rank, position – all that makes you proud! What have you done to deserve so many advantages? You have given yourself the trouble of being born, nothing more![56]

The play's cocktail of the satirical and the melodramatic, the sulphurous and the sublime, spiced with wicked humour, made it dangerous – too dangerous, it seemed, to be made public. Completed in 1778, it was not until 1781 that the Comédie-Française agreed to put it on. However, the verdict of no less a detractor than Louis XVI seemed to stop it in its tracks. The king had the play read to him by the queen's lady-in-waiting, Madame Campan. When she reached Figaro's famous monologue, the king rose in disgust:

[D]etestable! We would have to destroy the Bastille for the performance of this play not to be dangerously feckless. This man is making fun of everything that must be respected in a government . . . No, certainly, you can be sure [that it will never be performed]![57]

The king's brother, the comte de Provence, Keeper of the Seals Miromesnil and the *dévot* clan at court joined the royal chorus of disgust, and the archbishop of Paris prohibited his flock from seeing the play.

Louis was to prove quite as ineffectual over artistic censorship as he was over public policy. The queen's party, including the comte d'Artois, liked the play, and there was also a massive demand among the Parisian cognoscenti to have it read in the capital's literary salons. Soon Empress Catherine the Great of Russia was clamouring for a copy. In 1783, the Minister of the Maison du Roi, Breteuil, agreed to the Comédie-Française giving a semi-private performance in the Salle des Menus-Plaisirs at Versailles – only to have the king forbid it at the last moment. But the cause was gaining ground, and Artois had the play performed to the court in a private session. Changes to the text were made – the action was shifted from France to Spain, mention of the Bastille was removed, sundry anti-clerical taunts were withdrawn – and, following the eventual recruitment of a sympathetic censor (the sixth), the play opened at the Comédie-Française in Paris on 27 April 1784.

An unprecedented twelve curtain-calls signalled *Figaro*'s triumph. 'One laughs and laughs,' reported the *Correspondance secrète*.[58] The king's brothers were present at the opening, while the princesse de Lamballe led the Versailles female contingent, rattling their diamonds. Duchesses squatted on humble stools in the *parterre* rather than miss the event, and three unfortunate bystanders were killed in the crush outside the theatre to get tickets. Beaumarchais's tribulations were, however, not at an end. Unseemly rows with his critics in the newspapers led the king – casually breaking off a game of cards to sign a detention order on the back of a seven of spades – to have him briefly confined in the state reformatory at the Saint-Lazare monastery. Following a paradox which the entrepreneur in Beaumarchais was quick to exploit, and which highlighted the changed temper of cultural life, Louis's detestation was the play's best advertisement. By 1787, the play had run to an unheard-of 100 performances in Paris; amassed its author some 60,000 livres in royalties; enjoyed countless provincial stagings; and been translated into every major European language. By then too Mozart's opera, from Da Ponte's libretto, had made Figaro a stock character in the European cultural imaginary and set the whole of the Continent whistling Mozartian airs and chuckling at Figaresque humour.

Yet what, exactly, was the joke? Religious bigots had never found difficulty in laughing at Molière's *Tartuffe*, and noblemen and women were now among the most enthusiastic patrons of Beaumarchais's scandalous, but somehow charming, assault on their ilk. Contemporaries recorded how at the early performances, court aristocrats were seen playfully smacking their own cheeks to signal their thrilling mock-acceptance of the play's satire. Much of the niceness which audiences discovered in the play was, indeed, its naughtiness. The personal outrage of the king made each performance a micro-site of popular transgression. King, church, critics, censors, *lettres de cachet* and state prison had failed to silence either Figaro or his irrepressible author in what became a Frondeur (and *philosophe*) parable celebrating the triumph of wit and the vindication of public opinion. The play's fortunes literally dramatized the cause of freedom of speech, the issue of legal redress against arbitrary arrest and the character of state power which were playing out in more serious venues throughout the 1780s.

'There is no longer clergy, nobility or third estate in France,' Foreign Minister Vergennes had expostulated in 1781. 'The distinction is a fiction, a pure façade without any real meaning.' This was wishful thinking by a crown servant who signally overestimated the powers of the monarchy to reduce age-old divisions. At his next sentence – 'The monarch speaks, all are subjects and all obey'[59] – both Beaumarchais and Figaro could have been excused for convulsing with laughter. *The Marriage of Figaro* imbroglio semed to indicate that the monarch could not rule his own theatre troupe, his court or his family, let alone his kingdom. Besides its role as indicator of political repression, the play also contributed to a public questioning taking place more broadly within society about the social utility and state service of the nobility and the values of deference in a world increasingly inhabited by citizens rather than subjects.

Neither Beaumarchais nor his creation was against nobility as such. Figaro's aim in life is bourgeois respectability, which he hopes to achieve through his merits rather than by way of the barricades. Nor was Beaumarchais himself an obvious proponent of rank anti-nobilism: for he himself was a noble. A watch-maker by early vocation, his early forays on to the stage had been very much in the tradition of the bourgeois drama pioneered and theorized by Diderot: his 1770 play, *Les Deux Amis, ou le Négociant de Lyon* ('The Two Friends, or The Lyon Businessman'), was, he said, 'composed for businessmen and . . . to honour the Third Estate'.[60] Yet even prior to this he had utilized connections at court, where he had been appointed Royal Watch-maker, to build up a considerable personal fortune which allowed him to purchase ennobling office: in 1761, he paid ready cash for the post of secrétaire du Roi (King's Secretary), a straightforward means of achieving noble status, and he followed this up with a venal position as minor magistrate in the royal domains.

Beaumarchais (or Caron to give him his true patronymic: 'de Beaumarchais' had been added early in his career as a swanky piece of social climbing) was not alone in seeking the perquisites of noble status. There were maybe 4,000 offices – municipal, legal, administrative, military – which ennobled the owner, and though many of these were held by individuals who already enjoyed noble status, this constituted an important channel of bourgeois permeation of the noble order. The price of magistracies in the sovereign courts declined conspicuously over the century – partly no doubt as a result of uncertainty over their fate, and also because of a long-term reduction in the amount of legal business (and therefore potential fees and perquisites) they handled. Yet in general the market for ennobling office was highly buoyant, aided by speedier circulation of information in the country at large which encouraged the formation of national markets: ennobling offices were (like seigneurial and feudal titles) advertised alongside toothpowders, carriages, umbrellas and domestic pets in the national network of advertisers known as *Affiches*. The post of secrétaire du Roi which Beaumarchais had purchased (like Voltaire before him) was the most unproblematic means of social ascent, since the position entailed no duties whatever. Its price skyrocketed to 120,000 or more livres, yet there was no shortage of purchasers. The latter normally came from the ranks of rich merchants, manufacturers and financiers (along with the occasional successful author or eccentric like Sanson, the notorious public executioner). Around 6,000 commoners joined the nobility through purchase of ennobling office of some sort over the course of the century – not far off half of them in the short reign of Louis XVI alone. They composed between one-sixth and one-seventh of the total strength of the noble order of about 40,000 families.

Beaumarchais's acceptance of nobility was exemplary in another way too. The nobility enjoyed so much wealth, fortune, social esteem and cultural capital in the eighteenth century that it required the most self-denying of political principles or the moral fibre of a Rousseau to resist ennoblement if it was on offer and affordable. Those who enjoyed noble status comprised less than 1 per cent of the population, yet monopolized ministerial place (individuals like Necker being the rule-making exception), high administrative, financial and legal office, Royal Household positions, army high command and episcopal status. They owned between a fifth and a third of the country's cultivable land, and were in commanding positions in many sectors of the commercial and financial life of the nation. At each level of society – village, bourg, town, city, capital, court – nobles were invariably appreciably richer than co-resident commoners. They were also the most important patrons of the arts and the most conspicuous of cultural consumers.

'Instead of one nobility,' Talleyrand, aristocratic bishop (and, later, Revolutionary politician and arch-survivor), subsequently claimed, 'there were seven or eight',[61] before going on to consider some of the divisions – Robe and Sword, court and provincial, old and new, and so on. The noble order was certainly highly heterogeneous in terms of wealth. Leaving to one side the fifty or sixty hyper-rich court-based aristocratic dynasties, it numbered by the 1780s between 200,000 and 250,000 individuals, and could be divided into three rough groupings: two-fifths were extremely wealthy, a further two-fifths were comfortable, while a final one-fifth hovered on the edge of demotion into the Third Estate. Broadly speaking, the nobles who already had most in 1715 were in the strongest position to gain even more over the course of the century – in terms of wealth as well as in terms of their social, political and cultural position. Their extensive landholding allowed them to benefit disproportionately from the long-term rise in the prices of agricultural produce, and the concomitant increase in ground-rents. A fair number of middling and wealthy nobles made a disproportionate contribution to the growth of the economy as a whole. Noble estate-owners in the *pays de grande culture* of northern France, for example, were in the van of the move to import the new intensive farming technologies developed by the English and the Dutch. Mining – which, like glass manufacture, was viewed as part of estate management – was also noble-dominated, as was iron production. Numerous owners of textile and chemical factories were members of the second order, while in port cities like Nantes, Rouen and Bordeaux nobles and wealthy bourgeois formed a kind of mercantile oligarchy tapping into some of the fastest-growing sectors of the economy, notably colonial trade.

If the nobility was engaging more and more in the economic life of the nation this was partly at least because the principle of derogation no longer ruled it out. While the animated market for the purchase of office risked 'feudalizing' the bourgeoisie, the relaxation of the laws of *dérogeance* was working to bring nobles more into touch with market forces. A noble stood more chance of losing his status through not being able to pay the *capitation* tax than through engaging in 'demeaning' economic activity. Richelieu and Colbert had endlessly tried to get nobles involved in trading ventures, and by 1701 nobles were free to engage in wholesale and maritime trade, ship-chartering and construction and maritime insurance without losing their noble status, their sense of honour and their privileges. In 1767, manufacturing and banking were added to the list. Purchase of the post of secrétaire du Roi did not oblige the individual to renounce any form of economic activity. In Brittany, noble status could 'sleep', that is, a nobleman might engage in mercantile activity to recover his fortune, and resume his erstwhile status once he had done so. The father of the writer Chateaubriand, for example, had turned his hand to chartering shipping and dabbling in the slave trade to buttress his ancestral seat at Combourg. To demonstrate its commitment to the reconcilability of noble status and economic activity, the government also took to ennobling successful businessmen by royal letters patent, stressing the social utility and personal virtue which such individuals incarnated. From 1767, this was done on the basis of two ennoblements per year to successful traders and manufacturers – a modest rate, it is true, which even Turgot did not choose to accelerate.

The community of interest between business-oriented nobles and the upper sectors of the commercial bourgeoisie sometimes embarrassed the older nobility, who in theory prized blood and honour over the cash nexus. The intellectual heirs of aristocratic apologists like Boulainvilliers who stressed the primeval 'blood and soil' derivation of the noble order ended up claiming that noble businessmen and *anoblis* ('the ennobled') like Beaumarchais were simply not noble at all. In fact, there was a wide range of stratagems on offer (front-men, sleeping partnerships, etc.) to camouflage noble business involvement. Such coyness was, however, going out of style. Venal office acted as a lubricant for mergers of honour and money. And business partnerships were increasingly sealed by cross-class inter-marriage: the lovely daughter of an impoverished noble line counted for less in the noble marriage market than the ugly offshoot of a family loaded down with mercantile or financial wealth – as many a blue-blooded heir must have rued. The shared culture of the Enlightenment also smoothed the path to growing elite community: as we have seen, the bourgeois public sphere was full of nobles.[62]

There were still, however, zones of mutual distrust and non-cooperation between the status elite and the business classes, and it would be misleading to exaggerate the extent of nobles' involvement in economic expansion and their integration with the Third Estate. Despite the noble dominance in mining and metallurgy, in global terms noble involvement in industry was far outweighed by commoner activity. It also remained the case that the government invariably proved keener to establish a business nobility than the noble order itself. *Dérogeance* was more a cast of mind than legislative fiat. Around a quarter of the nobility upheld the order's claim to constitute the medieval category of *bellatores* by following a career in the armed forces, while between maybe 6 and 8 per cent had worthy legal careers. Many poorer nobles simply did not have the resources to invest in trade, industry or agricultural improvement. And countless generations of inbred snootiness insulated a considerable part of the order from engaging in forms of enrichment which it had traditionally shunned. Moreover, for every noble turning his back on economic activity, there was a bourgeois wishing to convert to a life of leisured idleness – a state generally known, significantly and perhaps (given the changes occurring within the second order) anachronistically enough, as 'living nobly' (*vivant noblement*).

Down to the time of Colbert it had been an implicit privilege of the bourgeoisie to engage in mercantile activity without competition from those in society with more capital, cash and connection than themselves. A century later, this had changed totally. Nobles at court and in government in particular were well-placed to benefit – by influence, connection and sheer propinquity – from the state's role in economic strategy. The government was the French economy's biggest client for manufactured goods: it maintained one of the largest armies in Europe; it developed what became, by the 1780s, a navy as big as the British; and it played the role of cultural Maecenas. The state was effectively a clearing-house for business contracts and economic regulations which could make or break firms, dynasties, nay, regions. The prosperity of parts of the Languedocian wool industry in the eighteenth century was based on the contracts for army uniforms which regional financial dynasties had carved out early in the century thanks to the influence of local boy-made-good, Cardinal Fleury. Similarly, when he was Navy Minister in the 1780s, the marquis de Castries proved able to secure important mining concessions from the crown to develop the industry in the Cévennes, which set him in rivalry with the industrious but less well-connected Tubeuf family (who ended up emigrating in disgust). The hyper-elitist duc de Croÿ, assiduous courtier and dependable general, developed the highly profitable coal mines of Anzin thanks to a string of state privileges (including a government ban on the import of competitive Belgian coal).

As its merchant critics often pointed out, the royal court was thus trading not simply in service and status rewards but in economic advantage. Greed seemed to be taking over from honour as the mechanism of court favour, as status perquisites became tradable commodities. The imposing presence of financiers in Paris and Versailles was also a factor stimulating noble business involvement. Court-based nobles tended not to compete against merchants in the form of family businesses, instead drawing on the capital available in the Parisian money market to invest in major capitalistic ventures: mining and metallurgy, but also new, dynamic areas like the chemical industry, colonial ventures, steam-driven manufactures, calicoes and the like. In a good many cases, moreover, noble 'involvement' amounted to little more than speculative gestures cognate to their beloved gambling.

Court favour produced resentment amongst the commoner business community. This was particularly evident in those parts of the industrial and service sectors where the state had established monopolies. Try as its merchants might, for example, the port of Sète never broke the exclusive rights to Levantine trading which Louis XIV had granted rival Marseille. The importance of the state in licensing access to lucrative markets was evident in the venality sector too. The non-ennobling venal offices which rose most sharply in value over the eighteenth century were in those fields which involved access to a market which could only be accessed through office. Whereas the price of offices which were not plugged into booming markets for services could be sluggish, that of offices which allowed one to work as a notary, attorney, usher, auctioneer, surgeon, wig-maker or hairdresser rose sharply. Major financial offices, which gave room for lucrative contacts in the money markets, were also among the most dynamic in the venal sector. Privilege gained at court and/or endorsed by government had thus become a means of sharing a corporate monopoly of access to markets, improving market share or providing an advantageous trading position.

On the issue of elites, the government was – as was typical of the vacillating Louis XVI – in two minds. On the one hand, it consistently championed the idea of a business nobility which would enrich itself as well as the nation, and itself played a key strategic role encouraging market dynamism wherever it found it. On the other hand, however, it never totally detached itself from a more traditionalist association with the values of its old nobility. Both Louis XV and Louis XVI prided themselves on being 'the first gentleman' of their kingdom, and wallowed luxuriantly in the archaic values of the old nobility where true, antique virtue and honour were to be found. The aristocratization of high office and restrictions on court presentations from mid-century was to the taste of both monarchs. This sometimes led to a depreciation of the value of the Robe nobility. The clash between Sword and Robe was still occurring in the court and ministries as we have seen, though outside Paris the division was less pronounced than under Louis XIV. Intermarriage between these wings of the noble order was important here, as was the influence of that generalized elite culture of the Enlightenment in which Sword and Robe both partook and which tended to blur social boundaries. In many provinces, high Robe and Sword had long become virtually indistinguishable. The magistrates of the Rennes Parlement, for example, were the oldest and most distinguished gentlemen in Brittany. Much the same was true in Provence: 61 per cent of Aix *parlement-*

aires were Sword nobles by the 1780s (as against 42 per cent in 1715).

The most significant bones of contention within the nobility focused on the country gentry on one hand and the newly ennobled – the *anoblis* – on the other. The division between rich and poor nobles was highlighted, especially from mid-century onwards, in impassioned public debates. The Parisian chronicler Barbier characterized the country gentry as individuals who educated their offspring alongside the children of rustics and who 'truly differ from peasants only because they wear a sword and call themselves gentlemen'.[63] We should beware of taking as concrete reality what became a literary topos: for even the most down-on-their-luck petty noble *hobereaux* ('little hawks') managed a servant or two. Nevertheless, it is true that this group tended to miss out on economic opportunities, depended critically on their tax exemptions for survival, lacked the wherewithal to engage in enlightened sociability, and risked going to the wall in the more commercial world of the eighteenth century. Many regions saw a sharp fall in the number of villages containing a nobleman, with some of the latter falling into the ranks of the peasantry, while others shifted to towns to seek their fortune (occasionally ending up on tax rolls as sedan-chair-carriers, muleteers, ditch-diggers . . .). A black sheep of the lofty ducal Saulx-Tavannes family – '*gentilhomme vagabond*', 'dressed in a tattered riding coat accompanied by a white hunting dog' – received police attention in Burgundy in the 1750s. Those nobles who clung on to residency often did so in desperate circumstances: Chateaubriand evoked Breton *chevaliers hauts et puissants* lording it over a dove-cote, a frog-marsh and a rabbit-warren.[64]

The country gentry had been the main focus of attention in a famous intellectual squabble of the 1750s which had pitted the abbé Coyer against the chevalier d'Arc.[65] Characteristically, the government had heeded both men. It responded to Coyer's proposal to remove all obstacles preventing the nobility from engaging in trade by further loosening, as we have seen, its stipulations regarding *dérogeance*. On the other hand, it also took very seriously Arc's call for greater efforts to channel the energies of the country gentry into the military careers which formed their historic vocation. The creation of the École militaire in Paris in 1751 had been targeted precisely at this group, and numerous related initiatives followed. Twelve ancillary provincial military schools were set up by War Minister Saint-Germain in 1776, for example, and analogous institutions were developed to provide young naval cadets with specialized training. The culmination of the trend was the 1781 Ségur ordinance, by which the War Minister prohibited access to the highest army grades to those who could not show four generations of nobility – a clear attempt to palliate the anger of the court nobility deprived by Saint-Germain of the right of purchasing army commissions. By that time, a copious literature had developed in the wake of the chevalier d'Arc, highlighting the role of dynasties of country gentlemen in fostering a professional service ethic which would make the army both more loyal to its monarch and more effective on the field of battle. Honour and virtue could only be maintained, it seemed, by renouncing commercial interest.

The state found itself facing two ways on the issue of noble virtue, locating it both in the archaic values of a warrior elite and then again in the rewardable merit of outstanding figures, noble or non-noble, who contributed to society's prosperity. The state was unwilling to stand back from the social order and allow its elite to be refashioned by market forces and changing *mentalités*. This would have identified it with the *anoblis* rather than the *noblesse de race*, a step which monarchs found difficult to take. This was evident in fiscal policy, for example, which tended to favour the older at the expense of the newer venal nobility. Since 1695, all nobles paid direct tax in the form of the *capitation*, and to this impost were added, over the course of the eighteenth century, sundry *vingtièmes*. The *parlements* had done a fairly effective job of blocking the state's efforts to introduce fairer and more proportionate means of assessing these direct taxes and to add the replacement of the *corvée* to the nobility's tax obligations. At the point of taxation, moreover, where local knowledge and connection mattered, *anoblis* were often less well placed to defend their position than the more solidly entrenched nobility. A Prince of the Blood or member of an ancient Sword dynasty could use patronage – and the threat of its withdrawal – as a means of remaining virtually tax-exempt. The personal fortunes of the Princes of the Blood were such that in theory they ought to have paid some 2.4 million livres in *vingtièmes*; they paid less than 0.2 million. 'I pay more or less what I like,' was the duc d'Orléans's airy comment.[66]

The grandees were among the greatest beneficiaries of state largesse too: Louis XVI not only winked at tax avoidance by his brothers, Artois and Provence, for example, he also cleared their gambling and other debts to the tune of 37 and 29 million livres respectively. Since Louis

XIV had created Versailles, the court had imposed on its denizens a prodigal style of life which could only be maintained, in most cases, by dependence on state pensions: three-quarters of Choiseul's income came from this source, while Marie-Antoinette's favourites, the Polignacs, lived like princes on account of the princely gift of 700,000 livres of annual income which the queen made them in 1780. Casualties might result: Choiseul died out of favour in 1785 with debts of 6 million livres; and the prince de Guémenée went bankrupt in 1781, owing his creditors some 32 million. Aggrieved country gentry joined in the generalized wailing over the way in which the court bailed out the profligacy of such 'vultures' and 'predators', yet in fact the state was merely observing a principle from which they too benefited, namely, that charity should be proportional to the place of an individual within the social hierarchy. Though it was the big pensions which were to attract the ire of the Revolutionary assemblies, three-quarters of the 25,000 royal pensions inherited from the Ancien Régime were worth less than 2,000 livres a year, and two-thirds of them went to soldiers, especially noble officers in fact, for 'services' or even 'the services of [their] ancestors'.[67] This skewing of royal bounty in terms of the needs of status tended not to favour newer, and especially venal, nobles. Indeed, the latter even had the indignity of having to pay levies specially created with them in mind: in 1771, for example, Controller-General Terray had enforced a confirmation fee of 10,000 livres on all nobles who had received their status since 1715 – a measure which raised 6 million livres.

Given the mixed messages which the government sent out concerning the desirability of either maintaining its existing social hierarchy or allowing it to be refashioned in the likeness of the emergent commercial society, it is unsurprising that there were tensions within the nobility as well as between the nobility and the commercial sector of the Third Estate. Whereas most provincial nobles could join in the broad general attack on the corrupt court nobility, all old nobles, rich and poor, vented their spleen on the *anobli*. Molière's *bourgeois gentilhomme* would have understood much of the latter debate, which focused on the comic tendency of the upwardly mobile Third Estate to ape the lifestyles of their social betters. *Anoblis*, it was claimed, tried desperately to wash themselves in the waters of Lethe to remove the stain of commoner origins or else gauchely rubbed shoulders with old nobles 'like iron seeking the influence of a magnet', in publicist Louis-Sébastien Mercier's words.[68] The quasi-egalitarian social mixing of the salon or the academy might soften relations between the groupings, but established traditions of social comedy proved more intractable outside these polite groupings. The archaic honorific symbols of social promotion – wearing a sword, having a coat of arms, erecting turrets on one's home, having one's tenants behave like deferential feudal vassals, maintaining a flotilla of lackeys, establishing one's correct place in the pecking order of processional precedence, or putting the *particule* before one's name (thus 'de' Beaumarchais) – were still taken seriously by the rising bourgeoisie. And they were still equally mocked by their social betters (and indeed by their plebeian inferiors too) for taking them seriously. The cultural frontier which set apart the 'true' noble from the pathetic bourgeois mimic (or the aspiring *anobli*) was still very much in place in 1789.

The dictum of Louis XIV's courtier-chronicler, Saint-Simon, to the effect that 'the king makes a noble, but not a gentleman'[69] was thus almost as true in 1789 as when it was uttered: the easiest thing about acceptance into the nobility was the juridical (and usually purely financial) step of acquiring noble status; the hardest was to gain the unaffected acceptance of the noble order as a whole. Upwardly mobile bourgeois invariably discovered that noble identity – as opposed to mere noble status – was a receding horizon. The symbols associated with nobility were therefore charged with heavy cultural freight, and the mildest sign of aristocratic exclusivity might be interpreted with rancour. Moves in many provincial *parlements* from the 1770s onwards to restrict access to magistracies to individuals with an acceptably ancient genealogy were largely ineffectual, while the 1781 Ségur ordinance was less successful at excluding commoners and *anoblis* than the country gentry hoped. But such signs of exclusivity, endorsed by the state, had a psychological impact on those seeking social promotion which should not be underestimated. By 1789, relations between nobility and bourgeoisie had become as much about cultural frustration as about social deprivation. Talleyrand, who was physically disabled himself (his crippled leg had ruled out any aristocratic career save the church) understood only too well how such symptoms of cultural impairment like the Ségur ordinance now worked: they were 'less a favour for the nobles than an insult [for the people]'.[70]

The Marriage of Figaro played very precisely into this ongoing cultural debate on the value and virtues of nobility. A good part of the noble order, as we have suggested, had changed drastically over the course of the century and seemed more than willing to embrace the commercial values of the century. Many nobles could therefore shrug off Beaumarchais's satire as playing upon discarded stereotypes. Beaumarchais, however, was inviting his audiences to believe that the noble leopard would never totally lose its spots. His play portrayed the trappings of noble power as a masquerade of vices: the law was an instrument of class power; feudal dues (notably the *ius primae noctis*) covered rape and raw sexual gratification; and distinguished aristocratic marriage was a sham. So transparent was noble vice that even his manservant could give Count Almaviva the run-around, thereby demonstrating the superiority of talent over birth. Even more subversively, moreover, *The Marriage of Figaro* had performed its cultural dissection both *con brio* and in the spirit of laughter. The joke was the nobility – for the nobility was a joke.

Napoleon Bonaparte's subsequent comment that the French Revolution dated not from the fall of the Bastille but from the first performance of *The Marriage of Figaro* was wrong. It underestimated the extent to which aristocratic culture could absorb and contain such humorous barbs, and overestimated the play's political impact. Equally, some commoners thought it shared the moral failings it mocked. All the same, one can understand what Bonaparte was getting at. By showing the nobility not as the repository of national honour and primeval virtues but as morally bankrupt and pathetic, the comedy played subtly into a more general process taking place in the 1780s of demonization of an aristocracy on whom the monarch continued to shower favours and privileges. And despite its good humoured conviction that in such affairs *tout finit par des chansons*, much of its largely middle-class audience took the anti-aristocratic political message home with them after the doors of the theatre shut.

8

Bourbon Monarchy on the Rack
(1784–8)

A) DIAMONDS: NOT A QUEEN'S BEST FRIEND

The scene had echoes of the last act of *The Marriage of Figaro*. It was midnight on the summery evening of 11 August 1784, in the 'Copse of Venus', a shadowy grove in palace grounds. A young woman in cloak and veil, in her hands a rose. A becloaked man approaches, his hat pulled over his face. He bows, kisses the hem of the woman's robe, takes the rose. A few muttered female words as sign of recognition: 'you may hope that the past will be forgotten'. Noises off. The two flee the spot, and each other.

This affair of furtive misrecognition, of misplaced passions of the heart, was the central incident – the 'sting' – in an elaborate piece of confidence trickery which, once revealed, would be the talk of France and Europe's fascination. A mildly amusing *fait divers* was transformed – by the king, ironically – into a political issue which, as it played out, would highlight the weakening of the bases of monarchical power, further blacken the image of the royal court and sully the reputation and honour of the queen, whose only fault in this rococo tale was to have loved diamonds too much.

Almost as much as she was known to love diamonds, Marie-Antoinette hated Louis, prince de Rohan, Grand Almoner to the king, cardinal bishop of Strasbourg. The causes of the hatred were inscrutable. Was it something Rohan had said or done while French ambassador in Vienna in the early 1770s? His known wariness about the Austrian alliance? His worldly air of the hedonistic prelate, notorious for his taste for foxhunting, ostentatious luxuries and beautiful women? His grandee's disdain and the wicked wit which castigated vulgarity even in

336

DIAMONDS: NOT A QUEEN'S BEST FRIEND

the courts of kings and (especially) queens? Or was it, maybe, that Rohan wanted power, wanted it palpably, wanted it so badly that it hurt? At all events, the cardinal realized that he was hated by the queen, and realized that the high office which he craved would never come his way while that hatred endured.

It was a down-at-heel aristocrat, one Jeanne de Saint-Rémy de Valois, Madame de La Motte, alleged descendant of illegitimate offspring of Henry II, who served him up with the idea that the way to Marie-Antoinette's heart might lie through her love for diamonds. The ingenious adventuress, who may have become Rohan's mistress, formed a plan to make her fortune out of the cardinal's passion for power and the queen's passion for gems. The mysterious midnight meeting in the 'Copse of Venus' was the focal point of an elaborate web of skulduggery, by which a woman whom Rohan mistook to be Marie-Antoinette (in fact it was a hired prostitute, Nicole Leguay) signalled 'her' forgiveness to the cardinal. By then, Madame de La Motte had already extorted considerable sums from the cardinal, allegedly to supply the queen with ready money. Then diamonds had appeared on the scene, in the form of a fabulous bejewelled necklace, which had originally been fashioned by court jewellers, Boehmer and Bossange, for Louis XV to give to Madame du Barry, but which had remained unsold. Rohan was persuaded by Madame de La Motte that the queen needed the clandestine services of a confidante to effect the purchase of this brilliant confection. Duly prompted, the cardinal sprang into the breach. The jewellers received the queen's purported purchase order, and Rohan's promise of the money – a cool 1.6 million livres.

The trickery was revealed when Boehmer went direct to Marie-Antoinette to query the first instalment of this massive sum, clutching the invoice on which was visible Marie-Antoinette's signature – or rather, its forgery. (By then in fact the necklace had been dismembered and its 500-odd stones were being sold on the Paris and London black-markets by La Motte's accomplices.) The ruse discovered, Marie-Antoinette went berserk with indignation. On 15 August 1785, Cardinal Rohan was arrested within the Versailles palace as he was preparing to say mass, interrogated personally by the king, placed under arrest and marched off in full cardinal's regalia through crowds of dumbfounded courtiers to the Bastille prison.

The whole thing had been, Louis wrote to Vergennes the following day, 'the most wretched and horrible affair that I've ever seen'.[1] In imprisoning the cardinal, the king seems to have been motivated by a sense of chivalric marital fidelity, freely agreeing to the queen's extraordinary demand that he would only discuss the affair with his ministers in her presence. 'The affair was concerted between myself and the king,' Marie-Antoinette told her brother, Emperor Joseph II. 'The ministers didn't know anything.'[2] Wily advisers such as Miromesnil and Vergennes stressed the need to separate royal responsibilities from marital *amour-propre*, but their warnings went unheeded. Louis listened instead to the Royal Household Minister, Breteuil, who used the occasion to boost his own influence at the expense of his fellow ministers. In particular, he promised the king that he would ensure that the Parlement produced a guilty verdict if and when the case was brought to trial.

Yet even an absolute monarch did not imprison a 'cousin' (a form of royal address to which Rohan, as cardinal and as luminary of one of France's most distinguished aristocratic families, was entitled) without causing profound political reverberations. On the first day of his imprisonment, Rohan was visited in the Bastille by a veritable Who's Who of the French aristocracy, headed by two Princes of the Blood. The outpouring of sympathy was not a mere flash in the pan. Rohan's cause was championed by much of the court nobility, most of the ecclesiastical establishment, and a public opinion which stubbornly refused to rally to the royal family's view of the incident. By the time the case came to trial, even the judges in the Parlement were displaying scepticism about Rohan's guilt. On 31 May 1786, following a roll-call in which each magistrate individually declared his view, the verdicts were handed down: Madame de La Motte was declared guilty, and was sentenced to branding and life imprisonment (she soon escaped); but, by a majority of 26 to 23, the Cardinal was declared innocent. The magistrates were mobbed by vivat-yelling crowds, some 10,000 of whom made their way to the Bastille where they clamoured for Rohan's release. The *Gazette de Leyde* rejoiced to see 'oppressed innocence triumph over fraud, artifice, imposture and ingratitude'.[3]

The queen was distraught at the verdicts, her husband furious. The king had totally misjudged the mood of the political elite and of public opinion. His imprisonment of Rohan by *lettre de cachet* was compared with the recent act of casual royal vindictiveness which had left Beaumarchais kicking his heels in the Saint-Lazare monastery.[4] After Rohan was acquitted, moreover, Louis had him exiled to a remote Auvergnat fastness, and dismissed him as Grand Almoner, following this up with a further act of pettiness, namely, the removal from the State Council of the aged political has-been, the marshal de Soubise, simply because he was a Rohan. By taking the affair out into the open and having a trial in the Parlement, Louis had placed his and his wife's reputation under public scrutiny. Vergennes and the new Lieutenant-General of Police, de Crosne, had worked overtime to censor a flurry of subversive productions by sundry hacks and caricaturists, but a great deal of damage was done to the queen's reputation in the ensuing pamphlet war. The legal substance of the affair meant that the main medium for debate – the *mémoire judiciaire*, or printed legal brief – was free from censorship. Pioneered by the Jansenists and dramatically exploited by Voltaire over the Calas affair, the *mémoire judiciaire* both appealed to the broader public, supreme tribunal of wrongs and rights, and also purported to embody that public and to constitute, as Malesherbes claimed, 'the last rampart of national liberty'.[5] The breakdown of the corporative structure of barristers in the Maupeou years had stimulated the advent of more aggressive and theatricalized forms of forensic address, making of court proceedings, as Le Paige put it, 'an arena of gladiators, who tear into each other with sharp teeth',[6] and the briefs of the Diamond Necklace case brought the melodramatic antics of the courtroom vividly into the public sphere. Rohan's defence counsel, Target, was one of the most acclaimed exponents of the art of the *mémoire judiciaire*, and his work on this case as well as the dozens of briefs produced by other counsel during the trial had print-runs of several thousands – over 20,000 in the case of the first defence brief for Marie-Antoinette look-alike Nicole Leguay.

The biggest casualty of Louis's profound misjudgement proved to be his wife's reputation, the protection of which had been one of his original reasons for being so personally involved in the issue. No longer were diamonds the queen's best friend. By judging that Rohan was a dupe rather than a criminal, the *parlementaires* implicitly accepted that it was plausible that the queen of France should have had nocturnal meetings and got involved in mildly erotic underhand dealings to procure herself ruinously expensive jewellery. That conclusion emerged not just from the sworn evidence but from the mountain of polemical writings which the affair had instigated. The Diamond Necklace affair spilled out into a much-extended public sphere, where pamphleteers and tyro barristers wanting to make a name or earn a few sous rubbed shoulders with all those who had a grudge against the queen, the court or the government.

Marie-Antoinette was no saint: her political meddling, her love of ostentation, her addiction to gambling, her mindless frivolity were already well known. It was not just pamphleteers but ultra-conventional courtiers like the marquis de Bombelles who were revolted by her model village at Trianon – the colossal sums of money which had gone into making the queen's 'cottage' look authentically impoverished should have been spent, the marquis fumed, on improving neighbouring peasant dwellings.[7] Yet she simply could not be as bad as she was painted in spleen-venting polemics by aristocratic outsiders to her court clique, Austrophobes, the tail of Maurepas's followers and others. Such writings took for granted Marie-Antoinette's unbridled lust, as chronicled in underground political pornography, and added a further portfolio of sins and vices: hard-hearted frivolity, deceit, corruption, vampiric greed. The stories told were all the more widely believed in that they played into narratives of class and gender circulating widely within political culture. Marie-Antoinette stood proxy for the indolent and corrupt aristocracy in that anti-noble, anti-court current of thinking already exploited in the *Marriage of Figaro* affair. To make matters worse, she was a woman. As we have seen, the Rousseauian view that politics should be the sole domain of virtuous males problematized the place of women in public life and strongly urged the confinement of women within the private sphere of domesticity. The failure of the queen to observe this gender boundary brought opprobrium upon her head – but was also implicitly reproof against her husband. The sacral aura of the absolutist monarch was insufficient protection against the telling Rousseauian charge that Louis had failed to keep even his own family in order. In the coded political language of the *mémoire judiciaire* this was tantamount to charging that the king, 'father of his peoples', was also failing in his wider patriarchal duties.

With its recurrent themes of queenly vice, regal weakness and court corruption, the Diamond Necklace affair highlighted the royal couple's major image problem, and openly broadcast that problem to a much extended audience. If, to some degree, the king had himself to blame for this state of affairs, he was also badly let down by his ministers. Breteuil had been foolish to encourage the king to take the matter so personally and to flush it into the public sphere. But the affair was more than his single responsibility, and to a degree Louis and Marie-Antoinette suffered the fall-out from disunity within the ministry after Maurepas's death. The advent of Calonne as Controller-General and Breteuil as Minister for the Royal Household in November 1783 meant that the ministry now contained (with Vergennes) three rivalrously ambitious ministers with conflicting philosophies and power bases. Vergennes's wish to succeed to Maurepas's supra-ministerial role was still intact, though following the d'Ormesson fiasco[8] his credit was rather low: he was unable to prevent the dissolution of the *comité des finances* through which he had monitored state expenditure and kept ministerial rivals in check. Breteuil had attained power through the influence of the queen's party and remained committed to the notion, which he had once shared with Austrian ambassador Mercy, of 'having the queen rule'.[9] In 1784, he saw through the purchase of the palace of Saint-Cloud from the duc d'Orléans as a residence for the queen. Plans for the internal operation of the residence – servants were to wear the queen's livery, for example, and orders were to be given 'In the Queen's Name' – shocked many contemporaries as utterly irregular. The idea of the queen's independent interests seemed extraordinary, while the heavy expense irked Controller-General Calonne on financial grounds. Breteuil thus had seen the Diamond Necklace affair as an opportunity to re-establish his credit with the royal couple at the expense of his two ministerial rivals.

Breteuil viewed the Diamond Necklace affair as a vehicle for his own advancement, with little thought for the potential damage which it might cause the royal couple. His misplaced confidence in securing a guilty verdict against Rohan underestimated the difficulty of the arts of parlementary management. Since the death of arch-fixer Maurepas, the Paris Parlement had begun to grow unruly again. Calonne's prior political record frightened the *parlementaires*, and he was also blamed for introducing initiatives in 1783–4 (which in the end came to nothing) to reform the Parlement, by cutting the enormous size of its area of jurisdiction, and also by rejigging its fee-system. Furthermore, shifts of power within the Parlement itself also made the task of management more difficult. Maurepas had always highlighted the need to keep sweet the most senior magistrates in the Grande Chambre. The obverse of this was the relative neglect of patronage among those not thought important enough to feature in the *parti ministériel*. This neglect was most marked in the subaltern chambers, where *parlementaires* with more radical and disenchanted views were to be found, as well as in provincial *parlements* which were proving even less docile than their Parisian counterpart. Although the Paris Parlement's junior chambers did not play a direct part in Cardinal Rohan's trial, which took place in the Grande Chambre, they contributed to public rumbustiousness surrounding the trial.

The anti-ministerialists received aid, moreover, from an unlikely source, namely the government itself. Breteuil's ministerial rivals, Vergennes and Calonne, were determined to prevent the affair from increasing his influence at their expense. Calonne had been appointed in 1783 largely through the good offices of Marie-Antoinette's connection, but had drifted away from the queen once in office, and the Saint-Cloud purchase alienated the two definitively. Calonne's career anyway marked him out as a loyal and orthodox servant of the king: he was known to have been Louis XV's scriptwriter for the so-called *Séance de la Flagellation* in 1766, had worked alongside the duc d'Aiguillon in the La Chalotais affair in Brittany in the late 1760s,[10] and then done a spell as Intendant in Flanders. He was soon collaborating with Vergennes and Keeper of the Seals Miromesnil to reduce the influence of Breteuil and the queen. While Breteuil did his best to bolster the *parti ministériel*, Calonne used all his wiles to boost the cause of those wishing to exculpate the cardinal. Austrian ambassador Mercy subsequently claimed that at least a dozen of those who had voted for Rohan's innocence were directly benefiting from Calonne's patronage.[11] Vergennes for his part – who in addition had close links of friendship and patronage with the Rohan clan – worked surreptitiously for the cardinal's cause, strengthening the defence case by having the forger of Marie-Antoinette's signature, for example, extradited from Geneva (where Breteuil would cheerfully have left him).

The Diamond Necklace case, with the Controller-General using royal patronage to frustrate the wishes of fellow ministers and the cause of the king, both highlighted and exacerbated the grave political situation in which the government now found itself. Following its post-Maupeou slumberings, the Paris Parlement seemed to be waking up to a political role. Miromesnil had always held that 'nothing disconcerts intriguers like unity amongst ministers and with the Premier President [of the Parlement]',[12] and now ministerial disunity acted as encouragement to opposition. The Paris Parlement issued seventeen sets of remonstrances under Calonne's ministry, and some of the provincial *parlements* were even more outspoken. It was also particularly worrying, moreover, that one of the areas on which magistrates were choosing to focus was state finance – and in particular Controller-General Calonne's policies.

Calonne was no miracle-worker. The trouble was, he claimed to be one. On coming to power, he was aware that he had only a limited time-window to get things right: in 1786, the third *vingtième* which Joly de Fleury had got past the Parlement in 1783 in the aftermath of the American War would run out, and the term on the General Farm's lease would also expire. He later claimed that he found the state treasury in far worse shape than Necker had claimed, with public confidence – boosted by Necker's *Compte Rendu* – his only asset. Consequently, he chose to refrain from contemplating new taxes or a bankruptcy (against which Louis XVI was anyway dead set). Instead of pleading poverty, he pleaded wealth. Witty, smooth-talking, beautifully mannered and affable, a Robin who got on well with the court aristocracy as well as being plugged into financial milieux, Calonne was a gambler by night, who slept off his excesses by day (even dozing, it was said, in the King's Council). From 1783 to 1786, as the financial solvency of the state eroded under his feet, he gambled on the future by continuing the easy money policy which Necker had instigated. Down to 1787 he borrowed more – 635 million livres – than the Genevan had managed between 1777 and 1781, adding thereby some 45 million of interest payments to the annual deficit. Necker had at least had the excuse that the state was at war. Even though the international state of affairs in the mid-1780s prohibited a thoroughgoing run-down of the military and naval establishments, Calonne was a peacetime minister.

Talleyrand remarked of Calonne that he had the air of 'an adroit steward to a bankrupt debauchee',[13] and it was the Controller-General's heavy expenditure on court cronies which had the highest profile and drew the greatest flak. His unwonted prodigality – around a half of all pensions granted in Louis XVI's reign were made under his stewardship – attracted to his side many of the erstwhile followers of the queen's party, led by the comte d'Artois, into whose pockets he was later said to have shovelled some 56 million livres. Although the big prizes went to court cronies, the Controller-General also gave generously to musicians and artists, adding to the air of *douceur de vivre* of these last years of absolute rule. He defended his bountifulness as forming part of a larger – economic – plan. France, he argued, was 'a kingdom where resources are increased by the very act of expenditure'.[14] He maintained that the air of stinginess which Necker had encouraged by his Household cuts, for example, had given the impression of unbecoming royal impecuniousness, which had deterred potential lenders to the state. Borrowing was absolutely essential to raise the capital which the economy of a great state like France required, Calonne argued, and if this necessitated laying on ostentatious shows of wealth, then so be it. In giving to the very wealthy, moreover, one was giving to the principal stakeholders in the kingdom. He took special care to ensure that the government looked like the kind of enterprise with which investors, national and international, would want to do business. Accordingly, he made sure that *rentes* were paid more promptly than under his predecessors, and he set up a 'sinking fund' (*caisse d'amortissement*), rescheduling the payment of past debts. He made a show of resisting stock-market speculation, forcing the Caisse d'escompte in 1784 to cut its dividends so as to dampen a flare-up in share prices. High rates of interest on government loans were intended to attract not only the wealthy within France but also disposable funds on the Dutch, Genoan and Swiss money markets. By the late 1780s, over one-quarter of investment in government loans was in foreign hands.

Calonne's instinct to spend his way out of financial trouble was not as mindless as was sometimes portrayed. His brains trust of advisers and publicists – men like the second-generation Physiocrat Dupont de Nemours, the Swiss banker Clavière, the Belgian banker Seneffe and the publicist Mirabeau *fils* – were less panicked by the scale of the problems in the state's financial structure than excited by the rosy potential for France's prosperity in the aftermath of the American War. The country's enormous landed wealth made its credit position much stronger, they argued, than the paper strength of rival England, which was still adjusting to its American losses. 'He who lends to England', puffed Sénac de Meilhan, 'lends to a gambler who can only pay back if he wins; he who lends to France lends to a man of real substance.'[15] Though England's industry was taking impressive strides, and its economy recovering remarkably swiftly from the American humiliation, France had more competitive wage rates and an unmatched record in the leading-edge technology. What was desperately needed in this moment of historic opportunity was the stimulation of home demand (and here Calonne had plans for attacking guild restrictiveness and protected markets) and above all the formation of capital. If these goals could be attained, went the argument, then there was no reason why France should not achieve in the economic sphere the kinds of successes which the country was enjoying diplomatically and culturally.

Calonne invested heavily in infrastructure projects which boosted industry, fine-tuned technology and improved communications. A major development, for example, was the huge naval centre constructed at Cherbourg, which Louis proudly visited in 1786, to popular rejoicings. The port was a boost to local industry, a laboratory for new marine technology and a military reminder to commercial rival England of the seriousness of France's global intentions. Calonne also approved major spending on urbanization projects in big commercial cities such as Lyon, Marseille and Bordeaux (as well as Paris), and provided additional credits for road- and canal-building projects. In 1785, his establishment of a new Indies Company (Compagnie des Indes) had been rather against England's wishes, but Calonne felt confident enough in France's economic potential to cooperate with the English as well, and in 1786 he drove through an Anglo–French Trade Treaty. The agreement was predicated on the assumption that the export of French wines and brandy would be matched by imports of English manufactured goods. The latter seemed to offer few dangers since, as zealous shoppers pointed out, it was possible to acquire most English knick-knacks in Parisian stores despite the embargoes which already existed.

Calonne postured as the industrialist's as well as the merchant's best friend, taking over Necker's interest in neo-Colbertian promotion of manufacturing industry. Where Necker had snubbed such individuals, Calonne proffered numerous state subventions, the incentive of cheap credit and, where helpful, support in poaching skilled workmen from international competitors – one of the most effective means of achieving technology transfers. The textiles and chemical industries benefited strongly from this aid, but Calonne's favour tended to go to heavy industry: in particular he made large investments in the Le Creusot industrial concentration in Burgundy which became in the 1780s Europe's most advanced iron foundry complex.

Like a traditional Controller-General, Calonne expected those who had bought into the state through venal office or tax farming to be wealthy and ready enough to provide the state with much of its credit requirements. What was new, however, was his more systematic attempt to encourage the state's creditors and its wealthiest pensionaries to engage in investment partnerships with government which boosted production and built up infrastructure. Continuing the aristocratic penchant for industrial investment noted earlier,[16] Artois set up chemical works at Javel and developed a porcelain works, while Orléans owned glassworks and printed cotton factories and showed boyish enthusiasm for the industrial potential of steam engines. Similarly, the Farmers General were egged on into investing in a customs wall around the city of Paris which would make its collection of indirect taxes more efficient (and Calonne squeezed an extra 16 million livres out of them on the basis of it in the renewal of their lease in 1786). A particularly striking exponent of such public–private partnership was Baudard de Saint-James, incumbent of the venal post of Navy Treasurer, who invested up to 7 million livres of his own money in industrial and infrastructure projects: besides 1.7 million in Le Creusot, he also had a colossal share-holding in the Company of the North, which traded with the Baltic, plus extensive investment in sailcloth in Angers, and mining in Navarre and on the Loire. He also was principal director of the Compagnie des Eaux, the Parisian water-supply company based on the engineering skills of the Périer brothers, and had slave plantations on Saint-Domingue.

The wave of investment which Calonne supervised and stimulated in the 1780s boosted consumer demand and encouraged industrial concentration, technological innovation, capital-formation and dynamism in important sectors of the economy. Growth rates were not unimpressive.[17] Yet ultimately advances were neither rapid enough nor well enough equilibrated to transform the condition of the state finances by the end of the time-window for reform with which he had been faced in 1783. Indeed by 1786 and 1787 there were ominous signs of speculative boom. Calonne had originally tried hard to keep under control a surge of speculation which the policy of easy money since the late 1770s had encouraged, but the task was daunting. The Caisse d'escompte – the discount bank which Calonne controlled increasingly closely – was above all 'a lending bank', as Isaac Panchaud remarked:[18] bankers borrowed from it at 4 to 5 per cent and then lent the money out at 5 or 6 per cent, or alternatively purchased state paper bearing anything between 6 and 10 per cent. Financial syndicates and bankers boosted share prices with their own personal enrichment in view, and a number of the trading companies – including Calonne's brainchild, the Compagnie des Indes – turned very little business.

Calonne had worked closely with a team of bankers and financiers led by the Belgian, Seneffe, who was also closely linked to Artois and to Genevan money in the Austrian Netherlands. (This gave the Controller-General's critics a new line to exploit: he was linked not just to leeches on the body social but to foreign leeches.) By 1785 and 1786, however, the group was far from running the show, and indeed Calonne seemed to be on the way to becoming the plaything of competing syndicates who were intent on making what they could out of the speculative bubble, which extended to widespread property speculation in Paris. The economy had started to overheat, and at the end of 1786, the public exposure of a counterfeiting racket of scarily indeterminate dimensions undermined the whole credit market, and triggered the worst money famine in the whole of the eighteenth century. With loans being called in as business confidence waned, and with the radical press gleefully linking Calonne and his cronies to this new revelation of financial shadiness, the bubble burst. Between January and June 1787, five of the biggest state financiers – including Baudard de Saint-James and his equally entrepreneurial counterpart at the Army Office, Mégret de Sérilly – faced liquidity crises so intense that they declared bankruptcy, triggering a host of minor business failures. Calonne's economic boom was running into the sand, leaving his fiscal policies high and dry. Short-term credit would be at a premium down to the storming of the Bastille on 14 July 1789.

Breteuil, who combined commercial and political rivalry with Calonne (they were even attached to different syndicates offering to supply water to Paris), worked tirelessly to make the deteriorating economic and financial position seem worse than it was. In particular, he had stories of the Controller-General's cronyism, corruption and incompetence leaked to court circles, magistrates in the Parlement and press publicists. Calonne's tarnished reputation for financial double-dealing and wanton prodigality was a particular impediment for him as regards his relations with the Paris Parlement. The Parlement had been willing to give the government the benefit of the doubt in agreeing loans in late 1783 and 1784, but made clear its preference for the kind of transparency in public accounting which Necker had offered in his *Compte Rendu*. (And Necker added fuel to the fire, condemning Calonne's methods in the self-serving *Traité de l'administration des finances* ('Treatise on the Adminstration of the Finances'), which he published in 1784.) Remonstrances fired warning shots across the Controller-General's bows, urging more prudent budgeting and greater accountability. When Calonne was obliged to return to the Parlement in December 1785 to seek authorization of a further loan, the magistrates frankly stated their disquiet over the Controller-General's stewardship of the state finances. Calonne survived this political storm – and indeed a further skirmish in March 1786 when the *parlementaires* implied that a financially prudent government measure to readjust the gold–silver ratio in coinage was motivated by a quest for personal profits. Calonne still enjoyed the support of the king. In a *lit de justice* which the king held on 23 December 1785 to enforce the loan legislation, Louis personally ripped out remonstrances from the Parlement's registers, sacked one of Calonne's most vociferous critics, *rapporteur du roi* Amécourt, and declared, 'I want it to be known that I am happy with my Controller-General.'[19] Such ringing declarations by a monarch well known for his vacillation cut little ice, and, instead, highlighted Calonne's shrinking options.

Calonne's triumph over Breteuil in the Diamond Necklace affair in mid-1786 was thus a pyrrhic victory. The Controller-General was now hopelessly boxed in. The annual deficit was running at around 100 million, and some kind of financial repackaging was essential. Yet his place within the ministry was undermined by rivalries and resentments which reduced his freedom of manoeuvre, while the Parlement, whose unruliness was partly at least a consequence of his divisive management strategies during the Diamond Necklace affair, was spoiling for a fight should he go back to it with plans for more loans or (worse still) new peacetime taxes. Cuts and economies were too slight a remedy for the state's ills, while the king stood as a watchdog against any thought of a bankruptcy. With the economy entering a sticky patch, and with panic seizing the credit market, Calonne the gambler gambled again: he proposed that the king should seek the endorsement of a reform package from a representative assembly, the Assembly of Notables, which had last met in 1626. Would, however, such an assembly find it easy to accept the blandishments of a minister whose reputation was increasingly besmirched by untrustworthiness? Much would depend on whether public opinion was willing to be wooed.

B) THE APPEARANCE OF LUXURY AND THE LUXURY OF APPEARANCES

In his *Confessions*, one of the best-sellers of the 1780s, Jean-Jacques Rousseau recalled how once, when a young man in 1731, he had got lost walking from Paris to Lyon and sought shelter at a rough peasant dwelling. The inhabitant offered him only crudely made barley bread and milk, but eventually, after careful scrutiny, determining that he was not an agent of the General Farm come to squeeze more tax out of him, opened a trap-door in his kitchen, and descended to bring up a white loaf, an appetizing haunch of ham and a good bottle of wine. Rousseau cursed the country where public oppression was such that a well-off farmer, to avoid the inquisitive eye of the tax-collector, 'dared not eat the bread which he had earned by the sweat of his brow, and could only avoid his ruin by displaying the same poverty as reigned all round him'.[20]

Rousseau's little story is a kind of parable about France's social and economic identity. Appearances were often highly misleading – and were indeed intended to mislead. Just as members of the labouring classes protected themselves against the tax-man by sporting the trappings of distress, so, at the other end of the scale, a Controller-General could consider, as we have seen, that the best way for France to re-establish itself as a great state was to appear as if it already was. Similarly, in the masquerade culture of the royal court, a duke might wallow in conspicuous ostentation so as to camouflage straitened purse-strings – while the regnant queen was dressing up as a milkmaid in her specially constructed 'village'. This paradoxical attitude towards shows of wealth and luxury gave French society a rather extreme, polarized look on which English travellers and commentators were prone to expatiate. France was the country of 'popery and wooden shoes', 'privileges and poverty', and lacked that *via media* in which every good Englishman and woman revelled. Proto-feminist Mary Wollstonecraft in 1794 was to attack the 'cast-like [sic] divisions' of French society, which were such, she claimed, that the French 'do not have a word in their vocabulary to express *comfort*' – clearly a middle-class and English notion.[21]

The snap chauvinistic judgements and unknowing jeremiads of tourists and travellers are an unreliable guide to the underlying structure of French society by the late eighteenth century. Although – inevitably – the gap between impoverished beggar or farm labourer and the ostentatious duke or peer was yawningly wide, the benefits of economic expansion were dispersed relatively widely within society, even despite the problems which the economy encountered in the 1780s. But in order to appreciate this, one needed to be able to decipher appearances often constructed to mislead.

The relative soundness of health of the economy in the reign of Louis XVI needs some special emphasis, moreover, since historians have generally found it difficult to resist the notion of a progressive worsening of economic indicators in that period and an erosion of gains made earlier in the century, preparing the way for the explosion of 1789, when France allegedly revealed its true, socially archaic and divided self. This pessimistic view is grounded in the statistical analyses of economic historian Ernest Labrousse, who in pioneering quantitative analyses from the 1930s onwards mapped long-term trends in prices, wages and rents, concluding that whereas agricultural prices rose by around 60 per cent between 1726–31 and the late 1770s to 1780s, nominal wages rose only by around a quarter over the same period, meaning a drop in purchasing power of between 15 and 25 per cent. While for Labrousse the poor got poorer, the rich got richer: over much the same period, land rents nearly doubled. Labrousse's judgement was particularly severe on the years from around 1778 through to 1787: low agricultural prices entailed a fall in agrarian profits and a slackening of demand which placed industrial as well as agricultural profits under the cosh. The crisis of 1787–9 had its roots in an economy characterized by chronic mass under-consumption.[22]

Although there is good deal of Labrousse's work which remains valuable, much of his picture of the economy is wrong. Despite his pessimism about living standards, average real wages seem to have fallen by less than 10 per cent in the half century before 1789 – a figure which compared favourably with most other European countries, England included – and this average, as we shall see, hid substantial variations around the mean. His view of the reign of Louis XVI as a phase of structural crisis is among the weakest parts of his work. Evidence abounds which suggests that many sectors of the economy prospered even until the very end of the 1780s (and in certain cases, beyond); and, bearing in mind short-term factors such as the crisis of credit triggered by the 1786 counterfeiting scandal, many aspects of the economic difficulties seem to have had more to do with unwise government policies than with problems gestating over the *longue durée*. These problems came, moreover, at the end of a century which had been characterized by growing consumption and expanding prosperity.

Over the century as a whole, the economy had done well enough to support a much expanded population without any of the demographic disasters which had marred the later years of Louis XIV's reign. For most of the century, political arithmeticians had been convinced that France was doomed to depopulation; from the 1770s onwards the recognition dawned that in fact population was growing, and growing fast. At just about any stage in history prior to this, a sharp fall in population could have been confidently predicted at the hands of war, disease or famine. Yet in the event, population continued to grow – even though signs began to appear that coitus interruptus was beginning to be used systematically to reduce family size. By 1789, population size was one-third greater than it had been in 1715 – 28.6 million as against 21.5 million. The national death rate fell from over 40 deaths per thousand head of the population in the first decades of the century to 35.5 in the ninth decade – a drop of over ten per cent. Life expectancy at birth rose between the 1740s and 1780s from 23.8 to 27.5 years for men, and from 25.7 to 28.1 for women. Uneven between the sexes, the improvement was socially and geographically diverse too: the life chances of the middle and upper classes improved faster than that of the rest of the population, while certain areas, notably the east, the north and the Massif Central, outshone others. The crisis of mortality was universally becoming a thing of the past. Even the very severe social crises of 1768–70 and 1787–9 triggered by appalling harvests were not accompanied by grave demographic consequences. Symptomatic of a lightening of the cultural atmosphere was a growing concern not with mortality but morbidity. French men and women, having forgotten how to die,[23] now learnt to be sick: a diverse cornucopia of forms of 'civilized' ill-health were highlighted by medical writers, ranging from nervous maladies to mental disturbances, and from children's illnesses to geriatric ailments.

The food required to feed the extra mouths was not produced as a result of the kind of agrarian revolution (scientific rotations, fodder crops, seed-drills, etc.) being pioneered in England and the Low Countries. There was, it is true, an anglophile craze for improving works on agronomy, triggered by Duhamel de Monceau's much reprinted *Traité de la culture des terres* (1750), yet its impact on popular attitudes was probably slight: 'everyone reads them', Voltaire ironized, 'except farmers'. The peasantry in the Hainaut managed to adapt the new techniques and achieve impressive yields, but in general, productivity on peasant land stayed sluggish – indeed, in certain areas such as the Vivarais, the Auvergne and the Pyrenees it was static. Particularly energetic efforts to experiment with new farming methods came from wealthy landowners (including many noblemen) on the big estates of the *pays de grande culture* in the north and north-east of the country. The business acumen of these landowners cut two ways. While some took the entrepreneurial route, raising productivity on their lands by introducing the new technology and sometimes enclosing common land, others regarded this as a subsidiary venture and took a more extractive approach, boosting profits merely by employing a more business-like approach to estate management. This included revision of seigneurial registers (*terriers*) and professional surveying and mapping of property. 'Gracchus' Babeuf, the future Revolutionary who worked as a feudal clerk in Picardy in the 1780s, reckoned that two-thirds of all seigneuries within France had been mapped out over the course of the century. The reimposition of feudal and seigneurial dues which had lain dormant for years was extremely unpopular with the peasantry. The ducal Saulx-Tavannes family in Burgundy even dug up and reimposed one due which had last been levied in the thirteenth century. Using such techniques, the comte de Provence boosted his seigneurial income from 0.3 to 1.9 million livres in a matter of years.

The ways in which more food was supplied to an expanding population continued to be extensive rather than intensive in character. They also bore the imprint of government encouragement. First, there was the diffusion of new crops which diversified farming: despite the best efforts of tuber impresario Parmentier and enlightened provincial Intendants, potatoes were regarded as fit only for pigs and Belgians, and made little headway into popular diet. Maize, however, did better, notably in the south-west. Second, more land was brought into cultivation. From the mid-1760s, government offered tax incentives for such measures, and the 600,000 hectares of reclaimed land down to 1789 represented some 2.5 per cent of total cultivable area. In places such as the Auvergne the movement was motivated by sheer need, with poverty-stricken communes extending farming to neglected and often sterile marginal lands. Elsewhere, however, where commercial profit was the spur, gains were more significant: Burgundy added between 8 and 10 per cent to its farming area. Government encouragement of the enclosure of common lands, urged by the Physiocrats, was also bringing more land under the plough: enabling legislation was passed between 1769 and 1781 to allow the division of common land in Alsace and Lorraine, Burgundy, Flanders, Artois and elsewhere.

The third way in which agricultural production continued to expand was through regional specialization. The reliably expanding demand for a variety of agricultural products in Paris, in the bigger cities and in the armed forces stimulated more and more regions to move away from customary polyculture and to concentrate on market crops. The Paris region disinvested in wine production and became even more mono-cereal in its output – knowing that it could import wine from the south, just as it increasingly drew its meat supply from Normandy, the Limousin and the Charolais and its butter and cheese from Bray, Auge and Bessin. Wine-growing was a particular feature of regional specialization. Rising prices over the century encouraged farmers both large and small to plant vines, and by the 1780s, the abbé Expilly reckoned that as many as 4.5 million people were dependent on the wine trade.[24] The growth in the sector was rather unbalanced, and a wine glut from the 1770s forced prices down and put pressure on smaller wine-growers. The areas of quality production, however – notably the Bordelais, Burgundy and Champagne (where the discovery of how to make wine fizz led to sparkling whites replacing the area's traditional reds) – had by then developed export outlets which protected them against the slump. Bordeaux's exports to Britain doubled in value in the 1780s. The prosperous, export-oriented brandy trade which Irish émigré families such as the Hennessys had helped to develop in the Charente area over the century also boomed as never before.

The development of a strong demand for quality wines and brandies abroad and in big cities like Paris could only be met because of improved communications which vastly extended the city's provisioning area. Better distribution was the fourth, and perhaps most significant, means by which the agrarian economy supplied the needs of additional population and enriched the economy. As we have suggested, more fluid exchange (commerce) was critical to the economy as well as to the philosophy of the age of Enlightenment. It was better transport – particularly the Canal du Midi linking the Mediterranean through the Garonne valley to the Atlantic, for example, but also the improved road system, on which Grand Tourists commented approvingly, which allowed regional specialization in the south-east. Transport costs fell by two-thirds, so that lower Languedoc could develop its wine trade, as well as olive-growing and woollen manufacturing, at the expense of grain cultivation, knowing that it could rely on speedy and cheap grain transfers. It left grain-growing to the increasingly commercialized grain sector in upper Languedoc. Business on the Canal du Midi tripled over the century, with its high point in 1780. The emphasis on contacts, communication and speed accelerated as the Revolution approached. The Ponts et Chaussées had provided France with some 30,000 kilometres of paved and maintained roads. Turgot's introduction of an improved haulage and transport system (the *messageries*) in the mid-1770s brought a sharp improvement in journey times and a reduction in transport costs. Between 1765 and the 1780s, the time taken to travel from Paris to Strasbourg, Marseille and Toulouse fell from 11, 12 and 15 days to 4, 8 and 7 days respectively – an astonishing social phenomenon in terms of market integration and the formation of national opinion.

Much-improved communications aided trade and industry as well as agriculture. Over the century, foreign trade increased fourfold and colonial trade tenfold, while internal trade (which constituted three-fifths of all commerce) also boomed as never before. The apogee of trade over the century as a whole was very precisely the 1780s. Business at the international fair in Beaucaire tripled between the 1750s and the late 1780s. Outside the port cities, urban growth was, in this context, somewhat modest: the share of the total population resident in towns rose from 15 to around 20 per cent over the century. Even where it was slow – Rouen developed from 64,000 to 73,000, Paris from 510,000 to 620–650,000 – these figures often obscured dynamic relations with the surrounding region: Rouen, for example, was a centre of domestic industry with some 60,000 individuals working in its surrounding villages. This form of complementarity was very widespread: proto-industrialization stimulated the thickening of the countryside rather than (or as well as) the growth of urban population.

France had bounced back impressively as a global power after the disastrous Seven Years War. The West Indies remained the jewel in

France's crown – Saint-Domingue in particular exported nearly half the world's sugar. Participation in the slave trade continued, drawing French interests ever deeper into west and central Africa. By defeating England in the American War, France seemed to be opening up the American mainland as well as the West Indies to commercial penetration. Losses in India in 1763 were followed by a trade boom with the East, including China, while although the expeditions of Bougainville and La Pérouse to the south seas in 1768 and 1785 were intended as essentially scientific projects, the potential interests of trade were also recognized.

France's international trade position was intricately involved with its industry, many sectors of which also continued to prosper in the 1770s and 1780s. The fate of older industries was mixed, some woollen and linen-producing areas experiencing decline from mid-century. But the new industries like cotton goods, coal, iron, glass and chemical industries on the whole did well. The fashion-driven production cycle perfected in the early part of the century still gave French goods the edge in many international markets.[25] In the mid-1780s, France had 115 cotton businesses (as against 111 in England) and produced 16 million metres of cloth (as against England's 12.4 million). The high technology and heavy investment iron industry registered a coup of international dimensions with the opening of the Le Creusot complex in the 1780s. Industries linked to France's booming overseas trade – sugar and tobacco refineries, tanneries for exotic hides – also prospered.

Many of the colonial imports were shipped out to meet Europe's needs, but much stayed within France, and began to percolate down the social scale, increasing home demand for exotic commodities. At the start of the century, sugar, coffee, tea, chocolate and tobacco had been luxury goods, used almost exclusively by the very rich and as much for medicinal purposes as for nutritional value. By the 1780s, despite some furious assaults by moralists and physicians on these new-fangled forms of indulgence, with help from 'fashion's empire', the substances were on their way to becoming integral parts of the middle-class and popular diet. Tobacco – taken as snuff or smoked in pipes – was issued as rations to troops and had become extremely widespread. D'Argenson reckoned that its consumption held up so well in times of high prices because the poor thought that it had nutritive value.[26] Coffee too had gone massively down-market: nearly half of Parisian homes had a coffee-pot, and *café au lait* had started to become the regular morning drink of the urban working classes. Sugar too was finding its way into more and more food and drinks – causing a mass rotting of teeth for which the birth of scientific dentistry from the 1720s was only partial compensation. Parisians consumed on average 10 pounds of sugar each per year. There would be sugar riots as well as grain riots in the 1790s, when provisions dried up and angry consumers took to the streets, showing how blurred the line between 'necessity' and 'luxury' was becoming.

This seeming democratization of luxury marked a commodification of material culture which was evident at all levels and which formed part of a transformation of living styles and standards. Though the taste for luxury often had an exotic, colonial flavour, domestic industries such as the drinks trade also benefited from rising levels of consumer demand. Domestic demand from middling as well as noble audiences for exotic semi-luxury imports such as cotton goods, porcelain and lacquer-ware was strong enough to stimulate moves towards import substitution. The extraordinary destiny of calicoes was accompanied by more modest development of cheaper china, and the use of papier-mâché as surrogate lacquer-ware – cheapish versions of cultural artifacts formerly categorized as luxury products which could be called semi-luxury, or 'populuxe' products.

The dynamic expansion of the home market for consumer goods above the line of raw necessity formed the backdrop for a 'revolution in objects'[27] which was quietly taking place in middle- and lower-class homes. To judge from the well-documented case of Paris, domestic interiors were transformed: space was more differentiated and specialized; beds became more ornate and showy, while the standard old linen-chest gave way to wardrobes, cupboards, chests of drawers and the like. On the walls, dusty tapestries were replaced by wallpaper, decorated with engravings, pictures and mirrors. Curtains took their place at windows, marking a new concern for intimacy. Showy furniture such as writing-tables, card-tables and coatstands became more common, as did cups, china and domestic utensils. The vogue for the decorative was a form of materialism in which the church, moreover, connived: 'holy objects' (crucifixes, pious engravings, rosaries, medallions, as well as religious books) constituted an important sector of the phenomenon. Personal appearance was now more soigné, to judge by the presence of snuffboxes, razors, umbrellas, chamberpots, jewellery, watches and the like. The handkerchief – one way of dealing with tobacco use – established itself in the pockets of poor and rich alike. *Pace* Mary Wollstonecraft,[28] comfort installed itself in numerous homes: stoves warmed and clarified the air, and there were always hotwater bottles and footwarmers for cold nights. People spent more money on clothes, with even the poorer categories having twice the number of garments at the end of the century than they had had at the beginning. Woollen garments worn year in, year out gave way to lighter and more diverse clothes. Though men tended to stick to sombre and reserved cuts and cloths, tidy breeches and stockings took over from workmen's trousers. Women indulged a vigorous interest in fashion, with clothes more varied in weight, colour and consistency. It was possible, by the 1780s, to mistake a dairy-maid for a duchess – a crisis of recognition which much exercised the indignation of those who preferred the society of orders to be inscribed on outward appearances. The call for new sumptuary legislation was, however, viewed as ridiculously anachronistic – Controller-General Silhouette's gesturing in that direction in 1759 had won him universal scorn.

Jean-Jacques Rousseau was among the grumblers, and the world had indeed changed since his encounter in 1731 with his prudent peasant. Appearance had become the emblem of a new reality, not a new decep-tion: Parisians increasingly looked different, behaved differently, had different tastes. 'The French are not in Paris,' Rousseau snorted indig-nantly about a city which he saw, like all others, as 'the abyss of the human species'.[29] His act of rebellion against trendy Parisian con-sumerism was to renounce modish clothes (he gave away his watch too), and to dress in archaic Armenian dress topped out with a beaver hat. The consumerist age would, however, have the last laugh: his taste for vestimentary simplicity initiated a fashion trend which ended up with Marie-Antoinette and her milkmaid dresses. In similar manner, a Rous-seauian attack on the use of rouge and other aristocratic cosmetics led to manufacturers developing beauty aids (such as 'vegetable rouge') which enabled the wearer to achieve a more 'natural' look.[30] Even transparency, it seemed, could be a market construct.

Paris was a glittering shopwindow for French wares, but was far from being the sole location for this consumer boom. Many contemporaries tended to draw a broad contrast between a supposedly rampant commer-cialism in England with a more subsistence-oriented France. Clearly most provincial markets cut a poor comparison when set against the world capital of shopping that was London. Yet though the density of demand for consumer goods was certainly stronger in England, the French home market outsized England's: 5.3 million lived in French towns, as against 2.3 million in England – an impressive lead, even if we accept that per capita disposable income was higher in the latter. Home demand for consumer goods was thus widely dispersed in French towns and even many countrysides. 'The most rustic peasant and his wife [are] agitated by the same vertiginous spirit', fulminated the urban chronicler of Toulouse, Pierre Barthès, at mid-century, 'the same luxury that I call the decay of the human spirit.'[31] Lyonnais weavers, Norman peasants and Limousin stone-cutters too all sported Sunday bests, with silver buttons, ornate shoebuckles and coloured ribbons. Appointed to a parish near to Le Mans, the *curé* François-Yves Besnard noted that fashions which had formerly taken more than five years to change were in a state of ceaseless oscillation, while he could only distinguish rich from poor by their dress on work-days.[32]

The modes of transmission of these styles of the modern were many and various. Domestic servants played an important role as cultural intermediaries. Most of these were peasants (90 per cent in Paris were from the provinces, for example), and their post-mortem inventories showed that they were more precocious in adopting the personalized material culture of their masters and mistresses. Fairs and markets boomed, serving as entrepots for rampant commercialism: the number of fairs increased by a third over the 1770s, and by the 1780s there were 16,000 fair-days throughout the country and 160,000 market-days. Pedlars, carrying the kind of knick-knacks which made peasants imagine they were being Parisian by owning them, relayed their efforts. In many localities, post-masters acted as retail outlets for larger enterprises, but a great many small towns were developing a retail shop sector: in 1715, the locality of Arcis-sur-Aube had contained only a few merchants, described as 'miserable paupers who sell pots and wooden clogs and have no proper shops'. Yet by 1775, the 2,000-odd inhabitants were regaled with 14 merchants, 4 general stores, 2 ironmongers, 1 grocer, 8 tailors, 4 wig-makers, 2 second-hand clothes-dealers and one linen-merchant.[33] Nor should the role of the press be underestimated: from the 1750s, a network of provincial advertiser news-sheets (*Affiches*) had been set up throughout the country, providing outlets for a dazzling array of commodities and services, and serving simultaneously the need 'for utility and pleasure' on the 'Great Chain of Buying'.[34]

The new taste for consumer goods seems to have had an impact on family organization as well as lifestyles. If the average real wage-rates of rural and urban workers were, as Labrousse suggested, in long-term decline, the presence of consumer goods in the homes of these individuals suggests not just changes of taste but also new work strategies. A great many families seem to have participated in what Jan de Vries has called an 'industrious revolution',[35] whereby family members engaged more systematically in waged work so as to package a joint income which could give them entrée into the market for consumer goods. In the Montpellier region, for example, the daily wage for agricultural work remained static from mid-century; yet workers earned more by getting up at 3 a.m. in the summer and completing the equivalent of two days work, going home with double pay in their pockets. The wide diffusion of proto-industry was especially significant in this tendency for more work to compensate for declining wage-rates. Proto-industry allowed women family members (and sometimes children too) to engage in spinning, weaving and other menial industrial tasks within their homes, and thereby to supplement the income their husbands and fathers derived from agricultural work. It is plausible that the spread of birth control among the middle and lower classes in this period is explicable in terms of such family strategies: restricting the number of children meant more could be spent on consumer goods and services for all family members – and it was in this period that children became the centre of great emotional as well as commercial investment by their parents.

As these examples show, the opportunities presented by commercial expansion were seized with alacrity by a wide range of social types. Clearly, the main agents and beneficiaries of economic growth were the established urban bourgeoisie, which grew rapidly in number – from 0.7 million to 2.3 million (and also in girth, to judge by the acres of fat on display in their portraits). Yet enterprise and initiative in seizing commercial opportunities did not comprise a bourgeois monopoly. As we have suggested,[36] a fraction of the nobility used their considerable social advantages to profit from expanding markets in industry and finance as well as on the land. The trend of rising prices for agricultural produce favoured many peasants too. Middling to large peasants who had enough grain to feed themselves and their families needed only a horse and cart and a sack of surplus grain to go to market and realize substantial gains. The buoyancy of wine prices was a godsend to small peasants too: in Alsace a peasant family needed 12 hectares of land planted in grain to support themselves, but only 2 hectares planted with vines.

The fact that large numbers of the popular classes were prominent among those who sought to benefit from the expansion of the economy should not blind us to the problems of commercial capitalism's uneven development over the century as a whole. This age of consumerism consumed lives and bodies, as well as adorning and enriching them. Those who had invented the term *bienfaisance* ('beneficence') woke up late to the fact that the major social problem of the late eighteenth century was not depopulation – that old spectre had been largely laid to rest by the 1770s – but the threat of mass pauperization in overcrowded and unhealthy cities and in disinherited rural outbacks. Industrial and agrarian entrepreneurs struggled to keep down the claims of labour on profits and rents, particularly at bad moments of the trade cycle, when the contrast between rich and poor sharpened. Russian nobleman Denis Fonvizine in the late 1770s was shocked by general levels of hygiene even in the consumerist shopwindow of Paris, which he concluded overall was 'just a whit cleaner than a pigsty' and where the most shocking contrasts were banal: 'one cannot take a step without coming across something absolutely excellent, which however is right next to something absolutely terrible and barbarous'.[37] 'Necessities' were dear while the trappings of luxury were remarkably cheap by international standards: 'lodging, food and carriage cost twice as much as in Saint-Petersburg, but baubles, dress, books and engravings are half as much or even cheaper'.[38]

Although governments affected an increasingly humanitarian rhetoric, they were singularly ineffective in staunching the running sore of poverty so evident even in its most illustrious site. Schemes of state beneficence such as charity workshops, disaster relief, pensions to needy gentlefolk, and medical aid programmes tended to be pinpricks rather than solutions. This was all the more depressing in that the financial position of most charitable institutions was worsening over the course of the century, as a result of growing demand for their services, inflationary institutional costs, and a marked decline in charitable donations. The biggest financial commitment made by the state was the creation of a network of a couple of score of *dépôts de mendicité* from the late 1760s to house vagrants. Subject to biting criticism, the institutions ended up as appallingly repressive and insanitary workhouse-cum-prisons housing a variegated population of the needy and distressed.

The voices of alarm and humanitarian concern were reaching a crescendo by the late 1780s. Yet it is difficult to draw a line between the appearances and the realities of distress – just as it is to distinguish between the appearances and the realities of 'luxury'. A downturn in agricultural prices in many regions from the late 1770s depressed rural incomes and left many peasants defenceless when the bad harvest of 1788 hit them. A serious drought in 1785 and 1786 caused a die-off of cattle, which ruined many peasant families, especially in the south. From 1786 and 1787, much of French industry was adversely affected by English competition following the 1786 Anglo–French Trade Treaty. The sum of even these serious problems did not add up to a structural crisis in the French economy. Parts of the latter were still doing very well – indeed the brilliant success of British manufactured goods' penetration of the French market after 1786 highlighted the continued buoyancy of domestic demand. Yet even though mass hunger was beginning to be seen in some rural areas, the economy did not appear to be in a state from which it would not have the resilience to bounce back after catastrophes.

Bad though it still was under Louis XVI, the problem of poverty had been far, far more severe under Louis XIV. Though the 1788–9 crisis hit hard, its significance as a social phenomenon was much amplified by the discursive context in which it now occurred. The Sun King's reign had not boasted the inquiries, reports, inquests, social analyses, quasi-ethnographic surveys and economic and demographic estimates of Louis XVI's reign. Ignorance had been bliss: knowledge of popular distress provoked guilty feelings and humane wishes that more should be done – and that the government should do it. A striking feature of the reign of Louis XVI was the extent to which both winners and losers on the commercial carousel looked to government for help and support – and were resentful and critical if and when they did not receive it.

A great deal rode on state policies. The winds of liberalization which swept through government bureaux from the 1750s and 1760s onwards had subjected the economy to the sometimes bracing, sometimes damaging effects of international competition. The extension of France's areas of commercial involvement left some traditional areas a little neglected, and others prey to international competition. Thus, in the 1770s and 1780s, both the Levant and the Baltic were being penetrated by English and to some extent Dutch traders, at French expense: the Languedocian wool trade, for example, which depended heavily on Levantine markets and which had been in crisis since the 1750s, never recovered its former buoyancy. Spain's prohibition of charcoal exports after 1769 consigned many Pyrenean mines and forges to irremediable decline. Similarly, in a move which underlined the limitations of the Family Compact, Charles III of Spain's embargo on French exports of silk and linen to the Iberian peninsula and the Spanish American colonies was a body blow to sectors of French textile manufacturing which hitherto had done exceptionally well.

Many sectors of France's trade and industry also lost out as a result of the government's dealings with England and its former American colonies after 1783. France lacked a colony in which there was a significant demand for home-produced manufactured articles, and many hoped that its American allies could be a good surrogate. French merchants lost all the tricks to their English counterparts, but a good deal of blame must also attach to government, which failed to show the flag in the New World in any meaningful way. The French ambassador complained about the 'unhealthily democratic environment'[39] of the new state. French red-tape and administrative torpor were further deterrents. Not only did the Americans not drift away from their English ambit, but they also began to penetrate French West Indian markets themselves.

If the spirit of liberalization had drawbacks as well as benefits attached to it, this was all the more the case in regard to domestic trade and industry. In 1759, the traditional ban on colour printing on cotton (designed to keep out English competition) was lifted and this spurred a prodigious boom in calicoes. Similarly, the decision in 1762 to allow industries to establish themselves outside the corporative framework of the guilds boosted proto-industrialization in a great many areas. Yet the government was only ever half-hearted about liberalizing the domestic economy: tolls remained numerous and costly, increasing distance times and haulage costs. Similarly, though Turgot had abolished trade guilds as a means of deregulating labour, his reforms, as we have seen, went off half-cock: a modified system of guilds was introduced by his successors which in some ways actually decreased mobility of labour, notably by generalizing the practice of the *livret*, or worker's passport. (Characteristically, government appreciated the guild system, since the sale of office within it brought it substantial cash benefits.) Then again, there was incoherence and inconsistency over the liberalization of the grain trade, with liberal measures in 1754, 1763–4, 1775 and then 1787 alternating with regulatory phases.

The stop-start nature of economic policies under Louis XVI owed something to the fragility of the post of Finance Minister – a position which, as the duc de Croÿ ruefully remarked, 'ought to be stable':[40] there were some seventeen incumbents between 1754 and 1789, ten of them in fifteen years of Louis XVI's reign. Government should not have been blamed for the existence of a real world in which French entrepreneurs had to compete – but it was. The welfarist discourse of power which the absolute monarchy increasingly deployed – legislative preambles became almost philosophical disquisitions on beneficence – set popular expectations high. So too the Enlightenment quest for solutions to social ills through purposive human action made French men and women particularly unforgiving for failings in the state, and they wilfully scapegoated government for a diverse range of ills. In this context, though trumpeted as the start of a new, more liberal era in foreign trade, Calonne's Anglo–French Trade Treaty was never going to be more than a mixed blessing. In the middle term, the economy might well have had the resilience to take the shock of English competition and turn it to advantage. But short-term difficulties were inevitable. Although the Bordelais was triumphant at the new English outlet for its wines, the textiles and iron industries were furious at the subsequent competition from English manufactured goods: imports of the latter rose from 16 million livres in 1784 to 23 million in 1787 and 27 million in 1788. Many of the loudest complainants – such as the Normandy linen and Montauban wool manufactures – had been in serious economic trouble even before 1786. Yet difficulties were now routinely ascribed to the state. Louis XVI's governments found it difficult enough to achieve the possible; by the late 1780s, as Calonne ruefully discovered, they were also having the impossible laid solemnly at their door.

C) SILENT REVOLUTION
IN AN AGE OF NOISE

Harlay de Champvallon, archbishop of Paris under Louis XIV, once remarked that 'the king does not like things which make a noise'.[41] Louis XVI's reign was, in contrast, most definitely, an age of noise, notably by an increasingly articulate and vociferous cacophony of competing discourses and debates, expressed as much in written as oral form, which royal and ecclesiastical institutions were losing their power to muzzle. Beneath the frothy, exuberant surface, however, a silent revolution was taking place.[42] A subtle, but widely ramified shift in *mentalités* signalled more individualized and less spiritually oriented attitudes towards life and death, while the emergence of the Great Chain of Buying demonstrated fundamental changes in ways of thinking, of believing, of behaving – and even of smiling.

It was in 1787, in fact, that a smile scandal rocked the public sphere. The smile in question was located on the face of Madame Vigée-Lebrun, in her self-portrait which was publicly displayed in the same year. 'An affectation which artists, art-lovers and persons of taste have been united in condemning,' noted Moufle d'Angerville's scabrous court messenger, the *Mémoires secrets*, 'and which finds no precedent among the Ancients, is that in smiling, [Madame Vigée-Lebrun] shows her teeth.'[43] To depict a toothy smile was not merely to cut across representational conventions in place since Antiquity, but also to contravene procedures for the artistic expression of emotion codified in the late seventeenth century by Charles Lebrun, First Painter and multi-purpose mythologizer of Louis XIV. Open mouths in paintings had denoted that an individual was grotesque (a point underlined by the accompanying revelation of disgustingly deformed teeth), demented, plebeian, or else subject to some highly extreme emotion. In polite society, facial extremes were simply unthinkable.

It is of course ridiculously glib to suggest that the impending financial bankruptcy of the Bourbon state in the late 1780s was being matched by a perceived bankruptcy in its role as arbiter of taste in emotional expression. Yet Madame Vigée-Lebrun's scandalously charming smile was indeed a token of a real enough shift which had taken place across the board in the sources of authority and legitimacy regarding aesthetic canons and modes of bodily presentation – and that shift would play into the character of the crisis of 1788–9. Whereas the royal court had once been viewed as the ultimate arbiter in such spheres, 'public opinion' had taken its place. The new toothy smile was of course predicated upon the emergence of a scientifically oriented dentistry from the 1720s onwards, plus the emergence of a corps of surgical experts capable of developing the tooth-puller's art into preventive and cosmetic dentistry. Yet the boom in smiles which the advent of the dentist in Western culture stimulated owed nothing to the royal court, which showed very little interest in the development. Louis XV had disfigured his smile by losing teeth, sound and decayed, to inexpert tooth-drawing (like his great-grandfather), and one of his early mistresses had been legendary for halitosis. Louis XVI, one of his pages later recalled, had 'a fine leg', but 'his teeth were badly arranged and made his smile rather ungraceful'. His brother, the comte d'Artois (future king Charles X), tended 'to have his mouth continually open, which gave his face a rather unintelligent appearance'.[44] The public sphere, in contrast to the royal court, was more than responsive. From mid-century onwards, newspapers were chockful of advertisements for tooth-pastes and powders, tooth-whitening agents, tooth-brushes, tooth-picks and tongue-scrapers, plus a multitude of dentures and other 'artificial pieces', attesting to the strength of the demand among consumers for new kinds of fashion which owed little or nothing to royal endorsement.

There were some who lamented the abdication by the royal court of its customary role in setting canons of taste. With the benefit of hindsight, the king's page, the comte d'Hézècques, was sure that the tendency of Louis XVI and his court to be indifferent to vestimentary splendour set a bad example, and reduced the respect his subjects owed a monarch.[45] Symptomatically, the unsmiling Louis XVI could not wait to get out of his massively heavy coronation robes in Reims in 1775, and he never wore them again, preferring lighter and less ceremonial dress at court which made it difficult for outsiders to pick him out from his aristocratic commensals. His wearing of the English riding-coat (*redingote*), popularized by his brothers and by the duc d'Orléans, showed that even the king of France seemed to have opted for the more bourgeois *luxe de subsistance* generally regarded as preferable to the court's traditional *luxe de décoration*.[46] Although Louis's queen did more than her fair share to keep the latter afloat, in general terms even

Versailles, increasingly viewed as sterile and out of touch, seemed to bow the knee, in matters fashionable and in lifestyle choices, to the energizing dynamo of public demand that was Paris. Louis XIV's solar temple had become, as Mercier put it, 'a satellite' round 'a whirlwind'.[47]

Whereas many sectors of the economy were experiencing problems in the 1780s, the market for cultural and leisure pursuits stayed highly buoyant. Parisian theatre audiences had grown fast from around 1760, and a developing national taste for drama and opera was reflected in the opening of splendid provincial theatres, especially in the 1780s. The brilliant success of *The Marriage of Figaro* highlighted audience reactions over which, as we have seen, royal opinion had no purchase. Public opinion rather than the ruler's cultural minions was increasingly seen as a determinant of aesthetic quality in painting too. The big audiences which since 1737 had visited the recurrent art exhibition in Paris known as the Salon ruffled the feathers of would-be connoisseurs, but undoubtedly influenced artistic practice. Whereas 7,000 individuals had visited the exhibition halls in 1755, over 21,000 were cramming in by 1788, forming, as one newspaper put it 'a vast theatre where neither rank, favour nor wealth can reserve a place for bad taste'.[48] That taste latterly took a classical republican turn, inspired by Jacques-Louis David's celebrated *Oath of the Horatii*, displayed in the 1785 Salon.

The death of the patriarchs of the classic Enlightenment occurred at this time: Voltaire and Rousseau died in 1778, d'Alembert in 1783, and Diderot in 1784, while leading salonnières Mesdames du Deffand and d'Épinay passed away in 1780 and 1783. Beneath this sombre necrology, important shifts were occurring in the workings of the public sphere and in the sites in which opinion was constructed. The Parisian salons and the provincial academies, which had played a pilot role in the arbitration of national taste during the classic phase of the Enlightenment, as we have seen, were being overtaken in importance by other forms and styles of sociability and opinion-formation. In addition, print increasingly replaced polite conversation as the prime medium of intellectual exchange, contesting the dominance of academies and salons.

The press was coming to play an even greater role in the Enlightenment project, joining up the points of light throughout the kingdom to produce a better, fairer, more inclusive and (hopefully) happier nation. In this context, buyers and sellers of the commodities which emblematized the triumph of consumerism merged imperceptibly into producers and consumers of ideas on the Great Chain of Buying, and the interactive and egalitarian polity this implied.[49] The ubiquity of the term *commerce* was significant in this respect, since it denoted both trade in goods and intellectual interchange: as the President de Brosses put it, 'exchange occurs for words as for other commodities'.[50] The editor of *Affiches de l'Orléanais* highlighted the periodical press's role in 'the communication and commerce of minds'. Newspapers certainly allowed the public to be increasingly responsive to political and cultural events: the circulation of the *Gazette de France* topped 12,000, for example, during the American War. We may speculate that a total newspaper circulation of 15,000 before 1750 rose to 60,000 by the mid-1780s. Newspapers reached a much wider audience than this, of course: reading rooms which developed from the 1760s onwards specialized in newspaper subscriptions (which were often too high for potential individual readers); so did coffee-houses and the embryonic clubs which began to spring up in the bigger cities in the 1780s in imitation of English and American models. Forms of collective readership – in the family or the workplace, for example – also multiplied the total number of readers, which we may conjecture was anything between a quarter and half a million individuals. The vocation of the newspaper as a marketplace overlapped, moreover, with the idea of it as a virtual public meeting or forum: the *Affiches de Limoges* fondly imagined the press network as 'a kind of confraternity, a sort of academy spread out throughout the kingdom', while, as Jacques-Pierre Brissot, moving spirit behind the Amis des Noirs ('Friends of the Blacks') abolitionist lobby, excitedly pointed out, a dynamic press network allowed the spirit of Athenian democracy to be replicated through the medium of print: 'One can teach the same truth at the same moment to millions of men; through the press, they can discuss it without tumult, decide calmly and give their opinion.'[51]

Increasing awareness of the democratizing potential of the press in the 1780s was accompanied by growing hopes pinned on the phenomenon of freemasonry. In 1744, there had been forty-four masonic lodges in France, and this grew to 165 by 1765 and some 400 at the death of Louis XV. By 1789, the number had increased prodigiously to nearly 1,000 lodges, spread throughout the country and comprising between 50,000 and 100,000 masons, making the masonic movement the largest voluntary organization in France except the church, with one urban male in twenty in its rolls. In the early days, Cardinal Fleury had repressed the secretive movement as dangerous for religion, monarchy and morals. Yet by 1780 Marie-Antoinette was writing to her sister that 'everyone belongs to it; everyone knows everything that takes place . . . It forms a society of beneficence and pleasure: they dine a lot, talk and sing – it's not at all a group of declared atheists, since, I'm told, God is in every mouth.'[52] There were indeed bishops and monks in masonic ranks, ignoring the pope's prohibition on membership. Not only ecclesiastics preferred the conviviality of the lodge to the spirituality of the religious confraternity. Freemasons were to be found in every walk of life including among the Princes of the Blood: the first Grand Master of French masonry was the duc d'Antin, while under Louis XVI the position was held by the duc de Chartres (succeeding as duc d'Orléans from 1785, the latter had taken over from the deceased Conti as leading dynastic troublemaker).

Though many lodges retained a hyper-exclusive stance and establishment ambience, in general the social composition of masonry was skewed towards the Third Estate. Whereas the first two orders (clergy, nobility) comprised one-fifth and two-fifths respectively of membership of academies, for example, the figures for masonry were 4 and 18 per cent. Over three-quarters of masons were commoners: with bourgeois rentiers and the professional classes (lawyers, medical men, state employees, etc.) particularly in evidence. What was also distinctive about the movement was the welcome it accorded the more mobile elements within society: around one-fifth of total membership was drawn from trade and business, while army officials and students were also particularly well represented. Artisans, shopkeepers and petty clerks who belonged to no other form of Enlightenment sociability were also to be found in the fraternal ranks of masonry. The masons were in addition younger and less socially staid than the academicians.

Despite their social mixing, freemasons faithfully reflected that distancing from the common people on which the *philosophes*, salonnières and academicians had founded the notion of a public. Implicit in masonic identity was a claim to moral nobility and virtuous respectability which excluded working men 'of the vilest kind' – and most women of any description. The question of whether women could be masons at all was hotly debated, and though many women did join, this was usually in affiliative 'lodges of adoption', which were restricted to a tokenist, decorative and spectatorial role. Freemasons were not alone in being prey to a growing anxiety about the role of women within the world of rational debate, which reflected Rousseau's rude republicanism, which had no room for female involvement in public affairs. The Genevan sage, it will be remembered, preferred his women in the bosom of the family, preferably breastfeeding their babies and submissively nurturing their menfolk.

The ambient Rousseauism of masonic culture which depreciated the role of workers and women was also hegemonic in new political clubs and societies (*musées*, *lycées*, clubs, etc.). Bourgeois males (plus some tame nobles) found it all too easy to get by without the female governance the salonnières had formerly provided. Women were passing from animators and facilitators of enlightened exchange to become outcasts from intellectual life. The cult of the quasi-spiritual healing of mesmerism in the same decade offered an interesting variation on this general theme. Attempts by the medical establishment to quash the experiments of the Austrian magus, Franz-Anton Mesmer, led to wealthy professionals and young liberal nobles championing his cause and developing a radical critique of the Enlightenment academy. Mesmerism was popular with women, but leading mesmerists regarded them as constituting too weak a vessel to play a part in the cult's organization.

Masonry and mesmerism thus exemplified a version of class and gender politics which was developing more broadly in the public sphere in the reign of Louis XVI. Masonry was exemplary too in seeking to create national networks of intellectual sociability which simultaneously embodied, represented and empowered public opinion. Moves by Condorcet in the 1760s and then in the early 1770s to establish a nationwide coordinating framework for the academies had foundered, partly at least on the fears of provincial institutions that they would be dominated and controlled from Paris. Yet the wish for closer federal contacts was strong, and in 1786 the initiative of Dubois de Fosseyeux, president of the Arras Academy (of which Robespierre was a member), to create a 'general correspondence office' for academies met with a warm reception, and encouraged fraternizing among the different bodies. Similarly, Vicq d'Azyr, the energetic secretary of the Royal Society of Medicine, the proto-academy for medicine created in 1778, was able to enlist the help of an enthusiastic medical profession throughout France as corresponding members to build up a national data-bank for meteorological, epidemiological and other observations. Even before this, steps had been taken to organize all French masons into a national body, the Grand Orient of France. Although some lodges, usually of a more mystical and radical tendency, refused to come in, the Grand Orient did provide greater national cohesion to the lodges and highlighted the late Enlightenment wish to use cultural networks more proactively.

Freemasons not only operated within nationwide parameters, they also celebrated an ethic of humanitarian egalitarianism. The Grand Orient had crystallized this approach in 1773 by establishing formal elections, principles of majority rule and representative governance for French masonry, while the Lodge of the Nine Sisters in Paris talked of fellow masons in the New World and the Old as 'citizens of the masonic democracy'.[53] Yet in general Marie-Antoinette's view that political and religious radicalism was not intrinsic to mainstream masonry was correct. Most masons were Christians (Protestants as well as Catholics) or Deists, and tolerance of different views was *de rigueur*: indeed, the student lodge in Montpellier was fairly characteristic in specifically banning members from talking either religion or politics. Conservative ideologues in the late 1790s searching out origins for the Revolution were to light on masonry as a Revolutionary creed, spawning Terrorism in its maw. Yet many masons probably enjoyed the singing, drinking and colourful rituals more than any putative political or even intellectual activity, and returned to life outside the masonic lodge with social prejudices confirmed rather than weakened. Although some of the more esoteric masonic sects experimented with daringly radical ideas, and elite Parisian and Versailles-based lodges dabbled in ministerial politicking, in general this was not masonry's cachet, and most lodges professed an integral loyalism. (If there would be former freemasons on the Committee of Public Safety during the Terror, they would be numbered too in the ranks of the *émigré* armies and counter-revolutionary Chouan rebels, and in tumbrils bound for the guillotine.)

If freemasons were thus far from constituting the leading cadres of a focused programme for political upheaval, they were still highly important as schools for the public-spirited, and as laboratories of citizenship. In striking contradiction with the formal principles of absolutism (or the stuffier academies and salons), the *cascade de mépris* characteristic of the society of orders did not apply in masonic circles. In theory at least, dukes and princes left their coronets at the door, and although there was ranking within lodges, this was based on service, seniority and merit rather than social position in the outside world. Enclaves of meritocratic and virtuous sociability, the lodges exuded, both through and beneath their mystical aura and bizarre ritualistic practices, a thoroughgoing meliorism. Masonic discourse highlighted how goodwill and an attention to social welfare (*bienfaisance*) was opening up a bright new future for mankind, and that social and political harmony could be achieved in an enlarged public sphere of rational debate. There was a particularly strong emphasis on self-improvement, which was seen as an essential prerequisite for moral and intellectual leadership within society.

The sizeable nationwide masonic network was also a telling symptom of a growing yearning within the bourgeois public sphere for the rituals of a more inclusive, more socially aware and fairer society. The heart of the masonic message that self-improvement was linked to the quest to improve society chimed with the development of a more exigent culturally based politics within other sites in the public sphere in the 1780s: in the Parisian salons of Madame Necker and Madame de Genlis, for example, both of which were more overtly political than their predecessors; in the academies, whose prize essay competitions veered away from literary and philosophical to social scientific and political issues; in the press, through *mémoires judiciaires* chronicling *causes célèbres* and a host of other polemical writings; in the work of interest groups such as the slave abolitionists; and in the new political clubs, *musées*, mesmerist groupings and the like.

The reign of Louis XVI thus saw the mood and the temper of public debate changing in important ways. Significantly, the concern for reform which was in line with enlightened principles and responsive to the promptings of the bourgeois public sphere also echoed at the heart of the state itself. Louis XVI professed the highest respect for public opinion; chose his ministers and policies with it in mind; allowed his ministers to use *philosophes* as policy consultants and propagandists; prefixed his laws with 'philosophic' preambles; had begun to dabble in new systems of political representation; and, in his private diaries and in legislative preambles, mythologized the transcendental virtues of public opinion quite as rhapsodically as any freemason or radical journalist. Jacques Peuchet, who wrote the volumes on *police* ('rational administration') for the *Encyclopédie méthodique* which appeared in 1789, articulated the rationale for this union between absolute monarchy and public opinion and contrived to make it sound anything but a shotgun marriage: 'public opinion', he stated, 'differs both from the spirit of obedience that must reign in a despotic state and the popular opinions which prevail in republican deliberations'.[54] In a disenchanted world in which society was less united than formerly around shared Christian values, the opportunity was there for the ruler to trade in his divine-right status for the chance of popularity in and dominance over the public sphere. By adapting himself to the promptings of the public, the king might be able to steer a middle course between despotism and anarchy and patriotically produce a more civilized and happier society. In a move which owed as much to Fénelon as to Rousseau, Louis could aim to restyle himself the first among citizens, viewing virtuous attachment to the public weal as his most important kingly duty.

As the financial and economic crisis of the late 1780s started to loom, however, Louis found himself uncomfortably straddling two horses. Was he first and foremost a Bourbon monarch in the line of the revered Louis XIV? Or was he first and foremost a patriotic citizen of the bourgeois public sphere? The dilemma partly reflected the king's astonishing propensity for vacillation and wishing to have everything both ways. He wavered between on the one hand posing as public opinion's champion, raining down attacks on the corporative shell of the society of orders on behalf of 'his' peoples, and on the other proving touchy about personal criticism, resisting egalitarian trends which had implications for his own position, and displaying haughty and aristocratophilic reflexes. Many contemporaries, as we have seen, viewed the extension of royal power as inimical to the public good. Symptomatically, for example, endless assurances over the century that changes to the tax system were designed to protect the poor and weak failed to diminish the almost universal view, seemingly borne out in practice, that greater state control over the tax system would mean heavier taxes for all.

Louis's havering between two political options was not simply a personal failing, however, nor a mere sign of insincerity. It also reflected a powerful line of schism opening up in the 1780s over the role of the state in serving social utility. The contours of that schism were often difficult to delineate – for the silent revolution had to be grasped through a babble of noise. Yet it was widely evident, not only within the sites of the burgeoning public sphere, but also increasingly amongst traditional privileged groupings ensconced within the society of orders. One of its outcrops, for example, was an impassioned debate about the role of professional competence in maximizing social utility, and how professional expertise could mesh effectively with the demands of a centralizing state on one hand and, on the other, a growing and more self-conscious public. Broadly speaking, two discourses of professionalism and public service were emerging. On one hand, there was a desire for change within the corporative framework, in ways which respected social hierarchy and vertical ties of dependence. In the case of the army, for example, post-Seven Years War reforms aimed to produce an effective and professional military force, Spartan (or possibly Prussian) in its virtues and operating within more bureaucratic and more hierarchical structures, with better training and clearer career pathways. Even the infamous Ségur ordinance of 1781 limiting military high command to *noblesse de race* was a professionalizing measure within this framework: the aim was not to exclude commoners rising on the basis of talent so much as to attack *anoblis* who had bought their posts, and yet who lacked the spirit of honour alleged to be inbred amongst the old nobility.

On the other hand, alongside this corporative discourse within the armed forces, there also developed a more overtly civic discourse of professionalism, which drew on both the equalizing rhetoric of enlightened absolutism and the more democratic values of the public sphere and which stressed horizontal and egalitarian bonds of mutual interdependence between citizens. The message echoing through a plethora of polemics and publications was that an army officer should not be hermetically sealed off by professional discipline from the wider society, but should be in some senses a citizen before he was a soldier. *Le Soldat-citoyen* – the 'soldier-citizen', to take the title of a 1780 pamphlet endorsing this view[55] – had no truck with the socially elitist (and implicitly 'unpatriotic') corporative professionalism espoused by fellow officers, who often couched their duties in terms of being 'subjects' of the king rather than 'citizens' within the 'nation'. 'Patriot' brother officers – often this turned out to be ambitious younger military men, eager to open up the hide-bound officer corps to wider social influences – prioritized allegiance to the nation above robotic obedience to their superiors.

Much the same discursive conflict between corporative and civic values was found within the church. Over the century, the clergy had emphatically adopted a classic Tridentine version of ecclesiastical professionalism grounded in accepting discipline from above, and emblematized by the wearing of the cassock 'uniform'. Yet by the time of Louis XVI's reign, a great many of the lower clergy in particular shifted towards grounding their version of professionalism in commitment to the nation rather than obedience to aristocratic prelates or worldly popes. Following the Dauphinois parish priest Henri Reymond, whose *Les Droits des curés* ('The Rights of Parish Priests') appeared in 1776, they saw themselves as 'citizen priests', for whom, as the Roman adage had it, 'the voice of the people is the voice of God'.[56] Though the initial episcopal opponents of the Unigenitus bull would have been appalled by the thought, Jansenism (and its sibling, Richerism) was stimulating a quasi-democratic call for a collective clerical say in fashioning ecclesiastical policy in the interests of the nation.

Advances in medical and surgical science over the eighteenth century had helped foster a civic discourse of medical professionalism in which the dedicated medical man was viewed as a lay equivalent to the *bon prêtre*, a self-sacrificing super-patriot fraternally dispensing the gift of life and good health to ailing fellow citizens. Yet the capacity to practise was viewed as being endlessly circumscribed by selfish corporatist privilege. The superior privileges of physicians over surgeons, who were more empirically oriented and more closely associated with key curative therapies such as smallpox inoculation, cataract-cutting and obstetrics, were viewed as anti-social and anti-utilitarian. Similarly, the Paris Medical Faculty's insistence that only trained Paris graduates could practise within the capital was a selfish restrictive practice from which the health of all Parisians suffered. A free field of medical practice would allow the demand for improved medical services to be met by a burgeoning supply of 'citizen officers of health' (*officiers de santé*). The state's repression of mesmerism led medical men who had championed the heterodox therapy to develop a full-scale attack on the academic, and by extension the political hierarchy, for it seemed only a short step from the 'academic aristocracy' to the aristocratic establishment.

The debate on professionalism was also found amongst numerous groups of state servants – and was given added pungency by broader critiques of government bureaucracy. A powerful blast of freedom was, it seemed, required to end the 'injurious separation which reigns between the administration and the Nation'.[57] The civil engineers of the Ponts et Chaussées service, for example, constituted the very cynosure of corporative professionalism, with their rigorous training programmes, punctilious bureaucratic regimes and unerring commitment to social utility. Yet they were increasingly criticized for technocratic arrogance and remoteness from civic concerns, and by the 1780s many younger members of the corps were stressing the need for greater attentiveness as regards the wishes of the 'nation' (rather than merely the orders of the king). Much the same was true in the ranks of the General Farm, widely criticized as an irresponsible leech on the body politic, despite its development of a corporative ethic of service and elegantly bureaucratic procedures of which Max Weber would have been proud.

These debates also spilled into the public discussion on venality of office. Venal officers had long defended themselves against the state's attacks by highlighting the status of their office as private property, defence of which was the king's constitutional duty. From the outside, this looked like selfishness and cronyism, and the monarchy was criticized for supporting a system which cut against market values purely in the state's fiscal interests, and in a way which placed enclaves of privilege and undeserved wealth close to the levers of power. As the century wore on, however, venal officers also justified their status in terms of the professional ethic they had developed within the corporative framework, and the contribution their honed expertise made to social welfare. Just as a good cobbler was more likely to produce good shoes than a good patriot, so the jurisprudential expertise of the most prominent of venal officers – the magistrates of the Paris Parlement – made a crucial contribution to wider social welfare, they held, by keeping the ruler within constitutional bounds.

Particularly vocal over issues of reform were professional groupings whose corporative lives were regulated by the state, and which were responsive not only to the new civic sociability of the public sphere but also – especially – to the booming markets for goods and services. Although members of the more market-oriented professions had always prided themselves as being above mere mercantile considerations, improved chances of enrichment as a result of growing demand for their services led many to embrace market values, which they regarded as fully consonant with civic duty. Their commitment to freedom in trade owed less to doctrinaire commitment to Enlightenment or Physiocratic precepts or to personal worries about the price of bread (the middle classes had reserves to fall back on) than to their experience of working in a situation in which they were frequently hampered by state under-pinning of corporative privilege. Strikingly, the price of venal offices went up fastest from mid-century in precisely those posts which gave access to dynamic markets for goods and services: attorneys, notaries, legal clerks, auctioneers and wig-makers. Many of these individuals appreciated the market edge which their post gave them, as well as the idea of protection from market dangers which state support promised. However, the erratic and extractive attitude of successive governments to venality, especially from the 1760s onwards, made more and more of these individuals disenchanted with state 'support' and willing to chance their arm in the world of the free market. This reflected a wavering between the benefits of freedom and those of state protection which many merchants and manufacturers also experienced.

The multi-tiered world of the law witnessed much the same range of corporative-vs-civic arguments. The magistrates of the *parlements* foregrounded their corporative legal expertise as a guarantee of consti-tutional rectitude, and resisted attempts to dilute their numbers or their rights, and the legal world as a whole was not short of individuals seeing in corporative privileges the foundation of professional expertise from which society necessarily benefited. Yet barristers and attorneys were probably the most vociferous of all social groupings in developing the discourse of civic professionalism. They did this in a wide range of venues, including political polemics (particularly during the years of the Maupeou crisis) and *mémoires judiciaires* in criminal and civil cases exposing the abuses of corporative and 'despotic' power. In addition, lawyers in Paris drew on the discourse of civic professionalism to revitalize a latent natural law tradition so as to defend journeymen against the 'tyranny' of the masters within their corporations. Their colleagues in eastern France did much the same as regards defending peasant communities against the imposition of feudal dues – a campaign which was given an added boost in 1780 when the Parlement of Besançon refused to register the royal decree abolishing serfdom. The acuity of clashes between civic and corporative notions of professionalism was sharpened in the 1780s, as throughout France barristers and attorneys, who hitherto had thrown themselves behind the corporatist *parlemen-taire* cause espoused by magistrates, began to develop independent attitudes which vaunted closer and more fruitful links with the wider society.

The corporative cells of the society of orders were thus by the 1780s engendering debates on the nature of professional service and identity within a modernized polity and a market economy, and these discussions interacted with polemics over the state and society being played out in the regenerated organs of the public sphere. Indeed, the fact that professionals – lawyers, medics, army officers, state employees – were amongst the most numerous members of masonic lodges, clubs, reading rooms and the like allowed new synergies and combinations to develop. By the 1780s, it was increasingly apparent that the bourgeois public sphere was not an entity encamped outside the royal citadel. On the contrary, many of its members were either within the state or already enjoyed its benefits, and contributed towards popularizing the contestatory interrogation of the aims and protocols of power. They set the tempo of debates in which the king was now player rather than umpire, participant rather than arbitrator. And they added their voices to the complaints of the business classes, financial milieux and tax-payers over the state's apparent mishandling of its finances and of the wider economy.

The most vocal proponents of the new mood of politics in the 1780s were thus individuals caught up in the triangulated crossfire between the regulatory power of the corporatist state; the attractions (and some of the dangers) of a still booming market for goods and services; and an enlarged and renovated public sphere of sociability and debate. The lawyers, medical men, state employees and other professionals who had become the voice of the 'public' were not Tocqueville's out-of-touch, politically naive and somewhat marginal intellectuals; nor yet were they the proto-industrial capitalists imagined by much of the Marxist tradition. Both characterizations predicate a separation between the state and civil society which was not a characteristic of the Bourbon polity. That kind of division would, however, become intrinsic to the political and social system to emerge from an impending Revolution, in which the lead was invariably taken by precisely these groupings.

D) THE ELUSIVE PUBLIC: FINANCIAL AND INSTITUTIONAL REFORM

The years 1787 and 1788 saw the collapse of France's high international standing in the aftermath of the American War. To France's long-acknowledged cultural hegemony in Europe, the Treaty of Versailles of 1783 had added a global diplomatic triumph which augured brilliantly for the future, and an economic boom stimulated by a government whose financial position was sound (or so Necker's *Compte Rendu* gave all to believe). Now, the monarchy seemed morally and financial bereft, the economy was in trouble and Bourbon diplomacy was in utter disarray, bordering on paralysis.

Diplomatic failures were both symptom and cause of government weakness. Vergennes had emerged from the American War determined to establish closer relations with the United Provinces, alongside whom France had fought, and whose naval strength and commercial power made an excellent counterweight against Britain. This was a delicate operation. First, the internal affairs of the Dutch were unstable at that time. Second, such a move risked alienating France's ally, Austria, which might feel that it threatened the adjacent Austrian Netherlands (or Belgium). Third, Joseph II, sole Austrian emperor since the death of Maria Theresa in 1780, was still restlessly seeking territorial aggrandisement. The river Scheldt had been closed to the shipping of the Austrian Netherlands at Utrecht in 1713 so as to protect the commercial interests of the neighbouring United Provinces. This measure had severely weakened Belgian Antwerp, and Joseph now urged the river's opening, following up with the suggestion that Austria should exchange its Belgian possessions for Bavaria. France joined with Prussia in blocking these moves and ironing out Austro–Dutch differences and in November 1785, Vergennes signed a defensive alliance with the Dutch. The urban 'Patriot' faction then dominant in the United Provinces was, however, engaged in a bitter dispute with the conservative and pro-British Stadtholder. The matter required careful handling, and Vergennes was hobbled by his fellow ministers Breteuil, representing Marie-Antoinette's pro-Austrian lobby, and Calonne. Even before Vergennes's death in February 1787, it was clear that France was losing out. In September 1787, following a personal assault on the Stadtholder's wife, who was sister to the new king of Prussia, Frederick William II, the latter sent in troops to overthrow the Patriots (many of whom fled the country) and, with England making threatening naval manoeuvres in his support, restored the Stadtholder's power. France thus lost the friendship of the Dutch, who next year entered into formal alliance with Prussia, while Austria was still smarting over French lack of commitment.

France had been brought to a depressing state of diplomatic nullity – a situation underlined in the East, where Vergennes's efforts to balance the friendship of both Turkey and Russia proved embarrassingly unsuccessful. British and Prussian intelligence sources had made it crystal clear to both governments that France had neither the resources nor the will to engage in military action in 1787–8. The government was simply too absorbed in domestic difficulties at the nub of which was, precisely, the country's ability to convert economic resources into armed might. Looking across the Channel at the 'prodigious' way in which the English built up their armed forces, Vergennes sagely noted that although France had 'more solid resources than England, [it is] far from being able to call them into play so easily. This is the result of [public] opinion, which cannot develop in an absolute monarchy to the extent that it can in a mixed monarchy.'[58] This was quite a compliment to how powerful public opinion had become, since earlier in the century English commentators such as Arthur Young had estimated that it was precisely the absolute monarch's ability to default on his debts which gave the French potential superiority over the British.[59] Now, however, things looked different. Credit, Necker's daughter, Madame de Staël, subsequently recorded him as saying, 'is only [public] opinion applied to financial affairs'.[60] This was an equation which, as Vergennes noted, boxed in even a putatively absolute ruler's financial options.

The years 1787–8 were to see this Anglo–French conundrum playing itself out. While Britain successfully restored its finances following its American humiliation, the French crown sought – with ever more difficulty – to put its financial affairs in order by seeking to come to an accommodation with public opinion. The government would find the public playing hard-to-get, and short-term credit hard to find. This was not simply because ministers introduced unpopular fiscal policies in an attempt to stimulate the economy and to fend off the growing threat of state bankruptcy. In addition, its new aura of military incapacity weakened its popular appeal. Military success was one of the most heavily resorted-to trump-cards of the great nation – territorial aggrandisement and international *gloire* had always been key components of the Bourbon dynasty's political project.[61] The need for defence of the realm justified higher taxes, while from mid-century, as we have seen, a kind of militaristic royal populism had developed in the public sphere. Louis XV had been 'Well-Beloved' at Metz in 1744 precisely because he had risked his life in flying to the frontier to lead his country. Even in spite of his later unpopularity, in practice he benefited from the patriotism whipped up in and after the Seven Years War. Louis XVI had built on this, notably by his success in the American War. His visit in 1786 to Cherbourg – whose naval defences were a kind of patriotic talisman in the anti-English struggle[62] – showed the potential force of royal populism. The state's financial incapacity, however, put mobilization of opinion around issues of war and peace beyond the scope of government at a moment when, in the context of serious financial crisis, it needed all the help it could get.

In order to institute the financial recovery of the state, Controller-General Calonne embarked upon what was to prove his last gamble. Certain that he would be unable to drive through the Parlement the drastic financial measures he estimated were essential to state solvency, he decided to call the Parlement's bluff. The magistrates' remonstrances invariably invoked their representative role vis-à-vis the public. Calonne now determined to present a package of wide-reaching reforms to a body which could be viewed as more representative of the wishes of the nation than the venal office-holding magistracy. He found this body – the Assembly of Notables – mothballed in the junk-room of absolutist monarchy. It had last met at Cardinal Richelieu's behest in 1626 very precisely so as to supply a more manageable form of public endorsement than the Parlement. It was to this archaic body, which customarily was handpicked by the king from the three estates of the realm, that Calonne chose to refer his reforms, which were set out in the *Précis d'un plan d'amélioration des finances* ('Outline of a Plan to Improve the Finances'), which he presented to the king in August 1786. The voice of the Assembly would, Calonne hoped, 'carry weight in the opinion of the public generally',[63] and smooth the way for financial redressment.

Calonne's programme was far more ambitious than merely finding an alternative to the third *vingtième*, which was scheduled to end by 1787.

The idea was to do away with the *vingtièmes* altogether, replacing them with a unitary land tax. This would be payable in kind, thus making it inflation-proof, and it would fall on all landowners irrespective of social rank. Unlike the *vingtièmes*, which had time-limits, it would be a permanent tax and would be graduated, according to property value. The assessment, banding and collection processes would be supervised, under the guidance of the local Intendant, by three tiers of local assemblies – at parish, district, and provincial levels. Calonne's network of provincial assemblies more closely resembled those formerly proposed by Turgot than the bodies instituted by Necker, in that they had an elective element and their membership was on the basis of landholding, without any division into three estates. More than a touch of Turgotian liberalism was evident too in ancillary reforms aimed to reactivate the economic boom on which Calonne's whole policy was predicated: the commutation of the *corvée*, the abolition of internal customs frontiers and the freeing-up of the circulation (and in most circumstances, the export) of grain.

In order to extricate the state from its severe financial plight, Calonne was thus bidding both to introduce a fairer and simpler system of tax-collection and, through proportional taxation, to draw more heavily on that wealthy elite which, after all, he had devoted the entirety of his tenure in office fattening up. Though the king was initially appalled by Calonne's programme – 'This is pure Necker!' he ejaculated[64] – he became enthused by the ethos of fairness about the reforms, which were designed to alleviate the lot of the common people, to whose welfare Louis was sentimentally attached. Though he was far from well-informed on the condition of his subjects, it was clear that economic difficulties were adding to the problems of the poor. The context for Calonne's innovations was thus rather impropitious, and his situation was further weakened in early 1787 during preparations for the Assembly of Notables. A chain of bankruptcies of major financiers, led by that of Navy Treasurer Baudard de Saint-James, undermined the Controller-General's borrowing facility. Working tirelessly on preparations for the Assembly, Calonne fell ill, and this delayed its opening, as did the unexpected death of Vergennes in February 1787. The latter was the minister whom Louis had found it easiest to trust. His support for Calonne had been crucial in shielding the Controller-General from the ire of the other ministers, Breteuil, Ségur and Castries, who were dead set against the convocation of the Assembly. These mishaps gave valuable time to the forces of opposition to gather and to frame their arguments for the moment when, on 22 February 1787, the Assembly opened.

Calonne's biggest asset for the success of his gamble was the whole-hearted support of his monarch. Louis opened the first session evoking the spirit of Good King Henry IV and calling for general interests to prevail over the sectional. 'This is my work', he stated in private, 'and I will see it through'.[65] Yet Calonne's powers of political management of the Assembly were to be no more effective than his record in parlementary management. He thunderstruck the assembled dignitaries by revealing from the start the extent of the annual deficit – some 112 million livres: quite a distance from the ten million livres *surplus* announced by Necker in 1781. Around 40 per cent of state expenditure was going on servicing past loans, with the army and navy taking a further 25 per cent. The state, it seemed, had been laid low by war and its debts. Yet as Keeper of the Seals Miromesnil informed the king, with more than a little collegial *schadenfreude*, most members of the Assembly 'fear that the deficit in your revenues has not been sufficiently demonstrated'.[66] Indeed, the deficit was so unexpectedly colossal that many deputies thought that they were being tricked by phony figures into agreeing to emergency measures.

Calonne had arranged for his proposals to be discussed in seven committees, each of which was chaired by a Prince of the Blood (to all of whom he had been amply generous over the previous years). Of all the chairs, only the comte d'Artois, Calonne's sometime partner in stock manipulation, did his job in winning the minister support. Although some of the proposals seemed acceptable in principle, the Assembly jibbed at the form in which they were presented – and the man who was presenting them. Calonne's reputation for financial double-dealing and corruption made him seem, one observer noted, 'a combination of the abuses he wanted to reform'.[67] Most of the political and social elite would have thought twice about buying a used cabriolet from him, let alone accepting the radical package of measures he was proposing. As Austrian ambassador Mercy privately noted, the whole 'rigmarole' seemed 'no more than a petty trick to raise more money'.[68]

Necker's many supporters in the Assembly felt that Calonne's claims about the deficit were less well founded than those of the Genevan maestro. Ecclesiastical representatives orchestrated by the ambitious protégé of Marie-Antoinette, archbishop Loménie de Brienne of Toulouse, expressed concern about the potential loss of historic church rights. Others worried about the provincial assemblies, which were seen as both too democratic (because they ignored distinctions of rank) and too despotic (because they would probably end up in the claws of provincial Intendants). It was the proposed land-tax, however, which drew most of the flak. The 150-strong Assembly was composed of individuals whose wealth lay in land – and who would be the first to suffer from such a tax: prelates, great nobles of Sword and Robe, representatives from the *pays d'état* and over a score of heads of municipal governments. Less selfishly, the members also picked up on parlementary discourses over taxation which had been maturing since the 1750s, highlighting the fear that the legal basis for the state was being overturned by 'despotic' direct executive agents of the ruler.[69] The kind of universal peacetime impost which overrode historic privileges which Calonne championed was implicitly, they maintained, unconstitutional. The idea that the authorization of such a tax required the assent of the Estates General – which had last met in 1614, and had a better claim to represent the nation than either the Assembly or the *parlements* – was initially floated, almost as a provocation, by the marquis de La Fayette, picking up a suggestion made by Malesherbes during the Maupeou crisis. It soon gathered a broad measure of support.

By early April, it was apparent that the whole exercise was failing disastrously to deliver what Calonne had wanted. The Assembly had simply not produced the answers for which it had been rigged, and indeed it had influenced the public more against the reforms than for them. The political establishment and the public sphere were so awash with suspicion of the whole 'rigmarole' that Calonne was finding it impossible to attract short-term credit. Desperate to rally potential creditors, he circulated a *supplément d'instruction* ('Supplement to the Instruction'), which made it explicit that the programme of reforms was wholly and unconditionally endorsed by the king. At the same time, he issued a rather demagogic document, the *Avertissement* ('Notice'), distributed gratis and read out in pulpits across the land, which argued that anyone opposing the reforms was motivated by selfish and sectional interests. This appeal to the Third Estate was both too little and too late (as well as being pretty unconvincing: after all, only two of the hand-picked members of the Notables did not enjoy noble status). Not even Louis's personal endorsement was enough to save his wobbling Controller-General now. Much to his regret, and after a standard measure of royal havering which included replacing Miromesnil as Keeper of the Seals by Lamoignon, the king dismissed Calonne. One of Calonne's aides, Bouvard de Fourqueux, was initially appointed as Controller-General, but this failed to work out, and the king was obliged to place his government in the hands of Calonne's most acerbic critic in the Assembly, Loménie de Brienne.

The appointment of Brienne, who was made *chef du conseil* on 1 May (and in August, *principal ministre*), was a triumph for his patron Marie-Antoinette, and marked the arrival of a queen as a major player in the Bourbon polity for the first time since Anne of Austria, Louis XIII's wife. This was a surprisingly swift about-turn, following Marie-Antoinette's wretched fortunes in the Diamond Necklace affair. She and 'her' ministers Breteuil, Castries and Ségur had not even been consulted over the convocation of the Assembly of Notables, and the sobriquet 'Madame Deficit' had started to be used about her in recognition of her extravagant ways. Her star now began to rise even as her husband's fell. The king took the departure of Calonne very hard: he had agreed with Calonne's policies, which he believed were in line with the wishes of his cherished public, and he felt he was being forced to dismiss him – probably the first time this had happened to a French king since the Frondeurs had forced the child Louis XIV to remove Mazarin in 1649. Louis distrusted 'priestly rabble' almost as much as 'Neckerite rabble',[70] and disliked Brienne's determination to convince the political nation that Calonne had been a crook. The king found the archbishop's chronic eczema repulsive and was shocked by the minister presumptuously resting his elbows on the council table. Louis went into a depression, growing ever more doom-laden: in one *lit de justice* over the summer he would be observed snoring. More important for Brienne than the king's disengagement and eeyorish bad temper, however, was the consistency of the queen's favour.

From these inauspicious beginnings, Brienne fashioned a remarkable reforming ministry which fell only in late 1788, a final victim to the financial bugbear with which, to all intents and purposes, it had by then become impossible to deal within the traditional template of Bourbon political culture. A political prelate with an excellent administrative record in the Languedoc Estates, Brienne had advanced 'philosophical' views – Louis had once turned him down as archbishop of Paris on the grounds that the primate of the French church should at least believe in God – and brought them into his ministry with him. Malesherbes was reintroduced as minister without portfolio, heading a ministerial think-tank which – to *dévot* disgust – included *philosophe* reinforcements, Condorcet and Morellet, as well as the Parisian magistrate, Adrien Duport, and the barrister Target. Breteuil, now sidelined in the queen's affections, was no longer a threat, and the cohesion of Brienne's team was increased by having his own brother, the comte de Brienne, appointed to the War Ministry, with Malesherbes's nephew, the comte de La Luzerne, taking on the Navy post. The new Keeper of the Seals, Lamoignon (Malesherbes's cousin), distinguished himself with a range of humane enlightened reforms, notably modernization of criminal procedure (including the removal of the last traces of judicial torture and rationaliz-ation of lower courts) and, in November 1787, the granting of civil status to France's 700,000 Protestants.

Brienne's assault on Calonne had been partly at least a means of career leverage for himself. As soon as he came to power, he realized that the state's financial situation was indeed dire – the deficit was running 20 to 30 per cent worse than even Calonne had stated. He therefore jettisoned his hostility to Calonne's reform package and tried to get the Notables to stomach a modified version of it. The Assembly refused to bite, and was dismissed. Brienne now had to essay a course of action from which Calonne had recoiled, namely, forcing substantial measures of reform through the recalcitrant Parlement. Free trade in grain and the commu-tation of the *corvée* did get through, as did the installation of provincial assemblies, though these now had the three orders reinstated, albeit with the number of Third Estate deputies doubled. As anticipated, however, the Parlement cut up rough over a new stamp duty on public and printed documents – which would have effectively been a tax on credit, since credit arrangements would necessarily be inscribed on stamped paper; and it also fired off against a revised version of the land tax, now to be collectable in cash, not kind. The measures were enforced by *lit de justice* on 6 August 1787, but when the Parlement objected even to this it was exiled for its pains to Troyes. Brienne carried on negotiating, however, and in late September came to an agreement whereby the two laws were withdrawn. In return, the restored Parlement agreed to the imposition of two *vingtièmes* for five years. The Prussian invasion of the United Provinces at this time highlighted France's weakened international position, and the crying need for structural reforms in the crown's finances.

On assuming power, Brienne had promised the king big savings through economies, and from the summer onwards he engaged in swingeing attacks on the Royal Household. War was declared on sinecures: the king's *porte-chaise d'affaires*, who carried the king's personal privy,[71] and sundry cravat-holders and royal wolf-hunters were cut. A single edict in January 1788 disposed of some 173 positions within the queen's household. Brienne linked up with the spirit of Necker's reforms in financial administration, streamlining the offices of the *Contrôle-générale* and effectively creating a unified state treasury which could – and did – produce overall statements of accounts. By themselves, however, such measures were never going to refloat the ship of state. Expenditure on the Household and on court pensions was actually falling over the century as a proportion of the total government spend: it represented around one-sixth in 1788 as against about one-quarter in 1726. Nevertheless, financial stringency in this domain had a powerful ideological effect in boosting creditors' confidence in the regime's fiscal management and in appeasing a public opinion increasingly critical, as we have seen, of court extravagance and economic parasitism.

Like all of Louis XVI's finance ministers, Brienne found himself caught between a rock and a hard place. The severity of the state's financial problems made an economy drive little more than window-dressing. Yet so profound was the general cynicism about the state's tax policies that even a new graduated tax dressed up in a rhetoric of social justice was universally assumed to mean heavier taxes for all. On the other hand, however, a squeeze on the state's creditors was also by now beset with political perils. The old days of scapegoating a few financiers were long gone – the Chambre de Justice option, for example, had looked ineffectual even in 1716. The state was so firmly bricked into networks of credit, which incorporated the king's own bureaucracy as well as national and international individuals and groupings, that any gesture in the direction of reducing interest payments on state annuities would be lambasted as 'despotic'. The Terray years (to which Louis had a strong personal aversion) had shown that such manoeuvres could be expected to lead on towards a political crisis which would damage confidence and worsen the negotiating terms under which the state borrowed money in the future. Furthermore, since the Regency, the state's creditors had become much more numerous and more socially mixed. The fiscal system worked not merely to pump the wealth of the monied and landed elite into the state's coffers; despite the disasters of the Law System, it also sucked in the savings of a formidable proportion of the rest of society. Early in the century around a quarter of solid wage-earners in Paris held government paper on their deaths; by the time of Louis XVI, the figure was up to two-thirds of the group. Ownership was as much a consumerist trait as possession of a wig, a coffee-pot or a shaving mirror. The financier and publicist Clavière reckoned that as many as 300,000 individuals throughout France were state creditors by the time of Louis XVI.[72] The great majority of these were also both tax-payers and fully paid-up members of the bourgeois public sphere. This meant that any government innovation regarding either taxation or manipulation of state credit would have immediate impact on and ramifications within the wider public, a fact which demonstrated the correctness of Necker's view that state credit was merely a financial incarnation of public opinion.[73]

Brienne's economy measures took time to bear fruit in terms of savings, and a shortage of short-term credit saw the Principal Minister knocking on the Parlement's door again on 19 November requesting authorization for further loans, and in return agreeing to the convocation of the Estates General in 1792, when the *vingtièmes* would expire. The king attended the session in person, but a procedural mix-up left the assembled worthies uncertain whether the king was forcibly registering the loans by *lit de justice* or whether he was assuming that his presence in the Parlement ensured there was no opposition to the proposal. When the duc d'Orléans stepped forward from the bench of peers to query the constitutionality of the proceedings, the king quashed him with disdain: 'It is legal because it is my will' ('*C'est légal parce que je le veux*') – as pure, unadulterated and politically insensitive a distillation of absolutist doctrine as ever came out of the mouth of a French king in public.

From the autumn of 1787 into early 1788, matters were delicately poised. The tough stance in the parlementary session of 19 November reaped dividends for Brienne's short-term position, particularly when followed up with the exile by *lettre de cachet* of Orléans and the arrest of two of his most prominent *parlementaire* supporters. 'The Archbishop is very steady to all his plans of economy,'[74] reported the British ambassador in Paris, the duke of Dorset, in November and the fact that the new loans were taken up by investors suggested growing confidence in the government's strategy. The Parlement felt on the defensive – in the new year rumours were about that Maupeou would soon be recalled to dish out further punishment. Within the Parlement, political initiative was passing to the younger and more radical magistrates. More strongly represented in the subaltern chambers, they began to sketch out an ideological position from which they might best defend themselves from royal assault. The councillor, Duval d'Eprémesnil, notorious for having privately urged the 'debourbonization' of France, was particularly vocal in the campaign for the convocation of the Estates General. The demand was the centrepiece of the 'Declaration of the Fundamental Laws of the Kingdom' which, on Duval's prompting, the Parlement issued on 3 May and which also attacked arbitrary arrest through *lettres de cachet*, and endorsed the irremovability of magistrates.

On 8 May 1788, the hammer blow fell. Brienne's 'May Edicts', forcibly registered by *lit de justice*, stipulated the reorganization of the higher courts, with the *parlements* losing much judicial authority to new subaltern appeal courts called *grands bailliages*; in addition, a Plenary Court (*cour plénière*) was created (though ministers tried to pass it off as the re-establishment of an ancient body) comprising the Paris Parlement's Grande Chambre plus all major ministers of the crown and high dignitaries of the realm. This would have responsibility for registering legislation, thus confining the *parlements* to a purely judicial role. A further decree placed all *parlements* on vacation. Dorset complacently reported to London that 'the storm, which threatened the internal tranquillity of this kingdom, will blow over'.[75] He could not have been more wrong.

The summer and early autumn of 1788 saw insubordination towards royal authority spreading throughout France, spearheaded by the nobility who, whilst vigorously defending their own privileges, prided themselves on protecting the nation from ministerial despotism. In Paris, it was the *parlementaires* who had fanned the flames of urban dissent, fitfully gaining noisy support from the legal world of barristers and legal clerks and from the popular classes. Much the same was now true of the main parlementary centres in the provinces. A handful of institutions had already been involved in political clashes under Louis XVI: Grenoble and Besançon in particular had put up a fight against the 1782 *vingtième* edict. From late 1787, many other *parlements* joined in, reviving the old arguments of the 'union of classes' which had been current in the 1760s and early 1770s. *Parlements* expressed fraternal support for the suspended Paris institution, and went on to oppose further financial edicts and the establishment of provincial assemblies, which they viewed as mouthpieces of central authority which would reduce rather than extend provincial particularism. The plans to remove power from the *parlements* to a Plenary Court – 'a senate of slaves' in one view[76] – met universal condemnation. The military mobilizations required to register the edicts in the provincial *parlements* were the occasion for ringing declarations of opposition to ministerial despotism, attacks on *lettres de cachet* and vigorous championing of provincial patriotism, while a number of bodies called for the Estates General as the only means of arbitrating the financial and political crisis. There were popular risings in support of the persecuted magistrates in Pau, Rennes and Grenoble. The 'Day of the Tiles' on 7 June saw inhabitants in the latter city raining projectiles from their rooftops on to the heads of the soldiery.

The temper of the resistance movement of 1788 was essentially aristocratic even if the nobility in this – as most other things – was often profoundly divided in its opinions and also drew other classes into its slipstream. The Frondeur intransigence of the Robe was applauded by many court nobles. A handful of peers made it clear to the king that they would not serve on the new Plenary Court, while Brienne found his position at court undermined by the score-settling of what he called 'that whole tribe of favourites who looked on the public treasury as an inexhaustible storehouse which I would not let them loot'.[77] The archbishop found himself attacked by his own order too: fellow aristocrats amongst the episcopacy led the assault on royal policies in the Assembly of Clergy which met over the summer of 1788. The usually docile discussions fixing the clergy's tax donation, the so-called *don gratuit*, turned into a farrago of recrimination, including complaints about the granting of civil status to Protestants, which some ecclesiastics saw as changing the spiritual basis of the regime. The rump of the *dévot* interest seemed to have no qualms about throwing in their lot with their erstwhile foes, the *parlements*, and in the end, the Assembly offered only a pitiful additional 1.8 million livres over two years instead of the 8 million which Brienne had requested. There was also a great deal of discontent with the ministry in that other noble-dominated arm of state, the army. Brienne's policy of economies had affected the livelihood of many career officers, while his brother's administrative reforms at the War Ministry, coming on top of Saint-Germain's reforms in the 1770s, also stirred up resentment. In a number of garrisons, notably at Rennes and Grenoble, there was vocal opposition among junior officers to the policing of riots caused by Brienne's May Edicts.

Turbulence also revolved around the new provincial assemblies, about a score of which had been established in the *pays d'élection* over the previous summer and autumn. It was the government's intention that these bodies should operate only under the authority of the Intendants, the king's local representatives: for in the view of the king himself, the monarchy was 'absolute because authority is not shared'.[78] Yet provincial opinion was often more hopeful: in Dauphiné, the comte de Virieu saluted this 'most complete and happiest of revolutions'. 'The hour is striking', he exclaimed, 'for us finally to think and talk for ourselves.'[79] One minor noble in the Anjou announced his intention in his local assembly of 'getting fat on the remains of the Intendant'.[80] Many Intendants did indeed view a reduction of their powers as inevitable, though others remained sure they could turn the assemblies into lapdogs. Just how local patterns of power would have been negotiated remained moot. For although the assemblies set to work fairly purposively, and functioned well alongside the district and municipal authorities created at the same time, the tergiversations of the summer of 1788 put the experiment on hold in most places. Besides their role in diffusing ideas and hands-on experience of local representative politics and administration, these assemblies were also significant for promoting moves for change regarding provincial estates. There were sometimes calls for an increase in the representation of the Third Estate in existing bodies in the *pays d'état*, along the lines of the provincial assemblies. Elsewhere there were demands for the reintroduction of estates in areas where these had been removed by the advance of absolutism.

The issue of provincial estates was given added acuity by political developments at the centre in July and August. Brienne found himself being outgunned by the advance of noble-led opposition and, even more pertinently, by a shortage of short-term credit to tide him through the crisis. Government normally had to rely on advances in respect of the following year's tax revenue. The problems of political crisis were exacerbated on one hand by the continuing money- and credit-famine consequent on the counterfeiting scandal of 1786, and on the other by poor weather over the summer of 1788 which augured ill for tax income in 1789. In these circumstances, financiers proved unwilling to offer credit, especially to a minister like Brienne whose policies were precisely based on reducing the state's dependence on financial cliques.

Under the cosh of noble intransigence, Brienne essayed a startling pirouette. First, he sought to utilize the promise of the Estates General as a means of mobilizing the bourgeois public sphere on the king's side. 'Since the nobility and the clergy abandon the king, who is their natural protector,' Brienne expostulated, then 'he must throw himself into the arms of the commons and use them to crush the other two.'[81] Accordingly, his edict of 5 July 1788 made an open appeal to all-comers to provide ideas and opinions on how exactly the Estates should be composed and run. Brienne had closed down political assemblies and societies and censored the press during the crisis of 1787, yet he now put government support behind a pamphlet campaign to undermine the historic and constitutional claims of the *parlements*. The second feature of Brienne's manoeuvre was to mobilize opinion in the provinces against the *parlements*. He had had a delegation of Breton nobles seeking a meeting of their local estates clapped into irons, but almost at once, in the summer of 1788, began to look more favourably on the return of provincial estates. His aim was to counterbalance *parlementaire* claims, and also to boost the Third Estate by promoting forms of organization (notably doubling of the numbers in the Third Estate, voting by head in a single assembly) favouring them. If there had to be representative organs, moreover, Brienne preferred them to be provincial ones, which would be more malleable. If by 1792 the new provincial bodies were working well, he cunningly calculated, this would obviate the need for a national body. In the autumn, authorization was consequently given for provincial estates in Dauphiné, Provence and Franche-Comté, where they had been either discontinued or politically neutered since 1628, 1639 and 1674 respectively. A blanket re-establishment of all such bodies in provinces was subsequently promised.

By appealing to the provinces and to the Third Estate to counterbalance what were already coming to be called the other two 'privileged orders' – as though privilege was not intrinsic to Bourbon public law and rampant in all three estates! – Brienne repeated Calonne's demagogic gesture of April 1787. Yet once more, however, the move was both too little and too late. Time was running out for the Principal Minister. Credit could not be commanded back to life: on 8 August, in a desperate attempt to rally public confidence, he agreed to the convocation of the Estates General on 1 May 1789, and suspended the operation of the Plenary Court until that time. The following week – on 16 August – he effectively defaulted on the state's obligations: treasury bills bearing 5 per cent interest were introduced for the payment of government creditors. The dreaded word 'bankruptcy' was on everyone's lips, and there was a rush on the Caisse d'escompte to cash paper holdings.

Brienne had not only been unable to acquire the confidence of the public; he had also destroyed state credit in the process. Since the aftermath of the John Law System in the 1720s, government had rejected a single credit source (on the lines of Britain's Bank of England) in favour of the utilization of the multiple corporate bodies within the state, adjudged more politically prudent. That credit was not forthcoming highlighted the scale of Brienne's alienation of the corporative nexus. His position was now impossible. Significantly, Marie-Antoinette, urged by Artois, shifted her backing from the archbishop to Necker, who, as ever, was waiting in the wings. On 26 August, Brienne was dismissed and the king, much to his personal disgust, was obliged to recall Necker as Director-General of Finances. This was the first ministerial recall of this order in the eighteenth century – normally ministers retired or were exiled.[82] In addition, the king granted the Genevan a place on the *conseil d'état* – a request for which had been the occasion of his dismissal in 1781 (though the 1787 toleration decree made this now a less problematic religious gesture). A ministerial reshuffle followed. Lamoignon, his judicial reforms in tatters, was replaced and went off and shot himself. Breteuil, who had shown sympathy with the provincial nobles over the summer, retired from the stage too, his favour with the queen now only a dim memory. But there were no illusions now about fresh starts. Necker saw his role less as budding political architect than as caretaker-cum-firefighter. He had to douse down the flames of noble and provincial unrest and keep the state in one piece until a full and satisfactory resolution of political imponderables could be attempted in the Estates General. He seems to have been genuinely worried that the country was on the brink of civil war, and his first gesture was to bring forward the meeting of the Estates General to 1 January 1789.[83] This pacificatory move – plus the political credit which he personally enjoyed – helped to stabilize the finances.

On his dismissal, Brienne's parting shot to the king had been to 'be sure to avoid an unconditional recall of the *parlements* or your monarchy will be destroyed and the state with it'.[84] Louis ignored him, recalling the *parlements* to the plenitude of their powers on 23 September. Would Brienne prove a prophet? Truth to tell, the omens for the monarchy did not look good. A whole set of recalls, reappearances and reoccurrences in 1787 and 1788 had highlighted the fragile state of the Bourbon polity: the first Assembly of Notables since 1626; the first Estates General since 1614; the first dismissal since the Fronde of a minister in whom the king had confidence (Calonne); the first Protestant in the *conseil d'état* (Necker) since long before the Revocation of the Edict of Nantes; the dissolution of the equation between confessional identity and citizenship established by that Revocation; a queen more powerful than any since Anne of Austria; the convocation of provincial estates which had last met under Richelieu and Colbert; the role of the Intendants more in question than at any other time since the reign of Louis XIII; and so on. The whole debate on the nature and forms of political legitimacy – given added piquancy by the concatenation of economic, financial and diplomatic disasters – made it appear that the most distinctive features of Bourbon absolutism were imperilled.

British envoy Daniel Hailes, reporting back to London on the completeness of the parlementary victory, noted: '[c]ertain it now is that these Bodies, which the Government has so long affected to despise, have at last raised themselves to a degree of consequence, from their negative authority that, if they choose to display it, nothing can withstand.'[85] Certainly the *parlements* were back – and back in style, as was witnessed by the street rejoicings which accompanied their return from exile, recalling the unanimous enthusiasm of 1775. Yet their triumph would flatter only to deceive. Within six months, the magistrates would be cravenly currying favour with ministers and offering to work with them against rising democratic forces.

When the turbulent magistrate Duval d'Eprémesnil had tauntingly urged the 'debourbonization' of France, he had in mind a return to an alleged aristocratic golden age pre-dating the arrival of Bourbon absolutism. But the rules of the political game – and the numbers of players – had changed since the Wars of Religion and the Fronde. Public opinion, the genie which Calonne and Brienne had tried so hard to coax out of its bottle for their own purposes, was from late 1788 defiantly establishing itself in the political arena. 'This deity of the modern age'[86] now appeared to express itself untrammelled by the promptings of government and threatened to prove as corrosive of parlementary pretensions as of the vestiges of life in the decaying body of Bourbon absolutism. 'Debourbonization' seemed now to threaten the powers of the *parlements* as well as of the dynasty. At the height of the May crisis of 1788, a Parisian lawyer had noted that

there are now in Paris and in the whole of the Kingdom the names of three parties: that of the royalists, that of the *parlementaires* and that of the Nationals. These latter two have made common cause [and] the Nationals hope that this alliance will be long.

Yet by the end of that year, the Swiss publicist, Mallet du Pan, would be announcing, 'The controversy has completely changed. King, despotism and constitution are now minor questions. The war is between the Third Estate and the other two orders.'[87]

9

Revolution in Political Culture
(1788–91)

A) IMAGINING THE NATION,
FEARING THE WORST

From late 1788 onwards, more and more participants in and observers of the French political scene were recording a belief that a political phenomenon of a radically new kind was emerging. It was generally agreed that the crisis would be much more than a replay of the Fronde, as had been widely believed down to the summer of 1788. The event which precipitated this transformation was the re-emergence of the Paris Parlement into political life following its return from exile in September 1788. On 25 September, with popular cheers still ringing in their ears, the newly restored magistrates expressed the wish that the Estates General should meet 'according to the forms observed in 1614'. It did not take long to register that this would involve the dominance of the First and Second Estates – the clergy and the nobility – over the Third Estate. In 1787–8, the *parlements* had led a movement of protest against government which had attracted a great deal of popular support within the public sphere. Now, the magistrates seemed intent on stabbing public opinion in the back. The impact of their action on their popularity was dramatic and sudden: they suddenly became part of the political problem rather than part of its solution.

The Parlement's stance – instantly excoriated as 'un-patriotic' and 'un-national' – seemed particularly retrograde when set against the much-talked-about example of the Dauphiné. Here debates in the late summer over the recall of provincial estates had led to a meeting at Vizille of deputies from the three estates and from all over the province which had called for the doubling of representatives from the Third Estate and for voting by head and in common – a programme which

Principal Minister Loménie de Brienne, in crafty pro-provincialist mood, endorsed. In many ways, the Vizille programme was not especially radical *per se*: certain provincial estates already had a larger Third Estate representation, while the recently created provincial assemblies had voting by head and in general assemblies as well. It was above all in the light of the Parlement's provocative predilection for 1614 forms that the Vizille programme – the doubling of the Third, voting by head – became a yardstick for those demanding serious reform at the national level.

The huge public outcry against the Paris Parlement in the late autumn of 1788 scared most magistrates out of their Frondeur wits. Though a few magistrates, led by councillor Adrien Duport, maintained a radical stance, the Parlement as a whole back-pedalled fast. Their meetings were altogether graver now, as though, one councillor noted, 'a dark veil had been drawn over the assembly'.[1] Attempts by magistrates to curry popular favour by measures condemning grain speculation were offset by their attacks on patriot political pamphlets. The king further weakened the Parlement's position by treating with contempt its claims to a political voice. The fiery ex-radical Duval d'Eprémesnil – erstwhile apostle of 'debourbonization' – was soon being hissed by the public as he walked through the Palais-Royal and cravenly promised the king that the Parlement would pass any financial edicts the government cared to introduce if he would deign to dissolve the Estates General.

The about-turn performed by the Parlement was a telling symptom of the seriousness of the political transformation taking place. In the past, the magistrates' strength had derived from their role as mouthpiece of popular grievance. The court constituted, Malesherbes had noted in 1787, 'the echo of Paris', and, he continued, 'the public of Paris is that of all the nation. It is the Parlement which speaks because it is the only body which has the right to speak . . . It is a question therefore of the whole nation.'[2] This mouthpiece role of the Parlement was eclipsed during the magistrates' exile, and other organs of expression emerged in their place. Clubs, driven underground by Brienne in 1787, came out into the open again. The duc d'Orléans's Palais-Royal – a city-centre pleasure-ground and political headquarters – hummed with activity. Throughout the land, informal committees and meetings sprang up in towns large and small; coffee-houses, reading rooms and the other institutions of the bourgeois public sphere were abuzz with lively debate; newspapers blossomed – there were forty creations in 1788 alone – and pamphlet production soared. 'Every day it's raining pamphlets and brochures,' exclaimed the Parisian publisher Nicolas Ruault in January 1789.[3] Promoted – or given pretext – by Brienne's edict of 5 July 1788 calling for the expression of views on the form in which the Estates General should meet, maybe as many as 4 million pieces of political commentary cascaded down on the French people from September 1788 to May 1789.

At no point back to the Fronde and the Wars of Religion had opinion been freer. Yet if everyone seemed to have his or her pet recommendation for the government, the latter constituted a silent, tranquil spot on a hyper-dynamic discursive map. Louis was increasingly subject to bouts of depression, worsened by anxieties about the health of his children. His fourth child, Sophie, died only a matter of months old in mid-1787, and the dauphin was chronically ailing. It can have hardly cheered the ruler, either, that his wife was widely rumoured to be conducting a sexual liaison with the comte de Fersen. Necker, who adopted an uncharacteristic wait-and-see attitude on his return to power, did nothing to remedy this eerie governmental paralysis. The Genevan's return had reassured state creditors – partly through the massive loans he made to the government out of his own fortune – but he wagered that his best option was to 'keep the administration of the finances in a kind of silence and obscurity'[4] until fundamental reform could be considered in the Estates General. Necker's position was worsened, moreover, by his weakness within the King's Councils, where Keeper of the Seals Barentin and Household Minister Laurent de Villedeuil were proving to be last-ditch defenders of root-and-branch absolutism. Nor was he helped by the growing influence on the king of Marie-Antoinette. The latter realized Necker was a political necessity, but personally detested him. Her cronies (the Polignacs, Fersen, etc.) led a whispering campaign against him.

Irritated by the Parlement's declaration for the forms of 1614, Necker decided to convoke a second meeting of the Assembly of Notables to seek advice on the procedures which the Estates General should adopt. This was not intended as a means of mobilizing public opinion, but rather as providing him with firmer authority within the political minefield that the Royal Council had become. In keeping with his new-found lack of political drive, he asked the Notables questions without offering much of a steer as regards the answers he wanted. His hands-off approach came a predictable cropper. The composition of the Assembly – which met from 6 November onwards – was much the same as Calonne's hand-picked body of 1787 (there were still, pitifully, less than half a dozen commoners amongst them). And the body stuck just as doggedly as its predecessor to the script of privilege and tradition, spiced with constitutional justifications. Though the Notables did accept that all orders should be equally obliged to pay taxes, they specifically opposed either the doubling of the Third Estate or voting by head. To make matters worse, five of the seven Princes of the Blood (Orléans and Provence were the exceptions) saw fit to submit to Louis a Memorandum on 12 December, just as the Assembly was breaking up. This document, whose content was soon widely known, attacked ministerial policies which were producing 'a revolution in the principles of government . . . through the fermentations of minds'. Fearful of a lurch towards either despotism or democracy, the Princes affirmed their belief that the Estates General should meet in the forms 'consecrated by laws and usages' and urged Louis to rely on 'that courageous, ancient and respectable nobility which has spilt so much blood for king and fatherland'.[5]

The king and Necker must have allowed themselves a wry smile at the spectacle of truculent sycophancy presented by a high Sword nobility which had only months before been leading a Frondeur-like assault on royal power, alongside a Robe magistracy now also zealously on the fast lane back towards political and social conservatism. However, these moves complicated rather than simplified the task of devising rules and regulations for how the Estates General should be elected and run, all the more in that the publication of the Memorandum of the Princes of the Blood caused a downturn in the take-up of government loans. Government resolutions, enshrined in a document curiously called 'Results of the Council', issued on 27 December, and then in the electoral regulations of 24 January 1789, were pitched midway between the Vizille programme and the wishes of the conservative nobility. There would be roughly 1,000 deputies, elected within the framework of the *bailliages* (not through the provincial estates, as many nobles had urged).[6] The number of deputies was to be proportional to an area's population and tax-base. And the size of the Third Estate deputation would match those of the other two orders combined: the 'doubling of the Third' had been conceded. The issue of voting procedures was, however, left up in the air – a significant concession to the nobility, and the occasion for a new hailstorm of popular pamphleteering.

The government's evident lack of clarity over its objectives for the Estates General boded ill for its ability to manage events. In a memorandum to the king, Malesherbes lamented that a king in the late eighteenth century should 'convoke the three Orders of the fourteenth century', instead of calling together 'the proprietors of a great nation renewed by its civilization'. 'Seize people's imagination with an institution which will surprise them and please them, that the nation will approve.'[7] Yet the call for a regenerative royal patriotism underestimated the torpor of the king and the deadlock which prevailed on the Royal Council. Rather than aim at imaginative innovation, as Malesherbes urged, so as to bring together the property-owning classes increasingly fractionalized by noble/commoner and aristocrat/*anobli* tensions, Louis seemed to opt for the divisively ersatz medievalism which he had favoured in his Reims coronation of 1775.[8]

In some senses it was ironic that in pamphlet and news-sheet, in discussion and debate, the nobility, along with the clergy, were being demonized as 'the privileged orders', egotistical obstacles standing in the way of serious reforms. For many individual nobles and clerics played a pivotal role in the crescendo of political criticism. One of the most active 'patriot' lobbies, for example, was the socially exclusive cross-class elite grouping called the 'Society of Thirty', which from late 1788 met several times a week at the house of the young *parlementaire*, Adrien Duport. The 'Thirty' (a numerical underestimate, incidentally: around seventy members have been identified) contained only a sprinkling, if a classy one, of non-nobles: men such as the barrister Target, commentators Lacretelle and abbé Siéyès and bankers Clavière and Panchaud. There was a Robe wing to the group drawn from the Paris Parlement, though much of this drifted off towards conservativism in early 1789. The bulk of the membership was formed by overlapping sets of 'patriot' nobles – dukes and peers (d'Aiguillon, Noailles, etc.), 'Americans' (like Lafayette and the Lameth brothers), other military officers plus liberals such as Condorcet, La Rochefoucauld-Liancourt, Dupont de Nemours, Roederer and Mirabeau.

These men were well habituated to politics – but politics of many sorts. They had been involved in a variety of reform projects in the past: Dupont de Nemours had worked with Calonne, for example, Lacretelle alongside Malesherbes, and Morellet with Brienne. The mere fact that such a variegated group had sunk their differences – or at least chosen to come together as a group to argue out strategy – highlighted a certain defensiveness in their posture towards a government which looked far more threatening to contemporaries than it usually has to historians. The threat of the government opting for a bankruptcy which would ruin the rentier class, destroy social and political bonds and leave the path open for a new, tyrannical state power which would make John Law's System look a plaything in comparison seemed real – and worryingly so.

The diversity of political experience on which the members of the Society of Thirty could draw – plus the fact that many were freemasons too, while a good number had belonged to the mesmerist movement – helped the group establish links and contacts in the nationwide dissemination of pamphlets and literature which the Society now undertook. 'Patriot' or 'national' literature, as it came to be known, called not merely for a patching-up of existing constitutional practices, but for the construction of a new, more truly national framework, encompassing a liberal constitutional regime, with a limited monarchy and a declaration of rights. The most powerful, as well as the most influential, text in this regard by one of the Society's members was the famous pamphlet *What is the Third Estate?*, published by the cleric abbé Siéyès in January 1789. The answer (and the emphasis) he provided to his own question – 'EVERYTHING' – was symptomatic of the radical changes afoot. Siéyès contrasted the enormity of the contribution of the Third Estate to the wealth and prosperity of the nation with the parasitic and selfish role of the two 'privileged orders'. Yet if in terms of production and utility, the Third Estate was 'everything', politically, in contrast, it amounted to 'NOTHING' – and this needed to change. In an act of transformative political will, the nation should look for a lead to representatives of the truly useful groups within society, which he itemized as agriculture, industry, the mercantile interest, 'services pleasant to the person' and the public services of the army, the law, the church and the bureaucracy – not a bad description, in fact, of the developing social constituency of the 'national' party. 'Subtract the privileged orders', he urged, in a phrase which combined arithmetical sophistication with great mobilizing shrewdness, 'and the nation would not be less but more.'[9]

No text played a greater role in the reassignment of meaning to the term 'privilege' than *What is the Third Estate?*. A sea-change in meaning which had been detectable in the polemics of the Maupeou years was now complete. 'Freedom' and 'liberty' were no longer the synonyms of 'privilege' but its antonyms. 'Privilege' now denoted a sectional and selfish right of possession prejudicial to the natural freedoms of fellow citizens who formed the nation. 'Each man must forget himself', urged Target, in phrases which evoked the debates over civic and corporative rights prior to 1789, '. . . detach himself from his individual existence, renounce all corporative spirit (*esprit de corps*), belong only to the greater society and be a child of the fatherland.'[10] Corporative privileges might have been 'useful against kings', but had become 'detestable against nations', as Mirabeau had it.[11] This semantic modulation was coextensive with a shift from historical justifications for rights to natural law traditions. Whereas noble groupings still tended to think historically and to elaborate myths of national origins debated from Boulainvilliers onwards, canny patriots like Siéyès had realized that this was an argument which only the nobility could win, and so began to edge towards a more functional approach which stressed the indefeasibility of individual rights in nature. History for Siéyès was 'the [dark] night of ferocity and barbarity'. As another pamphlet put it, 'we ought to distrust the mania for proving what ought to happen by what has occurred; for it's precisely what has occurred that we're complaining about'.[12] If there was a historical element to this type of argument it was to show that the French nation had somehow grown up to an age of reason since 1614: 'would the garment of 1614 fit us any better', demanded the Breton lawyer, Lanjuinais, 'than the garment of a child fits a man in the prime of life?'[13] The language of the pamphlets slipped from juridical terms, 'restoration' and 'revival', to the more biologically (or – significantly perhaps, considering the Jansenist roots of the patriot cause – theologically) 'natural' word 'regeneration'.

Popular caricatures circulating over the spring and summer of 1789 portrayed a nobleman and an ecclesiastic in fright at the sudden wakening of a slumbering lion – representing, of course, the Third Estate or, more generally, the People, breaking the chains of their former enslavement. The image is arresting in a number of ways: the *prise de conscience* of the Third Estate; all three orders seen as the principal players in the unfolding drama; the lion-like strength and virtue of the People; and the identification of the two 'privileged orders' as likely victims of popular awakening. Perhaps most striking of all, however, is an absence: that of the king. The only sovereign in sight is the king of the jungle – the awakening People. The body of the nation was no longer being viewed as inhering in the royal body, but as separate from it, and comprising three estates (or possibly – depending how hungry the lion was – a single, leonine body). The unfolding political and social struggle set class against class, with the monarch as bystander and, perhaps, endorser of popular victory over the privileged orders.

In the impassioned whirligig of pre-Estates General debate, the French Nation was being reimagined not as the corporative, vertically arranged society of orders but as a more egalitarian society of 'citizens' diffused throughout the public sphere. The triumph of civic discourses made corporate self-justifications appear unpatriotically selfish and sectional. A doom-laden question-mark now attached to those who had hitherto most enjoyed the illicit fruits of privilege. For the quixotic Languedocian nobleman the comte d'Antraigues, 'the Third Estate is the People, and the People are the Foundation of the State: it is the State itself, while the other orders are only parts of it'. Similarly, according to a Provençal pamphleteer in late 1788, the king's self-ascribed role as 'the nurturing father of the state' had passed from the monarch to the Third Estate.[14] There was no question as yet of republicanism being on the agenda, other than in the old, weak sense of a *res publica* or commonwealth to which both ruler and ruled owed allegiance. The fervent hope of all was that the monarch would follow the promptings of public opinion, and could be counted on against 'despotic' aristocratic cronies. A post-absolutist age seemed to be on the horizon.

In a sense, the construction of the nobility as a dangerous leech on the body politic in the electoral campaign of 1788–9 was Figaro's revenge. Images of the selfish aristocrat and courtier during the reign of Louis XVI had fanned the flames of diffuse anti-noble sentiment within society. Anti-nobilism was given added plausibility and edge, moreover, by sectional bitterness evident in provincial politicking in late 1788 and early 1789. The nobility might have started the process of reform, but – like the Paris Parlement – now seemed to be pulling the ladder up after themselves, and becoming more rather than less intransigent. The Memorandum of the Princes in December 1788 seemed less a whimper in the wings than a campaign platform for a resurgent nobility. The liberal 'Society of Thirty' found itself competing against the pro-aristocratic propaganda put out by a secretive conservative caucus, the

'Society of One Hundred', which was organized by turncoat Duval d'Eprémesnil, and which probably had more direct influence in many regions than the 'patriots'. In Dauphiné and Franche-Comté, nobles within the renovated provincial estates excluded any noble who did not have a fief from entering their ranks. Similar noble bloody-mindedness in the Breton estates caused *anoblis* to be driven out into the arms of the Third Estate. The hyper-wealthy merchant Jacques Cottin, ennobled by purchase of a venal royal secretaryship, for example, was excluded from the noble order – and went on to organize anti-noble lobbying in his native Nantes for elections to the Estates General. In nearby Rennes, inter-class tension led to street fighting in January 1789.

The nobility proved unable to master the electoral campaign. Framed for the sedate routines of the late medieval period, the rules of election, when adapted to the eighteenth century's communications networks, 'electrified' (that word was used) political opinion across the whole nation. Some 100,000 copies of the electoral procedures, agreed on 24 January 1789, were disseminated. They inaugurated the most ambitious exercise in political consultation in French history hitherto – indeed, in world history hitherto. It is easy from the vantage point of the twenty-first century to highlight the democratic deficit: a tripartite electoral process, the absence of women,[15] procedural shortcuts which disenfranchised many of the poor and so on. Even so, the process was extraordinarily wide-ranging. All nobles within each *bailliage* met together and chose their deputies for the Estates. Procedures for the First and Third Estates were more complicated. Monastic houses sent delegates to the clergy's *bailliage* assemblies, though bishops and the secular clergy attended in person. The system for the Third Estate was particularly complex. Beneath the level of 200-odd *bailliage* assemblies, there was a sprawling structure of preliminary assemblies: at parish level in the countryside, but with more ornate procedures for towns, including electoral meetings for professional associations and trade guilds as well as parishes and sections. There was no property franchise – any male over twenty-five years old could be involved in the procedures (as long as he was on the tax rolls and not a servant, an actor or a bankrupt). Even though many individuals either chose not to turn up to assemblies or else were shouldered aside by wealthier individuals within a community, the scale of consultation was extraordinarily wide.

This huge electorate was, moreover, positively urged to speak for itself. The electoral regulation of 24 January 1789 stated that 'His Majesty wishes that everyone, from the extremities of his realm and from the most remote dwelling places, may be assured that his desires and claims will reach Him.'[16] As well as electing delegates and deputies, each cell within this vast honeycombed structure was invited to express views on reforms needing to be undertaken. As far as we can judge, the clear majority of electoral assemblies availed themselves of the right to form 'books of grievances' (*cahiers des doléances*). Indeed, they often saw this part of the process as more important than the election of candidates to convey them onwards. A good proportion – about half of the general *cahiers* of the *bailliages* – were published at the expense of their collective authors.

The *cahiers de doléances* provide a matchless snapshot of the state of the nation's hopes and fears on the eve of major political transformation. It was emphatically not, however, an opinion poll, and it bore the marks of its immediate context as well as of longer-term attitudinal shifts and social structures. Elections were taking place in March and April 1789, when an economic crisis which had originated the previous summer was playing out, and this gave a powerful socio-economic twist to debates which hitherto had been largely political and constitutional. As we have seen, the 1780s had proved a tough decade for some sectors of the agrarian economy.[17] The 1787 harvest was poor, and its effects were amplified by an appalling hailstorm on 13 July 1788 which had destroyed crops from Normandy to the Toulousain. Grain, vines and orchards all suffered – only to suffer again in the winter from extremely cold weather, followed by a damaging thaw which inhibited circulation. The price of bread and firewood virtually doubled between September 1788 and February 1789, and though this meant there were speculative profits to be made by those producers who held a surplus, the number of individuals in that position was far lower than during other eighteenth-century crises. The money famine triggered by the counterfeiting scandal of 1786 also contributed to a slump in consumer demand for manufactured goods, which led to lay-offs and a spate of business failures. The downturn in many industries in the late 1780s initiated by the Anglo–French Trade Treaty had already reduced employment possibilities for urban and rural workers alike. By 1789, observers were reporting 25,000 unemployed silk workers in Lyon, 10–12,000 idle textiles workers in Rouen and Abbeville respectively, to whom were added thousands more in the surrounding villages. Half a century of market integration and communication improvement, plus the government's administrative experience at relief operations, ensured that the crisis remained at the level of dearth rather than outright famine. The countryside was not emptied of starving individuals as they had been in 1709, but remained full of hungry, angry and anxious peasants. Necker deployed a good deal of energy in buying grain abroad to alleviate hunger and shortages. Even so, there was a limit to what government could do. Rural paupers hit the road in large numbers, and the highways of France came to be covered by beggars and vagrants seeking work, hand-outs and shelter. A lot, therefore – including the social restabilization of rural France – was riding on the 1789 harvest.

Popular hopes for political reform were thus given an added charge by fears and anxieties deriving from the economic situation. This translated into grain- and bread-related disturbances on the pattern of the 1775 'Flour War'. Starting with attacks on bakers' shops in towns in Brittany in January, riots became widespread over the electoral period of March and April in Flanders in the north and, in the Midi, in Dauphiné, Provence, Languedoc and the Guyenne. To keep the peace, government deployed troops, and though the latter's morale started to fray, the army held good. The problem of order was exacerbated by the 'moral economy' convictions of many rioters, who demanded a fair price for bread and sought out local grain supplies through *taxation populaire*. They now claimed, moreover, that their actions had somehow been legitimized by the king. 'People everywhere are attacking priests, nobles and bourgeois,' Necker was informed by a worried Intendant of Provence (whose jurisdiction witnessed over fifty disturbances between March and June). 'Peasants ceaselessly proclaim that the destruction and pillaging is in line with the king's wishes.'[18] On 27–8 April, Paris was racked by the so-called 'Réveillon riots', in which a misinterpreted remark attributed to the eponymous wallpaper manufacturer to the effect that wages needed to come down sparked a severe bout of rioting in the industrial Faubourg Saint-Antoine area. It was put down by the Gardes-Françaises regiment with around fifty insurgents killed or wounded. (With telling lack of political acumen, the king blamed the Paris Parlement for the riot.)

The chance conjunction of grave economic crisis with the most extensive exercise in political consultation in the early modern period provided an explosive context for the framing of popular demands. The king had offered a dialogue with his people, and his people took him at his word, supplying a veritable logorrhoea of complaint: parish *cahiers* managed on average around forty *doléances*, nobles 158, Third Estate *bailliages* 234. Expressions of loyalty to the king suggested a good deal of strategic thinking, for one did not bite the hand that was promising to feed: 'it was necessary to be cautious', a Third Estate deputy later recalled, 'so as not to frighten despotism too much'.[19] Beneath a veneer of respect, however, the *cahiers* talked the language of citizens rather than subjects, and were more prone to preach the sacred rights of the nation then the sacred person of the monarch. True to his mood of inspirational torpor, Necker refrained from influencing the procedures, even chastising local royal officials who attempted to do so. Budding politicians did their best to shape popular opinion. Model *cahiers* were circulated widely to try to consolidate the culture of complaint, yet enjoyed relatively little success. Those which the duc d'Orléans had Siéyès write, and then had sent out in droves, seem not to have influenced even the peasant communities on his own domains, let alone anyone else, though some urban *cahiers* sent out into their rural hinterland did produce a measure of imitation. In general, however, peasant assemblies seem to have known how to discriminate between their own views and those which others wished to foist upon them.

Peasant *cahiers* were invariably the most localist of those drafted in the spring of 1789. The rights of provinces and the big political and constitutional issues debated *in extenso* at *bailliage* assemblies were outside the field of vision of most peasant *cahiers*, nor did the latter call for the overthrow of the local power of the nobility and the clergy (a programme they would actually enact within a matter of months through insurrectionary means). Peasants grasped that the *cahier* consultation was a 'weapon of the weak',[20] which dictated expressions of gratitude rather than threats of revolt. Consequently, they spoke the language of the parish pump, appearing most at ease with concretely itemizing their burdens and dramatizing their sufferings rather than exigently specifying the manner of their relief: 'We beg His Majesty to have pity on our farmland because of the hail we have had,' was the sweeping imprecation of the peasants of Menouville in the Paris basin.[21] Yet despite the deference and apparent conservatism of their demands, overall the peasant *cahiers* constituted a corrosive assault on the institutions and local beneficiaries of the Bourbon polity. Three-quarters of peasants' *cahiers* demanded an alleviation of royal, seigneurial or ecclesiastical impositions, and eight of the ten most frequently found demands related to tax burdens. Peasant attachment to a moral economy spilled over into a kind of moral fiscality. It was not the fact of state taxation which peasants opposed. Even though there were more demands for lower state taxes than any other complaint, linguistic analysis reveals a general equation between the terms 'citizen' and 'tax-payer'. Yet if tax-paying was taken for granted, what offended most was taxation whose imposition was arbitrary or erratic and which served to enrich intermediaries (the General Farm was a particular target in this respect). Even though much of their protest focused on the state, they were far more critical of nobles and clerics than their peasant forebears who had formulated *cahiers* in 1614. It was – again – the unfairness of seigneurs' exactions (which contrasted with the diminution of the services which seigneurs actually provided) which irritated the most. Symbolic of their resentments was the way in which insouciant lords allowed their pigeons and doves to ruin peasant crops, while prohibiting any right to resist.[22] By the same token, there were fewer complaints against the ecclesiastical tithe in localities in which the bulk of the monies stayed within the community and could be recirculated as charity or employment; it was when the crops simply disappeared off to the towns that peasants got upset. The peasantry were more than sufficiently attuned to the legalistic culture of the Bourbon polity not to call for the overthrow of the whole system. They did, however, look for substantial reforms, and urged either redemption or even (in around a quarter of cases) abolition of seigneurial levies of one sort or another. Under the same moralizing prism, the towns also sometimes came in for criticism as homes of usurious money-lenders, feudal lawyers and surveyors, and ruthless manufacturers profiting from exploitatively cheap rural labour.

The assemblies at which peasant *cahiers* were composed tended to be socially skewed towards the wealthier landowners – there were often few wage-earners present, while the very poor were routinely excluded in most places. This social filtration continued higher up in the consultation process too. The *bailliage* assemblies of the Third Estate were very much the creature of the urban bourgeoisie, plus any *anoblis* who had been ejected from the noble assemblies. The anti-urban complaints of many peasant communities came out in the wash, as did many anti-seigneurial grievances. This highlighted the fact that many urban bourgeois benefited from the seigneurial system, but was also in part a reflection of the Third Estate's wish that the targets of complaint should not be excessively parochial, and should link up to the broader concept of the 'nation'. The call for regular meetings of the Estates General with power over taxation issues was widespread. This often opened out into a more general attack on forms of privilege injurious to the bourgeoisie's status and careers or which were perceived as humiliatingly demeaning. Tax equality was also supported in many noble *cahiers*, but the Third Estate was more emphatic in its demands for equality before the law, the abolition of venality and equality in state careers such as the army. They also urged the removal of internal barriers to free trade (though, sensitive to the impact of the Anglo–French Trade Treaty, they enjoined protection from foreign competition). Peasant *cahiers* often showed impatience with the market; those of the Third Estate were impatient only with obstacles placed upon it.

If the content of the *cahiers* reflected a process of social filtration, this was even truer öf the composition of the delegations mandated by the *bailliage* electoral assemblies to convey their wishes to the Estates General in Versailles. The Third Estate delegation of 604 members contained not a single peasant or working man. Those actively engaged in economic activity (merchants and manufacturers for the most part) made up a solid corps of some ninety deputies, to whom could be added around forty landowners. These were far outnumbered by the more vocal and articulate professional bourgeoisie: there was a score of medical men, but lawyers made up no less than a quarter of the 648 deputies elected, and office-holders of one sort or another around a half. Altogether, the Third Estate deputies comprised the different elements of the educated upper fraction of the urban elite – a fact which did not escape the critical scrutiny of peasants and working men. 'Among the representatives chosen from the order of the Third Estate', wailed an anonymous Parisian pamphleteer in the *Complaints of the Poor People addressed to the Estates General* in late spring, 'there is not one from our class; and it seems as if everything has been done for the sake of rich men and property-owners.'[23] The indirect form of election to the Estates General for the Third Estate had thus papered over a major line of division – between the rich and poor.

Elections for the clergy and nobility were more direct, with the result that both the contents of their *cahiers* and their elected delegates were less ideologically and socially unified than those of the Third Estate. The clergy universally expected Catholicism to remain the centre of French life, and some felt that the toleration recently accorded to Protestants should be reversed. The biggest division showing up within the ecclesiastical order, however, was between the upper and the lower clergy. The numerical predominance of the latter ensured a more solid representation than they could ever dream of having at the prelate-dominated Assembly of the Clergy: around two-thirds of ecclesiastical deputies in the Estates General were parish priests, numbering 192 as against fifty-one bishops within a total delegation of 295. The nobility's *bailliage* assemblies were also marked by divisions. The exclusion of *anoblis* and the presence of large numbers of country gentry (around a quarter of the delegation as a whole) gave the meetings a very provincial and at times yokelish ethos. The most striking feature of the delegation as a whole was the triumph that it represented for the *noblesse de race*. Although maybe one-third of the nobility overall in 1789 had received their status since 1700, and another one-third since 1600, no fewer than 80 per cent of the Estates General delegation had been ennobled before 1600 (and nearly three-quarters overall in the Middle Ages). The Robe magistracy, who over the century had borne aloft the interests of the order in national politics, was sidelined as a result: the Sword outnumbered the Robe in the nobility's delegation eight to one. Around fifty of the 282 deputies in the delegation were liberal aristocrats (including a good admixture from the Society of Thirty), to whom could be added around forty liberal country gentlemen. Some seventy-five had served as soldiers, adding to the Estates General's professional orientation.

Noble *cahiers* reflected this degree of fragmentation. They often showed a good deal of consensus with the wishes of their local Third Estate assembly on constitutional, financial and personal freedom matters. Those assemblies where the gentry element dominated, however, tended to dig in their heels over the privilege issue, attached disproportionate importance to symbolic emblems of their superiority, which irritated the bourgeoisie (such as wearing swords and castellating their residences) and were recalcitrant to major reform of the seigneurial system. In contradistinction to Third Estate *cahiers*, the nobles spoke the language of 'preservation' and 'maintenance' rather than 'suppression' or 'abolition'. Careful content analysis of general *cahiers* suggests a pattern whereby there was relative consensus between the Third Estate and the nobility in the regions which were *pays d'élection* (and where thereby administrative centralization was more pronounced), which had been more profoundly penetrated by capitalism and improved communications, and whose economic life was dominated by smallish towns. In contrast, there were greater signs of conflict between the Second and Third Estates in big cities, in peripheral regions (including most *pays d'état*) where traditional elites retained a good deal of provincial power, and in regions in which capitalism had made fewer inroads.

Surveying this extraordinary scene of national decision-making, Gouverneur Morris, US envoy in Paris, felt that his host country could be compared with his own fledgling homeland: France was 'a nation which exists in hopes, prospects and expectations – the reverence for antient establishments gone, existing forms shaken to the very foundation and a new order of things about to take place, in which perhaps even to the very names, all former institutions will be disregarded'.[24] It was not mere reform which was on the cards, but wholesale political regeneration.

B) SUMMER LIGHTNING

The summer of 1789 should have been about communication. Everything about the convocation of the Estates General – the king's expressed wish to be 'enlightened' by his people, the remarkable consultation process incarnated in the *cahiers de doléances*, the considerable freedom accorded the press – made the deputies believe, on their way to Versailles for the historic opening, passing beggars and vagrants and the signs of widespread distress, that they were entering into a dialogue with their monarch over the future of France. That dialogue never happened: throughout the fateful summer of 1789, in which French politics and society were transformed beyond recognition, Louis XVI proved remarkably unwilling – maybe even unable – to communicate.

The Réveillon riots of April appear to have given the king the jitters, confirming the need to shift meetings of the Estates from Paris to tractable Versailles – a city, Arthur Young noted with some disgust, 'absolutely fed by the palace'.[25] Louis's mind was distracted by the sad and protracted tubercular agony of his eldest son, whose death on 4 June 1789 exacerbated his general moroseness. Marie-Antoinette proved scarcely able, even in public, to contain her contempt for the new assembly, while Louis's brothers, Artois and Provence, had started to combat the influence of Necker in the king's counsels. Horrified at popular exuberance, church elders and magistrates from that Paris Parlement – the latter now utterly weaned off its erstwhile incendiary ways – also pleaded with Louis to protect rather than undermine the status quo.

The welcome accorded the Third Estate in Versailles was consequently far from gracious. Anxious to stifle political creativity from the Estates, royal advisers had provided a setting for the meetings which – like the 1775 coronation – highlighted historic precedent and archaic pageantry. Court etiquette redolent of *la vieille France* was everywhere in evidence. At the religious service held on 4 May the deputies of the Third were peeved to find their own sombre black uniforms being outshone by the sparkling uniforms which the noble deputies had been required to wear. The snazzy plumes *à la Henri IV* with which the nobles' headgear was bedecked were a nice pre-Louis Quatorzian touch, but underestimated the extent to which such vestimentary marks of corporative (and, simultaneously, consumerist) privilege aggrieved the bourgeoisie. The aggressive traditionalism seemed, moreover, to go to the heads of many of the noble order. The Lyonnais Third Estate deputy Périsse du Luc was appalled that a fellow freemason from the noble order informed him quite seriously that he was 'in fact a member of another race with different blood'.[26] Herded round like cattle by ingratiating masters of ceremonies, sniggered over by their noble 'betters', expected to kneel in the presence of the monarch (which they refused), the commoner deputies found themselves growing increasingly resentful of the expectation that the historic ceremonial forms of the Bourbon polity could provide an appropriate framework for the task of national regeneration. All deputies were, it is true, momentarily dazzled by the official opening of the Estates on 5 May, though Thomas Jefferson's summation that it was as imposing as an opera tellingly betrayed a tendency to judge royal ceremony in the terms of the bourgeois public sphere.[27] Third Estate deputies were also disappointed to find the king's opening comments at the Estates General, voiced by Necker and Keeper of the Seals Barentin, still in the idiom of royal will, corporative particularism and popular deference. Their hackles were raised sufficiently, indeed, for them to refuse, the next day, to follow the king's orders to verify their credentials by order rather than in common assembly. Many deputies had been mandated by their electors to support voting by head rather than by order. While the noble and ecclesiastical orders went off to separate sessions, the deputies of the Third stood conspicuously firm – and by so doing deadlocked the course of events.

'Our Estates General do nothing', Poitou noble deputy the marquis de Ferrières reported a fortnight later: 'we spend the whole day in useless chatter and shouting, with no one listening to anyone else'.[28] The meetings of the Third Estate also presented a tableau of unedifying disorderliness. In the absence of a code of parliamentary procedures (which they would in time graft in from the English House of Commons), chaos appeared to rule: 'hundreds of deputies tried to speak', one witness recorded, 'sometimes all at once, other times one at a time; we cannot possibly identify the movers of motions'.[29] Yet the appearance of political incapacity was appearance only. By refusing to accept the corporative framework of the state even before the Estates met to deliberate, the deputies of the Third had thrown a mightily effective spanner into constitutional procedures. Royal aphasia and government repression proved unable, moreover, to choke the rising tide of vociferation which the political deadlock stimulated, notably in Paris. The complexity of the electoral procedures was such that the city's elections to the Estates were still taking place down to 20 May, and thus both reflected and were influenced by the political moves going on in Versailles. Though the clergy and the nobility met behind closed doors, the Third – or 'the Commons', as they were calling themselves – allowed the public to attend their sessions, thus ensuring that boisterous visiting Parisians got a whiff of the flavour of political crisis. The 'Commons' publicized their fruitless efforts to seek a way forward: the other two orders had accepted the royal command, and the king himself stayed studiously aloof, refusing to meet delegations. His government's efforts to keep a lid on discussion backfired too. The Provençal adventurer Mirabeau, for example, started a newspaper, the *États-Généraux*, to report events in the Estates, and was said to have over 10,000 Parisian subscribers within a day, but the government frowned on the venture and closed it down. Mirabeau countered by publishing the newspaper under the guise of letters to his constituents – a strategy beyond the reach of the censors. 'The business going forward at present in the pamphlet shops of Paris is incredible,' reported English agronomist Arthur Young on visiting the Palais-Royal, which had become the storm-centre of a popular radicalism which seemed to be getting out of control. Young was incredulous that 'while the press teems with the most levelling and even seditious principles that ... would overturn the monarchy, nothing in reply appears and not the least step is taken by the court to restrain the extreme licentiousness of publication'.[30]

By failing to give ear to the public debates raging over the previous few months and by neglecting to enter into a dialogue with the Third Estate once the Estates had met, the king cut himself off from a public opinion which had fallen in solidly behind the truculent 'Commons'. Royal incomprehension was at no moment better displayed than over the decision of the latter on 17 June to assume the name of 'National Assembly'. 'It's only a phrase,' the king pouted when told the news.[31] Yet this symbolic act – as subversive of the principle of corporate privilege as of respect for precedent-driven ceremonial – marked the moment at which the commoner deputies stopped the waiting game and, on the grounds that they constituted 'at least ninety-six one-hundredths of the nation', began the work of national regeneration on their own, with as many of the noble and clerical deputies as chose to join them. This new body alone, voting by head, would 'interpret and present the general will of the nation'.[32]

It says much about the suspicion and apprehension which the king's impassivity during the summer crisis had engendered in the new assembly that when on the morning of 20 June the deputies discovered the doors to their chamber locked, they immediately feared the worst. Anxious for their very lives, and assuming that a royal coup was imminent which would dispose of them, they repaired to a nearby hall, which had served as a tennis court. Under the direction of the scientist Bailly, one of the Parisian deputies, they took a solemn collective oath not to disperse until a new constitution had been properly established.

The Tennis Court Oath drama was based on a misreading of Louis's mind. The closure of the Assembly's hall had been merely an oversight: the King's Council had determined to hold a *séance royale* in which the king would attempt to end the deadlock by offering a reform programme to the fractious Estates, and it was felt that no further debates were necessary until then. In the event, when that session took place, on 23 June, the political mood had been immeasurably changed by the Tennis Court histrionics.

Louis XVI would look back on 23 June 1789 as the last time in his political life that he spoke freely and without duress. The reform programme he brought forward that day marked a moderately lucid compromise between conflicting views proffered on the royal council by Necker on one side, and by his royal brothers on the other. The decisions of the putative 'national assembly' were declared null and void, and the broad lineaments of a constitutional, noble-dominated political system were outlined. Mixed voting was promised on items of purely national business – all other affairs would be handled through meetings of the separate orders. There would be fiscal equality, a royal budget, national consent to new taxes, plus a greater measure of personal freedom (relaxation of *lettres de cachet*, less press censorship, etc.). There was, however, no mention of reform of feudalism, nor any major social change. The king had, it is true, finally broken his silence – but only to produce in turn a dismal silence from the usually loquacious Third Estate. It all seemed as though, glumly noted deputy Creuzé-Latouche, the king was choosing 'to draw up the constitution by himself', without any measure of consultation or negotiation.[33] The heavy military presence which accompanied the session made the deputies very uneasy. When the king finished, he summoned the different orders to withdraw separately to verify their powers and get on with meeting. But the putative Third Estate refused to budge, and when the royal master of ceremonies requested them to disperse, Mirabeau stepped forward to thunder that it would require bayonets to make them budge.

Louis's *séance royale* signally failed to kickstart the constitutional motor in the way he desired. Deadlock continued, and, as it did so, the position of the 'Commons' – or rather, the new National Assembly – grew ever stronger. The financial situation which had triggered the political crisis had not gone away: the state coffers were so bare that the king had to scrape around to find money to pay for masses to be said for the soul of his dear-departed dauphin. The *séance royale* caused government stocks to fall further. News coming in suggested an impending breakdown of order. A league or so from the Versailles palace, peasants were openly infringing the game laws and filling their stockpots with poached game, while from the provinces came reports of riots and rebellions triggered by high prices and continuing political instability. In Paris, the French Guards who had fired on the crowds in the Réveillon riots only weeks earlier were now disobeying their officers and fraternizing freely with turbulent civilians.

Behind the scenes at Versailles, moreover, political groupings and strategies were emerging to help structure events. Members of the 'Society of Thirty' continued to play a role in disseminating political propaganda. In addition, commoner deputies from Brittany – already hardened by tussles with the Breton nobility in 1788 – started informal evening meetings to coordinate action in the assembly the following day. These meetings of what was soon called the 'Breton Club' were attended by like-minded deputies from other delegations, notably the Artois grouping, among which numbered one Maximilien 'de' (as he still signed) Robespierre, an ambitious young lawyer. It was this group which had kept the new National Assembly together on 23 June, and, even before that, they had skilfully negotiated alliances with the fractions of the noble and clerical orders favourable to their cause. On 13 June, three *curés* from the Poitou had left the ecclesiastical chamber to join the 'Commons' to wild acclaim, and a sprinkling of their fellows followed in the next few days before on 25 June the majority of the clerics joined. On 22 June, a brace of noble deputies came too, to be followed on 26 June by some forty-seven nobles, led by the duc d'Orléans (whom many suspected of aiming for the crown for himself).

On 27 June, Louis performed what appeared to be a colossal climb-down. He ordered the rumps of the noble and clerical orders to join their *confrères* in the duly recognized National Assembly, and freed all deputies from the binding mandates their electors had placed upon them. Joy was momentarily unconfined. Arthur Young, who had been enraptured by the Parisian drama, judged this a good moment to leave the capital since, he felt, 'the revolution [was] now complete'.[34] Jefferson had much the same reaction: 'This great crisis now being over', he wrote home on 29 June, 'I shall not have matter interesting enough to trouble you with as often as I have done lately'.[35]

Such comments highlighted that what was occurring within France – though extraordinary – had not yet passed the threshold of the astonishing and the unprecedented. Jefferson himself had, after all, seen political revolution at first hand in the United States. A figure such as Young constantly harked back to Britain's 1688 'Glorious Revolution' – and was aware that political struggles were not rarities. Below the surface, however, things were moving ineluctably onwards. The wavering monarch, for example, had not ceased to waver. On the very same day that he seemed to give way, he called up the duc de Broglie ('a high flying aristocrat, cool and capable of every mischief', according to Jefferson),[36] to serve as generalissimo of all royal troops in the Parisian area. Soon tens of thousands of troops were on the march towards the capital, and though the official position was that these were to guard against the breakdown of order, most Parisians – by now inured to inferring the worst of a ruler who consistently failed to reveal his ideas – feared that a military crackdown was imminent. Those anxieties appeared to be founded when, on 11 July, the king dismissed Necker and his supporters on the Royal Council, replacing them by a new ministry which was generally viewed as brazenly counter-revolutionary, with Breteuil, the queen's quondam champion, in charge, and Broglie at the War Ministry. Assiduous efforts were made to erect roadblocks to prevent the news reaching Paris. They failed, and Paris was soon up in arms – indeed, in the midst of revolution.

The tale of 14 July 1789 has been painted into every storybook history of France, and the raw elements leading up to the attack on the Bastille, the day's centrepiece, need little recounting: how the news of Necker's dismissal provoked panic in Paris; how journalist Camille Desmoulins leapt on to a table at the Palais-Royal, crying 'To arms!'; how popular anxieties spread into attacks on the customs-posts in the Farmer Generals' wall surrounding Paris, blamed for keeping grain out and sending food prices rocketing; how the 407 Parisian Electors in the final stage of elections to the Estates General, who had been meeting unofficially since 25 June, transformed themselves into a city council which restored order; how preparations for urban defence were established by the call-up of the city's middle classes into a bourgeois militia (soon to be retitled National Guard); and how the search for arms and gunpowder to defend the city led to attacks on first the Invalides military pensioners hospital and then the Bastille. The picturesque and bathetic elements of the capture are also well known: the role of the renegade French Guardsmen in engineering the assault on the fortress; the women and children rushing up supplies and caring for the wounded; the exchange of fire and the smell of bloodshed; attempts to make a truce, followed by the botched capture of the fortress and the murder of the prison governor, de Launey, and many of the defenders; and the parading of severed heads around the city, alongside the (only) seven prisoners freed from the prison dungeons.

Even Louis XVI – never quick on the uptake – realized that the fall of the Bastille had changed everything. Some in his entourage, including the queen and Artois, had certainly been looking for military solutions: 'violence', Austrian ambassador, the comte de Mercy, had reported to Joseph II in early June, 'may be the only possible way to save the monarchy'.[37] Many deputies thought that a royal 'patriotic' coup, blustered through by Breteuil, and possibly on the lines of Gustavus III of Sweden's coup in 1772, would combine a state bankruptcy with their own dismissal. This was why one of the first things they did, on 12–13 July, was to prohibit any public authority or figure from even pronouncing the word, 'bankruptcy', thus effectively nationalizing the royal debt. All the same, it was (and remains) uncertain whether Louis himself was ever party to such violent plans. His silence was his undoing, however: he was hoist by the petard of his own taciturnity.

Paris in rebel hands posed a colossal challenge to the powers of repression, and Louis listened gloomily as the baron de Besenval, Broglie's lieutenant as army commander in the siege of Paris, informed him that he was unable to count on the loyalty of his troops, were battle to be joined with the rebels. Louis consequently entered the meeting of the Assembly dramatically to announce that he would disperse the troops and recall Necker – causing one excitable deputy to die of joy and a heart-attack. He determined, to general foreboding, to go in person to visit Paris. Unaccompanied save by the Versailles bourgeois militia, he entered the city on 17 July, making his way to the Hôtel de Ville (the city hall), where he confirmed Bailly as mayor of the municipal council and the marquis de Lafayette as commander of the Paris National Guard (as it now became). When he placed on his head the tricolour cockade imagined for this day of reconciliation – the city of Paris's red and blue emblematic colours set off by the Bourbon dynasty's white – a new era of social and political harmony seemed to be opening. And the king seemed definitely to be part of it.

Harmony was not, however, to prove characteristic of the following weeks. By mid-July it was becoming clear that the kind of municipal revolution instigated in Paris was being replicated throughout the land. Marseille had started the process in March, but in most other localities it required the political deadlock of the summer, followed by unaccountable troop movements and various varieties of turbulence, to stimulate urban elites into action. The form of their intervention varied, but usually an extraordinary committee of local business and professional elites – hitherto largely excluded from municipal power – either took over completely the running of urban affairs (as in Paris) or else came to a power-sharing arrangement with the established authorities. A particular feature of these changes was the creation of a bourgeois militia, both as a guarantee against noble or governmental counter-attack and also to ensure that law and order were maintained.

The countryside too was in upheaval. The period between grain stocks from the previous harvest running out and the harvesting beginning and putting fresh grain into the markets was always an emotionally fraught one for peasant families, especially following two such bad harvests as 1787 and 1788. Most rural areas were thus already on tenterhooks. The making of *cahiers des doléances* had also raised the threshold of popular expectation. The peasants had gone home from their parish assemblies, grumbled one legal official in Saumur, 'with the idea that henceforward they were free from tithes, hunting prohibitions and the payment of seigneurial dues'.[38] The political delays of the summer made many blame the court and the nobility for preventing reform from happening. Anti-noble and anti-seigneurial hostility was already well to the fore in peasant rebellions which had started in the spring: in Provence, Dauphiné and Franche-Comté from March, and in Hainaut and the Cambrésis in May. From 20 July to 6 August, the so-called 'Great Fear' – a set of panics, originating in around half a dozen starting-points – swept like lightning throughout France, immeasurably extending the area of peasant rebellion. The core of the message borne aloft in such panics was that nobles and noble-financed bands of brigands were touring the countryside ruining the crops and meting out death and destruction on those wanting reform.

The 'Great Fear' was grounded in fantasy – but understandable fantasy. No counter-revolutionary steps of the kind imagined were being taken. And the court faction most committed to violent solutions had broken up ignominiously post-Bastille, and Artois, Condé, Broglie and the Polignacs were already by 20 July leaving France for self-imposed exile. Yet the nobility's intransigence in Versailles, relayed in the provinces by local aristocrats, had certainly not passed unnoticed. In the mood of economic and political anxiety which reigned, moreover, any number of unusual occurrences – troop movements, the presence of vagrant bands of beggars, the formation of urban militias, and indeed the peasant rebellions already taking place – could be and were metamorphosed into components of a sinister conspiracy. The rural perambulations of agronomist Arthur Young were frequently interrupted by peasants who found it difficult to imagine his interests were purely scientific, and in the fastnesses of Auvergne he was accused of plotting with the queen, Artois and local aristocrats.[39] As in Paris, unattributable fears of counter-revolutionary action stimulated popular classes into militant action, with the Great Fear catalysing popular discontent – hunger riots, troubles over unemployment, anti-seigneurial hostility, rural crime – into a movement of radical social change. Very few areas were completely unaffected. In some localities (notably the Dauphiné, Flanders, lower Normandy, Mâconnais, Alsace), the Fear developed into violent peasant revolts involving château-burning, assaults on seigneurs and widespread looting. 'Brigandage and looting are going on everywhere,' reported the frightened estate steward of the duc de Montmorency from Normandy on 2 August. 'The populace attributes the dearness of grain to the kingdom's seigneurs, and is attacking everything belonging to them.' A band of peasants and brigands had, he reported, attacked the dove-cote of a neighbouring seigneur and taken away all the seigneurial documents from his archives, even having the audacity to 'give a receipt signed in the name of *the Nation*'.[40] This kind of action was in fact fairly characteristic of the movement: armed mobilization against a threat of noble action (which never transpired); use of the moment to make a collective move against local seigneurs; the selection of targets, both symbolic (the seigneurial dove-cote) and financial (registers of feudal rights); and claimed legitimation of radical action by the 'nation' or, sometimes, by the king.

In the movement of disturbances, which reached a climax at the end of July, all forms of authority – seigneurial, ecclesiastic, municipal, urban, social, economic – were potential targets of popular ire. The strongest thread running through the movement as a whole was anti-seigneurialism. Hatred of the seigneur was something which bound most members of a rural community together, even rich and poor who in other domains had antagonistic interests. Although the purchase of seigneuries by social-climbing bourgeois (including many deputies of the Third Estate) had been widespread over the eighteenth century, the assumption in most places was, nonetheless, that the interests of seigneurs and the nobility were identical. Unsurprisingly, many nobles blamed the whole movement on the commoner deputies of the Third Estate, who for their part too initially distanced themselves from it. 'One must work for the good of the people', the commoner deputy Duquesnoy had proclaimed, 'but the people must do nothing for it themselves.'[41] Some commoner deputies thought the peasant revolt – which was so very much more radical in its objectives than the wishes set out in the *cahiers* – further evidence of an aristocratic revolt aimed to thwart them in their task of creating a new constitution.

On 3 August, there were calls in the National Assembly for the restoration of law and order in the provinces and the continued payment of seigneurial dues, at least provisionally. In fact, by then deputies of the Breton Club caucus were seeking to devise a means of utilizing the peasant revolution as a way of strengthening the Assembly's authority. Accepting that peasant revolution could not be gone back on, they wagered that it was vital that the Assembly – rather than the king – should claim credit for it. Plans were duly hatched, and in a session on the evening of 4 August liberal aristocrats, led by the plutocratic young blue-bloods, the duc d'Aiguillon and the vicomte de Noailles, stepped forward to demand the abolition of seigneurial dues. The 'Night of 4 August' soon got out of hand, as the spirit of renunciation of the 'Ancien Régime' (a term which was beginning to be used at around this period) spread amongst the deputies. Rhetorical spontaneity overtook conspiratorial pre-planning, and vast swathes of institutions and practices with their roots far in French history were abolished under the name of 'feudalism': seigneurial and feudal dues, the ecclesiastical tithe, provincial and municipal 'liberties', venality of office . . . The list went on. Laws of 5–11 August would declare that the National Assembly had 'destroyed entirely the feudal regime'.[42]

Following the tergiversations of the July crisis and with the Artois faction in self-imposed exile, the king was in a state of uncommunicative depression. The way in which the National Assembly went about its business after 14 July depressed him more. He was, first, much irked by the Assembly's decision to prefix the blueprint for a new constitution with a declaration of rights, which it spent most of late July and August haggling over. The Declaration of the Rights of Man, agreed by the Assembly on 26 August, constituted a ringing invocation of individual natural rights, which at a stroke dissolved the corporative, privilege-riddled fabric of the Bourbon polity, and invested the nation rather than the ruler with political sovereignty.[43] Second, the king also resented efforts to eradicate the power and influence of the privileged orders: 'I shall never consent', he wrote confidentially on 5 August, 'to the despoliation of my clergy and my nobility' (a revealing use of the possessive adjective).[44] Third, he resented what seemed to be the Assembly's implicit republicanism: it, rather than he, claimed to represent the nation, and although he was willing to accept many of the anti-feudal reforms of 4 August, the deputies refused to brook even amendments of detail from him, so as to keep him entirely divorced from the legislative process.

Louis's opposition to the political drift was shared by a loose grouping within the Assembly known as the *monarchiens*, led by Mounier, Malouet and Lally-Tollendal, and linked to Mirabeau, who wished to strengthen royal power as the best bulwark against popular anarchy. Yet *monarchien* projects were consistently rejected by the Assembly, most notably on 10 September, when it massively rejected their proposal for a two-tier legislature, on the lines of the English houses of parliament and the American Congress, on the grounds that this risked reinstating noble intransigence at the heart of the political machine. And the following day, by a less striking majority, the Assembly also rejected *monarchien* plans for granting the king an absolute veto over Assembly legislation, agreeing only to a suspensive veto.

The baulking of the monarch's will led many to believe that Louis was planning either to flee to the provinces or else to attempt another counter-coup. These suspicions were fanned by the king's decision to call to Versailles, putatively for his own protection, the notoriously loyalist Flanders regiment. On 3 October, Parisians awoke to find their newspapers recounting horror-stories about how in a reception for the regiment at Versailles given by the king's bodyguard troops, drunken and overheated demonstration of personal loyalty to the king had merged with counter-revolutionary sentiments, with much symbolic stamping underfoot of national tricolour cockades. A royalist counter-coup seemed to be on the horizon. On 5 October, a British embassy official reported 'the ludicrous sight of a female army proceeding very clamorously but in ordered and determined step towards Versailles'.[45] The movement had originated as a demonstration of market women about bread prices (for the rural disturbances of the summer had profoundly disrupted normal commercial relations). Encouraged by radicals and journalists to beard the lion in its den, the demonstration turned into a plebeian political pilgrimage to the royal court – complete with cannon, pitchforks and rusty muskets – to protest about prices and about the Flanders regiment incident. Lafayette was press-ganged by his own National Guardsmen into going along. The mixed-sex demonstration developed overnight into a major political incident, as marauding gangs swept through the Versailles palace, threatening the life of queen and courtiers. Lafayette demobilized the crisis by getting the royal family to agree to relocate in Paris – and also to sanction the outstanding legislation regarding the abolition of feudalism and the Declaration of the Rights of Man. He then accompanied the royal convoy back to Paris, with the severed heads of slain bodyguards on pikes, and with the Assembly deputies following respectfully on, while the crowd chanted its contentment that 'the baker, the baker's wife and the baker's boy' were being brought to Paris: the transfer of king, queen and dauphin from Versailles to Paris was seen as the guarantee of the restoration of political order *and* affordable bread prices.

The events of 5–6 October had 'saved France by aborting an abominable conspiracy', Ménard de la Groye, deputy for Le Mans, wrote to his wife[46] – though here, as so often in 1789 and in following years, the substantial reality or non-reality of a political plot was less important than the mobilizing force of the fear of conspiracy. The king bore events with his customary diffidence, but was stung to the quick. This more than symbolic transfer, under duress, from Versailles to Paris was to bring him – but also the Assembly, which relocated to the Tuileries palace too – more directly under the influence of national and Parisian politics. A few days later, Louis penned a secret missive to his Bourbon cousin, King Charles IV of Spain, formally renouncing his sanction to 'all that has been done contrary to the royal authority this year'.[47] The Bourbon sphinx was developing further riddles.

c) THE TASK OF POLITICAL ARCHITECTURE

'It was not the Nation who made the Revolution,' opined physician-deputy Campmas. 'If it had been possible to keep the machine running [the Estates General] would never have been called.' The idea that the events of 1789 found their roots in the terminal decay of the Bourbon polity was echoed by the marquis de Ferrières: 'the French constitution was an ancient building. Stupidly, people tried to rebuild its foundations; the edifice collapsed.'[48]

The Revolutionaries bolstered their courage for the days ahead by stressing the elemental inevitability of the fall of the Bourbon regime. Yet their views do scant justice to the efforts of a variety of reforming ministers from the dark days of the Seven Years War onwards to 'popularize' the Bourbon polity, and to put it on a footing which harmonized with the social and cultural transformations of the century. The 'nation' was not the prime cause of the events of 1789, any more than those events were due to, as a Lyonnais deputy put it in July, 'the philosophy and Enlightenment which spread among all ranks of society'.[49] Yet the Bourbon polity did not fall simply because of its alleged superannuated caducity or of poorly executed repair-work but, rather, because of a quite unforeseeable fusion of financial and political crisis with social crisis. The fall of the Bourbon polity was not inevitable. It owed a great deal to the purposive action of particular groups: in particular, peasants and urban consumers mobilized by high prices, social distress and an unprecedented electoral process, and individuals within the newly expanded political elite who managed to turn the regime's instability to their own collective advantage in ways formerly unimaginable.

The commoner deputies of the Third Estate, now conjoined with the rumps of the noble and ecclesiastical orders in the National Constituent Assembly, enjoyed enthusiastic public support as a result of the vagaries of the summer crisis of 1789. The manner in which these men had handled the summer crisis of 1789 meant that they had a golden opportunity to refashion the political system from top to bottom in ways which began to be termed 'revolutionary'. Prior to 1789, the term 'revolution' had retained some traces of its classical meaning as a cyclical change or reversal of fortunes. It designated (especially when employed in the plural) significant vicissitudes which affected a political system (hence, 'the revolutions of England' in the 1640s, or the 'Maupeou revolution' of the 1770s). It was also used to evoke cultural transformation rooted in greater enlightenment and changed mores: in 1771, for example, Voltaire had written to d'Alembert that their age was witnessing 'a greater revolution . . . [in] people's minds than that of the sixteenth century' – and, moreover, it was a 'tranquil' one.[50] 1789 gave the term the sense of a major transformation which affected all aspects of life –

and which was in the process of volitional actualization. 'Revolution' was a political project opening up on a limitless future.

The 1200 deputies who now formed the National Constituent Assembly were aware that they had a unique and a golden opportunity for momentous political architecture. The transformation of the Estates General into the National Assembly had involved the dissolution of the binding mandates which their original electors had imposed on them, thus giving them full legislative freedom. The shipwreck of absolutism over the summer had reduced the constraints which royal power might pose. In addition, France was not at war nor in a situation of national emergency: despite occasional expressions of anxiety about foreign intervention, France's international rivals proved unenthusiastic about getting involved in French internal politics. Partly at least, this was because the Great Nation did not seem to be much of a threat: its attempt to back Spain in a conflict over Nootka Sound off the Californian coast in 1790, for example, was highly unconvincing, and the deputies eschewed coming to the aid of anti-Austrian rebels in the Austrian Netherlands who subscribed to the patriot cause.

In their epochal political task, the deputies also had freed themselves from the exigencies of history. We have seen how in the electoral campaign of 1788–9 the publicists supporting the Third Estate had shifted the grounds of political legitimacy from historical precedent, on which most anti-absolutist political action had been based hitherto, to rationally stated and universalizable precepts grounded in natural law. 'History is not our code,' claimed Languedocian Protestant pastor and deputy, Rabaut de Saint-Étienne.[51] Individuals rather than corporative groupings were invested with rights, and sovereignty was located not in the body of the dynast, but in the body of a nation of rights-bearing citizens. In Year One of Liberty, as 1789 came to be called, the tendency was to lump the past together in a single bloc, called variously 'the preceding regime', the 'old regime', and then, most durably, the 'former (ancien) regime'. The palimpsest of a rather undifferentiated but massively unjust past thus came to stand as a polar opposite to everything the Revolutionaries thought about the task they had in hand. This approach tended to erase consciousness of historical change prior to 1789. The Ancien Régime was 'the time of the seigneurs' (a phrase which remained in the popular memory until the twentieth century), unchanging, coercive and hierarchical, in contrast to the more dynamic, energetic and contractual age of the rights of men and citizens – which was the time of present and future. On 11 August 1789, the Assembly had, it is true, granted the king the title 'Restorer of French Liberties'. Yet this kind of historical quotation became increasingly rare. The Revolution would be about new beginnings, going forward rather than going back. In a new mythic present, France would be 'regenerated' from the torpid state of stagnancy and debility to which absolute monarchy had reduced it.[52]

The Declaration of the Rights of Man and the Citizen, passed on 26 August and sanctioned by the king on 6 October, provided, in the opinion of Rabaut de Saint-Étienne, 'the political alphabet' of this 'new world'.[53] The lineaments of that alphabet had been assembled over the previous half century as a result of processes which had impacted heavily on the consciousness of the deputies: a major shift in *mentalités*; the emergence of commercial capitalism, and the development of a strong tertiary and service sector; the growth of a bourgeois public sphere grounded in new forms of sociability and exchange; and a political and administrative system increasingly efficient at getting things done. The Declaration itself bore the imprint of its immediate context – the wish to restrict the powers of the monarch and to check backward steps towards 'despotism'. Yet it also transcended the circumstances of its drafting to provide an audacious boost to the emergence of a new political culture grounded in the ahistorical precepts of the philosophy of rights. 'Men', it opened, 'are born and remain free and equal in rights' – a lapidary Rousseauian statement which of itself implied the dissolution of the privilege-ridden corporatism of the absolutist polity. Sovereignty now rested not with the king, but with the nation (art. iii), and pre-1789 royal practices were specifically targeted in clauses which stipulated that arbitrary arrests and punishments were illegal (arts. vii, viii); that individuals were presumed innocent until proven guilty (art. ix); that made consent to taxation and accountability of public officials essential rights (arts. xiv, xv); that insisted on freedom of speech and the press (art. xi); and that predicated constitutionality on the separation rather than the conflation of powers (art. xvi). The pre-1789 church was the target for the proclamation of freedom of religious opinion (art. x). The purpose of government was stated to be the preservation of 'the natural and imprescriptible rights of man', itemized as 'liberty, property, security and resistance to oppression' (art. ii). All citizens had the right to participate in the legislative process and to have access to public office, and law was viewed as 'the expression of the general will' (art. vi).

The task of framing the new constitution around this political blueprint would take longer than was originally anticipated – it was only in September 1791 that it was complete and the deputies could hand on the torch to a newly elected legislature. Yet throughout these two years, their public pronouncements and private correspondence sang their collective enchantment with their epochal doing and making: 'the political system we have established', self-panegyrized Le Mans deputy Ménard de la Groye, '... is founded on the wisest, truest and most incontestable principles, and has as its only objective the common good'.[54] To achieve this end, the Revolutionaries spoke the language of creation and erasure, of regeneration and destruction. This was seen particularly clearly in one of their most lasting reforms, the replacement of the accreted patchwork of historic provinces by a rationally constructed ensemble of eighty-three departments. Though national unity was one of the watchwords of the new regime, the deputies were determined to cut back the centralization which they regarded as characteristic of the Ancien Régime. The abolition of the Intendants in December 1789 raised almost as loud a cheer as the final dissolution of the *parlements* a year later: election rather than royal appointment or purchase of office was to characterize the framework of local government. The carving-up of national territory gave rise to some lively debates: 'geometrists' wanting each region to be rectangular combated 'historicists', who advised observing wherever possible the frontiers of the ancient provinces. In the end a compromise was effected: there were to be eighty-three departments of roughly the same size – just large enough, it was claimed, for an individual to reach the departmental capital (or *chef-lieu*) in a day's travel. If the provincial boundaries were given measured respect, this was based on the assumption that the old provinces had tended to observe natural frontiers – and the Revolutionaries were especially keen to ground their new administrative map in nature. Hence the nomenclature of the departments was based on mountains, rivers and other natural features. 'Provence' vanished from the map, for example, but the area it covered was now filled, *grosso modo*, by the departments of the Bouches-du-Rhône, Basses-Alpes and Var.

THE TASK OF POLITICAL ARCHITECTURE

The departments were the bricks from which the edifice of the nation was to be constructed. They constituted a unitary form of adminis-tration, replacing the hodge-podge of different boundaries for indirect and direct taxes, military affairs, religion, justice and the rest which had characterized the Bourbon polity. Each department was endowed with the same internal framework: there were around half a dozen or so districts, which grouped the communes, which also had their own administrative structures. Tasks were shared out amongst the different levels – the departments, for example, had wide-ranging powers as regards schools, prisons, church maintenance, highways and canals and poor-relief.

The new structures were Janus-faced. On one hand, they were regarded as crucial expressions of local interests, and could be viewed as an agent of the decentralization of French political life. On the other, they owed their existence to the Revolution, formed a single chain of communication from the centre and had as their mission the regeneration of national spirit. Unlike the local particularism which had clung to many of the old provinces, the new public spirit was to be a fusion of energy: there was to be impulsion from on high, from the government, plus a supply of local vitality from below. It was significant that when the National Assembly sought to celebrate and commemorate the new spirit of national unity they chose to do so through the departmental framework: in the Fête de la Fédération, timed to be held in Paris on 14 July 1790, the first anniversary of the taking of the Bastille, the stars of the show were the delegations of National Guardsmen sent up by every department in France which proudly marched past the king under their local banners.

The best guarantee of transparency in all aspects of public life, and a means of protecting against departments becoming mouthpieces of sectional interests, was the electoral principle, which was present at every level. The right to participate in the electoral process was a badge of a new, patriotic citizenship which the Assembly gave out freely – but not without discrimination. Henceforward, it was property rather than birth or historical precedent which determined social and political entitlement – a point underlined by the abolition of noble titles in June 1790. From autumn 1789, the deputies introduced a tiered property franchise into electoral regulations which, as for the Estates General, were indirect. Although all French men enjoyed the civic rights enshrined in the Declaration of the Rights of Man, only those with fixed property-ownership were allowed to vote. Of maybe 7 million adult males, around 60 per cent (*c.* 4 million) had voting rights – a colossal figure when set against electoral practice elsewhere in Europe at the time, but still falling some way short of what universalist Revolutionary rhetoric seemed to imply. This distinction between so-called 'active' and 'passive' citizens marked a more general orientation of representation around property, which was marked by a stratified system of qualification for political responsibility. Thus, one needed to be wealthier than a simple active citizen to qualify for election as a municipal official or to serve in department-level administration, while to become a deputy one needed to pay in annual taxes the equivalent of a 'silver mark' (*marc d'argent*) – a considerable sum.[55]

The way in which the Assembly gave the universalism which it espoused a sectional spin was evidenced in other aspects of its laws on citizenship. An impressive openness was shown towards the inclusion of Protestants: they were given full electoral rights and in December 1789 were empowered to stand for public office too. Yet there was little generosity shown towards France's 40,000 Jews, nor much thought given to the idea of extending political rights either to women or to slaves. An abolitionist movement existed – the Amis des noirs ('Friends of the Blacks'), founded in 1788 and including Lafayette, abbé Grégoire, Siéyès, Lavoisier and Brissot among its patrons – but abolitionists were massively outnumbered in the Assembly: most deputies viewed the maintenance of France's colonial wealth through plantation slavery as an essential ingredient of national prosperity. The decision, late in September 1791, to end slavery in France was little more than a moral figleaf: the practice was maintained in the colonies. Earlier debates between Barnave, representing the Assembly's Colonial Committee, and the abolitionist lobby marshalled by Brissot over whether domestic freedom was compatible with imperial projects overseas which included enslavement of fellow humans was complicated by the question of whether free blacks from the Caribbean colonies should have the right to be represented in the new legislature. Debates were interwoven with violent clashes over the issue in the colonies themselves, and on 24 September 1791 the Assembly, adhering to the principle of order, deprived all blacks of any civic rights.

The extension of rights of citizenship and the quasi-fetishization of the electoral principle in the new system within France at least guaranteed public accountability and transparency. Two further freedoms expounded in the Declaration of the Rights of Man underpinned those ideals, namely, freedom of speech and freedom of assembly. Political issues were debated not only in the chamber and committees of the National Assembly but also in a wide variety of venues throughout the length and breadth of the land. Although there were property, race and gender limitations on Revolutionary inclusiveness, at least opinion was free – indeed had never been freer. If the Declaration of the Rights of Man clearly drew its inspiration from the philosophy of the Enlightenment, the political culture of the early years of the Revolution was a striking exemplification of the values of the Enlightenment public sphere. The measure of press freedom enjoyed since 1787–8 was extended enormously in 1789, and in the period down to 1791 the press enjoyed greater freedom than at any stage in French history, before or since. The vitality of the newspaper press was a useful proxy measure of transparency in public debate, a key Revolutionary value. Paris alone saw the appearance of 300 new titles in 1790, and a further 300 down to the end of the Constituent Assembly in September 1791, while the provinces provided some 200 additional titles over the same period. Marseille had had two newspapers in 1789; by 1791 it had fourteen. The comparable figures for Bordeaux were one and sixteen. The buoyant newspaper press made politics everybody's business, and schooled citizens in Revolutionary political culture.

The impact of the press was accentuated by greater freedom afforded political associations. Certain of the institutions of the pre-Revolutionary public sphere were, it is true, now frowned on: academies, for example, were increasingly viewed as hyper-exclusive nests of aristocrats, and they were eventually abolished in 1793; while salons and, to some degree, masonic lodges, whose semi-private status had in the past preserved them from the full force of state censorship, were seen as too secretive for the transparent and democratic atmosphere of the new regime. The characteristic institution of the Revolutionary public sphere was the political club. The archetype in some measure was the Assembly's own 'Breton Club', which, after the move to Paris in October, took the title 'Society of Friends of the Constitution'. It was better known as the Jacobin Club, after the Jacobin monastery in which it held its sessions. The Jacobins acted as a left-of-centre parliamentary pressure group, spending much of their time in coordinating the following day's business in the Assembly. They also drew non-deputies into their activities. From 1790, they opened their meetings to the general public, and they also acted as the centre for a vast correspondence and affiliation network of clubs similarly devoted to the success of the new political regime. The provincial clubs which affiliated to the Paris Club were meeting-places for local patriots, drawing in a largely middle-class clientele which they kept abreast of public affairs. They served as a training ground for budding politicians, but beyond that were also schools of political morality, sporting busts of Cato and Brutus, Voltaire, Rousseau and Ben Franklin on their walls, alongside framed copies of the Declaration of the Rights of Man. Their exact form varied according to locality and background: some sprang out of pre-existent literary societies; others had a strong admixture of freemasons; and most developed into political debating clubs like the Paris prototype. In early 1790, only a score or so of such clubs were linked to Paris; but by the summer over 100 had joined, and a year later the figure was close to 1,000. By then different types of club – radical and conservative, aristocratic and plebeian – were also emerging.[56]

Press and clubs worked most effectively when they worked together. They provided a continuous interactive commentary on and critique of the National Assembly's work of political architecture. They influenced as well as reflecting and recounting events. For deputies read the newspapers and were members of political clubs and also received a heavy post-bag. The Arras lawyer Robespierre won a national reputation for himself through speeches in both the Paris Jacobin Club and the National Assembly, speeches which he made sure were carried in newspapers. A good number of deputies would owe their election to their journalistic fame: Cérutti, editor of the specialist rural journal *La Feuille villageoise*, for example, and Brissot, of the *Patriote Français*, were elected to the Legislative Assembly in the summer of 1791, and there were numerous examples (Marat, Carra, Mercier, Gorsas, etc.) later in the decade.

The regeneration of national spirit infused liberty and equality into every domain of French life. Equality before the law implied that the law required more respect than it had mustered prior to 1789. The slow work began of national codification of laws (which would see its apotheosis in the Napoleonic Code of 1804). The penal code was simplified and humanized: degrading and cruel sentences, including torture, were abolished, and a tiered system of prisons introduced for punishing the persistent wrong-doer. This was complemented by the invention of a new and, it was said, highly humane form of capital punishment, which, its progenitor, the physician deputy Guillotin, assured his fellows would separate the head from the body 'in the twinkling of an eye' – 'one feels no more than a slight sensation of coolness at the back of the neck'.[57] (How Damiens would have cheered!) A functionally stratified system of courts was instituted too, with election of judges and (imported from England) the jury system and justices of the peace as means of making justice fairer, more transparent, and more oriented towards prevention and conciliation.

With the Ancien Régime yoke triumphantly lifted, and with public spirit regenerated through elections and the individual freedoms, deputies confidently expected a new era of prosperity and happiness to begin. The Rights of Man implied (though they did not make explicit) the freeing-up of the production, retailing and distribution of goods. The spirit of *laisser-faire* had been a hallmark of the *bailliage cahiers* of the Third Estate, and it dominated the Assembly's thinking on economic policy. The reforms of the night of 4 August entailed the removal of agricultural land from feudal constraints, and a similar spirit of freedom was evident in reforms in other areas of the economy. Freedom of trade now covered all goods: down to 1791, in piecemeal fashion, all indirect taxes, including the hated *gabelle*, were ended, and seigneurial and municipal tolls made illegal. (The unified internal market was, however, protected by a tariff wall against foreign competition, and as a sign of market caution, the export of grain was prohibited in 1790.) The attack on corporative privilege on 4 August had seemed to imply the abolition of trade guilds and corporations, though in the event these continued to subsist. Only on 2 March 1791 were they suppressed and state privileges formerly granted to manufacturers removed; while on 17 June 1791, the Le Chapelier law (named after the Breton deputy who introduced it, and actually aimed against political rather than workers' associations) had the effect of prohibiting workers and employers from forming associations – a law which made strike action illegal down to 1864.

The Constituent Assembly also began the work of reconstructing national finances, whose disastrous state had triggered the whole Revolutionary crisis. The privileged orders of the Ancien Régime could now be expected to pay their full tax allocation. If all individuals were now equal before the law, all were equally naked before the tax-man. When it came, the property tax which was the basis of the new fiscal regime was a unitary tax, payable by all, on lines which Calonne and Loménie de Brienne had preached. Measures aiming to centralize and bureaucratize the state's central finances on lines yearned for by reformist Controllers-General were also introduced, bringing greater economy and rationality to the Treasury. At the other end of the process, the removal of fiscal privilege brought transparency to the assessment and levying of taxation by democratically accountable local committees.

Such a system took time to introduce. The summer crisis of 1789, however, had caused tax revenue to plummet, while the removal of Ancien Régime taxes and agreement to new outgoings, such as compensation for venal offices, helped cause a real problem of short-term liquidity. The new Assembly just about held the line. Necker's return as Finance Minister after the fall of the Bastille helped, as did the Assembly's eschewing the road of state bankruptcy: it recognized the national debt and promised root and branch fiscal reform. On 6 October 1789, deputies called for a *contribution patriotique* (the associative word 'contribution' was thought to measure more accurately tax-payers' attitudes towards state demands than the more coercive-sounding Ancien Régime term, 'impost' or *impôt*): citizens were requested to make a one-off payment of a quarter of their income to help the new regime over the difficult circumstances of its birth, and there was indeed an emulative wave of conspicuous patriotic donation.

What provided most confidence in state credit in autumn 1789, however, was the decision to nationalize church property. By abolishing the tithe, the reforms of 4 August made the recasting of ecclesiastical finances inevitable. On 2 November, the state took over church land. Historians reckon this constituted between 6 and 10 per cent of the total cultivable land surface, though contemporaries thought it was even more. This was pending the state's reorganization of the funding of the church – which followed in the so-called Civil Constitution of the Clergy of 12 July 1790, which effectively made the church a sector of government administration. In the interim, from December 1790, state bonds known as *assignats*, interest-bearing treasury bills secured (or 'assigned') on church lands were issued. A start was also made at selling off the 'national lands' (*biens nationaux*) to the highest bidders. The Civil Constitution of the Clergy was perhaps the most ambitious piece of political architecture which the Constituent Assembly attempted. It was also the measure which caused the biggest headaches for it and its successors.

D) DEMOLITION PROBLEMS

The Bastille, arch-symbol of Revolutionary action, was turned into a demolition-site days after it was stormed, providing mass employment for Parisian building workers, visual entertainment for the leisured classes, and a fat profit for building entrepreneur Palloy, who added to his profits by selling off chunks of the fortress as patriotic memorabilia – an early example of Revolutionary commercialism. The 'Ancien Régime' (for the term was coming into use) did not, however, come down quite as easily. The work of political demolition proved altogether more intractable than the National Assembly, floating on a cloud of its own adrenaline and ceaselessly invoking the principle of unity in the political architecture of the new regime, was prepared to admit.

Writing to the US envoy in Paris in October 1789, the American President George Washington saluted the 'wonderful' revolution which had taken place in France, but expressed his fear that 'the revolution is of too great a magnitude to be effected in so short a space and with the loss of so little blood'. Shrewd government would be called for if 'the mortification of the king, the intrigues of the queen and the discontent of the princes and noblesse' were not to foment division and bloodshed.[58] Privilege – the prime target of Revolutionary legislation – had not been confined prior to 1789 to the so-called 'privileged orders' evoked by Washington, and its track-marks could be traced all over the corporative body of the Bourbon polity. Rabaut Saint-Étienne once sketched out the dilemma of any pre-1789 reforming minister 'who wants to disentangle the wires [of privilege, yet] does not know where to begin because as he touches them he makes the interest cry out to which they are attached'.[59] After 1789, the deputies in the Assembly found themselves in this very position. 'Everyone wants reform', sagely noted Ferrières, 'but when they themselves are affected, they complain.'[60] The sheer interconnectedness of so many features of the Bourbon polity ramified problems along crazily unpredictable zigzag paths. The reorganization of the church linked, for example, to the need to nationalize church lands so as to settle state finances – which were in turn affected by decisions on the slave colonies, decisions on which had implications on rights of citizenship. At each stage, decisions would be made which were popular with some, unpopular with others. There were, it is true, many individuals willing to sacrifice the benefits of pre-1789 privilege for the rights and freedoms guaranteed by the Revolution. Yet there would also be many – and not simply the powerful and ultra-privileged – who lost out, and whose discontent operated as a kind of political yeast, alimenting 'unpatriotic' thoughts and acts.

Much of that yeast stuck to the old 'privileged orders', for it was they who had most to lose from Revolutionary reforms and who often proved most recalcitrant at forming a patriotic identity. The Revolutionary melodrama of the summer crisis of 1789 had cast the privileged orders as stage villains – but the social groupings behind those personae were reluctant to leave the stage without a struggle. Deputy Adrien Duquesnoy was soon musing that the only individuals not to benefit 'enormously' from the Revolution were an unrepresentative sample of 'priests, nobility, magistrates and financiers'.[61] Yet his naive assumption that their importance had been snuffed out by a national tidal wave of patriotism proved well wide of the mark. In fact, these groups became the nodes around which opposition to the Revolution concentrated.

1789 had, moreover, much extended the sites in which resistance and protest could occur. Foremost in this respect was the Constituent Assembly itself, which was increasingly riven by division and dissension. 'Left' and 'Right' as terms designating particular political persuasions were coined precisely in this period, the 'patriot' deputies forming the habit of sitting to the left of the assembly's president in the Salle du Manège of the Tuileries palace, while the more monarchically inclined huddled to the right. The stars of the Right, which attracted a large following from the provincial nobility, were intransigents such as the abbé Maury, the eccentric Cazalès and Mirabeau's younger brother, the anorexically challenged Mirabeau-'Tonneau' ('Mirabeau the Barrel'). The *monarchiens* (now minus Mounier) had also regrouped and exploited the freedoms of the Assembly to continue to support a stronger role for the monarchy in the constitution-in-the-making. Furthermore, although the National Assembly rather than the monarch was now the cynosure of power, the royal court remained a significant political site, and factional and behind-the-scenes politicking continued. Jockeying to secure the king's ear was still prevalent, and extended from *émigré* leaders such as the comte d'Artois, through the leaders of the Right in the Assembly, through to even many of the individuals and groupings generally viewed as belonging to the 'Left'. The older Mirabeau, who had more than paid his patriotic dues during the summer crisis of 1789, passed covertly into the ranks of the king's advisers in spring 1790, while Layafette too sporadically made himself available for royal consultation.

Outside the Assembly too, the Right clustered under the protective wing of the freedoms guaranteed by the Rights of Man: the Revolutionary public sphere still encompassed the as yet indefeasible right to criticize the Revolution. Thus the patriot press had its counterpart in royalist sheets like abbé Royou's *L'Ami du Roi* and Rivarol's *Les Actes des Apôtres* which specialized in sarcasm and character assassination. Freedom to assemble was also utilized by the counter-revolutionaries for their own ends. *L'Ami du Roi* purported to be the mouthpiece of a nationwide network of 'Society of Friends of the King', roughly equivalent to the Jacobins' 'Society of Friends of the Constitution'. The comte d'Antraigues, who had once been a prominent supporter of the rights of the Third Estate,[62] was by now a brazenly counter-revolutionary plotter who helped organize mass royalist rallies in the Ardèche in late 1790 and early 1791. Courtiers also illicitly disbursed money among Parisians in order to secure 'spontaneous' collective demonstrations of support for the king. On several occasions, the Assembly debated whether more stringent policing of possible acts of treason required the violation of these individual freedoms in the interest of public safety, and indeed an Investigation Committee (Comité des recherches) was established in 1789. It was only a very pale foreshadowing, however, of the organs of Terror in 1792–4. The period down to the summer of 1791 was marked by the exercise of liberal freedoms even by the Revolution's avowed opponents.

'The people', Mirabeau once argued, 'have been promised more than can be promised; they have been given hopes that it will be impossible to realize . . . and in the final analysis the people will judge the Revolution by this fact alone: does it take more or less money?'[63] The judgement was, if crude and cynical, also shrewd. For the Revolution had accorded the popular classes not only a new horizon and expanded means of communication but also – as counter-revolutionaries could attest – a new language of political entitlement, which could be used to critique the universalist rhetoric of the National Assembly. The latter was thus squeezed between dual critiques from 'above' from the old privileged classes and from 'below' from the popular classes. Whereas deputies made great show of speaking in the interests of the entire nation, when the crunch came, moreover, they invariably gave a bourgeois gloss to universalist claims – as we have seen, for example, over the question of the tiered property franchise.[64] Economic freedoms were also divergent in their social impact: the introduction of free trade in grain from autumn 1789, for example, was massively unpopular with rural and urban consumers. Furthermore, the implementation of legislation regarding the abolition of feudalism involved the reintroduction of dues which many peasants had already renounced in the summer of 1789. The law of 15 March 1790 made a distinction between feudal dues imposed as a result of historical usurpation or personal violence (serfdom, hunting rights, corvées, banalités, etc.) and other seigneurial dues which were more contractual in nature. Whereas the former were adjudged to have been abolished outright on the Night of 4 August, the latter were to be redeemed by the peasantry over twenty to twenty-five years. This meant that seigneurs – both noble and bourgeois – were acting quite legally in taking errant peasants before the newly established network of lawcourts for arrears and payment of such rights. Even where seigneurs did accept the outright abolition of feudal dues, moreover, they invariably tried to compensate themselves by raising formal ground rents, and indeed the Assembly also permitted them to add the cost of the old tithe to rents.

The erasure of corporative privilege could, moreover, hit the low as well as the high. The abolition of pays d'état, for example, meant an instant tax-hike for all Bretons and Languedocians, whose privileged status had protected them from the full weight of royal fiscality. The tax load within the old province of Brittany may even have doubled. Many cities also lost out from the cull of privilege, especially if they failed to secure nomination as a departmental chef-lieu: Bayeux complained that the loss of ecclesiastical establishments as a result of the Civil Constitution lost the town 0.4 million livres annual income in wages and charities. The loss of their Ancien Régime superstructure of administrative, judicial and ecclesiastical establishments had, the inhabitants of Laon and Luçon stated, caused the towns to come face to face with likely 'annihilation' and 'nothingness'.[65] Other unlooked-for socio-economic effects caused by the Revolution included the collapse of the luxury trades, notably in Paris, as a result of the emigration of high nobles; and the inflation consequent on the Assembly's decision in spring 1790 to permit *assignats* to be used as legal currency (rather than, as originally planned, purely as an entitlement bond for the purchase of former church property).

Although the decent harvests of 1789 and 1790 at least helped keep grain prices within reach of working people again, the social and economic spin-offs of the transformation of political culture in the aftermath of 1789 ensured a continuing ferment of popular discontent. Most of this is probably best classified as *anti-* rather than *counter*-revolutionary – that is to say, it embraced the idea of the Revolution and wanted to improve it rather than reject it wholesale or plot its overthrow. The Assembly's legislation failed to end all outbreaks of popular violence – and indeed, some of its judgements even incited them. From December 1789 to mid-1790, many areas in the south-west (Quercy, Périgord, Limousin, the Albigeois, Rouergue) and part of Upper Brittany were involved in violent attacks against seigneurs who were continuing to demand feudal dues or else were utilizing the Assembly's moderate legislation on the abolition of feudalism to maintain their social authority. Subsistence riots continued to occur fitfully too, especially in northern France: disturbances in Paris in late October 1789 in which a baker, François, was murdered, led to the Assembly introducing martial law provisions. In some cities with a Protestant community, social protest took on a religious imprint: the *bagarre* ('brawl') of Nîmes in June 1790 pitched Catholic peasants and workers against Protestant local authorities and National Guard in street battles which left several hundreds (mainly Catholics) dead. Military garrisons were perilously involved in political activity too, the rank-and-file seeking to relive the 14 July experience and fraternize with their civilian co-citizens and criticize their largely aristocratic officers. In August 1790, the Nancy garrison in which the Royal Châteauvieux regiment was stationed experienced an acute crisis of military discipline, which was put down in draconian fashion by the local commander, the marquis de Bouillé, a notorious royalist. The Constituent Assembly supported the army high command, and the affair left a nasty taste in the mouth.

In many ways what was most striking about the degree of popular discontent and disillusion which subsisted through 1790 and into 1791 was the extent to which it was canalized within the framework of the new political culture established in 1789. Some peasants, urban workers and rank-and-file soldiers took direct action or resorted to illegality over the course of 1790 to express their disappointment that the high hopes of 1789 had not been met and that universal rights were not being properly implemented. But far more utilized the new court system to pursue their ends or petitioned the king and the Assembly for a redress of grievances. This adoption of the discourses and practices of Revolutionary citizenship by individuals and groups formally removed from the political process highlighted the expansion of the pre-revolutionary public sphere. Debate was particularly sharp over the issue of active and passive citizenship in autumn 1789. Were the 'active' citizens (popular speeches and pamphlets demanded) those crypto-royalists who passively accepted the outcome of 14 July 1789, or those putative 'passive' citizens who had actually stormed the Bastille? Women were another disenfranchized grouping to whom the new language of citizenship now began to be extended, in contradistinction to the intentions of the framers of the Declaration of the Rights of Man: indeed the term, 'citizen' (*citoyen*) acquired a female declension ('*citoyenne*, citizeness') for the first time in the word's history, and the maverick writer Olympe de Gouges penned a forcibly argued (and almost wholly disregarded) 'Declaration of the Rights of Woman' in 1791.

If freedom of the press allowed such arguments to be conducted in the public sphere, so too did freedom of assembly. The year 1790 saw the beginnings, notably in Paris, of popular clubs and societies whose procedures were based on those of the Jacobin Club but which extended membership to a much lowlier and less respectable clientele. The prototype here was the Cordeliers Club, or 'Society of Friends of the Rights of Man' which originated as a neighbourhood grouping on the Left Bank and which derived its name from the Cordeliers monastery in which it held its meetings. Admission costs were low, and membership included numerous artisans and shopkeepers, topped off with a talented crew of journalists and intellectuals including Georges Danton, Camille Desmoulins and Jean-Paul Marat. The latter's eponymous *L'Ami du People* proved a propaganda vehicle for the club, emphasizing its special role as the surveillance and denunciation of the public authorities. Women and workers were members too of the numerous Cordeliers-style fraternal societies which developed in the course of the 1790s.

From 1792, these were often within the new framework of forty-eight sections within which Paris was administered. There was also the more intellectual Cercle Social, founded by ex-cleric Claude Fauchet, in which many budding political figures (Bonneville, Brissot, Roland, Condorcet) cut their polemical teeth. The Cercle Social developed a left-wing critique of the Jacobin club, which was dominated by the moderate 'Triumvirate' – the Grenoblois barrister Barnave, the ex-*parlementaire* Adrien Duport and 'Americanist' career soldier Alexandre de Lameth (to whom was occasionally added Lameth's brother, Charles). The group also, along with the Cordeliers, attacked both the Paris municipality controlled by Bailly and the 'Society of 1789', which elitist opponents of the Triumvirate (notably Lafayette, Siéyès, Talleyrand and Bailly) established as a rival to the Jacobins in spring 1790. These popular discontents received support and endorsement, moreover, from within the Assembly itself – notably from Robespierre, who was fashioning himself quite a reputation as the whistle-blowing 'Incorruptible' and from a handful of other fellow-Jacobin radicals such as Pétion, Buzot and the abbé Grégoire.

The 'mortification' of the king in the summer of 1789 on which George Washington had remarked displayed itself thereafter as a characteristic political vacillation which made more difficult the Constituent Assembly's task of producing political harmony and tranquillity. Louis found it impossible to determine a means of both rallying to the Constituent Assembly and of supporting 'his' nobility and clergy. This tested the limits of his abandonment of the corporative format of political life with which he had grown up and his acceptance of the new, civic idiom of Revolutionary political culture. The venal Mirabeau dreamed of the king seizing the initiative and 'popularizing' monarchy so as to increase royal power. He reminded Louis that the abolition of the *parlements*, the provincial estates, the corporative privileges of nobility and clergy was an *oeuvre* of which even Richelieu would have been proud: 'several reigns of absolute government would not have done as much for royal authority as a single year of liberty'.[66] Sporadically at least Louis was alert to such opportunities for boosting his own popularity. In February 1790, for example, he went before the Assembly to express support for the work of the assembly, craftily combining this with a request to be more personally involved in its work. Nor did he baulk from playing a leading role in the Fête de la Féderation on 14 July 1790, or in December from publicly chiding the *émigrés* for their lack of patriotism.

It seems likely that all this amounted to little more than royal lip-service to the new political culture. The king inwardly harboured deeply felt hostility towards the new arrangements, which kept him in virtual imprisonment in the Tuileries, demoted him to mere executive agent of legislative power and drained away the power of his ministers into the hands of Assembly committees. Although he lacked the requisite intelligence and duplicitous steadfastness, he endeavoured to develop the kind of clandestine parallel diplomacy which his grandfather had cultivated through the *Secret du Roi*. His private letter to Charles IV of Spain in November 1789 renouncing the concessions he had made thus far was followed a year later by the equally secret grant of plenipotentiary diplomatic powers to the baron de Breteuil, central player in the ill-fated ministry of 11–14 July 1789, to negotiate with foreign courts. What held Louis back from more open counter-revolutionary sentiments was, first, a desire to avoid civil war and, second, a concern not to fall into a position of over-dependence towards the *émigré* nobility. After all, many of the latter had been responsible, by their acts in 1787–8, for getting him into his wretched position in the first place.

Louis's morose indecisiveness placed him increasingly in thrall to his wife, whose opposition to the Revolution was ferociously unconditional (and who, irritatingly, occasionally beat him at billiards). The queen used her champion, Fersen, and Austrian diplomatic envoy Mercy to keep in touch with her brothers, the Austrian emperors, Joseph II (down to his death in February 1790), then Leopold II (1790–92). These contacts gave rise to suspicions that she was running an 'Austrian Committee' which treasonously plotted with France's erstwhile ally. *L'Autrichienne* ('the Austrian bitch') became the target for public attacks which harmed the royal cause. In pornographic news-sheets and crude engravings she was portrayed as a kind of Habsburg Messalina, polluting the purity of French political life; while the disclosures of the so-called *Livre rouge* ('The Red Book') – the list of pensions which the king had disbursed before 1789 – revealed the extent of court extravagance for which the poor queen was widely held to be responsible. All ways out, Mirabeau was far less successful in 'popularizing' the monarchy at this critical stage than Marie-Antoinette in depopularizing it.

If the royal family attracted increasingly open attacks, this was even more true of the princes and the nobles whose 'discontent' Washington had evoked as a cause of potential political instability. The aristocracy worked to a considerable extent, as we have seen, within the legal framework of the new political culture – yet it also developed an extra-legal and openly counter-revolutionary character through the *émigré* princes, Artois (from July 1789) and Provence (from June 1791), and their exclusivist retinues. Over the course of the 1790s, perhaps 100,000 French men and women sought the road of emigration, particularly after 1791–2. Although only one in six of these was a noble, in the very early days the emigration was predominantly aristocratic and was driven by high politics (the fiasco of 14 July 1789, noble panics triggered by the Great Fear and the October Days) and anti-noble legislation (notably the end of feudalism and the abolition of noble titles). Artois appointed himself as a kind of clandestine regent in exile, petitioning the courts of Europe from his base in Turin for military and diplomatic aid against the Revolution, utilizing Antraigues and others to foment internal insurrectionary activity and seeking in all ways 'to serve the king and queen in spite of themselves'.[67] Yet by the end of 1790, nobles had achieved precious little for their pains, apart from irking popular opinion and maintaining the king in his state of endless vacillation. Their contention that they were not only defenders of their own privileges but also the tireless paladins of the rights of the French nation rang hopelessly hollow. What changed the fortunes of their cause was the reform of the Ancien Régime church in the Civil Constitution of the Clergy of 12 July 1790, whose unpopularity could be exploited for their own ends.

Root-and-branch reform of the Catholic church had been made indispensable by Revolutionary reforms (the abolition of tithes, the nationalization and sale of church property, etc.). Yet though the Constituent Assembly's handling of the ecclesiastical issue was to prove in the long run its most disastrous misjudgement, the church itself was, initially at least, far from the unwilling victim of ideologically driven or anti-clerical reforms. The anti-hierarchical lower clergy of the First Estate had been instrumental in ensuring the success of the Third Estate's manoeuvres during the summer crisis of 1789, and ecclesiastical deputies such as Talleyrand and the abbés Grégoire and Siéyès played important roles within the Constituent Assembly. The model of the 'citizen-priest' had been widely current among churchmen prior to 1789. Many of the Civil Constitution's stipulations – the stress on social utility, for example, and attacks on pluralism and absenteeism – were congruent with that model and were popular with dedicated clergy and lay-people alike. Nor were the Constituent Assembly's first steps to reorganize the church unwelcome: the prohibition of perpetual vows (October 1789) and the consequent reform of monasteries and convents (February 1790) – which allowed monks and nuns to leave their orders with a state pension or else to be regrouped in more economically run institutions – developed an anti-monastic current of thinking which had been evident among churchmen as well as *philosophes* prior to 1789.

Furthermore, the Civil Constitution appealed to a strong pre-1789 current of Jansenist and/or Gallican feeling among churchmen, by tying the national church much more closely to the state even than had been the case in the era of Divine Right absolutism. First, it made the diocesan framework identical with the departmental network which had just been established, consequently reducing the number of bishops from 136 to 83. Second, it provided for the payment of ecclesiastical salaries out of state coffers, setting parish priest salaries, for example, at a more generous level (1200 livres per annum) than that enjoyed by those on the *portion congrue* before 1790 (900 livres). Third, it stipulated the election rather than the appointment to benefices: thus parish priests were elected by members of the district assemblies, and bishops by those on the departmental assemblies, making it possible for Protestants and Jews to be amongst the electorate. (Ménard de la Groye expressed pleasure that henceforward 'we'll have to count the virtues of our bishops, rather than their degrees of nobility'.)[68] And finally it ended the 1516 Concordat of Bologna between Pope and the 'Most Christian King', by stating that the papacy had only the power to approve the election of bishops, rather than to share in their designation.

So consonant was the Civil Constitution with the reforming wishes of the absolute monarchy (as indeed of the *philosophes*) that it received the unreflecting assent of the monarch with an absence of fuss on 24 August 1790. However, both the papacy and the church itself soon stirred into hostile action and made him reconsider. Pope Pius VI was already much exercised over the papal enclave of Avignon and the Comtat Venaissin, which in June, after a plebiscite in favour of annexation into France, had indeed been incorporated into the revolutionary state, in a clear infringement of international law. The elective element in the Civil Constitution, the disrespect which it implied for church property and the growing toleration of other denominations were sufficient to excite the opposition of the pope, and from autumn 1790, Louis XVI began to receive papal warnings urging him not to agree to the reform. Although this injunction hit home with the king, many of the clergy could probably have lived fairly comfortably with papal disapprobation, such was the strength of Gallican sympathies in the church. Yet by the same token, they looked to a synodal meeting of the church as a whole to approve the reforms.

The Assembly's way around the problem, however, was not to submit the measure to a corporative decision, but to impose on the individual members of the church an oath of loyalty to the new measure. To have allowed the church to deliberate in that way seemed to deputies a denial of civic egalitarianism and a corporatist infringement of national sovereignty which they imagined the Night of 4 August had ended. Decided on 27 November 1790, this option of the oath was put into effect in December 1790 and January 1791. It revealed a church split almost down the middle: around 45 per cent of the parish clergy refused the oath (and were called 'refractory' or 'non-juring' clergy), and though 55 per cent did take it, around 6 per cent of the 'jurors' publicly retracted following the pope's public announcement of his opposition to the Civil Constitution in March 1791. There were higher numbers of refusals of the oath among other sectors of the clergy: only seven of 136 bishops took the oath, for example. Four of these were deputies in the Constituent Assembly, whose clerical membership was split from top to bottom by the oath.

Despite the individualistic, anti-corporative twist of the oath, the clergy did not vote in isolation. On the contrary, it would seem that they were under often intense pressure from their social environment. Parishioners appear to have viewed the oath as a chance to express through their local priest their attitude towards the Revolution thus far. The Civil Constitution poll thus served as a proxy measure of Revolutionary adherence mapping out – but also accentuating – a geography of Revolutionary and anti-revolutionary sentiment. The geography of resistance covered most of the west and much of the north-west of France, eastern France from the Vosges through Alsace to Picardy, and the southern fringe of the Massif Central. The strongholds of Revolutionism were more diffuse: the Paris basin, the Alpine region from Lyon to Nice, and a broad central swathe bounded in the north and north-east by Picardy, Champagne and Lorraine, and by Guyenne and the Massif Central in the south. A wide and complex range of factors influenced the clergy's choice on the matter, but it is noticeable that in many juring areas, the idea of the 'citizen-priest' had been current before 1789, and their *cahiers* had endorsed part of the programme of the Civil Constitution. There is an interesting correlation too between refractory areas and those non-French-speaking areas of western and south-western France which had been most antagonistic to centralization in the sixteenth and seventeenth centuries.

The Civil Constitution of the Clergy opened up a running sore at the heart of the polity which would suppurate throughout the 1790s, sapping the strength of the new regime. It dramatized the conflict between civic and corporative versions of the polity. And it sketched out a political geography rooted in the new Revolutionary culture which would be incredibly perdurable: non-juring areas in 1791 correspond closely to the strongholds of the Right in French politics down to the eve of the twenty-first century. The Assembly's handling of the issue only, moreover, comforted the king in his vacillatory and duplicitous stance towards the Revolution. He harkened to the pope's strictures, observed the negative attitude of the upper clergy whom he most respected and came to regard the constitutional clergy as heretical. From December 1790, moreover, he could see the Civil Constitution oath becoming the source of internecine conflicts in numerous regions: in refractory regions, the expulsion of non-jurors and their replacement by constitutional clerics triggered riots, threats to life, civil disobedience and other expressions of popular ill-will. In localities such as Paris, where a strong majority had taken the oath, the refractory minority was subject to vicious scapegoating: nuns from the Paris Hôtel-Dieu, for example, were subject to humiliating public spankings.

Louis's attitude towards the Assembly's religious policy exacerbated political divisions, especially when combined with his equivocal attitude towards the emigrated princes and nobility. It was soon generally known that the king preferred the refractory to the constitutional clergy for his own spiritual needs, and the view developed that he was biding his time to escape from Paris and raise the standard of revolt either in the provinces or from abroad. Fearing that the king's rupture from the Revolutionary cause would trigger civil war, the 'Triumvirate', the most influential political grouping in the Constituent Assembly in early 1791, put out secret feelers to the court and sought to placate the monarch by adopting more conservative policies. They got the Assembly to agree to the practice of public worship by refractory priests; to forbid collective petitioning in an effort to reduce the influence of anti-clerical and anti-monarchical political clubs; and to pass the Le Chapelier Law of 14 June against workers' associations. 'What we call the Revolution', 'Triumvir' Adrien Duport announced in the Assembly on 17 May, 'is over'.[69]

Initially at least, however, the Triumvirs failed to palliate the king or to dissipate a growing jitteriness in political life. In February, the emigration of the king's aged aunts, Adelaide and Victoire, to join Artois in Turin, had triggered a tremendous furore which was worsened by an imbroglio (the *'chevaliers du poignard'* ('knights of the dagger') affair) on 28 February in which a gang of young royalist noblemen were alleged to be plotting to kidnap the king. At Easter that year, matters worsened. On the Monday before Easter Day, 18 April, the king prepared to leave Paris for the royal palace at Saint-Cloud, where he planned to perform his Easter duties at the hands of a non-juror. Was this a cover so as to avoid having to receive communion from a Constitutional priest? Or was it, more darkly still, a pretext for royal flight? As his coach prepared to leave the Tuileries, Louis found his way blocked by hostile Parisian crowds and by National Guardsmen under a highly embarrassed Lafayette.

By confirming Louis in his feeling that he would remain effectively a political prisoner as long as he stayed in Paris, the Saint-Cloud incident determined the king to quit the capital. Secret preparations were made through Marie-Antoinette's knight errant, Fersen, and on 21 June 1791 Parisians awoke to discover the royal bird had flown, taking his family with him. Louis left behind him an open letter in which his petty rancours and inward resentments at all he had had to endure since 1789 were chronicled in graphic detail. The document also mapped out a programme of reform which reconnected with his views set out in the *séance royale* of 23 June 1789, that *nec plus ultra* of Bourbon reformism. It seemed, however, less a negotiating document than a piqued expression of royal wilfulness emanating from a political culture which had had its day. The king's declaration was made to look all the more inept, moreover, by the fact that the royal bird proved unable to quit its cage. Louis's aim seems to have been to effect a junction in eastern France with the royalist commander Bouillé, who would take over the fortress at Montmédy near the frontier. From there, it was planned that the king would negotiate constitutional change with the Assembly. But the king was not a great one for midnight swashbuckling or indeed for travel – he had only once been out of the Île-de-France in his entire life (to Cherbourg in 1786) – and the royal party lumbered along at a leisurely pace blithely assuming that the (pathetically transparent) disguise that they had adopted proofed them against discovery. However, Jean-Baptiste Drouet, humble postmaster of Saint-Ménéhould near Verdun, spied the king out, identifying the royal profile from a fifty-livre *assignat* he happened to have in his pocket. The bungling entourage was stopped at Varennes before it had achieved its objective.

An explosive situation which could well have lurched towards republicanism and civil war was stopped on the brink by 'Triumvir' Barnave. The latter was despatched to Varennes to collect the royal entourage and bring them back to Paris, and en route he brokered a deal with the king and (it was said) the queen. He held up to the pathetic monarch the prospect of his deposal and ensuing civil war in France as a spectre to frighten him into a more positive stance towards the Revolution. A line was agreed whereby the king would allow it to be known that he had been 'abducted' by counter-revolutionaries. In his journey through France he had come to understand that 'public opinion had decided in favour of the constitution', and he now wished to bow to 'the general will'.[70]

If Barnave had the king on side, it still remained to assemble a kind of party of order in the Assembly and secure a majority for the transparent 'kidnapping' fiction. Here the Triumvirs were helped by the utter disarray of the aristocratic faction, and by the sabre-rattling of the *émigrés*. Artois had moved his head-quarters to Coblentz, and his brother Provence joined him there following his successful escape from Paris (via Brussels) on 20 June. The flight to Varennes caused profound disillusionment amongst the noble-dominated army officer corps: in the following weeks, around half of them – some 6,000 men – left the service, some to join their *émigré* colleagues. For on the Rhine, Condé and Mirabeau-'Tonneau' had formed *émigré* legions at Worms ready for an invasion, and were stepping up pressure on Europe's crowned heads to join a counter-revolutionary crusade. These developments sent anxiety levels within France sky-rocketing. News of the king's flight had provoked a mini 'Great Fear' in many regions, leading on to pre-emptive mobilizations against feared military invasions and vengeful attacks on local aristocrats and non-juring priests. In Paris, while the Jacobins agonized, the Cordeliers and Parisian fraternal societies began to agitate noisily for the deposing of the king.

Paradoxically, the surge of popular anti-royalism served Barnave's intentions very well. He used the spectre of popular anarchy and civil and foreign war as a means of frightening his fellow deputies into accepting the Varennes fiction. 'One step further towards liberty must destroy the monarchy,' Barnave fulminated, 'one more step towards equality is an assault on private property.'[71] The deputies bought the package, formally stating on 16 July that the person of the monarch was inviolable, that Louis had indeed been 'abducted' on 20 June by Bouillé and that he should be reinstated as reigning monarch – but only when he had formally accepted the Constitution. The king now played his part in the drama, working assiduously with the Assembly over the summer on the Constitutional Act. He formally accepted this on 13–14 September, also agreeing for good measure to urge his brothers to return to France, and to oblige all émigrés to pay a triple tax load if they stayed abroad.

To be fully effective, however, the post-Varennes settlement still required the progress of popular republican sentiment to be stopped in its tracks – which duly occurred, in mid-July. Barnave's party of order seemed to be winning the arguments over the republicans in middle-class opinion, which preferred Barnave's recipe of 'finishing' the Revolution to the idea of initiating a second, more radical Revolution. The Cordeliers and the other Parisian popular societies were, however, still orchestrating republican demonstrations and petitions in mid-July. As a result of the kind of misunderstanding which occurs when both sides to a dispute are fearing the worst from the other, a mass republican demonstration on the Champ de Mars on 17 July led to the proclamation of martial law by mayor Bailly, and the crowd was fired on by Lafayette's National Guard, causing extensive casualties. A crack-down on political radicals ensued, entailing the infringement or limitation of forms of individual freedom hitherto taken as read. There was police harassment and imprisonment of popular militants, suppression of newspapers, the hounding of individual radicals such as Marat, Danton, Desmoulins and Hébert and new laws on seditious meetings and political associations. Barnave led the majority of moderate Jacobins out of the Paris club, forming a new Feuillant club which sought to rally the national Jacobin network behind Triumvirate policies.

Barnave carried the day – in the short run at least. Political republicanism had been checked; a majority was spatchcocked together in the Assembly to agree to the reincorporation of Louis XVI into the political nation; and the king himself was blackmailed into acceptance of the new constitution, to take effect from 1 October, when the members of the Constituent Assembly would retire from the fray and be replaced by a new legislature, the Legislative Assembly. The Constituent Assembly could congratulate itself on having achieved a colossally impressive work of political architecture. Gone for ever, however, was that 'great and wonderful majority of the early days' evoked nostalgically by deputy Camus as the deputies prepared to go home.[72] Political harmony had been maintained sufficiently to avoid major bloodshed of the kind predicted by George Washington in 1789. Yet the Assembly had far from demolished the dangerous relics of the Bourbon polity, which retained the active power to threaten everything which had been achieved. *Émigré* sabre-rattling would be the white noise against which the Revolutionary process would unfold through the 1790s.

The new Assembly would, moreover, bring new men into the political spotlight to face these difficult challenges. On 16 May – prior to the Varennes affair – 'Incorruptible' Robespierre had managed to persuade his fellow deputies to pass a self-denying ordinance whereby they excluded themselves from standing for election to the Legislative Assembly. The new men's efforts to patch up the broken unity of 1791 without major bloodshed would prove ineffectual. The Champ de Mars massacre would seem a veritable picnic in comparison with what would follow over the coming years. The deputies of the Constituent Assembly themselves would pay their pound of flesh: by the end of the decade nearly one in ten of them had been executed or murdered, one in five of the commoners spent time in gaol, and around a quarter sought the road to emigration. The initial architects of the Revolutionary nation would suffer copiously at the hands of their creation.

10

War and Terror
(1791–5)

A) *AUX ARMES, CITOYENS!*

'This assembly', Marie-Antoinette secretly confided to her beloved Fersen, '. . . is a gathering of scoundrels, madmen and fools.'[1] The queen's trenchant view of the Legislative Assembly, which met for the first time on 1 October 1791, augured ill for the spirit of conciliation which Barnave had enjoined upon the royal couple since Varennes. The summer elections under the property franchise of the new constitution (the latter a mere 'tissue of absurdities', as far as the queen could see)[2] had produced a kind of Second Coming of the Third Estate. Among the 745 new deputies, there were only a score of nobles, none of whom owned to flagrantly counter-revolutionary views and indeed most of whom the queen would regard as class renegades, like the *philosophe* marquis, Condorcet. There were precious few patrician prelates either – the only bishops among the twenty or so clerics elected were constitutional ones like former Cercle Social activist Fauchet. On the whole, the new delegation was young – but unflashily solid. 'New to glory', as Necker sourly remarked,[3] most were lawyers and middle-rank professionals, who owed their election to service in the lawcourts and bureaucracy of the new state. These men were the Revolution's children, beyond deference, versed in constitutionality, trained in Revolutionary rhetoric and committed to an ideal of social improvement formulated in the Enlightenment. Elected during the summer of Varennes, they cherished few illusions about the king – a fact which revived Orléans's dynastic hopes (though not for long). They took some time to get the hang of Parisian politics – 136 of them joined the famed Jacobin Club on arriving in Paris, but most left for the Feuillants when they were apprised of the post-Varennes split, leaving only around fifty hard-core Jacobins.

From the very start, foreign policy, which had hardly appeared on the radar of their predecessor, was at the heart of the preoccupations of the new deputies. The Constituent Assembly had tried to keep its nose clean in international company, deliberating on 22 May 1791 that the French nation renounced dynastic wars of conquest on the Ancien Régime model. But it was unable to avoid the need for careful, technically adept diplomacy required as a result of Avignon's quest for annexation into France and of the wish of German princes who had feudal and seigneurial rights within French frontiers to be exempted from their abolition on the Night of 4 August. It was less these inherited issues which dominated the minds of the new assembly, however, than the perceived threat to national security caused by the *émigrés*, who had set about winning military support for their cause from foreign powers. Following Varennes, the Austrian Emperor had wanted to show support for his sister and brother-in-law and agreed to the so-called Pillnitz Convention of 27 August, whereby he joined with Frederick William II of Prussia to threaten intervention in France if the royal family were harmed. The proviso which he attached – combined action on the part of the powers – in fact made the threat hollow, for it was evident that England would not commit to adventurism. Furthermore, the eastern states – Austria, Prussia and Russia – were more concerned with affairs in Poland, which they would partition between them in 1793 and 1795. Yet though Pillnitz was little more than a sop to the sensibilities of Marie-Antoinette and the *émigrés*, it fostered serious alarm and anxiety within France.

There was a similar discrepancy between reality and appearance as regards the *émigrés* themselves. As those who joined the *émigré* armies later attested, the forces – though some 20,000 strong at one time over the summer – were a pathetic assemblage. Chateaubriand, with nostalgic tenderness, later recalled them as 'a feudal levy . . . last image of a dying world', 'going back to their roots, and the roots of the monarchy . . . like an old man regressing to his childhood'.[4] Many *émigrés* vengefully planned the integral restoration of an Ancien Régime which had bestowed abundant privileges upon them, but many also served out of a sense of chivalric honour, suffering unlooked-for campaign hardships while their very identity was being effaced in their homeland. They were, moreover, poorly equipped and cared for by counter-revolutionary headquarters in Coblentz. Chateaubriand claimed he went through the entire 1792 campaign with a musket which was inoperable. The prince de Condé's equerry recounted that his fellow nobles served with 'patience, courage and gaiety', even though they had no sheets and half slept in their shirts and the other half in straw.[5]

The disproportionate anxiety which these raggle-taggle *émigré* forces caused within France derived as much from the links which they were held to have with secret counter-revolutionary networks throughout France as from their supposed military strength and diplomatic connections. The clandestine plotting of the comte d'Antraigues in the Midi and the web of royalist committees which the marquis de La Rouërie was discovered to have established throughout western France in 1791–2 tautened the Revolutionaries' sinews. The *émigrés* were also believed to be working in league with the refractory clergy – an association which did neither party any favours. Cardinal Rohan, of Diamond Necklace fame, and other ecclesiastics sat on Artois's council; refractories on the eastern frontier were said to be recruiting for Coblentz; while in the western Maine-et-Loire and Vendée departments, violence against the Constitutional clergy was becoming so fierce that there seemed a real risk of civil war and counter-revolution.

The new Assembly's response to this threat was to toughen its stance on the refractory clergy and to issue punitive legislation against the *émigrés*. On 14 October 1791, the king responded to the groundswell of opinion by formally inviting his brother, the comte de Provence, to return to France – and this was followed up on 31 October by an Assembly decree which stripped the count of his succession rights if he had not returned by the end of the year. A further decree of 9 November declared that *émigrés* who did not return to their homeland would be adjudged conspirators, subject to the death penalty and threatened with state sequestration of their property. The Assembly seemed to have no qualms about using the supposedly indefeasible rights of the individual for purposes of political leverage. For in a related move, on 29 November, the deputies declared that any refractory priest who did not come forward within a week to take the civic oath would be held to be a political suspect, placed under surveillance and, at his fellow citizens' request, exiled from his home. On the same day, the Assembly requested the rulers of Mainz and Trier to disperse the *émigré* formations within their territories.

The king's attitude towards these developments was characteristically sphinx-like. He was not as antagonistic to the new constitution as was

451

his wife: he told Navy Minister Bertrand de Molleville that he thought it flawed but would observe it in the hope that its defects would become so apparent that constitutional reform would ensue. Yet even though he dreaded becoming overly dependent on the *émigrés* for release from his Babylonian captivity, he still seems to have been hankering for a noble-dominated constitutional arrangement in which returned and reintegrated *émigrés* would have a leading part to play. He also felt that ties of kinship and loyalty barred him from acceding to the Assembly's punitive legislation against the *émigrés* and the refractory clergy, and he consequently imposed his veto.

The political temperature in a rapidly polarizing situation was raised by the deteriorating economic situation and by related financial problems which the state was facing. The 1791 harvest was poor, causing food prices to start rising by the turn of the year. Many localities in northern France experienced subsistence riots, which culminated in the murder of mayor Simmoneau of Étampes, just south of Paris, in early March 1792, for failing to agree to the fixing of bread prices. The capital itself was rocked by food riots in January and February 1792 over shortages of sugar (by now a staple of popular diet). This particular deficiency was caused by a deteriorating situation in the Caribbean colonies: after sporadic troubles earlier in the year, a full-scale slave revolt had begun in Saint-Domingue in August 1791, causing plantation production and profits to plummet. The consequences of crisis in colonial trade, which had been the most profitable sector of the eighteenth-century economy, were worsened by the slump in luxury trades caused by the emigration of wealthy noble plutocrats. The plight of workers thrown into unemployment by these changes was made all the more poignant by the erosion of poor relief provision. Many charitable institutions, including hospitals, monasteries and nursing communities, had lost out in the Night of 4 August, notably from the abolition of municipal tolls, and also as a consequence of related attacks on ecclesiastical privilege. Voluntary giving, which the church had always encouraged among the laity, seemed to dry up, worsening matters. The Constituent Assembly's Mendicity Committee sketched out a kind of embryonic welfare state which aimed to shift responsibility for relief of poverty away from the church – but the plans remained unimplemented. Short-term government credits and poorly funded charity workshops were insufficient to cope with the scale of the problems unfolding.

The agrarian sector of the economy was also experiencing problems. The implementation of the 'abolition' of feudalism in a way which secured respect for landed property was raising peasant hackles, and there were violent anti-seigneurial disturbances in early 1792 across the Midi in particular which took on an overtly political edge. 'We have no seigneur,' one peasant petition to the Assembly stated pointedly. 'He is in Coblentz.'[6] Peasant scepticism about the gains promised by the Revolution showed up with brutal clarity in the countryside's refusal to garner taxes following the introduction in 1791–2 of the new post-*taille* unitary direct tax, the *contribution foncière*. Fraud, non-payment, evasion and administrative confusion produced a national tax take nearly a quarter less than forecast. Reduced confidence in the credit of government in turn affected the success of the state-backed *assignat*, whose use as a paper money had driven much coinage off the marketplace. The *assignat* had traded at around 90 per cent of its face value in March 1791, but the political crisis, the state's continuing financial problems and the threat of counter-revolution caused its value to plummet. By the autumn, paper currency was at around 80 per cent of its face value, and by March 1792, around 50 per cent. In the Assembly in that month, the Jacobin Thuriot blamed popular disturbances on brigands in the pay of the likes of Bouillé, the villain of Varennes. Citing 'a great and determined conspiracy', he went on to blame the *émigrés* for speculating on currency and exporting coinage into Germany so that the country could not afford to pay for the grain imports essential for social harmony.[7]

The lineaments of the economic trajectory of the 1790s were already clearly discernible by late 1791 and early 1792: decay in the booming sectors of the pre-1789 economy; the government perennially harassed by shortage of money, which even the sale of church lands was unable to remedy; the running sore of a paper currency miserably failing to command public support; and a concomitant collapse of business confidence. Also apparent was a further factor which was both consequence of this sorry economic situation, and cause of its aggravation: namely, the growing articulacy of popular protest. Symptomatic in this respect were not only provincial subsistence and anti-seigneurial riots, but also popular protest within Paris. The radical Parisian press and the Cordeliers and popular societies scored a signal success, when in November 1791, their man, Pétion, formerly a radical deputy in the Constituent Assembly, defeated Lafayette in the contest to succeed Bailly (the other villain of the Champ de Mars massacre) as mayor of Paris. Lafayette's defeat tolled the knell for the influence of the 'Americans' on Revolutionary politics. More significant now was the voice of extra-parliamentary radicalism in the capital, which was clearly growing well-organized as well as articulate. Parisian popular pressure had contributed to the king's sense of being kept a prisoner in the city after October 1789. By early 1792, many deputies were also starting to feel a sense of entrapment, with popular militants pleading eloquently from the bar of the house, reacting noisily from the public galleries, from street-corners and every imaginable site of sociability, and also contributing to debates in print.

A distinctive culture of protest was emerging from the pullulating extra-parliamentary activities of the capital. Newspapers and clubs spoke of popular militants as *sans-culottes* ('no breeches') – signifying that they wore straight workmen's trousers rather than the knee-breeches which denoted gentility. This sparked a trend of political 'dressing down' which had its own vestimentary rules. One necessary fashion item for the dutiful *sans-culotte*, for example, was the red cap (*bonnet rouge*), which was alleged to recall the cap worn in Antiquity by emancipated slaves. The Paris publisher Ruault thought the mode – which was invariably accompanied by the sporting of a tricolour cockade – 'the height of vulgarity' and 'totally unnecessary'. Yet he noted how it spread like wildfire in late March 1792 – 'in the streets, in the squares, in the gardens and even at the theatre', so that it seemed destined to become 'the obligatory headgear of all French patriots'.[8] The language of patriotism now took on a rough demotic tone too in the burgeoning press associated with the popular movement. Prominent here was the *Père Duchesne*, eponymous newspaper of Jacques-René Hébert, whose brutally frank columns (to some extent modelled on scurrilous counter-revolutionary journalism) were littered with banteringly aggressive *bougres* and *foutres*. The swearwords were supposed to give *sans-culotte* language a raw plebeian authenticity – though readers probably found them more redolent of music-hall versions of popular speech. This playfulness was also evident in the poor typography and faded newsprint of such publications, which were specially 'roughed up' for their audience's delectation.

In a context in which the solutions to internal problems seemed to be situated outside French frontiers, Louis, more duplicitous by the hour, welcomed the prospect of a war in Europe. In a secret communication to the king of Prussia in early December 1791 he called for an alliance of the European powers, backed up by armed force, as a means of rectifying his sorry position. Yet as if to offset the impact of his use of the veto on anti-*émigré* legislation, he also made ever more forceful pronouncements against the Electors of Mainz and Trier, who were harbouring *émigré* formations. He made an enormous fuss of telling the German princelings to disperse the *émigrés* – whilst secretly intimating to Holy Roman Emperor Leopold II that he wished the opposite to happen. When the Electors did make a show of doing as requested, the king upped the ante by publicly demanding that the Emperor renounce any treaties which threatened French sovereignty – by which he meant the Pillnitz declaration of August 1791. 'The whole nation,' noted US envoy Gouverneur Morris in February 1792, 'though with different views, are desirous of war.'[9] An aggressive foreign policy was an issue on which king and Assembly – beset by external threat and internal turbulence – could unite, and deputies blissfully welcomed the king's apparent conversion to defence of the Revolution's interests, little suspecting his double game. The queen thought this drift to war full of black humour: 'the idiots don't see that it will help our cause,' she told Fersen, 'because . . . all the powers will have to become involved'.[10]

Bellicose sabre-rattling was the stock-in-trade of a grouping of deputies, revolving around Jacques-Paul Brissot, who seized the political initiative from the Feuillants in the early days of the Legislative Assembly. A journalist, hack writer and political campaigner who had founded the abolitionist *Amis des Noirs* (and who may well have turned his hand to spying for the Paris police when times were hard in the 1780s), Brissot developed a nexus of activists in Parisian municipal politics in 1790. This included many individuals in Fauchet's Cercle social plus the former factory inspector, Roland, whose wife, Manon Phlipon, ran a political salon for the group. In the Legislative Assembly, the Brissot grouping found soul-mates in delegates for the department of the Gironde, notably Vergniaud, Guadet, Gensonné and Grangeneuve. In an ensemble of electrifying performances within the Assembly, often replicated in the Jacobin Club, which they came to dominate, the Brissotins (or Girondins) argued for war with such persuasive force that the air was endlessly rent by cries of '*aux armes!*' ('To arms!'). War, it was claimed, would end the armed threat to the Revolution personified by the *émigrés* and would deter European powers from ill-considered adventurism. At home, it would clarify and hopefully tranquillize the political landscape by forcing waverers to declare for or against the Revolution, by bringing illicit counter-revolutionary activity into the open, and by making the king to quit havering and to join the Revolutionary ranks. The rhetoric not uncommonly got out of hand and the Brissotins went on to imagine a ring of sympathetic buffer states insulating France from Ancien Régime Europe, and they called for a crusade to spread Revolutionary principles throughout the world, to unshackle humanity from its feudal yoke. Robespierre was a biting critic of the latter argument, and strove to demonstrate that the logic of 1789 did not lead on ineluctably to violent aggression. Nobody, he reminded members of the Jacobin Club, likes 'armed missionaries'.[11] He suspected that the Brissotin calls for war were merely a platform for their own political elevation. Since war would also, he held, increase rather then diminish the powers of the executive over the legislature, it was more a threat to the Revolution than a promise of its consummation.

Robespierre, however, lost the debate, and the war issue developed into a roller-coaster which brooked no counter-argument. The Feuillant position upheld by ex-Triumvir Barnave was by now utterly outflanked. Barnave, who since Varennes had been acting as the royal family's secret adviser, was increasingly dismayed at the way in which his counsels were ignored, and he retired from politics in disgust in early 1792, thus removing an ideological brake on the gadarene rush into war. The Feuillants had soon lost the initiative in the Assembly too: their Paris headquarters failed to tempt the majority of provincial Jacobin clubs into their ranks, while many new recruits began to migrate either into the more Brissotin Jacobin Club, or towards the equally pro-war centrist faction headed by the ambitious Lafayette. The Brissotin cause received royal endorsement in early March 1792, when the king dismissed his Feuillant-oriented ministers and replaced them with a so-called 'Patriot Ministry' stuffed with Brissot's friends, including Roland as Interior Minister, former anti-Calonne speculator Clavière in Finance and the veteran soldier Dumouriez in the War Department. On 25 March, Louis came to the Assembly to issue a further ultimatum to Holy Roman Emperor Leopold II's successor, Francis II. On 20 April, he returned to declare that, because his ultimatum had been ignored, he regarded France as in a state of war with 'the king of Bohemia and Hungary'.[12] Only seven obscure deputies dared vote against a declaration of war which seemed to unify public opinion in a mood of revolutionary patriotism mixed with traditional Austrophobia. From Coblentz, Provence declared himself quite 'delighted' with the decision: the Revolutionaries seemed to be doing the *émigrés'* job for them.[13]

The Legislative Assembly had embraced the cause of war as a political convenience, an exit route out of the bafflingly intricate domestic situation in which the deputies found themselves. Most deputies imagined that they were embarking on a war of relatively restricted aims. History was to give them the lie. The next quarter of a century – with a few aberrant years of peace – would see France perpetually at war with Europe, with a total domestic casualty list which would amount to over a million and a half individuals. Despite the very many brilliant successes which France enjoyed and which inflated France's self-image as a great nation, and the role that war played in the formation of French national spirit, the state at the end of the period would have made no acquisitions beyond those of its 1792 borders. It would also have lost the colonial empire which had been the motor of its eighteenth-century wealth. War would also bear a heavy responsibility, as we shall see, for denaturing the Revolutionary process, dividing the nation, delegitimizing political opposition and, down to 1795, stimulating the frenetic crescendo of Terror.

The wisdom of hindsight was not, of course, on offer to those deputies making the momentous decision of 20 April 1792. And the momentous war began with sundry whimpers rather than a single bang. Lafayette, Rochambeau and Luckner, the three army commanders – all 'Americans' – soon realized that the men under them needed careful handling. The emigration of nearly half the officer corps, and the influx of over 100,000 enthusiastic volunteers, posed severe problems of military cohesion. Even those officers who remained in the force were suspect to the rank and file: as early as 29 April, for example, following an unsuccessful skirmish near Valenciennes, General Dillon was murdered by his own men. The state of military administration seemed appalling: 'I cannot imagine', Lafayette wrote to the War Office, 'how war could have been declared in such a state of unreadiness.'[14] Within a month, the three commanders were urging a truce – which scarcely seemed a viable political option. Continued fighting only produced reverses, engendering a growing sense of panic in Paris.

The king, who had placed himself at the head of a united nation on 20 April, proved chronically unable to maintain this posture. In the

Assembly, Brissot and Vergniaud launched bitter attacks on a putative 'Austrian committee' at court headed by Marie-Antoinette (who was, indeed, secretly passing classified military intelligence to her family in Austria). On 8 June, a proposed encampment near to Paris of some 20,000 provincial National Guardsmen (the so-called *fédérés*) was decreed, with the aim of offering a measure of protection to the capital if the enemy broke through the front. The king, however, vetoed the measure on 18 June. When the going got tough, the king got tender towards 'his' aristocratic servants and the refractory clergy, and he added further vetoes to a law of 27 May on the forced deportation of refractory priests and one on 29 May on a measure disbanding royal bodyguard troops. He dismissed the 'Patriot Ministry' in June, appointing in their stead insignificant political figures who failed to secure the confidence of the Assembly. Lafayette's call from the front for the Assembly to suppress political clubs only worsened matters for the king, and on 20 June a popular demonstration over the use of the royal veto led on to an invasion of the Tuileries palace. Louis was made to don the red cap – as if even an erstwhile absolutist monarch needed to be emancipated from his own enslavement – and to drink the health of the nation in scenes which were only broken up by the National Guard after many hours of pressure.

This extraordinary occasion – despite which, Louis stuck by his vetoes – produced something of a pro-monarchist backlash, both in the Assembly and in the country more generally. More significant than expressions of sympathy, however, was the fact that the king was being increasingly excluded from the decision-making process. On 2 July, for example, the *camp des fédérés* was decreed in open defiance of the royal veto, and a couple of days later a law on *la patrie en danger* ('the fatherland in danger') was passed, stipulating that when this state of affairs was decreed legislative and administrative authorities would assume emergency powers. On 11 July, as Prussian forces prepared to invade, *la patrie en danger* was duly declared, allowing the royal veto to be bypassed in the cause of national security. Significantly, even at this very late stage, such was the continuing tug of court prestige, that a number of Girondin deputies led by Vergniaud entered into secret negotiations with the king to see if there was some way of resuscitating the 'Patriot Ministry'. The sorcerer's apprentices seemed to be having second thoughts about the demiurgic powers they had unleashed. There proved not to be the basis for negotiation, however, and indeed as the military situation worsened, it was not simply the king but also the whole Legislative Assembly which appeared to be increasingly out of the loop.

The republican air which Paris had voiced following the flight to Varennes was now replayed on the national scale – and fortissimo. On 23 July, a petition originating from a group of *fédérés* – National Guardsmen called up to defend Paris, attend the third *Fête de la Fédération* on 14 July, and then to proceed to the front – called for the removal of the king. Within days, a coordinating committee representing popular societies and activists started meeting in the Hôtel-de-Ville to plan the king's overthrow. On 3 August, a petition from forty-seven of Paris's forty-eight sections demanded the removal of Louis – but the Assembly, fearful of starting a civil war, temporized. The progress of the war contributed to the sense of crisis. In early August, news filtered through to Paris of the Brunswick Manifesto, in which the allied commander-in-chief, the duke of Brunswick, threatened with death any citizen opposing the allied advance, and fulminated exemplary violence against the city of Paris if the royal family was harmed. In June, Louis had specifically requested his fellow monarchs not to allow the conflict to become like war between states: 'such conduct', the king maintained, 'would provoke civil war, endanger the lives of the king and his family [and] mean the overthrow of the throne, cause the royalists to be slaughtered and throw support behind the Jacobins'.[15] The Brunswick Manifesto ignored the king's warning – and proved him right.

The 'Revolutionary day' – or *journée* – of 10 August 1792 by which Louis XVI was overthrown was a defeat for the Legislative Assembly as well as the king. The Assembly's failure to do more than dither at this critical moment massively damaged its prestige. On 8 August, it refused Brissot's call for Lafayette's impeachment. The overthrow had to be planned within the Parisian popular movement. On 9 August, Parisian radicals established an insurrectionary committee to plan armed action on the following day. Though grounded in Parisian popular radicalism, the king's overthrow was more than a Parisian achievement, for provincial *fédérés* played a major role in it, especially the fearsome Marseille battalion, whose arrival in late July had boosted the republican movement (to which it also bestowed a national hymn, the 'War Song of the Army of the Rhine' by Rouget de l'Isle, soon to be better known as the

'Marseillaise'). A popular insurrection on the day of the 10th, involving fierce fighting after the king's Swiss guards opened fire on the demonstrating crowds and ending in the horrors of the guards' outright massacre, saw the Assembly bowing to popular pressure and voting the king's removal. The deputies also decreed the establishment of a new national assembly, the Convention, to be elected by universal manhood franchise rather than by property franchise. It was entrusted with the task of drawing up a new – republican – constitution.

Power was now hopelessly fragmented. The association of the Legislative Assembly with the disgraced king damaged the authority of the deputies, who were unable to prevent other sources of authority exercising wide-ranging powers. A Provisional Executive Council of 'Patriot' ministers – whose most dynamic figure proved to be the radical Danton at the Justice Ministry – claimed executive powers, while the new insurrectionary Paris Commune, to whom Robespierre and other popular luminaries were now added, also exerted great moral authority as a result of its role on 10 August. All three power sources acted to bolster national resistance, sending out commissioners into the departments to purge local administration of royalists, arrest suspects and set up patriotic committees to pursue the war effort.

While elections took place in this crisis situation, the worsening war situation set a frenzied tempo for political life, sparking new, terrifying symptoms of collective stress. Moves were made to enfranchise, motivate and rush out to the front hordes of volunteers. Parisian sections were allowed to sit in permanent session, the division between active and passive citizens was dissolved, and all citizens were admitted to the National Guard. Under the emergency conditions, the royalist press was closed down, all state functionaries, including priests, were made to take an oath of loyalty, and decrees were passed limiting the scope of public worship and tightening sanctions against the refractory clergy. Emergency legislation ended all seigneurial dues without indemnity, confiscated émigré property in the name of the nation, and allowed requisitioning for grain. The punitive dimension to political regeneration reached a sickening finale following the arrival of news about the fall on 1 September of Verdun, the last fortress remaining between the advancing allied troops and the capital. From 2 September, stimulated by (utterly ill-founded) rumours of a prison plot by noble detainees to break out and form a fifth column in the heart of Paris, vigilante groups started to form in the Paris sections, and these proceeded to tour the Parisian prisons massacring detainees. Between 1,100 and 1,500 inmates were killed over the next couple of days, sometimes with the travesty of trial, sometimes in an ambience of pure carnage. To these were added scores more caught up in similar butchery in provincial cities. The vast majority of victims were common criminals, though the cull also accounted for a handful of politicians and courtiers (Foreign Ministers de Lessart and Montmorin, the princesse de Lamballe, etc.) and a good number of refractory priests.

The pitiless killing of the king's Swiss guards on 10 August and the prison massacres of 2–5 September proved a bloody baptism for Paris's political movement, which had profited from the vacuum left by the king to set its own agenda. This was not the first time that popular violence by Parisians had inflected the course of the Revolution. Yet the *journées* of 14 July and 5–6 October 1789 had been far more moderate in their violence and had essentially pulled the National Assembly's chestnuts from the fire. On 10 August 1792, in contrast, the people in arms attacked the Legislative Assembly as well as the king. No other such event thus far had split the ranks of the Revolutionaries so emphatically. A Parisian bourgeois strolling past the Carmes prison with his wife and two children while the prison massacres were taking place reacted complacently on hearing the screams of the victims: 'It's ineffably sad,' he told his wife, 'but they are implacable enemies, and those who are ridding the fatherland of them are saving your life and the lives of our poor children.'[16] Yet on 5 September, in contrast, Brissotin salonnière Madame Roland expressed her fear at being 'under the knife' of Robespierre (who winked at the violence), Danton (who as Justice Minister should have stopped it) and Marat (who luridly justified it). 'You know my enthusiasm for the Revolution,' she wrote to the deputy Bancal des Issarts, 'well, I am ashamed of it! Its reputation is tarnished by these scoundrels, it is becoming hideous . . .'[17]

One of the most difficult political issues of the French Revolution was shaping up. The sanguinary power politics of August and September were not incompatible with high moral principle. The 'scoundrels' believed themselves to be acting in disinterested and patriotic ways. And the very kinds of people who committed the acts of bloody terror were also responsible for saving the nation from crushing military defeat. Over 20,000 volunteers left Paris for the front in the fortnight after the

September massacres. On 20 September 1792 – the same day that the Legislative Assembly met for the last time – French volunteers and regulars combined to check the allied advance in the so-called 'cannonade of Valmy'. The German writer Goethe, present at the battle with the Prussian forces, reflected to his fellows, 'This is the beginning of a new epoch in history, and you can claim to have witnessed it.'[18] The Revolutionaries could show their teeth to the wider world, not simply bare them in internecine internal bloodbaths. The *buveur de sang* was also the super-patriotic citizen in arms.

B) LOUIS CAPET BOWS OUT, TERROR BOWS IN

The new National Convention which met for the first time on 20 September 1792, following national elections by what was pretty much universal male suffrage, scrambled together in late August and early September, had as its task the establishment of a new constitution for a kingless state. Like their immediate predecessors, the 749 Conventionnels constituted a solidly homogeneous body drawn from the middling sort: there were only a handful of peasants and artisans, and nearly a half of the body were lawyers, a further third were professionals (55 clergymen, for example, 51 state bureaucrats, 46 medical men, 36 army officers, and so on), and around 10 per cent were businessmen.

Almost as a kind of unconscious intellectual homage to both Montesquieu and Rousseau, who had doubted the viability of a republican regime in large states like France, even ardent Revolutionaries after 10 August had somehow found it difficult to cut the Gordian knot and pronounce the word 'republic'. On 20–21 September, however, on abbé Grégoire's motion, the Conventionnels steeled themselves to abolish the monarchy and establish a republic, which they dubbed 'one and indivisible' in order to signal their hostility to any divisive federal scheming. Constitutional arrangements for the new state were referred to a committee chaired by Condorcet. By December, even advocating the restoration of the monarchy was punishable by death. The king, now a prisoner in the domestic calm of his immediate family in the gothic Temple prison at the heart of Paris, would not, however, go gently into any good night of the Convention's imaginings. One of the Assembly's most pressing tasks was to decide what to do with the person of the ex-ruler, Louis 'Capet'.

This fundamental issue had to be confronted, moreover, against a political background which had been transformed in three important ways. First, at the front, French armies were finding it possible to win battles. Once the Prussians had – at Valmy – tested French mettle and found it resistant, they reduced their military commitment, leaving inferior allied forces facing mass armies of French volunteers, shrewdly commanded and bursting with patriotic enthusiasm. On 6 November, some 40,000 men under Dumouriez defeated 13,000 Austrian troops at Jemappes and strode on to occupy Brussels. At the same time, Custine occupied the left bank of the Rhine, taking Mainz and a number of other German cities, while Anselme invaded Nice and Savoy. The *émigré* forces were breaking up in maximum disarray: 'we are beginning to be weary of this war', one *émigré* wrote home. 'We have to fight frontline troops, none of whom deserts, national volunteers, and armed peasants who either fire on us or murder anyone they find alone.' The *émigré* leaders had promised 'more butter than bread' but they looked foolish now.[19]

Military success was both consequence and cause of a swelling of popular patriotism, which was the second new factor complicating French political life in late 1792. Political muddles, electoral complexities, royalist abstentions, the demands of harvesting and other local factors had meant that the elections to the Convention mobilized less than one voter in five across the land, and there was still – as we shall see – a solid groundswell of popular opposition to the Revolution. Yet the summer crisis of 1792 had also given a tremendous boost to an increasingly vocal popular movement in the big cities, spearheaded by Paris's *sans-culottes*, which articulated widespread enthusiasm for the gains of the Revolution. And the hordes of volunteers who made their way eagerly to the front to fight for those gains highlighted the energy and scale of popular enthusiasm. By late summer, around 200,000 men were under arms, and plans were afoot to bring another quarter of a million men to join the fray.

The third characteristic feature of the political scene in the autumn of 1792 was a new level of political divisiveness at the heart of the political class. From the very earliest of the Convention's sessions, daggers were drawn between the 'Girondins' (the old Brissotin grouping plus some newcomers such as Buzot and Carra) and 'Montagnards' ('Mountain-eers': left-wing Jacobin deputies clustering at the top of the steeply graduated amphitheatre benches within the Convention). The division – which unaligned deputies of 'the Plain' watched with appalled fascin-ation – owed nothing to the social provenance of the two groups, which were split pretty evenly amongst the main socio-professional groupings which composed the Assembly as a whole. Although under the Conven-tion the Girondins would be increasingly vilified by the radical move-ment as 'aristocrats' and 'royalists', in fact the social background and political career of many Girondins did not differ markedly from their radical opponents. A number, for example, had been activists in Cercle Social and Cordelier circles in 1790–91 – alongside subsequent sans-culotte and Montagnard militants. Although the Girondins had former nobles – or ci-devants – among their ranks, such as the marquis de Condorcet, the Montagnards included Philippe-Égalité ('Philip Equality'), as the duc d'Orléans now called himself, the marquis de Lepeletier de Saint-Fargeau and others.

At issue between Girondins and Montagnards were matters of history and personality more than social origins or even political philosophy. Particularly pertinent was the line of blood drawn by the *buveurs de sang* in the September Massacres. Brissot, Roland and the Girondin deputies were not willing to forgive or forget threats to their lives in that sombre episode, and they came into the Convention bearing personal grudges against those they held responsible for their discomfiture. Almost at once, they launched vicious attacks against arch-*buveur de sang* Marat, against Robespierre (whose dictatorial laying-down of the law to the Legislative Assembly at the head of the Insurrectionary Commune had caused resentment) and against Danton (now also accused of fiddling the books as Justice Minister). They also tried to relaunch plans to establish a guard of *fédérés* near Paris to protect the assembly against the violence of the Parisian popular militants, whose continued impunity for the September atrocities infuriated them.

The Montagnards reacted by driving the Girondins out of the Paris Jacobin Club and seeking to blacken their names on the national club network. Yet the Girondins fought back spiritedly. They began the Convention with their orators the most listened to by the Plain, and with their friends in ministerial positions (Roland remained at the Interior while Girondin allies Lebrun-Tondu and Pache took over

Foreign Affairs and War). In August, Interior Minister Roland was granted 100,000 livres to propagandize in the provinces, and his Bureau de l'esprit public utilized Girondin papers such as Bonneville's *Chronique du mois*, Louvet's *Sentinelle* and the *Bulletin des Amis de la Vérité* to partisan effect: the news-sheets poured calumny on the heads of deputies associated with the Parisian popular movement and presented a picture of a patriotic and politically responsible Girondin leadership in peril of destruction by Jacobins and *sans-culottes*.

The atmosphere of hate and recrimination between the two sides was all the more regrettable in that on the two main issues of the day – the future of the war and the fate of the king – Girondin and Montagnard attitudes were surprisingly close. From late 1791, the Brissotins had been the most forceful supporters of war policy, and in the Convention the Montagnards followed their lead, embracing the patriotic cause with brio. The edict of 19 November 1792 promising fraternal aid to all peoples struggling to regain their liberty seemed merely to be a tardy enactment of Brissot's 1791 calls for a crusade for universal liberty. Similarly, on 15 December a further decree stipulated that Revolutionary legislation and reforms should be introduced in occupied territories – a programme which extended to the nationalization of church lands, the abolition of tithes and feudal dues, and the introduction of taxes and *assignats*. Though there were (increasingly half-hearted) efforts to orchestrate local consent to these innovations, these paled into insignificance against an annexationist reflex common to Girondins and Montagnards alike. In January 1793, for example, it was the Girondins' *bête noire*, Danton, who launched the overheated proposal that French frontiers should be fixed at the 'natural frontiers' of the Alps, the Pyrenees and the Rhine. Savoy had been incorporated into France in November 1792, followed by Nice in January 1793 and then Monaco and a scattering of German and Belgian territories. From November 1792, the river Scheldt was opened up to French shipping, breaking international conventions affirmed at Utrecht in 1713.

There is no reason to doubt that the Girondins had become any more monarchist or any less patriotic than their fellow Conventionnels – indeed, they were as rhapsodic as anyone at the declaration of the Republic, and several were to go to the scaffold defiantly singing the 'Marseillaise'. Yet their handling of the trial of the king became ever more arcane, obstructive and opportunistic, and their intemperate attacks on their Montagnard opponents led many disinterested observers in the assembly to wonder whether they might not revert to pro-monarchism if only to spike the guns of Montagnards who were becoming increasingly inflamed with expansionist rhetoric: 'Rolland [sic] and Brissot's party', British secret agent Colonel George Munro confidently asserted, 'are certainly struggling to save the king in order to humble Robespierre's party.'[20]

In early November, the knotty legal and constitutional issue of the means of determining the fate of Louis Capet was resolved when the Convention agreed that it alone should try him. Almost at once, the removal of the king became less a symbol of national unity than an awkward political football. Interior Minister Roland attempted to seize the initiative for the Girondins by rushing to the Convention on 20 November to announce the discovery of compromising political documents in a secret iron wallsafe in the Tuileries palace (the so-called *armoire de fer*). The coup blew up in Roland's face: the Montagnards accused him of removing documents which compromised the Girondins, whose negotiations with the king in July 1792 were also coming to be known. The tone for the debates was set by the uncompromising Robespierre and his adoring young acolyte, Saint-Just, whose chilling maiden speech proposed the axiom that 'no king rules innocently': the acts of the *journée* of 10 August had found Louis guilty and it only remained for the Convention to exterminate the tyrannicidal Capet.[21]

The Girondins were not the only deputies to be frightened by such scary political geometry, as trial proceedings began on 11 December. Defended by his doughty ex-minister, Malesherbes, Louis managed a pathetic dignity. But he stood no chance. The *armoire de fer* had sealed his fate – less perhaps as a result of its contents (which were not systematically analysed) than because of its symbolic value as a duplicitous infraction of the cherished values of political transparency. Just as everything seemed to be moving to a straightforward conclusion, however, the Girondins threw in a tactical manoeuvre. Expressing fears that the king's execution might trigger civil war and inflame Europe against France, they began to argue that the Convention's decision needed to be ratified by the country at large in primary assemblies. The reasoning for such an *appel au peuple* looked specious to most deputies, and in the context of the poor electoral turnout of September 1792 it was easy to believe that it might even result in a reprieve which would itself lead on to massive civil turbulence.

In the event, even a number of the Girondins swung round against the *appel au peuple* – highlighting the extent to which it had been an anti-Montagnard tactical manoeuvre – and the Convention embraced what to many seemed a historic mission. On 14 January, the deputies voted, nem. con., the guilt of the king, and rejected by roughly a two-thirds majority the *appel au peuple*. Between 16 and 20 January, they came to the rostrum one by one to cast, and to justify, their vote before their peers and in full view of the lowering *sans-culottes* cramming the public galleries. In this hypercharged existential moment, the deputies confronted their own political careers and the real possibility of their own death as a consequence of their decision – for whoever prevailed, their lives were on the line. Some 387 deputies (including Philippe-Égalité) eventually decided for the king's death – as against 334 who made some other proposal (imprisonment, exile, etc.). A call for a reprieve was definitively rejected by 380 votes to 310. The king's execution was carried out with great pomp and circumstance on 21 January 1793. A new line of blood had been traced at the heart of the Revolution: on one side stood the Montagnards, the regicidal deputies and the Parisian popular movement; on the other were not merely the forces of monarchical reaction but also the Girondin deputies and their supporters in the Convention and in the country at large.

The trial of Louis Capet had presented the unedifying spectacle of fellow republicans falling out for reasons of comparative political advantage. Matters did not end there. The spring of 1793 saw the exacerbation of political division under the pressure of three developments which, in different but obliquely interlocked ways, threatened the viability of the new Republic: war, counter-revolutionary civil turbulence and economic distress.

Post-Valmy military success had flattered only to deceive. Seeming to believe its own rhetoric, the Convention felt confident enough to extend the European conflict, declaring war against England and Holland on 1 February and Spain on 7 March 1793; by the autumn most of the rest of Europe was drawn into the conflict. Yet the army needed serious attention, many of the patriotic volunteers of summer 1792 having chosen to return to their homes over the winter. Dumouriez's advance into Holland was checked by an Austrian counter-attack, and defeat at

Neerwinden on 18 March led to the evacuation of Holland and Belgium. Things went badly on the eastern front too, where Custine lost control of the Rhineland to the duke of Brunswick, who besieged the French in Mainz. Lafayette-style, Dumouriez attempted a political coup, seeking to lead his army on Paris, with the aim of crushing the Jacobins and reinstituting the 1791 constitution. His army refused to follow his lead, however, and, after handing over to the enemy the four Conventionnels sent to arrest him, the errant general rode over to Austrian lines, with republican bullets whistling around his ears, taking with him Orléans's son, the duc de Chartres (the future king Louis-Philippe).

Betrayal was on everyone's lips. The plot mentality which had characterized the course of Revolutionary history back to the summer of the Great Fear of 1789 was, moreover, finding new – domestic – targets. The demands of external war had helped to catalyse a movement of resistance across the land which in the west developed into outright counter-revolution. To compensate for gaps in the ranks caused by returning volunteers, the Convention on 21 February issued the 'decree of 300,000 men', which envisaged the recruitment of these massive numbers by means left to the devices of local authorities. A measure which recalled the hated militia recruitment of the pre-revolutionary days was certain to be unpopular, and it sparked nationwide protests. In western France, moreover, from 11 March onwards, protest metamorphosed into thunderous waves of civil disobedience: attacks on National Guardsmen, republican mayors and Constitutional clergy and, above all, outright refusal to join the armed forces.

It was church rather than king which mobilized the rebels. Silence, possibly indifference, had greeted the edict which the comte de Provence issued on 28 January, a week after his brother's guillotining: whilst recognizing the young, imprisoned son Louis XVII as the rightful monarch, Provence assumed power himself as a regent and promised a return to the status quo ante 1789, and exemplary punishment for crimes committed since then. The rebellious western areas did not want an en bloc restoration of the Ancien Régime: they had fêted rather than lamented the passing of seigneurialism, and shrugged off the execution of their monarch. Yet the religious issue had really got under their skin. The missionary zeal of the Counter-Reformation in these regions had left deep marks on the mentalities of the peasantry, who had placed their clergymen under intense pressure to reject the Civil Constitution in

1791: Normandy, Brittany, Maine, Anjou and lower Poitou had been among the most solidly refractory zones over the oath issue, and these regions had seen a great deal of religious turbulence since then, including much 'juror-baiting'. The demand in early 1793 that local populations should send off cohorts to fight for a Revolution whose basic precepts were far from universally accepted led to the tocsin being sounded for counter-revolutionary action. This produced the complete collapse of government in a wide swathe of territory which became known as the 'military Vendée' – the area south of the river Loire to roughly the level of Fontenay-le-Comte, and covering parts of the departments of Maine-et-Loire, Loire-Inférieure and Deux-Sèvres as well as the Vendée.

This spontaneous peasant uprising soon produced levels of stomach-churning atrocity which stood comparison with the Parisian September massacres. The rebels liquidated republican officials in their takeover of towns such as Cholet and Machecoul (in which locality some 500 supporters of the Republic were coldly butchered). The initial leaders of the revolt, which grew daily in numbers and military sophistication, were drawn from humble social backgrounds – Cathelineau was a weaver, for example, Stofflet a gamekeeper. Though some of the region's most outstanding nobles had emigrated, there was a plethora of petty *hobereaux* whom it subsequently proved possible to draw in. Prominent amongst these was the comte de La Rochejacquelein, a former royal body-guard, who was appointed generalissimo of a 'Royal Catholic Army', which developed its own command structure, provisioning infrastructure, and insignia (prominent among which was the sacred heart) and which even issued *assignats* bearing the image of the infant Louis XVII.

The specifically royalist element in the Vendée revolt thus came in late. It owed nothing at all to *émigré* leaders, moreover, whose slowness to react to the counter-revolutionary potential revealed in the Vendée sprang from their conviction (shared by the British) that war was best conducted in classically conventional military style, and not by indisciplined hordes of pitchfork-wielding peasants. The latter, however, were able to exploit the relative depletion of republican troops in the interior as a result of the military crisis at the front to score signal early successes over raw National Guardsmen. The rebels seized Thouars on 5 May, before going on to take Parthenay and Fontenay later in the month.

Countenancing both a downturn in military fortunes at the front and the emergence of an obdurate zone of rebellion in the west, the

Convention also found itself in the midst of economic difficulties which mobilized Paris and caused widespread discontent throughout the land. The Civil Constitution and military recruitment issues exacerbated more generalized discontent about the economic impact of the Revolution. Though the scale of reforms since 1789 had been substantial, many French men and women were distinctly underwhelmed by the Revolution's palpable effects on their conditions of life. Tax relief had been slight; it had needed direct action from below to get successive national assemblies to liquidate seigneurialism; and in areas of widespread tenant-farming like the west the population was probably 30 per cent worse off in 1793 than in 1789. In addition, the new political class of townsmen had extended their influence and control over rural areas, notably by purchasing church lands, and they maintained their grip through town-based National Guards. The Revolutionary assemblies also proved unable to handle the deepening economic problems. The war with Europe was crippling foreign exchange, even before English naval blockade effectively wiped out valuable colonial trade. With the tax take still in the doldrums following fiscal and administrative reorganization, the only way the government could pay for war was by issuing ever more paper money, fuelling inflation and thereby undermining state credit. By February 1793, *assignats* were changing hands at around half of their face value. On the 12th of that month, the radical ex-*curé* Jacques Roux led a delegation from the Parisian faubourgs into the assembly demanding action to remedy popular distress; and a fortnight later, there were consumer riots in the capital, with much pillaging and enforced discount sales of colonial products (sugar, coffee, soap).

There was a chorus of disapproval within the Convention. Even deputies on the Left were unwilling to see the symptoms of economic distress as motivated by bread-and-butter issues rather than political principle. Marat felt that an aristocratic conspiracy must be behind riots over 'luxury goods', for example, while Robespierre chided the populace for 'unworthy' concern with 'paltry merchandise': 'the people', he orotundly declared, 'should rise not to collect sugar but to fell tyrants'.[22] Roux was, however, only one of an increasingly notorious group of so-called 'wild ones' (*enragés*) making their way in sectional politics and in radical journalism at this time. The grouping also included Jean Varlet, Théophile Leclerc and two feminist radicals, Claire Lacombe and Pauline Léon (Leclerc's partner). Although personal animosities complicated matters, their radical demands were close to those being peddled in the Paris Commune by 'Anaxagoras' Chaumette, the Commune's procurator, and by his deputy, Jacques Hébert, of *Père Duchêne* fame. Following news of Dumouriez's treason, Varlet set up a central coordinating committee based in the Évêché to follow events and to develop a distinctively *sans-culotte* programme, which was grounded in the conviction that sectional assemblies constituted a more authentic democratic expression of popular sovereignty than the elected Conventionnels. The economic dimension of this campaign included calls to eradicate hoarding and speculation (mainly through killing hoarders and speculators), plus a desire for the state to fix prices and enforce the legal value (the *cours forcé*) of *assignats*.

Under grave external threat, encumbered by internal counter-revolution, and harassed by a Parisian *sans-culotte* movement which seemed to be outflanking the Convention from the left, the deputies reacted strongly. On 18 March, they passed a law threatening the death penalty for anyone advocating the *loi agraire* – that is, the expropriation of the rich and the redistribution of their land to the needy. Yet in order to pre-empt popular radical agitation, they initiated a sweeping suspension of personal freedoms and natural rights, installing the dark machinery of state political terror: 'let us become terrible', Danton urged his fellows, in a grim nod towards the September massacres, 'so as to prevent the people from becoming so'.[23] On 10 March, a Revolutionary Tribunal was established to judge counter-revolutionary offences; on the 19th, summary execution was threatened for anyone rebelling against the nation; on the 21st, draconian legislation against non-juring priests was further tightened up; and on the 28th, anti-*émigré* legislation was codified and made more punitive. Particular attention was given to enforcement of this battery of Revolutionary measures. On 9 March, nearly 100 Conventionnels were despatched as 'deputies on mission' (*représentants en mission*) to call departmental authorities to account, supervise the arrest of suspects, ensure the grain trade functioned effectively and oversee conscription. On 21 March, communes were instructed to establish surveillance committees to vet strangers and to issue 'civic certificates' (*certificats de civisme*) to individuals of proven patriotism, while on 6 April, a Committee of Public Safety, composed of nine Conventionnels headed by Danton, was established to coordinate the war effort within France as well as at the front.

The Montagnards were among the most enthusiastic supporters of this battery of legislation, and increasingly laid claim to be the embodiment of Revolutionary opinion throughout France. Outside Paris, the Jacobin society was extending and consolidating its hold over provincial clubs. Whereas some 126 provincial clubs (notably in the west and south-west) expressed support for the Gironde in May 1793, 195 were paid-up supporters of the Paris Jacobins. The closure of Roland's Bureau de l'esprit public in January 1793 saw the initiative in political propaganda also passing to the Montagnard-Jacobin camp. In late March, restrictions were placed on press freedom, and many Montagnard deputies on mission used this as a pretext to impound pro-Girondin newssheets in the provinces for 'revolting partiality, and for their corruption of public opinion'.[24]

These developments troubled Girondin deputies, who were increasingly reflective about the direction in which the Revolution was headed, and into whose hands it was falling. Although they sometimes shivered at the consequences of the Terror which the Convention was busy designing, they were not counter-revolutionaries, and they wanted to win the war. Yet they found that their hated Montagnard rivals were more successful at presenting an energetic and patriotic posture against the threat to national security: the Montagnards were disproportionately highly represented, for example, among deputies on mission, who were proving to be the backbone of patriotic resistance. Girondin frustration was compounded by the failure of the Convention to accept the new constitution which their colleague, Condorcet, presented in February, and which came back on to the agenda in April. Resentful at being 'out-patriotized' by the Montagnards within the Convention, the Girondins also developed rampant anti-Parisian sentiment as a core value. One could understand why, for their loathing was amply reciprocated by the Parisian *sans-culottes*. Girondin unpopularity over the *appel au peuple* during the king's trial was exacerbated by the group's reiterated denunciations of Parisian radicalism. The Girondins also came to represent for militant *sans-culottes* the fiercest opponents of the directed economy which the radicals demanded. At bottom, the Girondins were no more and no less doctrinaire in political economy than the Montagnards, but they stuck to their *laisser-faire* guns more unbendingly just as, by April and May, the Montagnards began to show signs of pragmatically accepting the need for some of the economic controls called for by the *enragés*. The latter, in turn, began to assail individual Girondins as profiteers and hard-faced men doing well out of the war through alleged complicity with corrupt business interests. On 9–10 March a day of popular action (*journée*) saw militant crowds attacking the printshops responsible for producing leading Girondin newspapers (notably Gorsas's *Courrier des 83 départements* and Condorcet's *Chronique de Paris*). The action was contained but this did not prevent the *sansculottes* calling for the purge from the ranks of the Convention of twenty-two leading Girondins.

A few days later, the Girondin Vergniaud's thundering denunciation in the Convention of the events of 9–10 March inaugurated a vicious period of political fighting which would only end with the expulsion of many Girondin deputies on 2 June 1793. Vergniaud joined his attack on the radical Paris sections with reproaches against the Montagnards for maintaining popular effervescence at a time when tranquillity was called for, and making the return of despotism possible as the Revolution, 'like Saturn, devour[ed] its own children'.[25] The poisoning of relations with the Montagnards was consummated, as the latter started to embrace elements of the political and economic programme of the *enragés*. On 11 April, under Montagnard pressure, the Convention passed the *cours forcé* of the *assignat* and this was followed on 4 May by the 'First' Maximum, which regulated grain and bread prices in the consumers' interests. By late May, plans were afoot for a forced loan on the wealthy and for a scheme of public works.

As the Montagnards were coming to endorse *sans-culotte* demands for the expulsion of the Girondins, the latter realized that their necks were in the noose, and reacted by taking the battle to their avowed enemies on the increasingly Jacobin-dominated public sphere. Girondin supporters in the Paris sections endeavoured to counter the influence of the *enragés*; Girondin deputies urged the departments to protest against the domination of the popular movement over the Convention; moderate opponents of the Jacobins in provincial cities such as Lyon, Marseille and Bordeaux received Girondin support; and attempts were made to rejuvenate the Girondin press. Nor did the Girondins refrain from attempting to utilize the new machinery of Terror to try to pick off their opponents – a move which rebounded badly against them. On 14 April, benefiting from the absence *en mission* of many of their Montagnard opponents, the Girondins got the Convention to impeach Marat on

473

grounds of sedition. Marat gave himself up, and the ensuing trial before the new Revolutionary Tribunal turned into a Girondin fiasco: the 'Friend of the People' was acquitted and borne shoulder-high in triumph through the streets of Paris.

'It was they', Danton would later recall of the Girondins, 'who forced us to throw ourselves into the sans-culottery which devoured them'.[26] This was retrospective special pleading by a Montagnard who had long been in cahoots with the popular movement – yet he had a point. By their relentless attack on the Jacobins from autumn 1792 onwards, the Girondins left their opponents with less room for manoeuvre as regards the *sans-culottes* than the Montagnards would have liked. They also served up on a platter the mechanisms for their own indictment, by breaking the idea of the immunity of deputies in their campaign to nail Marat. And the shrillness and often partisan character of their anti-Jacobinism ended up disenchanting many centrist deputies of the Plain. With bad news from the front and from western France piling up, the Girondins preferred to garner their forces in Paris – and to complain about the Montagnards, even as the latter hurled themselves dae-monically into the war effort as deputies on mission. The Girondins' apparent lack of patriotism in war circumstances which – and the heavy irony was lost on no one – they had themselves energetically initiated, looked like appalling bad faith, and it drove many prominent moderates such as Couthon, Cambon, Lindet, Carnot and Barère into the arms of the Montagnards. As the physician-deputy Baudot later noted,

the Girondins wanted to halt the revolution with the bourgeoisie in power but at a time when it was both impossible and impolitic to do so: there was open war on the frontiers and civil war threatened; the foreign forces could only be repulsed by the masses; they had to be mobilized and given a stake in our fate.[27]

It was the *sans-culotte* spokespersons of these 'masses' of course on whom the Girondin deputies were launching their most vitriolic attacks.

This left the Girondins isolated when matters came to a head in late May. Their call for the maintenance of the rule of law, for the rights of the departments, and for the notion of national sovereignty embodied in the Convention were excellent in themselves. But they seemed frankly obstructive, out of touch and hypocritical. Attempts to appeal over the heads of the Parisians to provincial – and allegedly moderate – France by urging the relocation of the Convention in homely Bourges were combined with a new bout of aggression towards radical *sans-culottes*. On 18 May, the Convention established at their behest a 'Commission of Twelve' to investigate allegations of popular insurrectionary conspiracy, and its report on 25 May led to the arrest of Hébert, Varlet and a couple of other *sans-culotte* leaders – only for them to be released untried a few days later. The Girondin Isnard used his position as presiding chair of the Convention to launch a blistering attack on the *sans-culottes* for daring to threaten the Convention: if the deputies were harmed, he blustered, 'Paris will be annihilated and men will search the banks of the Seine for signs of the city' – a formulation whose similarity to the 1792 Brunswick Manifesto caused maximum offence.[28]

With the Montagnards in the Convention standing well back, the Parisian radicals began to organize for a new *journée* which would expel the Girondins from the Convention and inaugurate a full *sans-culotte* reform programme. On 31 May, the insurrectionary committee which Varlet had organized at the Évêché several days earlier took over the Paris Commune, and the Insurrectionary Commune appointed the radical ex-tax-clerk Hanriot to the post of National Guard Commander. A massive popular demonstration in the Convention urged the expulsion of the Girondin deputies, the suppression of the Commission of Twelve, sweeping arrests of hoarders and political suspects, and other radical welfare measures. The assembly agreed to the removal of the Twelve, but baulked at further action. Another day of insurrectionary action, on 2 June, however, forced them to go further. Although the deputies initially refused to renege on their fellows, their attempt to leave the assembly hall was frustrated by an encircling crowd of *sans-culottes* who refused to give them passage. As Hanriot threatened to order his National Guard cannoneers to open fire on the deputies, the latter meekly bowed to the fate mapped out for them: they returned to the assembly hall and voted the expulsion of some twenty-nine alleged Girondins (many of whom had already physically absented themselves from Paris). The *sans-culottes* had won a famous victory: though whether they – or the Montagnards – would reap the fuller rewards remained to be seen.

C) THE GLACIAL LOGIC
OF REPUBLICAN UNITY

There must be a single will. It must either be republican or royalist ... The internal dangers derive from the bourgeoisie; to overcome the bourgeoisie we must rally the people ... The people must ally themselves to the Convention and the Convention must make use of the people ... We must encourage enthusiasm for the republic by all possible means.[29]

These diarized meditations of Maximilien Robespierre date from early June 1793, when the Revolution was confronted by armed conflict on every front and by raging civil war. The 'Incorruptible' would emerge in the post-Girondin Convention as the principal ideologist of Terror, and from July 1793 as the leading spokesperson of the revitalized Committee of Public Safety (CPS). His musings contained a prescription for action. Given the dichotomization of the political map between republican Revolutionaries and crypto-royalist counter-revolutionaries, given the fact that even a good part of the bourgeoisie (represented by the Girondins) had gone over to the enemy, a single national and Revolutionary will was – in Robespierre's vision – imperative. It should be based, he held, on a symbiotic mobilizing alliance between Montagnard Conventionnels such as himself and the *sans-culottes* who had just, on 31 May–2 June, imposed their wishes on the assembly.

Terror, canalizing Revolutionary energy and enthusiasm within a crushing singleness of political purpose, would shape the destiny of French men and women, for better and for worse, for richer and for poorer, over the next year. These were to be, as Charles Dickens was later to reflect, simultaneously both 'the best of times [and] the worst of times'.[30] The Montagnard strategy involved enlisting widespread popular support so as to enact a programme of radical social, economic and political innovations which linked directly back to the Enlightenment project of societal amelioration, and sprang from equally high moral motives. At the same time, however, the threat of unflinching state violence hovered over the head of any individual or group – and these proved to be ever more legion – unlucky enough to be adjudged politically delinquent. As all deputies, with their classical educations, knew, the idea of Terror was an old Roman republican one: if a Roman legion did not do its duty, then indiscriminate punishment would be meted out. What was both terrifying and sobering about the Terror of 1793–4 was the aura of randomness which hovered over the violence it visited out – even when (or precisely because) it was being conducted by individuals of impeccable Latinate education and high moral principle.

The popular movement with which Robespierre and the Montagnards sought to ally was a social and political hybrid. The Parisian *sans-culottes* had redoubts in Bouchotte's War Ministry and in the Commune, but their characteristic milieu was the neighbourhood meeting of Paris's forty-eight sections and – in the capital and the provinces – the clubs, now called 'popular societies' (the most prominent of which in Paris was the Cordelier Club). The surveillance committees established in March 1793 drew on these reservoirs of patriotism and imprinted a strongly plebeian character on the implementation of Terror at local level. The movement as a whole comprised a mixture of the labouring classes and members of the petty bourgeoisie (artisans, shopkeepers, minor clerks, etc.) plus many individuals of modest wealth who in less socially deflationary times would have claimed gentility. The movement had more than its fair share of *déclassé* intellectuals and journalists too, plus the odd eccentric noble, such as the *ci-devant roué*, the marquis de Sade, who refashioned himself as a *sans-culotte* militant in the Section des Piques. The term *sans-culotte* was in fact something of a fashion pose: most eighteenth-century artisans and shopkeepers had worn knee-breeches before it had become politically correct to sport the plebeian trouser and the red cap of liberty.

The extent to which these Parisian radicals 'represented' the French people as a whole was very moot. Though they retained more of a separate identity in Paris, the demarcation line in the provinces separating them from the forces of Jacobinism was very porous. Indeed, in some measure, the *sans-culotte* movement was a Montagnard construct (albeit one which did develop a degree of autonomy). It proudly placed itself in the van of French people who stayed loyal to the Convention. Their numbers – and especially when added to the million or so men attracted to fight for the infant republic in the army in 1793–4 – constituted a very powerful force. In addition, there may have been as many as 20,000 surveillance committees in existence throughout the country, staffed by perhaps half a million men. Political clubs attracted as many as a million individuals during the Revolution. Attendance was most assiduous in this period: the 3,000 clubs in existence in 1793-4 may have included up to one adult male in ten. This level of popular participation would be regarded with envy by every radical social movement of nineteenth-century Europe.

Impressive though it undoubtedly was, it remained true that the popular movement was still very much a minority movement within France as a whole. A clear majority of the population did not feel much sympathy for either the *sans-culottes* or the Revolutionary government. Nine communes out of ten did not have a club, and the network was skewed towards town rather than countryside. Even in Paris, the proportion of adult males who attended sectional meetings was rarely above 10 per cent – elsewhere it was probably far less. At the other extreme, patriots were outgunned in areas of royalist rebellion such as the Vendée by open counter-revolutionaries, who were often more demotic and invariably more rural than they: the Vendéan armies were composed, claimed one of their number, of 'peasants like myself, wearing smocks or rough coats, armed with shotguns, pistols, muskets [and] often with tools – scythes, cudgels, axes, knives and roasting spits'.[31] It was such individuals who would bear the brunt of the military repression of the Vendée rising, while the Paris Revolutionary Tribunal would despatch twice as many peasants and workers to the scaffold as nobles and members of the upper bourgeoisie. Around 1 million individuals were imprisoned or brought under surveillance because of their political views in 1793-4 – roughly the same number as fought in the army. The Terror split the country down the middle, and the activists engaged ranged, on both sides of the struggle, from the top to the bottom of the social hierarchy.

The summer of 1793 saw a complex political dance occurring, as the Revolutionary government sought both to utilize the popular movement so as to frighten oppositional forces – yet at the same time to manoeuvre the *sans-culottes* into a position of subservience to the Montagnard project. In many ways, the Parisian radicals owed their importance less to the raw social forces they embodied than to the strategic advantage they possessed by being located in the seat of government – and, as the *journée* of 2 June had graphically illustrated – of being able to exert their power directly over the legislature. The raw political threat which they embodied was a useful means of deterring opposition in a country racked by political crisis. Much of France had found the *journées* of 31

May and 2 June indefensible. Over forty department administrations formally protested against them, and in around one-third of these, protests passed into active resistance in the so-called Federalist Revolt, which dragged on into the autumn. There was sullen obstructiveness in the Convention itself too: nearly 100 deputies formally protested against the expulsion of their Girondin colleagues, and throughout the summer kept up criticism of the policies of the CPS, the war-cabinet which the Montagnards were turning into the prime instrument of Terror (and on to which Robespierre was voted in July).

Although on 2 June 1793 the Convention had bowed to *sans-culotte* pressure, the Montagnards took time to embrace the popular movement's full economic, political and social message. Roux, now ensconced in the Commune, continued to ask for more, and was held to be behind soap riots in Paris in late June. 'Liberty is but a vain phantom', he berated the Convention on 25 June, 'when one class of men can starve another with impunity. Equality is but a vain phantom when the rich exercise the power of life and death over their fellows through monopolies.'[32] The assassination of the ailing Marat in his bath by the young Girondin supporter Charlotte Corday, on 13 July, left a niche in the Revolutionary pantheon for a new 'friend of the people', moreover, who would blow the whistle on the corruption of those in power. Contestants for the title were soon lining up and they included Roux's fellow-*enragé*, Varlet, and the *Père Duchesne*'s Hébert, deputy procurator of the Paris Commune, who shared a radical egalitarianism with his ally, Chaumette.

It took turbulent popular demonstrations in Paris on 5 September, triggered by news of the capitulation of the naval base at Toulon to the British navy, to make the Convention formally declare Terror 'the order of the day', and adopt much of the *enragé* programme: a General Maximum on all foodstuffs (enacted on 11 and 29 September); expansion of the Revolutionary Tribunal; the creation of 'people's armies' (*armées révolutionnaires*) to take Revolution out into the countryside and to engage in political and economic terrorism; a promise to step up the arrest of suspects (to be embodied in the Law of Suspects of 17 September, which vastly extended this category of political outsider); and an agreement to pay *sans-culottes* forty sous for attending sectional meetings. On 5–6 September, two radicals with known *sans-culotte* sympathies, Billaud-Varenne and Collot d'Herbois, were placed on the CPS.

Yet if the CPS was now putting on *enragé* clothes, it was also beginning to refashion the popular movement in its own image. In Hébert's *Père Duchesne*, the typical *sans-culotte* was represented as a demotically vulgar but endearingly good-hearted and patriotic soul who voiced vitriolic opinions on aristocrats and non-juring priests and who felt comfortable in the presence of fellow artisans, shopkeepers and petty clerks (but not their wives, whose job was to stay at home and bring up junior *sans-culottes*). The high-flown invocation of 'the people' in Montagnard discourse, in contrast, had an altogether more abstract, idealized, even sentimentalized tone. Robespierre and his ilk needed the popular movement to be an expression of sturdy virtue, embodied in politically and economically independent, public-spirited citizens. But they drew the line at hyper-critical *enragés* and putative post-Marat 'Friends of the People', whom they regarded as incipient misleaders of the people.

Idealization of the people thus provided ideological cover for Montagnard moves to bring the popular movement under control. The Montagnard project required the latter's strategic advantage on the streets of Paris outside the walls of the Convention to be terminated. On the very day – 5 September – that the Montagnards embraced *enragé* ideology, the government had Roux and Varlet arrested and put in gaol (where the former subsequently died). Among other radicals to feel the Terror's lash were women who had been involved in politics. In mid-October, queen Marie-Antoinette was guillotined, following a charade of a trial, and this was followed by an attack on women radicals. On 30 October, the Society of Female Revolutionary Republican Citizenesses, which *enragées* Claire Lacombe and Pauline Léon had founded to widen the movement's political base, was outlawed. This move formed part of a more sweeping political strategy aimed at confining women in Rousseauesque domesticity away from public life, which they were thought bound to pollute.[33]

The assault on the notion of women in political life was symptomatic of a more general campaign to forge a unitary (and highly masculine) notion of collective political identity which marked this phase of the Revolution. The Terror breathed a new urgency and cogency into calls for the Revolutionary process to produce a 'new nation' and a 'new man'. The rights-bearing citizen was now the red-capped *sans-culotte* and his pike, cogent symbol of the nation in arms. The French past was no longer available as a source of legitimate political reference, and Jacobins endlessly invoked the virtue of ancient Greece and Rome, as part of a programme of political regeneration. The eclipse of the church in public life, the war emergency and the removal of the king left gaps which the Convention sought to fill with its own distinctive cultural products. Political censorship may have reduced the range of publication, but government support for newspapers and tame pamphleteers meant that print massively extended the audience for the Revolutionary government's message. From early in the Revolution, the public festival had provided an ancillary means by which the regime could inculcate a regenerative message.[34] The first anniversary of the overthrow of the king saw the first totally secularized such ceremony, the Festival of Unity and Indivisibility on 10 August 1793. The new republican festivals sometimes retained much of the flavour of religious events: the ceremonies around the death of Marat in mid-1793 and the emergence of a cult of Revolutionary martyrs who had died defending the fatherland had clearly spiritual overtones. A more sombre form of political pedagogy was provided by public executions, which in the autumn of 1793 took on the character of classic pieces of educationally inspired political theatre: Marie-Antoinette's grim entourage of 13 October; the Girondins on the 31st (with Brissot and Vergniaud defiantly intoning the 'Marseillaise' on their ascent to the scaffold); 'Philippe-Égalité' on 6 November; and, six days later, ex-Mayor Bailly, with the guillotine melodramatically relocated for the occasion to the Champ de Mars, site of the infamous 1791 'massacre'.

The regime's regenerative aims were given added scope by the decision in October to introduce a Revolutionary calendar. A new, post-religious epoch in human history, it was claimed, had been opened up by the declaration of the Republic on 22 September 1792 (making October 1793 Year II already). The deputies thereby renounced reference to the historic past in favour of focusing on the cyclical, natural time of the mythic present in which Revolutionary political culture was immersed.[35] The year was divided up into twelve months renamed after the seasons (and with five *jours sans-culottides* added on for good luck); each month comprised three 'decades' of ten days – with the *décadi* replacing Sundays as a day of rest; and each day was reconsecrated to a natural product or farming tool or technique.

A velvet glove encased the Terror's punitive fist. The post-Girondin

Convention introduced a raft of populist measures buttressing its commitment to maintain popular living standards and radical welfare
reform. The *cours forcé* of the *assignat* stimulated the recovery of the
paper currency: it was down to a fifth of its face value over the 1793
summer crisis, but had risen to a (still unsatisfactory) 48 per cent by
Christmas. The peasant producer was the targeted beneficiary of certain
measures. Over the summer of 1793, legislation was introduced to sell
nationalized *émigré* land in small plots and with procedures which
favoured poor peasants, and a law of 10 June decreed the equitable
distribution of common lands. On 17 July, the Convention voted the
complete abolition of feudal dues without indemnity – the public bon-
fires of feudal titles provided a nice populist touch. A start was made
too on replacing the nation's crumbling stock of hospitals and poor-
houses. The so-called 'Laws of Ventôse' in March 1794 sought to
distribute the property of suspects among the poor. These were complemented by ambitious pensions schemes, including the institution of the
'Great Register of National Beneficence' on 11 May (22 Floréal II). On
a related tack, the Bouquier law of 19 December 1793 (29 Frimaire II)
established the principle of compulsory and free primary education. The
promise of an embryonic welfare state was an important ideological
plank in the Montagnard project of rallying the people – even though
little enduring was achieved in either education or poor relief.

Moves to tame unruly popular radicalism in Paris through a mixture
of political concession, radical welfare reforms, outright repression and
ideological bombardment allowed the government to focus on the task
of winning its wars, both foreign and civil. The institutions of Terror
created in the spring were cranked into action by a war government now
headed by a rejuvenated – and Robespierrized – CPS. The 'Incorruptible'
had entered the Committee in July, followed by Saint-Just. They drew
to their faction established members such as Couthon and Barère, as the
'Great Committee' began to form – the twelve Conventionnels who in
essence ruled France for the next year, pulled it through its military
disasters, and subjected it to a reign of political terror. Alongside them
from September were Billaud-Varenne and Collot d'Herbois, who represented *sans-culotte* influence, while at the other extreme, there were
the technicians of Terror, political moderates for the most part like
Robert Lindet, whom Robespierre dubbed the 'Fénelon of the Revolution' and whose national food commission, set up in October, policed

the Maximum; Prieur de la Côte d'Or, in charge of armaments and war supply; Prieur's fellow military engineer, Carnot, the military supremo later dubbed 'the organizer of victory'; and the Protestant pastor Jean Bon Saint-André, *de facto* Navy Minister for the duration of the Terror.

The CPS still had its critics – on both Left and Right – but worked insistently to extend its mission. The Convention had rushed through a new democratic constitution between 11 and 24 June, partly as a means of proving to pro-Girondin departments its commitment to the principles of 1789. The 1793 Constitution had an important totemic role in dismantling Federalism: it purported to demonstrate a Montagnard preference for democracy over authoritarianism, and gave its 1789 forebear a more egalitarian and welfare-oriented spin. But it was never implemented, on the grounds of the war emergency. Robespierre fought off moves to institute elections and on 10 October, at Saint-Just's prompting, the Convention decreed that the government should be 'revolutionary' (as opposed to constitutional) until peace was made. The Terror would be conducted in conditions of constitutional exceptionalism, with the CPS at the helm.

The armed forces were given the most careful attention. The *levée en masse* of 23 August 1793 extended the 300,000 levy of February, obliging every adult male to contribute to the war effort: single men between eighteen and twenty-five years old could be called to the colours and all other citizens were to expect to contribute to the war effort in some way through their labour and resources. The size of the army grew to 800,000 men, with over a million formally under military orders. A direction of civil labour unparalleled until the twentieth century was introduced, ranging through the collection of saltpetre in caves to make gunpowder to the production of arms and uniforms and the commandeering of food and livestock for military purposes. The Republic requisitioned science too: savants such as the chemists Hassenfratz and Chaptal and the mathematician Monge placed their expertise at the disposal of the government. At times, government requisitioning shaded into outright military looting – especially in occupied territories where, under the law of 15 December 1792, military administration was empowered to extract the army's means of subsistence from the local inhabitants.

The armed forces assembled by the CPS over the summer and autumn of 1793 proved devastatingly effective. The policy of 'amalgamation' adopted from early 1793 entailed the merger of volunteer and conscript troops with regular army units. The new army still lacked the training and expertise of its royal forebear, but compensated for this by enthusiasm for the cause of national defence. What General Hoche called 'fire, steel and patriotism' did the trick. French armies mixed the old linear formations with the kind of fighting in deep columns for which they became famous, throwing themselves with paralysing speed into hand-to-hand encounters with the enemy. Their strategy was not always crowned with success and the process was – of course – far from smooth. But the Revolutionary armies did often out-manoeuvre their opponents, and their role was vital in allowing the infant Republic to survive the summer crisis of 1793.

The most critical front was in the north, where fortunes oscillated dangerously: in mid-1793, British and Dutch forces were installed on French territory on the Belgian border, and although French successes at Hondschoote and Wattignies in the autumn gave some relief, matters were still evenly poised. In the east, the French surrender of Mainz in July caused the army to fall back well within France. But successive offensive waves orchestrated by Hoche from November cleared Alsace and allowed modest advances in the spring of 1794. By that time, French territory had been cleared of foreign invaders. The Spanish had also been pushed back across the Pyrenees, and preparations were being made to invade Savoy and Italy.

The only unadulterated failures were outside France. At sea, the English fleet instituted a blockade of French ports (and accepted the surrender of the French Mediterranean fleet at Toulon in August). The Royal Navy's naval superiority, though tested on a number of occasions over the decade, was not to be found wanting. It meant that to all intents and purposes France was cut off from its wealth-generating Caribbean colonies. The French islands had been racked by slave revolt from 1791. The English seized them in 1793, and though slave leaders Toussaint l'Ouverture and Victor-Hugues drove them out of Saint-Domingue and Guadeloupe respectively, this made no difference to the French: they had precious little contact with either island (and in 1801, Toussaint declared Saint-Domingue's independence as Haiti). France was losing its claims to be a global commercial power – but this paled into relative insignificance against vital continental successes.

The frightening volume of internal dissension within France during the summer of 1793 was also brought to an end. The Vendéan rebels had won a string of victories against raw recruits over the summer of 1793, and resistance spread into Normandy, where peasant royalists known as Chouans sprang to arms. Both movements, however, soon reached the limits of their military ambitions. An important victory by reinforced republican troops at Cholet on 17–18 October provided much-needed relief, forcing Vendéans and Chouans to move towards Granville in Normandy to effect a junction with the British fleet – which never happened. The Vendéans went on to be heavily defeated first in Le Mans and then at Savenay (23 December). The early months of 1794 would be spent with republican armies engaged in the region's 'pacification' – too sedate a word, in fact, for the vicious repression used. On 1 August 1793, the Convention had permitted its commanders there to introduce free-fire zones in troubled areas. 'My purpose', anti-Vendéan commander, Turreau, told the War Ministry in January 1794, 'is to burn everything.'[36]

By Christmas 1793, the Federalist revolt sparked by the purge of the Girondins had also been definitively crushed. Over the course of the summer, the Montagnards constructed an image of the Girondins as doctrinaire, decentralizing federalists which was far from the mark. Most Girondins were as in favour of the unitary indivisibility of the Republic as the Montagnards. It was essentially the threat from the Parisian popular movement which had caused them to appeal for assistance to the departments. This allowed them to be tarred with the Federalist brush. Even before 31 May, for example, Girondin support for an anti-Jacobin faction in Lyon had led to an anti-Parisian municipal coup in the city, and this kind of intra-city dispute was replicated in Marseille, Bordeaux and elsewhere. After 2 June, the anti-Parisian note became more desperately stentorian among those deputies who escaped arrest. In Normandy, proscribed Girondins Buzot, Barbaroux and Pétion attempted to raise an army against the Convention, but this dissolved in panic without a shot being fired at the 'battle' of Pacy-sur-Eure in July. The political outlaws fled to Bordeaux, where a more substantial resistance was forming.

Most areas which had protested against the *journées* of 31 May–2 June were brought into line as a result of government propaganda highlighting the new 1793 constitution. The areas which held out focused around a number of big cities in the south. Fortunately for the Montagnards, these areas were widely dispersed and never effected a junction of their forces. Avignon, then Marseille, fell to republican troops in late July and August, with Bordeaux following in September (leading to the collective suicide of the refugee Girondins). Following the recapture of Lyon in early October, Toulon was the only federalist locality still in arms. It eventually fell to republican action on 19 December which involved artillery bombardment in which a Jacobin lieutenant, the Corsican Napoleone Buonaparte, played a critical role.

Arguably as important as the role of republican generals in pulling France through the crisis of summer and autumn 1793 were the many deputies on mission sent out in waves to ensure that crucial Revolutionary war legislation was implemented. Whether purging hostile or tepid administrations, mobilizing armed defence, recruiting troops, securing food supplies, sending political suspects before revolutionary tribunals or acting as sources of government propaganda, the deputies were crucial liaison agents of Revolutionary government, articulating the objectives of the CPS with the popular energies of the provinces. They included many of the most overtly enthusiastic patriots among the Convention's rank and file – and quite a few from the radical fringe too. In July, the Convention had decreed that the edicts of its emissaries would be regarded as provisional laws, invested with all the sanctity of Revolutionary legislation, but such was the disarray of local administration anyway that the deputies effectively had *carte blanche* for the deployment of Terror on provincial populations both recalcitrant and compliant. They bolstered their efforts by drawing on local surveillance committees and clubs; appointed local commissaries with plenipotentiary powers; and formed 'people's armies' like those advocated by the Parisian *enragés* on 5 September. These *armées révolutionnaires* toured the countryside enforcing the Maximum, requisitioning supplies, executing Revolutionary laws and engaging in attacks on priests and other political suspects.

Deputies on mission were often chillingly repressive, notably in civil war zones. At Nantes, for example, Carrier complemented the reckless slaughters being carried out in the interior of the Vendée by General Turreau's 'infernal columns' with a hyperactive Revolutionary Tribunal. Alongside this, there were the infamous *noyades*: perhaps 2,000 alleged counter-revolutionaries strapped into barges were towed into the river Loire where the barges were scuppered, leaving the victims to drown. CPS stalwart Couthon was relatively mild in the punishment of Lyon (renamed 'Ville-Affranchie' ['Freed Town']) in October, but when Collot d'Herbois and Fouché replaced him, a veritable frenzy of repression occurred, with opponents being gunned down into open graves in the so-called *mitraillades*. At Marseille (now 'Ville Sans Nom' ['No Name Town']), Barras and Fréron also distinguished themselves by their draconian measures. Altogether, the areas of armed Federalism in the south and the Vendée in the west accounted for around three-quarters of direct victims of Revolutionary justice under the Terror.[37]

In all civil war zones, anti-clerical policies figured high on the agenda of the deputies on mission. Certain of their tasks – such as the melting-down of church bells for cannon and the requisitioning of gold and silver ecclesiastical ornaments for the war effort, and the enforcement of the Convention's laws regarding the deportation of non-jurors – inevitably brought them into conflict with religious personnel. There was scope, however, for more doctrinaire assaults on traditional religion, from which even the Constitutional clergy was not immune. Fouché, before 1789 a teacher attached to the Oratorian order, engaged in an extraordinary campaign of 'dechristianization' in his tour of duty in the department of the Nièvre in September: he forbade public worship, closed all churches, removed all vestiges of religious iconography, for-bade the wearing of religious costume and even secularized the cemeteries, which had all religious insignia removed and the slogan 'Death is an Eternal Sleep' emblazoned on their gates. Fouché also encouraged priests to abdicate their functions and either to marry or else to adopt a child or an old person as a gage of social utility. These practices spread quite widely thereafter: some 20,000 priests (roughly one-third of all *curés*) abdicated in the course of the Terror, around 6,000 of them marrying to boot. The objects and rituals of divine right monarchy were the target of particular ire: in Reims, Rühl took special pains ceremoniously to break the phial containing Clovis's sacred oil with which the kings of France were anointed; the statues of kings of Judah on the front of Notre-Dame cathedral in Paris were removed, carefully beheaded, and destroyed; and the tombs of generations of French monarchs at Saint-Denis were desecrated. Not all of France was subjected to this kind of dechristianizing auto-da-fé, whose highspots were the Paris basin, the Île-de-France, and the Rhône valley. But few areas were to escape its influence – or the divergent waves of revulsion and enthusiasm which it stimulated.

Just as the geographies of Terror and dechristianization were highly patchy, so was the role and function of the deputies on mission. Far more typical and numerically more characteristic than the Carriers, Collots and Fouchés were relatively unknown Conventionnels who utilized their missions to spread the humanitarian as well as the draconian message of Terror. Attacks on hoarders and big producers, for example, were integrated into a quest to seek fair shares for all those contributing to the war effort. Forced loans, the introduction of socially graduated tax rolls and the distribution of manageable lots of church and *émigré* lands were combined with a wide range of educational and welfare field trials: charity workshops, patriotic schools, pensions schemes, famine-relief measures and the like. For such deputies – the obscure Rouerguat physician Bo, for example, the Protestant attorney Ingrand, the cavalry-officer Roux-Fazillac and others – rallying the people was manifestly more than a narrowly political manoeuvre: it presaged the making of a new and fairer society. This regenerative impulse was often manifested in the cult of Revolutionary renaming. Locations with feudal, aristocratic, royal or religious names were 'revolutionized', while enthusiastic individuals also got into the swing of things, changing their own or their children's names in accordance with the Revolutionary Calendar. Fontenay-le-Comte became Fontenay-le-Peuple, for example, Roiville was transformed into Peuple-ville and Saint-Flour into Mont-Flour. General François-Amédée Doppet became Pervenche ('Periwinkle') Doppet, while Pierre-Gaspard Chaumette and François-Noel Babeuf took the names of the radicals of Antiquity, Anaxagoras and Gracchus.

Whatever their mode and intensity of action, the deputies on mission served the Convention well by helping to pull the country through the summer crisis of 1793. By the autumn, however, Robespierre and others were becoming concerned that their energetic commitment to regeneration was causing more problems than it solved. His anxieties crystallized around the issue of religion. Robespierre was a classic Enlightenment deist: a Voltairean belief in the social need for belief in an afterlife to encourage virtue and discourage vice was heavily overlaid with a Rousseauist openness to a creative Nature in which he recognized a Supreme Being. The Enlightenment project had, as we have seen,[38] sought to construct a moral social purpose for political action, steering a *via media* between revealed religion and a sceptical, individualized atheism, and Robespierre remained true to that inspiration. He had little hesitation in assuming that the Supreme Being would need to be subordinated to the supreme republic. He seems not to have doubted that the Revolution itself would become a cult which attracted more support than established Christianity, and which would be more grounded in the moral virtues at the heart of the Revolutionary project. In the interim, he urged an instrumentalist religious policy, striking hard against Catholicism only when and where it seemed to be impeding the progress of Revolutionary Virtue. Thus the CPS maintained legislation against non-jurors just as it did against *émigrés*, and buttressed this with increased levels of surveillance of both kinds of political suspects over the summer and autumn of 1793: from 26 August onwards, for example, all priests who had not taken the civic oath were liable to deportation.

Robespierre drew the line, however, at overly zealous dechristianizing campaigns by deputies on mission which smacked of atheism. Reports coming back to the CPS over the autumn suggested that the extreme measures being introduced in some areas were alienating the peasantry from the Revolution. Robespierre in fact probably underestimated the extent to which many regions had been prepared for dechristianizing activities by a generation or more of religious indifference. Like most of his colleagues on the CPS, he originated in the north of France, and found it difficult to comprehend the bitter acerbity caused by religious issues of many southern and western regions, some of which were receptive to and even spontaneously engaged in active dechristianization. Dechristianizing deputies on mission were often reacting to local circumstances, rather than whipping up irreligious frenzy as Robespierre claimed. Robespierre's suspicions about the movement were, however, fanned by the fact that dechristianization had been picked up by what he viewed as an unscrupulous horde of Parisian radicals, led by Chaumette, who had served alongside Fouché in the Nièvre, and whose Revolutionary credentials Robespierre profoundly distrusted. From late October, Chaumette led the Commune and the Cordeliers in a campaign to eradicate the outward signs of religion throughout Paris, to close churches and to prohibit public worship. On 7 November, the campaign staged something of a publicity stunt in which Gobel, Constitutional archbishop of Paris, abdicated his vocation and then married. Chaumette followed this up with the organization of a secular Festival of Reason on 10 November in a newly republicanized Notre-Dame cathedral. These noisy actions were combined with a left-wing attack on the CPS, involving calls for federations of popular societies to be allowed to express the 'popular will' and for a new purge of the Convention on the lines of 2 June 1793.

Robespierre had been the most consistent of all deputies in expressing fears that a war situation could lead to a military coup by an ambitious general. In the changed circumstances of 1793, the military threat seemed to be coming from what he saw as cynical and atheistic radicals leading a kind of armed revolutionary militia drawn on the Parisian sections and the provincial *armées révolutionnaires* (and probably secretly funded by William Pitt). He therefore expeditiously sought to bring under control the political extremism associated with dechristianization. In a speech in the Jacobin Club on 21 November he attacked atheism as both aristocratic and immoral, and he followed this up on 6 December, alongside Danton, Joseph Cambon, powerful chair of the Convention's Finance Committee, and many moderates, by formally reaffirming the principle of freedom of worship. By then, the CPS had also sought to tighten its controls over the more anarchic aspects of the Terror in the Law on Revolutionary Government of 14 Frimaire II (4 December 1793). The Law of 14 Frimaire provided a bureaucratic framework for Terror. The CPS was confirmed as the executive arm of government under the guidance of the Convention, with its subordinate Committee of General Security (CGS) in charge of all police matters. A new regularity of reporting procedures was introduced: a mountain of paperwork, sent to the CPS and CGS on a ten-day rota, would keep the 'committees of government' fully apprised of developments in the provinces. The role of the deputies on mission would be taken over by a plethora of government-appointed 'national agents' attached to districts and communes (departmental authorities were left out of the loop). Although the surveillance committees were maintained, there were to be no more provincial *armées révolutionnaires* (only the Parisian force was continued), no plenipotentiary underlings with their roving private armies, and no federative action by popular societies. Forced loans and other extreme social measures were prohibited, and all agents of Revolutionary government were henceforth enjoined to follow instructions to the letter.

The CPS move towards much stricter control over the agents of Revolutionary government was motivated by anxieties about a resurgent Right as well as a radical Left. While Hébert and other putative heirs of

Marat and Roux called for a redoubling of the policies of Terror, a group of more moderate deputies invoked a spirit of clemency. Although he had a more terroristic past than most, Danton appears to have become concerned by the ever-increasing centralization and bureaucratization to which the CPS was committed, and insinuated himself among the leaders of this moderate faction. According to some later accounts, his aim was to prick back into life an independent public opinion which the Terror had destroyed. He worked with the journalist Camille Desmoulins to use the latter's new newspaper venture, *Le Vieux Cordelier*, as a platform for political moderation. The 'Old Cordelier' used recollections of the Cordeliers Club of 1790–91 (in which Danton and Desmoulins had been prominent) against the allegedly extremist 'new' Cordeliers represented by Hébert and his followers, and called for greater clemency in government policy.

The CPS spent the winter and spring of 1794 endeavouring to enforce the Law of 14 Frimaire throughout France – and with Robespierre and his confidants becoming increasingly anxious that a plot was being hatched at the heart of the Convention which would bring the Republic down. Greater control was not, however, easy to impose, the fragmentation of authority in the summer crisis of 1793 having been to some degree magnified rather than diminished by the work of the deputies on mission. Many of the latter, moreover, were heartily opposed to the spirit of the Law of 14 Frimaire. Robespierre's diagnosis of ultra-revolutionary activities causing a backlash might have been correct for many areas, but it seemed perilously out of touch as regards the civil war zones. In post-Federalist Lyon, for example, Collot d'Herbois concluded that his colleague on the CPS had clearly lost his touch or else become part of a royalist plot, while Carrier at Nantes and Tallien at Bordeaux became similarly convinced that their recall was due to a dangerous relaxation in Revolutionary energy in Paris. Javogues, on mission in the Haute-Loire, fulminated against religious freedoms urged by the CPS: 'All the methods of coercion you employ against the chameleons who claim to be apostles of various sects will be evaded,' he scoffed. 'It would be much simpler to shoot them.'[39] He actively resisted recall to Paris, and continued his radical policies through to March, which was the high-water mark of dechristianizing activity nationally.

Attempts to bring under control *sans-culotte* radicals in Paris, extremist deputies on mission in the provinces and supporters of greater

'Indulgence' (clemency) near to the heart of government were thus creating new lines of division and a dizzyingly complex matrix of resentments and suspicions. The efforts of Robespierre, as principal ideologue in the ranks of the CPS, to master the situation drew antagonisms towards himself, which in turn exacerbated the well-known persecutory side to his character. From late autumn he had become increasingly responsive to gossip and rumour which claimed that the bitterness of factional politics was to be explained by a widely ramified foreign plot, hatched by England's William Pitt, to cause the overthrow of the Republic by setting republicans against republicans in fratricidal disputes. Informers fed him tales of the allegedly treasonous venality of Chaumette, Hébert and the cosmopolitan grouping associated with them (notably the Prussian 'Baron' de Clootz, the Austrians, Proli and the Frey brothers, and the Portuguese Jew, Pereira). Some of the *sans-culottes* ensconced within the War Ministry, such as Vincent and Ronsin, commander of Paris's *armée révolutionnaire*, were also whispered to be involved in the foreign plot and recipients of 'Pitt's gold'. The group's opportunistic adoption of doctrinaire anti-clericalism and their call, from early 1794, for a new purge of the Convention only deepened Robespierre's worry that, even as the Terror was producing outward political conformity, it was also nurturing the worm of old corruption in the bud of Revolutionary virtue. 'The Revolution is frozen,' Robespierre's ally, Saint-Just, privately remarked. 'All principles have weakened; nothing is left but red caps worn by intriguers. The use of Terror has desensitized crime, as strong liquors do the palate.'[40]

A dark struggle to ensure that the Montagnard project of unity of will prevailed over the swirl of faction and corruption thus began to take shape in the winter of 1793-4. Robespierre's initial move to support some of the ideas of 'Indulgence' promoted by the likes of Danton and Desmoulins against dechristianizing factionaries was checked by the return of Collot d'Herbois from Lyon in late December to defend the radicals' corner. In addition, Robespierre became more suspicious of the motives of Danton, who was as well known for personal corruption as for his doughty patriotic record. Danton's links to Fabre d'Eglantine in particular were held against him, as over the winter a financial scandal opened up which revealed that Fabre and a number of other deputies had profited personally from corrupt dealings in winding up the old Compagnie des Indes.

In March and April, the CPS acted to lance the festering abscess of factional corruption and to crush its critics on Left and Right who, beneath surface appearances, Robespierre held, were 'in cahoots like robbers in a wood'.[41] Coming in bewilderingly close succession, three show trials, each of them the result of complicated political manoeuvres only partly understood even now, saw the political erasure of a great many of the 'red caps worn by intriguers' criticized by Saint-Just. On 13 March (23 Ventôse II), the latter denounced before the Convention a plot, allegedly funded by foreign enemies, 'to destroy representative government by corruption'.[42] Around a score of radicals, including Hébert, Vincent and Ronsin, plus some foreigners like Clootz, were sent before the Revolutionary Tribunal, which duly convicted them. Their blood was scarcely cold on the guillotine when a new trial brought to the scaffold, on 5 April (16 Germinal), a motley crew including arch-Indulgents Danton and Desmoulins, alongside a range of critics of Revolutionary government and swindlers such as Fabre. Finally on 13 April (24 Germinal), in a trial of almost farcically trumped-up proportions, the tail of both groupings were despatched to their deaths: the widows of Hébert and Desmoulins, plus Chaumette, the dechristianized (and now happily married) ex-archbishop, Gobel, and others. The trials were accompanied by measures tightening up policing, reducing freedom of speech, and crushing the independence of the bastions of the popular movement, the Commune and the Cordeliers Club. The Paris *armée révolutionnaire* was dissolved, sectional societies wound up and Mayor Pache, known for Hébertist sympathies, was removed and replaced by Robespierrist yes-man Fleuriot-Lescot.

The CPS's efforts to liquidate faction by calculated destruction were designed to impose on the Revolution the glacial logic of unity invoked by Robespierre and Saint-Just. But the policy of Terror risked the political neutering of the Parisian popular movement, key player in Robespierre's project of rallying the people. It also – as Saint-Just had noted – risked driving opposition further underground, as a result of ever greater protestations of political conformity. On his way to the scaffold on 5 April, Danton had been heard to remark, 'What annoys me most is that I am dying six weeks before Robespierre.'[43] By spring 1794, the glacial logic of unity was in danger of thawing – to the considerable peril of the Montagnards who had initiated it.

D) KILLING ROBESPIERRE,
ENDING TERROR

In March 1794, at the same time that the CPS was bolstering its authority by liquidating Hébertists and Dantonists, the directors of Paris's armaments trade discovered that their musket-makers had defaced a poster recording one of the CPS's official decrees. At the end of a list of the names of Committee members, a plebeian hand had scrawled the words 'deceivers of the people, forever stupid brutes, thieves and assassins'. Specifically under the name of Robespierre was inscribed the word 'cannibal'.[44]

The putatively omnipotent mainspring of Revolutionary government, it seemed, could not silence nor keep in line workers in its own back yard, nor insulate Robespierre from targeted jeers. Even as the Committee was establishing a position above open criticism in the public sphere, it found its broader popularity in question. As the spring of 1794 wore on, more and more of the political nation would add their voices to a stifled chorus of discontent, and Robespierre would be increasingly represented as a figure who perpetuated and aggravated problems rather than resolved them. By the end of July, individuals from an extremely wide spectrum would unite in believing that the only way for the Revolution to progress involved the liquidation of 'the Incorruptible'.

The failure of the CPS's ever more ambitious pensions schemes and welfare programmes, integral part of Robespierre's strategy of 'rallying the people' within the Republic of Virtue was increasingly conspicuous. Beyond the airy rhetoric of 'beneficence', the financial demands of the war always won out over the needs of relief programmes, increasing popular ire. Police reports as well as anonymous graffiti highlighted the way the wind was blowing. 'We're dying of hunger', a police spy recorded a Parisian munitions worker as stating, 'and they mock us with pretty speeches'.[45] Despite the CPS's best efforts, the *assignat* was still running at around one-third of its face value, fuelling inflation and market disruption, and essential commodities were dear or non-existent. The abolition, in April, of the hoarding commissioners who had policed the Maximum, and the recall of deputies on mission who had been among the most vigorous proponents of economic terror made some believe that the CPS was considering a move towards more *laisser-faire* principles. In addition, the decision on 22 July to apply the Maximum on wages in Paris for the first time (the Maximum had hitherto only been applied to prices) implied a worsening of living standards for virtually all the Parisian trades. Social justice and republican virtue seemed to be losing out to a wish to reanimate profit.

It was difficult for the Revolutionary government to gauge the extent of popular discontent because it had destroyed most channels of independent expression. The Bourbon monarchs had at least had their *parlements* as mouthpieces of public opinion; the Revolutionary government lacked even that. Even before the Law of 14 Frimaire which had centralized power on the CPS spearheaded moves to outlaw dissent, there had been a marked shrinkage in the rights of free expression. Royalist newspapers had been closed down from the summer of 1792, and pro-monarchical, Feuillant, then Girondin clubs and salons were subsequently stopped from meeting or driven underground. The frank expression of dissenting private views risked falling foul of creeping surveillance laws. The lawcourts lost their erstwhile role as channels for popular grievance, and were subordinated to the interests of the Revolutionary Tribunal. The unitary Revolutionary will preached by Robespierre as a way out of the war emergency was meant to embody public opinion, rather than merely respond to it. These developments were part of a wholesale shrinkage in the scope and independence of the public sphere. The acme of political participation had been attained in the summer crisis of 1789, and the level of electoral involvement was unimpressive thereafter: between 20 and 30 per cent of the electorate participated in elections for the Legislative Assembly in 1791, and the comparable figure for elections to the Convention was a miserable 20 per cent. This recovered to a level of between 25 and 30 per cent in the plebiscite for the 1793 constitution in the summer of 1793,[46] but even so this still meant that the phase of the Revolution most associated with popular radical intervention witnessed a reduction in the use of the ballot box. There would be no elections under the Revolutionary government.

War and Terror had sucked any vitality out of public debate. Now, in the spring of 1794, the institutions of popular militancy were progressively muzzled, with sectional societies bullied into closure, the Paris *armée révolutionnaire* disbanded and the faceless CPS puppet, Fleuriot-Lescot, appointed Paris Mayor. A new chapter was opened in the government's commitment to centralized authoritarianism when on 16 April

Robespierre's ally, Saint-Just, forced through the Convention a police law which gave the CPS its own policing agency – a move which undercut the police monopoly enjoyed by the Committee of General Security (CGS). In addition, on 8 May, the powers of provincial courts and special commissions for judging counter-revolutionary crimes were transferred to the Paris Revolutionary Tribunal. This spelt the intensification as well as the centralization of the judicial machinery of Terror. The Law of 22 Prairial (10 June) introduced in the Convention by Saint-Just and driven through with Robespierre's support – in the context of 'the silence of the legislators rather than by their agreement', as Barère was later to recall[47] – diminished defendants' rights and speeded up trial proceedings. Its impact was immediate. In January and February combined, there had been 188 executions decreed. For June and July, the figure was 1,584 deaths. More than half the total number of the Tribunal's victims were despatched in these two months.

Robespierre's role as ideologist of Terror and as principal CPS spokesman in the Convention made him an obvious target for criticisms of government policy. His 'pretty speeches' were, moreover, becoming increasingly cryptic, as government veered unsteadily between the utopian-philanthropic and the coercive-authoritarian modes, and as Robespierre himself became ever more obsessed by fears of a foreign plot sapping Revolutionary resolve and compromising republican virtue. He devoted much energy to devising a means of 'regenerating' the nation, and creating an authentically new Revolutionary Man. He sought to achieve this through a more acceptable Revolutionary cult than either the dechristianizing atheism which the Hébertists had favoured, or a Catholicism still tarnished with counter-revolutionary sentiment. On 7 May (18 Floréal), he introduced a decree establishing a Cult of the Supreme Being, appending a long speech on the Principles of Political Morality in which he outlined the lineaments of civic virtue on which the Republic was to be grounded. He was acting president of the Convention on 8 June (20 Prairial), when the first festival of the new cult was held in Paris, and led the official procession clad stylishly in a sky-blue frockcoat, carrying a bunch of cornflowers.

'Look at the bugger!', one *sans-culotte* was heard to opine, *sotto voce*, about Robespierre's starring role in the ceremonies. 'It's not enough to be master, he wants to be God as well.'[48] Muffled demotic disrespect towards the 'cannibalistic' Incorruptible was seemingly infectious. The perpetrator of an attempt on the life of Collot d'Herbois in early May confessed he had Robespierre in his sights too, and a poor mad girl, Cécile Renault, was also discovered to have murderous intent towards him. Around the same time, police spies alighted on a Norman visionary, Catherine Théot, who was alleged to be claiming that Robespierre was the new Messiah. (Many Conventionnels must have allowed themselves a grim private smirk at the thought.) Growing numbers of Robespierre's colleagues were indeed having qualms at the prospect of both judicial terror and regeneratory, virtue-drenched rhetoric spinning out of control, with an increasingly intolerant Incorruptible at the controls. Robespierre had always cultivated moderates of the Plain in the Convention, and encouraged them to see in him a man to prevent the worst extremes: thus he had supported freedom of religious worship against the dechristianizers, for example, and claimed to have saved many of the supporters of the Girondins from the scaffold. In March, the Landais deputy, Dyzez, wrote of Robespierre that 'order and tranquillity are in his hands ... Public opinion invests him, and only him.'[49] Yet by June and July, any confidence that Robespierre was in touch with the public mood was eroding fast, while his role in building up the CPS's police powers, developing a personal cult and facilitating the workings of the Revolutionary Tribunal on 22 Prairial made moderate Conventionnels feel personally threatened.

The reservations of moderate Conventionnels were fortified by the improvement of the military situation, for it had been military disasters which – along with *sans-culotte* pressure – had provided the initial rationale for Terror. Victories at Tourcoing and Tournai in May, then, particularly emphatically, at Fleurus on 26 June (8 Messidor) relieved the northern front and allowed French armies under Pichegru to occupy Belgium and force their way into the Netherlands. Improvement was evident in the south too, with republican forces fighting their way into Catalonia. The English fleet defeated the French off Ushant on the 'Glorious First of June', but even here there was a silver lining: a sizeable convoy bringing American grain into France was able to slip past the British blockade and to provide a measure of relief to urban markets.

The anxiety about the direction the Terror was taking had spread, moreover, into the heart of the Revolutionary government. By the summer of 1794, the members of the CPS and the CGS had been living on their collective nerves for a year, holding the republic together under incredible pressure. The strain was telling – and seemed to be getting through to Robespierre, whose personal conduct grew ever more erratic. Boundary disputes between the two committees of government had amplified when the CPS developed its own police and spy apparatus, and then initiated a civic cult which some members of the CGS (such as the fervent atheist Vadier) found offensive and politically suspect. Joseph Cambon, chair of the Finance Committee, which retained a great deal of autonomy from the CPS, regarded the economic effects of Robespierre's policies as damaging, and his ill-feeling was amply recipro-cated. There was growing concern too, which was shared by the more politically conservative members of the CPS such as Carnot, Prieur de la Côte d'Or and Lindet, that Robespierre was allowing a personality cult to develop around him, backed up by devoted factionaries in the Revolutionary Tribunal and the state bureaucracy. In a scarcely collegial exchange in early June, Carnot called Robespierre 'a silly dictator' to his face.[50]

By the end of July, a range of very differing agendas was shaping up over the future course of Revolutionary government: a left-wing call for the state to deliver on its 'fair shares' welfare promises; a moderate wish for an alleviation of the Terror in the light of the improved security position; and a move to drive energetically onwards toward regeneratory virtue. The shadow of Robespierre's dark intentions hovered uncertainly over the Revolution's future, all the more as he was reputed to be compiling a list of patriots for preferment – and an accompanying list of candidates for proscription. Beneath the enforced ideological unity of the regime, faction was pullulating wildly. Whatever their political persuasions, no one in the Convention could feel safe: 'it was not', Conventionnel Baudot subsequently noted of the mood of his colleagues at this time, 'a question of principles; it was about killing'.[51]

On 27 July 1794 – 9 Thermidor II under the new dispensation – the killing was done. In the event, Robespierre brought it upon himself. The previous day, with tensions mounting, he had delivered a policy speech in the Convention calling for redoubled Revolutionary efforts, and had enigmatically alluded to a list of individuals to be proscribed. But he refused to announce to the nerve-racked Conventionnels, their stomachs churning, just whom he had in mind. That signal omission turned the proscription list into a suicide note. The same evening, individuals from all sectors of the political spectrum came together, under the guidance of dechristianizing former deputy on mission Fouché to plot his assassination. 'It is between Robespierre and myself,' prophesied an emotional Joseph Cambon, one of the conspirators, in a midnight letter to friends in Montpellier, 'tomorrow one or other of us will be dead.'[52] And so it came to pass. A Convention which had sat cowed and sullen through Robespierre's earlier pronouncements refused to come to his aid when the conspirators – in an impressive *coup de théâtre* – moved on to the offensive. Saint-Just was silenced in mid-sentence, and then Robespierre and his associates (notably Saint-Just and Couthon from the CPS, and, from the CGS, his brother Augustin and his ally Lebas) were ordered to be imprisoned as enemies of the state.

The fun was not yet, however, at an end. Robespierre and his cronies managed to evade the prison's lock. On the loose and desperate, they made an appeal, through the Commune, for the Parisian *sans-culottes* to come to their aid in a new show of popular sovereignty. The *sans-culottes*, whose vitality the Revolutionary government had spent months sapping, failed to pull Robespierre's chestnuts out of the fire. Despair overtook the outlaws. That night they were discovered bereft and disconsolate in a room in the Hôtel de Ville. The crippled Couthon had tried to kill himself by throwing himself down some stairs. Saint-Just was standing open-mouthed gawping at a poster of the Declaration of the Rights of Man. And Robespierre had tried to blow his brains out, but had succeeded only in almost detaching his jaw from his face – horridly apposite self-mutilation for one whose career had been grounded in his rhetorical skills. Shrieking in pain like a fatally wounded animal, he would be conveyed to the guillotine next day along with his allies. Over the next week, the executioner worked overtime, despatching around 100 alleged Robespierrists from the Commune and from the ministries.

Did killing Robespierre signify the end of the Terror? While many of those who conspired against him on 9 Thermidor, such as Fouché and Collot d'Herbois, felt that he stood in the way of advancement of the welfare and egalitarian ideals of Revolutionary government, many who welcomed his overthrow were all too eager to throw the Terrorist bathwater out with the Robespierrist baby. The months following Thermidor – as Year II became Year III[53] – saw a complex and shifting power-game being played out, with rival groupings contesting the meaning of what had just transpired. Robespierre's name now possessed a powerful charge of negative charisma. Whatever the future might hold, all seemed agreed that it should not include anything within the former vision of the deceased Incorruptible, at whose door even his closest colleagues were now happy to lay blame for the misdeeds of Year II. Mainspring of Revolutionary government, the CPS was now brought to a state of semi-paralysis. The Convention determined that the Committee's personnel should be renewed quarterly, and it soon voted off those with Robespierrist or *sans-culotte* associations. The CGS was similarly deRobespierrized. The new men at the helm included ex-Dantonists like Thuriot and Bréard, repentant Terrorists such as Tallien and former back-bench moderates. On 24 August, a new law revising the 14 Frimaire Law on Revolutionary government restricted the role of the CPS to war and diplomacy, and the hitherto obscure Committee of Legislation assumed a more prominent role in policy-formation and in appointment to administrative posts. The machinery as well as the personnel of Terror also received thoroughgoing reform. Revolutionary justice in particular was scaled down. The Law of 22 Prairial was repealed almost immediately, and the Revolutionary Tribunal was speedily reorganized, with Fouquier-Tinville, public prosecutor for all the political trials of Year II, arrested and, in May 1795, executed. Tighter and less inclusive definitions of political suspects helped bring the notion of a fair trial back into vogue. Prison doors were opened to release many of those arrested and detained often on the vaguest of pretexts – and the Convention further highlighted the mood of restitution by allowing back into its own ranks nearly eighty deputies who had been excluded for protesting against the purge of the Girondins in June 1793. In March 1795, proscribed Girondin deputies were allowed to take up their seats again.

With Terrorism increasingly a spent force, and with moderate republicans and political victims of Year II now back in circulation and free to express their views, the political mood was transformed. Thermidor had given the lie to the Robespierrist claim that the Revolutionary government embodied public opinion – indeed, the coup was to some extent public opinion's revenge on a government increasingly out of touch. Royalist views now still needed to be heavily coded, but on the Left, neo-Hébertist groupings, which had rallied together in the Electoral Club, produced newspapers such as Babeuf's *Le Tribun du Peuple*, which urged the immediate implementation of the radical Constitution of 1793.

The hope that Thermidor might unleash policies more amenable to the views of the *sans-culottes* did not, however, take long to dispel, and the radicals soon found themselves outgunned by the Right. Babeuf admitted he had been among the keenest to remove Robespierre, but, he added mournfully, 'I far from imagined that I was helping to build an edifice which . . . would be no less harmful to the people.'[54] Radicals were ousted by moderates in many Paris sections, and the tempo of the streets was no longer set by *sans-culottes* but by rowdy gangs of right-wing youths. Combining petty bourgeois, young professionals and deserters and draft-dodgers, the *jeunesse dorée* ('gilded youth'), as they were soon labelled, were coordinated by the Conventionnel Fréron, who was becoming as extremist in anti-Terrorism as he had been in Terrorism only months before. The gangs engaged in attacks on anything which smacked of the radical days of Year II: sectional personnel, symbols of popular radicalism, institutions of Terror. No person wearing the red cap of liberty on the streets of Paris could feel safe from a ragging at their hands. Theatres became the sites of brawls, as the *jeunesse*'s singing of 'Le Réveil du Peuple' ('The Re-Awakening of the People') strove to drown out the 'Marseillaise'. Publicly-displayed busts of 'martyred' Marat had to be taken down. On 12 November (22 Brumaire III), the youths achieved their greatest success, namely, the final closure of the Paris Jacobin Club, which was totally out of its element in the new political environment.

The Convention registered these seismic shifts in Parisian popular politics with a sharpening sense of revenge. The powers of the Paris Commune were cut back. The National Guard was reshaped so that it could be more loyal to government dictates and less responsive to street pressure. Former activists were rooted out of the Paris sections and the ministries. The Thermidorian spirit of revenge focused particularly on the most extreme – and most unrepentant – former Terrorists within the Convention. The first scapegoat was Carrier, of *noyades* infamy. Tried for terrorist crimes in November, he was executed in December. By then, the Thermidorians' sights were already trained on a further target, namely, 'the Four', as they became known: Billaud-Varenne, Collot d'Herbois and Barère from the old CPS and Vadier from the CGS. These ex-Terrorists had their fates debated in the Convention in December 1794, and they were indicted in March 1795.

The departments had needed no prompting from the top to begin the settling of scores. Initially there had been some uncertainty about what the Thermidor coup implied and in certain localities the policies of Terror actually intensified. But it did not take long for the Thermidorian penny to drop. Localities discovered that the removal of the figure most identified with the centralization of state power meant that the regime of endlessly obeying orders had passed. Popular radicalism was the first casualty. The powers and numbers of surveillance committees were reduced, and their coordination through correspondence was prohibited. Provincial outposts of Fréron's *jeunesse dorée* helped put local militants on the back foot, while the clandestine return of many non-juring priests and *émigrés* contributed to the local atmosphere of revenge. In the south-east, overtly anti-republican and pro-royalist groupings entered the picture. From the Haute-Loire through to the Bouches-du-Rhône department, semi-clandestine murder gangs known as the Companies of Jehu, of the Sun and of Jesus operated against Year II radicals and purchasers of national lands. Their task was facilitated by the law of 23 February 1795 (7 Ventôse III) which ordered every official discharged since 9 Thermidor to return to their home communes to remain under municipal surveillance. This was tantamount to sending radical activists back to face the fury of local vengeance. A spate of grisly massacres of political prisoners in the regions – Lyon, Nîmes, Marseille, Toulon, Aix, Tarascon – unfolded over the spring of 1795. Central government seemed unworried about such incidents. Indeed, certain deputies on mission in the region – notably ex-Girondin Isnard and Boisset – turned a blind eye to score-settling, and even tacitly encouraged it.

The forces of popular radicalism were further demoralized by the appalling social and economic conditions of the winter of 1794–5. Late autumnal downpours hit the harvest, and bitterly cold winter weather brought conditions which were widely compared with the terrible 1709–10 winter. Misery owed as much to men as to nature. The General Maximum's requisitioning had caused many farmers to cut back on their operations: there was little point of working hard to produce a surplus, if that surplus was only going to be expropriated. The effects of deliberate under-production were amplified by the gradual relaxation and then, in December 1794, the outright abolition of the Maximum. Economic deregulation encouraged the customary blights of the eighteenth-century economy: hoarding, speculation, and black-market operations. When grain and other prime commodities such as firewood and salt managed to reach the marketplace, moreover, consumers had to pay the high prices demanded either in specie or else in massively depreciated paper money. The *assignat*'s débâcle over this winter was frighteningly rapid. Trading at around one-third of its value at Robespierre's fall, it had fallen to 20 per cent in December 1794, 10 per cent in April 1795 and it subsequently spiralled remorselessly downwards to less than 1 per cent by the end of the year. Wary of the sullen resentment caused by such distress, but lacking guidance from a government keener on economic deregulation than welfare schemes, local authorities fell back on a variety of bread-dole and rationing programmes.

In ferocious social conditions which were producing high levels of mortality, malnutrition and epidemic disease, political activism became something of a luxury for which most people had neither time nor energy. Yet the Convention still remained nervous about the possibility of a *sans-culotte* come-back. In February 1795, Babeuf was imprisoned for calling for a 'peaceful insurrection' to provide food for the people and the introduction of the 1793 constitution. The latter document was in fact acquiring iconic status on the Left, which feared that a step away from the democratic values embodied in that unimplemented document was not far away. On 1 April (12 Germinal III), a rather aimless popular demonstration for 'bread and the 1793 constitution' spilled into the Convention hall. The deputies sat tight until it had run its course. They then agreed to establish a committee to revise the constitution, but also declared a state of siege and appointed General Pichegru Commander-in-Chief. The next day, they steeled themselves to deport the indicted 'Four' to Guiana, and went on to order arrests of other ex-Terrorists, including Amar, Thuriot and Cambon.

The '*journées* of Germinal' acted to stiffen the anti-Terrorist resolve of the majority in the Convention in a way likely to aggrieve the relics of the once-powerful *sans-culotte* movement. Conflict was sharpened by the provocative decision on 18 April to pack the 'Commission of Eleven' created to revise the 1793 constitution with moderate republicans and even a handful of known constitutional monarchists; and by reductions in bread-doles at the end of that month. On 20–21 May, the '*journées* of Prairial' (1–2 Prairial III) saw further poorly coordinated popular invasions of the Convention hall. The severed head of one deputy, Féraud, was waved rather unsteadily, on the end of a pike, in the face of the President of the Assembly, Boissy d'Anglas, who with considerable sangfroid doffed his hat at it. The pressure of the crowd was such that the vestigial Jacobin grouping of deputies leapt forward to propose measures in line with popular demands. By doing so, they put their own heads on the block. For the majority of the Convention subsequently cleared the hall, won back the initiative and three days later unleashed a bout of savage repression. The rebellious sections were overrun by troops who disarmed all activists, while the arrest was ordered of the ex-Jacobin Conventionnels who had compromised themselves by supporting the *journées*. Some had fled, but six were tried and sentenced to death. On their way to the guillotine on 17 June, they would attempt a collective suicide.

The stoical gesture of these 'martyrs of Prairial' highlighted the depths of impotence and despair to which the Left had been reduced within a year of 9 Thermidor. The Right was now firmly ensconced in power, and over the spring and summer of 1795, it continued its policy of dismantling of the machinery of Terror. The post of deputy on mission was abolished, for example, the Revolutionary Tribunal was wound up, and all political clubs were closed. From 12 June 1795 (24 Prairial III), it was forbidden to use the word 'revolutionary' in respect of any government institution. It was as if the Republic had become nervous of referring to its origins, for fear of inflaming 'extremists'.

The Right benefited as well from the much-improved domestic and international situations. The death in the Temple prison in Paris on 8 June 1795 of 'Louis XVII' – Louis XVI's young dauphin – served the Republic's interests very neatly. The succession passed to the *émigré* comte de Provence, who took the title of Louis XVIII. The new king's 'Verona Declaration' in June was massively misjudged: he promised – threatened was perhaps the word – the integral restoration of the Ancien Régime, with only vaguely denominated 'abuses' being corrected, plus the execution of the 'regicides' (those who had voted the execution of his brother). The glaring absence of an olive branch put compromise or negotiation out of the question. Affairs in western France had much the same effect. In the quest for pacification of this troubled area, General Hoche had been allying firmness and conciliation, and his efforts were crowned with some degree of success. Truces were signed with the remnants of the Vendéan forces and with the Chouan guerillas in Brittany, and an amnesty was agreed which also granted local freedom of worship even for non-juring priests – a concession only made for the rest of the country later in 1795. This seemed a badly chosen moment for the exiled pretender to undertake a military venture in the region. His plan, which involved coordinating an *émigré* landing with a further bout of local insurrection, was badly conceived, execrably implemented and duly turned out a fiasco: the invading royalist troops and their rebel allies were routed at Quiberon Bay in late June 1795.

The Republic was no longer under military pressure on the frontiers either. Indeed, the war of national defence of 1792–4 was mutating into a conflict in which it had become possible to envision not merely peace, but even peace with honour – and conquests. The battle of Fleurus (8 June 1794) had unlocked the door into the Low Countries, and by January 1795 Pichegru had begun to occupy part of Holland, capturing the Dutch fleet on the frozen Texel with a cavalry charge. The 1795 campaign in the east began well too, with General Jourdan advancing deep into Germany. Austria and England still stood fast, but their allies were beginning to crumble in the face of French successes. Prussia was preoccupied with developments in eastern Europe, where it was negotiating the third partition of Poland with Austria and Russia, and in April it came to terms of disengagement from the war with France. Treaties were subsequently signed with Holland in May and Spain in July. France agreed to the Prussian demand that it should evacuate the right bank of the Rhine, but secret clauses allowed the Republic to retain the left bank if and when peace eventuated. A regime whose watchword had all too recently been transparency seemed to be habituating itself to the byways of secret, Ancien Régime-style diplomacy: in the treaty with Holland, the Dutch agreed to finance the upkeep of 25,000 troops for the French cause; while in October, it was secretly determined that Belgium would be annexed into France.

Secure on the frontiers, triumphant over the forces of popular radicalism and authoritarian centralism, and happy beneficiary of the policy fiascos of the Bourbons, the Thermidorians profited from this fragile moment of stability to frame a new constitution. Their aim was to link up with the liberal spirit of 1791 – and to a considerable degree in fact with the *monarchien* project of the summer of 1789. The new regime should enshrine constitutional legality rather than Revolutionary exceptionalism. And it should avoid like the plague any hint of unified government which recalled the putatively democratic authoritarianism of Year

II, as well as the absolutist polity of the Bourbons. The Commission of the Eleven came up with a complex system of checks and balances tailored to avoid the perceived abuses of the recent, and not-so-recent past. The 'Constitution of Year III' (or 1795), instituted a *monarchien*-style bi-cameral legislature, based on a property franchise rather than universal manhood suffrage. Executive power was shared by a committee of five Directors, one of whom, designated by lot, would be replaced each year. The Thermidorians themselves looked to provide the careful handling which the new regime seemed to require: the Law of Two-Thirds decreed in August along with the new constitution stipulated that two-thirds of the new legislature would be drawn from the ranks of the Convention.

Ratification for the new constitution and the Law of Two-Thirds was sought in a plebiscite. Even though both decrees were passed, turnout was extremely low. Only 49,000 individuals voted against the new constitution, as against over 1 million in favour. Around 200,000 voted in favour of the Law of Two-Thirds, with over 100,000 against. The latter figures were arrived at, moreover, only after some dubious counting procedures: no fewer then forty-seven of Paris's forty-eight sections voted against the Law. Only days after its ratification was agreed in the Convention, there was a royalist rising of the Paris sections on 5 October (13 Vendémiaire IV) ostensibly in objection to it. The Convention was, however, developing intestinal fortitude in such cases: it appointed one of its members, Barras, to oversee its defence, and he used the military expertise of Napoleon Bonaparte to disperse the rioting crowds with – in Bonaparte's famous words – 'a whiff of grapeshot'. The Vendémiaire *journée* signalled the final act of one of the most dramatic periods of rule in French parliamentary history. In their final session, on 26 October (4 Brumaire IV), the Conventionnels offered a fitting gift to a Directorial regime whose destiny seemed to lie in the Right-to-centrist policies they had come round to espousing: a political amnesty. Yet those who were excluded from the amnesty – counterfeiters of *assignats*, the royalist rebels of Vendémiaire, all *émigrés*, and the deported ex-Conventionnels, Billaud-Varenne and Collot d'Herbois – were as revealing as those who were included. For they highlighted what would prove to be the continuing bugbears of the post-Terror republic: an economy shot to pieces by rampant inflation and currency depreciation, and men of violence on the Left and the Right.

II

The Unsteady Republic
(1795–9)

A) SHAKY FOUNDATIONS

The messy winding up of the Convention in October 1795 provided an inauspicious beginning for the new republican regime. The political chalice proffered by the Conventionnels which had disenchanted the electorate in the September plebiscite proved no more appetizing in the elections of the following month: only around a million citizens voted in primary assemblies, and the more restrictive second-level electoral assemblies delivered an unqualified raspberry to the new constitution. The Law of Two-Thirds had to be invoked to ensure that some 100 ex-Conventionnels were added to the 394 of their fellows elected. The Left lost heavily, and the new deputies had a strongly right-wing complexion: of 250 new men, 88 were outright counter-revolutionaries, and a further 73 could be qualified as moderate royalists. The continued domination of the ex-Conventionnels meant that the men chosen as Directors were all regicides. The politically supple ex-noble Barras, hero of the defeat of the Vendémiaire *journée*, was a popular choice, as was Carnot, acclaimed 'organizer of victory' in Year II (but now progressing towards moderate royalism), who stood in for Siéyès, who refused to serve. Their colleagues lacked political and personal sparkle: La Révellière-Lépeaux had little but worthy tedium to recommend him; Letourneur was a military engineer like Carnot; and Reubell, a diligent Alsatian lawyer of mildly leftish hue.

The first challenge awaiting the Directors was the continuing economic and social problems of the Republic – and the political agitation which that helped promote. Both factors brought under intense pressure the vaunted respect of the new regime for legality and constitutionality, after the Revolutionary exceptionalism of the Convention. The appalling

507

winter of 1794–5 augured exceeding ill for the first year of the Directory's power. The continuing depreciation of the *assignat* was worsening problems: in November and December, the currency's cash return dipped below 1 per cent of its face value, bringing a comic aspect to many exchanges and inducing street beggars to decline alms in paper form. Government benefited from the depreciation by paying off its debts, but conversely found the real value of its tax take dwindling almost to nothing. The Directors made a great show of abolishing the *assignat* as a currency, on 16 February 1796, formally breaking the overworked presses on which they had been printed. Yet problems persisted. The Directors rejected the proposal of Finance Minister Ramel to create a state bank – lingering memories of John Law still counted for something, and these were overlain with a continuing suspicion of the vulnerability of English-style dependence on public credit and foreign empire. In March 1796, the government simply introduced a new paper currency, the *mandat territorial*, which was fixed at the ratio of 1:30 against the old *assignats*. Wretchedly, however, it played out the *assignat*'s experience in fast-forward mode: within four months it had collapsed totally.

It was not simply a matter of the débâcle of paper currency over the winter and spring of 1795–6 worsening conditions for a great many individuals. What aggravated matters was that government showed rank insouciance towards popular suffering. The forced loan it tried to levy in December to compensate for a shrinking tax take aroused much indignation and little hard money. Although the state utilized devalued paper currency to pay its own debts, it also did its best to ensure that its own creditors paid in cash or kind: landowners, for example, were obliged to pay their taxes in grain or its cash equivalent. Economic deregulation was accompanied by boosts to private enterprise which scandalized aficionados of the controlled economy of Year II. The sale of national lands in return for devalued *assignats* provided a field day for property speculators, who went on to sell or lease in return for hard cash. Financial corruption seemed to characterize the government's growing use of the private sector: the private company established to wind up the *assignats* made huge profits, as did private contractors working for the army. The shabbiness of the regime was all the greater in that sleaze was matched by a new-found and brazen hedonism – in which Director Barras was up to his ears. The republic of vice seemed to have succeeded the Republic of Virtue.

Despite its reputation for the individual venality of leading figures, the regime worked hard to put the state's fiscality on to an even keel, in an appallingly difficult economic situation in which runaway inflation was being followed by plummeting deflation. Finance Minister Ramel – in post from February 1796 to July 1799 – was responsible for carrying through a partial state bankruptcy in September 1797 (Vendémiaire VI) following the *mandat territorial* fiasco. Although he dressed the measure up to disguise the fact, Ramel essentially repudiated two-thirds of the national debt – following this up in December by a parallel measure for the state's other financial commitments. These measures were hardly destined to improve the regime's popularity with the rentier class, which was propelled thereby more firmly to the right. But they did help the economy to recover from recent paroxysms. Ramel also overhauled the state's fiscal regime. First, he improved the collection system, introducing a Direct Tax Agency from November 1797 responsible to the Finance Minister. Second, he issued revised schedules for the main direct taxes, on land, on moveable wealth and on industry (the *patente*), and initiated a new tax on doors and windows. And, third, he brought back indirect taxation, from which the state had not profited since the onslaught on Farmers General, seigneurial and municipal tolls and the like in 1789. A stamp tax on paper and official documents was followed by municipal tolls (*octrois*) in Paris then other major cities, a tobacco tax and so on.

This patient work of state reconstruction failed to douse down political extremism. The opening of the Panthéon Club in November 1795, a successor to the closed Jacobins, marked the beginnings of the recovery of the extra-parliamentary Left, now reinforced by amnestied militants. Drawing together ex-Terrorists such as Amar, Pache, Darthé and Buonarroti, the Club called for more radical policies, and its message was taken up by Babeuf's *Tribun du Peuple*, and it also spread to the provinces where a network of neo-Jacobin groupings emerged. Director Barras had been giving subsidies to the anti-royalist press but now, as the Left began to consolidate its position, withdrew government aid, and in February 1796, closed down the Panthéon Club and its emulators. But by then the Left had begun to attract support from within the Directorial Councils.

'Gracchus' Babeuf's ideas about agrarian reform, symbolized by his adoption of a first name which honoured the radical land-reformer of the Roman Republic, included state ownership of all property, communism in distribution and small-scale direct democracy. He put much of this on hold, however, as he worked to give direction to the re-emerging Left. The Germinal and Prairial *journées* seemed to have demonstrated that the old kind of Revolutionary demonstration-cum-insurrection was no longer an effective option: bad living conditions demoralized rather than radicalized the people, while the disappearance of the old Parisian sections, following the rearrangement of municipal government, made organization much harder. In addition, the Right had far more support than at any time since 1791, while Vendémiaire showed that the government was now ready, if necessary, to meet force with superior force on the streets of Paris. Babeuf thus chose to target radical propaganda at key strategic sites – such as the Police Legion formed to take the place of the old National Guard. He combined this with the formation of a secret insurrectionary committee to organize a coup d'état to seize the levers of power, replace the Year III Constitution with that of 1793 and to go back to something like the closed economy of Year II.

Babeuf's 'Conspiracy of Equals' took shape from late March 1796. Those let into at least part of the secret tended to be the intellectual heirs of the Parisian *sans-culottes* (including members of the Police Legion), middling-sort radicals in the big provincial cities and a smattering of Left radicals from the Councils. The Directory had been deregulating the economy since Thermidor; but it had not cashiered the police spies on which the Terror had depended, and these allowed the government to keep abreast of the threat. A special Police Ministry was created in January under Merlin de Douai, who, as a Thermidorian CPS member, had won his reactionary spurs overseeing the closure of the Jacobin Club in November 1794. Press freedom was restricted, and on 16 April proposing the reintroduction of the 1793 constitution, the restoration of the monarchy or radical agrarian reforms was made punishable by death. At the end of the month, Merlin ordered the disbanding of the Police Legion, which had been infiltrated by the Babouvists. In a pre-emptive swoop on 10 May (21 Floréal V), Babeuf and many of his fellow 'Equals' were arrested, and sent to be tried for treason before the high court established in reassuringly out-of-the-way Vendôme.

The threat to the regime's political stability from the Left fizzled gently out over ensuing months. While nearly fifty putative 'Equals' were awaiting trial, the neo-Jacobin rump in Paris tried unsuccessfully to win over disgruntled soldiers encamped at nearby Grenelle. The attempt backfired, and special military commissions were set up to dispense summary justice over the would-be rebels. More than thirty death-sentences were carried out, including that on the wild ex-Conventionnel Javogues. The trial of Babeuf and his colleagues only got under way in February 1797. The conspiracy's secrecy made it difficult for the prosecution to establish the guilt of all but the ringleaders. Most of the accused were discharged, a handful were deported and only Babeuf and Darthé condemned to death: with due Roman stoicism they attempted to commit suicide on the way to the scaffold on 27 May 1797 (8 Prairial V). That their death caused nary a flicker of interest in Paris highlighted how remote the heirs of Year II radicalism had become from the popular classes whom they imagined themselves representing.

With the Left seemingly under control, the Directory could now endeavour to come to terms with the threat to political stability embodied by the resurgent Right. Fortunately for them, the royalists were split between moderates and extremists and their cause was also badly served by the unbudging refusal of their leader, Louis XVIII, to consider compromising his attachment to a restoration of the Ancien Régime. To a considerable extent, the mixed system of government instituted in Year III had been developed as a more attractive alternative to the form of unified government represented by the Bourbons. It was comforting, then, that the Bourbons fell into the trap. The Pretender was convinced that his native land had 'reverted to the end of the sixteenth century', and therefore needed more rather than less absolut-ism if it was to recover from religious and civil strife.[1] Though still smarting from the fiasco of Quiberon Bay, the émigrés tried another landing on the Île de Yeu off Brittany. It flopped, failing to reignite the forces of popular royalism in the west. The astute counter-insurgency work of the local republican commander, General Hoche, was also producing results here. Vendéan leaders Stofflet and Charette were captured and executed in early 1796, and within months the Vendéan rebels and the Breton Chouans had been neutralized.

The émigré position was also seriously affected by the course of the European war, for most of their European allies were beginning to disengage from the conflict, either from choice or under military pres-sure. Hoche's plan to use the Army of the West to invade Ireland and Wales came to nothing, and the Royal Navy's victory over the French at Cape Saint-Vincent in February 1797 confirmed English naval dominance. In continental Europe, the withdrawal of Prussia and Spain from the war in 1795 marked the beginning of a trend. Even though French fortunes in the German campaign of 1796 were mixed, many minor German states sought armistices.

The most striking successes were, however, the doing of General Bonaparte on the Italian front. The young Corsican had been a career artillery officer before 1789, springing to national prominence for his part in the capture of Toulon from the British in December 1793. A budding reputation as a Jacobin and friendship with Augustin Robespierre won him a spell in a Thermidorian gaol in August 1794. But he re-emerged to develop his career under the wing of Barras, whom he served in putting down the Vendémiaire rising. Marriage to one of Barras's protégées, the Créole widow Josephine de Beauharnais, was followed almost immediately by appointment to the Italian command. Bonaparte seized his opportunity with alacrity and, in a matter of months, had turned a military sideshow into the main focus of France's strategic efforts. In a whirlwind campaign strewn with brilliant victories, he knocked the kingdom of Savoy out of the war: the Armistice of Cherasco in April 1796 was followed by the Treaty of Paris in May, ceding Nice and Savoy to the French. Bonaparte's successes stimulated Jacobin radicals in Italian cities to demonstrate in France's favour, and the general turned the discomfiture of existing regimes to France's advantage. In December 1796, the duchy of Modena, including Reggio, was added to the papal territories of Bologna and Ferrara to form the new Cispadane ('this side of the Po') Republic, which was given a Directorial-style constitution. Bonaparte spent much of the autumn and winter of 1796–7 fighting the Austrians for control of the strategically key fortress of Mantua, and he inflicted a series of defeats upon them before the French took the city in February. With most of the states of the Italian peninsula falling into the hands of the young Frenchman, Austria decided to treat for terms. The Austro–French Peace Preliminaries signed at Leoben on 18 April were followed by the Treaty of Campo-Formio on 18 October 1797 (27 Vendémiaire VI).

Campo-Formio highlighted significant changes in France's international strategy and indeed its place in Europe. By forcing France's most formidable land foe to the conference table, Bonaparte ensured recognition of the Republic's annexations in the north (Belgium, the left bank of the Rhine) and in the south-east (Nice, Savoy). Yet his personal diplomacy – which extended French influence in Italy further than at any time in the previous 300 years – involved riding roughshod over the wishes of the Directors, who had wished to use Italian conquests as bargaining counters in a general peace with Austria and the Holy Roman Empire. The war of national defence of 1792–4 was turning into a conflict for expansion and conquest, recalling the dynastic manoeuvres of the Bourbon monarchy. Bonaparte had, moreover, displayed machiavellian cunning in utilizing pro-French agitation by local Jacobins as diplomatic leverage. Jacobin risings in the Venetian cities of Brescia and Bergamo served as the justificatory figleaf for him to work surreptitiously with the Austrians to partition the Venetian Republic: the Austrians took the lion's share, while Bonaparte's pickings were added to the conquered Lombardy and the Cispadane Republic so as to form the Cisalpine ('this side of the Alps') Republic.

Bonaparte's successes cancelled out the European threat associated with the *émigrés*, and allowed the regime to focus on devising a way of dealing with the growth of royalist sentiment within France itself. The Babeuf plot had caused a red scare (which the Directors helped orchestrate) which consolidated the popularity of the Right. The latter also benefited from the moderate religious *aggiornamento* which the Directory permitted: returned refractory priests did their utmost to prod their flocks towards opposing the regime. The Clichy Club in Paris became a rallying ground for royalist propaganda, allowing the fusion of moderate ex-Conventionnels such as Boissy d'Anglas and Henry La Rivière and returned *émigrés* such as Mathieu Dumas. Many Clichyens embraced the constitutional road, arguing that the working-through of the Law of Two-Thirds would allow the royalist majority in France to reassert itself democratically. Others on the Right, however, rejected such moderation. The *Institut philanthropique*, for example – a congeries of voluntary associations, located in most departments, which ostensibly sought to revive charity – developed as a front organization for insurrection. So did the 'Paris Agency' of abbé Brottier, reactionary journalist turned counter-revolutionary broker. Brottier's nationwide network of royalist agents had initially sought to persuade Louis XVIII to agree to a constitution and a political amnesty, but the abbé was turned towards insurrectionary methods by Louis's intransigence. Though Brottier's arrest in January 1797 reduced the influence of his 'Paris Agency', at much the

THE UNSTEADY REPUBLIC (1795-9)

same time, the eminent General Pichegru – dismissed from his post in early 1796 because of his political views – began to establish covert links with the exiled monarch. There seemed a real danger of the royalists frittering away their strong position in a welter of competing factions and crossed wires. Faction, the Achilles heel of the Bourbon polity, was the besetting vice of the emigration.

The Directory did its best to keep the royalists within the bounds of legality and to reduce their political *modus operandi*. The tightening of press censorship and the reorganization of political policing targeted the royalists as much as the Left. In March 1796, efforts had been made to shake royalists out of state service and administrative office by imposing on all functionaries an oath of hatred of royalty, and several weeks later the death penalty was reimposed for proposing the restoration of the monarchy. Among the Directors, Carnot in particular sought to find ways of winning over constitutional royalists to the cause of moderate republicanism, but for all his efforts he failed to devise a sufficiently attractive package. For example, had the Directors repealed the Therm-idorian law of 4 Brumaire IV (26 October 1795) which excluded *émigrés* and their relatives from any public office,[2] they would have alienated their supporters in the centre as well as on the Left. The latter was already weakened by the depredations of the White Terror in many areas. In the event, the Directors' efforts to placate the Right by attacking the Left through purging judicial, municipal and administrative posts dangerously strengthened the Right in the country as a whole and made more likely a further royalist victory at the polls in the spring of 1797.

The Directorial antagonism towards extremism of both the Right and the Left was generating an endless fight on two fronts which risked thinning support for the political centre and the principle of consti-tutionality which was the regime's touchstone. In April and May 1797, the fulcrum collapsed, and the inevitable occurred. The Year V elections to renew one-third of the Councils produced a royalist triumph: only thirteen of some 216 ex-Conventionnels who had put themselves up for consideration were elected, and even the workings of the Law of Two-Thirds could not forestall a massive shift to the Right in the Councils. The royalists, who included prominent figures such as Pichegru and Louis XVIII's political agent, Imbert-Colomès, were probably not far from a majority. In the first tests of strength, they had outgoing Director Letourneur replaced by the career diplomat and acknowledged rightist, Barthelémy, and Pichegru elected President of the Council of the Five Hundred.

Moderate republicans did not, however, take the royalist success lying down. In Paris, the Club de Salm emerged to orchestrate anti-royalism. One of their number, Siéyès, when asked what he had done during the Terror, famously replied 'J'ai vécu' ('I survived'). This *bon mot* could have been the collective watchword of the Club as a whole: it included figures such as former Terrorist Tallien, Girondinophiles Daunou and Garat, professional survival artistes such as Talleyrand, as well as the mutual admiration society that was the young Benjamin Constant and latterday salonnière Madame de Staël (the daughter of Necker). The Salmistes did their utmost to counter royalist propaganda, notably through their newspaper, *L'Éclair*, and also linked up with a developing network of 'constitutional circles' (*cercles constitutionnels*) which in larger cities were bringing together the provincial vestiges of Jacobinism.

The political situation after the Year V elections developed into a war of position between rival factions, with muffled insurrectionary noises off supplied by bellicose neo-Jacobins and sabre-rattling royalists. The seemingly unstoppable progress of the Right and the complaisance of Directors Carnot and Barthelémy was causing the remaining triumvirate on the Directory (Barras, Reubell and La Révellière-Lépeaux) to coordinate their views on the defence of the Republic. A significant – and in the event ominous – development was their desire to explore ways of profiting from the dazzling prestige in which the republican armies were now clothed. In July, a Directorial reshuffle ended the Clichyen complexion of the ministries, and Talleyrand was appointed Foreign Minister, with General Hoche offered the post of War Minister. To bring a military commander into the government was startling enough; but it was doubly so in that Hoche had been tipped off to bring his troops up within striking distance of Paris in case the Right took their protests to the streets.

In the event, Hoche's ministerial career was blocked by the realization that he was under the age requirement of forty for all ministers. The Right had, however, been thoroughly alarmed by the turn of events. In retrospect, it might have been in their interests to abandon a policy of caution. Yet divisions within their ranks continued to hobble their capacity for decisive action. Many moderate constitutionalist monarchists still urged a waiting game, with the electoral tide flowing so strongly in their favour. This was all the more the case after 27 June 1797 (9 Messidor V), when the Councils repealed the Law of 4 Brumaire IV, opening public office to *émigrés* and their families and ending persecution of refractory priests under 1792 and 1793 legislation. However, electoral success in Year V had stoked up the enthusiasm of the hardliners. They felt that the iron was hot enough to strike – but were divided over exactly when and how. Their dithering allowed their opponents to seize the initiative. The Triumvirs on the Directory – Barras, Reubell and La Révellière-Lépeaux – agreed to the Councils' wish to dissolve all political clubs, a move directed against the *cercles constitutionnels*. But they also put out feelers to the army to secure the aid of a sympathetic general. Barras won over his erstwhile client, Bonaparte, who sent the trustworthy General Augereau to Paris to be at the Triumvirate's disposal. Augereau harried the right-wing royalist youth gangs within the city, while Hoche circled the city menacingly with further troops. In an atmosphere crackling with political tension, the Triumvirs struck. On 4 September 1797 (18 Fructidor V), they ordered the military occupation of Paris and then went on to annul the Year V elections in forty-nine departments in which the Right had triumphed; to remove from the Councils nearly 200 deputies; and to deport over sixty leading royalists, including Carnot, Pichegru and Barthélemy.

The Fructidor coup d'état produced a sharp move back towards the political centre ground following months in which the Right had carried all before it. Barras, Reubell and La Révellière-Lépeaux took steps to effect an anti-royalist transformation of the political landscape. The two empty posts of Director were filled by ex-Police Minister, Merlin de Douai, and the technocratic François de Neufchâteau, who had been appointed Interior Minister in the July reshuffle. The Directors took on emergency powers so as to conduct purges over the next weeks at every level of public life, ejecting putative royalists in administrative, judicial and municipal posts. The law of 4 Brumaire IV – still very much the litmus test of factional contention – was reimposed, disbarring from public posts individuals from *émigré* families, while on 29 November 1797 former nobles were prohibited from public life. Any *émigré* who had returned to France without obtaining government consent was required to leave France forthwith, and the punitive laws of 1792–3 against refractory priests were reimposed, leading to the abandonment of the relative religious freedom which had developed prior to Fructidor.

All public officials, members of electoral assemblies and individuals serving on juries would henceforth swear an oath of hatred of royalty and anarchy (the latter a code-word for Jacobinism). A new press law forced the closure of much of the royalist and right-wing press, while military commissions were established with competence over returning *émigrés*, conspirators, bandits, rebels and highwaymen.

The Right was swift to denounce this wave of repression. Yet the 'Fructidorian Terror' was small beer when compared to the Terror of Year II (or indeed the White Terror of Year III). It disposed of political opponents mainly through the 'dry guillotine' of deportation rather than by physical liquidation. Some 1,600 priests were deported, for example, while the total number of capital victims of the military commissions down to 1799 was only around 150. This was far too mild to effect a durable sea-change in the political complexion of the country at large. Political clubs opened again, but levels of enthusiasm for the regime were not high. The methods which the Triumvirate had employed to carry out their coup caused a good deal of alarm and disenchantment. The Directory had prided itself on being the regime of legality in which the executive power was kept in check – in contradistinction to both the supra-legal personal absolutism of the Bourbon polity or the Revolutionary violence of Year II. Yet in Fructidor it used main force to override electoral decisions arrived at by constitutional means, and pressurized the judiciary into political sentencing.

Having stepped outside the charmed circle of constitutionality, moreover, the Fructidorians found it difficult to step back in, especially as it was soon apparent that they had far from depleted the strength of royalist opinion in the country as a whole. The attack on the Right had, moreover, triggered a compensatory resurgence of the Left. The early months of 1798 were spent in growing dread of the result of the Year VI elections from which both Right and Left could expect to make significant gains. The Directors worked hard on the electoral small print in order to deny their opponents too many advantages. Thus in February 1798, it was agreed that the outgoing (rather than incoming) Councils would choose the new Director each year; while political rights including participation in elections were denied to any individual who had discharged civil or military responsibilities with rebels. In March, the Directors began to encourage the idea of 'schismatic' electoral assemblies being formed in localities where it seemed likely that Left or Right candidates hostile to the regime might be elected. This gave them the scope for a choice of candidates to endorse when on 11 May (22 Floréal VI) the electoral results started to come in. They used this power especially against the Left – eighty-four of some 130 radicals or Jacobins were 'Floréalized', and replaced by pro-Directorial candidates from 'schismatic' assemblies. The process was, moreover, extended to other forms of elections taking place at this time: altogether around a quarter of legislative elections and a third of either judicial or administrative posts were affected by Directorial fiat.

The Directors were too engrossed in keeping their heads above the waters of political disillusionment at home to be able to control foreign policy. With Carnot and Barthélemy gone, they lacked a member with diplomatic nous and experience to resist the growing incursions of their generals in policy-making – at home as abroad. They consequently viewed with mixed feelings Bonaparte's development of his own personal diplomacy in Italy. If this threatened Directorial authority on one hand, at least it was a safety valve for ambitious energies which could prove explosive if they were brought home into the delicately poised atmosphere within France. The Corsican was still trailing clouds of glory for his role in Campo-Formio, and so the Directors listened attentively to his suggestion, from late 1797, that he should lead an expedition to Egypt, stepping-stone to British power in India. The widespread conviction that British imperial power was based on a wobbly system of public credit which might be pushed to the brink of collapse seemed to endorse this venture, especially as British naval power was shutting the French out of imperial battle theatres in the New World. The Directors also liked the proposal because it would bottle up Napoleon's ferocious energies in the Middle East – and might even put him in harm's way.

Under the provisions of Campo-Formio, further negotiations were to take place, involving France, Austria and the Holy Roman Empire, to settle a durable peace in Europe. The mood of the ensuing Congress of Rastadt was severely disturbed by continuing French gains, which further threatened the balance of power. Coups d'état performed by local Jacobins in Holland in January, then June, 1798 strengthened French influence in the 'Batavian Republic', which adopted a Directorial-style constitution. French military involvement on the Swiss frontier led to the annexation of Mulhouse (January 1798) and Geneva (April). Part of Switzerland had been merged into the Cisalpine Republic in 1797, and in spring 1798, the rump was formed into another 'sister republic', the Helvetic Republic. The unstable political situation after Campo-Formio also sucked the French further into the Italian peninsula. A riot in Rome in which the French general Duphot was murdered was pretext for French troops to invade and subsequently to organize a Roman Republic in February 1798. In November, troops from the kingdom of Naples attacked France's puppet regime, the Roman Republic. The riposte was so brusquely effective that within weeks, French commander Championnet had occupied Naples and – in direct contradiction to the wishes of the Directors – established a Neapolitan (or 'Parthenopean') Republic in the southern half of the peninsula

The Directors were aware that the personal diplomacy and war-mongering of Bonaparte and other generals were endangering the hopes for European peace. Yet they winked at the expansionism into which they were being drawn. The principal reason for this was the financial advantage which France derived from war. War was not without political costs. With the number of troops dwindling, and desertion spreading like an epidemic, the Jourdan Law of September 1798 was passed, introducing universal obligation to conscription for males over twenty years old. This was predictably unpopular. Yet the thought of ending war, bringing the armies back home and moving to a full peacetime economy promised even greater problems. For war had begun to pay for itself in a way that took pressure off tax-payers at home.

In the period of the Terror, the new mass armies, lacking bureaucratic support and maintenance, had resorted to an atavistic policy of plunder which the Finance supremo of Year II, Cambon, was happy to accept and to systematize. Field commanders were encouraged to seek ways of making conquered territories pay. Consequently, reforms trumpeted as Revolutionary – such as the nationalization of church property or the abolition of feudalism – in fact devolved into means of naked revenue-extraction. The instructions of 'organizer of victory' Carnot had been explicit as to both the substance and the motivation of such a policy: 'Strip our enemies of all their resources, all their means of existence. It is a great misfortune that we have to plunder, but it is still preferable to take destruction elsewhere than suffer it on one's own territory.'[3] From 1795 onwards, the same policy was imposed on the so-called 'sister republics'. After the latter received their new constitution, they signed a commercial treaty in which they undertook to make major contributions to the upkeep of troops. The Directors also adopted the practice of allowing the businessmen who served as army contractors a proportion of the tax take from conquered territories. The generals were playing the same game. Bonaparte in particular proved particularly adept at it, keeping a large proportion of money raised for the use of himself and his troops. He was also involved in measures of naked expropriation, notably of works of art. A good proportion of such booty also made its way back to Paris. Between 1796 and 1799, approximately one-quarter of the state's needs were met by income extorted from conquered territories. War had bricked itself into the Directory's financial and political architecture. Consequently, when in 1798–9 military strategy was to falter and France was faced again with the spectre of military defeat, the survival of the whole regime would be at stake.

B) REVOLUTION: A USER'S GUIDE

To the political class who had lived through the drama of the Terror, Thermidor gave the Revolution an historic second chance. The goal of the Thermidorians and Directorials was to put the Revolution back on the course on which it had set out so hopefully in 1789, linking up with the universalist assumptions embodied in the 1791 constitution of the Legislative Assembly, and the regenerative impulse at the heart of Revolutionary culture so as to make a 'new man'. Post-Thermidor politicians had still to work in the context of a European war which had brought down the 1791 constitution and had justified the patriotic outlook and practices apparent since 1792. They had to combine this with a thoroughgoing rejection of what they saw as both the excesses of the Convention and the hated spirit of the Ancien Régime.

The Directorials' endeavours to fulfil this ambitious programme were inhibited by a larger difficulty which dogged the Revolutionaries throughout the decade, namely, that of squaring the languages of individual rights with those of community interest. The Rights of Man and *la patrie* were talismanic terms in the lexicon of Revolution; but it proved very difficult to conjugate them together – never more than during the Terror when the very preservation of national identity seemed at threat from external and internal enemies, justifying a dizzyingly swift erosion of personal freedoms – and an equally rapid sanctification of the fatherland. The repressively communitarian politics of the Terror shocked liberal politicians, who stressed the inviolability of individual freedoms, and the Thermidorians sought to make individual rights properly respected. Yet for most Revolutionaries, it ran deeper than this. Many had acquiesced in the popular violence and lynchings of 14 July 1789, the Great Fear, and the overthrow of the monarchy. By the same token, the arch-ideologist of Terror, Robespierre, had been the most dogged defender of liberal freedoms, and a humane opponent of the death penalty, down to the outbreak of war. The clash between liberalism and national communitarianism divided patriots amongst themselves; but it was also a division that each Directorial nurtured within his own breast, a nagging conundrum which none could evade.

The conundrum was all the more intractable in that it linked to a moralism which lay at the heart of Revolutionary culture. The Directorials inherited a thoroughgoing rejection of the very notion of politics. Politics might have been, for Revolutionary legislators (to misquote W. H. Auden), their noon, their midnight, their talk, their song – but it was also something they thought was wrong, a morally indefensible notion which dared not speak its name. No harsher term existed in Revolutionary political life than 'the spirit of party', which denoted an un-Revolutionary attachment to sectional interest and private passion. 'I belong to no party,' postured the Girondin Conventionnel Boyer-Fonfrède on one highly charged occasion. 'I wish to belong to no one but my country and my conscience.'[4] Throughout the decade, Revolutionaries were certain that what they were doing transcended politics, and they strove to ascend sublime moral peaks with a firm sense of 'the public interest' or 'the national interest' in their intellectual knapsacks. Their aspiration was for an ethics of government, in which individuals rose above discord based on sectionalism, bad faith and privileged interests. The Constituent Assembly in June 1789 had released the deputies of the Estates General from the binding mandates of their electors precisely because they viewed themselves as representatives of the whole nation, not just a geographical or social splinter within it. Similarly, the Convention's proclamation of the 'Republic One and Indivisible' and the 1795 Constitution's stipulation that 'no individual or partial gathering of citizens may ascribe sovereignty to themselves' highlighted a determination to prevent the fissuring of political unity.[5]

The perceived redundancy of politics for adjudicating rival claims to authority was linked to a wider belief that 1789 had opened a new phase in the history of mankind in which totally new rules of social interaction applied. The legislators' guide would be Nature, touchstone of late Enlightenment sensibility, and Reason. The concomitant rejection of historic precedent as a source of political legitimacy had been arguably the most radical of the revolutionary shifts of 1789.[6] Enlightenment quarrels between pro-Frankish and pro-Gaulish factions were now a political curio, and only ancient Rome and Greece – so far removed in time and space that they seemed both utopian and achronic – provided any sort of positive historical referent. Cicero and Plutarch would be the most cited pre-revolutionary authors in the debates of the Assemblies: the combined number of references to their work was ten times larger than Montesquieu's *On Spirit of the Laws* and over twenty times larger than Rousseau's *Social Contract*.[7] The increasingly anti-clerical direction which the Revolution took from 1791-2 also removed another source of historically oriented authority – namely, the church – from the scope of Revolutionary discourse. The Revolutionary Calendar introduced in 1793 excised scripture from the recording of time, and gloriously proclaimed the certainty that the vagaries of French political life were of vital significance in the history of humankind. All that had gone before the Revolution could now be lumped together into one undifferentiated 'former state of things' or 'Ancien Régime'. Anything which recalled those ignoble days was irremediably *'ci-devant'* ('former'). There was no more dismissive (and, at times, more threatening) Revolutionary adjective.

Revolutionary anti-clericalism and anti-monarchicalism fused into a rejection of any kind of political patriarchalism. The master discourse of the Bourbon polity had been highly paternalistic: the execution of the king either ruled such a discourse out of court, or else displaced it towards filial respect for 'the fatherland' (*la patrie*). The Revolutionaries stressed horizontal rather than vertical ties of dependence in the form of fraternal self-help within the national family. (The adoption of *tutoiement* – the more intimate form of personal address – and the replacement of 'Monsieur' and 'Madame' by 'Citizen' had much the same intent.) It was a virile band of Revolutionary brothers who urged the regeneration of French society founded on what were seen as natural forms. There opened up a mythic present in which, rejecting any reference to the historic past, the Revolutionaries projected themselves into an unfurling utopian and putatively more natural future. 'Let us reconstitute nature', the abbé Grégoire urged his fellow Conventionnels in 1795, 'by giving it a new stamp.'[8] The wish to create something new through the application of human reason was consubstantial with the desire to ground it in the natural world.

In the early 1790s this sense of the rediscovery of the natural explained a widespread feeling that the public spirit was very little removed from the promptings of individuals' own political consciences. Enormous trust was placed on the principle of election in bringing the two forces in line with each other. It was not that elections were unknown in towns, villages, guilds and corporative bodies prior to 1789; indeed, the Bourbon monarchy was experimenting with representational forms from the 1760s onwards. The national mood stimulated into being by the elective process of 1789 was, however, something new – and something which Revolutionary political culture prized, indeed fetishized, as a symbol of democratic inclusiveness, transparency and accountability. There were elections for the national assembly in the summer of 1791; but before these had taken place, there had already been elections for communal, municipal, district and departmental administrative officials; for various kinds of judges and justices; and for priests and bishops. Electors at Rancon in the Haute-Vienne were called on to do their stuff on no fewer than twelve occasions between February 1790 and December 1792. Procedures were lengthy, quite complex and could get very tedious. Voting was done in the open by *appel nominal* (roll-call): it was feared that secret balloting would invite lobbying and the 'obscure manoeuvres of intriguing ambition'.[9]

The faith in the electoral process to deliver the legislators the loyal support of the national community gave them a feeling that they implicitly represented the general will of the whole community. Successive assemblies, it is true, believed that they had a duty to teach the people as well as to learn from them: 'The people are good', stated a Jacobin from Provins, 'but need educating.'[10] 'We must enlighten opinion,' agreed Charles de Lameth. 'We must rule over it so as to render it the benefits we derive from it.'[11] Yet it was anticipated that this would be an easy task, for what national assemblies were trying to do was not to impose alien standards on to a recalcitrant population, but – as Robespierre put it – 'to recall men to nature and to truth'.[12] The Revolutionary New Man lay in waiting in the conscience of the man of good faith, ready to be born again unto Revolution through the promptings of individual conscience and through the humanitarian obstetrics of true patriots. Happiness might be, as Saint-Just noted, 'a new idea in Europe';[13] but it was intelligible to all humankind precisely because it was a natural propensity.

Although the politics of the Revolutionary decade highlighted endless, sometimes murderous differences and divergences amongst those involved in public life, this sense of the Revolution as a regenerative process was widely shared throughout the period, representing as it did received wisdom inherited from the late Enlightenment vision of the possibility of making a better world. Human creativity could make that better world, guided by the light of public opinion, the supreme and impartial tribunal of rationality against which deeds and thoughts could be judged and measured. The Revolution witnessed the nation seizing sovereignty from the monarch, and allowing public opinion (or 'public spirit', as some Revolutionaries preferred to call it) to triumph over partisan views and interests. Prior to 1789, public opinion had had to make its way through the thickets of Ancien Régime censorship, privileged speech and corporative restriction; now it was a free agent, working for the betterment of society.

Before 1789, the king had controlled words; after 1789, words were king. Free and multi-lateral communication was viewed as crucial to the project of building an enlightened and dynamic national culture. In line with Enlightenment views, print technology was duly sanctified. It was, Condorcet once stated, 'through the printing process alone that discussion among a great people can truly be one', and the Declaration of the Rights of Man prefixed to the 1791 constitution had assured citizens that 'the free communication of thoughts and opinions is one of the most precious rights of man'.[14] The disappearance of the privileges of printers and publishers formerly subsidized by the king caused a mushrooming of publishing activity from 1789 onwards. The number of Parisian printers in work quadrupled over the Revolutionary period, and the number of booksellers and/or publishers tripled. Freedom in production and distribution massively amplified the place of politics in published output. While fiction was not particularly fashionable – news must have seemed more interesting – other genres proved better able to adapt to the taste for the political. Much science now came, for example, in bite-sized pieces of patriotic popularization. Revolutionary fervour also produced a politicization of established forms such as the almanach and the song. The number of political songs rose sharply, for example, expanding fivefold on 1789 levels by 1793, sixfold in 1794 and only falling away towards the end of the decade. There was also an explosion of prints and engravings, with cartoons and caricatures acting, in Lequinio's words, as 'the thermometer indicating the temperature of public opinion'.[15]

The popularity of these less canonical forms highlighted a point which Brissot made in his memoirs, namely, that Revolutionary enlightenment proceeded 'not through voluminous and well-reasoned works, because people do not read them, but through little works . . . through a journal which spread[s] light in every direction'.[16] A newspaper mailed to its subscribers was, the Girondin Louvet concurred, 'the easiest, most prompt and least costly way to spread the truth'.[17] More newspapers were established in a matter of months in 1789 than in the whole of the 1770s. The phenomenon was most striking in Paris: in 1789, there had been only one daily newspaper, the *Journal de Paris*, founded in 1777; by 1790, there were twenty-three dailies and as many appearing on a weekly or lesser tempo. The provinces were also affected: the number of provincial titles quadrupled down to 1791 alone, and newspapers flourished not only in big cities but also in relatively out-of-the-way localities. Well over 1,000 new titles appeared during the Revolutionary decade. Readership expanded massively: weekly circulation figures of the Parisian press rose sharply above pre-revolutionary levels of around 100,000 copies (60 per cent of which were sent into the provinces) to about 800,000 by 1794. Given collective reading habits, perhaps as many as 40 per cent of adult males had access to the Revolutionary (and, of course, the counter-revolutionary) press.

The print explosion of the 1790s, unthinkable without the prior impact of the Enlightenment on the politicians of the Revolutionary decade, imparted to the political culture they formulated one of its most striking characteristics: its loquacity. At first, this was not seen as a problem, for it was assumed that Revolutionary language would have a neutral, transparent value. The Revolutionaries of 1789 had seen themselves as having unmasked the cunning artifices of Ancien Régime power, and established a system in which unrhetorical Revolutionary language would allow individuals to have unmediated and sincere relations with each other, unaffected by institutional and inter-personal obstacles. The Revolutionaries prided themselves on a discursive style which rejected the flowery (and therefore, it was assumed, insincere) rhetoric of the Ancien Régime. The pure and transparent style was particularly prized in the Terror: 'Jacobins speak laconically,' as one Marseillais patriot stated (laconically).[18]

Yet this question looked totally different after Thermidor. For the period of the Terror seemed to have irrefutably demonstrated the dangers of too much speech and too much writing. In *The New Paris* of 1798, jaundiced sequel to his lively, pre-Revolutionary *Tableau de Paris*, for example, Louis-Sébastien Mercier painted a grim picture of 'this terrible chaos formed by writers in the Revolution, enormous mass of pages of journals, pamphlets and books, obscure and voluminous depository of conflicting discourses, torrent of invective and sarcasm, jumbled pile in which calumny has drowned itself', which he compared to an Egyptian plague bringing the nation to its knees.[19] This was more than an issue about the volume and variety of writings: print also transformed the nature of politics into a *'logomachie'* – a 'war of words'. The Terror had been a verbal delirium, in which words shook themselves loose from their referent and became the substance of conflict, not just conflict's expression. Just who was a 'Feuillant', a 'suspect', an 'aristocrat', a 'Brissotin', a 'moderate', a 'Jacobin'? At different times in the course of the 1790s, these were all words which – literally, as Michelet knew – could kill.

The Terror had been marked by a growing control over language, as part of a wider desire to control and manipulate public opinion. 'To take the pulse of the public spirit', Mercier ironized, in a shaft of Directorial hindsight, 'demands a very subtle touch'. Successive national assemblies had 'somehow got their fingers round the thermometer while consulting it, and [had mistaken] the temperature of their own hands for that of the surrounding air'.[20] The process of news management was undoubtedly accelerated by the demands of war, internal and external, on public morale. The Bureau de l'esprit public which worked under Girondin Interior Minister Roland in late 1792 set new standards of government sponsorship of propaganda and news management, which would be taken up enthusiastically by the Girondins' successors in government. Roland had grasped that, to be effective, the news and information which it supplied to the nation profited from some supplementary propagandistic spin. He and his successors would deny, even to themselves, that they were doing anything more than 'enlightening' the public. The declaration of Revolutionary government in October 1793, in particular by putting the electoral process on hold until peace was signed, removed the reality check that opinion could have on legislators claiming to represent it.

The growing sense of the need to 'enlighten' public opinion, when faced with internal and external war, had made the Conventionnels look increasingly askance at the institutions of voluntary sociability which had formerly served as relays and supports of public opinion. The secrecy and organizational privacy which had shielded these bodies from state interference within the Bourbon polity looked out of date after 1789. Thus the Revolution confirmed the demise, already prefigured by the 1780s, of the salon as a choice venue of opinion-formation. Indeed, the gatherings organized by would-be salonnières Madame de Staël, daughter of Necker, and of the Girondine Madame Roland were seen as revoltingly – maybe even treasonously – partisan. They were also socially elitist, a charge also levelled against academies, which were abolished in 1793 as nests of privileged 'aristocrats of science'. Freemasonic lodges, which had constituted one of the most dynamic fora of Enlightenment sociability in the 1780s, also underwent eclipse: the Grand Orient was closed down in 1793. A good number of individual lodges, their clandestine operations regarded as sinning against the prized value of transparency, metamorphosed into political clubs.

One location of political sociability came to triumph over all others after 1792, namely, the political club, affiliated to the Jacobins. The plethora of clubs of differing political complexions which sprang up in the early years of the Revolution did not survive the fall of the monarchy and the drift to war. Even before the electoral process was suspended under the Convention, the charge was frequently made – notably by Louis XVI in his letter when fleeing Paris in June 1791, by Lafayette and Dumouriez in seeking to lead their troops on Paris, and by hostile Girondins in 1792 and 1793 – that the Jacobins had fractured public opinion and subverted national spirit. From the vantage point of the Directory, Jacobin clubs seemed to have become institutions to suppress individual freedoms rather than to express opinion. The Parisian Jacobin Club had developed out of the political caucus, the Breton Club, in the early days of the Constituent Assembly, and following the Feuillant schism of July 1791 developed into a kind of counter-Assembly, in which first Brissot and the Girondins and then Robespierre and his grouping developed a critique of the moderate majority of the Legislative Assembly. Once the Republic was declared, however, the Jacobins housed the ultra-patriotic Montagnard grouping from the Convention, and made growing representative claims for itself. Robespierre's younger brother, Augustin, crowed in April 1793 that the Club was 'by its very nature incorruptible. It deliberates before an audience of 4,000 persons, so that its whole power lies in public opinion and it cannot betray the interests of the people.'[21] Similarly, the radical Dufourny argued that 'the National Assembly cannot be allowed to direct public opinion because they must be guided by it. Their task is to pass decrees and not to create the public spirit.'[22] The latter was clearly a job for the Jacobins. They – and provincial clubs under their tutelage – served as laboratories of patriotic apprenticeship for vast numbers of Frenchmen, spreading the Revolutionary good news, but also interpreting it and making it real and relevant for ordinary citizens.

The Jacobin club network was an important component of the Terrorist public sphere, which grew up on the ruins of the bourgeois public sphere triumphant in 1789. This aimed to instil a pedagogy of fear, emblematically through the use of the guillotine. A public execution was 'a tragedy ... meant to fill the spectator with awe',[23] a role which explained its hyper-theatricality – the charged tumbril making its way through Parisian streets, for example, the raising of the guillotine blade, the showing of the severed head to the crowds ... Yet the Terror scared Frenchmen and women into political conformity not simply by the public *mise-en-scène* of the apparatus of killing; after all, many had witnessed far worse prior to 1789 – the execution of Damiens, as well as a myriad of breakings on the wheel and judicial tortures. In fact, the guillotine was only one institution within a broader Terrorist public sphere comprising the Revolutionary government's committees, its clubs, its tribunals, its sponsored news-sheets, its orchestrated festivals. The category of political suspect – on which hung decisions of imprisonment, arraignment and, during the Great Terror, probable execution – could increasingly be applied on the basis of the most intimate and innermost thoughts. Speech was no longer free – one in ten victims of Revolutionary justice was executed for talking in a way which was adjudged counter-revolutionary. The press was heavily censored and cowed into conformism. The surveillance of informers and spies ensured that sociability was conducted only in formally approved gatherings such as Jacobin Clubs and Revolutionary festivals.

'If Terror is the order of the day for patriots,' noted the Jacobins at Metz in May 1794, 'that would be the end of liberty.'[24] Yet, ironically, this was precisely what was occurring at that very moment, in the shape of the repression of Dantonists, Hébertists and sans-culotte militants, followed by the infamous Law of 22 Prairial. By this time, moreover, the Revolutionary government was also increasingly sucking the vitality out of the Jacobin club network, changing the role of club from voluntary association to government agency. The clubs lost thereby their potential for expressing public opinion, a force which Robespierre argued, before a cowed Jacobin Club and Convention, was embodied within the Revolutionary government (and indeed increasingly in his own virtuous self).

A similar trajectory was traced by Revolutionary festivals, which, like the spread of Jacobin clubs, seemed initially to constitute comforting signs of public opinion's conformity with the Revolutionary project, but which by 1794 were increasingly locked into the apparatus of Terror. The Constituent and Legislative Assemblies had placed great store on developing forms and rituals which distanced the Revolution from the constitutional ceremonialism of the Bourbon polity. The transfer of the king from the Bourbon solar temple at Versailles to Paris, capital city of the bourgeois public sphere, had been only part of a larger rejection of existing types of monarchical ceremony. The sacred centre of state ritual was no longer the undying ceremonial body of the ruler. This left the field clear for a good deal of Revolutionary inventiveness, grounded in nature rather than history. New ritual forms strove to recapitulate – and to be born again into – that mythic moment of contract which had soldered together society and government. State ceremonies aimed to induce a sense of respectful awe and emotional surrender in participants by an increasingly orchestrated and theatrical ceremonialism.

'Man responds to impressions rather than reasoning,' Mirabeau had remarked. '[He] has to be moved rather than convinced.'[25] The apparently somewhat cynical, almost Louis-Quatorzian note of this comment overlay a conviction drawn direct from Lockean and Enlightenment empiricist premises. The new man was to be a kind of Revolutionary Émile, whose personality would be formed by the 'natural' and patriotic sensations with which the national sensorium was bombarded. A model in this respect was the Fête de la Fédération of 14 July 1790, commemorating the first anniversary of the fall of the Bastille. An enormous public amphitheatre was thrown together on the Champ de Mars in Paris, in which a quarter of a million Parisians witnessed a celebration of national unity, headed by the king, blessed by the church through a formal mass taking place on a prominent 'altar of the fatherland' (*autel de la patrie*), and with a stirring march-past by departmental delegations of the National Guard. Deprived of a commemorable history prior to 1789 – public history before that time was now viewed merely as the chronicle of the crimes of kings and priests – the Revolution's own past was appropriately festivized. Added to the memorialization of key Revolutionary *journées* was the use of the Pantheon church in Paris as a repository for the tombs of great men. Stately ceremonies accompanied a series of 'pantheonizations', many of them staged by the artist David, pageant-master extraordinaire to the Revolution, starting with Voltaire in July 1791, and including philosophers Descartes and Rousseau, Mirabeau (subsequently ignominiously ejected), and Marat and Lepeletier de Saint-Fargeau (both assassination victims), plus sundry patriotic heroes (such as the teenager Bara, who died heroically in a Vendéan ambush).

Festive culture associated with the Revolution's own sense of itself played an important role in the popularization of the Revolutionary cause, as a form of propaganda by the deed. It also registered the emergence of genuine patriotic sentiments at grass-roots level, which linked up with the evolution of open-air mass entertainments prior to 1789.[26] Like those, it was highly inclusive: the festivals' mass dimension was extended to include women and children as well as men, and the organizing principles were based on natural distinctions (the aged, children, widowed, etc.) rather than social hierarchies. The Fédération festivals which commemorated 14 July became popular and widespread from 1790 onwards, particularly the associated ceremony of swearing a civic oath on the altar of the fatherland. A similar combination of spontaneity and organization surrounded the act of planting a liberty tree, which started off as a peasant celebration in the Périgord in 1790 before becoming adopted more widely, with the associated act of singing of the 'Carmagnole'. Some 60,000 liberty trees were planted throughout the length and breadth of the country.

The growing discredit of the church led to the replacement of Christian Sundays by the Revolutionary Calendar's *décadis* for the celebration of the cult of the *patrie*. Yet efforts to fashion an authentically Revolutionary religion out of this failed to establish themselves, and became increasingly out of touch and sinister in their operations. The Paris Commune dechristianizers organized an infamous Festival of Reason at Notre-Dame cathedral in November 1793, but were stopped from developing this into a more substantial cult by Robespierre and Danton. The cult of Marat and other Revolutionary martyrs never really got much further than the placing of plaster busts of the 'Friend of the People' in sundry Jacobin clubs. Robespierre originated and did his best to popularize the Cult of the Supreme Being in spring 1794. Its apparent wish to dictate to consciences never won adherents, and it died with him.

The Terrorist public sphere evolving after 1792 derived much of its effect from the diffuse and subtle threat it imposed over private life and belief, dissolving the line which separated public from personal. This was evident in the Jacobin, then Revolutionary government's, wish for greater uniformity as regards individuals' use of Revolutionary symbols. A striking feature of the culture emergent in 1789 had been the extension of the images and symbols of Revolution into the paraphernalia of private life. The Bastille, for example, symbol of despotism, was metamorphosed into a symbol of the overthrow of that oppression, and turned up in countless paintings, engravings, sculptures and songs but also on buttons, plates, coffee-pots, razors, playing-cards, children's games, ladies' fans and wall-papers, testifying to a strong consumer demand for Revolutionary insignia. The latter increasingly mixed Revolutionary references – the tricolour cockade, the red cap, tablets with the Rights of Man inscribed on them – with other influences, popular (the Gallic cock), masonic (the set square symbolizing equality, the eye of vigilance), Antique (the fasces of union and authority) and so on. Contemporaries remarked on the alacrity with which individuals proclaimed their identification with the values of the Revolution by refashioning their appearances: sporting red caps, for example, cockades, *sans-culotte* trousers, unpowdered (and *ergo* unaristocratic) hairstyles and the like.

The political trust placed in symbols was, however, severely shaken at the height of the Terror. The wearing of the tricolour cockade had been made obligatory for adult males in July 1792, and this was reaffirmed on 3 April 1793 and extended to women in September. But there was a danger that this level of conformity would produce a backlash. Red

THE UNSTEADY REPUBLIC (1795–9)

caps could hide intriguers rather than patriots, as Saint-Just noted, and Revolutionary symbols could lose their status as emblems of adoptive political identity.[27] Consequently, the apparatus of Terror redoubled efforts to get beneath surface appearances and sought to attain the consciences of individuals, where good or bad faith could be adjudicated. Prosecutors for the Revolutionary Tribunal, for example, scrutinized the private letters of suspects with particular care, and even lukewarm sentiments towards the Revolution could lead to conviction, since the private letter still retained its Enlightenment function as a pure window into the heart. The archives of the Terror are full of individuals – in court, at a club, in a crowd, in print, before a charity committee – justifying themselves at extraordinary length, narrating their involvement with the Revolution in ways which purported to show, sometimes through the most serpentine of public manoeuvres, an adamantine faith in the Revolution.

By adopting policies and procedures which conflated public and private in this way, the adepts of Terror were entering a political and existential black hole. The quest to ensure loyalty and good faith in the hearts of individuals only redoubled anxiety about plots and conspiracies and stimulated exaggeration and deceit in equal measure. For by setting the Revolutionary bar at a such a height of translucent purity, the Revolutionary government ensured that even the warmest of patriots (let alone the politically antagonistic or apathetic) could not feel secure. There was a limit to the number of times even the most inventive of Revolutionary self-fashioners could 'make themselves another political virginity'.[28] In a world in which everyone was fast becoming a suspect, Robespierre's paranoia became perfectly intelligible.

The almost audible sigh of relief which greeted Thermidor among the political nation also marked a rediscovery of argument and information rather than force and deterrence as means of developing consensus. Characteristically, when Robespierre fell, one of the most telling charges against him was that he had sought 'to dominate public opinion'. Only public opinion', now opined Barère, post Thermidor, 'has the right to rule the nation.'[29] Thermidor was simultaneously the revenge of public opinion which had tired of being putatively embodied in the frame of the virtuous Incorruptible and the assertive reclamation by the conspirator deputies, from the Jacobin Club and the Committee of Public Safety, of the Convention's monopolistic right to represent public spirit. Given the role which the Jacobin Club played in the Terrorist public sphere, its closure in December 1794 could thus be represented to be a move for greater rather than less freedom of speech.

By seeking to reject the use of force and the threat of violence as prime instruments of Revolutionary regeneration, the Thermidorians and Directorials joined up with the spirit of the early part of the Revolution, and sought to replace the Terrorist public sphere with something more akin to the bourgeois public sphere of the Enlightenment. The desire to penetrate consciences evident in the Terror was dissipated, and distance once more emerged between private and public, allowing the re-emergence of the institutions of communication and sociability of the bourgeois public sphere. Thermidor released a fresh babble of exchange: despite the vagaries of government policy, for example, there were 190 new journals established in Year V alone, and newspaper readership stayed high at around 700,000 in 1799. New political clubs emerged which were no longer under the shadow of the Jacobins and which boasted pedigrees of both the Right and the Left (though these might be suppressed if they echoed the overweening claims of the old Jacobins). The Constitutional church re-emerged, along with – sporadically at least – refractory Catholicism and its confraternities. Coffee-houses prospered again, the conversations of their denizens less the object of police spying. Freemasonry recovered, with the Grand Orient resuming activity in 1796. Salons – out of style since the Legislative Assembly – also came back into being. They ranged from the studiously academic (Mesdames Helvétius, Condorcet and de Staël) through to the venal and hedonistic (Madame Récamier). Following the shipwreck of the Revolutionary government's plans for a pensions-based welfare state, private charitable organizations re-emerged, and alms-giving became respectable again.

With terror ruled out as a means of influencing opinion, greater emphasis was placed again on the principle of education. Even the Revolutionary government had argued that education had a key role to play in forming the new man. Just before his assassination in January 1793, the Montagnard ex-marquis Lepeletier de Saint-Fargeau had unveiled extremely ambitious plans for the recasting of the whole educational system and on 19 December 1793, the Bouquier Law established the principle of free primary schooling. Cash, however, was scarce for educational innovation at primary and secondary level while there was still a war to win, and little was achieved.

Madame de Staël was pretty representative of the post-Thermidorian mood in arguing that 'the Republic has forestalled the Enlightenment; we must hasten the work of time by all true means of public education'.[30] Yet the Directorials found that their efforts to resume the Enlightenment's work were frustratingly restricted by local dissension over the issue of private schools staffed by ex-religious, at both secondary and primary levels. Swings to the Left in Directorial policy were accompanied by sporadic harassment of pro-Catholic schoolteachers. The educational domain on which the Thermidorians and Directorials placed greater emphasis – and more funding – was the higher education and the research establishment. Although they still sought a moral basis in politics, the Directorials downplayed the feverish emotionalism which had fuelled Robespierre's regenerative efforts. Still holding a touching belief that their fellow citizens would listen to reason, they privileged scientific and rational inquiry as the basis of their approach to making a new man. Under the Terror, the scientific knowledge of numerous savants had been mobilized, but the regime had also been distrustful of 'aristocrats of science', and many of the old elitist scientific institutions of the Bourbon polity had been abolished or silenced. Post-Thermidorian governments revived the scientific establishment.[31]

The enlightening mission of the Directorials, like their predecessors back to 1789, was intended to 'electrify' (to cite a modish and much-utilized verb, which carried the desired connotations of energy, dynamism and scientific direction) the French nation with the spirit of liberty and equality. The Directorials thus renewed with the late Enlightenment desire to use human reason as a means of making life prosperous and comfortable as much as virtuous. They were far more relaxed than the Terrorists about the notion of 'luxury', but felt that something had to be done to restrict the exponentially expanding set of needs which commercial society brought in its train. They rejected material poverty and regarded begging and vagrancy as unseemly symptoms of aristocratic values. Viewing agriculture as enthusiastically as the Physiocrats as a source of national wealth, they waxed eulogistic about virtuous small farmers, developing a sense that a social structure grounded in the soil would act as a moral check on the expansion of wants and desires. At the same time, they also valorized all forms of manufacture and exchange, and highlighted the need for an infrastructure for them to flourish, such as road and canal building and better mail services.

If these educational and infrastructural reforms were going to be genuinely regenerative, it would be in the long rather than the short term – and time was what Thermidorians and Directorials most lacked. They therefore flanked their educational initiatives with a re-commitment to devising ceremonial forms and rituals which would have a pedagogic effect on all French men and women. From 1796, the Director La Révellière-Lépeaux threw his weight behind the cult of Theophilanthropy, a somewhat whimsical form of philosophical Deism. It failed either to find loyal adherents or to check the revival of Catholicism, and after the Fructidor coup in 1797, the Directors began to renew efforts to enracinate the decadal cult: on the *décadi* official uniforms were to be worn, liberty-trees to be planted, patriotic hymns were to be sung, recent laws to be read out and marriages to be celebrated.

It soon became clear, however, that Revolutionary festivals divided as much as they united the nation. For every locality enthusiastic about the *décadi* there was at least one sullenly formulaic and subversively conformist. And counter-revolutionaries took great pleasure in assailing the Revolution's festive and putatively unifying symbolic forms. In the White Terror, for example, *jeunesse dorée* and vigilante gangs not only launched personal attacks against Year II Terrorists, they also resisted the Revolution's festive culture on its own ground by loudly singing their theme tune, 'Le Réveil du Peuple' over the intonation of the 'Marseillaise'; by ostentatiously observing Sundays rather than *décadis* as a day of rest; by removing busts of Marat; and by chopping down, carving slogans on or urinating against trees of liberty. Rituals and symbols which in a more innocent past had sought to unify communities now alienated and fragmented them.

Most telling, perhaps, of the failure of efforts after Thermidor to forge a unifying national culture was the Right's subversion of what was probably the Revolution's most innovative contribution to political culture, namely, the act of election. In the early part of the Revolution, elections had affirmed the unified sense of community which lay at the heart of the new political culture and played a key role in civic pedagogy. As divisive issues became more envenomed, however, electoral procedures seemed to stimulate rather than allay local antagonisms, and to muddy the pristine waters of political transparency. This was probably a factor in growing voter apathy, highlighted by lower turnouts. Participation rates in 1790 had averaged nearly 50 per cent, though elections for the Legislative Assembly in 1791 attracted only around a quarter of voters, and in many locations voting for the Convention fell to under 10 per cent. The move away from the principle of election in the period of Revolutionary government was vigorously countered by the Thermidorians and Directorials. The 1795 Constitution actually stipulated elections on an annual basis. Yet voter response was little more than pathetic. The plebiscites in 1795 on the constitution and (in particular) the Two-Thirds Law attracted no enthusiasm. Annual turnout thereafter proved too demanding, especially as procedural changes made the electoral ritual even more laborious. Furthermore, as both constitutional royalists and, at the other extreme, ex-Terrorists anxious to protect their local position were quick to appreciate, declining participation opened the door to determined minorities imposing the sectional will. The constitutional royalists were spectacularly successful in the Year V (1797) elections.

The shock of counter-revolution defeating the Revolutionaries on their own hallowed ground of election was so great that, as we have seen,[32] the Directors reacted by launching the Fructidor coup, purging deputies, administrators and judges who were accounted to be on the Right. The forces of neo-Jacobinism may have rejoiced, but this illegal act in a regime which had stressed its foundation in constitutional rectitude rather than Revolutionary governmental force immensely damaged its overall credibility. The continuation of this kind of electoral game, in which sundry Directors, when they saw fit, played the coercive trump card could only lead to a further decrease in electoral enthusiasm and turnout. The regime of the rule of law had turned lawless, and seemed to encourage a sectionalism which the unifying political culture of the Revolution had always rejected.

c) ECONOMIC FORTUNES AND MISFORTUNES

The Directory's distinctive mélange of unexpected reverses, of changes of tack, and of a constantly evolving spectrum of political choices was set against economic upheavals of equally bewildering scale. These were linked to ongoing social and political transformations, but they were also shaped by the vagaries of war, civil and foreign, which affected individuals and social groupings in quite unforeseeable and sometimes catastrophic ways.

At the outset, most Revolutionaries had shown boundless confidence in the capacity of their emancipatory reforms to inaugurate an era of prosperity, by freeing the country from 'privileged classes', who were viewed as inhibitory and parasitic. From the reforms of the Constituent Assembly onwards, the framework of the kind of social and economic freedoms consonant with a successful capitalist economy were put in place. The abolition of seigneurial and ecclesiastical dues on the Night of 4 August boosted productive potential, while the nationalization, then sale, of church lands brought between 6 and 10 per cent of cultivable land out of ecclesiastical cold-storage. In addition, the abolition of venality removed a major source of non-productive investment. The removal of tolls and the generalization of free trade boosted circulation and distribution. The removal of economic privilege freed up the productive process, while the abolition of guilds, corporations and workers' associations (by the Allarde and Le Chapelier Laws of 2 March and 17 June 1791) removed labour restrictions much resented by manufacturers. Employers and workers entered an era of free contract. The move towards uniformity of weights and measures, begun by the Constituent Assembly and brought to fruition under the Thermidorian Convention, reduced transaction costs and provided benchmarks for a national market.

Despite this outstanding legislative achievement, early hopes were cruelly disappointed, and the economic position in 1799, after a decade of Revolution, seemed much poorer than it had been in the (hardly economically brilliant) year of 1789. In some ways, of course, it is silly to draw up a balance-sheet for the economic impact of the Revolution based on the single year of 1799. The dust was still settling after a decade of sometimes frenetic chopping and changing in state policy: the move to *laisser-faire* from 1789; the complete policy turn-around between 1792 and 1794–5 caused by the Revolutionary government's acceptance of the need for an authoritarian planned economy; and the return to economic freedom under the Directory. Many of the changes introduced over the decade were likely to have an impact in the longer rather than the shorter term, and in a real sense it was too soon to tell what the impact of the Revolution was. This was all the more the case in that some of what had occurred in the economy by 1799 might well have happened without a revolution taking place. That from 1792 France was at war is a further complicating factor, since disentangling the effects of war from those of Revolution is highly problematic.

Insofar as we are able to judge, it would appear that French GNP in 1799 was running at around 60 per cent of what it had been in 1789. Perhaps the most evident sign of deterioration was the collapse of the most dynamic sector of the eighteenth-century economy – colonial trade. Slave rebellion in Saint-Domingue in 1791 had severely shaken the jewel in France's colonial crown. But it was war, and in particular the economic blockade of France by the British navy after 1793, which did most damage. The number of sea-going vessels harboured in French ports shrank from around 2,000 to a mere 200 between 1789 and 1797, and over the same period, foreign trade slumped from representing 25 per cent of the national wealth to a mere 9 per cent. There was some degree of readjustment and adaptation, particularly under the Directory: American, Danish, Spanish and other neutral vessels allowed France to keep a trading lifeline out to the Caribbean and to the Indian Ocean. A reprise of privateering and contraband also helped the economy, as did military expansion into the Low Countries, Germany and Italy, which freed up land-based outlets. By 1799, however, French exports were still only around a half of 1789 levels.

The disruption and loss of foreign markets had a highly deleterious effect on those manufacturing sectors which had depended on the import of raw materials or which had specialized in exporting. The gamut of refining, finishing and ancillary industries which had grown up in and around the Atlantic ports suffered particularly badly: sugar-refining factories in Bordeaux fell like flies; up the Garonne at Tonneins, the number of rope-makers dropped from 700 to 200; while many tobacco plants and tanneries using imported hides went out of business. Many commercial cities experienced effective 'de-urbanization' – Bordeaux and Marseille, for example, shrank by 10 per cent (as did Paris) – and this also affected nearby rural areas formerly engaged in proto-industrialization. The traditional textiles industries were particularly badly affected. The output of linen in Brittany and Maine fell by a third, and the woollen industries had much the same experience: Carcassonne in Languedoc had produced 60,000 rolls of cloth in 1789; ten years later it was only producing 20,000. The story was identical in Dauphiné and on the Belgian border. Silk suffered too: the number of silkworkers in Nîmes dropped by half, while in Lyon the number of looms working fell from 16,000 to 5,000. Iron and coal extraction also experienced difficulties: the emigration of noble mine-owners and the nationalization of mines owned by the clergy complicated matters here. Production at the great Anzin complex was one-third less in 1800 than it had been in 1789. The vicissitudes of aristocratic owners also help explain the bad times suffered in many iron-works, which were also affected by worsening firewood shortages. Le Creusot, showcase of modernizing heavy industry before the Revolution, fell apart.

The Revolutionary decade was a pretty challenging time for business. The litany of complaints by industrialists was long and heartfelt. Besides disrupting foreign markets, war had led to a reduction in technology transfers from Britain, from now onwards the world's most highly industrialized nation. The luxury trades had been very badly hit by the emigration of wealthy noble consumers. The financial morass of the 1790s had an appalling effect on all businesses. Over-production of paper currency fuelled spiralling inflation down to 1797. When government then acted to right the situation, it initiated a severe and damaging period of deflation. This financial instability – plus the emigration and the practice of hoarding – made specie in short supply, while credit remained rare and dear. Two paper money débâcles within a single century – John Law's System and the *assignat* – gave Frenchmen an enduring distrust of the phenomenon. If war seemed to be paying for itself by the late 1790s, moreover, this did not alter industrialists' view that taxes were still punitively high. This was all the more irritating in that workers' wages appeared to have gone up over the 1790s: industrialists blamed the war for this, through potential workers being drawn away from the labour market into the army, allowing those who remained at home to be grasping and insubordinate. The business community was not always appreciative of the freedoms which the government had given them, and pined for a measure of the protection which the Bourbon state had formerly afforded.

Some of the problems of the 1790s would have occurred even without the dual impact of war and Revolution. Le Creusot, for example, had been a highly fragile creation. In addition, France was already by 1789 losing its competitiveness in many overseas markets, notably to the English.[33] Similarly, some of the problems of linen and woollen textiles and the silk industry pre-dated the Revolution, and they were to a considerable extent a reflection of changing consumer taste, which preferred cotton. And cotton did very well in the 1790s. Despite problems of supply of raw cotton, the cotton-works in Paris, Rouen, Alsace and the Lille area boomed. The Rouen factories were producing 32,000 kilos of cotton in 1800 where in 1789 they had managed 19,000. This was partly a result of improved mechanization, notably through the diffusion of the spinning jenny. Chemical works also prospered – dyes were used to make materials more colourful and attractive. The picture was far from bleak even in industries which overall were in decline: by 1799, the Anzin mines almost quadrupled their output against 1794 levels, while the coal-fields in the Gard were also by then starting to perform strongly again.

These developments demonstrated how, alongside the headaches, the Revolutionary decade provided new opportunities for enrichment. Revolutionary legislators had supplied businessmen with a superb institutional platform for economic development. In addition, the state's commitment to warfare offered a promising terrain for business: war might have damaged many merchants and industrialists, but it was a blessing for those who attached their fortunes to the military effort. Prior to 1792, the textiles manufactories at Montauban and Castres had been totally dependent on Levantine and Caribbean markets, for example. When these disappeared, they shifted into production of army uniforms and military blankets – and prospered. Iron-works which produced either cannon or small arms also boomed, stimulated by the efforts of Revolutionary government to equip the *levée en masse*. 'Let locksmiths cease to make locks,' had enthused Collot d'Herbois and Billaud-Varenne, in a CPS decree. 'The locks of liberty are bayonets and muskets.'[34] The Revolutionary government supplied not only capital and infrastructure but also manpower: semi-conscripted labour was supplied for war manufactories under the closed economy of Year II. In addition, contracts for army supply became a notorious source of enrichment, especially as government bureaucracy could be evaded (or, under the Directory, bribed), allowing much scope for embezzlement and racketeering. The *nouveaux riches* of the Directory more likely than not had their fingers in the army-contract pie. The millionaire Ouvrard had started the Revolution as a grocery clerk in Nantes, but made his money in paper-manufacturing in the early 1790s before landing the contract for provisioning the entire French navy (followed by the Spanish navy to boot) with all its requirements.

The national lands which came on to the market were also a real bonanza for businessmen, who bought in considerable numbers. In some cases, this merely represented the old bourgeois ethic of buying land to secure gentlemanly status and leave trade behind. In general, though, motives were mixed. Diversification of income streams made better sense in a period of economic difficulty, and land traditionally held its value better than other forms of investment – all the more so when purchased in hyper-depreciated *assignats*. Given the meagreness of credit mechanisms available, moreover, the purchase of land could be seen as a means of acquiring collateral for business development. Industrialists and merchants brought good business practice to the estates they purchased: the success of Bordeaux fine wines on the northern European markets owed a good deal to imported business acumen. Big town-based monasteries and convents also provided very handy ready-made spaces for factory production – as cotton masters in particular soon showed. The brother of the Toulouse Conventionnel Boyer-Fonfrède purchased an ex-monastery in his home city which he made into a cotton-works, employing orphans and foundlings from the local poor-house. (Two other Toulouse ex-monasteries were also hard at work in the city at the same time, producing cannons and bayonets.) The Boyer-Fonfrède case highlighted another advantage which the Revolution had brought to industrialists: by removing guild controls and deregulating labour, it made the industrial employment of small children (and of women for that matter) much more common and accepted. In addition, Boyer-Fonfrède relied on advice from a Yorkshireman who had chosen to stay in France even after war was declared, highlighting the continued possibility of cross-Channel technology transfers. Other businesses used English prisoners-of-war as a means of acquiring apprenticed skills from English workshops.

Although war had removed established foreign markets, internal demand had not collapsed as disastrously as might have been feared. The loss – as a result of exile, imprisonment, execution or intimidation – of the big spenders of the eighteenth-century economy on whom the luxury trades had relied was a heavy blow. Luxury might have been frowned upon in the virtuous days of the Terror, but after Thermidor – both in Paris and the other big cities – conspicuous consumption returned with a bang, a bang which caused intense annoyance to any remaining *sans-culottes*. Thermidorian Paris became – and remained – the byword for display. There were the mad fashions sported by the extraordinarily (by turns over- and under-) dressed *Incroyables* and *Merveilleuses*, the guzzling of champagne, and the ingestion of bountiful meals in smart restaurants (a recent invention). Though there was never to be a return to the kind of showy male styles popularized by the pre-1789 nobility – the enduring fashion for men was the dark business suit, with unpowdered hair – women's styles were more exuberant. Almost the first thing that happened to returning *émigrée* Madame de La Tour du Pin when she arrived in Mont de Marsan in 1796 was that the local hairdresser offered her 200 francs for her hair, which he could sell with profit to the Parisian wig-makers, who were crying out for beautiful hair for 'fair wigs'.[35] Haute couture was re-emerging. On top of their commitment to Directorial *dolce vita*, *arriviste* businessmen who were doing so well out of the war also showed an interest in artistic patronage: Ouvrard's favourite château at Raincy, near Paris, for example, had thirty-two Doric columns lining the vestibule and was decorated with outrageously wealthy and conspicuous taste.

The potential size of the internal market had not diminished. Many towns suffered a drop in population levels; nearly half a million men were lost in the Revolutionary wars; and maybe around 200,000 individuals emigrated (though many of these had started to return by 1800). Yet overall population size rose – from perhaps 28.6 million in 1790 to 29.1 million in 1800 – and the conquered territories also represented significant ancillary demand. Furthermore, an important effect of the British blockade had been to reduce competition from English manufactured goods, which had caused so much grief in the late 1780s: the French field had been effectively left free for the French manufacturers to exploit.

Sir Francis d'Ivernois, a perceptive observer of the French scene at century turn, felt that the transfer of incomes caused by the Revolution, 'from the class of consuming landowners to that of non-consuming [but landowning] farmers' produced real problems for France's manufacturing sector.[36] The expropriation and then sale of the estates of the church and of the *émigrés* had reduced demand at the luxury end of the market and also led to a fragmentation of the large properties on which agricultural improvement had often taken place since the 1750s. Yet though the structure of the rural economy had certainly experienced significant change, its impact on the overall pattern of demand was probably less than d'Ivernois thought. Many of the big estates still survived. Nor was the peasantry a broken reed in terms of demand for manufactured products.[37]

Although the return of top-end elite consumption after Thermidor constituted the most spectacular proof of the new buoyancy of demand, there was also abundant evidence of a recrudescence of middling and even quite humble tastes for fashionable objects. Manufacturers catered for this demand by using techniques of 'populuxe' cost-cutting and import substitution, around which, prior to 1789, a good deal of French industry had been orientated.[38] 'We need iron, not cotton,' proclaimed Saint-Just at the height of the Terror.[39] This rallying call only made sense in the context of the difficulty of the CPS to enforce its patriotic criteria over a public well inured to fashion and consumerism (and which had instigated sugar riots in Paris in the early 1790s). Despite its commitment to ascetic Spartan virtue, even the Revolutionary government made concessions to consumer change: the General Maximum fixed the prices of 'objects of first necessity', and extended that 'necessity' list to cover a veritable cornucopia of butters, cheeses, honeys, wines, *eaux-de-vie*, anchovies, almonds and figs plus nearly a score of different kinds of coffee, half a dozen sugars and as many tobaccos, plus tortoise shells, camel-hair and much else besides. After 1795, moreover, it was not just cotton that was *à la mode*: fashion was back in fashion too. The contemporary problems of the wool and linen industries, for example, owed a good deal to the fact that choosy consumers, including many peasants and workers, were preferring to purchase cotton goods – to the considerable benefit, as we have seen, of the cotton industry. Particularly strong recovery was evident in Directorial Paris for luxury and semi-luxury items popularized as *'articles de Paris'* – watches, ribbons, glasses, jewels, earthenware and sundry knick-knacks. Parisian shops and cafés were soon 'swimming in abundance'.[40] In the countryside, too, contemporary observer Jacques Peuchet noted, many peasants were picking up on new consumer habits such as hats, boots and shoes for the first time. As d'Ivernois commented, reflecting on the across-the-board increase in wages in the late 1790s, they were 'better dressed because they are better paid'.[41] Agricultural wages may have risen by 80 per cent on 1789 levels, and peasants remained within the outer fringes of the consumer markets which had been opened up over the course of the eighteenth century. Many English tourists who visited France in the brief respite of peace in

1802–3 would express surprise at the general levels of prosperity among the lower orders, which did not fit at all with the received propaganda about them being emaciated, blood-drinking wraiths. The peasantry were indeed, as we shall see, amongst the major beneficiaries of the new regime.

D) BOURGEOIS REVOLUTIONARIES . . .

An overview of the political trajectory and the economic outcomes of the Revolutionary decade from the vantage-point of 1799 presents certain continuities with the pre-Revolutionary era. What those elements of linkage were and how they were mixed together had been, however, almost totally unpredicted and unpredictable in 1789. This was partly because of the circumstances in which the Revolutionaries were obliged to operate, with new collective political actors (the peasantry, the urban *sans-culotterie*) elbowing their way into the picture, an international framework of warfare, and a wayward and erratic pattern of economic vicissitudes. Partly too it reflected the nature of Revolutionary politics throughout the 1790s, which was invariably a kind of inspired *bricolage*, which involved yoking together a wide range of pre-existent elements into an unanticipated and constantly changing salmagundi of political forms. Some of these elements were drawn from the Bourbon polity (such as the notion of indivisible sovereignty), while others (for example, the Enlightenment project of rational improvement, the deification of nature and the concept of public opinion) drew on the bourgeois public sphere which had emerged in the interstices of Bourbon absolutism.

Unpredictability extended to individual fortunes too. No one in 1789 could have anticipated the appalling fate of Louis XVI, ignominiously executed only a few years after having been recognized as divine-right absolute monarch and potential patriot king. At the other end of the spectrum, for example, who in 1789 could have begun to foretell the dazzling success story of the impoverished and ill-considered Corsican *hobereau* and artillery officer Napoleon Bonaparte, who ten years later would close the Revolutionary decade – and end the Revolution – by a coup d'état which promoted himself to ruler, and from 1804, Emperor of the French? Snooty royalists were not slow to point (complainingly) the scriptural moral that the first had been made last, and the last first.

The goddess Fortuna seemed to be working overtime in a period in which it mattered rather a lot to be on the right side – but when it was far from clear which the right side was. Successfully navigating choppy and changing political waters so as to stay on the right side involved a good deal of acumen – and a liberal dash of luck. So fast-moving was the Revolutionary torrent (as contemporaries themselves referred to it), that a certain nimbleness of wits was at a premium. Revolutionary political culture was both intensely pervasive and intensely invasive. Tranquil regions existed which suffered few counter-revolutionary guillotinings; yet even there army recruits had to be found, taxes paid, officials elected. Opting out of the Revolution was not an option.

The skills (and luck) required to survive and prosper in this teemingly fissiparous, diverse and high-pressure world were not spread evenly among any social grouping. Despite the counter-revolutionary dread of a World Turned Upside Down, or the apparently random, cut-throat world of individualistic risk and danger, in general it appears that overall it was the middling sort – a variegated group, which could reasonably be called the bourgeoisie – who did best over the course of the decade. Individuals who went into the Revolutionary maelstrom with very little usually gained little, while those who were comparatively most heavily burdened with wealth, fame and fortune were most at risk. Although of all social groups the bourgeoisie did best, this is not to say, of course, that many bourgeois did not lose – and lose heavily – over the Revolutionary decade. This group included many who had been deeply encysted within the corporative fabric of the Bourbon polity – plus many for whom the chips did not fall well. Yet in general it was the loose, middling-sort grouping who were best programmed to do well after 1789, possessing as they did sufficient social capital to cushion them against mishap (but not so much as to endanger their survival), prior exposure to the market, which had habituated them to negotiating risk, plus a good admixture of the requisite administrative and political skills. A way with words was also useful: an ability to handle the changing grammar of power helped individuals to adapt to the kaleidoscopic transformations of the political field.

The fortunes of the industrial and commercial sectors of the bourgeoisie were particularly mixed. Though many of those benefiting from state privilege were reluctant to see the Bourbon polity fall, a great many merchants and manufacturers had welcomed 1789 and the end of state-backed privilege – including the abolition of internal tolls and the dissolution of chartered trading companies and state manufactories – and they appreciated the strong winds of freedom the Revolution brought into the world of production, retailing and distribution. Yet hope was cruelly deceived. As we have noted,[42] the loss of colonial commerce, the dislocation of much intra-European trade and the resultant difficulties of industries dependent on the export market brought much ruin in their train. The wider context – the emigration of much of the luxury end of home demand, monetary chaos, the planned economy of Year II and systematic distrust in the period of Revolutionary government of the spirit of commerce – also took their toll. The institutionalization of warfare provided niches for enrichment, as we have seen, and the boom in cotton production highlighted the persistence of a buoyant home demand for fashionable commodities. But making a living required full-time effort over the 1790s, and it is not surprising that the proportion of merchants and industrialists engaged in national politics fell sharply over the decade: these groups had composed around 14 per cent of the membership of the Third Estate in 1789, but only 3 or 4 per cent of the Directorial Councils. They were stronger in local politics, and under the Directory they also inveigled themselves into the corridors of power. Their back-stairs influence and penchant for insider trading gave the whole regime a reputation for shocking venality and corruption, in everything relating to finance, army-contracting and speculative purchase of national land. In this respect, Directorial capitalists were not dissimilar to their pre-1789 forebears, who had a similarly Janus-faced attachment both to economic freedom and state support.

The best-represented group of the bourgeoisie at every level of politics were the professional groupings. Most prominent amongst these were men of law, who made up over two-thirds of the membership of the Third Estate in 1789 and around a half of the Convention. A quarter of the latter were other types of professionals, such as medical men, teachers and academics, petty clerks and soldiers. Politicians tended to be new men. Individuals who had been office-holders under the Ancien Régime dropped from around a quarter of the Third Estate in 1789 to a quarter of the Convention, to only an eighth of the Directorial Councils. What also increasingly characterized them was prior experience in lower branches of administration: 86 per cent of Conventionnels had held local office, especially at departmental level, while the figure for the Directorial Councils was only slightly less. Professionals were thus extremely well placed to benefit from the prizes – and also the perils – of political involvement.

Prior to 1789, the commercialization of the economy had brought most professional groupings into closer touch with the workings of markets for their services. State service and privilege had insulated some from commercial pressures, but to make a decent living most doctors and lawyers, for example, needed to ply their trade – and indeed they often showed real commercial zest. This situation within the wider public sphere had stimulated a wide-ranging debate on the nature of professionalism, which permeated all parts of the service sector of the economy.[43] A discourse of corporative professionalism emerged, which emphasized that the disciplined hierarchy of the society of orders offered an appropriate location for the development of different forms of expertise which could be placed at the disposal of the public. This view was challenged by a counter-discourse of civic professionalism, often with links to the institutions of the Enlightenment. It sought to transcend the corporative framework of the state and stressed that social utility was best served by professionals developing organic links with their fellow citizens within a more egalitarian and non-hierarchical polity. For civic professionals, one was a patriotic citizen first, a lawyer (say) second – whereas for the corporative professionals the order was reversed.

1789 marked the triumph for the discourse of civic professionalism. The professionals who dominated the Constituent Assembly exploded the pertinence of any version of corporatism (plus the venality of office which had often underpinned it), and introduced a realm of patriotic freedom within all sectors of society and the economy. The notion of the 'career open to talents' endorsed by article six of the Declaration of the Rights of Man was targeted at opening up professions to which privilege had restricted entry in the past, and it proved a sturdy weapon against all corporative occupational groupings. Just as mercantilist regulation was removed from trade and industry, so bodies which had formerly regulated professional markets were viewed as anathematic. Colleges of surgeons and physicians, for example, were suppressed as corporative groupings under the provisions of the Night of 4 August 1789, and universities, which almost joined them, came under attack as 'gothic' and elitist institutions. Some died out, though a few staggered on until they were finally suppressed in 1795. Even before this, academies and other learned societies were put on the defensive. 'Free nations do not require the services of speculative savants,' one speaker proclaimed, and in August 1793 all academies were closed down.[44] The introduction of the elective system within the judiciary changed the nature of magisterial office, while the extension of 'amateur' justices of the peace also struck against corporative legal professionalism. The Paris order of barristers disappeared on the grounds of its privileged status, and the status of attorney, following a measure of reform, was suppressed outright in October 1793.

By 1793, the language of civic professionalism had been given added potency by the declaration of war and the eulogization of patriotism. Civic professionalism was clearly ascendant in the army. The idea that soldiers were citizens before they were disciplined military automata had got some way before France went to war: the Nancy mutiny of 1791 had precisely concerned the issue of whether regular troops should enjoy the right to participate in political clubs. War changed the balance of forces. The emigration of the majority of the Ancien Régime officer corps cleared the way for greater egalitarianism. Though the practice of election of officers never really took hold, the soldier of Year II was the super-patriot, whose successes on the battlefield were held to owe more to his patriotic *élan* than to discipline or technical skills.

A similar development was evident in other professions. The notion of bureaucracy – and the word – had emerged in the last decades of the Ancien Régime to denote the machine-like operations of behind-the-scenes administrators. This grouping was hard hit by the suppression of venality of office in 1789. Most of the high nobles who had headed the administrative departments of Bourbon ministries resigned on political grounds or were dismissed. Many of their functions (and those of Intendants and their sub-delegates) had passed to the National Assembly and to elected officials at every level of national life from the commune upwards. Yet the outbreak of war, and the need to assemble prestissimo an army capable of keeping the European powers at bay, highlighted the case for a strong bureaucracy. The ministries' secretarial and clerical staff in 1789 had been less than 670, and this figure remained constant under the Constituent Assembly. Yet in mid-1794, the CPS alone had a staff of over 500, the CGS a further 150. By the end of the Convention, the committees were serviced by between 4,000 and 5,000 staff. Staff in the financial administration had numbered 264 in 1789; by 1795 they had grown to 1026, and by 1796 to 1246.

Finding reliable personnel in the tense circumstances of the Terror proved highly problematic. Reliance on past administrative skill would mean giving ex-nobles and ex-venal officers a chance, and this was difficult to swallow. Marat urged the War Minister to 'purge all the bureaux, which are infected with the most disgusting aristocracy, and replace them with tested patriots'.[45] The tendency was thus to opt for 'patriotic' appointments, on the assumption that enthusiasm for the Revolutionary cause was all a good administrator needed. Cambon, Montpellier-born chair of the Finance Committee, appointed a meridional mafia of proven political orthodoxy under him. At the War Ministry, first Pache, then Bouchotte, drew *sans-culottes* of the purest pedigree into the administration, and cashiered ex-nobles. One of the bureau chiefs had 'Call me citizen' posted on his office door and insisted on *tutoiement* just to drive the message home.[46]

Law and medicine were also affected by this patriotic trend. The abolition of barristers and attorneys opened the way for the *défenseur officieux*, the patriotic 'unofficial defender', who acted as counsel in criminal cases. No training or prior legal experience was required for individuals to offer themselves in a role which was less, as one judge put it, 'a position [*un état*] than a momentary service, a completely free service by a friend'.[47] At the same time, with their former regulatory bodies either dissolved or under a cloud, surgeons and physicians found themselves operating alongside self-appointed 'health officers' (*officiers de santé*), whose highest recommendation was their own patriotic estimation of themselves. The only credentials which either 'health officers' or 'unofficial defenders' required was a *certificat de civisme*.

By 1793–4, the professionals in the Convention – at the very time, moreover, that they were submitting the economy to the tightest controls it had ever experienced – were thus presiding over the development of a free field in professional practice. In the Terrorist public sphere, growing economic regulation accompanied professional deregulation. In a strange throw of fortune, however, the late 1790s were to see an exact reversal of this trend: economic *laisser-faire* was conjoined with professional re-regulation, as professionals in the legislature negotiated the perils as well as the pleasures of *laisser-faire*. Problems with the free field in professional practice were first signalled in the Convention on 4

December 1794. The physician Fourcroy, while paying lip-service to '*laissez-faire* [as] the great secret and the only road to success' (he was speaking a matter of weeks before the suppression of the General Maximum), launched an attack on unqualified medical charlatans ruining the health of soldiers at the front. He dramatically evoked the way in which 'murderous empiricism and ignorant ambition everywhere [now] hold out traps for trusting pain',[48] going on to get the Convention to agree to the creation of three new 'health schools', in Paris, Montpellier and Strasbourg. These medical faculties *avant la lettre* were soon certifying the talents of the 'health officers'. In the legal world, too, the tide began to turn against 'unofficial defenders'. The ex-Conventionnel Thibaudeau attacked the crooks and charlatans who had moved into this position and who exploited 'legal proceedings as if they were a branch of commerce'.[49] In the bureaucracy, there was a mass purge of *sans-culottes*, and the educational and social level of recruits went up, with recruiters expecting appointees to have prior administrative experience, not just patriotic opinions. In December 1794, CPS member Cambacérès defended the justice of appointing on the basis of talent, with no regard for noble pedigree: 'The man is of no import; it is his talent the Republic needs.'[50] Around one-third of the Directorial bureaucracy would have experience of government administration prior to 1789.

The latent authoritarianism in the Directorial regime – evident in its series of political coups, its electoral fixing, its deportation of political enemies – also manifested itself in the growth of the central bureaucracy at the expense of the elective principle. Even though the range of governmental tasks shrank when compared with the highly interventionist Jacobin state, government retained a supervisory and monitoring role over most aspects of social, economic, political and cultural life. A particularly significant innovation was the establishment of Directorial commissaries in each of the Departments to supervise local affairs – an institution which diminished local self-determination and simultaneously recalled the Bourbon Intendants and prefigured Napoleonic prefects. These men tended to evade the Directorial purges and provided a much-needed degree of administrative continuity for the regime. They also played an important part in the collection of data for the Ministry of the Interior which, particularly under François de Neufchâteau, started major statistical inquiries into the state of post-Revolutionary society and economy.

The Thermidorian and Directorial period thus saw a re-engagement with the problems of ensuring quality services in a maturing capitalist economy and state which were both professionally rigorous and also sufficiently imbued with patriotic public spirit. The conviction that patriotism by itself was insufficient as a guarantee of effective service was becoming universal, as was the perceived need for quality controls across the service sector. There was much hesitation, foot-dragging and changes of tack – in this as in most political domains in this troubled period – and the general trajectory would only be consummated under Bonaparte's regime. The new health schools dispensed medical training, and a full system of state approval for all medical practitioners was introduced in 1803. In hospitals too, the late 1790s saw a gradual reintegration of communities of religious nursing sisters who had been expelled at the height of dechristianization, but whose long-honed caring skills were regarded as more important than their private beliefs. The legal world also started to swing back in line. There were outspoken attacks on the free field in law from 1797 onwards, and lawyers were reintroduced in 1800, as was a state system of notarial certification in 1803. The bonds of patriotism became less forceful in the army in this period too. Military professionalization was now marked by tighter discipline, less expression of political opinions and greater loyalty towards generals (who often encouraged dependence by sharing the booty they plundered with their men) than towards the abstract notion of the Republic.

Although corporatism had been one of the principal targets of the Revolution from the earliest days, the Directory and Consulate were introducing a kind of neo-corporatism (even complemented by a light seasoning of venality as regards auctioneers and attorneys, who had to pay 'caution money' before acceding to a post). Institutions of professional training under the close surveillance of the state seemed to be the means by which the Directorials conjoined the requirements of patriotism and the exigencies of expertise. From the mid-1790s onwards, a range of new educational institutions was established, several of them recalling the spirit of the professional training institutions of the Bourbon monarchy. The Institut national des sciences et arts was created in October 1795 as a direct successor to the old national academies, and it operated as a government-funded research institute. Even prior to that, there had been a range of similar renewals. The royal botanical garden, the Jardin du Roi, was in June 1793 transformed into a 'Museum of Natural History' to dispense courses on this topic. In March 1794, a 'Central School for Public Works' was created, and on 22 October 1795, it was transformed into the École Polytechnique, which was linked to further training in civil engineering (like the old Ponts et Chaussées), mining and military engineering. In September 1794, a Conservatoire des arts et métiers for the artisanal arts was created, and in October, an École normale for teacher-training.

The social status and levels of wealth of professionals was also on the rise in the late 1790s. Professionals – with lawyers and officials in the van – were among the big buyers of national lands, endorsing thereby their commitment to the Revolution. 'Jacobins became buyers', as Michelet reflected, 'and buyers became Jacobins.'[51] They were also well placed to respond creatively to the resurgence of demand in the service sector of the economy in the late 1790s. In addition, the re-establishment of an academic hierarchy gave select savants employment and a salary, but also renewed cultural capital. It was significant, for example, that Bonaparte chose to take with him to Egypt a commission of savants which recalled the great scientific expeditions of the Bourbon monarchy. An Egyptian Institute on the lines of the new Institut in Paris was established, for 'the progress and the spreading of enlightenment in Egypt', and a range of archaeological, engineering, natural historical and linguistic researches were begun. Bonaparte clearly saw the professional intellectual as a rising force which he wished to attach to his wagon.

E) . . . AND THEIR OTHER(S)

The notion of national unity within Revolutionary culture involved the imposition of almost unrelenting unifying procedures on individuals and groupings, ranging from education, festive pedagogy and propaganda through to violence and terror. The pressure was such, however, that it ended up engendering opposition and fragmentation. There resulted the paradox of a political culture priding itself on its inclusiveness, yet fabricating a polarized opposition of outsiders and counter-revolutionary 'others'.

Polarization – 'othering' – became more intense when the Republic found itself facing the military might of the European powers. It focused on the English, target over the previous century of much anglophobia (but probably even more anglophilia). 'Perfidious Albion' was now viewed as being responsible for funding the war efforts of the European powers, and suborning French politics through bribery, corruption and every nefarious trick in Prime Minister William Pitt's book. British nationals found themselves receiving far more severe treatment than in any previous war. Sweeping laws (happily not much implemented, as far as can be seen) were passed, threatening English soldiers and sailors with summary execution if taken prisoner. England was the 'new Carthage', and Revolutionary orators lined up to play Cato. The demonization of the British, however, was matched by a sense of fraternal inclusiveness towards other Europeans. And it was perhaps less important for shaping the developing French nationalism than the way that the kinds of rhetorical strategies and ideological heat employed against enemies in war were turned inwards within France against putative opponents of the new regime. Revolutionary political culture had a fixation on unity and conspiracy which had not needed war as a trigger: it went back to 1788–9, and indeed had premonitory antecedents long before then. The Revolution's 'Other' consequently tended to be French rather than foreign. The French resumed their sense of civilized superiority over the rest of the world, but had now honed that sense of betterness within the political culture of the Revolution. The *mission civilisatrice* of the Great Nation, like charity, began at home.

The process of political othering was not simply a rhetorical consequence of the Revolution's own unifying political culture. 'Othering' also reflected the oscillations and reverses of the political quotidian, and it comprised groups and individuals whose opposition to the Revolutionary cause was anything but imaginary, and whose actions in turn helped shape the character and obsessions of the Revolutionaries. Nor were these interests squashed or eradicated by 1799. The scapegoats and the also-rans of Revolutionary political culture persisted as bearers of traditions and ideologies of diversity and resistance well into the following century. Their experiences, and their relationship to the Revolutionary project, are as important as the project itself in understanding post-Revolutionary France.

The Revolution had begun with the Third Estate setting itself up against the two 'privileged orders' of nobility and church. The trajectory of each over the course of the 1790s was rather different, but by 1799 both represented an other against which the Revolutionaries projected their dislike. Although 'aristocrat' had been not more than an academic term prior to the pre-Revolution, it emerged as a key term of hate in the Revolutionary lexicon. The word gave the semblance of homogeneity to noble groupings which were extremely divergent in their political views and social behaviour – indeed, which included many individuals who were political midwives to the birth of the Revolutionary nation in the 1789 crisis. From then onwards, 'aristocrat' both replaced the term 'noble' and was given the invariable meaning of opponent of the Revolution. This was especially the case when it was combined with another hate-term, *émigré*. Although a clear majority of these exiles were nobles and refractory ecclesiastics before the overthrow of the king, there was considerable change once war broke out. Over the decade as a whole, some 83 per cent of *émigrés* were non-nobles, and the grouping contained numerous peasants and workers. From 1793, moreover, the aristocracy of birth was joined by the aristocracy of wealth, who so exercised the venom of Jacques Roux and the Hébertists. By 1794, the term 'aristocrat' was being applied to full-blooded republicans – the Dantonists, the Hébertists, even the Robespierrists – who fell foul of the Revolutionary government.

Given this level of discursive demonization, it proved very difficult – though not impossible – for the nobility, brought up as top dogs in an unreflecting world of privilege, to adapt to the very different political culture and social world initiated in 1789. The wealthiest and the most aristocratic did worst of all. The only members of the royal family physically to survive the decade were those who ran away (Artois, Provence) or else (as, for example, in the case of Louis XVI's youngest daughter, Marie-Clotilde, exchanged with the Austrians in 1795 against French prisoners of war) who were political nullities. Even trading his Bourbon patronym for the epithet 'Equality' had been insufficient to save the skin of Philippe, duc d'Orléans. The higher one was up the political ladder of the pre-Revolutionary polity the greater the risks and dangers run – and the more the need to know when to keep one's head below the parapet. Thus the wealthiest group of private individuals under the Ancien Régime, the hated *anobli* Farmers General (including chemist Lavoisier), suffered the highest death-rate on the scaffold.

This was, however, the tip of the noble iceberg. Physical survival was less of a problem closer to the waterline. The vast majority of the pre-1789 noble order survived the Revolution living within France. Fewer than 1 per cent of the noble males – some 1,156 (around half of them in Paris), out of around 120,000 – were executed. More nobles took the road into emigration – some 16,431 in total, around one-third of whom were army officers. The democratization of politics in the Revolution had not liquidated the nobility – nor eradicated them definitively from public life. Although many *hobereaux* and impoverished nobles sank without trace into the commoner world once they had lost the oxygen of place and privilege, others proved altogether more resilient. Ex-nobles in national political life such as Barras or Talleyrand were rare after 1792–3, but at a subordinate level, lying low in their country estates proved a safe place of hibernation for a great many nobles, even those '*émigrés* of the heart' who harboured counter-revolutionary sentiments.[52] Many nobles who had emigrated were, moreover, returning to France in the late 1790s, and Napoleon would be even more welcoming. Prior to the Revolution, the nobility had owned between a fifth and a quarter of land, and their travails in the 1790s, including the expropriation and sale of *émigré* land, cut this sharply. The full impact of the sales was offset by a number of strategies, such as purchase of one's own property through front-men (*prête-noms*). In the department of the Meurthe around 15 per cent of *émigré* land was acquired by their relatives. Although there was an enormous amount of variation across the country, it would seem that overall the nobility lost around a half of their property over the Revolutionary period. The nobility re-emerged in national politics after 1799 (and especially after 1815, when the restored Bourbons would seek to be especially accommodating to reintegrated *émigrés*). But it only retained much local influence in conservative regions like the west. The abolition of feudalism had ended their unreflecting dominance over local politics, and the new elected municipal and village authorities established from 1790 proved more than capable of resisting their influence.

If 'aristocrat' was one of the key terms of hate in the Revolutionaries' lexicon, it was run close by 'fanatic' – a term which conventionally denoted any Catholic who had not rallied to the Revolution (and in some contexts any Catholic at all). Given the domination of Revolutionary institutions and language by the professional bourgeoisie, it is perhaps surprising – and it was certainly unpredicted – that the Catholic clergy should end the 1790s as a prime target of Revolutionary vituperation.

With the exception of the aristocratic upper clergy, stern upholders of discipline and corporative hierarchy within the church, most clerics in the Estates General had been firm supporters of the Third Estate in 1789 and in many respects were arch-professionals. The Revolutionaries were highly receptive to their integration within the Revolutionary project. It was Te Deums rather than civic festivals which celebrated great revolutionary events down to 1792 at least. At first sight, moreover, many of the measures in the Civil Constitution of the Clergy reforming the church – such as democratic procedures, rational hierarchies, better pay, a clear career structure, elective principles – conformed to the civic professional notions popularized before 1789 by 'citizen priests'. The oath on the Civil Constitution had, however, split the church from top to bottom. The zealous rejection of the oath by the refractory clergy smacked at best of atavistic commitment to corporatism, at worst as treachery to the *patrie*.

The advent of war made the more pessimistic estimations prevail. As the clergy became associated with emigration, civil unrest and, from early 1793, counter-revolution in the west, it proved increasingly difficult for most Revolutionary politicians to conjugate patriotism and Christianity. Despite the efforts of dwindling and demoralized Constitutional clerics to uphold the ethos of civic professionalism, republicans lost faith in the ability of the church to act as a medium for the Revolution's regenerative mission, and increasingly developed their own cults, withdrawing many customary functions from the hands of the clergy. From September 1792, for example, the registration of births, marriages and deaths was made a purely civil function, while legislation on divorce introduced at the same time was also entirely areligious. Dechristianizing Terror in 1793–4 completed the rout of the Constitutional clergy and the demonization of refractory Catholicism.

Furthermore, disestablishing the Catholic church in February 1795 essentially instituted a free field in religious belief. This lost Catholicism – in both its Constitutional and refractory versions – any semblance of a claim to special status, and also highlighted the gains which other religious formations had derived from the Revolution. Protestants, whom the crown had accorded a measure of tolerance in 1787, were unequivocally awarded full citizenship by the Declaration of the Rights of Man, and several Protestants, such as Rabaut de Saint-Étienne and Jean Bon Saint-André played a very full part in national political life, while in Protestant strongholds like the Lower Languedoc they took over local government. (Under the provisions of the Civil Constitution of the Clergy, they were even allowed to vote for their locality's priest.)

The early Assemblies were unsure what to make of France's 40,000-odd Jews, who were a divided grouping. The more vocal, wealthier and more integrated Sephardic community in Bordeaux was contemptuous of the poorer, less assimilated and, as they called them, 'mongrel' Ashkenazim community in Alsace and eastern France. On 28 January 1790, the Constituent Assembly granted the status of active citizen to Sephardic Jews with the required financial standing, but it was not until September 1791 that citizenship was formally extended to all Jews – a decision which the Legislative Assembly subsequently ratified. There were some vicious anti-Semites in the National Assembly, such as the Alsatian lawyer (and future Director) Reubell, who kept up a constant critique of the Ashkenazim. The group calling for Jewish rights was led by the abbé Grégoire, who in 1785 had won an essay prize organized by the Metz Academy on the best means of regenerating the Jews. The notion of regeneration was both strength and weakness of the pro-Jewish lobby. It conformed so closely to the general regeneratory mission of the Revolutionaries that it seemed apposite to be inclusive towards Jews. On the other hand, there was a strong sense, even among Grégoire and his allies, that the existing forms of Jewish organization and mores were part of a barbarian, superstitious and corporative past which should now be cast off. The fact that few Jews seemed keen to renounce their beliefs and their customary structures and enter the Revolutionary nation as regenerated individuals only made matters more problematic.

As political life polarized under the Legislative Assembly, then the Convention, and as organized religion fell more directly under the spotlight of Revolutionary suspicion, Protestant churches and Jewish communities came under increasing pressure. Both were subjected to iconoclastic attacks of the 'dechristianizing' type.[53] Protestant temples were sacked, and the church suffered real decline, with public worship starting again only very slowly in the late 1790s. Local and national authorities headed off peasant anti-Semitic pogroms in the east, but not without themselves subscribing to the language of hatred. Deputy on mission in the east Baudot threatened with 'regeneration by guillotine' any Jew 'placing cupidity in the place of love of the *patrie*, and their ridiculous superstitions in the place of Reason'.[54] Alsatian synagogues were smashed too, their treasures handed over for the war effort, and rabbis abjured their faith like Catholic priests, while observation of the sabbath (rather than the *décadi*) and the wearing of Jewish side-locks and beards were regarded as 'uncivic' offences.

The model of regenerative assimilationism which the Revolutionaries displayed towards the Jews was evident in regard to other groupings whose commitment to the patriotic cause was for whatever reason in doubt. This normative approach usually took a more anodyne form after the coercive episodes of the Terror. Aberrant behaviour could often to be ascribed to ignorance rather than error. Abbé Grégoire attacked the use of Yiddish in Ashkenazim communities, for example, but thought Jewish 'backwardness' required civic education rather than 'regeneration by guillotine'. An argument from utility was also made that linguistic unification would produce a more efficient commerce of ideas, just as uniform weights and measures helped in the commerce of commodities. Furthermore, the Revolutionaries viewed French – the pilot tongue of civilization and Enlightenment before 1789 – as the quintessential language of freedom, and thus far superior not only to Yiddish but also to any other tongue used within France. There were efforts early in the Revolution to spread the gospel of the Right of Man in other than its native French (in January 1790, for example, the Constituent Assembly agreed that all decrees should be translated into German and Flemish). The exhortatory tone turned more bullyingly intolerant of diversity as time went on. One Jacobin pamphleteer called for 'linguistic regeneration' to be made the order of the day.[55] Particular concern was shown towards the areas of federalism and counter-revolution, where local peasants were allegedly being kept in ignorance through their failure to manage the French language. 'Federalism and superstition', thundered Barère in January 1794, 'speak Breton; the emigration and hatred of the Republic speak German; the Counter-Revolution speaks Italian; and Fanaticism speaks Basque.'[56] The rhetorical thunder produced little lightning – no programme of linguistic terrorism was formulated, and after Thermidor, the Revolutionaries fell back on a vague belief in formal education as the best means of producing a single, French language. It would require the compulsory primary schooling of the Third Republic to make French the language of the French people.

The link which Barère made between linguistic diversity and peripheral areas of France was a characteristic one. The majority of the 6 million individuals who did not speak French, he reckoned, plus the 6 million others who could not sustain a conversation in it, were most likely to be peasants shut off from the civilizing current of urban Enlightenment. With the exception of the interlude of the Terror, when all adult males were accorded the franchise (although in the conditions of the Revolutionary government, they could not use them) only peasants who reached certain levels of landholding enjoyed full political rights. It was not, however, that all peasants were inevitably civically challenged. The peasant revolution of 1789 had marked them out as participatory members of the new nation and there was a constant panegyrization of the *bon cultivateur* in Revolutionary discourse, which stressed the involvement of the countryside in the forging of national unity. Newspapers were specially targeted at them – such as Cérutti's highly popular *La Feuille villageoise*, replaced under the Directory by the progressive Interior Minister, François de Neufchâteau, with the semi-official organ *La Feuille du cultivateur*. Clubs and societies penetrated into rural areas as well as in towns. In some areas in the south-east, nearly every village had a Jacobin club. There were rural Terrorists and dechristianizers as well as urban ones. François de Neufchâteau restarted agricultural societies (whose commitment to the cause of the potato, every town-dweller's idea of what peasants ought to be eating, remained undiminished). Moreover, all of France's 40,000 communes were equipped with elective local government, and maybe more than a million peasants profited from this widening of democratic space. In addition the new system of lawcourts dispensed a fairer, cheaper and more available justice than had been on offer to most rural communities prior to 1789.

Protective, patronizing and panegyric by turns, Revolutionary discourse turned nasty when peasants protested, resisted or showed they had minds of their own. The peasantry had to fight hard to gain the benefits from successive National Assemblies which they thought they had won for themselves in the 1789 insurrection. The Constituent Assembly's efforts to enforce the staged redemption of many seigneurial rights caused widespread peasant resistance. First the Legislative Assembly, then the Convention bowed to this grassroots pressure: the decree of 17 July 1793 definitively abolished all seigneurial rights without compensation. Peasant resistance also took the edge off the wish of the Revolutionary assemblies to impose Physiocratic-style agrarian reforms aimed at stimulating agrarian individualism. The hard-pressed legislators feared provoking further anti-revolutionary movements in the countryside which could push peasants into the arms of royalists and counter-revolutionaries. The Rural Code of 6 October 1791 was a timid document which left the initiative for enclosure, removal of use-rights, enclosure of common lands and the like in the hands of the rural community. It largely remained there for the remainder of the decade.

There was a strong tendency in the National Assembly to ascribe rural discontent to the manipulations of nobles and, particularly, priests. Peasant ignorance was the consequence of Catholic 'fanaticism' – a further item to add to the charge-sheet against the church. Around a fifth of known *émigrés* were peasants, as were about a quarter of known victims of Revolutionary justice during the Terror. To the latter number should be added the majority of the 200,000 individuals killed in civil war conditions in the Vendée, where after August 1793 Revolutionary commanders were given order to establish free fire zones as a means of establishing republican order among the rebellious peasantry. This civil strife underlined how strikingly the Revolution split social groupings.

Yet if peasants were amongst the most recalcitrant opponents of the political culture of the Revolution, they also figured amongst its principal beneficiaries of 1789. The benefits of Revolution were extremely diversely and unevenly spread, both geographically and socially within the rural community. Not all members of the rural community had benefited from the gains of 1789. The abolition of feudalism and the suppression of the tithe, hunting rights, seigneurial justice, labour services and the rest had removed significant claims on peasant surplus production. Yet the decision of the Constituent Assembly to allow landlords to add the amount of the tithe to their rents produced enormous resentment among all tenants, including sharecroppers. New national taxes increased many peasants' fiscal burden. The lot of many peasants engaged in proto-industrializing activity in their homes was worsened by the industrial crisis. The jewellery and precious metal industry in the Rouergue was just about wiped out, for example, while many home workers in the linen and wool trades in the hinterland behind the Atlantic ports also suffered badly. Additional impositions by the state tipped many areas into open revolt, notably over the imposition of the Constitutional clergy from 1791 in the numerous regions which were antagonistic to the oath of the Civil Constitution of the Clergy; and then from 1793, the obligation of military service.

Furthermore, the appalling experiences of the countryside from 1793 to 1797 alienated many rural areas from the Revolutionary cause.[57] Following the impositions of the planned economy of Year II, harvests between 1795 and 1798 were not bad, but they were framed by a poor one in 1799 and an appalling one in 1794–5. The requisitioning and dechristianization of the Terror of 1793–4 had led many peasants deliberately to reduce output so as to avoid generating a surplus which could be picked off by urban authorities and exigent *sans-culottes*. Post-Thermidorian deregulation of the grain trade caused bread prices to soar further, and the situation was worsened for most purchasers by the hyper-depreciation of the currency. The swelling of the ranks of beggars and vagrants caused by poor conditions in the countryside aggravated many peasants' plight. There was rural insecurity throughout the late 1790s, with rural brigandage and highway robbery on the increase.

The rural world passed through hell and high water during the 1790s. Significantly, however, even in the violently counter-revolutionary Vendée department there was little demand for the return of the Ancien Régime. Nostalgia for 'the time of the seigneurs' was kept at bay by an awareness of the Revolution's benefits to much of the rural community. Probably the main reason for any air of contentment detectable in the countryside by 1799 was that the previous decade had gone a long way to meeting the most pressing peasant demand in 1789, namely, land. Besides the abolition of seigneurial controls over peasant landownership, the dissolution of ecclesiastical and feudal authority stimulated peasants in many areas into a kind of land-grab on common lands and forests. Peasants were treating these, one authority in the department of the Aude complained, 'like their own garden cabbages',[58] as they continued the incremental extension of cultivable land surface which had characterized the eighteenth century. In addition, the nationalization and sale of church, and from 1793 *émigré*, property gave peasants an opportunity to enter or extend their holdings in the property market. The lion's share of church property from 1790 was snapped up by the urban bourgeoisie, causing a good deal of rural resentment. Some of this, however, had been purchased speculatively and was subsequently recycled back into the peasant pool. Procedures instituted for the sale of *emigré* land from 1793 onwards were more deliberately peasant-friendly. Sale in small lots was envisaged, for example, and though this practice was withdrawn after 1796, the fact that purchase could be made in depreciated *assignats* meant that anyone able to scrabble together a purchase price made a financial killing. Like John Law's system, the *assignat* experience cancelled much peasant indebtedness and left bigger farmers in particular well set for economic recovery.

Levels of agricultural production levels at the turn of the century were still well below 1789 levels. Yet recovery was in the air after 1796. Poor peasants might have lost out after 1796 in regard to acquisition of landed property, but they were compensated by the rise in agricultural incomes, while the Revolutionary decade overall had probably seen a rise of around one-third in the number of peasant owner-occupiers and an increase in the amount of land owned by the peasantry from around 30 to around 40 per cent. If rural involvement in the market still seemed somewhat problematical, this arguably owed less to a peasant reflex of seeking to fall back on low consumption patterns than to the material losses most had experienced, which required restocking and paying off debts. The appalling state of the marketing infrastructure was also a factor in this: canals had been left abandoned, road repair was nugatory, and the security of the main routes, infested with highway robbers and brigands, left much to be desired. The peasantry was certainly, moreover, proving adaptive in one sphere. Following the introduction of partible inheritance in 1793, peasants reacted by using systematic birth control for the first time so as to restrict the number of heirs among whom their property would have to be divided – causing a sharp and enduring drop in France's birth-rate. The peasantry seemed as adaptive as ever, and had not retreated into a shell. Their gains were not necessarily at the expense of the economy as a whole.

By 1799, the post-Thermidor deregulation of the economy had disenchanted most of the urban labouring classes from support for the Revolution. This group, like the peasantry, elicited ambiguous attitudes from the Revolutionary bourgeoisie. The urban worker could be both idealized as the icon of popular sovereignty, yet also condemned out of hand as a rapacious *buveur de sang*. The economic programme developed by the Parisian popular movement in 1793 had been adopted by the Montagnard Convention as the basis for its strategy of 'mobilizing the people', so as to win the war. But, as we have seen, no sooner had this been done than Revolutionary government was seeking to gaol the popular movement's leaders, draw its claws and subvert its notions and practices of direct democracy. After Thermidor, and with the sole exception of the image of the patriotic footsoldier, the *sans-culotte* of Year II was viciously vilified across the political spectrum. The Directory performed a U-turn from the Revolutionary government's commitment to welfare support for the poor and needy. The revival of private charity was insufficient to compensate for the losses experienced by the very poor over the Revolutionary decade.

The Directory's ambiguity towards the urban populations below the level of the bourgeoisie was particularly evident in disputes over the franchise, one of the flash-points in the area of tension marked out by a rhetoric of universal rights and a set of practices of exclusion. Disputes over the notion of active citizenship, which restricted political rights to significant property-holding, categorizing as passive citizen any male who failed to reach the requisite property-owning threshold, were ended with the overthrow of the king and the dissolution of the distinction. Universal male suffrage was an icon of popular republicanism – but not much of a working one, in that the period of Revolutionary government put on hold the exercise of the democratic rights outlined in the 1793 Constitution. The closure of Revolutionary government brought not the implementation of constitutionally guaranteed democratic rights but a move back to a property franchise which was deliberately intended to keep the property-poor under control and prevent a repeat of Year II.

Characteristically, perhaps, it was at the moment when political rights for the unpropertied were on the statute-books, but not enforced, that the Revolutionaries abolished slavery. The Constituent and Legislative Assemblies had proved unwilling to end plantation slavery, on which so much French prosperity depended. The token gesture of abolishing slavery within France was made on 28 September 1791. When finally in February 1794 Danton persuaded his fellow Conventionnels to agree to the abolition of slavery in the colonies, all contact with its Caribbean colonies had long been severed by England's naval blockade. It was a rhetorical gesture of a piece with the 1793 Constitution. Slavery would be reimposed by Napoleon.

Another grouping whose hopes for the enjoyment of full political rights did not achieve fruition were women. Women took advantage of the realm of freedom and equality mapped out by the Revolutionaries to play a significant and, on a global scale, highly precocious, role in the Revolutionary process over the 1790s, particularly before 1795. Such was the range of their activity that they invented and popularized the term 'citizeness' (*citoyenne*), to make a claim for political entitlement and in order to signify that the famed universalism of the Declaration of the Rights of Man (sic) should be gender-blind. There were women present and active in all the Revolutionary *journées* – and indeed they actually led one (5–6 October 1789). They benefited from the freedom of the press to write books, plays and (especially) pamphlets and to contribute to newspapers. The customary salonnière might be misprized, but the number of women contributing to the public sphere in print mushroomed from seventy-eight in the whole of the period from 1750 to 1789 to 330 in the Revolutionary decade. They also utilized the new-found freedom of association to attend and also to petition the meetings of representative bodies (including the National Assembly) and a wide range of clubs and societies, including the Paris Jacobin Club. They participated in the activities of certain mixed-sex clubs, such as Fauchet's Cercle social, and they also established their own associations, the most significant of which was the Society of Revolutionary Republican Citizenesses, established by *enragées* Claire Lacombe and Pauline Léon in May 1793. The outbreak of war amplified many activist women's conscious attachment to Revolutionary principles: not only did they look after their families in the absence of their volunteer husbands, they played a critical role in the enforcement of the Maximum by denouncing infringements and black-marketeering, and also knitted socks, collected clothes and gathered saltpetre for the war effort. Pauline Léon argued forcefully that women should be formally permitted to bear arms (and a handful of women did manage to fight at the front). Olympe de Gouges, author of the eloquently pointed *Declaration of the Rights of Woman* (1791), similarly contended that if women were extended the right to tread the steps of the scaffold, they should not be prevented from holding other rights (an ironic comment, in the light of her own execution in November 1793).

'Why should women, endowed with the faculty of feeling and expressing their views,' demanded an anonymous orator at a meeting of the Society for Revolutionary Republican Citizenesses, 'be excluded from public affairs?'[59] Why indeed? The natural law tradition adopted by the Revolutionaries, the stark break with the national past, the reduced influence of the clergy on public affairs in the 1790s and the challenge to patriarchalism comprised by the killing of the Father-King, all suggested that women might well benefit from the Revolution's inclusive universalism. There certainly were male participants in Revolutionary politics – most notably Condorcet, whose 'Essay on the Admission of Women to Political Rights' appeared in 1790[60] – who supported their political rights. And much of the legislation of the early 1790s showed consideration for the position of women: egalitarian inheritance laws, for example, and the introduction in 1792 of civil divorce (a measure which, far from being a Don Juan's charter, as had been predicted, was utilized by women in violent and unhappy marriages to give themselves a fresh start). Yet when it came to political involvement, women found themselves up against more than a generation of Rousseau-influenced texts which had argued the case for women being lovable (certainly), but essentially creatures of feeling and sensibility, physical weaklings who were constitutionally incapable of rational thought. An influential medical discourse evolved, furthering Rousseau's influence, which purported to confirm the biological inferiority of women. Pierre Roussel's popular *Système physique et morale de la femme* (1775) had assigned to women the production and care of children, and his influence is evident on the work of the Class of Moral and Political Sciences of the Institut after 1795. The symbolic figure of Marianne might emblematize the Republic on official seals and letter-heads; but there was no thought that any real woman could represent anything but her own feelings.

The fragility of the position of women contributing to public life in the 1790s was underlined by the extent to which femininity was utilized as a stock-in-trade of political insult. Even before the Revolution, Austrophobe court factions had assailed Marie-Antoinette – *l'Autrichienne* ('the Austrian bitch') – for unseemly interfering in politics, which had left, it was confidently reported, her poor husband limply impotent. The Diamond Necklace affair had seemed a Rousseauist parable, underlining the crucial importance of keeping women firmly under male control. This line of critique did not confine itself to Revolutionaries: counter-revolutionary propaganda routinely attacked the Revolution for allowing political space to beings who should by rights be confined within the cosier worlds of domesticity and maternity. But the way in which Revolutionaries' own self-presentation highlighted virile stoical actions – dramatized, for example, in David's taut characterization of the Tennis Court Oath – made this line of argument seem particularly relevant. They extended the gendered view of royal politics to suggest that all their opponents were somehow feminized and lacking good Revolutionary manliness. Berouged and beribboned aristocrats were assailed on these grounds as much as unreproductive ecclesiastics who spent their time consorting with females. This gendering of the public sphere became even more pronounced once war had been declared, and the virile republican became the pike-bearing *sans-culotte* or the patriotic musketeer. Political virtue and moral worth were thus gendered militaristically male – a tendency which Bonaparte's regime would strongly reinforce.

Such was the consensus across the political spectrum of the impropriety of women involving themselves in public life, that it seemed only a matter of time before the Revolutionaries drove the point home. Finally, in the autumn of 1793, the issue crystallized following clashes between members of the Society of Revolutionary Republican Citizenesses and Parisian market women over the issue of the compulsory wearing of the red cap. On 30 October 1793 (a fortnight after the execution of Marie-Antoinette, following a show trial which had melodramatized the dangers of letting a woman loose in national politics), Amar, spokesperson of the Committee of General Security, studding his speech with the clichés of Rousseauist sensibility, ordered the disbanding of the Society, and forbade such women's clubs in the future. Patriotic women, it appeared, displayed 'an over-excitation which would be deadly in public affairs'; they should stay at home and bring up young republicans.[61]

In some ways, Amar's order was an incidental spin-off from the Revolutionary government's campaign to control the *enragé* movement in Paris, to which both Léon and Lacombe subscribed, and it certainly triggered little comment or debate. Yet it represented a highly significant moment, for it marked the far limit of female political radicalism in the Revolutionary decade. The further marginalization of female activists followed easily from here onwards. On 20 March 1795, women were forbidden even from attending meetings of the Convention, and prohibited from assembling in groups in the streets, squares and marketplaces.

In the final analysis, the vast majority of male Revolutionaries found it impossible to break free from contemporary gender stereotyping, and to endow women with a part to play within the Revolutionary project save in decorative, supportive or reproductive roles. The late 1790s saw this rejection hardening even more. Particularly significant in this respect was the way that activist women came back into the political limelight, which was sure to win them republican disapprobation. For from the mid-1790s, women had begun to take a leading role in running the underground activities of the refractory Catholic church. They acted as defenders of their faith, obstructing the secular cults of republican officials, petitioning for the opening of churches, hiding 'suitcase *curés*' (itinerant under-cover priests) on their clandestine tours of their flocks, and organizing charity. The growth of religious indifference in the Enlightenment had been more marked among men than women, and iconoclastic dechristianization always seemed a more virile than feminine activity. By working hand in glove with the refractory clergy in this way, women seemed merely to confirm the weakness of their brains, by allowing themselves to be gulled by the 'fanatical' clergy. Though the French state (in Napoleon's Concordat with the pope in 1801) would relegitimize Catholicism and make it a state-approved cult, the conjoining of two of the Revolution's most hated 'others' – fanatical Catholics and 'public' women – would be a highly important legacy of the Revolution in the following century. The struggle between clericalism and anti-clericalism would be about gender as well as politics.

Conclusion: The Brumaire Leviathan and *la Grande Nation*

'Public opinion', mused Louis-Sébastien Mercier in 1798, 'no longer exists, because society is being torn apart.'[1] Certainly, the notion that public opinion had a unifying and harmonizing role looked comically malapropos in the politically turbulent Directorial period. A legacy of the Enlightenment project crystallized in the moment of the *Encyclopédie*, elaborated over the course of the eighteenth century in the developing bourgeois public sphere, it had lost its operational utility.

If public opinion no longer seemed a rudder for Revolutionaries to steer with, this was largely because, as we noted in the previous chapter, this paramount unifying and popularizing symbol of Revolutionary political culture generated rather than transcended division and discord. The Directorial regime registered the developing contradiction between unity and fragmentation in especially striking forms. As we have noted, the Directory's claims to legitimacy were endlessly, almost pathologically, fractured by oscillations both within the political elite and within the broader nation, summed up in the frenzied sectional atmosphere of electoral fixing. There were some Directorials who found this kind of instability acceptable within a constitutional regime: the moderate deputy Berlier, for example, regarded the electoral battles as 'simply a war of nuances among patriots of different degrees'.[2] Yet others wearied of them, and worried about the impact of such squabbling on popular support for the regime: attendance in primary elections on occasion dwindled to alarmingly meagre levels. Consequently, by 1798 and 1799, constitutional specialists such as Siéyès and idealistic intriguers like Madame de Staël and Benjamin Constant began to reflect on how the regime could be changed from the outside so as to reinject into the Revolutionary process a unity and a popularity which seemed to have evaded the Directory.

That even such enthusiasts for the rule of law as these individuals were willing to infringe constitutional legality for what they thought was the greater good underscored the regime's entropic state. Right and Left seemed to cancel each other out in a deadlock. The threat of royalist restoration had been much attenuated by 1798–9, but this was not so apparent to contemporaries, who retained that fear of conspiracy which was such a core feature of Revolutionary political culture. Louis XVIII had tried constitutional electoralism, peasant insurrection, clandestine intriguing and international lobbying: but he still found it impossible to secure a breakthrough in post-1789 public opinion. And no wonder. For Louis still rejected everything back to and including the work of the Constituent Assembly: the high-water mark of his political compromise was the programme outlined by Louis XVI in the *séance royale* of 23 June 1789 – 'the Ancien Régime minus the abuses', as the king-pretender put it.[3] The intransigence of royalist hawks – or *Purs* – was buttressed by a similar intractability among the counter-revolution's apologists and ideologists. The abbé Barruel's populist and popular *Mémoires pour servir à l'histoire du jacobinisme* ('Memoirs on the History of Jacobinism') (1797) ascribed the whole Revolution to a masonic plot with its roots in the Enlightenment. En bloc rejection of the Enlightenment project was also the hallmark of reactionary theoreticians such as Bonald and Joseph de Maistre, who unconditionally rejected the Revolution's commitment to natural rights, and journeyed down a Burkean path, seeking the answers to France's problems in a far-distant and highly idealized past.

If a royalist restoration was not really on the cards, there still existed within the political nation an irreducible core of supporters of the old Bourbon polity, impervious to Directorial propaganda, pedagogy and persuasion. These forces of counter-revolution had massive nuisance value in a regime as fragile as the Directory. The same was true of the Left. Though the Parisian popular movement had been muzzled, there still was a good deal of popular hostility towards the Directorial regime, underpinning the danger of a dictatorship of public safety imposing authoritarian and populist policies on every aspect of political life. One did not have to be a neo-Jacobin to appreciate the critical importance of the Montagnard mobilizing strategy of 1793–4 in protecting the gains of the Revolution when these were most under pressure from within and without. Yet overall, moderates preferred to consign such experiences to memory rather than actuality. Neo-Jacobin posturings frightened them as much as royalist fierceness.

For Siéyès and others in his circle, the way ahead appeared to be a strengthening of the executive arm over the legislature, in a way which avoided the extremes of Bourbon absolutism and Committee of Public Safety-style Terror. They could expect support from what Mercier called 'the minority of opinion composed of sensible folk who recognize the need for strong government'.[4] However, no one could expect the legislative Councils to approve their own weakening. Nor had the framers of the 1795 constitution made the task of revision easy: constitutional amendments involved tortuous and lengthy procedures which would be virtually impossible to get through the legislature, whatever its political complexion. To achieve anything, Siéyès reckoned, a 'sword' was essential – that is, a general who could be instrumental in a coup d'état which would allow change to be forced through. It was essential to Siéyès's developing plans that the general in question should be a political minnow, who would then stand aside and let the constitution be reworked under Siéyès's rational vision. In the event, Siéyès went fishing for a sword – but netted a leviathan. Politely demurring on his own account, General Joubert proposed Bonaparte to Siéyès: 'There's your man!' The coup d'état which Bonaparte engineered with Siéyès's assistance on 18 and 19 Brumaire VII (9–10 November 1799) installed a new regime, the Consulate, which brought the Directory to a close – and in the event also ended much of what had been distinctive about the the political culture of the previous decade.

The chequered course of the final political crisis of the Directory was intricately intertwined with the changing military and diplomatic position. War and Revolution, as always from 1792, were joined at the hip. Hopes for a Europe-wide peace in the aftermath of Campo-Formio had soon been dashed, with French generals finding it impossible to resist expansionism, notably in Italy. In April 1799, an untoward incident during the negotiations for a general peace being conducted at Rastadt saw the French envoys attacked by a hostile German crowd, and several of them murdered. This provided a convenient *casus belli* for the French, justifying the fact that military skirmishes were already taking place.

With Austria returning to the fray alongside England, France found itself pitted against its two most intractable foes – plus the relatively untried force of Russia, which had been stimulated into hostility by fears that Bonaparte's Egyptian ambitions might upset the balance of power in south-eastern Europe. The 1799 campaign went badly for the French almost at once. Jourdan led an army across the Rhine – but was soon beaten back by the reinvigorated Austrians. Meanwhile, the Royal Navy conveyed a British expeditionary force to Holland in order to link up with Russian troops and the allies managed to capture the Dutch fleet. In Italy too, theatre of so much French success since 1796, there were dramatic reverses. The Austrians and Russians defeated Schérer at Cassano in April, after the French had attempted to seize Tuscany. General Championnet evacuated the 'Parthenopean Republic' (Naples), so as to bring aid to his compatriots in the north. But he was defeated by the Russians at Trebbia. French armies were obliged to leave the peninsula altogether and to join up with the retreating forces from Germany to fight a holding battle at Zurich in June. By then, however, the entire network of pro-French regimes established since 1796 was collapsing like a house of cards.

Furthermore, the French now had new as well as old enemies on their hands. By the late 1790s, the soldier-in-arms of *la grande nation* had become less a fraternal liberator of Jacobin imaginings than a symbol of coercive extraction, and many of the populations to whom France prided itself on bringing a humane and emancipatory message had turned distinctly hostile. In addition, local Jacobins, particularly in the Italian cities, proved more radical than even the Directorial French, worsening social and political antagonisms. Some of the areas which had been brought directly under French rule – such as Belgium and the left bank of the Rhine, Mulhouse and Piedmont – were relatively shielded. But fighting zones and areas of French occupation were subject to brutal measures of looting and pillaging, and the fate of sister republics was often little better. The organization of the Batavian Republic, for example, was accompanied by the Dutch being forbidden to have links with their customary trading partners, the English; at the same time, high tariffs shut them out of the French market. Elsewhere it was the nationalization of church lands and anti-clerical policies conducted against refractory priests which produced high levels of popular resentment, particularly in Belgium and Italy. Attempts to introduce conscription under the Jourdan Law of 1798 triggered riots in Belgium which snowballed into outright peasant insurrection, along the lines of the

Vendée revolt of 1793. Peasant mobilization against the French was also in evidence in southern Italy. Cardinal Ruffo's peasant band, the 'Christian Army of the Holy Faith', swelled into a crusading host, wreaking vengeance on anyone who had dealings with the French Revolutionary Anti-Christ. The Republic had, moreover, added to its faults in Catholic eyes: following skirmishes in Italy, Pope Pius VI was taken prisoner by the French and in spring 1799 brought to France and imprisoned in Valence. (In August, he would die whilst still in prison.) This rankled with Catholics in France, where socio-religious and political opposition was re-emerging. Louis XVIII had been using his network of agents to rekindle revolt, and the conscription issue reactivated by the 1798 Jourdan Law helped to crystallize discontent. There was a peasant royalist rising at Montréjeau in the Haute-Garonne in August 1799, plus a spate of rebellions in Anjou, Normandy and Brittany.

Themselves divided, and faced with an irreducibly divided country plus the hostility of neighbouring populations, the Directors continued their customary balancing act. The leftist complexion of the Fructidorian Directory was being attenuated by the serendipities of replacement by lot. After the 1797 elections, Neufchâteau was replaced by the solid Treilhard, while the exit of moderate leftist Reubell in 1798 led to the election of Siéyès, whose critical views about the Year III Constitution were widely known. The air of uncertainty was amplified, moreover, by the tense military context in spring 1799 when the Year VII elections were held: the Directors deployed their administrative powers to take as many candidates as possible from the political extremes off the electoral slate. Even so, the patriotic feeling behind what had suddenly again become a war of national defence increased the proportion of left-wing candidates elected – even as the Directors themselves were sliding to the Right.

The Legislative Councils and Directors were almost at once at loggerheads. On 16 June, the Councils determined – against the Directors' wishes – to sit *en permanence*, evoking further memories of the 1793–4 war crisis. Then, on 18 June (30 Prairial VII), they acted to break the developing deadlock in a '*Journée* of the Councils'. A couple of days earlier they had had Treilhard removed as Director on the grounds that there were procedural problems about his election the previous year. The pro-Jacobin Gohier was put in his place and then, in the 30 Prairial *journée*, the Councils replaced Merlin de Douai and La Révellière-

Lépeaux with General Moulin and the Barras protégé Roger Ducos. A ministerial reshuffle followed, and pro-Directorial administrative personnel were also purged: significantly Robert Lindet, from the CPS of Year II, ex-Terrorist Fouché and General Bernadotte were chosen for the Ministries of Finance, Police and War respectively.

The Left shaped up to reinject some of the energy of the Revolutionary government into public affairs. The controls which the Directory had placed over freedom of expression in the aftermath of the Fructidor coup were lifted, and political newspapers started to open again. In Paris, the Manège Club was formed in July. Meeting in the site of Jacobin memory that was the Salle du Manège, where the National Convention had sat, it soon boasted over 3,000 members, including around 250 members of the Councils, alongside names from the Jacobin past including CPS stalwart Prieur de la Marne, ex-War Minister Bouchotte, post-master-cum-king-catcher Drouet, and Félix Lepeletier, the brother of Revolutionary martyr Lepeletier de Saint-Fargeau. Their call for *la patrie en danger* to be declared helped rally the forces of the Left more convincingly than at any time since 1794. They also helped to have an impact on national policy. An oath of hatred of royalty – but not, significantly, of 'anarchy' (Jacobinism's coded alias) – was imposed on all functionaries. The Jourdan Law was activated in its fullest form, involving the call-up of all young men between twenty and twenty-five years old, in a move which clearly recalled the *levée en masse*. The 'Law of Hostages' of 12 July allowed the authorities in departments adjudged to be in a state of rebellion to imprison as 'hostages' members of *émigré* families. These could be held personally financially liable for any damage caused by royalist disturbances. And after a degree of to-ing and fro-ing, a forced loan on the rich was decreed to compensate for lost revenue from conquered territories. When news came in of the royalist rising at Montréjeau and the landing of an Anglo–Russian expeditionary force in Holland, the Councils decreed that authorities could make visitations into the homes of suspects to seek incriminating evidence of counter-revolutionary activity or sentiments.

There were many who thrilled to this nostalgic trip down Terrorist memory lane. There were many more who did not. Patriotic overtures chilled rather than warmed the blood of much of the population. Those who looked unfondly back on 1793–4 found their spokesperson in the new Director, Siéyès, who did what he could to fire warning shots about the direction policy seemed to be taking. Brawls around the Manège Club involving the neo-Jacobins and rightist youths were used as a pretext for Police Minister Fouché to close the club down, and in September, tougher press laws led to the closure of many Left and Right newspapers. Siéyès then moved to have Bernadotte replaced as War Minister by the more flexible Dubois-Crancé, and coordinated opposition in the Councils to the Left's call for the declaration of *la patrie en danger*.

It was at this delicately poised moment that Bonaparte arrived back on the scene from Egypt. Since his embarkation on 19 May 1798, the Egyptian campaign which he had conceived and conducted had gone disastrously badly. He first smashed the native Mameluke army at the battle of the Pyramids on 21 July, and secured lower Egypt before leading an expedition into Syria against Turkish forces. The military value of the whole venture had, however, been brought into question almost straight away. In order to reach Egypt, Bonaparte had managed to slip the surveillance of Horatio Nelson's English fleet. Nelson doggedly tracked down his quarry, however, and on 1 August 1798 inflicted an appalling defeat on the French, sending most of their boats to the bottom of Aboukir Bay, just outside Cairo. The English then proceeded to offer support to Turkish resistance to the French invasion. Although Bonaparte was able to inflict a further defeat on the Turks at the battle of Aboukir on 25 July 1799, the project of turning Egypt into a 'sort of Islamic Milan'[5] had begun to pall. In later summer, Bonaparte heard the news of the loss of French control of Italy which he had done so much to establish. He determined to abandon the rump of the French forces in the Near East, and to return to France.

Bonaparte arrived at Fréjus on 9 October 1799 and within a week was back in Paris. The potential delicacy of his position – he had, after all, just abandoned his command to return home from a dreadful campaign – was overlooked. His cursus from Fréjus to Paris turned into a triumphal march, with whole towns and villages staging ceremonial *entrées* for him and cheering his passage. He had become, noted one Montpellier schoolteacher, 'this hero whose name is worth a whole army', 'a great man to whom France has turned its eyes as the object of its tenderest affections and dearest hopes'.[6]

This degree of panegyrization had its roots in Directorial festive culture, and testified to a subtle mutation which had been taking place in the tenor of public opinion. Prior to 1795, the heroes and great men which the Revolution had commemorated were civilians – or else tragic young soldiers such as Bara, the teenager hero voted the honours of the Pantheon in 1794. The festive culture of the Directory had become, however, less Revolutionary, more military and more nationalistic. Besides the decadal festivals honouring key Revolutionary anniversaries (14 July, 10 August, 9 Thermidor, etc.) or else for 'natural' categories (Spouses, Old Age, etc.) a new category of military and diplomatic festival now appeared. The town of Rodez, for example, had festivities for the victories of Lodi, Rivoli and Mantua in 1796–7. Toulouse fêted victory over Spain in 1795, over Austria in 1797 (with further celebrations for Campo-Formio) and the capture of Malta in 1798 – and there were also funerary services held for the deaths of Generals Hoche in 1797 and Joubert in 1799. Local officials noted that these chauvinistic events were the most enthusiastically received by the local populace: in Normandy in particular a good dose of anglophobia invariably made things go with a swing. Even in the civilian festivals, military glamour and nationalistic pride now prevailed over the evocation of civic and republican virtue. Soldierly parades with fife and drum were integral parts of the ceremonies. The 9 Thermidor fête held in Paris in 1797, moreover, had extensive sections which involved parading and glorying in the works of art plundered in the Italian campaigns. Directorial festive culture was being militarized. In addition, since most of these ancillary festivals had to do with the battles which Bonaparte had won and the peace he had helped secure, they also served the young general's popularity.

Bonaparte's return thus caused considerable alarm and excitement within the political nation which seemed to be enthusing less for Revolutionary principles and more for the expansionist glory of what was coming to be known as *la Grande Nation* ('the Great Nation'). The moment was particularly opportune because, although anxiety was still in the air, the military situation which had been the focus of preoccupation had begun to stabilize, and even improve. The English had been repulsed, and forced to evacuate Holland under the Convention of Alkmaar in October. French troops had also recovered their poise on the eastern front after some severe defeats, and they defeated the Austro–Russian force in a second battle of Zurich in late September. The Helvetic Republic was cleared, and the French went on to reoccupy the left bank of the Rhine, as a dispirited Czar Paul recalled Russian troops from western Europe. Within France too, royalist resistance to conscription and the Leftward swing of the Revolution had failed to ignite widespread revolt.

Yet if the military situation was being corrected, the state of politics had progressed to a point at which the decomposition of the regime seemed imminent. For several weeks after his arrival in Paris, Bonaparte held court in Paris, as interested parties and delegations from a variety of political groupings fawned over him. In every viable political pie, the finger of Siéyès was invariably to be found. The wily Director now set about assembling a conspiratorial team to revise a constitution which brooked no easy legal revision. His fellow conspirators included individuals drawn from the executive (Police Minister Fouché and Justice Minister Cambacérès as well as himself), the legislature (where Bonaparte's brother Lucien, who was President of the Council of the Five Hundred, played a crucial marshalling role), and the world of politics, high finance and state service (Talleyrand, Roederer, Chénier, Daunou, Cabanis).

By 18 Brumaire VII (9 November 1799), things were ready. On that day, by a prearranged signal, three of the Directors – Barras, Roger Ducos and Siéyès himself – resigned, forcing the hand of the more grudging Gohier and Moulin. The Councils were convened and informed of the existence of a ghastly Jacobin plot, and this served as justification for removing the Councils to out-of-the-way Saint-Cloud – plus Bonaparte's appointment as local commander-in-chief. The plotters had shown a little too much complacency, however, and the coordinated appearance of posters all over Paris declaring that the Republic had to be saved made many political insiders smell a rat. Next day, Bonaparte received a rude reception from the Councils, with cries of 'outlaw' and 'dictator' making themselves heard. Bonaparte was rattled, but his brother Lucien saved the day for him. He rallied the troops, forced the unruly neo-Jacobins out of the chambers at the end of bayonets, and inveigled the docile rump of the two Councils to agree that evening to a new regime, the Consulate. In a matter of months, Siéyès's 'sword' would marginalize the originator of constitutional revision, and skilfully craft a new constitution very much to his own measure. In the Constitution of Year VIII (13 December 1799/22 Frimaire VII), a new regime was established in which power was located much more firmly on the first of three consuls who composed the executive arm. The Napoleonic adventure was up and running.

Though having played the role of reformist zealot to a tee, the young Swiss Benjamin Constant had wonderfully lucid second thoughts about what had taken place on 18 Brumaire, and what the coup d'état might mean for the Revolutionary political culture to which he was so attached. 'I believe this is a decisive moment for liberty,' he wrote to Siéyès on the morning of 19 Brumaire.

[T]alk of adjourning the Councils . . . would seem disastrous to me at this time, since it would destroy the only barrier which could be set up against a man whom you associated with yesterday's events, but who is thereby only more of a threat to the Republic. His proclamations, in which he speaks only of himself and says that his return has raised hopes that in everything he does he sees nothing but his own elevation . . . [H]e has on his side the generals, the soldiers, aristocratic riffraff and everyone who surrenders enthusiastically embraces the appearance of strength . . .[7]

Constant's characterization of the three strongest supports of the regime in the making – the army, the right ('aristocratic riff-raff', in his disdainful prose) and supporters of a strong executive (those who 'embrace[d] the appearance of strength') – was just. Bonaparte needed military force to sweep aside the nay-sayers; the Right inevitably preferred a soldier in command to a republican ideologue like Robespierre; and much of the political nation had been won over to the idea of strengthening the executive. But Constant probably underestimated the strongest card in Bonaparte's hand – namely, his popularity. Public opinion, fractured and torn apart on all major issues within the Directorial regime, seemed to be on Bonaparte's side.

'We saw the frightful regime of terror gradually returning; then suddenly, the *journée* of 18 Brumaire displayed to us a less gloomy horizon.'[8] This comment by a bourgeois from Mende in the southern Massif captured fairly accurately the views of a solid wedge of middling France when confronted with Bonaparte's coup d'état. Whatever Bonaparte and his regime became, at the outset he had a great deal to recommend him to those who had benefited from the Revolution (or who did not wish to lose, by the continuation of political instability, more than they already had). That he was a military man was not excessively worrying, nor did it seem to predestine France for an inevitably militaristic future.

After all, George Washington had been generalissimo of the American colonists – and the United States of America had not turned into a military dictatorship. As the maker of Campo-Formio, moreover, Bonaparte was particularly associated with pacification with honour. He was an unusual figure, who had ostentatiously attended the Institut's sessions on his return to Paris, for example, as if to demonstrate his intellectual seriousness and his debts to Enlightenment science.

In addition, Bonaparte was living exemplification of the career open to talent, that talismanic precept of bourgeois Revolution. With his background, he would not have secured a military command before 1789, let alone have the kind of glorious career he had managed. His military career also made him a member of a professional grouping with which the Revolutionary cause was particularly associated. Without the super-patriotic soldier, the Revolution would not have lasted. Even Bonaparte's Jacobin past in the Terror – when the Revolution had seemed most at threat – probably did him no disfavours in that respect, for the army retained a reputation as a storm centre of fervent Revolutionary commitment. With the urban *sans-culottes* a busted flush, even most neo-Jacobins expected more in the way of radical commitment from the army than from the streets. Indeed, there were some – though neither Siéyès nor Benjamin Constant were of this number – who in 1799 would reflect that the professional soldier was more 'representative' of the spirit of the Revolution than the elected deputies who sat on the legislative Councils.

Historians of the Napoleonic regime have tended to exaggerate – so as excessively either to laud or to vilify – the putatively radical break which Bonaparte represented with the Revolutionary past. Bonaparte's declaration that 'the Revolution is over'[9] showed a determination to keep a firm control over many of those aspects of the 1790s which had created division rather than harmony – representative government, a strong legislature, the elective principle, a free press, personal freedoms. Yet this redrawing of the political map also signalled a commitment to draw a line under the Revolutionary experience in a way in which those who had benefited from it could enjoy their spoils. These individuals – property-owners and professionals for the most part, as we have seen – were looking for peace and security so that they could consolidate their gains – and Bonaparte seemed determined to satisfy them. The perpetuation of the political culture of the Revolution had seemed to produce only instability and apathy, and the Revolutionary mythic present inaugurated in 1789, which was such a cardinal feature of political culture, had become tiresome and lost its appeal. The bourgeoisie, which had provided the basis of the Revolutionary political class, was thus increasingly willing to surrender the rights outlined in the 1795 regime to a more authoritarian set-up which guaranteed them their more material gains.

Not, moreover, that there was much to surrender in certain areas, for much of Bonaparte's appeal was that he seemed to be continuing an existing but unfulfilled trend within Directorial government for a stronger executive power. The draconian views he soon exhibited on freedom of the press and freedom of association had already been prefigured by the Directory's repressive attitude towards newspapers and political associations on the fringes of the Left and Right. His reduction of the elective principle was less resented than might appear likely: the low ballots of the late 1790s suggested that the country could either take electoral democracy or leave it. Beneath the frothy oscillations of Directorial politicking, growing centralization through a Directorial bureaucracy more effective than anything that either the Bourbons or the earlier Revolutionaries had been able to assemble also prepared the way for the Napoleonic regime. The wide use of military justice under the Directory to control areas of brigandage and highway robbery, for example, presaged the tough policies of Napoleon in pacifying France and creating a kind of 'security state'.[10]

'Confidence comes from below,' Siéyès had opined, 'power comes from above.'[11] There was a telling Fénelonian echo in the comment which Bonaparte would have relished. The link between virtuous authority and a loyal and receptive population which Fénelon had posited as the basis of a moral polity found its consummation in the new First Consul. The source of his authority came not from the deity but from the public. 'I myself', he noted, 'am representative of the people.' The new system was, the *idéologue* Cabanis stated with no little satisfaction, 'democracy purged of all its inconveniences'.[12] That government was moreover made to Napoleonic measure. 'What's in the new constitution?' asked the wags as the Constitution of Year VIII succeeded that of Year III. 'Bonaparte,' was the reply. Liberal critics would accuse him of having hijacked public opinion, central myth of the Enlightenment project. Yet Bonaparte's claims to unify and represent public opinion, prefigured in the personal adulation and popular acclaim which had greeted him on his march from Fréjus to Paris, contrasted with the Directorial tendency to divide and fracture opinion.

There was still much uncertainty about what a Bonapartist regime would look like. Even Siéyès, whose more balanced constitutional schemes Napoleon put on ice, was uncertain whether Bonaparte would merely be a dictator in the old Roman republican sense, a frontman for a more representative scheme, or a continuator of a mixed system of government. Quite what Bonaparte's accession would mean for the international balance of power also remained uncertain. Would he be able to live up to his Campo-Formio reputation as a man of peace? Would he seek to recover the French colonies lost to England and to reposition France as a global colonial and commercial power? Or would he renounce Louis XV's conviction that France was a 'satisfied power' in Europe, and seek to make territorial gains like an old-fashioned eighteenth-century dynast?

There still seemed much that was uncertain, and much to play for in 1799. In a great many respects, 1715 seemed a very long way off. Despite Bonaparte's amputation or deformation of many of the cherished values of the Revolution, it would prove difficult to liquidate all elements of the political culture he inherited from the Revolutionary decade. Indeed, he would not seek to do so, and sought rather to transform that culture into one of the bases of his personal rule. Despite the uncertainties, many contemporaries grasped the point – underlined by the new constitution which now came forward – that Bonaparte was rewriting the political script in a way which personalized power more forcefully on an individual than anyone since the pre-Revolutionary reign of Louis XVI – with whom he would soon be comparing himself (to his own considerable advantage). An early portrait – by Gros in 1802 – even showed Bonaparte flaunting as fine a set of legs as the Sun King – a subliminal association which, given the First Consul's zealous dedication to propaganda and self-fashioning, was doubtless intentional. Power was represented in the body of the dynast again, and other representational claims were systematically downgraded. The eighteenth century closed therefore with a new, Bonapartist political tradition – which drew from Bourbon, Enlightenment and Revolutionary sources – establishing itself on the apparent ruins of Bourbon absolutism, constitutional monarchy, liberal republicanism and Jacobin authoritarianism. Its military orientation would, however, make fragile both the regime and its claim to greatness.

Notes

1: FRANCE IN 1715: THE KING'S LEG AND THE CHOREOGRAPHY OF POWER

1 Cited in R. Astier, 'Louis XIV, *Premier Danseur*', in D. L. Rubin (ed.), *Sun King: The Ascendancy of French Culture during the Reign of Louis XIV* (London, 1992), pp. 86–7.

2 Saint-Simon cited in J. M. Apostolides, *Le Roi-machine. Spectacle et politique au temps de Louis XIV* (Paris, 1981), p. 156.

3 A. Guéry and R. Descimon, 'Un État des temps modernes', in A. Burguière and J. Revel (eds.), *Histoire de la France. L'État et les pouvoirs* (Paris, 1989), p. 238.

4 Jacques-Bénigne Bossuet, *Politique tirée des propres paroles de l'Écriture sainte*, ed. J. Le Brun (Geneva, 1967), pp. 68, 185.

5 I have plundered this term from Lynn Hunt, *Politics, Culture and Class in the French Revolution* (London, 1984). See too below, chapter 11, section B.

6 *Manière de montrer les jardins de Versailles* (Paris, 1951 edn).

7 *Mémoires de Louis XIV* (2 vols.; Paris, 1860), vol. ii, p. 7.

8 P. Burke, *The Fabrication of Louis XIV* (London, 1992), p. 49.

9 N. Ferrier-Caverivière, *L'Image de Louis XIV dans la littérature française de 1660 à 1715* (Paris, 1981), p. 65.

10 Baron de Breteuil, *Mémoires*, ed. E. Lever (Paris, 1992), p. 330.

11 ibid., p. 328.

12 Henri IV, cited in J. Barbey, *Être roi. Le Roi et son gouvernement en France de Clovis à Louis XVI* (Paris, 1992), p. 146.

13 M. Bloch, *The Royal Touch. Sacred Monarchy and Scrofula in England and France* (London, 1973).

14 Bodin, *Les Six Livres de la République*, Book 1, ch. viii ('De la souveraineté').

15 There were ten *parlements* in existence on Louis XIV's birth: creations at Metz (1657), Besançon (1676) and Tournai (1686: changed to Douai in 1714)

brought the number up to thirteen in 1715. In the eighteenth century, Bastia (1768) and Nancy (1775) were added. In addition, there were twelve *cours des comptes* and four *cours des aides*, sovereign courts dealing with financial issues.

16 *Contrat de mariage du Parlement avec la ville de Paris* (Paris, 1649).

17 H. Leclercq, *Histoire de la Régence* (3 vols.; Paris, 1921), vol. i, p. 62.

18 Louis de Rouvroy, duc de Saint-Simon, *Mémoires de Saint-Simon*, eds. A. de Boislisle and L. Lecestre (43 vols.; Paris, 1879–1930), vol. xxvii, pp. 6–7.

19 W. J. Beik, *Absolutism and Society in Seventeenth-Century France: State Power and Provincial Aristocracy in Languedoc* (Cambridge, 1985), p. 265.

20 J. Klaits, *Printed Propaganda under Louis XIV. Absolute Monarchy and Public Opinion* (Princeton, NJ, 1976), p. 18.

21 See below, pp. 55–6.

22 *A Short Review of the Book of Jansenius* (n.p., 1710), 'Preface' (no pagination).

23 See below, chapter 3, section C.

24 Citations from R. Taveneaux, *Le Catholicisme dans la France classique (1610–1715)* (2 vols.; Paris, 1980), vol. i, pp. 326, 516.

25 C. Maire, *De la Cause de Dieu à la cause de la Nation. Le jansénisme au XVIIIe siècle* (Paris, 1998), p. 10.

26 M. Kwass, *Privilege and the Politics of Taxation in Eighteenth-Century France: Liberté, Égalité, Fiscalité* (Cambridge, 2000), p. 41.

27 Faydit's *La Télémaquomanie* was published in 1700. It is cited in V. Kapp, *'Télémaque' de Fénelon: la signification d'une oeuvre littéraire à la fin du siècle classique* (Paris and Tübingen, 1982), on which I have drawn heavily in this passage. Another equally mythical history being constructed as a weapon against absolutism was the 'Figurist' scriptural chronicle being devised by certain Jansenists: see below, pp. 102–3.

28 François de Fénelon, *Telemachus, Son of Ulysses*, ed. P. Riley (Cambridge, 1994), p. 60. (I have slightly altered the translation.)

29 ibid., p. 297.

30 See below, pp. 55–7.

31 Kapp, *'Télémaque' de Fénelon*, p. 205, n. 12.

32 G. Treca, *Les Doctrines et les réformes de droit public en réaction contre l'absolutisme de Louis XIV dans l'entourage du duc de Bourgogne* (Paris, 1909), p. 27.

33 *Lettres de Madame duchesse d'Orléans, née Princesse Palatine*, ed. O. Amiel (Paris, 1895), p. 352.

34 Full quote in Breteuil, *Mémoires*, p. 327.

35 *Mémoires de Saint-Simon*, vol. xxvii, p. 281. See also, on this episode, Breteuil, *Mémoires*, p. 328.

36 Pierre Narbonne, *Journal des règnes de Louis XIV et Louis XV (de l'année 1701 à l'année 1744)* (Paris, 1866), p. 44.

37 R. N. Nicolich, 'Sunset: the spectacle of the royal funeral and memorial services at the end of the reign of Louis XIV', in Rubin, *Sun King*, for the quotations and a full discussion. The physicians' autopsy is cited in full in A. Franklin, *La Vie privée d'autrefois. Les Chirurgiens* (Paris, 1893), pp. 290–91.

2: NEGOTIATING STORMY WEATHER: THE REGENCY AND THE ADVENT OF FLEURY (1715–26)

1 E. Faure, *La Banqueroute de Law (17 juillet 1720)* (Paris, 1977), p. 68.

2 Mathieu Marais, *Journal et mémoires sur la Régence et le règne de Louis XV (1715–37)* (4 vols.; Paris, 1863–8), vol. i, p. 180.

3 Louis-Antoine de Goudron, duc d'Antin, 'Mémoires', *Bibliothèque Nationale. Nouvelles Acquisitions Françaises* 23729–37: 23729, fol. 21. Compare this quotation with that from *Télémaque* above, p. 27.

4 Madame de Staal-Delaunay, *Mémoires*, ed. G. Doscot (Paris, 1970), p. 100.

5 See above, p. 27.

6 See below, p. 60ff.

7 d'Antin, 'Mémoires', *BN NAF* 23731, fols. 9ff.

8 See below, p. 113.

9 Marais, *Journal et mémoires*, vol. ii, p. 121.

10 See above, p. 21.

11 D'Antin is cited in J. C. Petitfils, *Le Régent* (Paris, 1986), p. 450. The incumbent of the post of Chancellor was immoveable. When not in favour or unable to work, his functions were carried out by the Keeper of the Seals (*Garde des Sceaux*).

12 For a fuller discussion of disputes over financial policy, see below, section E.

13 F. A. Isambert, *Recueil général des anciennes lois françaises* (29 vols.; Paris, 1821–33), vol. xxi, p. 147.

14 Retz called the ineffectual Conti 'un zéro', but added sardonically that one could nevertheless multiply by him because he was a Prince of the Blood. *Oeuvres*, ed. A. Feillet et al. (1870–96), vol. ii, p. 180.

15 Staal-Delaunay, *Mémoires*, pp. 101, 131 (an important source for the Maines' conspiracy).

16 *Lettres de M. *** à un homme de qualité* (no place or date of publication), pp. 43–4. This publication may be consulted, along with other pamphlets from the affair, in the British Library FR1.

17 *Lettres de Madame la duchesse d'Orléans née Princesse Palatine*, ed. O. Amiel (Paris, 1985): e.g. pp. 352, 409, 412, 422, etc.

18 Staal-Delaunay, *Mémoires*, p. 111.

19 See e.g. *Justification de M. le Président de *** sur la dispute des Princes* (n.p. 1717), p. 13. (British Library, FR1).

20 *Mémoires de Saint-Simon*, vol. xxvi, p. 280.

21 *Correspondance complète de Madame, duchesse d'Orléans*, ed. G. Binet (2 vols., Paris, 1866), vol. i, p. 453.

22 Marquis d'Argenson, *Journal et mémoires du règne de Louis XV* (9 vols.; Paris, 1859–67), vol. i, p. 23. Cf. on the same lines, d'Antin, 'Memoires', *BN NAF* 29,933, fol. 61.

23 Richer d'Aubé, 'Réflexions sur le Gouvernement de France', *Bibliothèque Nationale, Nouvelles Acquisitions Françaises* 9511, fols. 1–2.

24 France measured some 528 million square kilometres in the Revolution, and since then only a further 27,000 square kilometres have been added.

25 See below, chapter 4, section D.

26 Fénelon, *Lettre à Louis XIV*, ed. F. X. Cuche (Rezé, 1994), p. 44.

27 See above, pp. 19ff.

28 See above, chapter 1, section C.

29 Samuel Bernard, cited in M. and R. Bonney, *Jean-Roland Malet, premier historien des finances de la monarchie française* (Paris, 1993), p. 85.

30 Richer d'Aubé, 'Réflexions', fol. 57.

31 T. Kaiser, 'Money, despotism and public opinion in early eighteenth-century France: John Law and the debate on royal credit', *Journal of Modern History*, 63 (1991), p. 5.

32 John Law, *Oeuvres complètes*, ed. P. Harsin (3 vols.; Paris, 1934), vol. iii, p. 77.

33 Kaiser, 'Money, despotism and public opinion', p. 3.

34 *Correspondance complète de Madame, duchesse d'Orléans*, vol. ii, p. 72; Montesquieu, *Lettres persanes*, letter cxxxviii.

35 Law, *Oeuvres complètes*, vol. ii, p. 266.

36 J. de Flammermont, *Les Remontrances du parlement de Paris au XVIIIe siècle* (3 vols.; Paris, 1888–98), vol. i, p. 127.

37 Kaiser, 'Money, despotism and public opinion', p. 15.

38 ibid, p. 6.

39 Retz, *Oeuvres*, vol. iii, p. 358.

40 Marais, *Journal et mémoires*, vol. i, p. 319.

41 *Correspondance complète de Madame, duchesse d'Orléans*, vol. ii, p. 242 ('*en bon langage palatin*', she recorded).

42 E. F. J. Barbier, *Journal historique et anecdotique du règne de Louis XV* (4 vols.; Paris, 1847–56), vol. i, p. 69.

43 A. Murphy, *John Law, Economic Theorist and Policy Maker* (Oxford, 1997), p. 5.

44 See below, p. 158.

45 *De l'Esprit des Lois*, Book 2, ch. 2.

46 See below, chapter 4, section E.

47 The deaths in question: his father, mother, brother, then his great-grand-father before becoming king; then of Dubois and Orléans. The wedding was his own.

48 Barbier, *Journal historique et anecdotique*, vol. i, p. 70 (from December 1720).

49 A useful witness of Villeroy's eccentricities in this respect is Mehmed efendi, the Turkish envoy sent to France on an ambassadorial visit in 1721: see Mehmed efendi, *Le Paradis des infidèles. Un ambassadeur ottoman en France sous la Régence* (Paris, 1981), esp. pp. 95 ff.

50 M. Antoine, *Louis XV* (Paris, 1989), p. 25.

51 *Mémoires de Saint-Simon*, vol. vii, pp. 267–8.

52 Cf. Narbonne, *Journal*, p. 77.

53 Cited in Petitfils, *Le Régent*, p. 576.

54 Richer d'Aubé, 'Réflexions', fol. 1.

55 J. McManners, *Death and the Enlightenment. Changing Attitudes towards Death among Christians and Unbelievers in Eighteenth-Century France* (Oxford, 1981), p. 46.

56 Barbier, *Journal historique et anecdotique*, vol. i, p. 192.

57 Marais, *Journal et mémoires*, vol. iii, p. 187.

58 According to the duc de Bourbon: Antoine, *Louis XV*, p. 158.

59 Antoine, *Louis XV*, p. 162.

3: FLEURY'S FRANCE (1726–43)

1 Charles-Philippe Albert, duc de Luynes, *Mémoires sur la cour de Louis XV (1735–58)* (17 vols.; Paris, 1860–65), vol. iii, p. 209.

2 P. R. Campbell, *Power and Politics in Old Régime France (1720–45)* (London, 1996), p. 74.

3 René-Louis de Voyer de Paulmy, marquis d'Argenson, *Journal et mémoires*, ed. E. J. B. Rathery (9 vols.; Paris, 1859–67), vol. i, p. 265.

4 See e.g. Luynes, *Mémoires*, vol. ix, p. 288; vol. x, p. 311; etc.

5 Pierre Narbonne, *Journal des règnes de Louis XIV et Louis XV de l'année 1701 à l'année 1744* (Paris, 1866), p. 509.

6 'Journal de police sous Louis XV (1742–3)', in Barbier, *Chronique de la Régence et du règne de Louis XV (1718–66)* (8 vols.; Paris, 1857–66), vol.

viii. This journal is not included in the edition of Barbier which we have used elsewhere.

7 Richer d'Aubé, 'Réflexions sur le gouvernement de France', *Bibliothèque Nationale, Nouvelles Acquisitions Françaises* 9511, fo. 14.

8 Luynes, *Memoires*, vol. v, p. 92.

9 ibid., vol. iv, p. 167.

10 d'Argenson, *Journal et mémoires*, vol. i, p. 234. For economic recovery in this period, see chapter 4, section E.

11 ibid., vol. iii, p. 427.

12 Cited in F. Lebrun, *Être chrétien en France sous l'Ancien Régime, 1516–1790* (Paris, 1996), p. 128.

13 This is a contentious figure because it includes the dioceses located in the papal Comtat Venaissin as well as dioceses which extended outside the political frontiers. Territorial acquisitions plus some new creations caused the number of dioceses to rise to 136 by 1789.

14 Cited in B. Plongeron, *La Vie quotidienne du clergé français au XVIIIe siècle* (Paris, 1974), p. 75.

15 See above, pp. 33–4.

16 For the use of the term, see esp. M. Vovelle, *Piété baroque et déchristianisation. Attitudes provençales devant la mort au siècle des Lumières, d'après les clauses des testaments* (Paris, 1973).

17 Sauvageon's testimony is superbly examined in G. Bouchard, *Le Village immobile: Sennely-en-Sologne au XVIIIe siècle* (Paris, 1972): see esp. pp. 339, 341, etc.

18 G. Hardy, *Le Cardinal Fleury et le mouvement janséniste* (Paris, 1925), pp. 9–10.

19 Citations in E. Appolis, *Le Jansénisme dans le diocèse de Lodève au XVIIIe siècle* (Albi, 1952), p. 105. For similar remarks from Fleury to the pope in 1730, see Campbell, *Power and Politics.* p. 240.

20 See above, p. 75.

21 B. R. Kreiser, *Miracles, Convulsions and Ecclesiastical Politics in Early Eighteenth-Century Paris* (Princeton, NJ, 1978), p. 59.

22 Cited in C. Maire, *De la Cause de Dieu à la cause de la nation. Les jansénistes au XVIIIe siècle* (Paris, 1998), p. 138.

23 See above, pp. 26–7.

24 See above, p. 45.

25 *Nouvelles ecclésiastiques*, 1728, cited in Maire, *De la Cause de Dieu*, p. 225.

26 See above, p. 93.

27 Campbell, *Politics and Power*, p. 212.

28 Maire, *De la Cause de Dieu*, p. 385.

29 M. Antoine, *Louis XV* (Paris, 1989), p. 284.

30 E. J. F. Barbier, *Journal historique et anecdotique du règne de Louis XV*, ed. A. de La Villegille (4 vols.; Paris, 1847–56), vol. ii, p. 430.

31 Fénelon, 'Examen de conscience sur les devoirs de la royauté', in id., *Oeuvres*, ed. J. Le Brun (Paris, 1983), vol. ii, p. 977.

32 According to the analyses of historical demographers, France's population passed from 24.5 to 25.7 million between 1750 and 1760: see J. Dupâcquier, *Histoire de la population française. ii. De la Renaissance à 1789* (Paris, 1988), p. 61. See also below, pp. 157–8.

33 F. de Dainville, *La Cartographie reflet de l'histoire* (Geneva, 1986), p. 279.

34 The Parisian police official Le Maire, writing in 1770, as cited in M. Raeff, 'The well-ordered police state and the development of modernity in seventeenth- and eighteenth-century Europe: an attempt at a comparative approach', *American Historical Review*, 80 (1975), p. 1,235n.

35 M. Fogel, *L'État dans la France moderne (de la fin du XVe au milieu du XVIIIe siècle)* (Paris, 1992), p. 372.

36 d'Argenson, *Journal et mémoires*, vol. iii, p. 103.

37 Along with clocks. See the list in R. Briggs, 'The Académie royale des Sciences and the pursuit of utility', *Past and Present*, 131 (1991).

38 Antoine, *Louis XV*, p. 325.

39 D. Roche, 'Censorship and the publishing industry', in id. and R. Darnton (eds.), *Revolution in Print: The Press in France, 1775–1800* (Berkeley, Ca., 1989), p. 22; R. Chartier, *The Cultural Origins of the French Revolution.* (Durham, NC, 1991), p. 50.

40 M. N. Bourguet, *Déchiffrer la France. La statistique départementale à l'époque napoléonienne* (Paris, 1989), p. 32.

41 D. Bell, *Lawyers and Citizens. The Making of a Political Elite in Old Régime France* (Oxford and New York, 1994), p. 4.

42 Barbier, *Journal historique*, vol. ii. p. 148.

43 As told to d'Argenson, *Journal et mémoires*, vol. i, p. 133.

44 Cited in Bell, *Lawyers and Citizens*, p. 7.

45 *Bibliothèque de l'Arsenal, Paris*: ms. 10159: police report, 17 September 1729.

46 d'Argenson, *Journal et mémoires*, vol. ii, p. 178.

47 See below, chapter 5, section E.

48 Campbell, *Politics and Power*, p. 147.

49 Cf. d'Argenson, *Journal et mémoires*, vol. i, p. 284; Luynes, *Mémoires*, vol. ii, p. 232.

50 Luynes, *Mémoires*, vol. ii, p. 431; d'Argenson, *Journal et mémoires*, vol. iii, p. 171.

51 Marc-Pierre de Voyer, comte d'Argenson (1696–1764) should be distinguished from his elder brother René-Louis de Voyer (1694–1757), marquis d'Argenson, the author of the *Journal et mémoires* on which we have drawn

in this account. They were sons of Marc-René de Voyer, comte, then marquis d'Argenson (1652–1721), who as Lieutenant Général of Police served the Regent well on the changeover of power in 1715, then in 1718 became Keeper of the Seals.

52 Antoine, *Louis XV*, p. 301.

53 Barbier, *Journal*, vol. ii, p. 189.

54 ibid., vol. iii, p. 333.

55 Barbier, *Chronique de la Régence et du règne de Louis XV* [sic], p. 216.

56 id., *Journal*, vol. ii, p. 157.

4: UNSUSPECTED GOLDEN YEARS (1743–56)

1 M. Antoine, *Louis XV* (Paris, 1989), p. 353.

2 Louis to Noailles: ibid, p. 355.

3 Richer d'Aubé, 'Réflexions sur le Gouvernement de France', *Bibliothèque Nationale. Nouvelles Acquisitions Françaises*, 9515, fo. 556. Cf. E. J. F. Barbier, *Journal historique et anecdotique du règne de Louis XV*, ed. A. de La Villegille (4 vols.; Paris, 1857–64), vol. ii, pp. 402ff.; Charles-Philippe Albert, duc de Luynes, *Mémoires sur la cour de Louis XV (1735–58)*, (17 vols; Paris, 1860–5), vol. vi, p. 48.

4 René-Louis Voyer de Paulmy, marquis d'Argenson, *Journal et mémoires*, ed. E. J. B. Rathery (9 vols., Paris, 1959–67), vol. iv, p. 106.

5 Barbier, *Journal historique*, vol. iii, p. 296.

6 P. Narbonne, *Journal des règnes de Louis XIV et Louis XV (de l'année 1701 à l'année 1744)* (Paris, 1866), p. 502.

7 This was according to d'Argenson (who detested her): *Journal et mémoires*, vol. vii, p. 282. See C. Jones, *Madame de Pompadour. Images of a Mistress* (London, 2002).

8 See above, p. 120.

9 Barbier, *Journal historique*, vol. iii, p. 242.

10 See below, pp. 137–9.

11 Jacques-Louis Ménétra, *Journal of My Life*, ed. D. Roche (New York, 1986), p. 22. The event is recorded and commented on in all the memorialists of the reign, and is well covered in A. Farge and J. Revel, *The Vanishing Children of Paris: Rumor and Politics before the French Revolution* (Cambridge, Mass., 1991).

12 Barbier, *Journal historique*, vol. iii, p. 296.

13 d'Argenson, *Journal et mémoires*, vol. vi, p. 219.

14 See above, p. 22.

15 See above, chapter 3, Section E.

16 Cited in J. Black, 'Mid Eighteenth Century Conflict with Particular Reference to the Wars of the Polish and Austrian Succession', in id. (ed.), *The Origin of War in Early Modern Europe* (Edinburgh, 1987), p. 228. This was a familiar British fantasy.

17 d'Argenson, *Journal et mémoires*, vol. iv, p. 135; Antoine, *Louis XV*, p. 400.

18 ibid.

19 M. S. Anderson, *The War of the Austrian Succession, 1740–8* (London, 1995), p. 35; Maurice, comte de Saxe, *Mes Rêveries* (2 vols.; Amsterdam and Leipzig, 1757), vol. ii, p. 148.

20 See below, p. 228.

21 Cited in Daniel Roche, *Histoire des choses banales: Naissance de la consommation (XVIIe–XIXe siècle)* (Paris, 1997), p. 248.

22 See below, next section.

23 See above, p. 55

24 Example from 1637 cited in F. Lebrun, 'Les Crises démographiques en France aux XVIIe et XVIIIe siècles', *Annales ESC*, 35 (1980), p. 216.

25 See above, p. 55–6.

26 The concept is developed in O. Hufton's outstanding *The Poor of Eighteenth-Century France (1750–89)* (Oxford, 1974).

27 See below, pp. 275, 281, 297, etc.

28 See M. Sonenscher, 'Fashion's empire: trade and power in early eighteenth-century France', in R. Fox and A. Turner (eds.), *Luxury Trades and Consumerism in Ancien Régime Paris: Studies in the History of the Skilled Workforce* (Aldershot, 1998).

29 M. Berg, 'French Fancy and Cool Britannia: The Fashion Markets of Early Modern Europe', *Proceedings of the Istituto internazionale di storia economica 'F. Datini'* (Prato, 2001), p. 532; John Law, *Oeuvres complètes*, ed. P. Harsin (3 vols.; Paris, 1934), vol. ii, pp. 115–16.

30 Cited in L. Hilaire-Pérez, *L'Expérience de la mer: Les Européens et les espaces maritimes au XVIIIe siècle* (Paris, 1997), p. 16.

31 Abbé Galiani, *Correspondance*, eds. L. Perey and G. Maugras (2 vols.; Paris, 1890), vol. i, p. 247.

32 Mehmed efendi, *Le Paradis des infidèles. Un ambassadeur ottoman en France sous la Régence* (Paris, 1981), p. 79; Arthur Young, *Travels in France in the Years 1787, 1788 and 1789*, ed. C. Maxwell (Cambridge, 1929), p. 58.

33 Cited in M. Filion, *Maurepas, ministre de Louis XV, 1715–49* (Montreal, 1967), p. 43.

34 François-Vincent Toussaint, *Anecdotes curieuses de la cour de France sous le règne de Louis XV*, ed. P. Fould (Paris, 1908), p. 66. The work first appeared in 1745 with coded names.

35 Letter to her husband, 18 August 1739, cited in A. M. Wilson, *French Foreign Policy during the Administration of Cardinal Fleury* (Cambridge, Mass., 1936), p. 55.

36 'Situation du Commerce Exterieur du Roiaume exposée à Sa Majesté par M. le Comte de Maurepas' (1730): cited in full in Filion, *Maurepas*, p. 159.

5: AN ENLIGHTENING AGE

1 *Encyclopédie, ou Dictionnaire raisonné des sciences, des arts et des métiers, par une société de gens de lettres* (Paris, 1751–72).

2 See below, p. 192.

3 *Encyclopédie*, vol. i, p. 716 (article, 'art').

4 ibid., vol. v, p. 641 (article, 'Encyclopédie').

5 Diderot, cited in R. Darnton, 'Philosophers trim the tree of knowledge: the epistemological strategy of the *Encyclopédie*', in id., *The Great Cat Massacre and Other Episodes in French Cultural History* (New York, 1985), p. 199.

6 'Prospectus de l'Encyclopédie', in D. Diderot, *Oeuvres complètes*, eds. H. Dieckman and J. Varloot (5 vols., Paris, 1975), vol. v, p. 88.

7 *Encyclopédie*, vol. v, p. 635 (article, 'Encyclopédie').

8 'Avertissement' to *Encyclopédie*, vol. iii, p. iv.

9 *Encyclopédie*, vol. v, p. 636 (article, 'Encyclopédie').

10 As noted in R. Darnton, *The Business of Enlightenment: A Publishing History of the Encyclopédie, 1775–1800* (Cambridge, Mass., 1979), p. 8.

11 *Encyclopédie*, vol. v, p. 642 (article, 'Encyclopédie).

12 ibid., vol. v, p. 637 (article, 'Encyclopédie').

13 Montesquieu, *Lettres persanes* (1721), letter lxxiii.

14 Louis-Sébastien Mercier, *Tableau de Paris* (12 vols; Amsterdam, 1782–8), vol. i, pp. 227–8.

15 Bouhier, cited by D. Goodman, *The Republic of Letters. A Cultural History of the French Enlightenment* (Ithaca, NY, 1994), p. 17.

16 See above, p. 166.

17 *Réponse d'un artiste à un homme de Lettres qui lui avait écrit sur les waux-halls* (Amsterdam, 1769), cited in G. A. Langlois, ' "Les Charmes de l'égalité": éléments pour une urbanistique des loisirs publics à Paris de Louis XV à Louis-Philippe', *Histoire urbaine*, 1 (2000), p. 12.

18 For women, see below, pp. 195ff. The commoner representation would undoubtedly be even higher in all cases if we counted non-noble clerics involved in the various activities.

19 Cited in S. Schaffer, 'Enlightened Automata', in W. Clark, J. Golinski and S. Schaffer (eds.), *The Sciences in Enlightened Europe* (Chicago, 1999), p. 129.

20 As cited in M. Hulliung, *The Autocritique of Enlightenment. Rousseau and the Philosophes* (Cambridge, Mass., 1994), p. 38.

21 Voltaire as cited in K. Baker, *Inventing the French Revolution. Essays on French Political Culture in the Eighteenth Century* (Cambridge, 1990) p. 214; René-Louis Voyer de Paulmy, marquis d'Argenson, *Journal et mémoires*, ed. E. J. B. Rathery (9 vols.; Paris, 1959–67), vol. vi, p. 464.

22 See above, p. 26. For the political uses of historical research, see section E below.

23 *Encyclopédie*, vol. viii, p. 220 (article, 'histoire').

24 *De l'Esprit des lois*, 'Préface'.

25 Voltaire, *Le Siècle de Louis XIV*, ch. 1.

26 *Encyclopédie*, vol. v, p. 641 (article, 'Encyclopédie').

27 *Lettres persanes*, lettre xxiv; N. Ferrier-Caverivière, *Le Grand Roi à l'aube des lumières, 1715–51* (Paris, 1985), p. 48.

28 *Lettres philosophiques*, in Voltaire, *Oeuvres*, ed. P. Naves (Paris, 1988), p. 45.

29 Voltaire, *Zaïre* (1736): '*seconde épître dédicatoire*'.

30 See above, p. 169.

31 Voltaire, cited in D. Roche, *France in the Enlightenment* (Cambridge, Mass., 1998), p. 566.

32 ibid.

33 Voltaire to the chevalier du Coudray, 8 March 1773: *Correspondance complète*, ed. T. Besterman (101 vols.; Geneva, 1953–77), vol. xxxix, letter 18236, p. 327.

34 *De l'Esprit des lois*, book 20, ch. 1.

35 *Encyclopédie*, vol. ix, pp. 769–70 (article, 'luxe').

36 In fact, Mirabeau, who used the term in 1756, saw religion rather than trade and exchange as crucial to the process of civilization. The term soon took on a more materialist and progressivist flavour: see discussion in J. Starobinski, *Blessings in Disguise, or the Morality of Evil* (Cambridge, 1993), esp. p. 3.

37 J.-J. Rousseau, *Oeuvres complètes* (5 vols.; Paris, 1959–95), eds. M. Raymond and B. Gagnebin, vol. i, p. 388.

38 Voltaire, *Correspondance*, vol. xxvii, p. 230 (letter 5,792).

39 ibid., vol. xlii, p. 134 (letter 8,238).

40 For further discussion of Rousseau's politics, see below, pp. 221ff.

41 Readers' fan mail cited in Darnton, *Great Cat Massacre*, esp. pp. 236–8.

42 *Émile* in *Oeuvres* (5 vols.; 1964–95), vol. iv, p. 267.

43 ibid., vol. v, p. 703.

44 ibid., vol. iv, p. 736.

45 *Encyclopédie*, vol. vi, p. 471.

46 Rousseau, 'First Discourse', in *Oeuvres*, vol. iii, p. 21n.

47 As explored in L. Steinbrügge, *The Moral Sex: Women's Nature in the French Enlightenment* (Oxford, 1995).

48 'Lettre à d'Alembert', in *Oeuvres*, vol. iii, pp. 45 and 1,135 n. 5.

49 Pierre Roussel, *Système physique et moral de la femme, ou Tableau philosophique de la constitution, de l'état organique, du tempérament, des moeurs et des fonctions propres au sexe* (Paris, 1775), p. 103.

50 N. Hampson, *The Enlightenment* (Harmondsworth, 1968), p. 131.

51 Diderot, *Correspondance*, ed. G. Roth (16 vols.; Paris, 1955–70), vol. iv, pp. 176–7 (29 Sept 1762).

52 Voltaire, *Oeuvres*, vol. cxxxiv, pp. 399, 403.

53 Cited in J. de Viguerie, *Histoire et dictionnaire du temps des Lumières, 1715–99* (Paris, 1995), p. 284.

54 See above, pp. 97–8.

55 See above, pp. 33–4.

56 See above, p. 98.

57 Diderot, *Correspondance*, vol. iv, p. 98 (letter of 12 August 1762). For the expulsion of the Jesuits, see below, p. 247ff.

58 D'Holbach, *Système de la nature* (3 vols; London, 1770) vol. ii, pp. 397–8.

59 Cited by J. Roger, *Buffon* (Paris, 1989), p. 566.

60 *Encyclopédie*, vol. xi, p. 8.

61 B. M. Stafford, *Artful Science. Enlightenment Entertainment and the Eclipse of Visual Education* (Cambridge, Mass., 1994), p. 234.

62 D. C. Charlton, *New Images of the Natural in France. A Study in European Cultural History, 1750–1800* (Cambridge, 1984), p. 79.

63 Roland de la Platière, husband of the future Girondin salonnière. The citation which comes from 1785 is in Roche, *France in the Enlightenment*, p. 246.

64 M. Foucault, *The Order of Things. An Archaeology of the Human Sciences* (New York, 1971).

65 L. Daston, in Clark, Golinski and Schaffer (eds.), *The Sciences in Enlightened Europe* (Chicago, 1999), p. 347.

66 ibid., pp. 355, 357.

67 *Émile*, in *Oeuvres*, vol. i, p. 277.

68 In his *Confessions: Oeuvres*, vol. i, p. 116.

69 Mercier, *Tableau de Paris*, vol. i, pp. 25–8.

70 Abbé Galiani and Madame d'Épinay, *Correspondance*, ed. G. Dulac (5 vols.; Paris, 1992), vol. ii, p. 259.

71 In his *Fragments sur les institutions républicaines* (3rd fragment).

72 See below, p. 268.

73 1778 edn, cited in J. Sgard, *Dictionnaire des journaux, 1600–1789* (Paris, 1991), vol. ii, p. 137.

74 De Viguerie, *Histoire et dictionnaire*, p. 314.

75 See above, p. 147.

76 I am drawing heavily here on the tripartite division elaborated in K. M. Baker, *Inventing the French Revolution* (Cambridge, 1990).

77 See above, p. 191.

78 Cited in J. Proust, *Diderot et l'Encyclopédie* (Paris, 1962), p. 451, n.7.

79 See esp. below, over the Calas Affair, pp. 270–71.

80 Montesquieu, *De l'Esprit des lois*, ch. xix.

81 Rousseau to Mirabeau, 26 July 1767:, in id., *Correspondance*, ed. R. A. Leigh et al. (51 vols.; Oxford, 1972–99), vol. xxxiii, p. 243.

82 See above, p. 193.

83 *Esquisse d'un tableau historique des progrès de l'esprit humain* (Paris, 1988), p. 188.

84 *Encyclopédie*, vol. xi, pp. 506ff (article, 'opinion').

85 See above, pp. 48–9, 52, 102.

86 See esp. below, p. 308.

6: FORESTALLING DELUGE (1756–70)

1 D. Van Kley, *The Damiens Affair and the Unravelling of the Ancien Régime, 1750–1770* (Princeton, NJ, 1984), p. 23.

2 ibid., p. 36.

3 ibid., p. 43.

4 J. de Flammermont, *Les Remontrances du parlement de Paris au XVIIIe siècle* (3 vols.; Paris, 1888–98), vol. i, p. 523. This phrase was all the more annoying for the crown in that it had first been used by the Parlement in 1527 and therefore could not be presented as dangerously innovatory.

5 E. F. J. Barbier, *Journal historique et anecdotique du règne de Louis XV*, ed. A. de La Villegille (4 vols.; Paris, 1857–64), vol. iv, p. 198.

6 For an account of the scene based on contemporary accounts, see the opening pages of Michel Foucault, *Discipline and Punish. The Birth of the Prison* (London, 1977).

7 Cited in J. Rogister, *Louis XV and the Parlement of Paris, 1737–55* (Cambridge, 1995), p. 231.

8 M. Antoine, *Louis XV* (Paris, 1989), p. 579.

9 L. A. Le Paige, *Lettres historiques sur les fonctions essentielles du Parlement* (Amsterdam, 1753), p. 320.

10 Flammermont, *Les Remontrances du parlement*, vol. ii, p. 26.

11 See above, p. 106

12 *De l'Esprit des lois*, book 2, ch. 4.

13 René-Louis de Voyer de Paulmy, marquis d'Argenson, *Journal et mémoires*, ed. E. J. B. Rathery (9 vols.; Paris, 1859-67), vol. iii, p. 153. In conciliar theory, a council of the church universal had spiritual precedence over the authority of the pope.

14 ibid., p. 315.

15 J. Egret, *Louis XV et l'opposition parlementaire, 1715–74* (Paris, 1970), p. 84. Some of Le Paige's fellow polemicists in the 1750s followed Conciliarist logic to the conclusion of seeing the highest expression of sovereignty as not king, nor even the *parlements*, but the Estates General, which the emergence of absolutism had consigned to mothballs. This was as yet, however, only a minority view.

16 Flammermont, *Les Remontrances du parlement*, vol. ii, p. 138 (22 August 1756).

17 J. Merrick, *The Desacralization of the French Monarchy in the Eighteenth Century* (Baton Rouge, La., 1990), pp. 94–5.

18 D. Van Kley, *The Damiens Affair*, p. 115.

19 See next section.

20 L. Kennett, *The French Army in the Seven Years War* (Durham, NC, 1967), p. x.

21 J. D. Woodbridge, *Revolt in Prerevolutionary France: The Prince de Conti's Conspiracy against Louis XV 1755–7* (Baltimore, Md, 1995), p. 135.

22 M. S. Anderson, *The War of Austrian Succession, 1740–8* (London, 1995), p. 63.

23 See above, p. 137.

24 See above, p. 139.

25 T. C. W. Blanning, *The Origins of the French Revolutionary Wars* (London, 1986), p. 41.

26 P. Mansel, *Louis XVIII* (Stroud, 1981), p. 40.

27 d'Argenson, *Journal et mémoires*, vol. ix, p. 340. For the debate on Conti, see Woodbridge, *Revolt in Prerevolutionary France*.

28 The comparison was the Président Hénault's, according to Kennett, *The French Army in the Seven Years War*, p. 6.

29 M. Antoine, *Louis XV* (Paris, 1989), p. 748.

30 M. Sonenscher, 'The Nation's Debt and the birth of the modern republic: The French fiscal deficit and the politics of the Revolution of 1789', *History of Political Thought*, 18 (1997), p. 94, n. 85.

31 See esp. below, chapter 8, section B.

32 See below, p. 246.

33 J. Barbey, *Être roi. Le roi et son gouvernement en France de Clovis à Louis XVI* (Paris, 1992), p. 183.

34 Barbier, *Journal historique*, vol. iv, p. 453.

35 id., *Chronique de la Régence et du règne de Louis XV (1718–63)*, ed. Charpentier (8 vols.; Paris, 1857), vol. vii, p. 77, n. 1.

36 id., *Journal historique*, vol. iv, pp. 447, 460.

37 D. Van Kley, *The Jansenists and the Expulsion of the Jesuits from France, 1757–65* (New Haven, 1975), p. 28.

38 id., *The Religious Origins of the French Revolution from Calvin to the Civil Constitution, 1560–1791* (New Haven, 1996), p. 158.

39 J. Swann, *Politics and the Parlement of Paris under Louis XV* (Cambridge, 1995), p. 216.

40 ibid., p. 241.

41 Antoine, *Louis XV*, p. 799.

42 *Mémoires et lettres de François-Joachim de Pierre, cardinal de Bernis (1715–58)*, ed. F. Masson (2 vols.; Paris, 1878), vol. ii, p. 61.

43 Swann, *Politics and the Parlement of Paris*, pp. 49–50.

44 J. Bérenger and J. Meyer, *La France dans le monde au XVIIIe siècle* (Paris, 1993), p. 240.

45 See above, pp. 251–2.

46 I owe this formulation to C. C. Gillispie, *Science and Polity at the End of the Old Régime* (Princeton, NJ, 1980), p. 309.

47 See above, p. 115.

48 A. M. Le Boursier du Coudray, *Abrégé de l'art des accouchements* (Paris, 1759), cited in N. R. Gelbart, *The King's Midwife: The History and Mystery of Madame du Coudray* (Berkeley, Ca., 1998), p. 76.

49 Cited in S. L. Kaplan, *Bread, Politics and Political Economy in the Reign of Louis XV* (2 vols.; The Hague, 1976), p. 117. Cf. above, pp. 219–20.

50 See below, pp. 327ff.

51 M. Bordes, *La Réforme municipale du contrôleur-général Laverdy et son application* (Toulouse, 1967), p. 18.

52 *Journal et mémoires de Christophe Collé*, ed. H. Bonhomme (3 vols; Paris, 1868), vol. iii, p. 16. My account of the impact of the plays draws heavily on this source, and on A. Boes, 'La lanterne magique de l'histoire: essai sur le théâtre historique en France de 1750 à 1789', *Studies on Voltaire and the Eighteenth Century*, p. 231 (1982).

53 D. Bell, 'Jumonville's death: war propaganda and national identity in eighteenth-century France', in C. Jones and D. Wahrman (eds.), *An Age of Cultural Revolution: England and France, 1750–1820* (Berkeley, Ca., 2002), esp. pp. 45ff.

54 Cited in W. Kraus, ' "Patriote", "patriotique", "patriotisme" à la fin de l'Ancien Régime', in W. H. Barber et al., *The Age of Enlightenment. Studies Presented to Theodore Bestermann* (Edinburgh, 1969), p. 393.

55 Louis-Sébastien Mercier, *2440* (2 vols.; Paris, Year V), vol ii, p. 610. (This is a later edition.)

56 K. Baker, *Inventing the French Revolution*: see esp. 'Controlling French history: the ideological arsenal of Jacob-Nicolas Moreau', pp. 59–85.

57 See above, p. 25.

58 Barbier, *Journal historique*, vol. iv, p. 236.

59 See above, pp. 116–17, 213.

60 Cited in Egret, *Louis XV et l'opposition parlementaire*, p. 181.

61 Flammermont, *Les Remontrances du parlement*, vol. ii, pp. 557–8.

62 D. Roche, *France in the Enlightenment* (Cambridge, Mass., 1998), p. 421.

63 See above, chapter 4, section A.

64 D. Bien, *The Calas Affair: Persecution, Toleration and Heresy in Eighteenth-Century Toulouse* (Princeton, NJ, 1960), p. 68; D. Van Kley, *Jansenists and the Expulsion of the Jesuits*, p. 156.

65 Barbier, *Chronique de la Régence et du règne de Louis XV (1718–63)*, ed. A. de La Villegille (8 vols.; Paris, 1866), vol. vii, p. 237.

66 See above, pp. 172, 213.

67 See above, p. 245.

68 J. Riley, *The Seven Years War and the Old Regime in France: The Economic and Financial Toll* (Princeton, NJ, 1986), p. 192.

69 Egret, *Louis XV et l'opposition parlementaire*, p. 132: the quotation is from Necker, future Royal Finance Minister. See also above, p. 113.

70 Cited in R. Chartier, *The Cultural Origins of the French Revolution* (Durham, NC, 1991), pp. 31–2. See also above, ch. 5.

71 *Le Comte de Creutz. Lettres inédites de Paris, 1766–70*, ed. M. Molander (Paris, 1987), p. 361.

72 A. Young, *Travels in France in the Years 1787, 1788 and 1789*, ed. C. Maxwell (Cambridge, 1929), p. 114 (19 September 1788).

73 See above, p. 250.

74 See above, p. 263.

75 Egret, *Louis XV et l'opposition parlementaire*, p. 159.

76 Antoine, *Louis XV*, p. 857.

77 Egret, *Louis XV et l'opposition parlementaire*, p. 101.

78 See above, p. 229.

79 Bordes, *La Réforme municipale*, p. 142.

80 Swann, *Politics and the Parlement of Paris*, p. 328.

81 Antoine, *Louis XV*, p. 911.

82 Flammermont, *Les Remontrances du parlement*, vol. iii, pp. 153–7.

83 Antoine, *Louis XV*, p. 923.

84 ibid., p. 92.

7: THE TRIUMVIRATE AND ITS AFTERMATH
(1771–84)

1 See esp. A. Cobban, *A History of Modern France. Vol. 1: 1715–99* (Harmondsworth, 1957).

2 J. F. Bosher, 'The French crisis of 1770', *History*, 57 (1972), p. 19.

3 Voltaire, *Correspondance complète*, ed. T. Bestermann (101 vols.; Geneva, 1953–77), vol. lxxiv, p. 202 (letter 15,258).

4 W. Doyle, *Venality. The Sale of Offices in Eighteenth-Century France* (Oxford, 1996), p. 119.

5 M. Kwass, *Privilege and the Politics of Taxation in Eighteenth-Century France* (Cambridge, 2000), p. 42, n. 57.

6 J. de Flammermont, *Les Remontrances du parlement de Paris au XVIIIe siècle* (3 vols.; Paris, 1888–98), vol. iii, p. 204.

7 D. Echeverria, *The Maupeou Revolution: A Study in the History of Libertarianism. France 1770–4* (Baton Rouge, La, 1985), p. 27.

8 Voltaire, *Correspondance*, vol. lxxix, p. 79 (letter 16,094).

9 Citations from N. R. Gelbart, *Feminine and Opposition Journalism in Old Regime France: 'Le Journal des Dames'* (Berkeley, Ca, 1987), p. 152; and D. Van Kley, 'The religious origins of the patriote and ministerial parties in pre-Revolutionary France: controversy over the Chancellor's constitutional coup. 1771–5', *Historical Reflections/Réflexions historiques*, 18 (1992), p. 52.

10 [Mathieu-François Pidansat de Mairobert], *Journal historique de la révolution opérée dans la constitution de la monarchie françoise par M. de Maupeou, Chancelier de France* (7 vols; London, 1774–6), vol. ii, p. 351 (20 January 1771).

11 See above, p. 47.

12 See above, p. 12.

13 Abbé Galiani, *Correspondance*, eds. L. Perey and G. Maugras (2 vols.; Paris, 1881), vol. ii, p. 88.

14 See above, pp. 221ff.

15 M. Antoine, *Louis XV* (Paris, 1989), p. 986. For Metz, see above, pp. 126–7.

16 Duc de Croÿ, *Journal inédit du duc de Croÿ, 1718–84*, eds. vicomte de Grouchy and P. Cottin (4 vols.; Paris, 1906–7), vol. iii, pp. 134–5.

17 Cited in J. de Viguerie, *Histoire et dictionnaire du temps des Lumières, 1715–89* (Paris, 1995), p. 344.

18 Galiani, *Correspondance*, vol. ii. pp. 334–5.

19 de Croÿ, *Journal inédit*, vol. iii, p. 153.

20 Cited in Viguerie, *Histoire et dictionnaire*, p. 359.

21 J. M. Augeard, *Mémoires secrets de J. M. Augeard, secrétaire des command-*

ements de la reine Marie-Antoinette, 1760–1800, ed. E. Bavoux (Paris, 1866), p. 77.

22 J. Hardiman, *French Politics, 1774–89: From the Accession of Louis XVI to the Fall of the Bastille* (London, 1995), p. 232.

23 Echeverria, *The Maupeou Revolution*, p. 32 (quoting Pidansat de Mairobert). The king doubtless did not spot the potentially Rousseauian implications of his phrase, 'general will'.

24 C. C. Gillispie, *Science and Polity in Old Regime France* (Princeton, NJ, 1980), p. 3.

25 Galiani, *Correspondance*, pp. 345–6.

26 *Oeuvres de Turgot*, ed. G. Schell (5 vols.; Paris, 1913–23), vol. iv, p. 204.

27 Flammermont, *Les Remontrances du parlement*, vol. iii, p. 279.

28 See above, p. 255.

29 J. Hardman, *Louis XVI* (London, 2000), p. 18.

30 D. Dakin, *Turgot and the Ancien Régime* (London, 1939), p. 131.

31 Jean-Louis Soulavie, *Mémoires historiques et politiques du règne de Louis XVI, depuis son mariage jusqu'à sa mort* (6 vols.; Paris, 1801), vol. iii, p. 147.

32 M. Price, *Preserving the Monarchy. The Comte de Vergennes, 1774–87* (Cambridge, 1995), p. 49.

33 For the episode, and all citations, see J. Le Goff, 'Reims, ville du sacre' in P. Nora (ed.), *Les Lieux de mémoire* (3 vols.; Paris, 1997), vol. i; and H. Weber, 'Le sacre de Louis XVI', in *Le Règne de Louis XVI* (Dourgne, 1977).

34 De Croÿ, *Journal inédit*, vol. iii, p. 125.

35 F. Y. Besnard, *Souvenirs d'un nonagénaire* (2 vols.; Paris, 1880), vol. ii, p. 129.

36 *Souvenirs-portraits du duc de Lévis*, ed. J. Dupâcquier (Paris, 1993), p. 160.

37 J. Hardman and M. Price (eds.), *Louis XVI and the Comte de Vergennes: Correspondence, 1774–87* (Oxford, 1998), p. 250.

38 ibid., p. 237.

39 Comte de Mercy-Argenteau, *Correspondance secrète entre Marie-Thérèse et le comte de Mercy-Argenteau*, ed. A. d'Arneth and M. Geoffroy (3 vols.; Paris, 1874), vol. i, pp. 225–6.

40 J Grieder, *Anglomania in France, 1740–89. Fact, Fiction and Political Discourse* (Geneva, 1985), pp. 19–20.

41 See above, pp. 259–61.

42 S. Schama, *Citizens: A Chronicle of the French Revolution* (New York, 1989), p. 37; S. M. Hardy, *Mes Loisirs*, ed. M. Tourneux and M. Vitrac (Paris, 1912), p. 410.

43 J. Merrick, 'The Body Politics of French absolutism' in S. E. Melzer and

K. Norberg (eds.), *From the Royal to the Republican Body. Incorporating the Political in Seventeenth- and Eighteenth-Century France* (Berkeley, Ca., 1998), pp. 17–18.

44 de Viguerie, *Histoire et dictionnaire*, p. 355.

45 For the puzzle of the king's sexuality, see esp. D. Beales, *Joseph II. Vol. 1. In the Shadow of Maria Theresa, 1741–80* (Cambridge, 1987), pp. 371–5.

46 K. M. Baker, *Inventing the French Revolution* (Cambridge, 1989), p. 344, n. 99.

47 Price, *Preserving the Monarchy*, p. 52.

48 Hardman, *Louis XVI*, p. 87.

49 Cited in D. Jarrett, *The Begetters of Revolution. England's Involvement with France, 1759–89* (London, 1973), pp. 160–1.

50 Price, *Preserving the Monarchy*, p. 54.

51 Croÿ, *Journal inédit*, vol. iv, pp. 230, 234.

52 Hardman, *French Politics*, p. 55.

53 Price, *Preserving the Monarchy*, p. 56.

54 Marquis de Bombelles, *Journal*, eds. J. Grassion and F. Durif (2 vols.; Geneva, 1978–82), vol. i, p. 204.

55 *La Folle Journée, ou le Mariage de Figaro*, 'Préface'.

56 Acte v, scène iii.

57 Madame Campan, *Mémoires sur la vie privée de Marie-Antoinette* (3 vols., Paris, 1822), vol. i, p. 278.

58 C. Petitfrère, *1784: Le Scandale du 'Mariage de Figaro'. Prélude à la Révolution française* (Brussels, 1989), p. 9.

59 Price, *Preserving the Monarchy*, p. 57.

60 J. Lough, *An Introduction to Eighteenth-Century France* (London, 1960), p. 94.

61 Talleyrand, *Mémoires*, ed. duc de Broglie (5 vols.; Paris, 1891–2), vol. i, pp. 117–18.

62 See above, p. 184.

63 Barbier, *Chronique*, vol. v, p. 15.

64 R. Forster, *The House of Saulx-Tavannes: Versailles and Burgundy, 1700–1830* (Baltimore, Md, 1971), pp. 34–5; François de Chateaubriand, *Mémoires d'Outre-Tombe*, ed. J. C. Berchet (Paris, 1989), p. 129.

65 See above, pp. 255ff.

66 G. Chaussinand-Nogaret, *The French Nobility in the Eighteenth Century. From Feudalism to Enlightenment* (Cambridge, 1985), p. 51.

67 Tim Le Goff, 'Essai sur les pensions royales', in M. Açerra et al., *État, marine et société. Hommage à Jean Meyer* (Paris, 1995), esp. p. 261.

68 Louis-Sébastien Mercier, *Tableau de Paris* (12 vols., Amsterdam, 1780–88), vol. vii, ch. dc.

69 Cited in P. Goubert, *The Ancien Régime, French Society, 1600–1750* (London, 1969), p. 179.

70 Talleyrand, *Mémoires*, vol. i, p. 119.

8: BOURBON MONARCHY ON THE RACK (1784–8)

1 J. Hardman and M. Price, *Louis XVI and the Comte de Vergennes: Correspondence, 1774–87* (Oxford, 1998), p. 376.

2 *Marie-Antoinette, Joseph II und Leopold II: Ihr Briefwechsel*, ed. A. von Arneth (Leipzig, 1866), p. 94.

3 J. D. Popkin, *News and Politics in the Age of Revolution: Jean Luzac's 'Gazette de Leyde'* (Ithaca, NY, 1989), p. 195.

4 See above, p. 324.

5 Cited in D. A. Bell, *Lawyers and Citizens. The Making of a Political Elite in Old Regime France* (New York, 1994), p. 157.

6 ibid., p. 153.

7 Marquis de Bombelles, *Journal*, eds. G. Grassion and F. Durif (2 vols.; Geneva, 1978–93), vol. i, p. 293.

8 See above, pp. 321–2.

9 F. C., comte de Mercy-Argenteau, *Correspondance secrète entre Marie-Thérèse et le comte de Mercy-Argenteau*, eds. A. d'Arneth and M. Geoffroy (3 vols.; Paris, 1889–91), vol. iii, p. 36.

10 See above pp. 273ff.

11 F. C., comte de Mercy-Argenteau, *Correspondance secrète du comte de Mercy-Argenteau avec l'empereur Joseph II et le prince de Kaunitz*, eds. A. d'Arneth and J. Flammermont (2 vols.; Paris, 1889–91), vol. ii, pp. 32–4.

12 W. Doyle, *Officers, Nobles and Revolutionaries. Essays on Eighteenth-Century France* (London, 1995), p. 30.

13 *Mémoires du prince de Talleyrand*, ed. duc de Broglie (5 vols.; Paris, 1891–2), vol. i, p. 104.

14 J. Hardman, *French Politics, 1774–89: From the Accession of Louis XVI to the Fall of the Bastille* (London, 1995), p. 153.

15 D. Jarrett, *The Begetters of Revolution. England's Involvement with France, 1759–89* (London, 1973), p. 220.

16 See above, pp. 327ff.

17 See below, pp. 350ff.

18 Cited by Pierre Léon in F. Braudel and E. Labrousse (eds.), *Histoire économique et sociale de la France, ii. 1660–1789* (Paris, 1970), pp. 317–18.

19 M. Price, *Preserving the Monarchy. The Comte de Vergennes, 1774–87* (Cambridge, 1995), p. 159.

20 J.-J. Rousseau, 'Confessions', in id., *Oeuvres complètes*, eds. B. Gagnebin and M. Raymond (5 vols.; Paris, 1959), vol. i, pp. 163–4.

21 Mary Wollstonecraft, *An Historical and Moral View of the Origins of the French Revolution and the Effects It Has Produced in Europe* (London, 1794), vol. i, pp. 511 and vii.

22 See esp. C. E. Labrousse, *Esquisse du mouvement des prix et des revenus en France au XVIIIe siècle* (Paris, 1933); id., *La Crise de l'économie française à la fin de l'Ancien Régime et au début de la Révolution* (Paris, 1944).

23 See above, p. 201.

24 Expilly, *Tableau de la population de la France* (1780).

25 See above, p. 162.

26 René Louis de Voyer de Paulmy, marquis d'Argenson, *Journal et mémoires du marquis d'Argenson*, ed. E. J. B. Rathery (9 vols.; 1859–67), vol. vii, p. 9.

27 J. Cornette, 'La Révolution des objets: le Paris des inventaires après decès (XVIIe–XVIIIe siècles)', *Revue d'histoire moderne et contemporaine*, 36 (1989). This is a useful summary of work by Daniel Roche, Annik Pardailhé-Galabrun and others, references to which are given in the bibliography.

28 See above, p. 349.

29 M. Hulliung, *The Autocritique of Enlightenment. Rousseau and the Philosophes* (Cambridge, Mass., 1994), pp. 151, 178.

30 See Morag Martin's unpublished Ph.D. dissertation, 'Consuming Beauty: The Commerce of Cosmetics in France', University of California, Irvine, 2000.

31 R. A. Schneider, *The Ceremonial City. Toulouse Observed, 1738–80* (Princeton, NJ, 1995), p. 47. Despite the religious grumbling, the church connived in the new consumerism: see below, p. 356.

32 F. Y. Besnard, *Souvenirs d'un nonagénaire* (2 vols.; Paris, 1880), vol. i, pp. 137, 303.

33 C. C. Fairchilds, 'Marketing the Counter-Reformation: religious objects and consumerism in early modern France', in C. Adams, J. R. Censer and L. J. Graham (eds.), *Visions and Revisions of Eighteenth-Century France* (Philadelphia, 1997), p. 50.

34 C. Jones, 'The Great Chain of Buying: medical advertisement, the bourgeois public sphere and the origins of the French Revolution', *American Historical Review* 103 (1996): one of the *Affiches'* catch phrases was their concern for 'l'utile et l'agréable'.

35 See esp. J. de Vries, 'Between purchasing power and the world of goods: understanding the household economy in early modern Europe', in J. Brewer and R. Porter (eds.), *Consumption and the World of Goods* (London, 1993).

36 See above, pp. 327ff.

37 Denis Fonvizine, *Lettres de France, 1777–8* (Paris, 1995), ed. H. Grose et al., pp. 144, 105.

38 ibid., p. 119.

39 Peter P. Hill, *French Perceptions of the Early American Republic, 1783–93* (Philadelphia, 1988), p. 3.

40 Duc de Croÿ, *Journal inédit du duc de Croÿ*, eds. vicomte de Gourchy and P. Cottin (Paris, 1906–7), vol. iv, p. 279.

41 R. Taveneaux, *Le Catholicisme dans la France classique, 1610–1715* (2 vols.; Paris, 1980), p. 323.

42 See above, ch. 5, esp. section C.

43 Moufle d'Angerville, *Mémoires secrets*, vol. xxiv (18 September 1787), pp. 351–2. Cited in C. Jones, 'Pulling Teeth in Eighteenth-Century Paris', *Past and Present*, 163 (2000).

44 Félix, comte d'Hézècques, *Souvenirs d'un page à la cour de Louis XVI* (Paris, 1904), pp. 6, 60.

45 He actually thought it was the cause of the Revolution: *Souvenirs d'un page*, pp. 190–91.

46 See above, p. 191.

47 L. S. Mercier, *Tableau de Paris* (12 vols.; Amsterdam, 1782–8), vol. iv, ch. cccxlvi, p. 258.

48 Louis de Carmontelle, writing in 1785, cited in T. E. Crow, *Painters and Public Life in Eighteenth-Century Paris* (New Haven, Ct, 1985), p. 18.

49 See above, chapter 5, section C.

50 Cited in D. Roche, *France in the Enlightenment* (Cambridge, Mass., 1998), p. 361 (my translation).

51 Jones, 'Great Chain of Buying', p. 24; and J. D. Popkin, in R. Darnton and D. Roche (eds.), *Revolution in Print, 1770–1800* (Princeton, NJ, 1989), p. 145.

52 *Louis XVI, Marie-Antoinette et Madame Elisabeth. Lettres et documents inédits*, ed. F. Feuillet de Conches (6 vols.; Paris, 1864), vol. i, p. 137.

53 M. Jacob, *Living the Enlightenment. Freemasonry and Politics in Eighteenth-Century Europe* (New York, 1991), p. 151.

54 Jacques Peuchet, 'Discours préliminaire', *Encyclopédie méthodique: Jurisprudence. ix. Police et municipalités* (1789). Cited in K. M. Baker, *Inventing the French Revolution. Essays on French Political Culture in the Eighteenth Century* (Cambridge, 1990), p. 196.

55 Joseph Servan, *Le Soldat Citoyen* (1780).

56 T. Tackett, *Priest and Parish in Eighteenth-Century France: A Social and Political Study of the Curé in a Diocese of Dauphiné, 1750–91* (Princeton, NJ, 1977). See also above, p. 200.

57 V. Azimi, '1789: L'echo des employés, ou le nouveau discours administratif', *XVIIIe siècle*, 21 (1989), p. 134.

58 Hardman and Price, *Louis XVI and the comte de Vergennes*, p. 103.

59 As noted in M. Sonenscher, 'The Nation's Debt and the birth of the modern republic: the French fiscal deficit and the politics of the Revolution of 1789', *History of Political Thought*, 18 (1997), p. 66.

60 Madame de Staël, *Considérations sur la Révolution française*, ed. J. Godechot (Paris, 1983), p. 79.

61 See above, pp. 7ff.

62 See above, p. 345.

63 J. Egret, *The French Pre-Revolution, 1787–8* (Chicago, 1977), p. 6.

64 J. de Viguerie, *Histoire et dictionnaire du temps des Lumières, 1715–89* (Paris, 1995), p. 403.

65 J. Hardman, *Louis XVI* (London, 1993), p. 114.

66 id., *The French Revolution Sourcebook* (London, 1999), p. 43.

67 Malouet, cited in Egret, *The French Pre-Revolution*, p. 30.

68 Cited in Price, *Preserving the Monarchy*, p. 225.

69 See above, pp. 217, 266–7.

70 Louis, cited in N. Aston, *The End of an Elite. The French Bishops and the Coming of the Revolution, 1786–90* (Oxford, 1992), p. 64 ('prêtraille', 'Neckeraille').

71 d'Hézècques, *Souvenirs d'un page*, p. 211.

72 D. Roche, *The People of Paris. An Essay in Popular Culture in the Eighteenth Century* (Leamington Spa, 1987); H. Root, *The Fountain of Privilege. Political Foundations of Markets in Old Regime France and England* (Berkeley, Ca., 1994), p. 203n. The discrepancy between Parisian and provincial levels should be noted.

73 See above, p. 379.

74 *Despatches from Paris, 1784–88*, ed. O. Browning (London, 1909), p. 263.

75 *Despatches from Paris, 1788–90*, ed. O. Browning (London, 1910), p. 44.

76 Weber, cited in Aston, *The End of an Elite*, p. 104.

77 Egret, *The French Pre-Revolution*, p. 185.

78 ibid., p. 255n.

79 Citations from Baker, *Inventing the French Revolution*, p. 216; J. Nicolas, *La Révolution française dans les Alpes, Dauphiné et Savoie, 1789–99* (Toulouse, 1989), p. 46.

80 P. M. Jones, *Reform and Revolution in France. The Politics of Transition, 1774–91* (Cambridge, 1995), p. 142.

81 Egret, *The French Pre-Revolution*, p. 179.

82 Maurepas – dismissed in 1749, recalled in 1774 – was the arch-exception in this respect.

83 Subsequently postponed to May 1789: see below, chapter 9, section A.

84 Hardman, *French Politics*, p. 98.

85 *Despatches from Paris, 1788–90*, p. 105.

86 Cited by R. Birn in H. Chisick (ed.), *The Press in the French Revolution* (Oxford, 1991), p. 67.

87 D. Bell, *The Cult of the Nation in France: Inventing Nationalism 1680–1800* (Cambridge, Mass., 2001), p. 72; Mallet du Pan, cited in G. Lefebvre, *The Coming of the French Revolution* (Princeton, NJ, 1947), p. 45.

9: REVOLUTION IN POLITICAL CULTURE (1788–91)

1 Cited in J. Egret, *The French Pre-Revolution, 1787–8* (Chicago, 1977), p. 202.

2 ibid., p. 98.

3 N. Ruault, *Gazette d'un parisien sous la Révolution*, eds. A. Vassal and C. Rimbaud (Paris, 1976), p. 121.

4 Egret, *The French Pre-Revolution*, p. 189.

5 *Archives parlementaires*, vol. i, pp. 487–8.

6 Elections were, however, within provincial boundaries in Béarn, Navarre and Dauphiné.

7 Egret, *The French Pre-Revolution*, p. 188.

8 See above, p. 301.

9 Siéyès, *Qu'est-ce que le Tiers État?* (1788 – and much reprinted thereafter). As the nobility had a minus value, their subtraction from the nation made two negatives – and consequently a positive value.

10 Cited in D. L. Wick, *A Conspiracy of Well-Intentioned Men. The Society of Thirty and the French Revolution* (New York, 1987), p. 267.

11 Egret, *The French Pre-Revolution*, p. 195.

12 'Considérations sur le Tiers État', cited in Wick, *A Conspiracy of Well-intentioned Men*, p. 259.

13 Cited in S. Schama, *Citizens. A Chronicle of the French Revolution* (Cambridge, Mass., 1989), p. 300.

14 Antraigues, cited in Wick, *A Conspiracy of Well-Intentioned Men*, p. 272; *Catéchisme du Tiers État*, cited in M. Cubells, *Les Horizons de la liberté. Naissance de la Révolution en Provence, 1787–9* (Aix-en-Provence, 1987), p. 38.

15 Women might attend as representatives of nunneries in the First Order (though they usually sent male proxies), and as heads of household or workshops in parish and guild assemblies.

16 A. Brette, *Recueil de documents relatifs à la convocation des États Généraux de 1789* (4 vols.; 1894–1915), vol. i, p. 66.

17 See above, p. 361.

18 Cubells, *Les Horizons de la liberté*, p. 107.

19 T. Tackett, 'Nobles and Third Estate in the Revolutionary dynamic of the National Assembly, 1789–90', *American Historical Review* (1989), p. 276.

20 J. C. Scott, *Weapons of the Weak: Everyday Forms of Peasant Resistance* (New Haven, Ct, 1985).

21 E. Mallet (ed.), *Les Elections du bailliage secondaire de Pontoise en 1789* (no place or date of publication), p. 329.

22 According to the extensive sampling done by John Markoff, pigeons were the fourteenth most frequently found complaint in peasant cahiers. The issue ranked higher than an Estates General veto on taxes (seventeenth), regular meetings of the Estates General (nineteenth) and voting by head in the Estates General (fortieth)! J. Markoff, *The Abolition of Feudalism: Peasants, Lords and Legislators in the French Revolution* (Philadelphia, 1996), pp. 30–32.

23 C. L. Chassin, *Les Elections et les cahiers de Paris en 1789* (2 vols.; Paris, 1888), vol. ii, pp. 589–90.

24 *Gouverneur Morris: A Diary of the French Revolution*, ed. B. C. Davenport (2 vols.; Boston, Mass., 1939 [1972 reprint]), vol. i, pp. xlii–xliii.

25 A. Young, *Travels in France in the Years 1787, 1788 and 1789*, ed. C. Maxwell (Cambridge, 1929), p. 151.

26 T. Tackett, *Becoming a Revolutionary. The Deputies of the French National Assembly and the Emergence of a Revolutionary Culture, 1789–91* (Princeton, NJ, 1996), pp. 109–10.

27 *The Papers of Thomas Jefferson*, eds. J. P. Boyd et al. (27 vols.; Princeton, NJ, 1950–97), vol. xv, pp. 104–5.

28 Marquis de Ferrières, *Correspondance inédite (1789, 1790, 1791)*, ed. H. Carré (Paris, 1932), p. 47.

29 The Anjou deputies, cited in E. H. Lemay and A. Patrick, *Revolutionaries at Work. The Constituent Assembly. 1789–91* (Oxford, 1996), p. 5.

30 Young, *Travels in France*, p. 134 (9 June).

31 J. Hardman, *Louis XVI* (London, 1993), p. 150.

32 *Réimpression de l'Ancien Moniteur*, vol. i, pp. 82–3.

33 J. A. Creuzé-Latouche, *Journal des Etats-Généraux du début de l'Assemblée nationale*, ed. J. Marchant, p. 139.

34 Young, *Travels in France*, p. 159.

35 *Papers of Thomas Jefferson*, vol. xv, p. 223

36 ibid., pp. 267–8. Jefferson used the italianate form 'de Broglio'.

37 *Correspondance secrète du comte de Mercy-Argenteau avec l'empereur Joseph II et le prince de Kaunitz*, eds. A. d'Arneth and J. Flammermont (2 vols.; Paris 1889–91), vol. ii, p. 248.

38 P. M. Jones, *The Peasantry in the French Revolution* (Cambridge, 1988), p. 66.

39 Young, *Travels in France*, pp. 207–9, 215–16 (the latter case allegedly involving local nobleman, the comte d'Antraigues, now viewed as a counter-revolutionary).

40 J. M. Roberts, *French Revolution Documents. Vol. 1* (Oxford, 1966), pp. 144–5.

41 G. Lefebvre, *The Coming of the French Revolution* (New York, 1947), p. 84.

42 *Archives parlementaires*, vol. viii, p. 397.

43 See below, pp. 423ff.

44 E. Lever, *Louis XVI* (Paris, 1985), p. 524.

45 *Despatches from Paris, 1788–90*, p. 263.

46 F. Ménard de la Groye, *Correspondance (1789–91)*, ed. F. Mirouse (Le Mans, 1989), pp. 123–4.

47 Hardman, *Louis XVI*, p. 174.

48 Campmas cited in Tackett, *Becoming a Revolutionary*, p. 303; Ferrières, *Correspondance*, p. 137

49 Tackett, *Becoming a Revolutionary*, p. 48.

50 Voltaire, *Correspondance complète*, ed. T. Besterman, (101 vols.; Geneva, 1953–77), vol. xxxvii, p. 439.

51 Cited by D. Van Kley in id., (ed.), *The French Idea of Freedom. The Old Régime and the Declaration of Rights of 1789* (Stanford, Ca., 1994), p. 93.

52 For Louis XIV's mythic present, see above, chapter 1, esp. section A. Cf. L. Hunt, *Politics, Culture and Class in the French Revolution* (Berkeley, Ca., 1994).

53 Cited in J. P. Jessenne, *Révolution et Empire, 1783–1815* (Paris, 1993), p. 80.

54 Ménard de la Groye, *Correspondance*, p. 256.

55 The regulations on the *marc d'argent* were lightened in the summer of 1791.

56 See below, pp. 438–9.

57 Guillotin, cited in D. Arasse, *The Guillotine and the Terror* (London, 1989), p. 17.

58 *The Diaries and Letters of Gouverneur Morris*, vol. i, pp. 373–4.

59 C. B. A. Behrens, *The Ancien Régime* (London, 1967), p. 179.

60 Ferrières, *Correspondance*, p. 327.

61 *Journal d'Adrien Duquesnoy sur l'Assemblée Constituante*, ed. R. de Crèvecoeur (2 vols.; Paris, 1894), pp. 286, 411.

62 See above, p. 402.

63 Schama, *Citizens*, p. 537.

64 See above, p. 427ff.

65 T. W. Margadant, *Urban Rivalries in the French Revolution* (Princeton, NJ, 1992), pp. 123, 125.

66 Hardman, *The French Revolution Sourcebook*, p. 113.

67 W. Doyle, *The Oxford History of the French Revolution* (Oxford, 1989), p. 146.

68 Ménard de la Groye, *Correspondance*, p. 342.

69 *Archives parlementaires*, vol. xxvi, p. 149.

70 ibid., vol. xxvii, p. 553.

71 ibid., vol. xxviii, p. 330.

72 Le May, *Revolutionaries at Work*, p. 106.

10: WAR AND TERROR (1791–5)

1 R. M. Klincköwstrom (ed.), *Le comte de Fersen et la cour de France* (2 vols.; Paris, 1877), vol. i, p. 208.

2 *Marie-Antoinette et Barnave. Correspondance secrète (juillet 1791–janvier 1792)*, ed. A. Söderhjelm (Paris, 1934), p. 71n.

3 C. J. Mitchell, *The French Legislative Assembly of 1791* (Leiden, 1988), p. 43.

4 Chateaubriand, *Mémoires d'outre-tombe*, ed. J. C. Berchet (4 vols.; Paris, 1989), vol. i, p. 508.

5 ibid., vol. i, p. 509; P. Vaissière, *Lettres d' 'aristocrates': La Révolution racontée par des correspondances privées (1789–94)* (Paris, 1907), p. 354.

6 Mitchell, *The French Legislative Assembly*, p. 63.

7 J. M. Roberts, *French Revolution Documents, Vol. 1* (Oxford, 1966), p. 423.

8 N. Ruault, *Gazette d'un parisien sous la Révolution*, eds. A. Vassal and C. Rimbaud (Paris, 1976), pp. 279–80.

9 Gouverneur Morris, *A Diary of the French Revolution* (2 vols.; Westport, Ct, 1972), pp. 355–6.

10 F. S. Feuillet de Conches (ed.), *Marie-Antoinette et Madame Elisabeth. Lettres et documents inédits* (6 vols.; 1864–73), p. 344.

11 Robespierre, *Oeuvres*, eds. M. Bouloiseau, G. Lefebvre and A. Soboul (5 vols.; Paris, 1950–67), vol. ii, p. 81.

12 It was phrased in this way because the Habsburg Francis II had not yet been elected Holy Roman Emperor.

13 P. Mansell, *Louis XVIII* (London, 1981), p. 67.

14 H. G. Brown, *War, Revolution and the Bureaucratic State. Politics and Army Administration in France, 1791–99* (Oxford, 1995), p. 30.

15 Cited in Buchez and Roux, *Histoire parlementaire*, vol. xiv, p. 423.

16 P. Caron, *Les Massacres de septembre* (Paris, 1935), p. 146, n. 1.

17 Manon Roland, *Correspondance politique (1790–3)* (Paris, 1995), p. 127.

18 'Campagne in Frankreich 1792', in *Goethes Werke*, eds. L. Blumenthal and W. Loos (Hamburg, 1981), pp. 234–5.

19 J. P. Bertaud, *Valmy. La démocratie en armes* (Paris, 1970), p. 114.

20 *The Despatches of Earl Gower*, ed. O. Browning (Cambridge, 1888), p. 258.

21 M. Walzer, *Regicide and Revolution* (Cambridge, 1974), p. 124.

22 J. Hardman, *The French Revolution Sourcebook* (London, 1999), p. 161; P. Higonnet, *Goodness beyond Virtue. Jacobins during the French Revolution* (Cambridge, Mass., 1998), p. 53.

23 *Archives parlementaires*, vol. lx, p. 63.

24 H. Gough, *The Newspaper Press in the French Revolution* (London, 1988), p. 95.

25 S. Schama, *Citizens. A Chronicle of the French Revolution* (Cambridge, Mass., 1989), p. 714.

26 N. Hampson, *Danton* (London, 1978), p. 137.

27 M. A. Baudot, *Notes historiques sur la Convention nationale, le Directoire, l'Empire et l'exil des votants* (Paris, 1893), p. 158.

28 *Archives parlementaires*, vol. lxv, p. 320.

29 *Papiers inédits trouvés chez Robespierre, Saint-Just, Payan, etc supprimés ou omis par Courtois* (3 vols.; Paris, 1828), vol. i, pp. 15–16.

30 Charles Dickens, *A Tale of Two Cities*, opening pages.

31 R. Secher, *Le Génocide franco-français: La Vendée-Vengé* (Paris, 1986), p. 129

32 'Manifeste des enragés': Jacques Roux, *Scripta et acta*, ed. W. Markov (Berlin, 1969), p. 141.

33 See below, pp. 564ff.

34 See below, pp. 579ff.

35 For the mythic present, see below, pp. 521ff.

36 H. Wallon, *Les Représentants en mission et la justice révolutionnaire dans les départements en l'an II (1793–4)* (5 vols.; Paris, 1889–90), vol. i, p. 220.

37 See below, pp. 564–5.

38 See above, p. 425.

39 Hardman, *French Revolution Sourcebook*, p. 189.

40 Buchez and Roux, *Histoire parlementaire*, vol. xxxv, p. 290.

41 F. Brunel, *Thermidor. La chute de Robespierre* (Brussels, 1989), p. 20.

42 *Archives parlementaires*, vol. lxxxviii, p. 434.

43 Ruault, *Gazette d'un parisien*, p. 350.

44 K. Alder, *Engineering the Revolution. Arms and Enlightenment in France,*

1763–1815 (Princeton, NJ, 1997), p. 253. See also the picture on p. 254. (I differ from Alder in the attribution of epithets.)

45 ibid, p. 272.

46 See below, p. 535.

47 B. Barère, *Mémoires*, ed. H. Carnot and P. J. David (4 vols.; 1842–4), vol. ii, pp. 202–3.

48 Vilate, cited in Buchez and Roux, *Histoire parlementaire*, vol. xxxiii, p. 177.

49 P. Gueniffey, *La Politique de la Terreur. Essai sur la violence révolutionnaire, 1789–94* (Paris, 2000), p. 273.

50 Brunel, *Thermidor*, p. 27.

51 Baudot, *Notes*, p. 125.

52 J. Duval-Jouve, *Montpellier pendant la Révolution* (Montpellier, 1879), p. 188n.

53 1 Vendémiaire III, the first day of Year III in the Revolutionary calendar, was 22 September 1794.

54 Cited in D. Woronoff, *The Thermidorean Regime and the Directory, 1794–9* (Cambridge, 1972), p. 7.

11: THE UNSTEADY REPUBLIC (1795–9)

1 Louis to the duc d'Harcourt, cited in E. Sparrow, *British Agents in France, 1792–1815* (Woodbridge, 1999), p. 60.

2 See above, p. 506.

3 F. Aftalion, *The French Revolution. An Economic Interpretation* (Cambridge, 1990), p. 158.

4 D. Outram, *The Body in the French Revolution: Sex, Class and Political Culture* (London, 1989), p. 83.

5 Article 18 of the Declaration of Rights and Duties (sic) of Man and the Citizen in the 1795 Constitution.

6 See above, pp. 401, 424–5.

7 H. T. Parker, *The Cult of Antiquity in the French Revolution* (Chicago, 1937), pp. 18–19.

8 L. Hunt, *Politics, Culture and Class in the French Revolution* (Berkeley, Ca., 1984), p. 2.

9 To cite from the 1795 balloting procedures: as noted by I. Woloch, *The New Regime. Transformations of the French Civic Order, 1789–1820s* (London, 1994), p. 99.

10 P. Higonnet, *Goodness beyond Virtue. Jacobins during the French Revolution* (Cambridge, Mass., 1998), p. 207.

11 N. Hampson, 'The Heavenly City of the French Revolutionaries', in C. Lucas (ed.), *Rewriting the French Revolution* (Oxford, 1991), p. 55.

12 Speech on 18 Floréal II, cited by M. H. Huet, *Mourning Glory. The Will of the French Revolution* (Philadelphia, 1997), p. 27.

13 See above, p. 212.

14 G. Kates, *The Cercle Social, the Girondins and the French Revolution* (Princeton, NJ, 1985), p. 180; and article xi of the Declaration of the Rights of Man and the Citizen prefixed to the 1791 Constitution.

15 Lequinio, cited by R. Reichardt, 'Prints: Images of the Bastille', in R. Darnton and D. Roche (eds.), *Revolution in Print. The Press in France, 1775–1800* (Berkeley, Ca., 1989), p. 225.

16 Cited in C. Hesse, 'Economic upheavals in publishing', in Darnton and Roche, *Revolution in Print*, p. 97.

17 Kates, *The Cercle Social*, p. 228.

18 Isoard, cited in J. Guilhaumou, 'Rhétorique et antirhétorique à l'époque de la Révolution française', in *La Légende de la Révolution* (Clermont-Ferrand, 1988), p. 151.

19 Louis-Sébastien Mercier, *Le Nouveau Paris* (Paris, n.d. [=1797–8]), vol. iii, pp. 39–40 and ii, 112; for 'logomachie', see p. ii, 111.

20 Mercier, *Le Nouveau Paris*, vol. iv, p. 52.

21 M. J. Sydenham, *The French Revolution* (London, 1965), p. 130.

22 Higonnet, *Goodness beyond Virtue*, p. 158.

23 Huet, *Mourning Glory*, p. 33.

24 Higonnet, *Goodness beyond Virtue*, p. 181.

25 'Sur les fêtes politiques', as cited in J. de Viguerie, *Les Deux patries: Essai historique sur l'idée de la patrie en France* (Paris, 1998), p. 106.

26 See above, p. 183.

27 See above, p. 492.

28 A favourite saying of Richard Cobb: see his *Paris and its Provinces* (Oxford, 1975), pp. 97–8.

29 Higonnet, *Goodness beyond Virtue*, pp. 209, 126.

30 Staël's *Des Circonstances actuelles qui peuvent terminer la Révolution*, cited in F. Furet, *The French Revolution, 1770–1814* (Oxford, 1992), p. 204.

31 See above, p. 53.

32 See above, p. 516.

33 See above, p. 361–2.

34 K. Alder, *Engineering the Revolution. Arms and Enlightenment in France, 1763–1815* (Princeton, NJ, 1997), p. 262.

35 Madame de La Tour du Pin, *Memoirs* (London, 1999), p. 299.

36 F. Crouzet, *De la Supériorité de l'Angleterre sur la France. L'économique et l'imaginaire, XVIIe–XXe siècle* (Paris, 1985), p. 254.

37 See below.

38 See above, pp. 356ff.

39 L. Bergeron, 'L'économie française et la Révolution', in H. Berding et al. (eds.), *La Révolution, la France et l'Allemagne: deux modèles opposés de changement social?* (Paris, 1989), p. 89.

40 According to a visit in 1801 recorded in H. Meister, *Souvenirs de mon dernier voyage à Paris (1795)* (Paris, 1910), p. 234.

41 Crouzet, *De la Supériorité de l'Angleterre sur la France*, p. 276.

42 See previous section.

43 See above, p. 372ff.

44 F. Pontheil, *Histoire de l'enseignement, 1789–1965* (Paris, 1966), pp. 70–71.

45 H. G. Brown, *War, Revolution and the Bureaucratic State: Politics and Army Administration in France, 1791–9* (Oxford, 1995), p. 31.

46 ibid., p. 45. ('Call me citizen' is my translation of '*Ici on se tutoie.*')

47 Woloch, *The New Regime*, p. 495, n. 5.

48 L. Brockliss and C. Jones, *The Medical World of Early Modern France* (Oxford, 1997), p. 819.

49 Woloch, *The New Regime*, p. 328.

50 Brown, *War, Revolution and the Bureaucratic State*, p. 170.

51 Michelet, *Histoire de la Révolution française*, ed. G. Walter (2 vols.; Paris, 1952), vol. i, p. 752.

52 The phrase comes from Archives Nationales, W 342 (no. 648). Thanks to Tom Kaiser for letting me have this reference.

53 The term seems hardly apposite for Jews, of course.

54 P. Girard, *La Révolution et les juifs* (Paris, 1989), p. 224.

55 Higonnet, *Goodness beyond Virtue*, p. 221.

56 *Archives parlementaires*, vol. lxxxiii, p. 715.

57 See above, esp. pp. 502ff.

58 Bergeron, 'L'économie française et la Révolution', p. 81.

59 W. H. Sewell, 'Le citoyen/la citoyenne: activity, passivity and the Revolutionary concept of citizenship', in C. Lucas, *The Political Culture of the French Revolution* (vol. 2 of *The French Revolution and the Creation of Modern Political Culture*) (Oxford, 1988), p. 115.

60 'Essai sur l'admission des femmes au droit de cité' (1790) in *Oeuvres de Condorcet*, eds. A. Condorcet O'Connor and M. F. Arago (12 vols.; Paris, 1847), vol. x.

61 Amar, cited in D. G. Levy, H. B. Applewhite and M. D. Johnson (eds.), *Women in Revolutionary Paris, 1789–95* (Urbana, Ill., 1979), p. 216.

CONCLUSION: THE BRUMAIRE LEVIATHAN AND
LA GRANDE NATION

1 L. S. Mercier, *Le Nouveau Paris* (Paris, n.d. [=1797–8]), 'Avant-Propos', vol. i, p. xvii.

2 I. Woloch, *Napoleon and his Collaborators: The Making of a Dictatorship* (London, 2001), p. 8.

3 Cf. above, p. 511.

4 Mercier, *Le Nouveau Paris*, vol. i, p. xvii.

5 F. Furet, *The French Revolution, 1770–1814* (Oxford, 1992), p. 199.

6 R. Laurent and G. Gavignaud, *La Révolution française dans le Languedoc méditerranéen, 1789–99* (Toulouse, 1987), p. 313.

7 N. King and E. Hofman, 'Les Lettres de Benjamin Constant à Siéyès', *Annales Benjamin Constant*, 3 (1983), pp. 96–7.

8 Laurent and Gavignaud, *La Révolution française dans le Languedoc méditerranéen*, p. 316.

9 B. J. Buchez and P. C. Roux, *Histoire parlementaire de la Révolution française, ou Journal des Assemblées nationales depuis 1789 jusqu'en 1815* (40 vols.; Paris, 1834–8), vol. xxxviii, p. 301.

10 H. G. Brown, 'From organic society to security state: the war on brigandage in France, 1797–1802', *Journal of Modern History*, 69 (1997).

11 J. Tulard, *Le 18 Brumaire: comment terminer une révolution* (Mesnil-sur-l'Estrée, 1999).

12 F. Bluche, *Le Bonapartisme: aux origines de la droite autoritaire (1800–50)* (Paris, 1980), pp. 29, 28n.

Further Reading

A full bibliography, which highlights works published in English, may be located under *http://www.warwick.ac.uk/staff/Colin.Jones*. Works, mainly in English, which provide a helpful introduction to or overview of the period include the following:

M. Antoine, *Louis XV* (Paris, 1989)

K. M. Baker, *Inventing the French Revolution: Essays on French Political Culture in the Eighteenth Century* (Cambridge, 1990)

K. M. Baker et al. (eds.), *The French Revolution and the Creation of Modern Political Culture* (4 vols.; Oxford, 1987–94)

D. Bell, *The National and the Sacred: Religion and the Origins of Nationalism in Eighteenth-Century France* (Cambridge, Mass., 2002)

J. Black, *From Louis XIV to Napoleon. The Fate of a Great Power* (London, 1999)

T. C. W. Blanning, *The French Revolutionary Wars, 1787–1802* (London, 1996)

P. M. Campbell, *Power and Politics in Old Régime France, 1720–43* (London, 1996)

R. Chartier, *The Cultural Origins of the French Revolution* (Durham, N.C., 1991)

A. Cobban, *A History of Modern France. vol. 1. Old Regime and Revolution, 1715–99* (Harmondsworth, 1957)

J. B. Collins, *The State in Early Modern France* (Cambridge, 1995)

W. Doyle, *The Oxford History of the French Revolution* (Oxford, 1989)

W. Doyle, *The Origins of the French Revolution* (3rd edn; Oxford, 1999)

W. Doyle (ed.), *Old Régime France* (Oxford, 2001)

J. Egret, *The French Pre-Revolution, 1787–8* (Chicago, 1977)

F. Furet and M. Ozouf, *A Critical Dictionary of the French Revolution* (London, 1989)

P. Goubert, *The Ancien Régime* (New York, 1970)

P. Higonnet, *Goodness beyond Virtue: Jacobins during the French Revolution* (Cambridge, Mass., 1998)

L. Hunt, *Politics, Culture and Class in the French Revolution* (Berkeley, Ca., 1984)

C. Jones, *The Longman Companion to the French Revolution* (London, 1989)

C. Jones, *Madame de Pompadour: Images of a Mistress* (London, 2002)

E. Le Roy Ladurie, *The Ancien Régime. A History of France, 1610–1774* (Oxford, 1996)

M. Lyons, *Napoleon Bonaparte and the Legacy of the French Revolution* (London, 1994)

S. Maza, *Private Lives and Public Affairs. The Causes Célèbres of Pre-Revolutionary France* (Berkeley, Ca., 1993)

J. McManners, *Church and Society in Eighteenth-Century France* (2 vols.; Oxford, 1998)

R. Porter, *The Englightenment* (2nd edn; London, 1999)

D. Roche, *France in the Enlightenment* (Cambridge, Mass., 1996)

R. Schechter (ed.), *The French Revolution: Essential Readings* (Oxford, 2001)

D. Sutherland, *France, 1789–1815: Revolution and Counter-Revolution* (London, 1985)

J. Swann, *Politics and the Parlement of Paris under Louis XV, 1754–74* (Cambridge, 1995)

T. Tackett, *Religion, Revolution and Regional Culture in Eighteenth-Century France. The Ecclesiastical oath of 1790–91* (Princeton, N.J. 1986)

D. Van Kley, *The Religious Origins of the French Revolution* (New Haven, Conn., 1996)

J. de Viguerie, *Histoire et dictionnaire du temps des Lumières, 1715–89* (Paris, 1995)

Index

Abbeville 271, 404

absolutism 18, 26–7, 370; critics
20–21, 23; Enlightenment 218,
221; Louis XIV 2, 7–8, 12–14,
24, 36, 40–41, 43–4, 49, 52, 56,
59, 77, 81, 102, 105, 110, 114,
125, 231, 263–4; Louis XV 148,
218, 245, 247 262–5, 273–4,
280, 288, 290–91; Louis XVI
338, 340, 343, 363, 371, 373,
379–80, 387, 390, 393–4, 397,
580; Regency 67–8, 72, 77–8, 81,
145 ; Revolution 402, 424–5,
439, 442, 458, 506; Directory
511, 517, 544, 570

Aboukir, battle of 574

Aboukir Bay 574

Academies 117, 176, 179–81, 184,
186, 191, 206–7, 209–11, 257–8,
262, 334, 366, 368–71, 527, 548,
551, 557; Academy of Agriculture
115; Academy of Architecture 5,
114; Académie Française 5, 43,
114, 131, 176, 179, 186;
Academy for Inscriptions and
Belles-Lettres 5, 114; Academy of
Music 5; Academy of Naval
Affairs 115; Academy of Painting
and Sculpture 5, 114; Academy of

Sciences 5, 114, 117; Academy of
Surgery 115

Acadians 139

Adelaide, Madame 445

Affaires de l'Angleterre 308

Affiches 182, 325, 358

Affiches de Limoges 367

Affiches de l'Orléanais 367

Africa 53, 65, 160, 355

agriculture 149–51, 153, 157, 167,
327, 351, 352–4, 359–61, 453,
471, 510, 534, 542–3, 559,
561–2; *see also* peasantry

Aguesseau, Henri François d' 3,
22–3, 25, 45, 87, 116, 119–20

Aiguillon, duc d' 273–4, 276–7,
279–80, 282–3, 285–6, 291–3,
303, 342, 399, 420

Aix-en-Provence 101, 233, 256,
330, 502

Aix-la-Chapelle, Treaty of 131,
137–8, 146, 169, 244–5

Alary, abbé d' 117

Alberoni, Cardinal 50–51

Albigeois 437

Alembert, Jean-Baptiste le Rond d'
171–2, 174–6, 178–80, 188, 193,
213, 366, 423

Alfort 257